The
Mercer
Reader

Second Edition

Copley Custom Textbooks

An imprint of XanEdu Custom Publishing

ISBN 13: 978-1-58152-662-2
ISBN 10: 1-58152-662-8

Printed on recycled paper with soy ink.

Copley Custom Textbooks
An imprint of XanEdu Custom Publishing
138 Great Road
Acton, MA 01720
800-562-2147

Contents

FYS 101: The Core of the Self

Composing the Self

iv

Bridging the Self and the World

FYS 102: The Core of the World

Engaging the World

The Mercer Ethic

Themes

Art and Imagination

Conscience and Selfhood

Education

Family

Friendship and Love

Global Perspectives

Nature/Stewardship

Social Justice

Race, Class, and Gender Identities

Religion

Virtue and Ethics

Editors

(2009–2012 Edition)

Chris Grant
Associate Professor of Political Science

Fernando Palacios
Assistant Professor of Spanish

Gordon Johnston
Associate Professor of English

Deneen Senasi
Assistant Professor of English

Andrew Silver
Associate Professor of English

Anya Silver
Associate Professor of English

With contributions from the Mercer University First Year Seminar Faculty and the Mercer University Faculty at Large

Cover design by Craig Coleman, Assistant Professor of Art, and Katy Olmsted

(2006–2008 Edition)

Sarah Gardner
Associate Professor of History

Gordon Johnston
Associate Professor of English

Andrew Silver
Associate Professor of English

Charlotte Thomas
Associate Professor of Philosophy

Dear First-Year Student,

I am pleased to have this opportunity to welcome you to university life and to briefly share my reflections on the First Year Seminar. Unlike a survey course, a seminar requires participants to share responsibility for learning. You will be a stakeholder in your class and will be expected to reveal and defend your thoughts on a range of issues. FYS 101 (Composing the Self) begins with an interrogation of identity, and FYS 102 (Engaging the World) shifts focus to reflect on the relationships we have with others. Each course provides opportunities for you to improve your craft of writing and to develop your proficiency in oral communication.

The dual objectives of the two FYS courses are to foster the habits of critical thinking, speaking, and writing vital to success in university study and to bring students into the educational community at Mercer University. *The Mercer Reader* provides a diverse group of texts that present arguments for how we should understand ourselves and how we should relate to the world. As you read these texts, you will be asked to judge the arguments advanced and to reveal the moral reasoning you utilized to arrive at your assessment. At stake in these discussions will be an understanding of how we know what we know and also a sense of what obligations we have to others. It almost goes without saying that the more energy and passion you bring to class the more rewarded you will be.

I am very excited to serve as the director of the First Year Seminar program, and I am confident that these two courses are vital to creating and sustaining the educational community of Mercer University. I hope the next four years challenge you to become more aware of who you are, what you can be, and what that may mean for others. The First Year Seminar exists to introduce you to that purpose and your commitment to learning will help it to continue to be a definitive part of the Mercer experience.

In Service,

Kevin J. Cummings

Director, First Year Seminar

Introduction to
The Mercer Reader

The fairest thing we can experience is the mysterious. It is the fundamental emotion which stands at the cradle of true art and true science.

Albert Einstein
The World As I See It

This is not the first revolution the human race has dealt with.

Doris Lessing
"On Not Winning the Nobel Prize"

Beginnings can be a bit mysterious. Coming to a new place filled with unknown faces and unfamiliar expectations is like stepping into another world. What will happen here, in this "new world" of the university? Who, among these strangers' faces, will I come to know? What will I learn, and who will I come to be? If, as Albert Einstein suggests, "the fairest thing we can experience is the mysterious," then beginnings are one of the primary ways most of us encounter it.

This then is a book of beginnings, a text that has been created for you and your First Year Seminar with the mystery of such beginnings in mind. Yet as I sit here, writing this Introduction (itself a kind of beginning) I pause, thinking of the ironies of introducing this book to you when, as the American poet, Adrienne Rich, describes it, "this is no place you ever knew me" ("An Atlas of the Difficult World" 62). I will come to know some, but probably not all, of you. You, in turn, may come to know some, but perhaps not all, of the Mercer faculty who have been part of this book's creation. Yet as Rich also writes, "this is a map of our country" (78). This book is both: a "country"—a landscape of ideas, issues, and images—*and* a "map" or rather, many maps—a collection of pathways, passages, and possible journeys. Within this textual terrain, all of us, faculty and students alike, may meet, and like Christopher Columbus and Galileo (two of the historical figures you will encounter in this text) set out on an experience that is unique to each one of us, yet shared within a spirit of mutual exploration and discovery.

Beginnings can also be revolutionary. Consider the story of the Luther Bible. During his stay at Wartburg Castle in 1522, Martin Luther began his translation of the New Testament into German in order to make the text more accessible, a place where the widest possible range of German-speakers could encounter God's word. While at Wartburg, the story goes, Luther often left the castle and traveled into the towns and markets in the surrounding countryside in order to listen to the everyday speech of the people, which he then used in his translation. Luther's path, from the text to the world (and the selves he encountered within it) and back again, turned out to be "revolutionary" in several senses of the word. The completed translation of both testaments, published in 1534, is not only a foundational text of the Reformation but is also thought to have been instrumental in the development of the modern German language. In this story, the scholar leaves his ivory tower and goes out into the world to engage with it, and then he carries it back into the text that he creates. On a more modest scale, of course, *The Mercer Reader* works to follow Luther's path, from the text to the self, to the world, and back again. It is our hope that this book will serve as an instrument of engagement, a tidal pool of smaller tributary texts leading beyond the boundaries of the book itself to the oceanic expanses of human knowledge and experience. A voyage out that is also a passage within, thus a revolution in the truest sense of the word.

In fact, the history of the book is a history of revolutions. In her Nobel Prize lecture (also featured in the *The Mercer Reader*), British novelist, Doris Lessing, emphasizes this relationship between the book, the self, and the world. She reminds us that the technological advances of our own century are not "the first revolution the human race has dealt with" and that the earlier printing revolution "transformed our minds and ways of thinking." The potential for transformation that Lessing points to lies at the heart of the First Year Seminar program you are about to begin. An education, like the selves that experience it, is composed of a series of such revolutions. Within your own education, the courses you take will engage your thoughts and imagination through both their content and their form, an experience that is defined by not only *what* you learn but also *how* you learn it. The First Year Seminar is remarkable for both. The term "seminar" is derived from another word, "seminary," which was originally a piece of ground where seeds were sown. Eventually, it came to also be defined as "a place of origins and early development; a place or thing in which something (e.g., an art or science, a virtue or vice) is developed or cultivated, or from which it is propagated abundantly," literally, a place of beginnings. Throughout the First Year Seminar experience, we will ask ourselves what it means to have or be a "self"; we will ask whether we make the world or the world makes us, and we will listen for the answers that come from you. It is the contemplation of such questions and the actions that such contemplation gives rise to that *The Mercer Reader* works to "propagate abundantly" in those who participate in it. Welcome to the revolution.

Deneen Senasi

Chair of The Mercer Reader Committee, on behalf of The Mercer Reader Committee and the First Year Seminar Faculty

11 May 2009

Michael Cass, Pollock Professor of English and Interdisciplinary Studies, was one of the architects of the First Year Seminar program at Mercer University, singer of the first and only FYS theme song ("We won't stop tryin' 'til we create disturbance in your mind"), and the first FYS Director. Below are his notes for a speech to the first convocation of First Year Semnar students and faculty in 1997. Samples from these handwritten notes appear on the cover of The Mercer Reader.

Notes for Inaugural First Year Seminar Speech, August 1997

*Michael Cass, Professor of English
and Interdisciplinary Studies*

Mercer was already a year old when Abe Lincoln entered politics, 11 yrs old when Marx met Engels.

Mercer is one yr older than the Univ. of Brussels, 12 yrs older than the Naval Academy, 32 yrs older than MIT, & 43 yrs older than Johns Hopkins Univ. Mercer is 4 yrs older than the state of Michigan, 18 yrs older than the New York Times, 21 yrs older than the Republican Party, 36 years older than intercollegiate football, 43 yrs older than the National League and the telephone, 53 years older than Coca Cola, and 87 years older than radio.

We've been here awhile . . . we're serious.

Dean Douglas Steeples, on CLA's Web page, says that here you can gain "A premier liberal arts education," and that's what we want FYS to be the first building-block for.

Plenty of precedents for FYS, but still, this is the first time we're trying this.

Purpose: coherence; same texts; talking to each other during the semester, and after the semester, and later courses building on your having had the same texts.

Purpose: critical thinking.

Critical thinking: not thinking simplistically. (We all think simplistically some of the time, but the goal is to do it less of the time.)

Critical thinking: looking past the surfaces into the depths of things and events and people.

Critical thinking: sometimes against the grain of the culture.

"Be not conformed to this world, but be transformed in the renewal of your mind" (Romans 12).

Prophetic: to look deeply into the present, into this culture: "Prophetic dialectics."

Purpose: writing skills.

Purpose: speaking skills.

Preceptors: "to take beforehand," in its Latin roots--to advise, to instruct, to order, to give rules to. Your preceptors are your liaisons with the teacher, if you need liaison; they are your companions, your older brothers and sisters in the community of learning we're trying to establish.

I was like you in the Fall of 1959, not sure this would be right for me; I was from a family in which going to college was not the standard—father one year, mother not at all, no other relatives except some distant cousins.

But I remember one night in October or November when I was RUNNING TO THE LIBRARY, so eager I was to get there to study, and so full of the enjoyment of my running. Without knowing yet that I had found a place to belong deeply to, I was belonging and was celebrating that belonging. I thought to myself, at the moment, "Look at me! I'm running to the library because I'm in such a rush to study!" I wish that joy of learning, that enthusiasm, that pleasure of knowing you belong, for each one of you.

I'm about to close. When I do close—If you haven't met your teacher yet, I urge you to go up to her or him now, extend your hand, and introduce yourself. But first:

Proverbs 25:2 says, recognizing the mystery of being and the privilege of being human, "It is the glory of God to conceal things, but the glory of kings is to search them out." You were told at Convocation Friday afternoon that you can be presidents, and I tell you now that you are the kings that Proverbs speaks of.

It is your glory to search out the truth. Go search!

FYS 101: The Core of the Self

Winslow Homer. *The Gulf Stream.* (1899)

René Magritte. *La Condition Humaine.* (1933)

from **Allegory of the Cave (400 B.C.E.)**

Plato

Book VII: On Shadows and Realities in Education

(Socrates, Glaucon.)

And now, I said, let me show in a figure how far our nature is enlightened or unenlightened: Behold! human beings living in an underground den, which has a mouth open toward the light and reaching all along the den; here they have been from their childhood, and have their legs and necks chained so that they cannot move, and can only see before them, being prevented by the chains from turning round their heads. Above and behind them a fire is blazing at a distance, and between the fire and the prisoners there is a raised way; and you will see, if you look, a low wall built along the way, like the screen which marionette-players have in front of them, over which they show the puppets.

I see.

And do you see, I said, men passing along the wall carrying all sorts of vessels, and statues and figures of animals made of wood and stone and various materials, which appear over the wall? Some of them are talking, others silent.

You have shown me a strange image, and they are strange prisoners.

Like ourselves, I replied; and they see only their own shadows, or the shadows of one another, which the fire throws on the opposite wall of the cave?

True, he said; how could they see anything but the shadows if they were never allowed to move their heads?

And of the objects which are being carried in like manner they would only see the shadows?

Yes, he said.

And if they were able to converse with one another, would they not suppose that they were naming what was actually before them?

Very true.

And suppose further that the prison had an echo which came from the other side, would they not be sure to fancy when one of the passers-by spoke that the voice which they heard came from the passing shadow?

No question, he replied.

To them, I said, the truth would be literally nothing but the shadows of the images.

That is certain.

And now look again, and see what will naturally follow if the prisoners are released and disabused of their error. At first, when any of them is liberated and compelled suddenly to stand up and turn his neck round and walk and look toward the light, he will suffer sharp pains; the glare will distress him, and he will be unable to see the realities of which in his former state he had seen the shadows; and then conceive someone saying to him, that what he saw before was an illusion, but that now, when he is approaching nearer to being and his eye is turned toward more real existence, he has a clearer vision—what will be his reply? And you may further imagine that his instructor is pointing to the objects as they pass and requiring him to name them—will he not be perplexed? Will he not fancy that the shadows which he formerly saw are truer than the objects which are now shown to him?

Far truer.

And if he is compelled to look straight at the light, will he not have a pain in his eyes which will make him turn away to take refuge in the objects of vision which he can see, and which he will conceive to be in reality clearer than the things which are now being shown to him?

True, he said.

And suppose once more, that he is reluctantly dragged up a steep and rugged ascent, and held fast until he is forced into the presence of the sun himself, is he not likely to be pained and irritated? When he approaches the light his eyes will be dazzled, and he will not be able to see anything at all of what are now called realities.

Not all in a moment, he said.

He will require to grow accustomed to the sight of the upper world. And first he will see the shadows best, next the reflections of men and other objects in the water, and then the objects themselves; then he will gaze upon the light of the moon and the stars and the spangled heaven; and he will see the sky and the stars by night better than the sun or the light of the sun by day?

Certainly.

Last of all he will be able to see the sun, and not mere reflections of him in the water, but he will see him in his own proper place, and not in another; and he will contemplate him as he is.

Certainly.

He will then proceed to argue that this is he who gives the season and the years, and is the guardian of all that is in the visible world, and in a certain way the cause of all things which he and his fellows have been accustomed to behold?

Clearly, he said, he would first see the sun and then reason about him.

And when he remembered his old habitation, and the wisdom of the den and his fellow-prisoners, do you not suppose that he would felicitate himself on the change, and pity him?

Certainly, he would.

And if they were in the habit of conferring honors among themselves on those who were quickest to observe the passing shadows and to remark which of them went before, and which followed after, and which were together; and who were therefore best able to draw conclusions as to the future, do you think that he would care for such honors and glories, or envy the possessors of them? Would he not say with Homer,

"Better to be the poor servant of a poor master,"

and to endure anything, rather than think as they do and live after their manner?

Yes, he said, I think that he would rather suffer anything than entertain these false notions and live in this miserable manner.

Imagine once more, I said, such a one coming suddenly out of the sun to be replaced in his old situation; would he not be certain to have his eyes full of darkness?

To be sure, he said.

And if there were a contest, and he had to compete in measuring the shadows with the prisoners who had never moved out of the den, while his sight was still weak, and before his eyes had become steady (and the time which would be needed to acquire this new habit of sight might be very considerable), would he not be ridiculous? Men would say of him that up he went and down he came without his eyes; and that it was better not even to think of ascending; and if anyone tried to loose another and lead him up to the light, let them only catch the offender, and they would put him to death.

No question, he said.

This entire allegory, I said, you may now append, dear Glaucon, to the previous argument; the prison-house is the world of sight, the light of the fire is the sun, and you will not misapprehend me if you interpret the journey upward to be the ascent of the soul into the intellectual world according to my poor belief, which, at your desire, I have expressed—whether rightly or wrongly, God knows. But, whether true or false, my opinion is that in the world of knowledge the idea of good appears last of all, and is seen only with an effort; and, when seen, is also inferred to be the universal author of all things beautiful and right, parent of light and of the lord of light in this visible world, and the immediate source of reason and truth in the intellectual; and that this is the power upon which he who would act rationally either in public or private life must have his eye fixed.

I agree, he said, as far as I am able to understand you.

Moreover, I said, you must not wonder that those who attain to this beatific vision are unwilling to descend to human affairs; for their souls are ever hastening into the upper world where they desire to dwell; which desire of theirs is very natural, if our allegory may be trusted.

Yes, very natural.

And is there anything surprising in one who passes from divine contemplations to the evil state of man, misbehaving himself in a ridiculous manner; if, while his eyes are blinking and before he has become accustomed to the surrounding darkness, he is compelled to fight in courts of law, or in other places, about the images or the shadows of images of justice, and is endeavoring to meet the conceptions of those who have never yet seen absolute justice?

Anything but surprising, he replied. Anyone who has common-sense will remember that the bewilderments of the eyes are of two kinds, and arise from two causes, either from coming out of the light or from going into the light, which is true of the mind's eye, quite as much as of the bodily eye; and he who remembers this when he sees anyone whose vision is perplexed and weak, will not be too ready to laugh; he will first ask whether that soul of man has come out of the brighter life, and is unable to see because unaccustomed to the dark, or having turned from darkness to the day is dazzled by excess of light. And he will count the one happy in his condition and state of being, and he will pity the other; or, if he have a mind to laugh at the soul which comes from below into the light, there will be more reason in this than in the laugh which greets him who returns from above out of the light into the den.

That, he said, is a very just distinction.

But then, if I am right, certain professors of education must be wrong when they say that they can put a knowledge into the soul which was not there before, like sight into blind eyes.

They undoubtedly say this, he replied.

Whereas, our argument shows that the power and capacity of learning exists in the soul already; and that just as the eye was unable to turn from darkness to light without the whole body, so too the instrument of knowledge can only by the movement of the whole soul be turned from the world of becoming into that of being, and learn by degrees to endure the sight of being, and of the brightest and best of being, or, in other words, of the good.

Very true.

And must there not be some art which will effect conversion in the easiest and quickest manner; not implanting the faculty of sight, for that exists already, but has been turned in the wrong direction, and is looking away from the truth?

Yes, he said, such an art may be presumed.

And whereas the other so-called virtues of the soul seem to be akin to bodily qualities, for even when they are not originally innate they can be implanted later by habit and exercise, the virtue of wisdom more than anything else contains a divine element which always remains, and by this conversion is rendered useful and profitable; or, on the other hand, hurtful and useless. Did you never observe the narrow intelligence flashing from the keen eye of a clever rogue—how eager he is, how clearly his paltry soul sees the way to his end; he is the reverse of blind, but his keen eyesight is forced into the service of evil, and he is mischievous in proportion to his cleverness?

Very true, he said.

But what if there had been a circumcision of such natures in the days of their youth; and they had been severed from those sensual pleasures, such as eating and drinking, which, like leaden weights, were attached to them at their birth, and which drag them down and turn the vision of their souls upon the things that are below—if, I say, they had been released from these impediments and turned in the opposite direction, the very same faculty in them would have seen the truth as keenly as they see what their eyes are turned to now.

Very likely.

Yes, I said; and there is another thing which is likely, or rather a necessary inference from what has preceded, that neither the uneducated and unin-formed of the truth, nor yet those who never make an end of their edu-cation, will be able ministers of the State; not the former, because they have no single aim of duty which is the rule of all their actions, private as well as public; nor the latter, because they will not act at all except upon compulsion, fancying that they are already dwelling apart in the islands of the blessed.

Very true, he replied.

Then, I said, the business of us who are the founders of the State will be to compel the best minds to attain that knowledge which we have already shown to be the greatest of all—they must continue to ascend until they arrive at the good; but when they have ascended and seen enough we must not allow them to do as they do now.

What do you mean?

I mean that they remain in the upper world: but this must not be allowed; they must be made to descend again among the prisoners in the den, and partake of their labors and honors, whether they are worth having or not.

But is not this unjust? he said; ought we to give them a worse life, when they might have a better?

You have again forgotten, my friend, I said, the intention of the legislator, who did not aim at making any one class in the State happy above the rest; the happiness was to be in the whole State, and he held the citizens together by persuasion and necessity, making them benefactors of the State, and therefore benefactors of one another; to this end he created them, not to please themselves, but to be his instruments in binding up the State.

True, he said, I had forgotten.

Observe, Glaucon, that there will be no injustice in compelling our philosophers to have a care and providence of others; we shall explain to them that in other States, men of their class are not obliged to share in the toils of politics: and this is reasonable, for they grow up at their own sweet will, and the government would rather not have them. Being self-taught, they cannot be expected to show any gratitude for a culture which they have never received. But we have brought you into the world to be rulers of the hive, kings of yourselves and of the other citizens, and have educated you far better and more perfectly than they have been educated, and you are better able to share in the double duty. Wherefore each of you, when his turn comes, must go down to the general underground abode, and get the habit of seeing in the dark. When you have acquired the habit, you will see ten thousand times better than the inhabitants of the den, and you will know what the several images are, and what they represent, because you have seen the beautiful and just and good in their truth. And thus our State, which is also yours, will be a reality, and not a dream only, and will be administered in a spirit unlike that of other States, in which men fight with one another about shadows only and are distracted in the struggle for power, which in their eyes is a great good. Whereas the truth is that the State in which the rulers are most reluctant to govern is always the best and most quietly governed, and the State in which they are most eager, the worst.

Quite true, he replied.

And will our pupils, when they hear this, refuse to take their turn at the toils of State, when they are allowed to spend the greater part of their time with one another in the heavenly light?

Impossible, he answered; for they are just men, and the commands which we impose upon them are just; there can be no doubt that every one of them will take office as a stern necessity, and not after the fashion of our present rulers of State.

Yes, my friend, I said; and there lies the point. You must contrive for your future rulers another and a better life than that of a ruler, and then you may have a well-ordered State; for only in the State which offers this, will they rule who are truly rich, not in silver and gold, but in virtue and wisdom, which are the true blessings of life. Whereas, if they go to the administration of public affairs, poor and hungering after their own private advantage, thinking that hence they are to snatch the chief good, order there can never be; for they will be fighting about office, and the civil and domestic broils which thus arise will be the ruin of the rulers themselves and of the whole State.

Most true, he replied.

And the only life which looks down upon the life of political ambition is that of true philosophy. Do you know of any other?

Indeed, I do not, he said.

And those who govern ought not to be lovers of the task? For, if they are, there will be rival lovers, and they will fight.

No question. Who, then, are those whom we shall compel to be guardians? Surely they will be the men who are wisest about affairs of State, and by whom the State is best administered, and who at the same time have other honors and another and a better life than that of politics?

They are the men, and I will choose them, he replied.

The Loss of the Creature (1958)

Walker Percy

I

Every explorer names his island Formosa, beautiful. To him it is beautiful because, being first, he has access to it and can see it for what it is. But to no one else is it ever as beautiful—except the rare man who manages to recover it, who knows that it has to be recovered.

Garcia López de Cárdenas discovered the Grand Canyon and was amazed at the sight. It can be imagined: One crosses miles of desert, breaks through the mesquite, and there it is at one's feet. Later the government set the place aside as a national park, hoping to pass along to millions the experience of Cárdenas. Does not one see the same sight from the Bright Angel Lodge that Cárdenas saw?

The assumption is that the Grand Canyon is a remarkably interesting and beautiful place and that if it had a certain value P for Cárdenas, the same value P may be transmitted to any number of sightseers—just as Banting's discovery of insulin can be transmitted to any number of diabetics. A counterinfluence is at work, however, and it would be nearer the truth to say that if the place is seen by a million sightseers, a single sightseer does not receive value P but a millionth part of value P.

It is assumed that since the Grand Canyon has the fixed interest value P, tours can be organized for any number of people. A man in Boston decides to spend his vacation at the Grand Canyon. He visits his travel bureau, looks at the folder, signs up for a two-week tour. He and his family take the tour, see the Grand Canyon, and return to Boston. May we say that this man has seen the Grand Canyon? Possibly he has. But it is more likely that what he has done is the one sure way not to see the canyon.

Why is it almost impossible to gaze directly at the Grand Canyon under these circumstances and see it for what it is—as one picks up a strange object from one's back yard and gazes directly at it? It is almost impossible because the Grand Canyon, the thing as it is, has been appropriated by the symbolic complex which has already been formed in the sightseer's mind. Seeing the canyon under approved circumstances is seeing the symbolic complex head on. The thing is no longer the thing as it confronted the Spaniard; it is rather that which has already been

15

formulated—by picture postcard, geography book, tourist folders, and the words *Grand Canyon*. As a result of this preformulation, the source of the sightseer's pleasure undergoes a shift. Where the wonder and delight of the Spaniard arose from his penetration of the thing itself, from a progressive discovery of depths, patterns, colors, shadows, etc., now the sightseer measures his satisfaction *by the degree to which the canyon conforms to the preformed complex*. If it does so, if it looks just like the postcard, he is pleased, he might even say, "Why it is every bit as beautiful as a picture postcard!" He feels he has not been cheated. But if it does not conform, if the colors are somber, he will not be able to see it directly; he will only be conscious of the disparity between what it is and what it is supposed to be. He will say later that he was unlucky in not being there at the right time. The highest point, the term of the sightseer's satisfaction, is not the sovereign discovery of the thing before him; it is rather the measuring up of the thing to the criterion of the preformed symbolic complex.

Seeing the canyon is made even more difficult by what the sightseer does when the moment arrives, when sovereign knower confronts the thing to be known. Instead of looking at it, he photographs it. There is no confrontation at all. At the end of forty years of preformulation and with the Grand Canyon yawning at his feet, what does he do? He waives his right of seeing and knowing and records symbols for the next forty years. For him there is no present; there is only the past of what has been formulated and seen and the future of what has been formulated and not seen. The present is surrendered to the past and the future.

The sightseer may be aware that something is wrong. He may simply be bored; or he may be conscious of the difficulty: that the great thing yawning at his feet somehow eludes him. The harder he looks at it, the less he can see. It eludes everybody. The tourist cannot see it; the bellboy at the Angel Lodge cannot see it: For him it is only one side of the space he lives in, like one wall of a room; to the ranger it is a tissue of everyday signs relevant to his own prospects—the blue haze down there means that he will probably get rained on during the donkey ride.

How can the sightseer recover the Grand Canyon? He can recover it by any number of ways, all sharing in common the stratagem of avoiding the approved confrontation of the tour and the Park Service.

It may be recovered by leaving the beaten track. The tourist leaves the tour, camps in the back country. He arises before dawn and approaches the South Rim through a wild terrain where there are no trails and no railed-in lookout points. In other words, he sees the canyon by avoiding all the facilities for seeing the canyon. If the benevolent Park Service hears about this fellow and thinks he has a good idea and places the following notice in the Bright Angel Lodge: *Consult ranger for information on getting off the beaten track*—the end result will only be the closing of another access to the canyon.

It may be recovered by a dialectical movement which brings one back to the beaten track but at a level above it. For example, after a lifetime of avoiding the beaten track and guided tours, a man may deliberately seek out the most beaten track of all, the most commonplace tour imaginable: he may visit the canyon by a Greyhound tour in the company of a party from Terre Haute—just as a man who has lived in New York all his life may visit the Statue of Liberty. (Such dialectical savorings of the familiar as the familiar are, of course, a favorite stratagem of *The New Yorker* magazine.) The thing is recovered from familiarity by means of an exercise in familiarity. Our complex friend stands behind the fellow tourists at the Bright Angel Lodge and sees the canyon through them and their predicament, their picture taking and busy disregard. In a sense, he exploits his fellow tourists; he stands on their shoulders to see the canyon.

Such a man is far more advanced in the dialectic than the sightseer who is trying to get off the beaten track—getting up at dawn and approaching the canyon through the mesquite. This stratagem is, in fact, for our complex man the weariest, most beaten track of all.

It may be recovered as a consequence of a breakdown of the symbolic machinery by which the experts present the experience to the consumer. A family visits the canyon in the usual way. But shortly after their arrival, the park is closed by an outbreak of typhus in the south. They have the canyon to themselves. What do they mean when they tell the home folks of their good luck: "We had the whole place to ourselves"? How does one see the thing better when the others are absent? Is looking like sucking: the more lookers, the less there is to see? They could hardly answer, but by saying this they testify to a state of affairs which is considerably more complex than the simple statement of the schoolbook about the Spaniard and the millions who followed him. It is a state in which there is a complex distribution of sovereignty, of zoning.

It may be recovered in a time of national disaster. The Bright Angel Lodge is converted into a rest home, a function that has nothing to do with the canyon a few yards away. A wounded man is brought in. He regains consciousness; there outside his window is the canyon.

The most extreme case of access by privilege conferred by disaster is the Huxleyan novel of the adventures of the surviving remnant after the great wars of the twentieth century. An expedition from Australia lands in Southern California and heads east. They stumble across the Bright Angel Lodge, now fallen into ruins. The trails are grown over, the guard rails fallen away, the dime telescope at Battleship Point rusted. But there is the canyon, exposed at last. Exposed by what? By the decay of those facilities which were designed to help the sightseer.

This dialectic of sightseeing cannot be taken into account by planners, for the object of the dialectic is nothing other than the subversion of the efforts of the planners.

The dialectic is not known to objective theorists, psychologists, and the like. Yet it is quite well known in the fantasy-consciousness of the popular arts. The devices by which the museum exhibit, the Grand Canyon, the ordinary thing, is recovered have long since been stumbled upon. A movie shows a man visiting the Grand Canyon. But the moviemaker knows something the planner does not know. He knows that one cannot take the sight frontally. The canyon must be approached by the stratagems we have mentioned: the Inside Track, the Familiar Revisited, the Accidental Encounter. Who is the stranger at the Bright Angel Lodge? Is he the ordinary tourist from Terre Haute that he makes himself out to be? He is not. He has another objective in mind, to revenge his wronged brother, counterespionage, etc. By virtue of the fact that he has other fish to fry, he may take a stroll along the rim after supper and then we can see the canyon through him. The movie accomplishes its purpose by concealing it. Overtly the characters (the American family marooned by typhus) and we the onlookers experience pity for the sufferers, and the family experience anxiety for themselves; covertly and in truth they are the happiest of people and we are happy through them, for we have the canyon to ourselves. The movie cashes in on the recovery of sovereignty through disaster. Not only is the canyon now accessible to the remnant: the members of the remnant are now accessible to each other; a whole new ensemble of relations becomes possible—friendship, love, hatred, clandestine sexual adventures. In a movie when a man sits next to a woman on a bus, it is necessary either that the bus break down or that the woman lose her memory. (The question occurs to one: Do you imagine there are sightseers who see sights just as they are supposed to? A family who live in Terre Haute, who decide to take the canyon tour, who go there, see it, enjoy it immensely, and go home content? A family who are entirely innocent of all the barriers, zones, losses of sovereignty I have been talking about? Wouldn't most people be sorry if Battleship Point fell into the canyon, carrying all one's fellow passengers to their death, leaving one alone on the South Rim? I cannot answer this. Perhaps there are such people. Certainly a great many American families would swear they had no such problems, that they came, saw, and went away happy. Yet it is just these families who would be happiest if they had gotten the Inside Track and been among the surviving remnant.)

It is now apparent that as between the many measures which may be taken to overcome the opacity, the boredom, of the direct confrontation of the thing or creature in its citadel of symbolic investiture, some are less authentic than others. That is to say, some stratagems obviously serve other purposes than that of providing access to being—for example, various unconscious motivations which it is not necessary to go into here.

Let us take an example in which the recovery of being is ambiguous, where it may under the same circumstances contain both authentic and unauthentic components. An American couple, we will say, drives down into Mexico. They see the usual sights and have a fair time of it. Yet they are never without the sense of missing something. Although Taxco and Cuernavaca are interesting and picturesque as advertised, they fall short of "it." What do the couple have in mind by "it"? What do they really hope for? What sort of experience could they have in Mexico so that upon their return, they would feel that "it" had happened? We have a clue: Their hope has something to do with their own role as tourists in a foreign country and the way in which they conceive this role. It has something to do with other American tourists. Certainly they feel that they are very far from "it" when, after traveling five thousand miles, they arrive at the plaza in Guanajuato only to find themselves surrounded by a dozen other couples from the Midwest.

Already we may distinguish authentic and unauthentic elements. First, we see the problem the couple faces and we understand their efforts to surmount it. The problem is to find an "unspoiled" place. "Unspoiled" does not mean only that a place is left physically intact; it means also that it is not encrusted by renown and by the familiar (as in Taxco), that it has not been discovered by others. We understand that the couple really want to get at the place and enjoy it. Yet at the same time we wonder if there is not something wrong in their dislike of their compatriots. Does access to the place require the exclusion of others?

Let us see what happens.

The couple decide to drive from Guanajuato to Mexico City. On the way they get lost. After hours on a rocky mountain road, they find themselves in a tiny valley not even marked on the map. There they discover an

Indian village. Some sort of religious festival is going on. It is apparently a corn dance in supplication of the rain god.

The couple know at once that this is "it." They are entranced. They spend several days in the village, observing the Indians and being themselves observed with friendly curiosity.

Now may we not say that the sightseers have at last come face to face with an authentic sight, a sight which is charming, quaint, picturesque, unspoiled, and that they see the sight and come away rewarded? Possibly this may occur. Yet it is more likely that what happens is a far cry indeed from an immediate encounter with being, that the experience, while masquerading as such, is in truth a rather desperate impersonation. I use the word *desperate* advisedly to signify an actual loss of hope.

The clue to the spuriousness of their enjoyment of the village and the festival is a certain restiveness in the sightseers themselves. It is given expression by their repeated exclamations that "this is too good to be true," and by their anxiety that it may not prove to be so perfect, and finally by their downright relief at leaving the valley and having the experience in the bag, so to speak—that is, safely embalmed in memory and movie film.

What is the source of their anxiety during the visit? Does it not mean that the couple are looking at the place with a certain standard of performance in mind? Are they like Fabre, who gazed at the world about him with wonder, letting it be what it is; or are they not like the overanxious mother who sees her child as one performing, now doing badly, now doing well? The village is their child and their love for it is an anxious love because they are afraid that at any moment it might fail them.

We have another clue in their subsequent remark to an ethnologist friend. "How we wished you had been there with us! What a perfect goldmine of folkways! Every minute we would say to each other, if only you were here! You must return with us." This surely testifies to a generosity of spirit, a willingness to share their experience with others, not at all like their feelings toward their fellow Iowans on the plaza at Guanajuato!

I am afraid this is not the case at all. It is true that they longed for their ethnologist friend, but it was for an entirely different reason. They wanted him, not to share their experience, but to certify their experience as genuine.

"This is it" and "Now we are really living" do not necessarily refer to the sovereign encounter of the person with the sight that enlivens the mind and gladdens the heart. It means that now at last we are having the acceptable experience. The present experience is always measured by a prototype, the "it" of their dreams. "Now I am really living" means that now I am filling the role of sightseer and the sight is living up to the prototype of sights. This quaint and picturesque village is measured by a Platonic ideal of the Quaint and the Picturesque.

Hence their anxiety during the encounter. For at any minute something could go wrong. A fellow Iowan might emerge from an adobe hut; the chief might show them his Sears catalog. (If the failures are "wrong" enough, as these are, they might still be turned to account as rueful conversation pieces: "There we were expecting the chief to bring us a churinga and he shows up with a Sears catalog!") They have snatched victory from disaster, but their experience always runs the danger of failure.

They need the ethnologist to certify their experience as genuine. This is borne out by their behavior when the three of them return for the next corn dance. During the dance, the couple do not watch the goings-on; instead they watch the ethnologist! Their highest hope is that their friend should find the dance interesting. And if he should show signs of true absorption, an interest in the goings-on so powerful that he becomes oblivious of his friends—then their cup is full. "Didn't we tell you?" they say at last. What they want from him is not ethnological explanations; all they want is his approval.

What has taken place is a radical loss of sovereignty over that which is as much theirs as it is the ethnologist's. The fault does not lie with the ethnologist. He has no wish to stake a claim to the village; in fact, he desires the opposite: He will bore his friends to death by telling them about the village and the meaning of the folkways. A degree of sovereignty has been surrendered by the couple. It is the nature of the loss, moreover, that they are not aware of the loss, beyond a certain uneasiness. (Even if they read this and admitted it, it would be very difficult for them to bridge the gap in their confrontation of the world. Their consciousness of the corn dance cannot escape their consciousness of their consciousness, so that with the onset of the first direct enjoyment, their higher consciousness pounces and certifies: "Now you are doing it! Now you are really living!" and, in certifying the experience, sets it at nought.)

Their basic placement in the world is such that they recognize a priority of title of the expert over his particular department of being. The whole horizon of being is staked out by "them," the experts. The highest satisfaction of the sightseer (not merely the tourist but any layman seer of sights) is that his sight should be certified as genuine. The worst of this impoverishment is that there is no sense of impoverishment. The surrender of title is so complete that it never even occurs to one to reassert title. A poor man may envy the rich man, but the sightseer does not envy the expert. When a caste system becomes absolute, envy disappears. Yet the caste of lay-man-expert is not the fault of the expert. It is due altogether to the eager surrender of sovereignty by the layman so that he may take up the role not of the person but of the consumer.

I do not refer only to the special relation of layman to theorist. I refer to the general situation in which sovereignty is surrendered to a class of privileged knowers, whether these be theorists or artists. A reader may surrender sovereignty over that which has been written about, just as a consumer may surrender sovereignty over a thing which has been theorized about. The consumer is content to receive an experience just as it has been presented to him by theorists and planners. The reader may also be content to judge life by whether it has or has not been formulated by those who know and write about life. A young man goes to France. He too has a fair time of it, sees the sights, enjoys the food. On his last day, in fact as he sits in a restaurant in Le Havre waiting for his boat, something happens. A group of French students in the restaurant get into an impassioned argument over a recent play. A riot takes place. Madame la concierge joins in, swinging her mop at the rioters. Our young American is transported. This is "it." And he had almost left France without seeing "it"!

But the young man's delight is ambiguous. On the one hand, it is a pleasure for him to encounter the same Gallic temperament he had heard about from Puccini and Rolland. But on the other hand, the source of his pleasure testifies to a certain alienation. For the young man is actually barred from a direct encounter with anything French excepting only that which has been set forth, authenticated by Puccini and Rolland—those who know. If he had encountered the restaurant scene without reading Hemingway, without knowing that the performance was so typically charmingly French, he would not have been delighted. He would only have been anxious at seeing things get out of hand. The source of his delight is the sanction of those who know.

This loss of sovereignty is not a marginal process, as might appear from my example of estranged sightseers. It is a generalized surrender of the horizon to those experts within whose competence a particular segment of the horizon is thought to lie. Kwakiutls are surrendered to Franz Boas; decaying Southern mansions are surrendered to Faulkner and Tennessee Williams. So that, although it is by no means the intention of the expert to expropriate sovereignty—in fact he would not even know what sovereignty meant in this context—the danger of theory and consumption is a seduction and deprivation of the consumer.

In the New Mexican desert, natives occasionally come across strange-looking artifacts which have fallen from the skies and which are stenciled: Return to *U.S. Experimental Project, Alamogordo Reward*. The finder returns the object and is rewarded. He knows nothing of the nature of the object he has found and does not care to know. The sole role of the native, the highest role he can play, is that of finder and returner of the mysterious equipment.

The same is true of the layman's relation to *natural* objects in a modern technical society. No matter what the object or event is, whether it is a star, a swallow, a Kwakiutl, a "psychological phenomenon," the layman who confronts it does not confront it as a sovereign person, as Crusoe confronts a seashell he finds on the beach. The highest role he can conceive himself as playing is to be able to recognize the title of the object, to return it to the appropriate expert, and have it certified as a genuine find. He does not even permit himself to see the thing—as Gerard Hopkins could see a rock or a cloud or a field. If anyone asks him why he doesn't look, he may reply that he didn't take that subject in college (or he hasn't read Faulkner).

This loss of sovereignty extends even to oneself. There is the neurotic who asks nothing more of his doctor than that his symptoms should prove interesting. When all else fails, the poor fellow has nothing to offer but his own neurosis. But even this is sufficient if only the doctor will show interest when he says, "Last night I had a curious sort of dream; perhaps it will be significant to one who knows about such things. It seems I was standing in a sort of alley—" (I have nothing else to offer you but my own unhappiness. Please say that it, at least, measures up, that it is a proper sort of unhappiness.)

II

A young Falkland Islander walking along a beach and spying a dead dogfish and going to work on it with his jackknife has, in a fashion wholly unprovided in modern educational theory, a great advantage over the Scarsdale high-school pupil who finds the dogfish on his laboratory desk. Similarly the citizen of Huxley's *Brave New World* who stumbles across a volume of Shakespeare in some vine-grown ruins and squats on a potsherd to read it is in a fairer way of getting at a sonnet than the Harvard sophomore taking English Poetry II.

The educator whose business it is to teach students biology or poetry is unaware of a whole ensemble of relations which exist between the student and the dogfish and between the student and the Shakespeare sonnet. To put it bluntly: A student who has the desire to get at a dogfish or a Shakespeare sonnet may have the greatest difficulty in salvaging the creature itself from the educational package in which it is presented. The great difficulty is that he is not aware that there is a difficulty; surely, he thinks, in such a fine classroom, with such a fine textbook, the sonnet must come across! What's wrong with me?

The sonnet and the dogfish are obscured by two different processes. The sonnet is obscured by the symbolic package which is formulated not by the sonnet itself but by the *media* through which the sonnet is transmitted, the media which the educators believe for some reason to be transparent. The new textbook, the type, the smell of the page, the classroom, the aluminum windows and the winter sky, the personality of Miss Hawkins—these media which are supposed to transmit the sonnet may only succeed in transmitting themselves. It is only the hardiest and cleverest of students who can salvage the sonnet from this many-tissued package. It is only the rarest student who knows that the sonnet must be salvaged from the package. (The educator is well aware that something is wrong, that there is a fatal gap between the student's learning and the student's life: The student reads the poem, appears to understand it, and gives all the answers. But what does he recall if he should happen to read a Shakespeare sonnet twenty years later? Does he recall the poem or does he recall the smell of the page and the smell of Miss Hawkins?)

One might object, point out that Huxley's citizen reading his sonnet in the ruins and the Falkland Islander looking at his dogfish on the beach also receive them in a certain package. Yes, but the difference lies in the fundamental placement of the student in the world, a placement which makes it possible to extract the thing from the package. The pupil at Scarsdale High sees himself placed as a consumer receiving an experience-package; but the Falkland Islander exploring his dogfish is a person exercising the sovereign right of a person in his lordship and mastery of creation. He too could use an instructor and a book and a technique, but he would use them as his subordinates, just as he uses his jackknife. The biology student does not use his scalpel as an instrument; he uses it as a magic wand! Since it is a "scientific instrument," it should do "scientific things."

The dogfish is concealed in the same symbolic package as the sonnet. But the dogfish suffers an additional loss. As a consequence of this double deprivation, the Sarah Lawrence student who scores A in zoology is apt to know very little about a dogfish. She is twice removed from the dogfish, once by the symbolic complex by which the dogfish is concealed, once again by the spoliation of the dogfish by theory which renders it invisible. Through no fault of zoology instructors, it is nevertheless a fact that the zoology laboratory at Sarah Lawrence College is one of the few places in the world where it is all but impossible to see a dogfish.

The dogfish, the tree, the seashell, the American Negro, the dream, are rendered invisible by a shift of reality from concrete thing to theory which Whitehead has called the fallacy of misplaced concreteness. It is the mistaking of an idea, a principle, an abstraction, for the real. As a consequence of the shift, the "specimen" is seen as less real than the theory of the specimen. As Kierkegaard said, once a person is seen as a specimen of a race or a species, at that very moment he ceases to be an individual. Then there are no more individuals but only specimens.

To illustrate: A student enters a laboratory which, in the pragmatic view, offers the student the optimum conditions under which an educational experience may be had. In the existential view, however—that view of the student in which he is regarded not as a receptacle of experience but as a knowing being whose peculiar property it is to see himself as being in a certain situation—the modern laboratory could not have been more effectively designed to conceal the dogfish forever.

The student comes to his desk. On it, neatly arranged by his instructor he finds his laboratory manual, a dissecting board, instruments, and a mimeographed list:

Exercise 22: Materials

> 1 dissecting board
> 1 scalpel
> 1 forceps
> 1 probe
> 1 bottle india ink and syringe
> 1 specimen of *Squalus acanthias*

The clue to the situation in which the student finds himself is to be found in the last item: 1 specimen of *Squalus acanthias*.

The phrase *specimen of* expresses in the most succinct way imaginable the radical character of the loss of being which has occurred under his very nose. To refer to the dogfish, the unique concrete existent before him, as a "specimen of *Squalus acanthias*" reveals by its grammar the spoliation of the dogfish by the theoretical method. This phrase, *specimen of*, example of, instance of, indicates the ontological status of the individual creature in the eyes of the theorist. The dogfish itself is seen as a rather shabby expression of an ideal reality, the species *Squalus acanthias*. The result is the radical devaluation of the individual dogfish. (The *reductio ad absurdum* of Whitehead's shift is Toynbee's employment of it in his historical method. If a gram of NaCl is referred to by the chemist as a "sample of" NaCl, one may think of it as such and not much is missed by the oversight of the act of being of this particular pinch of salt, but when the Jews, and the Jewish religion are understood as—in Toynbee's favorite phrase—a "classical example of" such and such a kind of *Voelkerwanderung*, we begin to suspect that something is being left out.)

If we look into the ways in which the student can recover the dogfish (or the sonnet), we will see that they have in common the stratagem of avoiding the educator's direct presentation of the object as a lesson to be learned and restoring access to sonnet and dogfish as beings to be known, reasserting the sovereignty of knower over known.

In truth, the biography of scientists and poets is usually the story of the discovery of the indirect approach, the circumvention of the educator's presentation—the young man who was sent to the *Technikum* and on his way fell into the habit of loitering in book stores and reading poetry; or the young man dutifully attending law school who on the way became curious about the comings and goings of ants. One remembers the scene in *The Heart Is a Lonely Hunter* where the girl hides in the bushes to hear the Capehart in the big house play Beethoven. Perhaps she was the lucky one after all. Think of the unhappy souls inside, who see the record, worry about scratches, and most of all worry about whether they are *getting it*, whether they are bona fide music lovers. What is the best way to hear Beethoven: sitting in a proper silence around the Capehart or eavesdropping from an azalea bush?

However it may come about, we notice two traits of the second situation: (1) an openness of the thing before one—instead of being an exercise to be learned according to an approved mode, it is a garden of delights which beckons to one; (2) a sovereignty of the knower—instead of being a consumer of a prepared experience, I am a sovereign wayfarer, a wanderer in the neighborhood of being who stumbles into the garden.

One can think of two sorts of circumstances through which the thing may be restored to the person. (There is always, of course, the direct recovery: A student may simply be strong enough, brave enough, clever enough to take the dogfish and the sonnet by storm, to wrest control of it from the educators and the educational package.) First by ordeal: The Bomb falls;

when the young man recovers consciousness in the shambles of the biology laboratory, there not ten inches from his nose lies the dogfish. Now all at once he can see it, directly and without let, just as the exile or the prisoner or the sick man sees the sparrow at his window in all its inexhaustibility; just as the commuter who has had a heart attack sees his own hand for the first time. In these cases, the simulacrum of everydayness and of consumption has been destroyed by disaster; in the case of the bomb, literally destroyed. Secondly, by apprenticeship to a great man: One day a great biologist walks into the laboratory; he stops in front of our student's desk; he leans over, picks up the dogfish, and ignoring instruments and procedure, probes with a broken fingernail into the little carcass. "Now here is a curious business," he says, ignoring also the proper jargon of the specialty. "Look here how this little duct reverses its direction and drops into the pelvis. Now if you would look into a coelacanth, you would see that it—" And all at once the student can see. The technician and the sophomore who loves his textbooks are always offended by the genuine research man because the latter is usually a little vague and always humble before the thing; he doesn't have much use for the equipment or the jargon. Whereas the technician is never vague and never humble before the thing; he holds the thing disposed of by the principle, the formula, the textbook outline; and he thinks a great deal of equipment and jargon.

But since neither of these methods of recovering the dogfish is pedagogically feasible—perhaps the great man even less so than the Bomb—I wish to propose the following educational technique which should prove equally effective for Harvard and Shreveport High School. I propose that English poetry and biology should be taught as usual, but that at irregular intervals, poetry students should find dogfishes on their desks and biology students should find Shakespeare sonnets on their dissection boards. I am serious in declaring that a Sarah Lawrence English major who began poking about in a dogfish with a bobby pin would learn more in thirty minutes than a biology major in a whole semester; and that the latter upon reading on her dissecting board

> That time of year Thou may'st in me behold
> When yellow leaves, or none, or few, do hang
> Upon those boughs which shake against the cold—
> Bare ruin'd choirs where late the swee t birds sang.

might catch fire at the beauty of it.

The situation of the tourist at the Grand Canyon and the biology student are special cases of a predicament in which everyone finds himself in a modern technical society—a society, that is, in which there is a division between expert and layman, planner and consumer, in which experts and planners take special measures to teach and edify the consumer. The measures taken are measures appropriate to the consumer: The expert and the planner *know* and *plan*, but the consumer *needs* and *experiences*.

There is a double deprivation. First, the thing is lost through its packaging. The very means by which the thing is presented for consumption, the very techniques by which the thing is made available as an item of need-satisfaction, these very means operate to remove the thing from the sovereignty of the knower. A loss of title occurs. The measures which the museum curator takes to present the thing to the public are self-liquidating. The upshot of the curator's efforts are not that everyone can see the exhibit but that no one can see it. The curator protests: Why are they so indifferent? Why do they even deface the exhibit? Don't they know it is theirs? But it is not theirs. It is his, the curator's. By the most exclusive sort of zoning, the museum exhibit, the park oak tree, is part of an ensemble, a package, which is almost impenetrable to them. The archaeologist who puts his find in a museum so that everyone can see it accomplishes the reverse of his expectations. The result of his action is that no one can see it now but the archaeologist. He would have done better to keep it in his pocket and show it now and then to strangers.

The tourist who carves his initials in a public place, which is theoretically "his" in the first place, has good reasons for doing so, reasons which the exhibitor and planner know nothing about. He does so because in his role of consumer of an experience (a "recreational experience" to satisfy a "recreational need") he knows that he is disinherited. He is deprived of his title over being. He knows very well that he is in a very special sort of zone in which his only rights are the rights of a consumer. He moves like a ghost through schoolroom, city streets, trains, parks, movies. He carves his initials as a last desperate measure to escape his ghostly role of consumer. He is saying in effect: I am not a ghost after all; I am a sovereign person. And he establishes title the only way remaining to him, by staking his claim over one square inch of wood or stone.

Does this mean that we should get rid of museums? No, but it means that the sightseer should be prepared to enter into a struggle to recover a sight from a museum.

The second loss is the spoliation of the thing, the tree, the rock, the swallow, by the layman's misunderstanding of scientific theory. He believes that the thing is *disposed* of by theory, that it stands in the Platonic relation of being a *specimen* of such and such an underlying principle. In the transmission of scientific theory from theorist to layman, the expectation of the theorist is reversed. Instead of the marvels of the universe being made available to the public, the universe is disposed of by theory. The loss of sovereignty takes this form: As a result of the science of botany, trees are not made available to every man. On the contrary. The tree loses its proper density and mystery as a concrete existent and, as merely another *specimen* of a species, becomes itself nugatory.

Does this mean that there is no use taking biology at Harvard and Shreveport High? No, but it means that the student should know what a fight he has on his hands to rescue the specimen from the educational package. The educator is only partly to blame. For there is nothing the educator can do to provide for this need of the student. Everything the educator does only succeeds in becoming, for the student, part of the educational package. The highest role of the educator is the maieutic role of Socrates: to help the student come to himself not as a consumer of experience but as a sovereign individual.

The thing is twice lost to the consumer. First, sovereignty is lost: It is theirs, not his. Second, it is radically devalued by theory. This is a loss which has been brought about by science but through no fault of the scientist and through no fault of scientific theory. The loss has come about as a consequence of the seduction of the layman by science. The layman will be seduced as long as he regards beings as consumer items to be experienced rather than prizes to be won, and as long as he waives his sovereign rights as a person and accepts his role of consumer as the highest estate to which the layman can aspire.

As Mounier said, the person is not something one can study and provide for; he is something one struggles for. But unless be also struggles for himself, unless he knows that there is a struggle, he is going to be just what the planners think he is.

Servant, Birthright (2004)

Pattiann Rogers

If god was a cow, I could lead him
by a rope through a ring in his nose,
hang a bell around his neck, always
hear him wherever he was, even alone
in the open night. I could feed him
and fatten him. I could take him to clover
and fields of new grasses, put hay
on the snow for him in winter. I could
walk him to shelter out of hailstones
and thunderstorms, through the smoke
of summer fires, past trailing wolves, free him
from thorny bramble and cactus patches.

If god was a cow, I could slaughter him.
I could bludgeon him in the head
between the eyes with a hammer,
crack his skull, see his brains seeping.
I could watch his legs crumple under him
as he sank to the ground. I could feel
in the shake of the earth, and remember,
the weight of him as he fell.

I could eat him, drain his blood,
cook his blood and spoon it in
like soup. I could roast him, savor
his flanks and ribs and simmering
fat, absorb his fragrances, the perfumes
of his waft and smoke. I could skin him
and tan his hide and fashion his hide
and wear his hide as shoes, as hat,
as weskit, be covered by the pelt
of god, walk inside of god.

I could say, "I know you, god.
It was I who named you *cow*.
I have kept you, prepared you,

honored you, watched over you.
I have borne witness to you. After all,
I butchered you with care and skill.
I cut you open to the core. I uncovered
your parts. I touched all of your parts,
your secret parts. I have tasted you,
chewed you up, swallowed you,
sucked your bones and spit them out,
bleached your empty skull and hung it
high on my wall. I have wanted
you. I have needed you. You
have become and forsaken me.
In this we must both be satisfied."

The Summer Day (1990)

Mary Oliver

Who made the world?
Who made the swan, and the black bear?
Who made the grasshopper?
This grasshopper, I mean—
the one who has flung herself out of the grass,
the one who is eating sugar out of my hand,
who is moving her jaws back and forth instead of up and down—
who is gazing around with her enormous and complicated eyes.
Now she lifts her pale forearms and thoroughly washes her face.
Now she snaps her wings open, and floats away.
I don't know exactly what a prayer is.
I do know how to pay attention, how to fall down
into the grass, how to kneel down in the grass,
how to be idle and blessed, how to stroll through the fields,
which is what I have been doing all day.
Tell me, what else should I have done?
Doesn't everything die at last, and too soon?
Tell me, what is it you plan to do
with your one wild and precious life?

Manifesto: The Mad Farmer Liberation Front (1973)

Wendell Berry

Love the quick profit, the annual raise,
vacation with pay. Want more
of everything ready-made. Be afraid
to know your neighbors and to die.
And you will have a window in your head.
Not even your future will be a mystery
any more. Your mind will be punched in a card
and shut away in a little drawer.
When they want you to buy something
they will call you. When they want you
to die for profit they will let you know.
So, friends, every day do something
that won't compute. Love the Lord.
Love the world. Work for nothing.
Take all that you have and be poor.
Love someone who does not deserve it.
Denounce the government and embrace
the flag. Hope to live in that free
republic for which it stands.
Give your approval to all you cannot
understand. Praise ignorance, for what man
has not encountered he has not destroyed.
Ask the questions that have no answers.
Invest in the millennium. Plant sequoias.
Say that your main crop is the forest
that you did not plant,
that you will not live to harvest.
Say that the leaves are harvested
when they have rotted into the mold.
Call that profit. Prophesy such returns.
Put your faith in the two inches of humus
that will build under the trees
every thousand years.
Listen to carrion—put your ear

33

close, and hear the faint chattering
of the songs that are to come.
Expect the end of the world. Laugh.
Laughter is immeasurable. Be joyful
though you have considered all the facts.
So long as women do not go cheap
for power, please women more than men.
Ask yourself: Will this satisfy
a woman satisfied to bear a child?
Will this disturb the sleep
of a woman near to giving birth?
Go with your love to the fields.
Lie easy in the shade. Rest your head
in her lap. Swear allegiance
to what is nighest your thoughts.
As soon as the generals and the politicos
can predict the motions of your mind,
lose it. Leave it as a sign
to mark the false trail, the way
you didn't go. Be like the fox
who makes more tracks than necessary,
some in the wrong direction.
Practice resurrection.

The Unknown Citizen (1940)

W. H. Auden

To JS/07/M/378
This Marble Monument Is Erected by the State

He was found by the Bureau of Statistics to be
One against whom there was no official complaint,
And all the reports on his conduct agree
That, in the modern sense of an old-fashioned word, he was a saint,
5 For in everything he did he served the Greater Community.
Except for the War till the day he retired
He worked in a factory and never got fired,
But satisfied his employers, Fudge Motors Inc.
Yet he wasn't a scab or odd in his views,
10 For his Union reports that he paid his dues,
(Our report on his Union shows it was sound)
And our Social Psychology workers found
That he was popular with his mates and liked a drink.
The Press are convinced that he bought a paper every day
15 And that his reactions to advertisements were normal in every way.
Policies taken out in his name prove that he was fully insured,
And his Health-card shows he was once in hospital but left it cured.
Both Producers Research and High-Grade Living declare
He was fully sensible to the advantages of the Installment Plan
20 And had everything necessary to the Modern Man,
A phonograph, a radio, a car and a frigidaire.
Our researchers into Public Opinion are content
That he held the proper opinions for the time of year;
When there was peace, he was for peace; when there was war, he
       went.
25 He was married and added five children to the population,
Which our Eugenist says was the right number for a parent of
       his generation,
And our teachers report that he never interfered with their education.
Was he free? Was he happy? The question is absurd:
29 Had anything been wrong, we should certainly have heard.

Composing the Self

This Is What It Means to Say Phoenix, Arizona (1993)

Sherman Alexie

Just after Victor lost his job at the Bureau of Indian Affairs, he also found out that his father had died of a heart attack in Phoenix, Arizona. Victor hadn't seen his father in a few years, had only talked to him on the telephone once or twice, but there still was a genetic pain, which was as real and immediate as a broken bone. Victor didn't have any money. Who does have money on a reservation, except the cigarette and fireworks salespeople? His father had a savings account waiting to be claimed, but Victor needed to find a way to get from Spokane to Phoenix. Victor's mother was just as poor as he was, and the rest of his family didn't have any use at all for him. So Victor called the tribal council.

"Listen," Victor said. "My father just died. I need some money to get to Phoenix to make arrangements."

"Now, Victor," the council said, "you know we're having a difficult time financially."

"But I thought the council had special funds set aside for stuff like this."

"Now, Victor, we do have some money available for the proper return of tribal members' bodies. But I don't think we have enough to bring your father all the way back from Phoenix."

"Well," Victor said. "It ain't going to cost all that much. He had to be cre-mated. Things were kind of ugly. He died of a heart attack in his trailer and nobody found him for a week. It was really hot, too. You get the picture."

"Now, Victor, we're sorry for your loss and the circumstances. But we can really only afford to give you one hundred dollars."

"That's not even enough for a plane ticket."

"Well, you might consider driving down to Phoenix."

"I don't have a car. Besides, I was going to drive my father's pickup back up here."

38

"Now, Victor," the council said, "we're sure there is somebody who could drive you to Phoenix. Or could anybody lend you the rest of the money?"

"You know there ain't nobody around with that kind of money."

"Well, we're sorry Victor, but that's the best we can do."

Victor accepted the tribal council's offer. What else could he do? So he signed the proper papers, picked up his check, and walked over to the Trading Post to cash it.

While Victor stood in line, he watched Thomas Builds-the-Fire standing near the magazine rack talking to himself. Like he always did. Thomas was a storyteller whom nobody wanted to listen to. That's like being a dentist in a town where everybody has false teeth.

Victor and Thomas Builds-the-Fire were the same age, had grown up and played in the dirt together. Ever since Victor could remember, it was Thomas who had always had something to say.

Once, when they were seven years old, when Victor's father still lived with the family, Thomas closed his eyes and told Victor this story: "Your father's heart is weak. He is afraid of his own family. He is afraid of you. Late at night, he sits in the dark. Watches the television until there's nothing but that white noise. Sometimes he feels like he wants to buy a motorcycle and ride away. He wants to run and hide. He doesn't want to be found."

Thomas Builds-the-Fire had known that Victor's father was going to leave, known it before anyone. Now Victor stood in the Trading Post with a one-hundred-dollar check in his hand, wondering if Thomas knew that Victor's father was dead, if he knew what was going to happen next.

Just then, Thomas looked at Victor, smiled, and walked over to him.

"Victor, I'm sorry about your father," Thomas said.

"How did you know about it?" Victor asked.

"I heard it on the wind. I heard it from the birds. I felt it in the sunlight. Also, your mother was just in here crying."

"Oh," Victor said and looked around the Trading Post. All the other Indians stared, surprised that Victor was even talking to Thomas. Nobody talked to Thomas anymore because he told the same damn stories over and over again. Victor was embarrassed, but he thought that Thomas might be able to help him. Victor felt a sudden need for tradition.

"I can lend you the money you need," Thomas said suddenly. "But you have to take me with you."

"I can't take your money," Victor said. "I mean, I haven't hardly talked to you in years. We're not really friends anymore."

"I didn't say we were friends. I said you had to take me with you."

"Let me think about it."

Victor went home with his one hundred dollars and sat at the kitchen table. He held his head in his hands and thought about Thomas Builds-the-Fire, remembered little details, tears and scars, the bicycle they shared for a summer, so many stories.

Thomas Builds-the-Fire sat on the bicycle, waiting in Victor's yard. He was ten years old and skinny. His hair was dirty because it was the Fourth of July.

"Victor," Thomas yelled. "Hurry up. We're going to miss the fireworks."

After a few minutes, Victor ran out of his family's house, vaulted over the porch railing, and landed gracefully on the sidewalk.

Thomas gave him the bike and they headed for the fireworks. It was nearly dark and the fireworks were about to start.

"You know," Thomas said, it's strange how us Indians celebrate the Fourth of July. It ain't like it was our independence everybody was fighting for."

"You think about things too much," Victor said. "It's just supposed to be fun. Maybe Junior will be there."

"Which Junior? Everybody on this reservation is named Junior."

The fireworks were small, hardly more than a few bottle rockets and a fountain. But it was enough for two Indian boys. Years later, they would need much more.

Afterward, sitting in the dark, fighting off mosquitoes, Victor turned to Thomas Builds-the-Fire.

"Hey," Victor said. "Tell me a story."

Thomas closed his eyes and told this story: "There were these two Indian boys who wanted to be warriors. But it was too late to be warriors in the old way. All the horses were gone. So the two Indian boys stole a car and drove to the city. They parked the stolen car in the front of the police station and then hitchhiked back home to the reservation. When they got back, all their friends cheered and their parents' eyes shone with pride. 'You were very brave,' everybody said to the two Indian boys. 'Very brave.'"

"Ya-hey," Victor said. "That's a good one. I wish I could be a warrior."

"Me too," Thomas said.

Victor sat at his kitchen table. He counted his one hundred dollars again and again. He knew he needed more to make it to Phoenix and back. He knew he needed Thomas Builds-the-Fire. So he put his money in his wallet and opened the front door to find Thomas on the porch.

"Ya-hey, Victor," Thomas said. "I knew you'd call me."

Thomas walked into the living room and sat down in Victor's favorite chair.

"I've got some money saved up," Thomas said. "It's enough to get us down there, but you have to get us back."

"I've got this hundred dollars," Victor said. "And my dad had a savings account I'm going to claim."

"How much in your dad's account?"

"Enough. A few hundred."

"Sounds good. When we leaving?"

When they were fifteen and had long since stopped being friends, Victor and Thomas got into a fistfight. That is, Victor was really drunk and beat Thomas up for no reason at all. All the other Indian boys stood around and watched it happen. Junior was there and so were Lester, Seymour, and a lot of others.

The beating might have gone on until Thomas was dead if Norma Many Horses hadn't come along and stopped it.

"Hey, you boys," Norma yelled and jumped out of her car. "Leave him alone."

If it had been someone else, even another man, the Indian boys would've just ignored the warnings. But Norma was a warrior. She was powerful.

She could have picked up any two of the boys and smashed their skulls together. But worse than that, she would have dragged them all over to some tepee and made them listen to some elder tell a dusty old story.

The Indian boys scattered, and Norma walked over to Thomas and picked him up.

"Hey, little man, are you O.K.?" she asked.

Thomas gave her a thumbs-up.

"Why they always picking on you?"

Thomas shook his head, closed his eyes, but no stories came to him, no words or music. He just wanted to go home, to lie in his bed and let his dreams tell the stories for him.

•   •   •

Thomas Builds-the-Fire and Victor sat next to each other in the airplane, coach section. A tiny white woman had the window seat. She was busy twisting her body into pretzels. She was flexible.

"I have to ask," Thomas said, and Victor closed his eyes in embarrassment.

"Don't," Victor said.

"Excuse me, miss," Thomas asked. "Are you a gymnast or something?"

"There's no something about it," she said. "I was first alternate on the 1980 Olympic team."

"Really?" Thomas asked.

"Really."

"I mean, you used to be a world-class athlete?" Thomas asked.

"My husband thinks I still am."

Thomas Builds-the-Fire smiled. She was a mental gymnast too. She pulled her leg straight up against her body so that she could've kissed her kneecap.

"I wish I could do that," Thomas said.

Victor was ready to jump out of the plane. Thomas, that crazy Indian storyteller with ratty old braids and broken teeth, was flirting with a beautiful Olympic gymnast. Nobody back home on the reservation would ever believe it.

"Well," the gymnast said. "It's easy. Try it."

Thomas grabbed at his leg and tried to pull it up into the same position as the gymnast's. He couldn't even come close, which made Victor and the gymnast laugh.

"Hey," she asked. "You two are Indian, right?"

"Full-blood," Victor said.

"Not me," Thomas said. "I'm half magician on my mother's side and half clown on my father's."

They all laughed.

"What are your names?" she asked.

"Victor and Thomas."

"Mine is Cathy. Pleased to meet you all."

The three of them talked for the duration of the flight. Cathy the gymnast complained about the government, how they screwed the 1980 Olympic team by boycotting the games.

"Sounds like you all got a lot in common with Indians," Thomas said.

Nobody laughed.

After the plane landed in Phoenix and they had all found their way to the terminal, Cathy the gymnast smiled and waved goodbye.

"She was really nice," Thomas said.

"Yeah, but everybody talks to everybody on airplanes," Victor said.

"You always used to tell me I think too much," Thomas said. "Now it sounds like you do."

"Maybe I caught it from you."

"Yeah."

Thomas and Victor rode in a taxi to the trailer where Victor's father had died.

"Listen," Victor said as they stopped in front of the trailer. "I never told you I was sorry for beating you up that time."

"Oh, it was nothing. We were just kids and you were drunk."

"Yeah, but I'm still sorry."

"That's all right."

Victor paid for the taxi, and the two of them stood in the hot Phoenix summer. They could smell the trailer.

"This ain't going to be nice," Victor said. "You don't have to go in."

"You're going to need help."

Victor walked to the front door and opened it. The stink rolled out and made them both gag. Victor's father had lain in that trailer for a week in hundred-degree temperatures before anyone had found him. And the only reason anyone found him was the smell. They needed dental records to identify him. That's exactly what the coroner said. They needed dental records.

"Oh, man," Victor said. "I don't know if I can do this."

"Well, then don't."

"But there might be something valuable in there."

"I thought his money was in the bank."

"It is. I was talking about pictures and letters and stuff like that."

"Oh," Thomas said as he held his breath and followed Victor into the trailer.

When Victor was twelve, he stepped into an underground wasps' nest. His foot was caught in the hole and no matter how hard he struggled, Victor couldn't pull free. He might have died there, stung a thousand times, if Thomas Builds-the-Fire had not come by.

"Run," Thomas yelled and pulled Victor's foot from the hole. They ran then, hard as they ever had, faster than Billy Mills, faster than Jim Thorpe, faster than the wasps could fly.

Victor and Thomas ran until they couldn't breathe, ran until it was cold and dark outside, ran until they were lost and it took hours to find their way home. All the way back, Victor counted his stings.

"Seven," Victor said. "My lucky number."

•   •   •

Victor didn't find much to keep in the trailer. Only a photo album and a stereo. Everything else had that smell stuck in it or was useless anyway. "I guess this is all," Victor said. "It ain't much."

"Better than nothing," Thomas said.

"Yeah, and I do have the pickup."

"Yeah," Thomas said. "It's in good shape."

"Dad was good about that stuff."

"Yeah, I remember your dad."

"Really?" Victor asked. "What do you remember?"

Thomas Builds-the-Fire closed his eyes and told this story: "I remember when I had this dream that told me to go to Spokane, to stand by the falls in the middle of the city and wait for a sign. I knew I had to go there but I didn't have a car. Didn't have a license. I was only thirteen. So I walked all the way, took me all day, and I finally made it to the falls. I stood there for an hour waiting. Then your dad came walking up. 'What the hell are you doing here?' he asked me. I said, 'Waiting for a vision.' Then your father said, 'All you're going to get here is mugged.' So he drove me over to Denny's, bought me dinner, and then drove me home to the reservation. For a long time, I was mad because I thought my dreams had lied to me. But they hadn't. Your dad was my vision. *Take care of each other* is what my dreams were saying. *Take care of each other.*"

Victor was quiet for a long time. He searched his mind for memories of his father, found the good ones, found a few bad ones, added it all up, and smiled.

"My father never told me about finding you in Spokane," Victor said.

"He said he wouldn't tell anybody. Didn't want me to get in trouble. But he said I had to watch out for you as part of the deal."

"Really?"

"Really. Your father said you would need the help. He was right."

"That's why you came down here with me, isn't it?" Victor asked.

"I came because of your father."

Victor and Thomas climbed into the pickup, drove over to the bank, and claimed three hundred dollars in the savings account.

T homas Builds-the-Fire could fly.

Once, he jumped off the roof of the tribal school and flapped his arms like a crazy eagle. And he flew. For a second he hovered, suspended above all the other Indian boys, who were too smart or too scared to jump too.

"He's flying," Junior yelled, and Seymour was busy looking for the trick wires or mirrors. But it was real. As real as the dirt when Thomas lost altitude and crashed to the ground.

He broke his arm in two places.

"He broke his wing, he broke his wing, he broke his wing," all the Indian boys chanted as they ran off, flapping their wings, wishing they could fly too. They hated Thomas for his courage, his brief moment as a bird. Everybody has dreams about flying. Thomas flew.

One of his dreams came true for just a second, just enough to make it real.

V ictor's father, his ashes, fit in one wooden box with enough left over to fill a cardboard box.

"He always was a big man," Thomas said.

Victor carried part of his father out to the pickup, and Thomas carried the rest. They set him down carefully behind the seats, put a cowboy hat on the wooden box and a Dodgers cap on the cardboard box. That was the way it was supposed to be.

"Ready to head back home?" Victor asked.

"It's going to be a long drive."

"Yeah, take a couple days, maybe."

"We can take turns," Thomas said.

"O.K.," Victor said, but they didn't take turns. Victor drove for sixteen hours straight north, made it halfway up Nevada toward home before he finally pulled over.

"Hey, Thomas," Victor said. "You got to drive for a while."

"O.K."

Thomas Builds-the-Fire slid behind the wheel and started off down the road. All through Nevada, Thomas and Victor had been amazed at the lack of animal life, at the absence of water, of movement.

"Where is everything?" Victor had asked more than once.

Now, when Thomas was finally driving, they saw the first animal, maybe the only animal in Nevada. It was a long-eared jackrabbit.

"Look," Victor yelled. "It's alive."

Thomas and Victor were busy congratulating themselves on their discovery when the jackrabbit darted out into the road and under the wheels of the pickup.

"Stop the goddamn car," Victor yelled, and Thomas did stop and backed the pickup to the dead jackrabbit.

"Oh, man, he's dead," Victor said as he looked at the squashed animal.

"Really dead."

"The only thing alive in this whole state and we just killed it."

"I don't know," Thomas said. "I think it was suicide."

Victor looked around the desert, sniffed the air, felt the emptiness and loneliness, and nodded his head.

"Yeah," Victor said. "It had to be suicide."

"I can't believe this," Thomas said. "You drive for a thousand miles and there ain't even any bugs smashed on the windshield. I drive for ten seconds and kill the only living thing in Nevada."

"Yeah," Victor said. "Maybe I should drive."

"Maybe you should."

Thomas Builds-the-Fire walked through the corridors of the tribal school by himself. Noone wanted to be anywhere near him because of all those stories. Story after story.

Thomas closed his eyes and this story came to him: "We are all given one thing by which our lives are measured, one determination. Mine are the stories that can change or not change the world. It doesn't matter which, as long as I continue to tell the stories. My father, he died on Okinawa in World War II, died fighting for this country, which had tried to kill him for years. My mother, she died giving birth to me, died while I was still inside her: She pushed me out into the world with her last breath. I have no brothers or sisters. I have only my stories, which came to me before I even had the words to speak. I learned a thousand stories before I took my first thousand steps. They are all I have. It's all I can do."

Thomas Builds-the-Fire told his stories to all those who would stop and listen. He kept telling them long after people had stopped listening.

Victor and Thomas made it back to the reservation just as the sun was rising. It was the beginning of a new day on earth, but the same old shit on the reservation.

"Good morning," Thomas said.

"Good morning."

The tribe was waking up, ready for work, eating breakfast, reading the newspaper, just like everybody else does. Willene LeBret was out in her garden, wearing a bathrobe. She waved when Thomas and Victor drove by.

"Crazy Indians made it," she said to herself and went back to her roses.

Victor stopped the pickup in front of Thomas Builds-the-Fire's HUD house. They both yawned, stretched a little, shook dust from their bodies.

"I'm tired," Victor said.

"Of everything," Thomas added.

They both searched for words to end the journey. Victor needed to thank Thomas for his help and for the money, and to make the promise to pay it all back.

"Don't worry about the money," Thomas said. "It don't make any difference anyhow."

"Probably not, enit?"

"Nope."

Victor knew that Thomas would remain the crazy storyteller who talked to dogs and cars, who listened to the wind and pine trees. Victor knew that he couldn't really be friends with Thomas, even after all that had happened. It was cruel but it was real. As real as the ash, as Victor's father, sitting behind the seats.

"I know how it is," Thomas said. "I know you ain't going to treat me any better than you did before. I know your friends would give you too much shit about it."

Victor was ashamed of himself. Whatever happened to the tribal ties, the sense of community? The only real thing he shared with anybody was a bottle and broken dreams. He owed Thomas something, anything.

"Listen," Victor said and handed Thomas the cardboard box that contained half of his father. "I want you to have this."

Thomas took the ashes and smiled, closed his eyes, and told this story: "I'm going to travel to Spokane Falls one last time and toss these ashes into the water. And your father will rise like a salmon, leap over the bridge, over me, and find his way home. It will be beautiful. His teeth will shine like silver, like a rainbow. He will rise, Victor, he will rise."

Victor smiled.

"I was planning on doing the same thing with my half," Victor said. "But I didn't imagine my father looking anything like a salmon. I thought it'd be like cleaning the attic or something. Like letting things go after they've stopped having any use."

"Nothing stops, cousin," Thomas said. "Nothing stops."

Thomas Builds-the-Fire got out of the pickup and walked up his driveway. Victor started the pickup and began the drive home.

"Wait," Thomas yelled suddenly from his porch. "I just got to ask one favor."

Victor stopped the pickup, leaned out the window, and shouted back.

"What do you want?" he asked.

"Just one time when I'm telling a story somewhere, why don't you stop and listen?" Thomas asked.

"Just once?"

"Just once."

Victor waved his arms to let Thomas know that the deal was good. It was a fair trade. That's all Thomas had ever wanted from his whole life. So Victor drove his father's pickup toward home while Thomas went into his house, closed the door behind him, and heard a new story come to him in the silence afterward.

from Nichomachean Ethics (350 B.C.E.)

Aristotle

Book VIII

1

After what we have said, a discussion of friendship would naturally follow, since it is a virtue or implies virtue, and is besides most necessary
with a view to living. For without friends no one would choose to live,
though he had all other goods; even rich men and those in possession of
office and of dominating power are thought to need friends most of all;
for what is the use of such prosperity without the opportunity of beneficence, which is exercised chiefly and in its most laudable form towards
friends? Or how can prosperity be guarded and preserved without
friends? The greater it is, the more exposed is it to risk. And in poverty
and in other misfortunes men think friends are the only refuge. It helps
the young, too, to keep from error; it aids older people by ministering to
their needs and supplementing the activities that are failing from weakness; those in the prime of life it stimulates to noble actions—'two going
together'—for with friends men are more able both to think and to act.
Again, parent seems by nature to feel it for offspring and offspring for
parent, not only among men but among birds and among most animals;
it is felt mutually by members of the same race, and especially by men,
whence we praise lovers of their fellowmen. We may even in our travels
how near and dear every man is to every other. Friendship seems too to
hold states together, and lawgivers to care more for it than for justice; for
unanimity seems to be something like friendship, and this they aim at
most of all, and expel faction as their worst enemy; and when men are
friends they have no need of justice, while when they are just they need
friendship as well, and the truest form of justice is thought to be a
friendly quality.

But it is not only necessary but also noble; for we praise those who love
their friends, and it is thought to be a fine thing to have many friends; and
again we think it is the same people that are good men and are friends.

Not a few things about friendship are matters of debate. Some define it as
a kind of likeness and say like people are friends, whence come the sayings 'like to like', 'birds of a feather flock together', and so on; others on

the contrary say 'two of a trade never agree'. On this very question they inquire for deeper and more physical causes, Euripides saying that 'parched earth loves the rain, and stately heaven when filled with rain loves to fall to earth', and Heraclitus that 'it is what opposes that helps' and 'from different tones comes the fairest tune' and 'all things are produced through strife'; while Empedocles, as well as others, expresses the opposite view that like aims at like. The physical problems we may leave alone (for they do not belong to the present inquiry); let us examine those which are human and involve character and feeling, e.g. whether friendship can arise between any two people or people cannot be friends if they are wicked, and whether there is one species of friendship or more than one. Those who think there is only one because it admits of degrees have relied on an inadequate indication; for even things different in species admit of degree. We have discussed this matter previously.

2

The kinds of friendship may perhaps be cleared up if we first come to know the object of love. For not everything seems to be loved but only the lovable, and this is good, pleasant, or useful; but it would seem to be that by which some good or pleasure is produced that is useful, so that it is the good and the useful that are lovable as ends. Do men love, then, the good, or what is good for them? These sometimes clash. So too with regard to the pleasant. Now it is thought that each loves what is good for himself, and that the good is without qualification lovable, and what is good for each man is lovable for him; but each man loves not what is good for him but what seems good. This however will make no difference; we shall just have to say that this is 'that which seems lovable'. Now there are three grounds on which people love; of the love of lifeless objects we do not use the word 'friendship'; for it is not mutual love, nor is there a wishing of good to the other (for it would surely be ridiculous to wish wine well; if one wishes anything for it, it is that it may keep, so that one may have it oneself); but to a friend we say we ought to wish what is good for his sake. But to those who thus wish good we ascribe only goodwill, if the wish is not reciprocated; goodwill when it is reciprocal being friendship. Or must we add 'when it is recognized'? For many people have goodwill to those whom they have not seen but judge to be good or useful; and one of these might return this feeling. These people seem to bear goodwill to each other; but how could one call them friends when they do not know their mutual feelings? To be friends, then, they must be mutually recognized as bearing goodwill and wishing well to each other for one of the aforesaid reasons.

3

Now these reasons differ from each other in kind; so, therefore, do the corresponding forms of love and friendship. There are therefore three kinds of friendship, equal in number to the things that are lovable; for with respect to each there is a mutual and recognized love, and those who love each other wish well to each other in that respect in which they love one another. Now those who love each other for their utility do not love each other for themselves but in virtue of some good which they get from each other. So too with those who love for the sake of pleasure; it is not for their character that men love ready-witted people, but because they find them pleasant. Therefore those who love for the sake of utility love for the sake of what is good for themselves, and those who love for the sake of pleasure do so for the sake of what is pleasant to themselves, and not in so far as the other is the person loved but in so far as he is useful or pleasant. And thus these friendships are only incidental; for it is not as being the man he is that the loved person is loved, but as providing some good or pleasure. Such friendships, then, are easily dissolved, if the parties do not remain like themselves; for if the one party is no longer pleasant or useful the other ceases to love him.

Now the useful is not permanent but is always changing. Thus when the motive of the friendship is done away, the friendship is dissolved, inasmuch as it existed only for the ends in question. This kind of friendship seems to exist chiefly between old people (for at that age people pursue not the pleasant but the useful) and, of those who are in their prime or young, between those who pursue utility. And such people do not live much with each other either; for sometimes they do not even find each other pleasant; therefore they do not need such companionship unless they are useful to each other; for they are pleasant to each other only in so far as they rouse in each other hopes of something good to come. Among such friendships people also class the friendship of a host and guest. On the other hand the friendship of young people seems to aim at pleasure; for they live under the guidance of emotion, and pursue above all what is pleasant to themselves and what is immediately before them; but with increasing age their pleasures become different. This is why they quickly become friends and quickly cease to be so; their friendship changes with the object that is found pleasant, and such pleasure alters quickly. Young people are amorous too; for the greater part of the friendship of love depends on emotion and aims at pleasure; this is why they fall in love and quickly fall out of love, changing often within a single day. But these people do wish to spend their days and lives together; for it is thus that they attain the purpose of their friendship.

Perfect friendship is the friendship of men who are good, and alike in virtue; for these wish well alike to each other qua good, and they are good themselves. Now those who wish well to their friends for their sake are most truly friends; for they do this by reason of own nature and not incidentally; therefore their friendship lasts as long as they are good—and goodness is an enduring thing. And each is good without qualification and to his friend, for the good are both good without qualification and useful to each other. So too they are pleasant; for the good are pleasant both without qualification and to each other, since to each his own activities and others like them are pleasurable, and the actions of the good are the same or like. And such a friendship is as might be expected permanent, since there meet in it all the qualities that friends should have. For all friendship is for the sake of good or of pleasure—good or pleasure either in the abstract or such as will be enjoyed by him who has the friendly feeling—and is based on a certain resemblance; and to a friendship of good men all the qualities we have named belong in virtue of the nature of the friends themselves; for in the case of this kind of friendship the other qualities also are alike in both friends, and that which is good without qualification is also without qualification pleasant, and these are the most lovable qualities. Love and friendship therefore are found most and in their best form between such men.

But it is natural that such friendships should be infrequent; for such men are rare. Further, such friendship requires time and familiarity; as the proverb says, men cannot know each other till they have 'eaten salt together'; nor can they admit each other to friendship or be friends till each has been found lovable and been trusted by each. Those who quickly show the marks of friendship to each other wish to be friends, but are not friends unless they both are lovable and know the fact; for a wish for friendship may arise quickly, but friendship does not.

4

This kind of friendship, then, is perfect both in respect of duration and in all other respects, and in it each gets from each in all respects the same as, or something like what, he gives; which is what ought to happen between friends. Friendship for the sake of pleasure bears a resemblance to this kind; for good people too are pleasant to each other. So too does friendship for the sake of utility; for the good are also useful to each other.

Among men of these inferior sorts too, friendships are most permanent when the friends get the same thing from each other (e.g. pleasure), and not only that but also from the same source, as happens between ready-witted people, not as happens between lover and beloved. For these do not take pleasure in the same things, but the one in seeing the beloved and the other in receiving attentions from his lover; and when the bloom of youth is passing the friendship sometimes passes too (for the one finds no pleasure in the sight of the other, and the other gets no attentions from the first); but many lovers on the other hand are constant, if familiarity has led them to love each other's characters, these being alike. But those who exchange not pleasure but utility in their amour are both less truly friends and less constant. Those who are friends for the sake of utility part when the advantage is at an end; for they were lovers not of each other but of profit.

For the sake of pleasure or utility, then, even bad men may be friends of each other, or good men of bad, or one who is neither good nor bad may be a friend to any sort of person, but for their own sake clearly only good men can be friends; for bad men do not delight in each other unless some advantage come of the relation.

The friendship of the good too and this alone is proof against slander; for it is not easy to trust any one talk about a man who has long been tested by oneself; and it is among good men that trust and the feeling that 'he would never wrong me' and all the other things that are demanded in true friendship are found. In the other kinds of friendship, however, there is nothing to prevent these evils arising. For men apply the name of friends even to those whose motive is utility, in which sense states are said to be friendly (for the alliances of states seem to aim at advantage), and to those who love each other for the sake of pleasure, in which sense children are called friends. Therefore we too ought perhaps to call such people friends, and say that there are several kinds of friendship—firstly and in the proper sense that of good men qua good, and by analogy the other kinds; for it is in virtue of something good and something akin to what is found in true friendship that they are friends, since even the pleasant is good for the lovers of pleasure. But these two kinds of friendship are not often united, nor do the same people become friends for the sake of utility and of pleasure; for things that are only incidentally connected are not often coupled together.

Friendship being divided into these kinds, bad men will be friends for the sake of pleasure or of utility, being in this respect like each other, but good men will be friends for their own sake, i.e. in virtue of their goodness. These, then, are friends without qualification; the others are friends incidentally and through a resemblance to these.

5

As in regard to the virtues some men are called good in respect of a state of character, others in respect of an activity, so too in the case of friendship; for those who live together delight in each other and confer benefits on each other, but those who are asleep or locally separated are not performing, but are disposed to perform, the activities of friendship; distance does not break off the friendship absolutely, but only the activity of it. But if the absence is lasting, it seems actually to make men forget their friendship; hence the saying 'out of sight, out of mind'. Neither old people nor sour people seem to make friends easily; for there is little that is pleasant in them, and no one can spend his days with one whose company is painful, or not pleasant, since nature seems above all to avoid the painful and to aim at the pleasant. Those, however, who approve of each other but do not live together seem to be well-disposed rather than actual friends. For there is nothing so characteristic of friends as living together (since while people who are in need desire benefits, even those who are supremely happy desire to spend their days together; for solitude suits such people least of all); but people cannot live together if they are not pleasant and do not enjoy the same things, as friends who are companions seem to do.

The truest friendship, then, is that of the good, as we have frequently said; for that which is without qualification good or pleasant seems to be lovable and desirable, and for each person that which is good or pleasant to him; and the good man is lovable and desirable to the good man for both these reasons. Now it looks as if love were a feeling, friendship a state of character; for love may be felt just as much towards lifeless things, but mutual love involves choice and choice springs from a state of character; and men wish well to those whom they love, for their sake, not as a result of feeling but as a result of a state of character. And in loving a friend men love what is good for themselves; for the good man in becoming a friend becomes a good to his friend. Each, then, both loves what is good for himself, and makes an equal return in goodwill and in pleasantness; for friendship is said to be equality, and both of these are found most in the friendship of the good.

6

Between sour and elderly people friendship arises less readily, inasmuch as they are less good-tempered and enjoy companionship less; for these are thought to be the greatest marks of friendship productive of it. This is why, while men become friends quickly, old men do not; it is because men do not become friends with those in whom they do not delight; and similarly sour people do not quickly make friends either. But such men may bear goodwill to each other; for they wish one another well and aid one another in need; but they are hardly friends because they do not spend their days together nor delight in each other, and these are thought the greatest marks of friendship.

One cannot be a friend to many people in the sense of having friendship of the perfect type with them, just as one cannot be in love with many people at once (for love is a sort of excess of feeling, and it is the nature of such only to be felt towards one person); and it is not easy for many people at the same time to please the same person very greatly, or perhaps even to be good in his eyes. One must, too, acquire some experience of the other person and become familiar with him, and that is very hard. But with a view to utility or pleasure it is possible that many people should please one; for many people are useful or pleasant, and these services take little time.

Of these two kinds that which is for the sake of pleasure is the more like friendship, when both parties get the same things from each other and delight in each other or in the things, as in the friendships of the young; for generosity is more found in such friendships.

Friendship based on utility is for the commercially minded. People who are supremely happy, too, have no need of useful friends, but do need pleasant friends; for they wish to live with some one and, though they can endure for a short time what is painful, no one could put up with it continuously, nor even with the Good itself if it were painful to him; this is why they look out for friends who are pleasant. Perhaps they should look out for friends who, being pleasant, are also good, and good for them too; for so they will have all the characteristics that friends should have.

People in positions of authority seem to have friends who fall into distinct classes; some people are useful to them and others are pleasant, but the same people are rarely both; for they seek neither those whose pleasantness is accompanied by virtue nor those whose utility is with a view to noble objects, but in their desire for pleasure they seek for ready-witted people, and their other friends they choose as being clever at doing what they are told, and these characteristics are rarely combined. Now we have said that the good man is at the same time pleasant and useful; but such a man does not become the friend of one who surpasses him in station, unless he is surpassed also in virtue; if this is not so, he does not establish equality by being proportionally exceeded in both respects. But people who surpass him in both respects are not so easy to find.

However that may be, the aforesaid friendships involve equality; for the friends get the same things from one another and wish the same things for one another, or exchange one thing for another, e.g. pleasure for utility; we have said, however, that they are both less truly friendships and less permanent.

But it is from their likeness and their unlikeness to the same thing that they are thought both to be and not to be friendships. It is by their likeness to the friendship of virtue that they seem to be friendships (for one of them involves pleasure and the other utility, and these characteristics belong to the friendship of virtue as well); while it is because the friendship of virtue is proof against slander and permanent, while these quickly change (besides differing from the former in many other respects), that they appear not to be friendships; i.e. it is because of their unlikeness to the friendship of virtue.

7

But there is another kind of friendship, viz. that which involves an inequality between the parties, e.g. that of father to son and in general of elder to younger, that of man to wife and in general that of ruler to subject. And these friendships differ also from each other; for it is not the same that exists between parents and children and between rulers and subjects, nor is even that of father to son the same as that of son to father, nor that of husband to wife the same as that of wife to husband. For the virtue and the function of each of these is different, and so are the reasons for which they love; the love and the friendship are therefore different also. Each party, then, neither gets the same from the other, nor ought to seek it; but when children render to parents what they ought to render to those who brought them into the world, and parents render what they should to their children, the friendship of such persons will be abiding and excellent. In all friendships implying inequality the love also should be proportional, i.e. the better should be more loved than he loves, and so should the more useful, and similarly in each of the other cases; for when the love is in proportion to the merit of the parties, then in a sense arises equality, which is certainly held to be characteristic of friendship.

But equality does not seem to take the same form in acts of justice and in friendship; for in acts of justice what is equal in the primary sense is that which is in proportion to merit, while quantitative equality is secondary, but in friendship quantitative equality is primary and proportion to merit secondary. This becomes clear if there is a great interval in respect of virtue or vice or wealth or anything else between the parties; for then they are no longer friends, and do not even expect to be so. And this is most manifest in the case of the gods; for they surpass us most decisively in all good things. But it is clear also in the case of kings; for with them, too, men who are much their inferiors do not expect to be friends; nor do men of no account expect to be friends with the best or wisest men. In such cases it is not possible to define exactly up to what point friends can remain friends; for much can be taken away and friendship remain, but when one party is removed to a great distance, as God is, the possibility of friendship ceases. This is in fact the origin of the question whether friends really wish for their friends the greatest goods, e.g. that of being gods; since in that case their friends will no longer be friends to them, and therefore will not be good things for them (for friends are good things). The answer is that if we were right in saying that friend wishes good to friend for his sake, his friend must remain the sort of being he is, whatever that may be; therefore it is for him only so long as he remains a man that he will wish the greatest goods. But perhaps not all the greatest goods; for it is for himself most of all that each man wishes what is good.

8

Most people seem, owing to ambition, to wish to be loved rather than to love; which is why most men love flattery; for the flatterer is a friend in an inferior position, or pretends to be such and to love more than he is loved; and being loved seems to be akin to being honoured, and this is what most people aim at. But it seems to be not for its own sake that people choose honour, but incidentally. For most people enjoy being honoured by those in positions of authority because of their hopes (for they think that if they want anything they will get it from them; and therefore they delight in honour as a token of favour to come); while those who desire honour from good men, and men who know, are aiming at confirming their own opinion of themselves; they delight in honour, therefore, because they believe in their own goodness on the strength of the judgement of those who speak about them. In being loved, on the other hand, people delight for its own sake; whence it would seem to be better than being honoured, and friendship to be desirable in itself. But it seems to lie in loving rather than in being loved, as is indicated by the delight mothers take in loving; for some mothers hand over their children to be brought up, and so long as they know their fate they love them and do not seek to be loved in return (if they cannot have both), but seem to be satisfied if they see them prospering; and they themselves love their children even if these owing to their ignorance give them nothing of a mother's due. Now since friendship depends more on loving, and it is those who love their friends that are praised, loving seems to be the characteristic virtue of friends, so that it is only those in whom this is found in due measure that are lasting friends, and only their friendship that endures.

It is in this way more than any other that even unequals can be friends; they can be equalized. Now equality and likeness are friendship, and especially the likeness of those who are like in virtue; for being steadfast in themselves they hold fast to each other, and neither ask nor give base services, but (one may say) even prevent them; for it is characteristic of good men neither to go wrong themselves nor to let their friends do so. But wicked men have no steadfastness (for they do not remain even like to themselves), but become friends for a short time because they delight in each other's wickedness. Friends who are useful or pleasant last longer; i.e. as long as they provide each other with enjoyments or advantages. Friendship for utility's sake seems to be that which most easily exists between contraries, e.g. between poor and rich, between ignorant and learned; for what a man actually lacks he aims at, and one gives something else in return. But under this head, too, might bring lover and beloved, beautiful and ugly. This is why lovers sometimes seem ridiculous, when they demand to be loved as they love; if they are equally lovable their claim can perhaps be justified, but when they have nothing lovable about them it is ridiculous. Perhaps, however, contrary does not even aim at contrary by its own nature, but only incidentally, the desire being for what is intermediate; for that is what is good, e.g. it is good for the dry not to become wet but to come to the intermediate state, and similarly with the hot and in all other cases. These subjects we may dismiss; for they are indeed somewhat foreign to our inquiry.

9

Friendship and justice seem, as we have said at the outset of our discussion, to be concerned with the same objects and exhibited between the same persons. For in every community there is thought to be some form of justice, and friendship too; at least men address as friends their fellow-voyagers and fellowsoldiers, and so too those associated with them in any other kind of community. And the extent of their association is the extent of their friendship, as it is the extent to which justice exists between them. And the proverb 'what friends have is common property' expresses the truth; for friendship depends on community. Now brothers and comrades have all things in common, but the others to whom we have referred have definite things in common—some more things, others fewer; for of friendships, too, some are more and others less truly friendships. And the claims of justice differ too; the duties of parents to children, and those of brothers to each other are not the same, nor those of comrades and those of fellow-citizens, and so, too, with the other kinds of friendship. There is a difference, therefore, also between the acts that are unjust towards each of these classes of associates, and the injustice increases by being exhibited towards those who are friends in a fuller sense; e.g. it is a more terrible thing to defraud a comrade than a fellow-citizen, more terrible not to help a brother than a stranger, and more terrible to wound a father than any one else. And the demands of justice also seem to increase with the intensity of the friendship, which implies that friendship and justice exist between the same persons and have an equal extension.

Now all forms of community are like parts of the political community; for men journey together with a view to some particular advantage, and to provide something that they need for the purposes of life; and it is for the sake of advantage that the political community too seems both to have come together originally and to endure, for this is what legislators aim at, and they call just that which is to the common advantage. Now the other communities aim at advantage bit by bit, e.g. sailors at what is advantageous on a voyage with a view to making money or something of the kind, fellow-soldiers at what is advantageous in war, whether it is wealth or victory or the taking of a city that they seek, and members of tribes and demes act similarly (Some communities seem to arise for the sake or pleasure, viz. religious guilds and social clubs; for these exist respectively for the sake of offering sacrifice and of companionship. But all these seem to fall under the political community; for it aims not at present advantage but at what is advantageous for life as a whole), offering sacrifices and arranging gatherings for the purpose, and assigning honours to the gods, and providing pleasant relaxations for themselves. For the ancient sacrifices and gatherings seem to take place after the harvest as a sort of first-fruits, because it was at these seasons that people had most leisure. All the communities, then, seem to be parts of the political community; and the particular kinds friendship will correspond to the particular kinds of community.

10

There are three kinds of constitution, and an equal number of deviation-forms—perversions, as it were, of them. The constitutions are monarchy, aristocracy, and thirdly that which is based on a property qualification, which it seems appropriate to call timocratic, though most people are wont to call it polity. The best of these is monarchy, the worst timocracy.

The deviation from monarchy is tyrany; for both are forms of one-man rule, but there is the greatest difference between them; the tyrant looks to his own advantage, the king to that of his subjects. For a man is not a king unless he is sufficient to himself and excels his subjects in all good things; and such a man needs nothing further; therefore he will not look to his own interests but to those of his subjects; for a king who is not like that would be a mere titular king. Now tyranny is the very contrary of this; the tyrant pursues his own good. And it is clearer in the case of tyranny that it is the worst deviation-form; but it is the contrary of the best that is worst. Monarchy passes over into tyranny; for tyranny is the evil form of one-man rule and the bad king becomes a tyrant. Aristocracy passes over into oligarchy by the badness of the rulers, who distribute contrary to equity what belongs to the city—all or most of the good things to themselves, and office always to the same people, paying most regard to wealth; thus the rulers are few and are bad men instead of the most worthy. Timocracy passes over into democracy; for these are coterminous, since it is the ideal even of timocracy to be the rule of the majority, and all who have the property qualification count as equal. Democracy is the least bad of the deviations; for in its case the form of constitution is but a slight deviation. These then are the changes to which constitutions are most subject; for these are the smallest and easiest transitions.

One may find resemblances to the constitutions and, as it were, patterns of them even in households. For the association of a father with his sons bears the form of monarchy, since the father cares for his children; and this is why Homer calls Zeus 'father'; it is the ideal of monarchy to be paternal rule. But among the Persians the rule of the father is tyrannical; they use their sons as slaves. Tyrannical too is the rule of a master over slaves; for it is the advantage of the master that is brought about in it. Now this seems to be a correct form of government, but the Persian type is perverted; for the modes of rule appropriate to different relations are diverse. The association of man and wife seems to be aristocratic; for the man rules in accordance with his worth, and in those matters in which a man should rule, but the matters that befit a woman he hands over to her. If the man rules in everything the relation passes over into oligarchy; for in doing so he is not acting in accordance with their respective worth, and not ruling in virtue of his superiority. Sometimes, however, women rule, because they are heiresses; so their rule is not in virtue of excellence but due to wealth and power, as in oligarchies. The association of brothers is like timocracy; for they are equal, except in so far as they differ in age; hence if they differ much in age, the friendship is no longer of the fraternal type.

Democracy is found chiefly in masterless dwellings (for here every one is on an equality), and in those in which the ruler is weak and every one has licence to do as he pleases.

11

Each of the constitutions may be seen to involve friendship just in so far as it involves justice. The friendship between a king and his subjects depends on an excess of benefits conferred; for he confers benefits on his subjects if being a good man he cares for them with a view to their well-being, as a shepherd does for his sheep (whence Homer called Agamemnon 'shepherd of the peoples'). Such too is the friendship of a father, though this exceeds the other in the greatness of the benefits conferred; for he is responsible for the existence of his children, which is thought the greatest good, and for their nurture and upbringing.

These things are ascribed to ancestors as well. Further, by nature a father tends to rule over his sons, ancestors over descendants, a king over his subjects. These friendships imply superiority of one party over the other, which is why ancestors are honoured. The justice therefore that exists between persons so related is not the same on both sides but is in every case proportioned to merit; for that is true of the friendship as well. The friendship of man and wife, again, is the same that is found in an aristocracy; for it is in accordance with virtue the better gets more of what is good, and each gets what befits him; and so, too, with the justice in these relations. The friendship of brothers is like that of comrades; for they are equal and of like age, and such persons are for the most part like in their feelings and their character. Like this, too, is the friendship appropriate to timocratic government; for in such a constitution the ideal is for the citizens to be equal and fair; therefore rule is taken in turn, and on equal terms; and the friendship appropriate here will correspond.

But in the deviation-forms, as justice hardly exists, so too does friendship. It exists least in the worst form; in tyranny there is little or no friendship. For where there is nothing common to ruler and ruled, there is not friendship either, since there is not justice; e.g. between craftsman and tool, soul and body, master and slave; the latter in each case is benefited by that which uses it, but there is no friendship nor justice towards lifeless things. But neither is there friendship towards a horse or an ox, not to a slave qua slave. For there is nothing common to the two parties; the slave is a living tool and the tool a lifeless slave. Qua slave then, one cannot be friends with him. But qua man one can; for there seems to be some justice between any man and any other who can share in a system of law or be a party to an agreement; therefore there can also be friendship with him in so far as he is a man. Therefore while in tyrannies friendship and justice hardly exist, in democracies they exist more fully; for where the citizens are equal they have much in common.

12

Every form of friendship, then, involves association, as has been said. One might, however, mark off from the rest both the friendship of kindred and that of comrades. Those of fellow-citizens, fellow-tribesmen, fellow-voyagers, and the like are more like mere friendships of association; for they seem to rest on a sort of compact. With them we might class the friendship of host and guest. The friendship of kinsmen itself, while it seems to be of many kinds, appears to depend in every case on parental friendship; for parents love their children as being a part of themselves, and children their parents as being something originating from them. Now (1) parents know their offspring better than their children know that they are their children, and (2) the originator feels his offspring to be his own more than the offspring do their begetter; for the product belongs to the producer (e.g. a tooth or hair or anything else to him whose it is), but the producer does not belong to the product, or belongs in a less degree. And (3) the length of time produces the same result; parents love their children as soon as these are born, but children love their parents only after time has elapsed and they have acquired understanding or the power of discrimination by the senses. From these considerations it is also plain why mothers love more than fathers do. Parents, then, love their children as themselves (for their issue are by virtue of their separate existence a sort of other selves), while children love their parents as being born of them, and brothers love each other as being born of the same parents; for their identity with them makes them identical with each other (which is the reason why people talk of 'the same blood', 'the same stock', and so on). They are, therefore, in a sense the same thing, though in separate individuals. Two things that contribute greatly to friendship are a common upbringing and similarity of age; for 'two of an age take to each other', and people brought up together tend to be comrades; whence the friendship of brothers is akin to that of comrades. And cousins and other kinsmen are bound up together by derivation from brothers, viz. by being derived from the same parents. They come to be closer together or farther apart by virtue of the nearness or distance of the original ancestor.

The friendship of children to parents, and of men to gods, is a relation to them as to something good and superior; for they have conferred the greatest benefits, since they are the causes of their being and of their nourishment, and of their education from their birth; and this kind of friendship possesses pleasantness and utility also, more than that of strangers, inasmuch as their life is lived more in common. The friendship of brothers has the characteristics found in that of comrades (and especially when these are good), and in general between people who are like each other, inasmuch as they belong more to each other and start with a love for each other from their very birth, and inasmuch as those born of the same parents and brought up together and similarly educated are more akin in character; and the test of time has been applied most fully and convincingly in their case.

Between other kinsmen friendly relations are found in due proportion. Between man and wife friendship seems to exist by nature; for man is naturally inclined to form couples—even more than to form cities, inasmuch as the household is earlier and more necessary than the city, and reproduction is more common to man with the animals. With the other animals the union extends only to this point, but human beings live together not only for the sake of reproduction but also for the various purposes of life; for from the start the functions are divided, and those of man and woman are different; so they help each other by throwing their peculiar gifts into the common stock. It is for these reasons that both utility and pleasure seem to be found in this kind of friendship. But this friendship may be based also on virtue, if the parties are good; for each has its own virtue and they will delight in the fact. And children seem to be a bond of union (which is the reason why childless people part more easily); for children are a good common to both and what is common holds them together.

How man and wife and in general friend and friend ought mutually to behave seems to be the same question as how it is just for them to behave; for a man does not seem to have the same duties to a friend, a stranger, a comrade, and a schoolfellow.

13

There are three kinds of friendship, as we said at the outset of our inquiry, and in respect of each some are friends on an equality and others by virtue of a superiority (for not only can equally good men become friends but a better man can make friends with a worse, and similarly in friendships of pleasure or utility the friends may be equal or unequal in the benefits they confer). This being so, equals must effect the required equalization on a basis of equality in love and in all other respects, while unequals must render what is in proportion to their superiority or inferiority. Complaints and reproaches arise either only or chiefly in the friendship of utility, and this is only to be expected. For those who are friends on the ground of virtue are anxious to do well by each other (since that is a mark of virtue and of friendship), and between men who are emulating each other in this there cannot be complaints or quarrels; no one is offended by a man who loves him and does well by him—if he is a person of nice feeling he takes his revenge by doing well by the other. And the man who excels the other in the services he renders will not complain of his friend, since he gets what he aims at; for each man desires what is good. Nor do complaints arise much even in friendships of pleasure; for both get at the same time what they desire, if they enjoy spending their time together; and even a man who complained of another for not affording him pleasure would seem ridiculous, since it is in his power not to spend his days with him.

But the friendship of utility is full of complaints; for as they use each other for their own interests they always want to get the better of the bargain, and think they have got less than they should, and blame their partners because they do not get all they 'want and deserve'; and those who do well by others cannot help them as much as those whom they benefit want.

Now it seems that, as justice is of two kinds, one unwritten and the other legal, one kind of friendship of utility is moral and the other legal. And so complaints arise most of all when men do not dissolve the relation in the spirit of the same type of friendship in which they contracted it. The legal type is that which is on fixed terms; its purely commercial variety is on the basis of immediate payment, while the more liberal variety allows time but stipulates for a definite quid pro quo. In this variety the debt is clear and not ambiguous, but in the postponement it contains an element of friendliness; and so some states do not allow suits arising out of such agreements, but think men who have bargained on a basis of credit ought to accept the consequences. The moral type is not on fixed terms; it makes a gift, or does whatever it does, as to a friend; but one expects to receive as much or more, as having not given but lent; and if a man is worse off when the relation is dissolved than he was when it was contracted he will complain. This happens because all or most men, while they wish for what is noble, choose what is advantageous; now it is noble to do well by another without a view to repayment, but it is the receiving of benefits that is advantageous. Therefore if we can we should return the equivalent of what we have received (for we must not make a man our friend against his will; we must recognize that we were mistaken at the first and took a benefit from a person we should not have taken it from—since it was not from a friend, nor from one who did it just for the sake of acting so—and we must settle up just as if we had been benefited on fixed terms).

Indeed, one would agree to repay if one could (if one could not, even the giver would not have expected one to do so); therefore if it is possible we must repay. But at the outset we must consider the man by whom we are being benefited and on what terms he is acting, in order that we may accept the benefit on these terms, or else decline it.

It is disputable whether we ought to measure a service by its utility to the receiver and make the return with a view to that, or by the benevolence of the giver. For those who have received say they have received from their benefactors what meant little to the latter and what they might have got from others—minimizing the service; while the givers, on the contrary, say it was the biggest thing they had, and what could not have been got from others, and that it was given in times of danger or similar need. Now if the friendship is one that aims at utility, surely the advantage to the receiver is the measure. For it is he that asks for the service, and the other man helps him on the assumption that he will receive the equivalent; so the assistance has been precisely as great as the advantage to the receiver, and therefore he must return as much as he has received, or even more (for that would be nobler). In friendships based on virtue on the other hand, complaints do not arise, but the purpose of the doer is a sort of measure; for in purpose lies the essential element of virtue and character.

14

Differences arise also in friendships based on superiority; for each expects to get more out of them, but when this happens the friendship is dissolved. Not only does the better man think he ought to get more, since more should be assigned to a good man, but the more useful similarly expects this; they say a useless man should not get as much as they should, since it becomes an act of public service and not a friendship if the proceeds of the friendship do not answer to the worth of the benefits conferred. For they think that, as in a commercial partnership those who put more in get more out, so it should be in friendship. But the man who is in a state of need and inferiority makes the opposite claim; they think it is the part of a good friend to help those who are in need; what, they say, is the use of being the friend of a good man or a powerful man, if one is to get nothing out of it?

At all events it seems that each party is justified in his claim, and that each should get more out of the friendship than the other—not more of the same thing, however, but the superior more honour and the inferior more gain; for honour is the prize of virtue and of beneficence, while gain is the assistance required by inferiority.

It seems to be so in constitutional arrangements also; the man who contributes nothing good to the common stock is not honoured; for what belongs to the public is given to the man who benefits the public, and honour does belong to the public. It is not possible to get wealth from the common stock and at the same time honour. For no one puts up with the smaller share in all things; therefore to the man who loses in wealth they assign honour and to the man who is willing to be paid, wealth, since the proportion to merit equalizes the parties and preserves the friendship, as we have said. This then is also the way in which we should associate with unequals; the man who is benefited in respect of wealth or virtue must give honour in return, repaying what he can. For friendship asks a man to do what he can, not what is proportional to the merits of the case; since that cannot always be done, e.g. in honours paid to the gods or to parents; for no one could ever return to them the equivalent of what he gets, but the man who serves them to the utmost of his power is thought to be a good man. This is why it would not seem open to a man to disown his father (though a father may disown his son); being in debt, he should repay, but there is nothing by doing which a son will have done the equivalent of what he has received, so that he is always in debt. But creditors can remit a debt; and a father can therefore do so too. At the same time it is thought that presumably no one would repudiate a son who was not far gone in wickedness; for apart from the natural friendship of father and son it is human nature not to reject a son's assistance. But the son, if he is wicked, will naturally avoid aiding his father, or not be zealous about it; for most people wish to get benefits, but avoid doing them, as a thing unprofitable. So much for these questions.

from Confessions (398)

St. Augustine

Book Two

Chapter I

1. I wish now to review in memory my past wickedness and the carnal corruptions of my soul—not because I still love them, but that I may love thee, O my God. For love of thy love I do this, recalling in the bitterness of self-examination my wicked ways, that thou mayest grow sweet to me, thou sweetness without deception! Thou sweetness happy and assured! Thus thou mayest gather me up out of those fragments in which I was torn to pieces, while I turned away from thee, O Unity, and lost myself among "the many." For as I became a youth, I longed to be satisfied with worldly things, and I dared to grow wild in a succession of various and shadowy loves. My form wasted away, and I became corrupt in thy eyes, yet I was still pleasing to my own eyes—and eager to please the eyes of men.

Chapter II

2. But what was it that delighted me save to love and to be loved? Still I did not keep the moderate way of the love of mind to mind—the bright path of friendship. Instead, the mists of passion steamed up out of the puddly concupiscence of the flesh, and the hot imagination of puberty, and they so obscured and overcast my heart that I was unable to distinguish pure affection from unholy desire. Both boiled confusedly within me, and dragged my unstable youth down over the cliffs of unchaste desires and plunged me into a gulf of infamy. Thy anger had come upon me, and I knew it not. I had been deafened by the clanking of the chains of my mortality, the punishment for my soul's pride, and I wandered farther from thee, and thou didst permit me to do so. I was tossed to and fro, and wasted, and poured out, and I boiled over in my fornications—and yet thou didst hold thy peace, O my tardy Joy! Thou didst still hold thy peace, and I wandered still farther from thee into more and yet more barren fields of sorrow, in proud dejection and restless lassitude.

3. If only there had been someone to regulate my disorder and turn to my profit the fleeting beauties of the things around me, and to fix a bound to

their sweetness, so that the tides of my youth might have spent themselves upon the shore of marriage! Then they might have been tranquilized and satisfied with having children, as thy law prescribes, O Lord— O thou who dost form the offspring of our death and art able also with a tender hand to blunt the thorns which were excluded from thy paradise! For thy omnipotence is not far from us even when we are far from thee. Now, on the other hand, I might have given more vigilant heed to the voice from the clouds: "Nevertheless, such shall have trouble in the flesh, but I spare you," and, "It is good for a man not to touch a woman,"and, "He that is unmarried cares for the things that belong to the Lord, how he may please the Lord; but he that is married cares for the things that are of the world, how he may please his wife." I should have listened more attentively to these words, and, thus having been "made a eunuch for the Kingdom of Heaven's sake," I would have with greater happiness expected thy embraces.

4. But, fool that I was, I foamed in my wickedness as the sea and, forsaking thee, followed the rushing of my own tide, and burst out of all thy bounds. But I did not escape thy scourges. For what mortal can do so? Thou wast always by me, mercifully angry and flavoring all my unlawful pleasures with bitter discontent, in order that I might seek pleasures free from discontent. But where could I find such pleasure save in thee, O Lord—save in thee, who dost teach us by sorrow, who woundest us to heal us, and dost kill us that we may not die apart from thee. Where was I, and how far was I exiled from the delights of thy house, in that sixteenth year of the age of my flesh, when the madness of lust held full sway in me—that madness which grants indulgence to human shamelessness, even though it is forbidden by thy laws—and I gave myself entirely to it? Meanwhile, my family took no care to save me from ruin by marriage, for their sole care was that I should learn how to make a powerful speech and become a persuasive orator.

Chapter III

5. Now, in that year my studies were interrupted. I had come back from Madaura, a neighboring city where I had gone to study grammar and rhetoric; and the money for a further term at Carthage was being got together for me. This project was more a matter of my father's ambition than of his means, for he was only a poor citizen of Tagaste. To whom am I narrating all this? Not to thee, O my God, but to my own kind in thy presence—to that small part of the human race who may chance to come upon these writings. And to what end? That I and all who read them may understand what depths there are from which we are to cry unto thee.

For what is more surely heard in thy ear than a confessing heart and a faithful life? Who did not extol and praise my father, because he went quite beyond his means to supply his son with the necessary expenses for a far journey in the interest of his education? For many far richer citizens did not do so much for their children. Still, this same father troubled himself not at all as to how I was progressing toward thee nor how chaste I was, just so long as I was skillful in speaking—no matter how barren I was to thy tillage, O God, who art the one true and good Lord of my heart, which is thy field.

6. During that sixteenth year of my age, I lived with my parents, having a holiday from school for a time—this idleness imposed upon me by my parents' straitened finances. The thornbushes of lust grew rank about my head, and there was no hand to root them out. Indeed, when my father saw me one day at the baths and perceived that I was becoming a man, and was showing the signs of adolescence, he joyfully told my mother about it as if already looking forward to grandchildren, rejoicing in that sort of inebriation in which the world so often forgets thee, its Creator, and falls in love with thy creature instead of thee—the inebriation of that invisible wine of a perverted will which turns and bows down to infamy. But in my mother's breast thou hadst already begun to build thy temple and the foundation of thy holy habitation—whereas my father was only a catechumen, and that but recently. She was, therefore, startled with a holy fear and trembling: for though I had not yet been baptized, she feared those crooked ways in which they walk who turn their backs to thee and not their faces.

7. Woe is me! Do I dare affirm that thou didst hold thy peace, O my God, while I wandered farther away from thee? Didst thou really then hold thy peace? Then whose words were they but thine which by my mother, thy faithful handmaid, thou didst pour into my ears? None of them, however, sank into my heart to make me do anything. She deplored and, as I remember, warned me privately with great solicitude, "not to commit fornication; but above all things never to defile another man's wife." These appeared to me but womanish counsels, which I would have blushed to obey. Yet they were from thee, and I knew it not. I thought that thou wast silent and that it was only she who spoke. Yet it was through her that thou didst not keep silence toward me; and in rejecting her counsel I was rejecting thee—I, her son, "the son of thy handmaid, thy servant." But I did not realize this, and rushed on headlong with such blindness that, among my friends, I was ashamed to be less shameless than they, when I heard them boasting of their disgraceful exploits—yes, and glorying all the more the worse their baseness was. What is worse, I

took pleasure in such exploits, not for the pleasure's sake only but mostly for praise. What is worthy of vituperation except vice itself? Yet I made myself out worse than I was, in order that I might not go lacking for praise. And when in anything I had not sinned as the worst ones in the group, I would still say that I had done what I had not done, in order not to appear contemptible because I was more innocent than they; and not to drop in their esteem because I was more chaste.

8. Behold with what companions I walked the streets of Babylon! I rolled in its mire and lolled about on it, as if on a bed of spices and precious ointments. And, drawing me more closely to the very center of that city, my invisible enemy trod me down and seduced me, for I was easy to seduce. My mother had already fled out of the midst of Babylon and was progressing, albeit slowly, toward its outskirts. For in counseling me to chastity, she did not bear in mind what her husband had told her about me. And although she knew that my passions were destructive even then and dangerous for the future, she did not think they should be restrained by the bonds of conjugal affection—if, indeed, they could not be cut away to the quick. She took no heed of this, for she was afraid lest a wife should prove a hindrance and a burden to my hopes. These were not her hopes of the world to come, which my mother had in thee, but the hope of learning, which both my parents were too anxious that I should acquire—my father, because he had little or no thought of thee, and only vain thoughts for me; my mother, because she thought that the usual course of study would not only be no hindrance but actually a furtherance toward my eventual return to thee. This much I conjecture, recalling as well as I can the temperaments of my parents. Meantime, the reins of discipline were slackened on me, so that without the restraint of due severity, I might play at whatsoever I fancied, even to the point of dissoluteness. And in all this there was that mist which shut out from my sight the brightness of thy truth, O my God; and my iniquity bulged out, as it were, with fatness!

Chapter IV

9. Theft is punished by thy law, O Lord, and by the law written in men's hearts, which not even ingrained wickedness can erase. For what thief will tolerate another thief stealing from him? Even a rich thief will not tolerate a poor thief who is driven to theft by want. Yet I had a desire to commit robbery, and did so, compelled to it by neither hunger nor poverty, but through a contempt for well-doing and a strong impulse to iniquity. For I pilfered something which I already had in sufficient measure, and of much better quality. I did not desire to enjoy what I stole, but only the

theft and the sin itself. There was a pear tree close to our own vineyard, heavily laden with fruit, which was not tempting either for its color or for its flavor. Late one night—having prolonged our games in the streets until then, as our bad habit was—a group of young scoundrels, and I among them, went to shake and rob this tree. We carried off a huge load of pears, not to eat ourselves, but to dump out to the hogs, after barely tasting some of them ourselves. Doing this pleased us all the more because it was forbidden. Such was my heart, O God, such was my heart—which thou didst pity even in that bottomless pit. Behold, now let my heart confess to thee what it was seeking there, when I was being gratuitously wanton, having no inducement to evil but the evil itself. It was foul, and I loved it. I loved my own undoing. I loved my error—not that for which I erred but the error itself. A depraved soul, falling away from security in thee to destruction in itself, seeking nothing from the shameful deed but shame itself.

Chapter V

10. Now there is a comeliness in all beautiful bodies, and in gold and silver and all things. The sense of touch has its own power to please and the other senses find their proper objects in physical sensation. Worldly honor also has its own glory, and so do the powers to command and to overcome: and from these there springs up the desire for revenge. Yet, in seeking these pleasures, we must not depart from thee, O Lord, nor deviate from thy law. The life which we live here has its own peculiar attractiveness because it has a certain measure of comeliness of its own and a harmony with all these inferior values. The bond of human friendship has a sweetness of its own, binding many souls together as one. Yet because of these values, sin is committed, because we have an inordinate preference for these goods of a lower order and neglect the better and the higher good—neglecting thee, O our Lord God, and thy truth and thy law. For these inferior values have their delights, but not at all equal to my God, who hath made them all. For in him do the righteous delight and he is the sweetness of the upright in heart.

11. When, therefore, we inquire why a crime was committed, we do not accept the explanation unless it appears that there was the desire to obtain some of those values which we designate inferior, or else a fear of losing them. For truly they are beautiful and comely, though in comparison with the superior and celestial goods they are abject and contemptible. A man has murdered another man—what was his motive? Either he desired his wife or his property or else he would steal to support himself or else he was afraid of losing something to him; or else, having been injured, he

was burning to be revenged. Would a man commit murder without a motive, taking delight simply in the act of murder? Who would believe such a thing? Even for that savage and brutal man [Catiline], of whom it was said that he was gratuitously wicked and cruel, there is still a motive assigned to his deeds. "Lest through idleness," he says, "hand or heart should grow inactive." And to what purpose? Why, even this: that, having once got possession of the city through his practice of his wicked ways, he might gain honors, empire, and wealth, and thus be exempt from the fear of the laws and from financial difficulties in supplying the needs of his family—and from the consciousness of his own wickedness. So it seems that even Catiline himself loved not his own villainies, but something else, and it was this that gave him the motive for his crimes.

Chapter VI

12. What was it in you, O theft of mine, that I, poor wretch, doted on— you deed of darkness , in that sixteenth year of my age? Beautiful you were not, for you were a theft. But are you anything at all, so that I could analyze the case with you? Those pears that we stole were fair to the sight because they were thy creation, O Beauty beyond compare, O Creator of all, O thou good God—God the highest good and my true good. Those pears were truly pleasant to the sight, but it was not for them that my miserable soul lusted, for I had an abundance of better pears. I stole those simply that I might steal, for, having stolen them, I threw them away. My sole gratification in them was my own sin, which I was pleased to enjoy; for, if any one of these pears entered my mouth, the only good flavor it had was my sin in eating it. And now, O Lord my God, I ask what it was in that theft of mine that caused me such delight; for behold it had no beauty of its own—certainly not the sort of beauty that exists in justice and wisdom, nor such as is in the mind, memory senses, and the animal life of man; nor yet the kind that is the glory and beauty of the stars in their courses; nor the beauty of the earth, or the sea—teeming with spawning life, replacing in birth that which dies and decays. Indeed, it did not have that false and shadowy beauty which attends the deceptions of vice.

13. For thus we see pride wearing the mask of high-spiritedness, although only thou, O God, art high above all. Ambition seeks honor and glory, whereas only thou shouldst be honored above all, and glorified forever. The powerful man seeks to be feared, because of his cruelty; but who ought really to be feared but God only? What can be forced away or withdrawn out of his power—when or where or whither or by whom? The enticements of the wanton claim the name of love; and yet nothing is

more enticing than thy love, nor is anything loved more healthfully than thy truth, bright and beautiful above all. Curiosity prompts a desire for knowledge, whereas it is only thou who knowest all things supremely. Indeed, ignorance and foolishness themselves go masked under the names of simplicity and innocence; yet there is no being that has true simplicity like thine, and none is innocent as thou art. Thus it is that by a sinner's own deeds he is himself harmed. Human sloth pretends to long for rest, but what sure rest is there save in the Lord? Luxury would fain be called plenty and abundance; but thou art the fullness and unfailing abundance of unfading joy. Prodigality presents a show of liberality; but thou art the most lavish giver of all good things. Covetousness desires to possess much; but thou art already the possessor of all things. Envy contends that its aim is for excellence; but what is so excellent as thou? Anger seeks revenge; but who avenges more justly than thou? Fear recoils at the unfamiliar and the sudden changes which threaten things beloved, and is wary for its own security; but what can happen that is unfamiliar or sudden to thee? Or who can deprive thee of what thou lovest? Where, really, is there unshaken security save with thee? Grief languishes for things lost in which desire had taken delight, because it wills to have nothing taken from it, just as nothing can be taken from thee.

14. Thus the soul commits fornication when she is turned from thee, and seeks apart from thee what she cannot find pure and untainted until she returns to thee. All things thus imitate thee—but pervertedly—when they separate themselves far from thee and raise themselves up against thee. But, even in this act of perverse imitation, they acknowledge thee to be the Creator of all nature, and recognize that there is no place whither they can altogether separate themselves from thee. What was it, then, that I loved in that theft? And wherein was I imitating my Lord, even in a corrupted and perverted way? Did I wish, if only by gesture, to rebel against thy law, even though I had no power to do so actually—so that, even as a captive, I might produce a sort of counterfeit liberty, by doing with impunity deeds that were forbidden, in a deluded sense of omnipotence? Behold this servant of thine, fleeing from his Lord and following a shadow! O rottenness! O monstrousness of life and abyss of death! Could I find pleasure only in what was unlawful, and only because it was unlawful?

Chapter VII

15. "What shall I render unto the Lord" for the fact that while my memory recalls these things my soul no longer fears them? I will love thee, O Lord, and thank thee, and confess to thy name, because thou hast put

away from me such wicked and evil deeds. To thy grace I attribute it and to thy mercy, that thou hast melted away my sin as if it were ice. To thy grace also I attribute whatsoever of evil I did not commit—for what might I not have done, loving sin as I did, just for the sake of sinning? Yea, all the sins that I confess now to have been forgiven me, both those which I committed willfully and those which, by thy providence, I did not commit. What man is there who, when reflecting upon his own infirmity, dares to ascribe his chastity and innocence to his own powers, so that he should love thee less—as if he were in less need of thy mercy in which thou forgivest the transgressions of those that return to thee? As for that man who, when called by thee, obeyed thy voice and shunned those things which he here reads of me as I recall and confess them of myself, let him not despise me—for I, who was sick, have been healed by the same Physician by whose aid it was that he did not fall sick, or rather was less sick than I. And for this let him love thee just as much—indeed, all the more—since he sees me restored from such a great weakness of sin by the selfsame Saviour by whom he sees himself preserved from such a weakness.

Chapter VIII

16. What profit did I, a wretched one, receive from those things which, when I remember them now, cause me shame—above all, from that theft, which I loved only for the theft's sake? And, as the theft itself was nothing, I was all the more wretched in that I loved it so. Yet by myself alone I would not have done it—I still recall how I felt about this then—I could not have done it alone. I loved it then because of the companionship of my accomplices with whom I did it. I did not, therefore, love the theft alone—yet, indeed, it was only the theft that I loved, for the companionship was nothing. What is this paradox? Who is it that can explain it to me but God, who illumines my heart and searches out the dark corners thereof? What is it that has prompted my mind to inquire about it, to discuss and to reflect upon all this? For had I at that time loved the pears that I stole and wished to enjoy them, I might have done so alone, if I could have been satisfied with the mere act of theft by which my pleasure was served. Nor did I need to have that itching of my own passions inflamed by the encouragement of my accomplices. But since the pleasure I got was not from the pears, it was in the crime itself, enhanced by the companionship of my fellow sinners.

Chapter IX

17. By what passion, then, was I animated? It was undoubtedly depraved and a great misfortune for me to feel it. But still, what was it? "Who can

understand his errors?" We laughed because our hearts were tickled at the thought of deceiving the owners, who had no idea of what we were doing and would have strenuously objected. Yet, again, why did I find such delight in doing this which I would not have done alone? Is it that no one readily laughs alone? No one does so readily; but still sometimes, when men are by themselves and no one else is about, a fit of laughter will overcome them when something very droll presents itself to their sense or mind. Yet alone I would not have done it—alone I could not have done it at all.

Behold, my God, the lively review of my soul's career is laid bare before thee. I would not have committed that theft alone. My pleasure in it was not what I stole but, rather, the act of stealing. Nor would I have enjoyed doing it alone—indeed I would not have done it! O friendship all unfriendly! You strange seducer of the soul, who hungers for mischief from impulses of mirth and wantonness, who craves another's loss without any desire for one's own profit or revenge—so that, when they say, "Let's go, let's do it," we are ashamed not to be shameless.

Chapter X

18. Who can unravel such a twisted and tangled knottiness? It is unclean. I hate to reflect upon it. I hate to look on it. But I do long for thee, O Righteousness and Innocence, so beautiful and comely to all virtuous eyes—I long for thee with an insatiable satiety. With thee is perfect rest, and life unchanging. He who enters into thee enters into the joy of his Lord, and shall have no fear and shall achieve excellence in the Excellent. I fell away from thee, O my God, and in my youth I wandered too far from thee, my true support. And I became to myself a wasteland.

from Meditations (170–180)

Marcus Aurelius

The First Book

I. Of my grandfather Verus I have learned to be gentle and meek, and to refrain from all anger and passion. From the fame and memory of him that begot me I have learned both shamefastness and manlike behaviour. Of my mother I have learned to be religious, and bountiful; and to forbear, not only to do, but to intend any evil; to content myself with a spare diet, and to fly all such excess as is incidental to great wealth. Of my great-grandfather, both to frequent public schools and auditories, and to get me good and able teachers at home; and that I ought not to think much, if upon such occasions, I were at excessive charges.

II. Of him that brought me up, not to be fondly addicted to either of the two great factions of the coursers in the circus, called Prasini, and Veneti: nor in the amphitheatre partially to favour any of the gladiators, or fencers, as either the Parmularii, or the Secutores. Moreover, to endure labour; nor to need many things; when I have anything to do, to do it myself rather than by others; not to meddle with many businesses; and not easily to admit of any slander.

III. Of Diognetus, not to busy myself about vain things, and not easily to believe those things, which are commonly spoken, by such as take upon them to work wonders, and by sorcerers, or prestidigitators, and impostors; concerning the power of charms, and their driving out of demons, or evil spirits; and the like. Not to keep quails for the game; nor to be mad after such things. Not to be offended with other men's liberty of speech, and to apply myself unto philosophy. Him also I must thank, that ever I heard first Bacchius, then Tandasis and Marcianus, and that I did write dialogues in my youth; and that I took liking to the philosophers' little couch and skins, and such other things, which by the Grecian discipline are proper to those who profess philosophy.

IV. To Rusticus I am beholding, that I first entered into the conceit that my life wanted some redress and cure. And then, that I did not fall into the ambition of ordinary sophists, either to write tracts concerning the common theorems, or to exhort men unto virtue and the study of philosophy by public orations; as also that I never by way of ostentation did affect to show myself an active able man, for any kind of bodily exercises. And that I gave over the study of rhetoric and poetry, and of elegant neat language. That I did not use to walk about the house in my long robe, nor to do any such things. Moreover I learned of him to write letters without any affectation, or curiosity; such as that was, which by him was written to my mother from Sinuessa: and to be easy and ready to be reconciled, and well pleased again with them that had offended me, as soon as any of them would be content to seek unto me again. To read with diligence; not to rest satisfied with a light and superficial knowledge, nor quickly to assent to things commonly spoken of: whom also I must thank that ever I lighted upon Epictetus his Hypomnemata, or moral commentaries and commone-factions: which also he gave me of his own.

V. From Apollonius, true liberty, and unvariable steadfastness, and not to regard anything at all, though never so little, but right and reason: and always, whether in the sharpest pains, or after the loss of a child, or in long diseases, to be still the same man; who also was a present and visible example unto me, that it was possible for the same man to be both vehement and remiss: a man not subject to be vexed, and offended with the incapacity of his scholars and auditors in his lectures and expositions; and a true pattern of a man who of all his good gifts and faculties, least esteemed in himself, that his excellent skill and ability to teach and persuade others the common theorems and maxims of the Stoic philosophy. Of him also I learned how to receive favours and kindnesses (as commonly they are accounted) from friends, so that I might not become obnoxious unto them, for them, nor more yielding upon occasion, than in right I ought; and yet so that I should not pass them neither, as an unsensible and unthankful man.

VI. Of Sextus, mildness and the pattern of a family governed with paternal affection; and a purpose to live according to nature: to be grave without affectation: to observe carefully the several dispositions of my friends, not to be offended with idiots, nor unseasonably to set upon those that are carried with the vulgar opinions, with the theorems, and tenets of philosophers: his conversation being an example how a man might accommodate himself to all men and companies; so that though his company were sweeter and more pleasing than any flatterer's cogging and fawning; yet was it at the same time most respected and reverenced: who also had a proper happiness and faculty, rationally and methodically to find out, and set in order all necessary determinations and instructions for a man's life. A man without ever the least appearance of anger, or any other passion; able at the same time most exactly to observe the Stoic Apathia, or unpassionateness, and yet to be most tender-hearted: ever of good credit; and yet almost without any noise, or rumour: very learned, and yet making little show.

VII. From Alexander the Grammarian, to be un-reprovable myself, and not reproachfully to reprehend any man for a barbarism, or a solecism, or any false pronunciation, but dextrously by way of answer, or testimony, or confirmation of the same matter (taking no notice of the word) to utter it as it should have been spoken; or by some other such close and indirect admonition, handsomely and civilly to tell him of it.

VIII. Of Fronto, to how much envy and fraud and hypocrisy the state of a tyrannous king is subject unto, and how they who are commonly called [Eupatridas Gk.], i.e. nobly born, are in some sort incapable, or void of natural affection.

IX. Of Alexander the Platonic, not often nor without great necessity to say, or to write to any man in a letter, 'I am not at leisure'; nor in this manner still to put off those duties, which we owe to our friends and acquaintances (to every one in his kind) under pretence of urgent affairs.

X. Of Catulus, not to contemn any friend's expostulation, though unjust, but to strive to reduce him to his former disposition: freely and heartily to speak well of all my masters upon any occasion, as it is reported of Domitius, and Athenodotus: and to love my children with true affection.

XI. From my brother Severus, to be kind and loving to all them of my house and family; by whom also I came to the knowledge of Thrasea and Helvidius, and Cato, and Dio, and Brutus. He it was also that did put me in the first conceit and desire of an equal commonwealth, administered by justice and equality; and of a kingdom wherein should be regarded nothing more than the good and welfare of the subjects. Of him also, to observe a constant tenor, (not interrupted, with any other cares and distractions,) in the study and esteem of philosophy: to be bountiful and liberal in the largest measure; always to hope the best; and to be confident that my friends love me. In whom I moreover observed open dealing towards those whom he reproved at any time, and that his friends might without all doubt or much observation know what he would, or would not, so open and plain was he.

XII. From Claudius Maximus, in all things to endeavour to have power of myself, and in nothing to be carried about; to be cheerful and courageous in all sudden chances and accidents, as in sicknesses: to love mildness, and moderation, and gravity: and to do my business, whatsoever it be, thoroughly, and without querulousness. Whatsoever he said, all men believed him that as he spake, so he thought, and whatsoever he did, that he did it with a good intent. His manner was, never to wonder at anything; never to be in haste, and yet never slow: nor to be perplexed, or dejected, or at any time unseemly, or excessively to laugh: nor to be angry, or suspicious, but ever ready to do good, and to forgive, and to speak truth; and all this, as one that seemed rather of himself to have been straight and right, than ever to have been rectified or redressed; neither was there any man that ever thought himself undervalued by him, or that could find in his heart, to think himself a better man than he. He would also be very pleasant and gracious.

XIII. In my father, I observed his meekness; his constancy without wavering in those things, which after a due examination and deliberation, he had determined. How free from all vanity he carried himself in matter of honour and dignity, (as they are esteemed) his laboriousness and assiduity, his readiness to hear any man, that had aught to say tending to any common good: how generally and impartially he would give every man his due; his skill and knowledge, when rigour or extremity, or when remissness or moderation was in season; how he did abstain from all unchaste love of youths; his moderate condescending to other men's occasions as an ordinary man, neither absolutely requiring of his friends, that they should wait upon him at his ordinary meals, nor that they should of necessity accompany him in his journeys; and that whensoever any business upon some necessary occasions was to be put off and omitted before it could be ended, he was ever found when he went about it again, the same man that he was before. His accurate examination of things in consultations, and patient hearing of others. He would not hastily give over the search of the matter, as one easy to be satisfied with sudden notions and apprehensions. His care to preserve his friends; how neither at any time he would carry himself towards them with disdainful neglect, and grow weary of them; nor yet at any time be madly fond of them. His contented mind in all things, his cheerful countenance, his care to foresee things afar off, and to take order for the least, without any noise or clamour. Moreover how all acclamations and flattery were repressed by him: how carefully he observed all things necessary to the government, and kept an account of the common expenses, and how patiently he did abide that he was reprehended by some for this his strict and rigid kind of dealing. How he was neither a superstitious worshipper of the gods, nor an ambitious pleaser of men, or studious of popular applause; but sober in all things, and everywhere observant of that which was fitting; no affecter of novelties: in those things which conduced to his ease and convenience, (plenty whereof his fortune did afford him,) without pride and bragging, yet with all freedom and liberty: so that as he did freely enjoy them without any anxiety or affectation when they were present; so when absent, he found no want of them. Moreover, that he was never commended by any man, as either a learned acute man, or an obsequious officious man, or a fine orator; but as a ripe mature man, a perfect sound man; one that could not endure to be flattered; able to govern both himself and others. Moreover, how much he did honour all true philosophers, without upbraiding those that were not so; his sociableness, his gracious and delightful conversation, but never unto satiety; his care of his body within bounds and measure, not as one that desired to live long, or over-studious of neatness, and elegancy; and yet not as one that did not regard it: so that through his own care and providence, he seldom needed any inward physic, or outward applications: but especially how ingeniously he would yield to any that had obtained any peculiar faculty, as either eloquence, or the knowledge of the laws, or of ancient customs, or the like; and how he concurred with them, in his best care and endeavour that every one of them might in his kind, for that wherein he excelled, be regarded and esteemed: and although he did all things carefully after the ancient customs of his forefathers, yet even of this was he not desirous that men should take notice, that he did imitate ancient customs. Again, how he was not easily moved and tossed up and down, but loved to be constant, both in the same places and businesses; and how after his great fits of headache he would return fresh and vigorous to his wonted affairs. Again, that secrets he neither had many, nor often, and such only as concerned public matters: his discretion and moderation, in exhibiting of the public sights and shows for the pleasure and pastime of the people: in public buildings, congiaries, and the like. In all these things, having a respect unto men only as men, and to the equity of the things themselves, and not unto the glory that might follow. Never wont to use the baths at unseasonable hours; no builder; never curious, or solicitous, either about his meat, or about the workmanship, or colour of his clothes, or about anything that belonged to external beauty. In all his conversation, far from all inhumanity, all boldness, and incivility, all greediness and impetuosity; never doing anything with such earnestness, and intention, that a man could say of him, that he did sweat about it: but contrariwise, all things distinctly, as at leisure; without trouble; orderly, soundly, and agreeably. A man might have applied that to him, which is recorded of Socrates, that he knew how to want, and to enjoy those things, in the want whereof, most men show themselves weak; and in the fruition, intemperate: but to hold out firm and constant, and to keep within the compass of true moderation and sobriety in either estate, is proper to a man, who hath a perfect and invincible soul; such as he showed himself in the sickness of Maximus.

XIV. From the gods I received that I had good grandfathers, and parents, a good sister, good masters, good domestics, loving kinsmen, almost all that I have; and that I never through haste and rashness transgressed against any of them, notwithstanding that my disposition was such, as that such a thing (if occasion had been) might very well have been committed by me, but that It was the mercy of the gods, to prevent such a concurring of matters and occasions, as might make me to incur this blame. That I was not long brought up by the concubine of my father; that I preserved the flower of my youth. That I took not upon me to be a man before my time, but rather put it off longer than I needed. That I lived under the government of my lord and father, who would take away from me all pride and vainglory, and reduce me to that conceit and opinion that it was not impossible for a prince to live in the court without a troop of guards and followers, extraordinary apparel, such and such torches and statues, and other like particulars of state and magnificence; but that a man may reduce and contract himself almost to the state of a private man, and yet for all that not to become the more base and remiss in those public matters and affairs, wherein power and authority is requisite. That I have had such a brother, who by his own example might stir me up to think of myself; and by his respect and love, delight and please me. That I have got ingenuous children, and that they were not born distorted, nor with any other natural deformity. That I was no great proficient in the study of rhetoric and poetry, and of other faculties, which perchance I might have dwelt upon, if I had found myself to go on in them with success. That I did by times prefer those, by whom I was brought up, to such places and dignities, which they seemed unto me most to desire; and that I did not put them off with hope and expectation, that (since that they were yet but young) I would do the same hereafter. That I ever knew Apollonius and Rusticus, and Maximus. That I have had occasion often and effectually to consider and meditate with myself, concerning that life which is according to nature, what the nature and manner of it is: so that as for the gods and such suggestions, helps and inspirations, as might be expected from them, nothing did hinder, but that I might have begun long before to live according to nature; or that even now that I was not yet partaker and in present possession of that life, that I myself (in that I did not observe those inward motions, and suggestions, yea and almost plain and apparent instructions and admonitions of the gods,) was the only cause of it. That my body in such a life, hath been able to hold out so long. That I never had to do with Benedicta and Theodotus, yea and afterwards when I fell into some fits of love, I was soon cured. That having been often displeased with Rusticus, I never did him anything for which afterwards I had occasion to repent. That it being so that my mother was to die young, yet she lived with me all her latter years. That as often as I had a purpose to help and succour any that either were poor, or fallen into some present necessity, I never was answered by my officers that there was not ready money enough to do it; and that I myself never had occasion to require the like succour from any other. That I have such a wife, so obedient, so loving, so ingenuous. That I had choice of fit and able men, to whom I might commit the bringing up of my children. That by dreams I have received help, as for other things, so in particular, how I might stay my casting of blood, and cure my dizziness, as that also that happened to thee in Cajeta, as unto Chryses when he prayed by the seashore. And when I did first apply myself to philosophy, that I did not fall into the hands of some sophists, or spent my time either in reading the manifold volumes of ordinary philosophers, nor in practising myself in the solution of arguments and fallacies, nor dwelt upon the studies of the meteors, and other natural curiosities. All these things without the assistance of the gods, and fortune, could not have been.

XV. In the country of the Quadi at Granua, these. Betimes in the morning say to thyself, This day I shalt have to do with an idle curious man, with an unthankful man, a railer, a crafty, false, or an envious man; an unsociable uncharitable man. All these ill qualities have happened unto them, through ignorance of that which is truly good and truly bad. But I that understand the nature of that which is good, that it only is to be desired, and of that which is bad, that it only is truly odious and shameful: who know moreover, that this transgressor, whosoever he be, is my kinsman, not by the same blood and seed, but by participation of the same reason, and of the same divine particle; How can I either be hurt by any of those, since it is not in their power to make me incur anything that is truly reproachful? or angry, and ill affected towards him, who by nature is so near unto me? for we are all born to be fellow-workers, as the feet, the hands, and the eyelids; as the rows of the upper and under teeth: for such therefore to be in opposition, is against nature; and what is it to chafe at, and to be averse from, but to be in opposition?

XVI. Whatsoever I am, is either flesh, or life, or that which we commonly call the mistress and overruling part of man; reason. Away with thy books, suffer not thy mind any more to be distracted, and carried to and fro; for it will not be; but as even now ready to die, think little of thy flesh: blood, bones, and a skin; a pretty piece of knit and twisted work, consisting of nerves, veins and arteries; think no more of it, than so. And as for thy life, consider what it is; a wind; not one constant wind neither, but every moment of an hour let out, and sucked in again. The third, is thy ruling part; and here consider; Thou art an old man; suffer not that excellent part to be brought in subjection, and to become slavish: suffer it not to be drawn up and down with unreasonable and unsociable lusts and motions, as it were with wires and nerves; suffer it not any more, either to repine at anything now present, or to fear and fly anything to come, which the destiny hath appointed thee.

XVII. Whatsoever proceeds from the gods immediately, that any man will grant totally depends from their divine providence. As for those things that are commonly said to happen by fortune, even those must be conceived to have dependence from nature, or from that first and general connection, and concatenation of all those things, which more apparently by the divine providence are administered and brought to pass. All things flow from thence: and whatsoever it is that is, is both necessary, and conducing to the whole (part of which thou art), and whatsoever it is that is requisite and necessary for the preservation of the general, must of necessity for every particular nature, be good and behoveful. And as for the whole, it is preserved, as by the perpetual mutation and conversion of the simple elements one into another, so also by the mutation, and alteration of things mixed and compounded. Let these things suffice thee; let them be always unto thee, as thy general rules and precepts. As for thy thirst after books, away with it with all speed, that thou die not murmuring and complaining, but truly meek and well satisfied, and from thy heart thankful unto the gods.

Gryphon (1985)

Charles Baxter

On Wednesday afternoon, between the geography lesson on ancient Egypt's hand-operated irrigation system and an art project that involved drawing a model city next to a mountain, our fourth-grade teacher, Mr. Hibler, developed a cough. This cough began with a series of muffled throat-clearings and progressed to propulsive noises contained within Mr. Hibler's closed mouth. "Listen to him," Carol Peterson whispered to me. "He's gonna blow up." Mr. Hibler's laughter—dazed and infrequent—sounded a bit like his cough, but as we worked on our model cities we would look up, thinking he was enjoying a joke, and see Mr. Hibler's face turning red, his cheeks puffed out. This was not laughter. Twice he bent over, and his loose tie, like a plumb line, hung down straight from his neck as he exploded himself into a Kleenex. He would excuse himself, then go on coughing. "I'll bet you a dime," Carol Peterson whispered, "we get a substitute tomorrow."

Carol sat at the desk in front of mine and was a bad person—when she thought no one was looking she would blow her nose on notebook paper, then crumple it up and throw it into the wastebasket—but at times of crisis she spoke the truth. I knew I'd lose the dime.

"No deal," I said.

When Mr. Hibler stood us in formation at the door just prior to the final bell, he was almost incapable of speech. "I'm sorry, boys and girls," he said. "I seem to be coming down with something. "

"I hope you feel better tomorrow, Mr. Hibler," Bobby Kryzanowicz, the faultless brown-noser, said, and I heard Carol Peterson's evil giggle. Then Mr. Hibler opened the door and we walked out to the buses, a clique of us starting noisily to hawk and laugh as soon as we thought we were a few feet beyond Mr. Hibler's earshot.

Since Five Oaks was a rural community, and in Michigan, the supply of substitute teachers was limited to the town's unemployed community college graduates, a pool of about four mothers. These ladies fluttered, provided easeful class days, and nervously covered material we had mastered weeks earlier. Therefore it was a surprise when a woman we had never seen came into the class the next day, carrying a purple purse, a checkerboard lunchbox, and a few books. She put the books on one side of Mr. Hibler's desk and the lunchbox on the other, next to the Voice of Music phonograph. Three of us in the back of the room were playing with Heever, the chameleon that lived in a terrarium and on one of the plastic drapes, when she walked in.

She clapped her hands at us. "Little boys," she said, "why are you bent over together like that?" She didn't wait for us to answer. "Are you tormenting an animal? Put it back. Please sit down at your desks. I want no cabals this time of the day." We just stared at her. "Boys," she repeated, "I asked you to sit down."

I put the chameleon in his terrarium and felt my way to my desk, never taking my eyes off the woman. With white and green chalk, she had started to draw a tree on the left side of the blackboard. She didn't look usual. Furthermore, her tree was outsized, disproportionate, for some reason.

"This room needs a tree," she said, with one line drawing the suggestion of a leaf. "A large, leafy, shady, deciduous . . . oak."

Her fine, light hair had been done up in what I would learn years later was called a chignon, and she wore gold-rimmed glasses whose lenses seemed to have the faintest blue tint. Harold Knardahl, who sat across from me, whispered, "Mars," and I nodded slowly, savoring the imminent weirdness of the day. The substitute drew another branch with an extravagant arm gesture, then turned around and said, "Good morning. I don't believe I said good morning to all of you yet."

Facing us, she was no special age—an adult is an adult—but her face had two prominent lines, descending vertically from the sides of her mouth to her chin. I knew where I had seen those lines before: *Pinocchio*. They were marionette lines. "You may stare at me," she said to us, as a few more kids from the last bus came into the room, their eyes fixed on her, "for a few more seconds, until the bell rings. Then I will permit no more staring. Looking I will permit. Staring, no. It is impolite to stare, and a sign of bad breeding. You cannot make a social effort while staring."

Harold Knardahl did not glance at me, or nudge, but I heard him whisper "Mars" again, trying to get more mileage out of his single joke with the kids who had just come in.

When everyone was seated, the substitute teacher finished her tree, put down her chalk fastidiously on the phonograph, brushed her hands, and faced us. "Good morning," she said. "I am Miss Ferenczi, your teacher for the day. I am fairly new to your community, and I don't believe any of you know me. I will therefore start by telling you a story about myself."

While we settled back, she launched into her tale. She said her grandfather had been a Hungarian prince; her mother had been born in some place called Flanders, had been a pianist, and had played concerts for people Miss Ferenczi referred to as "crowned heads." She gave us a knowing look. "Grieg," she said, "the Norwegian master, wrote a concerto for piano that was . . ." —she paused—"my mother's triumph at her debut concert in London." Her eyes searched the ceiling. Our eyes followed. Nothing up there but ceiling tile. "For reasons that I shall not go into, my family's fortunes took us to Detroit, then north to dreadful Saginaw, and now here I am in Five Oaks, as your substitute teacher, for today, Thursday, October the eleventh. I believe it will be a good day: all the forecasts coincide. We shall start with your reading lesson. Take out your reading book. I believe it is called *Broad Horizons*, or something along those lines."

Jeannie Vermeesch raised her hand. Miss Ferenczi nodded at her. "Mr. Hibler always starts the day with the Pledge of Allegiance," Jeannie whined.

"Oh, does he? In that case," Miss Ferenczi said, "you must know it very well by now, and we certainly need not spend our time on it. No, no allegiance pledging on the premises today, by my reckoning. Not with so much sunlight coming into the room. A pledge does not suit my mood." She glanced at her watch. "Time *is* flying. Take out *Broad Horizons*."

She disappointed us by giving us an ordinary lesson, complete with vocabulary and drills, comprehension questions, and recitation. She didn't seem to care for the material, however. She sighed every few minutes and rubbed her glasses with a frilly handkerchief that she withdrew, magician-style, from her left sleeve.

After reading we moved on to arithmetic. It was my favorite time of the morning, when the lazy autumn sunlight dazzled its way through ribbons of clouds past the windows on the east side of the classroom and crept across the linoleum floor. On the playground the first group of children, the kindergartners, were running on the quack grass just beyond the monkey bars. We were doing multiplication tables. Miss Ferenczi had made John Wazny stand up at his desk in the front row. He was supposed to go through the tables of six. From where I was sitting, I could smell the Vitalis soaked into John's plastered hair. He was doing fine until he came to six times eleven and six times twelve. "Six times eleven," he said, "is sixty-eight. Six times twelve is . . ." He put his fingers to his head, quickly and secretly sniffed his fingertips, and said, " . . . seventy-two." Then he sat down.

"Fine," Miss Ferenczi said. "Well now. That was very good. "

"Miss Ferenczi!" One of the Eddy twins was waving her hand desperately in the air. "Miss Ferenczi! Miss Ferenczi!"

"Yes?"

"John said that six times eleven is sixty-eight and you said he was right!"

"*Did* I?" She gazed at the class with a jolly look breaking across her marionette's face. "Did I say that? Well, what *is* six times eleven?"

"It's sixty-six!"

She nodded. "Yes. So it is. But, and I know some people will not entirely agree with me, at some times it is sixty-eight."

"When? When is it sixty-eight?"

We were all waiting.

"In higher mathematics, which you children do not yet understand, six times eleven can be considered to be sixty-eight." She laughed through her nose. "In higher mathematics numbers are . . . more fluid. The only thing a number does is contain a certain amount of something. Think of water. A cup is not the only way to measure a certain amount of water, is it?" We were staring, shaking our heads. "You could use saucepans or thimbles. In either case, the water *would be the same*. Perhaps," she started again, "it would be better for you to think that six times eleven is sixty-eight only when I am in the room."

"Why is it sixty-eight," Mark Poole asked, "when you're in the room?"

"Because it's more interesting that way," she said, smiling very rapidly behind her blue-tinted glasses. "Besides, I'm your substitute teacher, am I not?" We all nodded. "Well, then, think of six times eleven equals sixty-eight as a substitute fact."

"A substitute fact?"

"Yes." Then she looked at us carefully. "Do you think," she asked, "that anyone is going to be hurt by a substitute fact?"

We looked back at her.

"Will the plants on the windowsill be hurt?" We glanced at them. There were sensitive plants thriving in a green plastic tray, and several wilted ferns in small clay pots. "Your dogs and cats, or your moms and dads?" She waited. "So," she concluded, "what's the problem?"

"But it's wrong," Janice Weber said, "isn't it?"

"What's your name, young lady?"

"Janice Weber."

"And you think it's wrong, Janice?"

"I was just asking."

"Well, all right. You were just asking. I think we've spent enough time on this matter by now, don't you, class? You are free to think what you like. When your teacher, Mr. Hibler, returns, six times eleven will be sixty-six again, you can rest assured. And it will be that for the rest of your lives in Five Oaks. Too bad, eh?" She raised her eyebrows and glinted herself at us. "But for now, it wasn't. So much for that. Let us go on to your assigned problems for today, as painstakingly outlined, I see, in Mr. Hibler's lesson plan. Take out a sheet of paper and write your names on the upper left-hand corner."

For the next half hour we did the rest of our arithmetic problems. We handed them in and then went on to spelling, my worst subject. Spelling always came before lunch. We were taking spelling dictation and looking at the clock. "Thorough," Miss Ferenczi said. "Boundary." She walked in the aisles between the desks, holding the spelling book open and looking down at our papers. "Balcony." I clutched my pencil. Somehow, the way she said those words, they seemed foreign, mis-voweled and mis-conso-nanted. I stared down at what I had spelled. *Balconie.* I turned the pencil upside down and erased, my mistake. *Balconey.* That looked better, but still incorrect. I cursed the world of spelling and tried erasing it again and saw the paper beginning to wear away. *Balkony.* Suddenly I felt a hand on my shoulder.

"I don't like that word either," Miss Ferenczi whispered, bent over, her mouth near my ear. "It's ugly. My feeling is, if you don't like a word, you don't have to use it." She straightened up, leaving behind a slight odor of Clorets.

At lunchtime we went out to get our trays of sloppy joes, peaches in heavy syrup, coconut cookies, and milk, and brought them back to the classroom, where Miss Ferenczi was sitting at the desk, eating a brown sticky thing she had unwrapped from tightly rubber-banded waxed paper. "Miss Ferenczi," I said, raising my hand. "You don't have to eat with us. You can eat with the other teachers. There's a teacher's lounge," I ended up, "next to the principal's office."

"No, thank you," she said. "I prefer it here."

"We've got a room monitor," I said. "Mrs. Eddy." I pointed to where Mrs. Eddy, Joyce and Judy's mother, sat silently at the back of the room, doing her knitting.

"That's fine," Miss Ferenczi said. "But I shall continue to eat here, with you children. I prefer it," she repeated.

"How come?" Wayne Razmer asked without raising his hand.

"I talked to the other teachers before class this morning," Miss Ferenczi said, biting into her brown food. "There was a great rattling of the words for the fewness of the ideas. I didn't care for their brand of hilarity. I don't like ditto-machine jokes."

"Oh," Wayne said.

"What's that you're eating?" Maxine Sylvester asked, twitching her nose. "Is it food?"

"It most certainly *is* food. It's a stuffed fig. I had to drive almost down to Detroit to get it. I also brought some smoked sturgeon. And this," she said, lifting some green leaves out of her lunchbox, "is raw spinach, cleaned this morning. "

"Why're you eating raw spinach?" Maxine asked.

"It's good for you," Miss Ferenczi said. "More stimulating than soda pop or smelling salts." I bit into my sloppy joe and stared blankly out the window. An almost invisible moon was faintly silvered in the daytime autumn sky. "As far as food is concerned," Miss Ferenczi was saying, "you have to shuffle the pack. Mix it up. Too many people eat . . . well, never mind."

"Miss Ferenczi," Carol Peterson said, "what are we going do this afternoon?"

"Well," she said, looking down at Mr. Hibler's lesson plan, "I see that your teacher, Mr. Hibler, has you scheduled for a unit on the Egyptians." Carol groaned. "Yesssss," Miss Ferenczi continued, "that is what we will do: the Egyptians. A remarkable people. Almost as remarkable as the

Americans. But not quite." She lowered her head, did her quick smile, and went back to eating her spinach.

After noon recess we came back into the classroom and saw that Miss Ferenczi had drawn a pyramid on the blackboard close to her oak tree. Some of us who had been playing baseball were messing around in the back of the room, dropping the bats and gloves into the playground box, and Ray Schontzeler had just slugged me when I heard Miss Ferenczi's high-pitched voice, quavering with emotions. "Boys," she said, "come to order right this minute and take your seats. I do not wish to waste a minute of class time. Take out your geography books." We trudged to our desks and, still sweating, pulled out *Distant Lands and Their People*. "Turn to page forty-two." She waited for thirty seconds, then looked over at Kelly Munger. "Young man," she said, "why are you still fossicking in your desk?"

Kelly looked as if his foot had been stepped on. "Why am I what?"

"Why are you . . . burrowing in your desk like that?"

"I'm lookin' for the book, Miss Ferenczi."

Bobby Kryzanowicz, the faultless brown-noser who sat in the first row by choice, softly said, "His name is Kelly Munger. He can't ever find his stuff. He always does that."

"I don't care what his name is, especially after lunch," Miss Ferenczi said. *"Where is your book?"*

"I just found it." Kelly was peering into his desk and with both hands pulled at the book, shoveling along in front of it several pencils and crayons, which fell into his lap and then to the floor.

"I hate a mess," Miss Ferenczi said. "I hate a mess in a desk or a mind. It's . . . unsanitary. You wouldn't want your house at home to look like your desk at school, now, would you?" She didn't wait for an answer. "I should think not. A house at home should be as neat as human hands can make it. What were we talking about? Egypt. Page forty-two. I note from Mr. Hibler's lesson plan that you have been discussing the modes of Egyptian irrigation. Interesting, in my view, but not so interesting as what we are about to cover. The pyramids, and Egyptian slave labor. A plus on one side, a minus on the other." We had our books open to page forty-two, where there was a picture of a pyramid, but Miss Ferenczi wasn't looking at the book. Instead, she was staring at some object just outside the window.

"Pyramids," Miss Ferenczi said, still looking past the window. "I want you to think about pyramids. And what was inside. The bodies of the pharaohs, of course, and their attendant treasures. Scrolls. Perhaps," Miss Ferenczi said, her face gleeful but unsmiling, "these scrolls were novels for the pharaohs, helping them to pass the time in their long voyage through the centuries. But then, I am joking." I was looking at the lines on Miss Ferenczi's skin. "Pyramids," Miss Ferenczi went on, "were the repositories of special cosmic powers. The nature of a pyramid is to guide cosmic energy forces into a concentrated point. The Egyptians knew that; we have generally forgotten it. Did you know," she asked, walking to the side of the room so that she was standing by the coat closet, "that George Washington had Egyptian blood, from his grandmother? Certain features of the Constitution of the United States are notable for their Egyptian ideas."

Without glancing down at the book, she began to talk about the movement of souls in Egyptian religion. She said that when people die, their souls return to Earth in the form of carpenter ants or walnut trees, depending on how they behaved—"well or ill"—in life. She said that the Egyptians believed that people act the way they do because of magnetism produced by tidal forces in the solar system, forces produced by the sun and by its "planetary ally," Jupiter. Jupiter, she said, was a planet, as we had been told, but had "certain properties of stars." She was speaking very fast. She said that the Egyptians were great explorers and conquerors. She said that the greatest of all the conquerors, Genghis Khan, had had forty horses and forty young women killed on the site of his grave. We listened. No one tried to stop her. "I myself have been in Egypt," she said, "and have witnessed much dust and many brutalities." She said that an old man in Egypt who worked for a circus had personally shown her an animal in a cage, a monster, half bird and half lion. She said that this monster was called a gryphon and that she had heard about them but never seen them until she traveled to the outskirts of Cairo. She wrote the word out on the blackboard in large capital letters: GRYPHON. She said that Egyptian astronomers had discovered the planet Saturn but had not seen its rings. She said that the Egyptians were the first to discover that dogs, when they are ill, will not drink from rivers, but wait for rain, and hold their jaws open to catch it.

"She lies."

We were on the school bus home. I was sitting next to Carl Whiteside, who had bad breath and a huge collection of marbles. We were arguing. Carl thought she was lying. I said she wasn't, probably.

"I didn't believe that stuff about the bird," Carl said, "and what she told us about the pyramids? I didn't believe that, either. She didn't know what she was talking about."

"Oh yeah?" I had liked her. She was strange. I thought I could nail him. "If she was lying," I said, "what'd she say that was a lie?"

"Six times eleven isn't sixty-eight. It isn't ever. It's sixty-six, I know for a fact."

"She said so. She admitted it. What else did she lie about?"

"I don't know," he said. "Stuff."

"What stuff?"

"Well." He swung his legs back and forth. "You ever see an animal that was half lion and half bird?" He crossed his arms. "It sounded real fakey to me."

"It could happen," I said. I had to improvise, to outrage him. "I read in this newspaper my mom bought in the IGA about this scientist, this mad scientist in the Swiss Alps, and he's been putting genes and chromosomes and stuff together in test tubes, and he combined a human being and a hamster." I waited, for effect. "It's called a humster."

"You never." Carl was staring at me, his mouth open, his terrible bad breath making its way toward me. "What newspaper was it?"

The National Enquirer," I said, "that they sell next to the cash registers." When I saw his look of recognition, I knew I had him. "And this mad scientist," I said, "his name was, um, Dr. Frankenbush." I realized belatedly that this name was a mistake and waited for Carl to notice its resemblance to the name of the other famous mad master of permutations, but he only sat there.

"A man and a hamster?" He was staring at me, squinting, his mouth opening in distaste. "Jeez. What'd it look like?"

When the bus reached my stop, I took off down our dirt road and ran up through the backyard, kicking the tire swing for good luck. I dropped my books on the back steps so I could hug and kiss our dog, Mr. Selby. Then I hurried inside. I could smell brussels sprouts cooking, my unfavorite vegetable. My mother was washing other vegetables in the kitchen sink, and my baby brother was hollering in his yellow playpen on the kitchen floor.

"Hi, Mom," I said, hopping around the playpen to kiss her. "Guess what?"

"I have no idea."

"We had this substitute today, Miss Ferenczi, and I'd never seen her before, and she had all these stories and ideas and stuff."

"Well. That's good." My mother looked out the window in front of the sink, her eyes on the pine woods west of our house. That time of the afternoon her skin always looked so white to me. Strangers always said my mother looked like Betty Crocker, framed by the giant spoon on the side of the Bisquick box. "Listen, Tommy," she said. "Would you please go upstairs and pick your clothes off the floor in the bathroom, and then go outside to the shed and put the shovel and ax away that your father left outside this morning?"

"She said that six times eleven was sometimes sixty-eight!" I said. "And she said she once saw a monster that was half lion and half bird." I waited. "In Egypt."

"Did you hear me?" my mother asked, raising her arm to wipe her forehead with the back of her hand. "You have chores to do."

"I know," I said. "I was just telling you about the substitute."

"It's very interesting," my mother said, quickly glancing down at me, "and we can talk about it later when your father gets home. But right now you have some work to do."

"Okay, Mom." I took a cookie out of the jar on the counter and was about to go outside when I had a thought. I ran into the living room, pulled out a dictionary next to the TV stand, and opened it to the Gs. After five minutes I found it. *Gryphon*: variant of griffin. *Griffin*: "a fabulous beast with the head and wings of an eagle and the body of a lion." Fabulous was right. I shouted with triumph and ran outside to put my father's tools in their proper places.

Miss Ferenczi was back the next day, slightly altered. She had pulled her hair down and twisted it into pigtails, with red rubber bands holding them tight one inch from the ends. She was wearing a green blouse and pink scarf, making her difficult to look at for a full class day. This time there was no pretense of doing a reading lesson or moving on to arithmetic. As soon as the bell rang, she simply began to talk.

She talked for forty minutes straight. There seemed to be less connection between her ideas, but the ideas themselves were, as the dictionary would say, fabulous. She said she had heard of a huge jewel, in what she called the antipodes, that was so brilliant that when light shone into it at a certain angle it would blind whoever was looking at its center. She said the biggest diamond in the world was cursed and had killed everyone who owned it, and that by a trick of fate it was called the Hope Diamond. Diamonds are magic, she said, and this is why women wear them on their fingers, as a sign of the magic of womanhood. Men have strength, Miss Ferenczi said, but no true magic. That is why men fall in love with women but women do not fall in love with men: they just love being loved. George Washington had died because of a mistake he made about a diamond. Washington was not the first *true* President, but she didn't say who was. In some places in the world, she said, men and women still live in the trees and eat monkeys for breakfast. Their doctors are magicians. At the bottom of the sea are creatures thin as pancakes who have never been studied by scientists because when you take them up to air, the fish explode.

There was not a sound in the classroom, except for Miss Ferenczi's voice, and Donna DeShano's coughing. No one even went to the bathroom.

Beethoven, she said, had not been deaf; it was a trick to make himself famous, and it worked. As she talked, Miss Ferenczi's pigtails swung back and forth. There are trees in the world, she said, that eat meat: their leaves are sticky and close up on bugs like hands. She lifted her hands and brought them together, palm to palm. Venus, which most people think is the next closest planet to the sun, is not always closer, and, besides, it is the planet of greatest mystery because of its thick cloud cover. "I know what lies underneath those clouds," Miss Ferenczi said, and waited. After the silence, she said, "Angels. Angels live under those clouds." She said that angels were not invisible to everyone and were in fact smarter than most people. They did not dress in robes as was often claimed but instead wore formal evening clothes, as if they were about to attend a concert. Often angels *do* attend concerts and sit in the aisles, where, she said, most people pay no attention to them. She said the most terrible angel had the shape of the Sphinx. "There is no running away from that one," she said. She said that unquenchable fires burn just under the surface of the earth in Ohio, and that the baby Mozart fainted dead away in his cradle when he first heard the sound of a trumpet. She said that someone named Narzim al Harrardim was the greatest writer who ever lived. She said that planets control behavior, and anyone conceived during a solar eclipse would be born with webbed feet.

"I know you children like to hear these things," she said, "these secrets, and that is why I am telling you all this." We nodded. It was better than doing comprehension questions for the readings in *Broad Horizons*.

"I will tell you one more story," she said, "and then we will have to do arithmetic." She leaned over, and her voice grew soft. "There is no death," she said. "You must never be afraid. Never. That which is, cannot die. It will change into different earthly and unearthly elements, but I know this as sure as I stand here in front of you, and I swear it: you must not be afraid. I have seen this truth with these eyes. I know it because in a dream God kissed me. Here." And she pointed with her right index finger to the side of her head, below the mouth where the vertical lines were carved into her skin.

Absentmindedly we all did our arithmetic problems. At recess the class was out on the playground, but no one was playing. We were all standing in small groups, talking about Miss Ferenczi. We didn't know if she was crazy, or what. I looked out beyond the playground, at the rusted cars piled in a small heap behind a clump of sumac, and I wanted to see shapes there, approaching me.

On the way home, Carl sat next to me again. He didn't say much, and I didn't either. At last he turned to me. "You know what she said about the leaves that close up on bugs?"

"Huh?"

"The leaves," Carl insisted. "The meat-eating plants. I know it's true. I saw it on television. The leaves have this icky glue that the plants have got smeared all over them and the insects can't get off 'cause they're stuck. I saw it." He seemed demoralized. "She's tellin' the truth."

"Yeah."

"You think she's seen all those angels?"

I shrugged.

"I don't think she has," Carl informed me. "I think she made that part up."

"There's a tree," I suddenly said. I was looking out the window at the farms along County Road H. I knew every barn, every broken windmill, every fence, every anhydrous ammonia tank, by heart. "There's a tree that's . . . that I've seen . . ."

"Don't you try to do it," Carl said. "You'll just sound like a jerk."

I kissed my mother. She was standing in front of the stove. "How was your day?" she asked.

"Fine."

"Did you have Miss Ferenczi again?"

"Yeah."

"Well?"

"She was fine. Mom," I asked, "can I go to my room?"

"No," she said, "not until you've gone out to the vegetable garden and picked me a few tomatoes." She glanced at the sky. "I think it's going to rain. Skedaddle and do it now. Then you come back inside and watch your brother for a few minutes while I go upstairs. I need to clean up before dinner." She looked down at me. "You're looking a little pale, Tommy." She touched the back of her hand to my forehead and I felt her diamond ring against my skin. "Do you feel all right?"

"I'm fine," I said, and went out to pick the tomatoes.

Coughing mutedly, Mr. Hibler was back the next day, slipping lozenges into his mouth when his back was turned at forty-five-minute intervals and asking us how much of his prepared lesson plan Miss Ferenczi had followed. Edith Atwater took the responsibility for the class of explaining to Mr. Hibler that the substitute hadn't always done exactly what he, Mr. Hibler, would have done, but we had worked hard even though she talked a lot. About what? he asked. All kinds of things, Edith said. I sort of forgot. To our relief, Mr. Hibler seemed not at all interested in what Miss Ferenczi had said to fill the day. He probably thought it was woman's talk: unserious and not suited for school. It was enough that he had a pile of arithmetic problems from us to correct.

For the next month, the sumac turned a distracting red in the field, and the sun traveled toward the southern sky, so that its rays reached Mr. Hibler's Halloween display on the bulletin board in the back of the room, fading the pumpkin head scarecrow from orange to tan. Every three days I measured how much farther the sun had moved toward the southern horizon by making small marks with my black Crayola on the north wall, ant-sized marks only I knew were there.

And then in early December, four days after the first permanent snowfall, she appeared again in our classroom. The minute she came in the door, I felt my heart begin to pound. Once again, she was different: this time, her hair hung straight down and seemed hardly to have been combed. She hadn't brought her lunchbox with her, but she was carrying what seemed to be a small box. She greeted all of us and talked about the weather. Donna DeShano had to remind her to take her overcoat off.

When the bell to start the day finally rang, Miss Ferenczi looked out at all of us and said, "Children, I have enjoyed your company in the past, and today I am going to reward you." She held up the small box. "Do you know what this is?" She waited. "Of course you don't. It is a Tarot pack."

Edith Atwater raised her hand. "What's a Tarot pack, Miss Ferenczi?"

"It is used to tell fortunes," she said. "And that is what I shall do this morning. I shall tell your fortunes, as I have been taught to do."

"What's fortune?" Bobby Kryzanowicz asked.

"The future, young man. I shall tell you what your future will be. I can't do your whole future, of course. I shall have to limit myself to the five-card system, the wands, cups, swords, pentacles, and the higher arcanes. Now who wants to be first?"

There was a long silence. Then Carol Peterson raised her hand.

"All right," Miss Ferenczi said. She divided the pack into five smaller packs and walked back to Carol's desk, in front of mine. "Pick one card from each one of these packs," she said. I saw that Carol had a four of cups and a six of swords, but couldn't see the other cards. Miss Ferenczi studied the cards on Carol's desk for a minute. "Not bad," she said. "I do not see much higher education. Probably an early marriage. Many children. There's something bleak and dreary here, but I can't tell what. Perhaps just the tasks of a housewife life. I think you'll do very well, for the most part." She smiled at Carol, a smile with a certain lack of interest. "Who wants to be next?"

Carl Whiteside raised his hand slowly.

"Yes," Miss Ferenczi said, "let's do a boy." She walked over to where Carl sat. After he picked his five cards, she gazed at them for a long time. "Travel," she said. "Much distant travel. You might go into the army. Not too much romantic interest here. A late marriage, if at all. But the Sun in your major arcana, that's a very good card." She giggled. "You'll have a happy life."

Next I raised my hand. She told me my future. She did the same with Bobby Kryzanowicz, Kelly Munger, Edith Atwater, and Kim Foor. Then she came to Wayne Razmer. He picked his five cards, and I could see that the Death card was one of them.

"What's your name?" Miss Ferenczi asked.

"Wayne."

"Well, Wayne," she said, "you will undergo a great metamorphosis, a change, before you become an adult. Your earthly element will no doubt leap higher, because you seem to be a sweet boy. This card, this nine of swords, tells me of suffering and desolation. And this ten of wands, well, that's a heavy load."

"What about this one?" Wayne pointed at the Death card.

"It means, my sweet, that you will die soon." She gathered up the cards. We were all looking at Wayne. "But do not fear," she said. "It is not really death. Just change. Out of your earthly shape." She put the cards on Mr. Hibler's desk. "And now, let's do some arithmetic."

At lunchtime Wayne went to Mr. Faegre, the principal, and informed him of what Miss Ferenczi had done. During the noon recess, we saw Miss Ferenczi drive out of the parking lot in her rusting green Rambler American. I stood under the slide, listening to the other kids coasting down and landing in the little depressive bowls at the bottom. I was kicking stones and tugging at my hair right up to the moment when I saw Wayne come out to the playground. He smiled, the dead fool, and with the fingers of his right hand he was showing everyone how he had told on Miss Ferenczi.

I made my way toward Wayne, pushing myself past two girls from another class. He was watching me with his little pinhead eyes.

"You told," I shouted at him. "She was just kidding."

"She shouldn't have," he shouted back. "We were supposed to be doing arithmetic."

"She just scared you," I said. "You're a chicken. You're a chicken, Wayne. You are. Scared of a little card," I singsonged.

Wayne fell at me, his two fists hammering down on my nose. I gave him a good one in the stomach and then I tried for his head. Aiming my fist, I saw that he was crying. I slugged him.

"She was right," I yelled. "She was always right! She told the truth!" Other kids were whooping. "You were just scared, that's all!"

And then large hands pulled at us, and it was my turn to speak to Mr. Faegre.

In the afternoon Miss Ferenczi was gone, and my nose was stuffed with cotton clotted with blood, and my lip had swelled, and our class had been combined with Mrs. Mantei's sixth-grade class for a crowded afternoon science unit on insect life in ditches and swamps. I knew where Mrs. Mantei lived: she had a new house trailer just down the road from us, at the Clearwater Park. She was no mystery. Somehow she and Mr. Bodine, the other fourth-grade teacher, had managed to fit forty-five desks into the room. Kelly Munger asked if Miss Ferenczi had been arrested, and Mrs. Mantei said no, of course not. All that afternoon, until the buses came to pick us up, we learned about field crickets and two-striped grasshoppers, water bugs, cicadas, mosquitoes, flies, and moths. We learned about insects' hard outer shell, the exoskeleton, and the usual parts of the mouth, including the labrum, mandible, maxilla, and glossa. We learned about compound eyes, and the four-stage metamorphosis from egg to larva to pupa to adult. We learned something, but not much, about mating. Mrs. Mantei drew, very skillfully, the internal anatomy of the grasshopper on the blackboard. We learned about the dance of the honeybee, directing other bees in the hive to pollen. We found out about which insects were pests to man, and which were not. On lined white pieces of paper we made lists of insects we might actually see, then a list of insects too small to be clearly visible, such as fleas; Mrs. Mantei said that our assignment would be to memorize these lists for the next day, when Mr. Hibler would certainly return and test us on our knowledge.

Genesis 1–3 (Tenth–Sixth Century B.C.E.)

The Bible

Genesis 1

In the beginning when God created the heavens and the earth, **2** the earth was a formless void and darkness covered the face of the deep, while a wind from God swept over the face of the waters. **3** Then God said, "Let there be light"; and there was light. **4** And God saw that the light was good; and God separated the light from the darkness. **5** God called the light Day, and the darkness he called Night. And there was evening and there was morning, the first day.

6 And God said, "Let there be a dome in the midst of the waters, and let it separate the waters from the waters." **7** So God made the dome and separated the waters that were under the dome from the waters that were above the dome. And it was so. **8** God called the dome Sky. And there was evening and there was morning, the second day.

9 And God said, "Let the waters under the sky be gathered together into one place, and let the dry land appear." And it was so. **10** God called the dry land Earth, and the waters that were gathered together he called Seas. And God saw that it was good. **11** Then God said, "Let the earth put forth vegetation: plants yielding seed, and fruit trees of every kind on earth that bear fruit with the seed in it." And it was so. **12** The earth brought forth vegetation: plants yielding seed of every kind, and trees of every kind bearing fruit with the seed in it. And God saw that it was good. **13** And there was evening and there was morning, the third day.

14 And God said, "Let there be lights in the dome of the sky to separate the day from the night; and let them be for signs and for seasons and for days and years, **15** and let them be lights in the dome of the sky to give light upon the earth." And it was so. **16** God made the two great lights— the greater light to rule the day and the lesser light to rule the night—and the stars. **17** God set them in the dome of the sky to give light upon the earth, **18** to rule over the day and over the night, and to separate the light from the darkness. And God saw that it was good. **19** And there was evening and there was morning, the fourth day.

20 And God said, "Let the waters bring forth swarms of living creatures, and let birds fly above the earth across the dome of the sky." **21** So God created the great sea monsters and every living creature that moves, of every kind, with which the waters swarm, and every winged bird of every kind. And God saw that it was good. **22** God blessed them, saying, "Be fruitful and multiply and fill the waters in the seas, and let birds multiply on the earth." **23** And there was evening and there was morning, the fifth day.

24 And God said, "Let the earth bring forth living creatures of every kind: cattle and creeping things and wild animals of the earth of every kind." And it was so. **25** God made the wild animals of the earth of every kind, and the cattle of every kind, and everything that creeps upon the ground of every kind. And God saw that it was good.

26 Then God said, "Let us make humankind in our image, according to our likeness; and let them have dominion over the fish of the sea, and over the birds of the air, and over the cattle, and over all the wild animals of the earth, and over every creeping thing that creeps upon the earth."

27 So God created humankind in his image, in the image of God he created them; male and female he created them.

28 God blessed them, and God said to them, "Be fruitful and multiply, and fill the earth and subdue it; and have dominion over the fish of the sea and over the birds of the air and over every living thing that moves upon the earth." **29** God said, "See, I have given you every plant yielding seed that is upon the face of all the earth, and every tree with seed in its fruit; you shall have them for food. **30** And to every beast of the earth, and to every bird of the air, and to everything that creeps on the earth, everything that has the breath of life, I have given every green plant for food." And it was so. **31** God saw everything that he had made, and indeed, it was very good. And there was evening and there was morning, the sixth day.

Genesis 2

Thus the heavens and the earth were finished, and all their multitude. **2** And on the seventh day God finished the work that he had done, and he rested on the seventh day from all the work that he had done. **3** So God blessed the seventh day and hallowed it, because on it God rested from all the work that he had done in creation.

4 These are the generations of the heavens and the earth when they were created. In the day that the Lord God made the earth and the heavens, **5** when no plant of the field was yet in the earth and no herb of the field had yet sprung up—for the Lord God had not caused it to rain upon the earth, and there was no one to till the ground; **6** but a stream would rise from the earth, and water the whole face of the ground—**7** then the Lord God formed man from the dust of the ground, and breathed into his nostrils the breath of life; and the man became a living being. **8** And the Lord God planted a garden in Eden, in the east; and there he put the man whom he had formed. **9** Out of the ground the Lord God made to grow every tree that is pleasant to the sight and good for food, the tree of life also in the midst of the garden, and the tree of the knowledge of good and evil.

10 A river flows out of Eden to water the garden, and from there it divides and becomes four branches. **11** The name of the first is Pishon; it is the one that flows around the whole land of Havilah, where there is gold; **12** and the gold of that land is good; bdellium and onyx stone are there. **13** The name of the second river is Gihon; it is the one that flows around the whole land of Cush. **14** The name of the third river is Tigris, which flows east of Assyria. And the fourth river is the Euphrates.

15 The Lord God took the man and put him in the garden of Eden to till it and keep it. **16** And the Lord God commanded the man, "You may freely eat of every tree of the garden; **17** but of the tree of the knowledge of good and evil you shall not eat, for in the day that you eat of it you shall die."

18 Then the Lord God said, "It is not good that the man should be alone; I will make him a helper as his partner." **19** So out of the ground the Lord God formed every animal of the field and every bird of the air, and brought them to the man to see what he would call them; and whatever the man called each living creature, that was its name. **20** The man gave names to all cattle, and to the birds of the air, and to every animal of the field; but for the man there was not found a helper as his partner. **21** So the Lord God caused a deep sleep to fall upon the man, and he slept; then he took one of his ribs and closed up its place with flesh. **22** And the rib that the Lord God had taken from the man he made into a woman and brought her to the man. **23** Then the man said,

> "This at last is bone of my bones
>   and flesh of my flesh;
> this one shall be called Woman,
>   for out of Man this one was taken."

24 Therefore a man leaves his father and his mother and clings to his wife, and they become one flesh. **25** And the man and his wife were both naked, and were not ashamed.

Genesis 3

Now the serpent was more crafty than any other wild animal that the Lord God had made. He said to the woman, "Did God say, 'You shall not eat from any tree in the garden'?" **2** The woman said to the serpent, "We may eat of the fruit of the trees in the garden; **3** but God said, "You shall not eat of the fruit of the tree that is in the middle of the garden, nor shall you touch it, or you shall die.'" **4** But the serpent said to the woman, "You will not die; **5** for God knows that when you eat of it your eyes will be opened, and you will be like God, knowing good and evil." **6** So when the woman saw that the tree was good for food, and that it was a delight to the eyes, and that the tree was to be desired to make one wise, she took of its fruit and ate; and she also gave some to her husband, who was with her, and he ate. **7** Then the eyes of both were opened, and they knew that they were naked; and they sewed fig leaves together and made loincloths for themselves.

8 They heard the sound of the Lord God walking in the garden at the time of the evening breeze, and the man and his wife hid themselves from the presence of the Lord God among the trees of the garden. **9** But the Lord God called to the man, and said to him, "Where are you?" **10** He said, "I heard the sound of you in the garden, and I was afraid, because I was naked; and I hid myself." **11** He said, "Who told you that you were naked? Have you eaten from the tree of which I commanded you not to eat?" **12** The man said, "The woman whom you gave to be with me, she gave me fruit from the tree, and I ate." **13** Then the Lord God said to the woman, "What is this that you have done?" The woman said, "The serpent tricked me, and I ate." **14** The Lord God said to the serpent,

> "Because you have done this,
>   cursed are you among all animals
>   and among all wild creatures;
> upon your belly you shall go,
>   and dust you shall eat
>   all the days of your life.
> **15** I will put enmity between you and the woman,
>   and between your offspring and hers;
> he will strike your head,
>   and you will strike his heel."
> **16** To the woman he said,
> "I will greatly increase your pangs in childbearing;
>   in pain you shall bring forth children,
> yet your desire shall be for your husband,
>   and he shall rule over you."

17 And to the man he said,
"Because you have listened to the voice of your wife,
   and have eaten of the tree
about which I commanded you,
   'You shall not eat of it',
cursed is the ground because of you;
   in toil you shall eat of it all the days of your life;
18 thorns and thistles it shall bring forth for you;
   and you shall eat the plants of the field.
19 By the sweat of your face
   you shall eat bread
until you return to the ground,
   for out of it you were taken;
you are dust,
   and to dust you shall return."

20 The man named his wife Eve, because she was the mother of all who live. 21 And the Lord God made garments of skins for the man and for his wife, and clothed them.

22 Then the Lord God said, "See, the man has become like one of us, knowing good and evil; and now, he might reach out his hand and take also from the tree of life, and eat, and live for ever"—23 therefore the Lord God sent him forth from the garden of Eden, to till the ground from which he was taken. 24 He drove out the man; and at the east of the garden of Eden he placed the cherubim, and a sword flaming and turning to guard the way to the tree of life.

Ecclesiastes 1–2 (Fourth Century B.C.E.)

The Bible

Ecclesiastes 1

The words of the Teacher, the son of David, king in Jerusalem.
2 Vanity of vanities, says the Teacher,
  vanity of vanities! All is vanity.
3 What do people gain from all the toil
  at which they toil under the sun?
4 A generation goes, and a generation comes,
  but the earth remains forever.
5 The sun rises and the sun goes down,
  and hurries to the place where it rises.
6 The wind blows to the south,
  and goes round to the north;
round and round goes the wind,
  and on its circuits the wind returns.
7 All streams run to the sea,
  but the sea is not full;
to the place where the streams flow,
  there they continue to flow.
8 All things are wearisome;
  more than one can express;
the eye is not satisfied with seeing,
  or the ear filled with hearing.
9 What has been is what will be,
  and what has been done is what will be done;
  there is nothing new under the sun.
10 Is there a thing of which it is said,
  "See, this is new"?
It has already been,
  in the ages before us.
11 The people of long ago are not remembered,
  nor will there be any remembrance
of people yet to come
  by those who come after them.

12 I, the Teacher, when king over Israel in Jerusalem, **13** applied my mind to seek and to search out by wisdom all that is done under heaven; it is an unhappy business that God has given to human beings to be busy with. **14** I saw all the deeds that are done under the sun; and see, all is vanity and a chasing after wind.

15 What is crooked cannot be made straight,
  and what is lacking cannot be counted.

16 I said to myself, "I have acquired great wisdom, surpassing all who were over Jerusalem before me; and my mind has had great experience of wisdom and knowledge." **17** And I applied my mind to know wisdom and to know madness and folly. I perceived that this also is but a chasing after wind.

18 For in much wisdom is much vexation,
and those who increase knowledge increase sorrow.

Ecclesiastes 2

I said to myself, "Come now, I will make a test of pleasure; enjoy yourself." But again, this also was vanity. **2** I said of laughter, "It is mad", and of pleasure, "What use is it?" **3** I searched with my mind how to cheer my body with wine—my mind still guiding me with wisdom—and how to lay hold on folly, until I might see what was good for mortals to do under heaven during the few days of their life. **4** I made great works; I built houses and planted vineyards for myself; **5** I made myself gardens and parks, and planted in them all kinds of fruit trees. **6** I made myself pools from which to water the forest of growing trees. **7** I bought male and female slaves, and had slaves who were born in my house; I also had great possessions of herds and flocks, more than any who had been before me in Jerusalem. **8** I also gathered for myself silver and gold and the treasure of kings and of the provinces; I got singers, both men and women, and delights of the flesh, and many concubines.

9 So I became great and surpassed all who were before me in Jerusalem; also my wisdom remained with me. **10** Whatever my eyes desired I did not keep from them; I kept my heart from no pleasure, for my heart found pleasure in all my toil, and this was my reward for all my toil. **11** Then I considered all that my hands had done and the toil I had spent in doing it, and again, all was vanity and a chasing after wind, and there was nothing to be gained under the sun.

12 So I turned to consider wisdom and madness and folly; for what can the one do who comes after the king? Only what has already been done. **13** Then I saw that wisdom excels folly as light excels darkness.

14 The wise have eyes in their head,
  but fools walk in darkness.

Yet I perceived that the same fate befalls all of them. **15** Then I said to myself, "What happens to the fool will happen to me also; why then have I been so very wise?" And I said to myself that this also is vanity. **16** For there is no enduring remembrance of the wise or of fools, seeing that in the days to come all will have been long forgotten. How can the wise die just like fools? **17** So I hated life, because what is done under the sun was grievous to me; for all is vanity and a chasing after wind.

18 I hated all my toil in which I had toiled under the sun, seeing that I must leave it to those who come after me **19** —and who knows whether they will be wise or foolish? Yet they will be master of all for which I toiled and used my wisdom under the sun. This also is vanity. **20** So I turned and gave my heart up to despair concerning all the toil of my labors under the sun, **21** because sometimes one who has toiled with wisdom and knowledge and skill must leave all to be enjoyed by another who did not toil for it. This also is vanity and a great evil. **22** What do mortals get from all the toil and strain with which they toil under the sun? **23** For all their days are full of pain, and their work is a vexation; even at night their minds do not rest. This also is vanity.

24 There is nothing better for mortals than to eat and drink, and find enjoyment in their toil. This also, I saw, is from the hand of God; **25** for apart from him who can eat or who can have enjoyment? **26** For to the one who pleases him God gives wisdom and knowledge and joy; but to the sinner he gives the work of gathering and heaping, only to give to one who pleases God. This also is vanity and a chasing after wind.

The Rug Maker (2003)

Stephen Bluestone

Tattooed on my hands and wrists, the knotted patterns
repeat themselves, as I tie the warps to the heddle,
to form the frame. Sometimes I sit at the horizontal loom,
the tripod above my head, and lift the alternate warps,
running wefts beneath from the shuttle in my hand.
Or else, seated at a standing loom, between cross beams
and upright posts, I unfurl drawings as the work goes;
these contain designs to guide me as I knot the yarn.
Once I sat in a workshop, in rows with others,
while the master weaver called out changes of color.
That was mechanical, though, and now even men and boys,
ordinary laborers, will weave in shops, on looms
they've never built, running yarn they've never strung.
These days I work in a room in my house, in the dark,
not needing light, or just enough to see the pile,
the hooks and metal combs, and the clippings at my feet.
In this space that feels like a yurt, I remember
the songs I learned from my mother and grandmother,
as our rugs grew like melodies, like the dowries
of beautiful brides contained in fields of endless light.

As the knot counts rise, yet remain the same,
the patterns flow, each line advancing toward the edge.
I always use the sketches, but, as I work,
the details matter less and less, and the pile lifts,
like woven air, up from the loom, towards a brightness
beyond the deepest madder-dyes or the finest silk
or the surface float of gold or silver thread.
And when this happens, my heart will soar
like a young wife's, into the holy distance above me,
into the space between my husband's head and the stars.
And this, too, I learned as a girl, during instruction
in the countless ways there are to plait a fringe.

Hearing stories of ancient palace carpets,
I also learned that every knot is equal to the eye,
yet the eye, always at the same distance from each knot,

must wander like a vine, mirroring and doubling,
into fields more rich than beds of real gardens.
So I gather and separate, combine and divide,
until there is, or seems to be, no end of meandering.
With each arabesque, I scroll through enclosures
of lilies and peonies, peacocks and cypresses,
until, like sand for water to wash with in the desert,
this wandering, too, cleanses for prayer.

More and more, though, my heart is empty.
The daughters of my daughters have kept me alive,
but now, in the cities, where they live among strangers,
their weaving is shallow market stuff,
and their own daughters have other things to learn.
In the great carpet of the mosque at Ardabil,
the central medallion is a golden rosette of the sun,
around which are sixteen almond-shaped pendants,
which enclose, within that light, four lotus blossoms,
the divine source of water, on a gray-blue field.
The earth's boundless tendrils go everywhere,
and the world is as alive as the fingers that knot it,
as the voice of its weaver chattering and singing,
as the look in the eye of a young girl listening.

Cathedral (1983)

Raymond Carver

This blind man, an old friend of my wife's, he was on his way to spend the night. His wife had died. So he was visiting the dead wife's relatives in Connecticut. He called my wife from his in-laws'. Arrangements were made. He would come by train, a five-hour trip, and my wife would meet him at the station. She hadn't seen him since she worked for him one summer in Seattle ten years ago. But she and the blind man had kept in touch. They made tapes and mailed them back and forth. I wasn't enthusiastic about his visit. He was no one I knew. And his being blind bothered me. My idea of blindness came from the movies. In movies, the blind moved slowly and never laughed. Sometimes they were led by seeing-eye dogs. A blind man in my house was not something I looked forward to.

That summer in Seattle she had needed a job. She didn't have any money. The man she was going to marry at the end of the summer was in officer's training school. He didn't have any money, either. But she was in love with the guy, and he was in love with her, etc. She'd seen something in the paper: Help Wanted—Reading for Blind Man, and a telephone number. She phoned and went over, was hired on the spot. She'd worked with this blind man all summer. She read stuff to him, case studies, reports, that sort of thing. She helped him organize his little office in the county social service department. They'd become good friends, my wife and the blind man. How do I know these things? She told me. And she told me something else. On her last day in the office, the blind man asked if he could touch her face. She agreed to this. She told me he ran his fingers over every part of her face, her nose—even her neck! She never forgot it. She even tried to write a poem about it. She was always writing a poem. She wrote a poem or two every year, usually after something really important had happened to her.

When we first started going out together, she showed me the poem. In the poem she recalled his fingers and the way they had moved around over her face. In the poem she talked about what she had felt at the time, about what went through her mind as he touched her nose and lips. I can recall I didn't think much of the poem. Of course I didn't tell her that. Maybe I just don't understand poetry. I admit it's not the first thing I reach for when I pick up something to read.

Anyway, this man who'd first enjoyed her favors, the officer-to-be, he'd been her childhood sweetheart. So okay. I'm saying that at the end of the summer she let the blind man run his hands over her face, said good-bye to him, married her childhood etc., who was now a commissioned officer, and she moved away from Seattle. But they'd kept in touch, she and the blind man. She made the first contact after a year or so. She called him up one night from an Air Force base in Alabama. She wanted to talk. They talked. He asked her to send him a tape and tell him about her life. She did this. She sent the tape. On the tape she told the blind man about her husband and about their life together in the military. She told the blind man she loved her husband but she didn't like it where they lived and she didn't like it that he was a part of the military-industrial complex. She told the blind man she'd written a poem and he was in it. She told him that she was writing a poem about what it was like to be an Air Force officer's wife in the Deep South. The poem wasn't finished yet. She was still writing it. The blind man made a tape. He sent her the tape. She made a tape. This went on for years. My wife's officer was posted to one base and then another. She sent tapes from Moody AFB, McGuire, McConnell, and finally Travis, near Sacramento, where one night she got to feeling lonely and cut off from people she kept losing in that moving-around life. She balked, couldn't go it another step. She went in and swallowed all the pills and capsules in the medicine cabinet and washed them down with a bottle of gin. Then she got into a hot bath and passed out.

But instead of dying she got sick. She threw up. Her officer—Why should he have a name? He was the childhood sweetheart, and what more does he want?—came home from a training mission, found her, and called the ambulance. In time, she put it on the tape and sent the tape to the blind man. Over the years she put all kinds of stuff on tapes and sent the tapes off lickety-split. Next to writing a poem every year, I think it was her chief means of recreation. On one tape she told the blind man she'd decided to live away from her officer for a time. On another tape she told him about her divorce. She and I began going out, and of course she told her blind man about this. She told him everything, so it seemed to me. Once she asked me if I'd like to hear the latest tape from the blind man. This was a year ago. I was on the tape, she said. So I said okay, I'd listen to it. I got us drinks and we settled down in the living room. We made ready to listen. First she inserted the tape into the player and adjusted a couple of dials. Then she pushed a lever. The tape squeaked and someone began to talk in this loud voice. She lowered the volume. After a few minutes of harmless chitchat, I heard my own name rasped out by this stranger, this man I didn't even know! And then this: "From all you've said about him,

I can only conclude—" But we were interrupted, a knock at the door, something, and we didn't get back to the tape. Maybe it was just as well. I'd heard enough, anyway.

Now this same blind stranger was coming to sleep in my house.

"Maybe I could take him bowling," I said to my wife. She was at the draining board doing scalloped potatoes. She put down the knife she was using on the onion and turned around.

"If you love me," she said, "you can do this for me. If you don't love me, okay. But if you had a friend, any friend, and the friend came to visit, I'd make him feel comfortable." She wiped her hands with the dish towel.

"I don't have any blind friends," I said.

"You don't have any friends," she said. "Period. Besides," she said, "god-damnit, his wife's just died! Don't you understand that? The man's lost his wife!"

I didn't answer. She'd told me a little about the blind man's wife. The wife's name was Beulah. Beulah! That's a name for a colored woman.

"Was his wife a Negro?" I asked.

"Are you crazy?" my wife said. "Have you just flipped or something?" She picked up the onion. I saw it hit the floor, then roll under the stove. "What's wrong with you?" she said. "Are you drunk?"

"I'm just asking," I said.

Right then my wife filled me in with more detail than I cared to know. I made a drink and sat at the kitchen table to listen. Pieces of the story began to fall into place.

Beulah had gone to work for the blind man the summer after my wife had stopped working for him. Pretty soon Beulah and the blind man had themselves a church wedding. It was a little wedding—who'd be anxious to attend such a wedding in the first place?—just the two of them, and the minister and the minister's wife. But it was a church wedding just the same. What Beulah had wanted, he'd said. But even then Beulah must have been carrying cancer in her lymph glands. After they had been insep-arable for eight years—my wife's word, inseparable—Beulah's health went into a rapid decline. She died in a Seattle hospital room, the blind man sitting beside the bed and holding on to her hand. They'd married, lived and worked together, slept together—had sex, sure—and then the blind man buried her. All this without his having ever seen what the god-damned woman looked like. It was beyond my understanding. Hearing this, I felt sorry for the blind man for a minute. And then I found myself thinking what a pitiful life this woman must have led. Imagine a woman who could never see herself reflected in the eyes of her loved one. A woman who could go on day after day and never receive the smallest compliment from her beloved. A woman whose husband would never read the expression on her face, be it misery or something better. Someone who could wear make-up or not—what difference to him? She could, if she wanted, wear green eye shadow around one eye, a straight pin in her nostril, yellow slacks and burgundy pumps, no matter. And then to slip off into death, the blind man's hand on her hand, his blind eyes streaming tears—I'm imagining now—her last thought maybe this: that her beloved never knew what she looked like, and she on an express to the grave. Robert was left with a small insurance policy and half of a twenty-peso Mexican coin. The other half of the coin went into the box with her. Pathetic.

So when the time rolled around, my wife went to the rail station. With nothing to do but wait—and sure, I blamed him for that—I was having a drink and watching TV when I heard the car pull into the drive. I got up from the sofa with my drink and went to the window to have a look.

I saw my wife laughing as she parked the car. I saw her get out of the car and shut the door. She was still wearing a smile. Just amazing. She went around to the other side of the car to where the blind man was already starting to get out. This blind man, feature this, he was wearing a full beard! A beard on a blind man! Too much, I say. The blind man reached into the back seat and dragged out a suitcase. My wife took his arm, shut the car door, and, talking all the way, moved him down the drive and then up the steps to the front porch. I turned off the TV. I finished my drink, rinsed the glass, dried my hands. Then I went to the door.

My wife said, "I want you to meet Robert. Robert, this is my husband. I've told you all about him." She closed the porch screen. She was beaming. She had this blind man by his coat sleeve.

The blind man let go of his suitcase and up came his hand.

I took it. He squeezed hard, held my hand, and then he let it go.

"I feel like we've already met," he boomed.

"Likewise," I said. I didn't know what else to say. Then I said, "Welcome. I've heard a lot about you." We began to move then, a little group, from the porch into the living room, my wife guiding him by the arm. He carried his suitcase in his other hand. My wife said things like, "To your left here, Robert. That's right. Now watch it, there's a chair. That's it. Sit down right here. This is the sofa. We just bought this sofa two weeks ago."

I started to say something about the old sofa. I'd liked that old sofa. But I didn't say anything. Then I wanted to say something else, small talk, about the scenic Hudson River. How going to New York, sit on the right-hand side of the train, and coming from New York, the left-hand side.

"Did you have a good train ride?" I said. "Which side of the train did you sit on, by the way?"

"What a question, which side!" my wife said. "What's it matter which side?" she said.

"I just asked," I said.

"Right side," the blind man said. "For the sun. Until this morning," the blind man said, "I hadn't been on a train in nearly forty years. Not since I was a kid. With my folks. That's been a long time. I'd nearly forgotten that sensation. I have winter in my beard now," he said. "So I've been told, anyway. Do I look distinguished, my dear?" he said to my wife.

"You look distinguished, Robert," she said. "Robert," she said.

"Robert, it's just so good to see you." My wife finally took her eyes off the blind man and looked at me.

I had the distinct feeling she didn't like what she saw. I shrugged.

I've never met or personally known anyone who was blind. This blind man was late forties, a heavyset, balding man with stooped shoulders, as if he carried a great weight there. He wore brown slacks, brown cordovan shoes, a light brown shirt, a tie, a sports coat. Spiffy. He also had this full beard. But he didn't carry a cane and he didn't wear dark glasses. I'd always thought dark glasses were a must for the blind. Fact was, I wished he had a pair. At first glance, his eyes looked like anyone else's eyes. But if you looked close there was something different about them. Too much white in the iris, for one thing, and the pupils seemed to move around in the sockets without his knowing it or being able to control it. Creepy. As I stared at his face, I saw the left pupil turn in toward his nose, while the other made a futile effort to keep in one place. But it was only an effort, for that eye was on the roam without his knowing it or wanting it to be.

I said, "Let me get you a drink. What's your pleasure? We have a little of everything. It's one of our pastimes."

"Bub, I'm a Scotch man myself," he said fast enough, in this big voice.

"Right," I said. Bub! "Sure you are. I knew it."

He let his fingers touch his suitcase, which was sitting alongside the sofa. He was taking his bearings. I didn't blame him for that.

"I'll move that up to your room," my wife said.

"No, that's fine," he said loudly. "It can go up when I go up."

"A little water with the Scotch?" I said.

"Very little," he said.

"I knew it," I said.

He said, "Just a tad. The Irish actor, Barry Fitzgerald? I'm like that fellow. When I drink water, Fitzgerald said, I drink water. When I drink whiskey, I drink whiskey." My wife laughed. The blind man brought his hand up under his beard. He lifted his beard slowly and let it drop.

I did the drinks, three big glasses of Scotch with a splash of water in each. Then we made ourselves comfortable and talked about Robert's travels. First the long flight from the West Coast to Connecticut, we covered that. Then from Connecticut up here by train. We had another drink concerning that leg of the trip.

I remembered having read somewhere that the blind didn't smoke because, speculation had it, they couldn't see the smoke they exhaled. I thought I knew that much and that much only about blind people. But this blind man smoked his cigarette down to the nubbin and then lit another one. This blind man filled his ashtray and my wife emptied it.

When we sat down to the table for dinner we had another drink. My wife heaped Robert's plate with cube steak, scalloped potatoes, green beans. I buttered him up two slices of bread. I said, "Here's bread and butter for you." I swallowed some of my drink. "Now let us pray," I said, and the blind man lowered his head. My wife looked at me, her mouth agape. "Pray the phone won't ring and the food doesn't get cold," I said.

We dug in. We ate everything there was to eat on the table. We ate like there was no tomorrow. We didn't talk. We ate. We scarfed. We grazed that table. We were into serious eating. The blind man had right away located his foods, he knew just where everything was on his plate. I watched with admiration as he used his knife and fork on the meat. He'd cut two pieces of meat, fork the meat into his mouth, and then go all out for the scalloped potatoes, the beans next, and then he'd tear off a hunk of buttered bread and eat that. He'd follow this up with a big drink of milk. It didn't seem to bother him to use his fingers once in a while, either. He used his bread to scoop beans.

We finished everything, including half of a strawberry pie. For a few moments we sat as if stunned. Sweat beaded on our faces. Finally, we got up from the table and left the dirty plates. We didn't look back. We took ourselves into the living room and sank into our places again. Robert and my wife sat on the sofa. I took the big chair. We had us two or three more drinks while they talked about the major things that had transpired for them in the past ten years. For the most part, I just listened. Now and then I joined in. I didn't want him to think I'd left the room, and I didn't want her to think I was feeling left out. They talked of things that had happened to them—to them!—these past ten years. I waited in vain to hear my name on my wife's sweet lips: "And then my dear husband came into my life"—something like that. But I heard nothing of the sort. More talk of Robert. Robert had done a little of everything, it seemed, a regular blind jack-of-all-trades. But most recently he and his wife had had an Amway distributorship, from which, I gathered, they'd earned their living, such as it was. The blind man was also a ham radio operator. He talked in his loud voice about conversations he'd had with fellow operators in Guam, the Philippines, Alaska, even Tahiti. He said he'd have a lot of friends there if he ever wanted to go visit those places. From time to time he'd turn his blind face toward me, put his hand under his beard, ask me something. How long had I been at my present position? (Three years.) Did I like my work? (I didn't.) Was I going to stay with it? (What were the options?)

Finally, when I thought he was beginning to run down, I got up and turned on the TV.

My wife looked at me with irritation. She was heading toward a boil. Then she looked at the blind man and said, "Robert, do you have a TV?"

The blind man said, "My dear, I have two TVs. I have a color set and a black-and-white thing, an old relic. It's funny, but if I turn the TV on, and I'm always turning it on, I turn the color set on. Always. It's funny."

I didn't know what to say to that. I had absolutely nothing to say about that. No opinion. So I watched the news program and tried to listen to what the announcer was saying.

"This is a color TV," the blind man said. "Don't ask me how, but I can tell."

"We traded up a while ago," I said.

The blind man had another taste of his drink. He lifted his beard, sniffed it, and let it fall. He leaned forward on the sofa. He positioned his ashtray on the coffee table, then put the lighter to his cigarette. He leaned back on the sofa and crossed his legs at the ankles.

My wife covered her mouth, and then she yawned. She stretched. She said, "I think I'll go upstairs and put on my robe. I think I'll change into something else. Robert, you make yourself comfortable," she said.

"I'm comfortable," the blind man said.

"I want you to feel comfortable in this house," she said.

"I am comfortable," the blind man said.

After she'd left the room, he and I listened to the weather report and then to the sports roundup. My wife had been gone so long I didn't know if she was going to come back. I thought she might have gone to bed. I wished she'd come back downstairs. I didn't want to be left alone with a blind man. I asked him if he wanted another drink, and he said sure. Then I asked if he wanted to smoke dope with me. I said I'd just rolled a number. I hadn't, but I planned to do so in about two shakes.

"I'll try some with you," he said.

"Damn right," I said. "That's the stuff."

I got our drinks and sat down on the sofa with him. Then I rolled us two fat numbers. I lit one and passed it. I brought it to his fingers. He took it and inhaled.

"Hold it as long as you can," I said. I could tell he didn't know the first thing.

My wife came back downstairs wearing her robe and pink slippers. "What do I smell?" she said.

"We thought we'd have us some cannabis," I said.

My wife gave me a purely savage look. Then she looked at him and said, "Robert, I didn't know you smoked."

He said, "I do now, my dear. First time for everything," he said. "But I don't feel anything yet."

"This stuff is pretty mellow," I said. "This stuff is mild. It's dope you can reason with. It doesn't mess you up."

"Not much it doesn't, bub," he said, and laughed.

My wife sat on the sofa between the blind man and me. I passed her the number. She took it and inhaled and then passed it back to me. "Which way is this going?" she said. Then she said, "I shouldn't be smoking this. I can hardly keep my eyes open as it is. That dinner did me in. I should-n't have eaten so much."

"It was the strawberry pie," the blind man said. "That's what did it," he said, and he laughed his big laugh. Then he shook his head.

"There's more strawberry pie," I said.

"Do you want some more, Robert?" my wife asked.

"Maybe in a little while," he said.

We gave our attention to the TV. My wife yawned again. She said, "Your bed is made up when you feel like going to bed, Robert. I know you must have had a long day. When you're ready to go to bed, say so." She pulled his arm. "Robert?"

He came to and said, "I've had a real nice time. This beats tapes, doesn't it?"

I said, "Coming at you," and I put the number between his fingers. He inhaled, held the smoke, and then let it go. It was like he'd been doing it since he was nine years old.

"Thanks, bub," he said. "But I think this is all for me. I think I'm begin-ning to feel it," he said. He held the burning roach out for my wife.

"Same here," she said. "Ditto. Me too." She took the roach and passed it to me. "I may just sit here for a while between you two guys with my eyes closed. But don't let me bother you, okay? Either one of you. If it bothers you, say so. Otherwise, I may just sit here with my eyes closed until you're ready to go to bed," she said. "Your bed's made up, Robert, when you're ready. It's right next to our room at the top of the stairs. We'll show you up when you're ready. You wake me up now, you guys, if I fall asleep." She said that and then she closed her eyes and went to sleep.

The news program ended. I got up and turned the channel. I sat back down on the sofa. I wished my wife hadn't pooped out. Her head lay across the back of the sofa, her mouth open. She'd turned so that her robe had slipped away from her legs, exposing a juicy thigh. I reached to draw her robe over the thigh, and it was then I glanced at the blind man. What the hell! I flipped the robe open again.

"You say when you want some strawberry pie," I said.

"I will," he said.

I said, "Are you tired? Do you want me to take you up to your bed? Are you ready to hit the hay?"

"Not yet," he said. "No, I'll stay up with you, bub. If that's all right. I'll stay up until you're ready to turn in. We haven't had a chance to talk. Know what I mean? I feel like me and her monopolized the evening." He lifted his beard and he let it fall. He picked up his cigarettes and his lighter.

"That's all right," I said. Then I said, "I'm glad for the company." And I guess I was. Every night I smoked dope and stayed up as long as I could before I fell asleep. My wife and I hardly ever went to bed at the same time. When I did go to sleep, I had these dreams. Sometimes I'd wake up from one of them, my heart going crazy.

Something about the Church and the Middle Ages, narrated by an Englishman, was on the TV. Not your run-of-the-mill TV fare. I wanted to watch something else. I turned to the other channels.

But there was nothing on them, either. So I turned back to the first channel and apologized.

"Bub, it's all right," he said. "It's fine with me. Whatever you want to watch is okay. I'm always learning something. Learning never ends. It won't hurt me to learn something tonight. I got ears," he said.

We didn't say anything for a time. He was leaning forward with his head turned at me, while his right ear was aimed in the direction of the set. Very disconcerting. Now and then his eyelids drooped and then they snapped open again. Now and then he put his fingers into his beard and tugged, as if thinking about something he was hearing on the television.

On the screen a group of men wearing cowls was being set upon and tormented by men dressed in skeleton costumes and men dressed as devils. The men dressed as devils wore devil masks, horns, and long tails. This pageant was part of a procession. The Englishman said it all took place in

Málaga, Spain, once a year. I tried to explain to the blind man what was happening.

"Skeletons," he said. "I know about skeletons," he said, and he nodded.

The TV showed Chartres Cathedral. Then there was a long slow look at Sainte-Chapelle. Finally the picture switched to Notre-Dame, with its flying buttresses, its spires reaching toward clouds. The camera pulled away to show the whole of the cathedral rising above the skyline.

There were times when the Englishman who was telling the thing would shut up, would simply let the camera move around over the cathedrals. Or else the camera would tour the countryside, men in fields walking behind oxen. I waited as long as I could. Then I felt I had to say something. I said, "They're showing the outside of this cathedral now. Gargoyles. Little statues carved to look like monsters. Now I guess they're in Italy. Yeah, they're in Italy. There's fresco paintings on the walls of this one church."

"What's fresco painting, bub?" he asked, and he sipped from his drink.

I reached for my glass. But it was empty. I tried to remember what I could remember about frescoes. "You're asking me what are frescoes?" I said. "That's a good question. I don't know."

The camera moved to a cathedral outside Lisbon, Portugal. The differences in the Portuguese cathedral compared with the French and Italian were not that great. But they were there. Mostly the interior stuff. Then something occurred to me and I said, "Something has occurred to me. Do you have an idea what a cathedral is? What they look like, that is? Do you follow me? If somebody says *cathedral* to you, do you have any notion what they're talking about? Do you know the difference between that and a Baptist church, say? Or that and a mosque, or synagogue?"

He let the smoke issue from his mouth. "I know they took hundreds of workers fifty or a hundred years to build," he said. "I just heard the man say that, of course. I know generations of the same families worked on a cathedral. I heard him say that, too. The men who began their life's work on them, they never lived to see the completion of their work. In that wise, bub, they're no different from the rest of us, right?" He laughed. Then his eyelids drooped again. His head nodded. He seemed to be snoozing. Maybe he was imagining himself in Portugal. The TV was showing another cathedral now. This one was in Germany. The Englishman's voice droned on. "Cathedrals," the blind man said. He sat up and rolled his head back and forth. "If you want the truth, bub, that's about all I know. What I just said. What I heard him say. But maybe you could describe one to me? I wish you'd do it. I'd like that. If you want to know, I really don't have a good idea."

I stared hard at the shot of the cathedral on the TV. It held a minute. Then it was gone, and the view was of the inside with rows of benches and high windows. How could I even begin to describe it? But say my life depended on it. Say my life was being threatened by an insane Turkish bey.

They took the camera outside again. I stared some more at the cathedral before the picture flipped off into the countryside. There was no use. I turned to the blind man and said, "To begin with, they're very tall. Very, very tall." I was looking around the room for clues. I tried again. "They reach way up. Up and up. Toward the sky. They soar. They're like poetry, that's what they're like. They're so big, some of them, they have to have these supports. To help hold them up, so to speak. These supports are called buttresses. They remind me of viaducts for some reason. But maybe you don't know viaducts, either? Sometimes the cathedrals have devils and such carved into the front. Sometimes great lords and ladies. Don't ask me why this is," I said. He was nodding. The whole upper part of his body seemed to be moving back and forth. "I'm not doing so good, am I?" I said.

He stopped nodding and leaned forward on the edge of the sofa. As he listened to me, he was running his fingers through his beard. I wasn't getting through to him though, I could see that. But he waited for me to go on just the same. He nodded, as if trying to encourage me. I tried to think what else I could say. "They're really big. They're massive. They're built of stone. Marble, too, sometimes. In those old days, when they built cathedrals, men aspired to be close to God. In those days God was an important part of everyone's life. This was reflected in their cathedral building. I'm sorry," I said, "but it looks like that's the best I can do for you. I'm just no good at it."

"That's all right, bub," he said. "Hey, listen. I hope you don't mind my asking you. Can I ask you something? Let me ask you a simple question, yes or no. I'm just curious and there's no offense. You're my host. But let me ask if you are in any way religious? You don't mind my asking?"

I shook my head. He couldn't see that, though. A wink is the same as a nod to a blind man. "I guess I'm agnostic or something. No, the fact is, I don't believe in it. Anything. Sometimes it's hard. You know what I'm saying?"

"Sure, I do," he said.

"Right," I said.

The Englishman was still holding forth. My wife sighed in her sleep. She drew a long breath and continued with her sleep.

"You'll have to forgive me," I said. "But I can't tell you what a cathedral looks like. It just isn't in me to do it. I can't do any more than I've done." The blind man sat very still, his head down, as he listened to me. "The truth is, cathedrals don't mean anything special to me. Nothing. Cathedrals. They're something to look at on late-night TV. That's all they are."

It was then he cleared his throat. He brought something up. He took a handkerchief from his back pocket. In a minute he said, "I get it, bub. It's okay. It happens. Don't worry about it," he said. "Hey, listen to me. Will you do me a favor? I got an idea. Why don't you find us some heavy paper? And a pen. We'll do something. An experiment. Sure, you can do it. You can. We'll draw one together. Get us a pen and some heavy paper. Go on, bub, get the stuff," he said.

So I went upstairs. My legs felt like they didn't have any strength in them. They felt like they did sometimes after I'd run a couple miles. In my wife's room I looked around. I found some ballpoints in a little basket on her table. And then I tried to think where to look for the kind of paper he was talking about.

Downstairs, in the kitchen, I found a shopping bag with onion skins in the bottom of the bag. I emptied the bag and shook it. I brought it into the living room and sat down with it near his legs. I moved some things, smoothed the wrinkles from the bag, spread it out on the coffee table. The blind man got down from the sofa and sat next to me on the carpet.

He ran his fingers over the paper. He went up and down the sides of the paper and the edges, top and bottom. He fingered the corners. "All right," he said. "All right. Let's do her."

He found my hand, the hand with the pen. He closed his hand over my hand. "Go ahead, bub, draw," he said. "Draw. You'll see. I'll follow along with you. It'll be all right. Just begin now, like I'm telling you. You'll see. Draw," he said.

So I began. First I drew a box that resembled a house. It could have been the house I lived in. Then I put a roof on the house. At either end of the roof I drew spires. Crazy.

"Swell," he said. "Terrific. You're doing fine," he said. "Never thought anything like this could happen in your lifetime, did you? Well, it's a strange life, bub, we all know that. Go on now. Keep it up."

I put in windows with arches. I drew flying buttresses. I hung great doors. I couldn't stop. The TV station went off the air. I put down the pen and closed and opened my fingers. The blind man felt around over the paper. He moved the tips of his fingers slowly over the paper, over what I'd drawn, and he nodded. "Doing fine," he said.

I took up the pen, and he found my hand once more. I kept at it. I'm no artist. But I kept drawing just the same.

My wife opened her eyes and gazed at us. She sat up on the sofa, her robe hanging open. She said, "What are you doing? What in the world are you doing?"

I didn't answer her. The blind man said, "We're drawing a cathedral, dear. Me and him are working on something important. Press hard now," he said to me. "That's right. That's good," he said. "Sure. You got it, bub. I can tell. You didn't think you could. But you can, can't you? You're cooking with Crisco now. You'll see. Know what I'm saying? We're going to have us something here in a minute. How's the old arm?" he said. "Put some people in there now. What's a church without people, bub?"

"What's going on?" my wife said. "Robert, what are you doing? What's going on?"

"It's all right," he said to her. "Close your eyes now, bub," he said.

I did that. I closed them just like he said.

"Are they closed?" he said, "Don't fudge."

"They're closed," I said.

"Keep them that way," he said. He said, "Don't stop now." So we kept on with it. His fingers rode my fingers as my hand went over the rough paper. It was like nothing else in my life up to now.

In a minute he said, "I think that's enough. I think you got the idea," he said. "Take a look. What do you think?"

But I had my eyes closed. I thought I'd keep them closed a little longer. I thought it was something I ought not to forget.

"Well?" he said. "Are you looking?"

My eyes were still closed. I was in my house and I knew that. But I did-n't feel inside anything.

"It's really something," I said.

An Account of My Hut (1212)

Kamo no Chōmei

The flow of the river is ceaseless and its water is never the same. The bubbles that float in the pools, now vanishing, now forming, are not of long duration: so in the world are man and his dwellings. It might be imagined that the houses, great and small, which vie roof against proud roof in the capital remain unchanged from one generation to the next, but when we examine whether this is true, how few are the houses that were there of old. Some were burnt last year and only since rebuilt; great houses have crumbled into hovels and those who dwell in them have fallen no less. The city is the same, the people are as numerous as ever, but of those I used to know, a bare one or two in twenty remain, They die in the morning, they are born in the evening, like foam on the water.

Whence does he come, where does he go, man that is born and dies? We know not. For whose benefit does he torment himself in building houses that last but a moment, for what reason is his eye delighted by them? This too we do not know. Which will be first to go, the master or his dwelling? One might just as well ask this of the dew on the morning-glory. The dew may fail and the flower remain—remain, only to be withered by the morning sun. The flower may fade before the dew evaporates, but though it does not evaporate, it waits not the evening.

The Great Fire

In the forty and more years that have passed since first I became aware of the meaning of things, I have witnessed many terrible sights. It was, I believe, the twenty-eighth day of the fourth month of 1177, on a night when the wind blew fiercely without a moment of calm, that a fire broke out toward nine o'clock in the southeast of the capital and spread north-west. It finally reached the gates and buildings of the palace, and within the space of a single night all was reduced to ashes. The fire originated in a little hut where a sick man lodged.

The fire fanned out as the shifting wind spread it, first in one direction and then another. Houses far away from the conflagration were enveloped in the smoke, while the area nearby was a sea of flames. The ashes were blown up into the sky, which turned into a sheet of crimson from the reflected glare of the fire, and the flames, relentlessly whipped by the wind, seemed to fly over two or three streets at a time. Those who were caught in the midst could not believe it was actually happening: some collapsed, suffocated by the smoke, others surrounded by flames died on the spot. Still others barely managed to escape with their lives, but could not rescue any of their property: all their treasures were turned into ashes. How much had been wasted on them!

Sixteen mansions belonging to the nobility were burnt, not to speak of innumerable other houses. In all, about a third of the capital was destroyed. Several thousand men and women lost their lives, as well as countless horses and oxen. Of all the follies of human endeavor, none is more pointless than expending treasures and spirit to build houses in so dangerous a place as the capital.

The Whirlwind

Again, on the twenty-ninth day of the fourth moon of 1180, a great whirlwind sprang up in the northeast of the capital and violently raged as far south as the Sixth Ward. Every house, great or small, was destroyed within the area engulfed by the wind. Some were knocked completely flat, others were left with their bare framework standing. The tops of the gates were blown off and dropped four or five hundred yards away, and fences were swept down, making neighboring properties one. Innumerable treasures from within the houses were tossed into the sky; roofs of bark or thatch were driven like winter leaves in the wind. A smoke-like dust rose, blindingly thick, and so deafening was the roar that the sound of voices was lost in it. Even so must be the blasts of Hell, I thought.

Not only were many houses damaged or destroyed, but countless people were hurt or crippled while repairing them. The whirlwind moved off in a southwesterly direction, leaving behind many to bewail its passage. People said in wonder, "We have whirlwinds all the time, but never one like this. It is no common case—it must be a presage of terrible things to come."

The Moving of the Capital

In the sixth month of the same year the capital was suddenly moved, a most unexpected occurrence. It had been hundreds of years since the reign of the Emperor Saga when the capital was fixed in Kyoto.[1] The site of the capital was not a thing lightly to be changed without sufficient reason, and the people were excessively agitated and worried by the news.

However, complaints served no purpose and everyone moved, from the Emperor, his ministers, and the nobility on downward. Of all those who served the court, not a soul was left in the old capital. Those who had ambitions of office or favors to ask of the Emperor vied to be the first to make the move. Only those who, having lost their chances of success, were superfluous in the world and had nothing to hope for, remained behind, although with sorrow. The mansions whose roofs had rivaled one another fell with the passing days to rack and ruin. Houses were dismantled and floated down the Yodo River, and the capital turned into empty fields before one's eyes. People's ways changed completely—now horses were prized and oxcarts fell into disuse. Estates by the sea in the south or west were highly desired, and no one showed any liking for manors in the east or the north.[2]

About this time I happened to have business which took me to the new capital. The site was so cramped that there was not even enough space to divide the city into the proper number of streets.[3] To the north the land rose up high along a ridge of hills and to the south sloped down to the sea. The roar of the waves made a constant din, and the salt winds were of a terrible severity. The palace was in the mountains and, suggesting as it did the log construction of the ancient palaces, was not without its charms.

I wondered where they could have erected the houses that were daily dismantled and sent down the river so thick as to clog it. There were still many empty fields, and few houses standing. The old capital was now desolate but the new one had yet to be finished. Men all felt uncertain as drifting clouds. Those people who were natives of the place lamented the loss of their land, and those who now moved there complained over the difficulties of putting up houses. I could see on the roads men on horseback who should have been riding in carriages; instead of wearing court robes they were in simple service dress. The manners of the capital had suddenly changed and were now exactly like those of rustic soldiers.

Everywhere people could be heard wondering if future disorders were portended, and indeed, with the passage of the days, the country came to be torn by disturbances and unrest. The sufferings of the people were not, however, entirely in vain—in the winter of the same year the capital was returned to Kyoto. But what had happened to the dismantled houses? They could not all have been re-erected in their former grandeur.

Some faint reports have reached my ears that in the wise reigns of former days the country was ruled with clemency. Then the Imperial palace was thatched with straw, and not even the eaves were aligned.[4] When the

Emperor saw that the smoke rising from the kitchen fires was thin, he went so far as to remit the taxes, although they were not excessive. That was because he loved his people and sought to help them. If we compare present conditions with those of ancient times, we may see how great is the difference.

The Famine

Again, about 1181—it is so long ago that I cannot remember for certain— there was a famine in the country which lasted two years, a most terrible thing. A drought persisted through the spring and summer, while the autumn and winter brought storms and floods. One disaster followed another, and the grains failed to ripen. All in vain was the labor of tilling the soil in spring or planting in summer, for there was none of the joy of the autumn reaping or winter harvest. Some of the people as a result abandoned their lands and crossed into other provinces; some forgot their homes and went to live in the mountains. All manner of prayers were begun and extraordinary devotions performed, but without the slightest effect.

The capital had always depended on the countryside for its needs, and when supplies ceased to come it became quite impossible for people to maintain their composure. They tried in their desperation to barter for food one after another of their possessions, however cheaply, but no one desired them. The rare person who was willing to trade had contempt for money and set a high value on his grain. Many beggars lined the roads, and their doleful cries filled the air.

Thus the first year of the famine at last drew to a close. It was thought that the new year would see an improvement, but it brought instead the additional affliction of epidemics, and there was no sign of any amelioration. The people were starving, and with the passage of days approached the extremity, like fish gasping in insufficient water. Finally, people of quality, wearing hats and with their legs covered,[5] were reduced to going from house to house desperately begging. Overwhelmed by misery, they would walk in a stupor, only presently to collapse. The number of those who died of starvation outside the gates or along the roads may not be reckoned. There being no one even to dispose of the bodies, a stench filled the whole world, and there were many sights of decomposing bodies too horrible to behold. Along the banks of the Kamo River there was not even room for horses and cattle to pass.

The lower classes and the wood-cutters were also at the end of their strength, and as even firewood grew scarce those without other resources broke up their own houses and took the wood to sell in the market. The amount obtainable for all that a man could carry, however, was not enough to sustain life a single day. Strange to relate, among the sticks of firewood were some to which bits of vermilion or gold and silver leaf still adhered. This, I discovered, came about because people with no other means of living were robbing the old temples of their holy images or breaking up the furnishings of the sacred halls for firewood. It was because I was born in a world of foulness and evil that I was forced to witness such heartbreaking sights.

There were other exceedingly unhappy occurrences. In the case of husbands and wives who refused to separate, the ones whose affections were the stronger were certain to die first. This was because, whether man or woman, they thought of themselves second and gave to their beloved whatever food they occasionally managed to get. With parents and children it inevitably happened that the parents died first. Sometimes an infant, not realizing that its mother was dead, would lie beside her, sucking at her breast.

The Abbot Ryūgyō of the Ninnaji, grieving for the countless people who were dying, gathered together a number of priests who went about writing the letter A on the forehead of every corpse they saw, thus establishing communion with Buddha.[6] In an attempt to determine how many people had died, they made a count during the fourth and fifth months, and found within the boundaries of the capital over 42,300 corpses lying in the streets. What would the total have been had it included all who died before or after that period, both within the city and in the suburbs? And what if all the provinces of Japan had been included?

I have heard that a similar disaster occurred in 1134, during the reign of the Emperor Sutoku, but I did not myself experience what happened then. Of all that has passed before my eyes, this famine was the strangest and saddest of all disasters.

The Earthquake

Then there was the great earthquake of 1185, of an intensity not known before. Mountains crumbled and rivers were buried, the sea tilted over and immersed the land. The earth split and water gushed up; boulders were sundered and rolled into the valleys. Boats that rowed along the shores were swept out to sea. Horses walking along the roads lost their footing. It is needless to speak of the damage throughout the capital—not a single mansion, pagoda, or shrine was left whole. As some collapsed and others tumbled over, dust and ashes rose like voluminous smoke.

The rumble of the earth shaking and the houses crashing was exactly like that of thunder. Those who were in their houses, fearing that they would presently be crushed to death, ran outside, only to meet with a new cracking of the earth. They could not soar into the sky, not having wings. They could not climb into the clouds, not being dragons. Of all the frightening things of the world, none is so frightful as an earthquake.

Among those who perished was the only child of a samurai family, a boy of five or six, who had made a little house under the overhanging part of a wall and was playing there innocently when the wall suddenly collapsed, burying him under it. His body was crushed flat, with only his two eyes protruding. His parents took him in their arms and wailed uncontrollably, so great was the sorrow they experienced. I realized that grief over a child can make even the bravest warrior forget shame—a pitiable but understandable fact.

The intense quaking stopped after a time, but the after-tremors continued for some while. Not a day passed without twenty or thirty tremors of a severity which would ordinarily have frightened people. After a week or two their frequency diminished, and there would be four or five, then two or three a day; then a day might be skipped, or there be only one tremor in two or three days. After-tremors continued for three months.

Of the four great elements, water, fire, and wind are continually causing disasters, but the earth does not normally afflict man. Long ago, during the great earthquake of the year 855, the head of the Buddha of the Tōdaiji fell off, a terrible misfortune, indeed, but not the equal of the present disaster. At the time everyone spoke of the vanity and meaninglessness of the world, and it seemed that the impurities in men's hearts had somewhat lessened, but with the passage of the months and the days and the coming of the new year people no longer even spoke in that vein.

Hardships of Life in the World

All is as I have described it—the things in the world which make life difficult to endure, our own helplessness and the undependability of our dwellings. And if to these were added the griefs that come from place or particular circumstances, their sum would be unreckonable.

When a man of no great standing happens to live next door to a powerful lord, however happy he may be he cannot celebrate too loudly; however grief-stricken, he cannot raise his voice in lamentations. He is uneasy no matter what he does; in his every action he trembles like a swallow approaching a falcon's nest. The poor man who is the neighbor of a wealthy family is always ashamed of his wretched appearance, and makes his entrances and exits in bursts of flattery. And when he sees how envious his wife and children and his servants are, or hears how the rich family despises him, his mind is incessantly torn by an agitation that leaves not a moment's peace. If a man's house stands in a crowded place and a fire breaks out in the neighborhood, he cannot escape the danger. If it stands in a remote situation, he must put up with the nuisance of going back and forth to the city, and there is always a danger of robbers.

Those who are powerful are filled with greed; and those who have no protectors are despised. Possessions bring many worries; in poverty there is sorrow. He who asks another's help becomes his slave; he who nurtures others is fettered by affection. He who complies with the ways of the world may be impoverished thereby; he who does not, appears deranged. Wherever one may live, whatever work one may do, is it possible even for a moment to find a haven for the body or peace for the mind?

Renunciation of the World

I inherited the house of my father's grandmother and for a long time lived there. Afterward I lost my position and fell on hard times.[7] Many things led me to live in seclusion, and finally, unable longer to remain in my ancestral home, in my thirties I built after my own plans a little cottage. It was a bare tenth the size of the house in which I had lived, and being intended just as a place where I might stay it had no pretensions about it. An earthen wall was, it is true, raised around it, but I lacked the means to put up an ornamental gate. I also built a rough shed of bamboo posts for my carriage. I must confess that when the snow fell or gales blew, I could not but feel alarmed; and since the house was near the Kamo River, there was considerable danger of flooding as well as the threat of bandits.

For over thirty years I had tormented myself by putting up with all the things of this unhappy world. During this time each stroke of misfortune had naturally made me realize the fragility of my life. In my fiftieth year, then, I became a priest and turned my back on the world. Not having any family, I had no ties that would make abandoning the world difficult. I had no rank or stipend—what was there for me to cling to? How many years had I vainly spent among the cloud-covered hills of Ohara?[8]

The Hut Ten Feet Square

Now that I have reached the age of sixty, and my life seems about to evaporate like the dew, I have fashioned a lodging for the last leaves of my years. It is a hut where, perhaps, a traveler might spend a single night; it is like the cocoon spun by an aged silkworm. This hut is not even a hundredth the size of the cottage where I spent my middle years.

Before I was aware, I had become heavy with years, and with each remove my dwelling grew smaller. The present hut is of no ordinary appearance. It is a bare ten feet square and less than seven feet high. I did not choose this particular spot rather than another, and I built my house without consulting any diviners.[9] I laid a foundation and roughly thatched a roof. I fastened hinges to the joints of the beams, the easier to move elsewhere should anything displease me. What difficulty would there be in changing my dwelling? A bare two carts would suffice to carry off the whole house, and except for the carter's fee there would be no expenses at all.

Since first I hid my traces here in the heart of Mount Hino, I have added a lean-to on the south and a porch of bamboo. On the west I have built a shelf for holy water, and inside the but, along the west wall, I have installed an image of Amida. The light of the setting sun shines between its eyebrows.[10] On the doors of the reliquary I have hung pictures of Fugen and Fudō.[11] Above the sliding door that faces north I have built a little shelf on which I keep three or four black leather baskets that contain books of poetry and music and extracts from the sacred writings. Beside, them stand a folding koto and a lute.

Along the east wall I have spread long fern fronds and mats of straw which serve as my bed for the night. I have cut open a window in the eastern wall, and beneath it have made a desk. Near my pillow is a square brazier in which I burn brushwood. To the north of the hut I have staked out a small plot of land which I have enclosed with a rough fence and made into a garden. I grow many species of herbs there.

This is what my temporary hut is like. I shall now attempt to describe its surroundings. To the south there is a bamboo pipe which empties water into the rock pool I have laid. The woods come close to my house, and it is thus a simple matter for me to gather brushwood. The mountain is named Toyama. Creeping vines block the trails and the valleys are overgrown, but to the west is a clearing, and my surroundings thus do not leave me without spiritual comfort.[12] In the spring I see waves of wistaria like purple clouds, bright in the west. In the summer I hear the cuckoo call, promising to guide me on the road of death. In the autumn the voice of the evening insects fills my ears with a sound of lamentation for this cracked husk of a world. In winter I look with deep emotion on the snow, piling up and melting away like sins and hindrances to salvation.

When I do not feel like reciting the *nembutsu*[13] and cannot put my heart into reading the Sutras, no one will keep me from resting or being lazy, and there is no friend who will feel ashamed of me. Even though I make no special attempt to observe the discipline of silence, living alone automatically makes me refrain from the sins of speech; and though I do not necessarily try to obey the Commandments, here where there are no temptations what should induce me to break them?

On mornings when I feel myself short-lived as the white wake behind a boat,[14] I go to the banks of the river and, gazing at the boats plying to and fro, compose verses in the style of the Priest Mansei. Or if of an evening the wind in the maples rustles the leaves, I recall the river at Jinyō, and play the lute in the manner of Minamoto no Tsunenobu.[15] If still my mood does not desert me, I often tune my lute to the echoes in the pines, and play the "Song of the Autumn Wind," or pluck the notes of the "Melody of the Flowing Stream," modulating the pitch to the sound of the water. I am but an indifferent performer, but I do not play to please others. Alone I play, alone I sing, and this brings joy to my heart.

At the foot of this mountain is a rough-hewn cottage where the guardian of the mountain lives. He has a son who sometimes comes to visit me. When I am bored with whatever I am doing, I often go for a walk with him as my companion. He is sixteen and I sixty: though our ages greatly differ we take pleasure in each other's company.

Sometimes I pick flowering reeds or the wild pear, or fill my basket with berries and cress. Sometimes I go to the rice fields at the foot of the mountain and weave wreaths of the fallen ears. Or, when the weather is fine, I climb the peak and look out toward Kyoto, my old home, far, far away. The view has no owner and nothing can interfere with my enjoyment.

When I feel energetic and ready for an ambitious journey, I follow along the peaks to worship at the Iwama or Ishiyama Temple. Or I push through the fields of Awazu to pay my respects to the remains of Semimaru's hut, and cross the Tanagami River to visit the tomb of Sarumaru.[16] On the way back, according to the season, I admire the cherry blossoms or the autumn leaves, pick fern-shoots or fruit, both to offer to the Buddha and to use in my house.

If the evening is still, in the moonlight that fills the window I long for old friends or wet my sleeve with tears at the cries of the monkeys.[17] Fireflies in the grass thickets might be mistaken for fishing-lights off the island of Maki; the dawn rains sound like autumn storms blowing through the leaves. And when I hear the pheasants' cries, I wonder if they call their father or their mother; when the wild deer of the mountain approach me unafraid, I realize how far I am from the world. And when sometimes, as is the wont of old age, I waken in the middle of the night, I stir up the buried embers and make them companions in solitude.

It is not an awesome mountain, but its scenery gives me endless pleasure regardless of the season, even when I listen in wonder to the hooting of the owls.[18] How much more even would the sights mean to someone of deeper thought and knowledge!

When I first began to live here I thought it would be for just a little while, but five years have already passed. My temporary retreat has become rather old as such houses go: withered leaves lie deep by the eaves and moss has spread over the floor. When, as chance has had it, news has come to me from the capital, I have learned how many of the great and mighty have died since I withdrew to this mountain. And how to reckon the numbers of lesser folk? How many houses have been destroyed by the numerous conflagrations? Only in a hut built for the moment can one live without fears. It is very small, but it holds a bed where I may lie at night and a seat for me in the day; it lacks nothing as a place for me to dwell. The hermit crab chooses to live in little shells because it well knows the size of its body. The osprey stays on deserted shores because it fears human beings. I am like them. Knowing myself and the world, I have no ambitions and do not mix in the world. I seek only tranquillity; I rejoice in the absence of grief.

Most people do not build houses for their own sake. Some build for their families or their relatives; some for their friends and acquaintances. Some build for their masters or teachers, and some even to hold their possessions or beasts. I have built for myself and not for others. This is because in times like these, being in the position I am, I have no companion and no servant to help me. Supposing that I had built a spacious house, whom should I have lodged? Whom should I have had live there?

A man's friends esteem him for his wealth and show the greatest affection for those who do them favors. They do not necessarily have loves for persons who bear them warm friendship or who are of an honest disposition. It is better to have as friends music and the sights of nature. A man's servants crave liberal presents and are deferential to those who treat them generously. But however great the care and affection bestowed on them, they do not care the slightest for their master's peace and happiness. It is best to be one's own servant.

If there is something which must be done, I naturally do it myself. I do sometimes weary of work, but I find it simpler to work than to employ a servant and look after him. If some errand requires walking, I do the walking myself. It is disagreeable at times, but it is preferable to worrying about horse-trappings or an oxcart. I divide my body and make two uses of it: my hands are my servants, my feet my vehicle, and they suit me well. When my mind or body is tired, I know it at once and I rest. I employ my servants when they are strong. I say "employ," but I do not often overwork them. If I do not feel like working, it does not upset me. And is it not true that to be thus always walking and working is good for the body? What would be the point in idly doing nothing? It is a sin to cause physical or mental pain: how can we borrow the labor of others?

My clothing and food are as simple as my lodgings. I cover my nakedness with whatever clothes woven of wistaria fiber and quilts of hempen cloth come to hand, and I eke out my life with berries of the fields and nuts from the trees on the peaks. I need not feel ashamed of my appearance, for I do not mix in society and the very scantiness of the food gives it additional savor, simple though it is.

I do not prescribe my way of life to men enjoying happiness and wealth, but have related my experiences merely to show the differences between my former and present life. Ever since I fled the world and became a priest, I have known neither hatred nor fear. I leave my span of days for Heaven to determine, neither clinging to life nor begrudging its end. My body is like a drifting cloud—I ask for nothing, I want nothing. My greatest joy is a quiet nap; my only desire for this life is to see the beauties of the seasons.

The Three Worlds are joined by one mind.[19] If the mind is not at peace, neither beasts of burden nor possessions are of service, neither palaces nor pavilions bring any cheer. This lonely house is but a tiny hut, but I somehow love it. I naturally feel ashamed when I go to the capital and must beg, but when I return and sit here I feel pity for those still attached to the world of dust. Should anyone doubt the truth of my words, let him look to the fishes and the birds. Fish do not weary of the water, but unless one is a fish one does not know why. Birds long for the woods, but unless one is a bird one does not know why. The joys of solitude are similar. Who could understand them without having lived here?

Now the moon of my life sinks in the sky and is close to the edge of the mountain. Soon I must head into the darkness of the Three Ways:[20] why should I thus drone on about myself? The essence of the Buddha's teaching to man is that we must not have attachment for any object. It is a sin for me now to love my little hut, and my attachment to its solitude may also be a hindrance to salvation. Why should I waste more precious time in relating such trifling pleasures?

One calm dawning, I thought over the reasons for this weakness of mine, I told myself that I had fled the world to live in a mountain forest in order to discipline my mind and practice the Way. "And yet, in spite of your monk's appearance, your heart is stained with impurity. Your hut may take after Jōmyō's,[21] but you preserve the Law even worse than Handoku. If your low estate is a retribution for the sins of a previous existence, is it right that you afflict yourself over it? Or should you permit delusion to come and disturb you?" To these questions my mind could offer no reply. All I could do was to use my tongue to recite two or three times the *nembutsu*, however inacceptable from a defiled heart.

It is now the end of the third moon of 1212, and I am writing this at the hut on Toyama.

Notes

[1] The capital was actually established at Kyoto by Saga's father, the Emperor Kammu, in 794.

[2] Oxcarts were the traditional vehicles of the court nobility, who now were changing to military ways. Estates near the new capital of Fukuhara (by the Inland Sea) were desirable, but those near the center of Minamoto power in the east and north were dangerous.

[3] According to the *yin-yang* system of Chinese divination, a capital should have nine streets running east-west and eight streets running north-south, as was observed in the building of Kyoto.

[4] A description combining the virtues of the legendary Chinese Emperor Yao with the Japanese Emperor Nintoku.

[5] Ordinary beggars would have been bareheaded and barelegged.

[6] In Shingon Buddhism, of which the Ninnaji was a center, great significance is given to *A*, the first letter of the Sanskrit alphabet, the beginning of things, and it is believed that all afflictions can be ended by contemplating this letter.

[7] Kamo no Chōmei's family enjoyed a hereditary position as Shinto priests at the Kamo Shrine, but in his generation this privilege was rescinded.

[8] Chōmei felt that even the simplicity of his cottage was still not a suitable life; he had to become a true hermit.

[9] Normally the site of a house was selected after consulting *yin-yang* diviners, but for a Buddhist priest one place was as good as another.

[10] The Buddha was said to have emitted light between his eyebrows.

[11] Fugen (Sanskrit, Samantabhadra) is the highest of the bodhisattvas. Fudō Myōō (Sanskrit, Acalanātha) is the chief of the Guardian Kings.

[12] The west is the direction of Paradise and it was thus auspicious that it should have been clear in that direction. The purple cloud is the one on which Amida Buddha descends to guide the believer to the Western Paradise.

[13] The invocation to Amida Buddha practiced particularly by believers in Jōdo Buddhism.

[14] From a poem by the Priest Mansei. See page 93.

[15] Reference to the famous "Lute Song" (*P'i-p'a Chi*) by Po Chü-i. Minamoto no Tsunenobu (1016–1097) was a famous musician and poet.

[16] Semimaru was a poet of the Heian Period who lived in a hut near the Barrier of Ausakayama. See page 92. Sarumaru-dayū was an early Heian poet, but nothing is known about him. For a later description of roughly the same area, see Bashō's "Unreal Dwelling," page 374.

[17] This paragraph is full of allusions to old poems which it would be tedious to explain.

[18] From a poem by Saigyō: "The mountain is remote; I do not hear the voices of the birds I love, but only the eerie cries of the owl."

[19] From the Avatamska Sutra. The Three Worlds may be interpreted as the past, the present, and the future.

[20] The three paths in the afterworld leading to different types of hells.

[21] Jōmyō (Vimalakirti) was a priest of Sakyamuni's time who built himself a stone hut much like Chōmei's. Handoku (Panthaka) was the most foolish of Sakyamuni's disciples.

What Sort of Despotism Democratic Nations Have to Fear (1835)

Alexis de Tocqueville

I had remarked during my stay in the United States that a democratic state of society, similar to that of the Americans, might offer singular facilities for the establishment of despotism; and I perceived, upon my return to Europe, how much use had already been made by most of our rulers, of the notions, the sentiments, and the wants engendered by this same social condition, for the purpose of extending the circle of their power. This led me to think that the nations of Christendom would perhaps eventually undergo some sort of oppression like that which hung over several of the nations of the ancient world.

A more accurate examination of the subject, and five years of meditations, have not diminished my apprehensions, but they have changed the object of them.

No sovereign ever lived in former ages so absolute or so powerful as to undertake to administer by his own agency, and without the assistance of intermediate powers, all the parts of a great empire: none ever attempted to subject all his subjects indiscriminately to strict uniformity of regulation, and personally to tutor and direct every member of the community. The notion of such an undertaking never occurred to the human mind; and if any man had conceived it, the want of information, the imperfection of the administrative system, and above all, the natural obstacles caused by the inequality of conditions, would speedily have checked the execution of so vast a design.

When the Roman emperors were at the height of their power, the different nations of the empire still preserved manners and customs of great diversity; although they were subject to the same monarch, most of the provinces were separately administered; they abounded in powerful and active municipalities; and although the whole government of the empire was centred in the hands of the emperor alone, and he always remained, upon occasions, the supreme arbiter in all matters, yet the details of social life and private occupations lay for the most part beyond his control. The emperors possessed, it is true, an immense and unchecked power, which allowed them to gratify all their whimsical tastes, and to employ for that purpose the whole strength of the State. They frequently abused that power arbitrarily to deprive their subjects of property or of life; their tyranny was extremely onerous to the few, but it did not reach the greater number, it was fixed to some few main objects, and neglected the rest, it was violent, but its range was limited.

But it would seem that if despotism were to be established amongst the democratic nations of our days, it might assume a different character; it would be more extensive and more mild; it would degrade men without tormenting them. I do not question, that in an age of instruction and equality like our own, sovereigns might more easily succeed in collecting all political power into their own hands, and might interfere more habitually and decidedly within the circle of private interests, than any sovereign of antiquity could ever do. But this same principle of equality which facilitates despotism, tempers its rigour. We have seen how the manners of society become more humane and gentle in proportion as men become more equal and alike. When no member of the community has much power or much wealth, tyranny is, as it were, without opportunities and a field of action. As all fortunes are scanty, the passions of men are naturally circumscribed,—their imagination limited, their pleasures simple. This universal moderation moderates the sovereign himself, and checks within certain limits the inordinate stretch of his desires.

Independently of these reasons drawn from the nature of the state of society itself, I might add many others arising from causes beyond my subject; but I shall keep within the limits I have laid down to myself.

Democratic governments may become violent and even cruel at certain periods of extreme effervescence or of great danger; but these crises will be rare and brief. When I consider the petty passions of our contemporaries, the mildness of their manners, the extent of their education, the purity of their religion, the gentleness of their morality, their regular and industrious habits, and the restraint which they almost all observe in their vices no less than in their virtues, I have no fear that they will meet with tyrants in their rulers, but rather guardians.

I think then that the species of oppression by which democratic nations are menaced is unlike anything which ever before existed in the world: our contemporaries will find no prototype of it in their memories. I am trying myself to choose an expression which will accurately convey the whole of the idea I have formed of it, but in vain; the old words despotism and tyranny are inappropriate: the thing itself is new; and since I cannot name it, I must attempt to define it.

I seek to trace the novel features under which despotism may appear in the world. The first thing that strikes the observation is an innumerable multitude of men all equal and alike, incessantly endeavouring to procure the petty and paltry pleasures with which they glut their lives. Each of them, living apart, is as a stranger to the fate of all the rest,—his children and his private friends constitute to him the whole of mankind; as for the rest of his fellow-citizens, he is close to them, but he sees them not;—he touches them, but he feels them not; he exists but in himself and for himself alone; and if his kindred still remain to him, he may be said at any rate to have lost his country.

Above this race of men stands an immense and tutelary power, which takes upon itself alone to secure their gratifications, and to watch over their fate. That power is absolute, minute, regular, provident, and mild. It would be like the authority of a parent, if, like that authority, its object was to prepare men for manhood; but it seeks on the contrary to keep them in perpetual childhood: it is well content that the people should rejoice, provided they think of nothing but rejoicing. For their happiness such a government willingly labours, but it chooses to be the sole agent and the only arbiter of that happiness: it provides for their security, foresees and supplies their necessities, facilitates their pleasures, manages their principal concerns, directs their industry, regulates the descent of property, and subdivides their inheritances—what remains, but to spare them all the care of thinking and all the trouble of living?

Thus it every day renders the exercise of the free agency of man less useful and less frequent; it circumscribes the will within a narrower range, and gradually robs a man of all the uses of himself. The principle of equality has prepared men for these things: it has predisposed men to endure them, and oftentimes to look on them as benefits.

After having thus successively taken each member of the community in its powerful grasp, and fashioned them at will, the supreme power then extends its arm over the whole community. It covers the surface of society with a network of small complicated rules, minute and uniform, through which the most original minds and the most energetic characters cannot penetrate, to rise above the crowd. The will of man is not shattered, but softened, bent, and guided: men are seldom forced by it to act, but they are constantly restrained from acting: such a power does not destroy, but it prevents existence; it does not tyrannize, but it compresses, enervates, extinguishes, and stupefies a people, till each nation is reduced to be nothing better than a flock of timid and industrious animals, of which the government is the shepherd.

I have always thought that servitude of the regular, quiet, and gentle kind which I have just described, might be combined more easily than is commonly believed with some of the outward forms of freedom; and that it might even establish itself under the wing of the sovereignty of the people.

Our contemporaries are constantly excited by two conflicting passions; they want to be led, and they wish to remain free: as they cannot destroy either one or the other of these contrary propensities, they strive to satisfy them both at once. They devise a sole, tutelary, and all-powerful form of government, but elected by the people. They combine the principle of centralization and that of popular sovereignty; this gives them a respite: they console themselves for being in tutelage by the reflection that they have chosen their own guardians. Every man allows himself to be put in leading strings, because he sees that it is not a person or a class of persons, but the people at large that holds the end of his chain.

By this system the people shake off their state of dependence just long enough to select their master, and then relapse into it again. A great many persons at the present day are quite contented with this sort of compromise between administrative despotism and the sovereignty of the people; and they think they have done enough for the protection of individual freedom when they have surrendered it to the power of the nation at large. This does not satisfy me: the nature of him I am to obey signifies less to me than the fact of extorted obedience.

I do not however deny that a constitution of this kind appears to me to be infinitely preferable to one, which, after having concentrated all the powers of government, should vest them in the hands of an irresponsible person or body of persons. Of all the forms which democratic despotism could assume, the latter would assuredly be the worst.

When the sovereign is elective, or narrowly watched by a legislature which is really elective and independent, the oppression which he exercises over individuals is sometimes greater, but it is always less degrading; because every man, when he is oppressed and disarmed, may still imagine, that whilst he yields obedience it is to himself he yields it, and that it is to one of his own inclinations that all the rest give way. In like manner I can understand that when the sovereign represents the nation, and is dependent upon the people, the rights and the power of which every citizen is deprived, not only serve the head of the state, but the state itself; and that private persons derive some return from the sacrifice of their independence which they have made to the public. To create a representation of the people in every centralized country is, therefore, to diminish the evil which extreme centralization may produce, but not to get rid of it.

I admit that by this means room is left for the intervention of individuals in the more important affairs; but it is not the less suppressed in the smaller and more private ones. It must not be forgotten that it is especially dangerous to enslave men in the minor details of life. For my own part, I should be inclined to think freedom less necessary in great things than in little ones, if it were possible to be secure of the one without possessing the other.

Subjection in minor affairs breaks out every day, and is felt by the whole community indiscriminately. It does not drive men to resistance, but it crosses them at every turn, till they are led to surrender the exercise of their will. Thus their spirit is gradually broken and their character enervated; whereas that obedience, which is exacted on a few important but rare occasions, only exhibits servitude at certain intervals, and throws the burden of it upon a small number of men. It is in vain to summon a people, which has been rendered so dependent on the central power, to choose from time to time the representatives of that power; this rare and brief exercise of their free choice, however important it may be, will not prevent them from gradually losing the faculties of thinking, feeling, and acting for themselves, and thus gradually falling below the level of humanity.

I add that they will soon become incapable of exercising the great and only privilege which remains to them. The democratic nations which have introduced freedom into their political constitution, at the very time when they were augmenting the despotism of their administrative constitution, have been led into strange paradoxes. To manage those minor affairs in which good sense is all that is wanted,—the people are held to be unequal to the task; but when the government of the country is at stake, the people are invested with immense powers; they are alternately made the playthings of their ruler, and his masters—more than kings, and less than men. After having exhausted all the different modes of election, without finding one to suit their purpose, they are still amazed, and still bent on seeking further; as if the evil they remark did not originate in the constitution of the country far more than in that of the electoral body.

It is, indeed, difficult to conceive how men who have entirely given up the habit of self-government should succeed in making a proper choice of those by whom they are to be governed; and no one will ever believe that a liberal, wise, and energetic government can spring from the suffrages of a subservient people.

A constitution, which should be republican in its head and ultra-monarchical in all its other parts, has ever appeared to me to be a short-lived monster. The vices of rulers and the ineptitude of the people would speedily bring about its ruin; and the nation, weary of its representatives and of itself, would create freer institutions, or soon return to stretch itself at the feet of a single master.

from The Prophet (1923)

Kahlil Gibran

Then Almitra spoke again and said, And what of Marriage, master?
And he answered saying:
You were born together, and together you shall be forevermore.
You shall be together when the white wings of death scatter your days.
Aye, you shall be together even in the silent memory of God.
But let there be spaces in your togetherness,
And let the winds of the heavens dance between you.

• • •

Love one another, but make not a bond of love:
Let it rather be a moving sea between the shores of your souls.
Fill each other's cup but drink not from one cup.
Give one another of your bread but eat not from the same loaf.
Sing and dance together and be joyous, but let each one of you be alone,
Even as the strings of a lute are alone though they quiver with the same music.
Give your hearts, but not into each other's keeping.
For only the hand of Life can contain your hearts.
And stand together yet not too near together:
For the pillars of the temple stand apart,
And the oak tree and the cypress grow not in each other's shadow.

And a man said, Speak to us of Self-Knowledge.
And he answered, saying:
Your hearts know in silence the secrets of the days and the nights.
But your ears thirst for the sound of your heart's knowledge.
You would know in words that which you have always known in thought.
You would touch with your fingers the naked body of your dreams.

• • •

And it is well you should.

The hidden well-spring of your soul must needs rise and run murmuring to the sea;

And the treasure of your infinite depths would be revealed to your eyes.

But let there be no scales to weigh your unknown treasure;

And seek not the depths of your knowledge with staff or sounding line.

For self is a sea boundless and measureless.

Say not, "I have found the truth," but rather, "I have found a truth."

Say not, "I have found the path of the soul." Say rather, "I have met the soul walking upon my path."

For the soul walks upon all paths.

The soul walks not upon a line, neither does it grow like a reed.

The soul unfolds itself, like a lotus of countless petals.

And a youth said, Speak to us of Friendship.

And he answered, saying:

Your friend is your needs answered.

He is your field which you sow with love and reap with thanksgiving.

And he is your board and your fireside.

For you come to him with your hunger, and you seek him for peace.

•   •   •

When your friend speaks his mind you fear not the "nay" in your own mind, nor do you withhold the "ay."

And when he is silent your heart ceases not to listen to his heart;

For without words, in friendship, all thoughts, all desires, all expectations are born and shared, with joy that is unacclaimed.

When you part from your friend, you grieve not;

For that which you love most in him may be clearer in his absence, as the mountain to the climber is clearer from the plain.

And let there be no purpose in friendship save the deepening of the spirit.

For love that seeks aught but the disclosure of its own mystery is not love but a net cast forth: and only the unprofitable is caught.

•   •   •

And let your best be for your friend.

If he must know the ebb of your tide, let him know its flood also.

For what is your friend that you should seek him with hours to kill?
Seek him always with hours to live.

For it is his to fill your need, but not your emptiness.

And in the sweetness of friendship let there be laughter, and sharing of pleasures.

For in the dew of little things the heart finds its morning and is refreshed.

from Notes on the State of Virginia, Query XVII. Religion (1784)

Thomas Jefferson

The first settlers in this country were emigrants from England, of the English Church, just at a point of time when it was flushed with complete victory over the religious of all other persuasions. Possessed, as they became, of the powers of making, administering, and executing the laws, they showed equal intolerance in this country with their Presbyterian brethren, who had emigrated to the northern government. The poor Quakers were flying from persecution in England. They cast their eyes on these new countries as asylums of civil and religious freedom; but they found them free only for the reigning sect. Several acts of the Virginia assembly of 1659, 1662, and 1693, had made it penal in parents to refuse to have their children baptized; had prohibited the unlawful assembling of Quakers; had made it penal for any master of a vessel to bring a Quaker into the state; had ordered those already here, and such as should come thereafter, to be imprisoned till they should abjure the country; provided a milder punishment for their first and second return, but death for their third; had inhibited all persons from suffering their meetings in or near their houses, entertaining them individually, or disposing of books which supported their tenets. If no execution took place here, as did in New-England, it was not owing to the moderation of the church, or spirit of the legislature, as may be inferred from the law itself; but to historical circumstances which have not been handed down to us. The Anglicans retained full possession of the country about a century. Other opinions began then to creep in, and the great care of the government to support their own church, having begotten an equal degree of indolence in its clergy, two-thirds of the people had become dissenters at the commencement of the present revolution. The laws, indeed, were still oppressive on them, but the spirit of the one party had subsided into moderation, and of the other had risen to a degree of determination which commanded respect.

The present state of our laws on the subject of religion is this. The convention of May 1776, in their declaration of rights, declared it to be a truth, and a natural right, that the exercise of religion should be free; but when they proceeded to form on that declaration the ordinance of government, instead of taking up every principle declared in the bill of rights, and guarding it by legislative sanction, they passed over that which asserted our religious rights, leaving them as they found them. The same convention, however, when they met as a member of the general assembly in October 1776, repealed all *acts of Parliament* which had rendered criminal the maintaining any opinions in matters of religion, the forbearing to repair to church, and the exercising any mode of worship; and suspended the laws giving salaries to the clergy, which suspension was made perpetual in October 1779. Statutory oppressions in religion being thus wiped away, we remain at present under those only imposed by the common law, or by our own acts of assembly. At the common law, *heresy* was a capital offence, punishable by burning. Its definition was left to the ecclesiastical judges, before whom the conviction was, till the statute of 1 El. c. 1 circumscribed it, by declaring, that nothing should be deemed heresy, but what had been so determined by authority of the canonical scriptures, or by one of the four first general councils, or by other council, having for the grounds of their declaration the express and plain words of the scriptures. Heresy, thus circumscribed, being an offence against the common law, our act of assembly of October 1777, c. 17, gives cognizance of it to the general court, by declaring that the jurisdiction of that court shall be general in all matters at the common law. The execution is by the writ *De haeretico comburendo*. By our own act of assembly of 1705, c. 30, if a person brought up in the Christian religion denies the being of a God, or the Trinity, or asserts there are more Gods than one, or denies the Christian religion to be true, or the scriptures to be of divine authority, he is punishable on the first offence by incapacity to hold any office or employment ecclesiastical, civil, or military; on the second by disability to sue, to take any gift or legacy, to be guardian, executor, or administrator, and by three years' imprisonment without bail. A father's right to the custody of his own children being founded in law on his right of guardianship, this being taken away, they may of course be severed from him, and put by the authority of a court into more orthodox hands. This is a summary view of that religious slavery under which a people have been willing to remain, who have lavished their lives and fortunes for the establishment of their civil freedom.

The error seems not sufficiently eradicated, that the operations of the mind, as well as the acts of the body, are subject to the coercion of the laws. But our rulers can have no authority over such natural rights, only as we have submitted to them. The rights of conscience we never submitted, we could not submit. We are answerable for them to our God. The legitimate powers of government extend to such acts only as are injurious to others. But it does me no injury for my neighbor to say there are twenty gods, or no god. It neither picks my pocket nor breaks my leg. If it be said, his testimony in a court of justice cannot be relied on, reject it then, and be the stigma on him. Constraint may make him worse by making him a hypocrite, but it will never make him a truer man. It may fix him obstinately in his errors, but will not cure them. Reason and free inquiry are the only effectual agents against error. Give a loose to them, they will support the true religion by bringing every false one to their tribunal, to the test of their investigation. They are the natural enemies of error, and of error only. Had not the Roman government permitted free inquiry, Christianity could never have been introduced. Had not free inquiry been indulged at the era of the reformation, the corruptions of Christianity could not have been purged away. If it be restrained now, the present corruptions will be protected, and new ones encouraged. Was the government to prescribe to us our medicine and diet, our bodies would be in such keeping as our souls are now. Thus in France the emetic was once forbidden as a medicine, and the potato as an article of food. Government is just as infallible, too, when it fixes systems in physics. Galileo was sent to the inquisition for affirming that the earth was a sphere; the government had declared it to be as flat as a trencher, and Galileo was obliged to abjure his error. This error, however, at length prevailed, the earth became a globe, and Descartes declared it was whirled round its axis by a vortex. The government in which he lived was wise enough to see that this was no question of civil jurisdiction, or we should all have been involved by authority in vortices. In fact, the vortices have been exploded, and the Newtonian principle of gravitation is now more firmly established, on the basis of reason, than it would be were the government to step in, and to make it an article of necessary faith. Reason and experiment have been indulged, and error has fled before them. It is error alone which needs the support of government. Truth can stand by itself. Subject opinion to coercion: whom will you make your inquisitors? Fallible men; men governed by bad passions, by private as well as public reasons. And why subject it to coercion? To produce uniformity. But is uniformity of opinion desirable? No more than of face and stature. Introduce the bed of Procrustes then, and as there is danger that the large men may beat the small, make us all of a size, by lopping the former and stretching the latter. Difference of opinion is advantageous in religion. The several sects perform the office of a Censor morum over each other. Is uniformity attainable? Millions of innocent men, women, and children, since the introduction of Christianity, have been burnt, tortured, fined, imprisoned; yet we have not advanced one inch towards uniformity. What has been the effect of coercion? To make one half the world fools, and the other half hypocrites. To support roguery and error all over the earth. Let us reflect that it is inhabited by a thousand millions of people. That these profess probably a thousand different systems of religion. That ours is but one of that thousand. That if there be but one right, and ours that one, we should wish to see the 999 wandering sects gathered into the fold of truth. But against such a majority we cannot effect this by force. Reason and persuasion are the only practicable instruments. To make way for these, free inquiry must be indulged; and how can we wish others to indulge it while we refuse it ourselves. But every state, says an inquisitor, has established some religion. No two, say I, have established the same. Is this a proof of the infallibility of establishments? Our sister states of Pennsylvania and New York, however, have long subsisted without any establishment at all. The experiment was new and doubtful when they made it. It has answered beyond conception. They flourish infinitely. Religion is well supported; of various kinds, indeed, but all good enough; all sufficient to preserve peace and order; or if a sect arises, whose tenets would subvert morals, good sense has fair play, and reasons and laughs it out of doors, without suffering the State to be troubled with it. They do not hang more malefactors than we do. They are not more disturbed with religious dissensions. On the contrary, their harmony is unparalleled, and can be ascribed to nothing but their unbounded tolerance, because there is no other circumstance in which they differ from every nation on earth. They have made the happy discovery, that the way to silence religious disputes, is to take no notice of them. Let us too give this experiment fair play, and get rid, while we may, of those tyrannical laws. It is true, we are as yet secured against them by the spirit of the times. I doubt whether the people of this country would suffer an execution for heresy, or a three years' imprisonment for not comprehending the mysteries of the Trinity. But is the spirit of the people an infallible, a permanent reliance? Is it government? Is this the kind of protection we receive in return for the rights we give up? Besides, the spirit of the times may alter, will alter. Our rulers will become corrupt, our people careless. A single zealot may commence persecutor, and better men be his victims. It can never be too often repeated, that the time for fixing every essential right on a legal basis is while our rulers are honest, and ourselves united. From the conclusion of this war we shall be going down hill. It will not then be necessary to resort every moment to the people for support. They will be forgotten, therefore, and their rights disregarded. They will forget themselves, but in the sole faculty of making money, and will never think of uniting to effect a due respect for their rights. The shackles, therefore, which shall not be knocked off at the conclusion of this war, will remain on us long, will be made heavier and heavier, till our rights shall revive or expire in a convulsion.

from Poetry and Professing (2005)

Gordon Johnston

The teacher doesn't identify truth so much as show students how others have found it and what the tools of the search and their proper uses are. The most important lesson isn't *Here is the truth*. It is *The truth must be found*. . . From this course of study there is no graduation, because there is always another, fuller knowledge at which to arrive—and another, fuller selfhood as well. . . . Ideally, teaching is bringing students to preparation not for careers but for the endless dialectics of their lives.

Before students can say anything for themselves or pursue free decisions made in the light of their own thinking, they must become self-conscious. My first experience of this self-consciousness came about in my freshman year of college when I read "Allegory of the Cave" in Sara Wingard's English class and not only became aware of the many removes that separate the individual from the "true light of day" but was forced by my professor to locate myself among these removes. Was I a prisoner chained in the pit of the cave, mistaking shadows for real things? A freed prisoner squinting in pain at the fire that made the shadows? A man in the outside air looking up at the sun? For the first time I found myself thinking about myself thinking—and I repeatedly identified with the prisoner who, on being brought from deep shadow to roaring fireside, turns away from the painful light. The battle between the natural physical reflex of shutting the eyes to light and the intellectual and spiritual compulsion to comprehend that same light became my image for opposibility. My junior year of college Dr. Wingard assigned me the reading of John Henry Cardinal Newman's *The Idea of a University*, in which I underlined these sentences: "Education . . . gives a man a clear, conscious view of his own opinions and judgments, a truth in developing them, an eloquence in expressing them, and a force in urging them. It teaches him to see things as they are, to go right to the point, to disentangle a skein of thought, to detect what is sophistical, and to discard what is irrelevant." I have been disentangling skeins of thought ever since, and arriving again and again at a renewed sense of who I am. I couldn't become a self until I had a conscious view of my own opinions and judgments and an awareness that they were often formulated or acculturated into me without my choosing to embrace them. Once I became conscious of my own limitations in intellect, sympathy, and experience, chiefly by reading and rereading widely,

I began (and continue) to try to transcend those limitations, which in turn led to my developing "just" opinions and judgments rather than unduly prejudiced ones. In my own experience with students I find that they, too, often need Newman's conscious view before they can embark on the journey to selfhood. While they need to see things as they are in the empirical world, their more urgent need is to see them as they are in their own minds, colored by countless subtle human prejudices. Then they can go about identifying and eliminating the sophistical and the irrelevant, which they will continue to do for the rest of their lives. . . . There is always another, fuller personhood at which to arrive.

Awakenings (1996)

Susan Monk Kidd

"That's How I Like to See a Woman"

It was autumn, and everything was turning loose. I was running errands that afternoon. Rain had fallen earlier, but now the sun was out, shining on the tiny beads of water that clung to trees and sidewalks. The whole world seemed red and yellow and rinsed with light. I parked in front of the drugstore where my daughter, Ann, fourteen, had an after-school job. Leaping a puddle, I went inside.

I spotted her right away kneeling on the floor in the toothpaste section, stocking a bottom shelf. I was about to walk over and say hello when I noticed two middle-aged men walking along the aisle toward her. They looked like everybody's father. They had moussed hair, and they wore knit sportshirts the color of Easter eggs, the kind of shirts with tiny alligators sewn at the chest. It was a detail I would remember later as having ironic symbolism.

My daughter did not see them coming. Kneeling on the floor, she was intent on getting the boxes of Crest lined up evenly. The men stopped, peering down at her. One man nudged the other. He said, "Now that's how I like to see a woman—on her knees."

The other man laughed.

Standing in the next aisle, I froze. I watched the expression that crept into my daughter's eyes as she looked up. I watched her chin drop and her hair fall across her face.

Seeing her kneel at these men's feet while they laughed at her subordinate posture pierced me through.

For the previous couple of years I had been in the midst of a tumultuous awakening. I had been struggling to come to terms with my life as a woman—in my culture, my marriage, my faith, my church, and deep inside myself. It was a process not unlike the experience of conception and labor. There had been a moment, many moments really, when truth seized me and I "conceived" myself as woman. Or maybe I reconceived

154

myself. At any rate, it had been extraordinary and surprising to find myself—a conventionally religious woman in my late thirties—suddenly struck pregnant with a new consciousness, with an unfolding new awareness of what it means to be a woman and what it means to be spiritual as *a woman*.

Hard labor had followed. For months I'd inched along, but lately I'd been stuck. I'd awakened enough to know that I couldn't go back to my old way of being a woman, but the fear of going forward was paralyzing. So I'd plodded along, trying to make room for the new consciousness that was unfolding in my life but without really risking change.

I have a friend, a nurse on the obstetrical floor at a hospital, who says that sometimes a woman's labor simply stalls. The contractions grow weak, and the new life, now quite distressed, hangs precariously. The day I walked into the drugstore, I was experiencing something like that. A stalled awakening.

Who knows, I may have stalled interminably if I had not seen my daughter on her knees before those laughing men. I cannot to this day explain why the sight of it hit me so forcibly. But to borrow Kafka's image, it came like an ice ax upon a frozen sea, and suddenly all my hesitancy was shattered. Just like that.

The men's laughter seemed to go on and on. I felt like a small animal in the road, blinded by the light of a truck, knowing some terrible collision is coming but unable to move. I stared at my daughter on her knees before these men and could not look away. Somehow she seemed more than my daughter; she was my mother, my grandmother, and myself. She was every woman ever born, bent and contained in a small, ageless cameo that bore the truth about "a woman's place."

In the profile of my daughter I saw the suffering of women, the confining of the feminine to places of inferiority, and I experienced a collision of love and pain so great I had to reach for the counter to brace myself.

This posture will not perpetuate itself in her life, I thought.

Still I didn't know what to do. When I was growing up, if my mother had told me once, she'd told me a thousand times, "If you can't say something nice, don't say anything at all." I'd heard this from nearly everybody. It was the kind of thing that got cross-stitched and hung in kitchens all over my native South.

I'd grown up to be a soft-voiced, sweet-mouthed woman who, no matter how assailing the behavior before me or how much I disagreed with it, responded nicely or else zip-locked my mouth shut. I had swallowed enough defiant, disputatious words in my life to fill a shelf of books.

But it occurred to me that if I abandoned my daughter at that moment, if I simply walked away and was silent, the feminine spirit unfolding inside her might also become crouched and silent. Perhaps she would learn the *internal* posture of being on her knees.

The men with their blithe joke had no idea they had tapped a reservoir of pain and defiance in me. It was rising now, unstoppable by any earthly force.

I walked toward them. "I have something to say to you, and I want you to hear it," I said.

They stopped laughing. Ann looked up.

"This is my daughter," I said, pointing to her, my finger shaking with anger. "You may like to see her and other women on their knees, but we don't belong there. *We don't belong there!*"

Ann rose to her feet. She glanced sideways at me, sheer amazement spread over her face, then turned and faced the men. I could hear her breath rise and fall with her chest as we stood there shoulder to shoulder, staring at their faces.

"Women," one of them said. They walked away, leaving Ann and me staring at each other among the toothpaste and dental floss.

I smiled at her. She smiled back. And though we didn't say a word, more was spoken between us in that moment than perhaps in our whole lives.

I left the drugstore that day so internally jolted by the experience that everything in me began to shift. I sat in the car feeling like a newborn, dangled upside down and slapped.

Throughout my awakening, I'd grown increasingly aware of certain attitudes that existed in our culture, a culture long dominated by men. The men in the drugstore had mirrored one attitude in particular, that of seeking power over another, of staying up by keeping others down.

Sitting in my car replaying my statement back to those men—that women did not belong on their knees—I knew I had uttered my declaration of intent.

That night Ann came to my room. I was sitting in bed reading. She climbed up beside me and said, "Mama, about this afternoon in the drugstore. . ."

"Yeah?"

"I just wanted to say, thanks."

Conceiving the Feminine Self

Poet Maxine Kumin wrote, "When Sleeping Beauty wakes up, she is almost fifty years old." I wasn't fifty when my awakening began, but I was nearing forty. I'd lived just long enough for the bottom to start falling out of my notions of womanhood.

It all started when I was thirty-eight, two years before I walked into the drugstore. I was a full-time writer, spending many hours immersed in books. I lived in a nice house with a man I'd been married to for eighteen years, and we had two children, Bob and Ann, both in early adolescence. I went to church regularly and was involved in the social life of the small, Southern town where we lived. The last thing I expected was an encounter with feminist spirituality.

Feminist. What a word to deal with. I felt a secret sympathy for the underlying cause of feminism—what it might do for women—but I was uncomfortable with the word, uncomfortable with the images it carried. Overall, I'd kept a discreet distance from it. In fact, if there had been a contest for Least Likely to Become a Feminist, I probably could have made the finals on image alone.

But then one September night, I fell asleep and dreamed a momentous dream:

> While sitting on the sand at the edge of the ocean, I am amazed to see that I am nine months pregnant and starting labor. I took around for help but I am on an island by myself. Well, I think. I'll just have to deliver the baby myself. As the labor begins, I rub my abdomen and breathe deeply. I scoop up water as the waves flow ashore and bathe my abdomen and face. The pain comes and goes. Sometimes I cry and feel I might faint, but then the pain subsides. Finally I start to push. I give birth to a healthy baby girl. I hold her up, laughing with joy. I bring her close and look into her eyes. I am shocked to see I have given birth to myself, that I am the baby and the mother both.

I woke abruptly. You know how some dreams are so vivid you have to spend a few moments after you wake assuring yourself it didn't really happen? That's how I felt, like I needed to look around in the sheets for a newborn. I felt awed, like something of import and worthy of great reverence had taken place.

For years I'd written down my dreams, believing, as I still do, that one of the purest sources of knowledge about our lives comes from the symbols and images deep within. So, being careful not to wake my husband, I slipped out of bed, crept through the darkness into my study, and wrote down the dream.

At breakfast I took my tea to the patio and stared at the morning, wondering about this baby girl who was myself. What new potential did she represent? Who would she grow up to be? The dream was a mystery in many ways, but somehow I knew clearly that it was about my life as a woman.

Despite that realization, it didn't quite sink in that this dream was signaling the beginning of a profound new journey. I didn't know then that the child in the dream would turn my world upside down. That she would eventually change every fundamental relationship in my life: my way of being religious and spiritual, my way of being a woman in the world, my marriage, my career, and my way of relating to other women, to the earth, and even to myself.

At forty (or sometimes thirty or sixty), women grow ripe for feminist spiritual conception. By then we've been around long enough to grow disenchanted with traditional female existence, with the religious experience women have been given to live out.

Nearing forty, I needed to rethink my life as a "man-made woman." To take back my soul. Gradually I began to see what I hadn't seen before, to feel things that until then had never dared to enter my heart. I became aware that as a woman I'd been on my knees my whole life and not really known it. Most of all, I ached for the woman in me who had not yet been born, though I couldn't have told you then the reason for the ache.

When this disenchantment, this ripeness, begins, a woman's task is to conceive herself. If she does, the spark of her awakening is struck. And if she can give that awakening a tiny space in her life, it will develop into a full-blown experience that one day she will want to mark and celebrate.

Conception, labor, and birthing—metaphors thick with the image and experiences of women—offer a body parable of the process of awakening. The parable tells us things we need to know about the way awakening works—the slow, unfolding, sometimes hidden, always expanding nature of it, the inevitable queasiness, the need to nurture and attend to what inhabits us, the uncertainty about the outcome, the fearful knowing that once we bring the new consciousness forth, our lives will never be the same. It tells us that and more.

I've given birth to two children, but bringing them into the world was a breeze compared to birthing myself as woman. Bringing forth a true, instinctual, powerful woman who is rooted in her own feminine center, who honors the sacredness of the feminine, and who speaks the feminine language of her own soul is never easy. Neither is it always welcomed. I discovered that few people will rush over to tie a big pink bow on your mailbox.

Yet there is no place so awake and alive as the edge of becoming. But more than that, birthing the kind of woman who can authentically say, "My soul is my own," and then embody it in her life, her spirituality, and her community is worth the risk and hardship.

Today, eight years after my waking began, I realize that the women who are bringing about this kind of new female life are brand new beings among us. I keep meeting them; I keep hearing their stories. They confirm my own experience, that somewhere along the course of a woman's life, usually when she has lived just long enough to see through some of the cherished notions of femininity that culture holds out to her, when she finally lets herself *feel* the limits and injustices of the female life and admits how her own faith tradition has contributed to that, when she at last stumbles in the dark hole made by the absence of a Divine Feminine presence, then the extraordinary thing I've been telling you about will happen. This woman will become pregnant with herself, with the symbolic female-child who will, if given the chance, grow up to reinvent the woman's life.

This female-child is the new potential we all have to become women grounded in our own souls, women who discover the Sacred Feminine way, women who let loose their strength. In the end we will reinvent not only ourselves, but also religion and spirituality as they have been handed down to us.

Nobel Prize-winning novelist Toni Morrison wrote of her character Pilate that "when she realized what her situation in the world was she threw away every assumption she had learned and began at zero." With her new awareness, Pilate conceived herself and birthed a new way of being woman.

When my dream came, the potential to do the same rose up. Only it would take a long time to shed my old assumptions and begin at zero.

The Deep Sleep

The dream left me with a vague kind of anticipation, a sense of restlessness. Two things happened as a result. First, I made plans to go away two months later for a solitary retreat at a Benedictine monastery, which

I typically did when something was stirring inside. The second thing involved a journal.

Writing is not only my career, it's my compulsion. I keep voluminous journals, normally beginning a new one each January, so it was revealing that soon after the dream, even though it was September, even though I already had a nice journal with months of pages left, I went out and bought a new one. I bought a pink one.

Many mornings throughout October, I sat by the windows in the den before the children awoke, before my husband, Sandy, came in and started the coffee ritual. I sat there thinking about my life as a woman.

So much of it had been spent trying to live up to the stereotypical formula of what a woman should be—the Good Christian Woman, the Good Wife, the Good Mother, the Good Daughter—pursuing those things that have always been held out to women as ideals of femininity.

One morning I wrote about something that had happened several months earlier. I'd been inducted into a group of women known as the Gracious Ladies. I'm not exactly sure what the criteria was, except one needed to portray certain ideals of womanhood, which included being gracious and giving of oneself unselfishly. During a high-lace ceremony, standing backstage waiting to be inducted, I felt a stab of discomfort. I thought about the meticulous way we were coiffed and dressed, the continuous smiling, the charm that fairly dripped off us, the sweet, demure way we behaved, like we were all there to audition for the Emily Poster Child. We looked like the world's most proper women.

What am I doing here? I thought. Lines from the poem "Warning," by Jenny Joseph, popped into my head and began to recite themselves.

> When I am an old woman, I shall wear purple / with a red hat that doesn't go, and doesn't suit me. . . . / I shall go out in my slippers in the rain / And pick the flowers in other people's gardens / And learn to spit.

I turned to a woman beside me and said, "After we're Gracious Ladies, does that mean we can't wear purple with a red hat or spit?" She smiled but appeared vaguely dismayed that someone who'd managed to get into the group had just said the word *spit*.

"It's from a poem," I explained.

"I see," she said. Still smiling.

It occurred to me on that October morning that living the female life under the archetype of Gracious Lady narrowed down the scope of it considerably. It scoured away a woman's natural self, all the untamed juices of the female life. It would be many years before I read Clarissa Pinkola Estés's words, "When a woman is cut away from her basic source, she is sanitized," but somehow even then, in the most rudimentary way, I was starting to know it.

In my spiritual life I was also a sanitized woman. I had always been very spiritual and very religious, too, so as I wrote in my journal I began trying to put my womanhood together with my spirituality and religion.

I wrote that I was mainstream orthodox. It sounded very dull, but actually it hadn't been dull at all. I'd pursued a spiritual journey of depth and meaning, but—and this was the big realization for me—I'd done so safely within the circle of Christian orthodoxy. I would no more have veered out of that circle than a child would have purposely drawn outside the lines in her coloring book.

I had been raised in the Southern Baptist Church, and I was still a rather exemplary member of one, but beginning in my early thirties I'd become immersed in a journey that was rooted in contemplative spirituality. It was the spirituality of the "church fathers," of the monks I'd come to know as I made regular retreats in their monasteries. I was influenced by Meister Eckhart and Julian of Norwich, who did, now and then, refer to "God our Mother," but this had never really sunk in. It was nice poetry. Now I wondered: What did "God our Mother" really mean?

Morning after morning I wrote, starting to realize how my inner journey had taken me into the airy world of intellect and the fiery realm of spirit, places that suddenly seemed very removed. I thrived on solitude, routinely practicing silent meditation as taught by the monks Basil Pennington and Thomas Keating. Because I visited monasteries and practiced the spirituality they were built upon, people often asked me, "Why do you like monasteries so much?" I would grin and say, "Well, what do you expect? My middle name *is* Monk." Like the Gracious Lady, Monk was an archetype—a guiding inner principle—I lived by.

I'd read many of the classics of Christian contemplative literature, the church fathers and the great mystics of the church. For years I'd studied Thomas Merton, John of the Cross, Augustine, Bernard, Bonaventure, Ignatius, Eckhart, Luther, Teilhard de Chardin, *The Cloud of Unknowing*, and others. Why had it never seemed peculiar that they were all men?

I often went to Catholic mass or Eucharist at the Episcopal church, nourished by the symbol and power of this profound feeding ritual. It never occurred to me how odd it was that women, who have presided over the domain of food and feeding for thousands of years, were historically and routinely barred from presiding over it in a spiritual context. And when the priest held out the host and said, "This is my body, given for you," not once did I recognize that it is women in the act of breast-feeding who most truly embody those words and who are also most excluded from ritually saying them.

When those particular thoughts struck me one morning as I was writing, they pricked a bubble of anger I didn't know I had, and I surprised myself by throwing my pen across the room. It landed inside the fireplace in a pile of soot. I had to go get the pen and clean it off. There had been so many things I hadn't allowed myself to see, because if I fully woke to the truth, then what would I do? How would I be able to reconcile myself to it? The truth may set you free, but first it will shatter the safe, sweet way you live.

The thoughts and memories I was collecting in the journal were random, disjointed. Frankly, I couldn't see what any of them had to do with the dream. It was as if I were walking around and around some secret enclosure, trying to find a way into it. I sometimes wondered what good my pacing was doing.

But after leaving the process for a few days, I would be back in the den, picking up where I'd left off, trying to make sense of things. I wrote about how odd it was that at the same time I was making these retreats in monasteries, going to Eucharist, and meditating on the words of Merton and St. Francis, I was going to a Baptist church—not just on Sunday mornings, but also on Sunday and Wednesday evenings—where the emphasis was not on symbol and silence and God in the soul but on evangelizing and preaching and God in the word. I was a contemplative in an evangelical church, which is sort of like trying to squeeze a round soul into a square slot. It was all I could do to hold the tension between them. I had one foot on shore and the other in a boat that had started to drift.

But despite the inner tension, I kept trying to adapt. The Southern Baptist Church had been the fabric of my religious existence since childhood. And if that wasn't enough, I was married to a Southern Baptist minister who was a religion teacher and chaplain on a Baptist college campus. That alone was enough to keep me securely tethered to the flock. So I taught Sunday school and brought dishes to all manner of potlucks and tried to adjust the things I heard from the pulpit to my increasingly incongruent faith.

I filled pages about my life as a Baptist.

I recorded the time Ann, then eight, tugged on my dress during a church service while the minister was ordaining a new set of deacons. "When are they going to do the women?" she asked.

"The women?" I echoed.

She nodded. Her assumption of equality was earnest and endearing. These days you will find a few female deacons in the more moderate Southern Baptist churches, but not so much then. I'd felt like a harbinger of cruel truth when I told her, "They don't ordain women, honey. Only men."

She had frowned, truly puzzled.

That day in church, the words *only men, only men, only men* went on echoing in my head for a good five minutes, but it soon passed. With a little more ripeness, I might have conceived a new female life that long-ago day, but then I was too consumed with staying in line and being a good and proper woman, something that renders you fairly sterile as far as feminine journeys go.

Writing down that memory reminded me of the time *I* was eight and had my own first encounter with "cruel truth." I was in the church yard during Vacation Bible School. It was hot. Georgia hot. The girls sat under a tree, making tissue paper corsages, while the boys climbed the limbs above us. I could not remember how it started, only that a quarrel broke out—one of those heated boys-are-better-than-girls or girls-are-better-than-boys arguments that eight year olds have with such verve. Finally one of the boys told us to shut up, and, of course, we wanted to know who'd made him our boss. "God!" he said. "God made us the boss."

So we girls marched inside to the teacher and asked her point-blank if this was so. We asked her with the same earnest and endearing assumption of equality with which Ann had posed her question to me. And, like me, the teacher was slow to answer. "Well. . . actually technically, I guess I have to say the Bible does make men the head."

"The head?" we asked.

"That means in charge," she said and looked at us as if to say, I know, I know, it's a blow, but that's the way it is.

I stared at her, amazed. I had never heard anything like this before, and I was sure it had to be a mistake. A *big* mistake. I mean, if this were true, then women, girls, me—we were not at all what I thought. At eight I couldn't have expressed it fully, but on some level I knew what this meant. That we were less than males and that we were going to spend the rest of our lives obeying and asking permission or worrying if we didn't. That event and others like it would eventually limit everything I ever thought about freedom and dreams and going where they took me. But worse, those events said something about the female gender itself—that it simply wasn't up to par. It had to be subdued, controlled, ruled over.

For girls there is always a moment when the earnest, endearing assumption of equality is lost, and writing about it in my journal thirty years later made me want to take those two eight year olds into my arms—myself and Ann, both.

October was nearly spent before I finally got around to reflecting on my life as a "Christian writer," which was how I was often identified. I'd been a prolific contributor to an inspirational magazine with millions of readers. I'd written articles for religious journals and magazines, books about my contemplative spirituality. It always surprised me where my readers turned up. One time I called L. L. Bean to order Sandy a denim shirt, and the operator said she was reading one of my books. I got lots of mail from readers. I spoke at Christian conferences, in churches. As a result, it seemed people expected me to be a certain way. Of course, I expected me to be a certain way, too. And that way had nothing remotely to do with feminist spirituality.

After a month of journal writing, one morning I sat as usual in the den. The light was coming up in the backyard, and the maple, at the height of fall color, appeared to be on fire. As I gazed at it, I understood that while I had gone through a lot of spiritual transformation and written about it, my changes had not deviated much from what were considered safe, standard, accepted Christian tenets. I had never imagined any kind of internal reformation that would call into question the Orthodox Christian Woman, the Good Daughter to the Church, or the Monk who lived high in the spiritual tower of her head. The risk of doing so seemed much too high for lots of reasons, but certainly paramount among them was that it might jeopardize my marriage and my career. I finally came to this:

As a woman, I've been asleep. The knowing rose in me, fast and brilliant, like the light coming now across the grass. I closed the journal and put it away.

A woman in Deep Sleep is one who goes about in an unconscious state. She seems unaware or unfazed by the truth of her own female life, the truth about women in general, the way women and the feminine have been wounded, devalued, and limited within culture, churches, and families. She cannot see the wound or feel the pain. She has never acknowledged, much less confronted, sexism within the church, biblical interpretations, or Christian doctrine. Okay, so women have been largely missing from positions of church power, we've been silenced and relegated to positions of subordination by biblical interpretations and doctrine, and God has been represented to us as exclusively male. So what? The woman in Deep Sleep is oblivious to the psychological and spiritual impact this has had on her. Or maybe she has some awareness of it all but keeps it sequestered nicely in her head, rarely allowing it to move down into her heart or into the politics of her spirituality.

The awarenesses about my female life that emerged during that month were sketchy, thin, and incomplete. A memory here, a thought there, a recognition, an insight—all of them sifting around like vapor. I knew as a woman I'd been asleep, but I had no idea exactly how. I knew I was waking up, but I didn't possess a clue about what I might be waking up to. All I knew was that there was this tiny female life inside, some part of me waking up and wanting to be born. She was rousing me out of years of somnambulance, and something had to be done with her.

The Rights of Conscience
Inalienable (1791)

John Leland

. . . The question is, "Are the rights of conscience alienable, or inalienable?"

The word conscience signifies common science, a court of judicature which the Almighty has erected in every human breast; a censor morum over all his actions. Conscience will ever judge right when it is rightly informed, and speak the truth when it understands it. But to advert to the question—"Does a man upon entering into social compact surrender his conscience to that society to be controlled by the laws thereof, or can he in justice assist in making laws to bind his children's consciences before they are born?" I judge not, for the following reasons:

1. Every man must give an account of himself to God, and therefore every man ought to be at liberty to serve God in that way that he can best reconcile it to his conscience. If government can answer for individuals at the day of judgment, let men be controlled by it in religious matters; otherwise let men be free.

2. It would be sinful for a man to surrender that to man which is to be kept sacred for God. A man's mind should be always open to conviction, and an honest man will receive that doctrine which appears the best demonstrated; and what is more common than for the best of men to change their minds? Such are the prejudices of the mind, and such the force of tradition, that a man who never alters his mind is either very weak or very stubborn. How painful then must it be to an honest heart to be bound to observe the principles of his former belief after he is convinced of their imbecility? And this ever has and ever will be the case while the rights of conscience are considered alienable.

3. But supposing it was right for a man to bind his own conscience, yet surely it is very iniquitous to bind the consciences of his children; to make fetters for them before they are born is very cruel. And yet such has been the conduct of men in almost all ages that their children have been bound to believe and worship as their fathers did, or suffer shame, loss, and sometimes life; and at best to be called dissenters, because they dissent from that which they never joined voluntarily. Such conduct in parents is

worse than that of the father of Hannibal, who imposed an oath upon his son while a child never to be at peace with the Romans.

4. Finally, religion is a matter between God and individuals, religious opinions of men not being the objects of civil government nor any ways under its control.

It has often been observed by the friends of religious establishment by human laws, that no state can long continue without it; that religion will perish, and nothing but infidelity and atheism prevail.

Are these things facts? Did not the Christian religion prevail during the three first centuries, in a more glorious manner than ever it has since, not only without the aid of law, but in opposition to all the laws of haughty monarchs? And did not religion receive a deadly wound by being fostered in the arms of civil power and regulated by law? These things are so.

From that day to this we have but a few instances of religious liberty to judge by; for in almost all states civil rulers (by the instigation of covetous priests) have undertaken to steady the ark of religion by human laws; but yet we have a few of them without leaving our own land.

The state of Rhode Island has stood above 160 years without any religious establishment. The state of New York never had any. New Jersey claims the same. Pennsylvania has also stood from its first settlement until now upon a liberal foundation; and if agriculture, the mechanical arts and commerce, have not flourished in these states equal to any of the states I judge wrong.

It may further be observed, that all the states now in union, saving two or three in New England, have no legal force used about religion, in directing its course or supporting its preachers. And moreover the federal government is forbidden by the constitution to make any laws establishing any kind of religion. If religion cannot stand, therefore, without the aid of law, it is likely to fall soon in our nation, except in Connecticut and Massachusetts.

To say that "religion cannot stand without a state establishment" is not only contrary to fact (as has been proved already) but is a contradiction in phrase. Religion must have stood a time before any law could have been made about it; and if it did stand almost three hundred years without law it can still stand without it.

The evils of such an establishment are many.

1. Uninspired fallible men make their own opinions tests of orthodoxy, and use their own systems, as Procrustes used his iron bedstead, to stretch and measure the consciences of all others by. Where no toleration is granted to non-conformists either ignorance and superstition prevail or persecution rages; and if toleration is granted to restricted non-conformists the minds of men are biased to embrace that religion which is favored and pampered by law (and thereby hypocrisy is nourished) while those who cannot stretch their consciences to believe any thing and every thing in the established creed are treated with contempt and opprobrious names; and by such means some are pampered to death by largesses and others confined from doing what good they otherwise could by penury. The first lie under a temptation to flatter the ruling party, to continue that form of government which brings the sure bread of idleness; the last to despise that government and those rulers that oppress them. The first have their eyes shut to all further light that would alter the religious machine; the last are always seeking new light, and often fall into enthusiasm. Such are the natural evils of establishment in religion by human laws.

2. Such establishments not only wean and alienate the affections of one from another on account of the different usages they receive in their religious sentiments, but are also very impolitic, especially in new countries; for what encouragement can strangers have to migrate with their arts and wealth into a state where they cannot enjoy their religious sentiments without exposing themselves to the law? When at the same time their religious opinions do not lead them to be mutinous. And further, how often have kingdoms and states been greatly weakened by religious tests! In the time of the persecution in France not less than twenty thousand people fled for the enjoyment of religious liberty.

3. These establishments metamorphose the church into a creature, and religion into a principle of state; which has a natural tendency to make men conclude that bible religion is nothing but a trick of state. Hence it is that the greatest part of the well informed in literature are overrun with deism and infidelity: nor is it likely it will ever be any better while preaching is made a trade of emolument. And if there is no difference between bible religion and state religion I shall soon fall into infidelity.

4. There are no two kingdoms or states that establish the same creed or formularies of faith (which alone proves their debility). In one kingdom a man is condemned for not believing a doctrine that he would be condemned for believing in another kingdom. Both of these establishments cannot be right—but both of them can be, and surely are, wrong.

5. The nature of such establishments, further, is to keep from civil office the best of men. Good men cannot believe what they cannot believe; and they will not subscribe to what they disbelieve, and take an oath to maintain what they conclude is error: and as the best of men differ in judgment there may be some of them in any state: their talents and virtue entitle them to fill the most important posts, yet because they differ from the established creed of the state they cannot—will not fill those posts. Whereas villains make no scruple to take any oath.

If these and many more evils attend such establishments—what were and still are the causes that ever there should be a state establishment of religion?

The causes are many—some of them follow.

1. The love of importance is a general evil. It is natural to men to dictate for others; they choose to command the bushel and use the whip-row, to have the halter around the necks of others to hang them at pleasure.

2. An over-fondness for a particular system or sect. This gave rise to the first human establishment of religion, by Constantine the Great. Being converted to the Christian system, he established it in the Roman empire, compelled the pagans to submit, and banished the Christian heretics, built fine chapels at public expence, and forced large stipends for the preachers. All this was done out of love to the Christian religion: but his love operated inadvertently; for he did the Christian church more harm than all the persecuting emperors did. It is said that in his day a voice was heard from heaven, saying, "Now is the poison spued into the churches." If this voice was not heard, it nevertheless was a truth; for from that day to this the Christian religion has been made a stirrup to mount the steed of popularity, wealth, and ambition.

3. To produce uniformity in religion. Rulers often fear that if they leave every man to think, speak and worship as he pleases, that the whole cause will be wrecked in diversity; to prevent which they establish some standard of orthodoxy to effect uniformity. But is uniformity attainable? Millions of men, women and children, have been tortured to death to produce uniformity, and yet the world has not advanced one inch towards it. And as long as men live in different parts of the world, have different habits, education and interests, they will be different in judgment, humanly speaking.

Is conformity of sentiments in matters of religion essential to the happiness of civil government? Not at all. Government has no more to do with the religious opinions of men than it has with the principles of the mathematics. Let every man speak freely without fear—maintain the principles that he believes—worship according to his own faith, either one God, three Gods, no God, or twenty Gods; and let government protect him in so doing, i.e. see that he meets with no personal abuse or loss of property for his religious opinions. Instead of discouraging him with proscriptions, fines, confiscation or death; let him be encouraged, as a free man, to bring forth his arguments and maintain his points with all boldness; then if his doctrine is false it will be confuted, and if it is true (though ever so novel) let others credit it. When every man has this liberty what can he wish for more? A liberal man asks for nothing more of government.

The duty of magistrates is not to judge of the divinity or tendency of doctrines, but when those principles break out into overt acts of violence then to use the civil sword and punish the vagrant for what he has done and not for the religious phrenzy that he acted from.

It is not supposable that any established creed contains the whole truth and nothing but truth; but supposing it did, which established church has got it? All bigots contend for it—each society cries out "The temple of the Lord are we." Let one society be supposed to be in possession of the whole—let that society be established by law—the creed of faith that they adopt be so consecrated by government that the man that disbelieves it must die—let this creed finally prevail over the whole world. I ask what honor truth gets by all this? None at all. It is famed of a Prussian, called John the Cicero, that by one oration he reconciled two contending princes actually in war; but, says the historian, "It was his six thousand horse of battle that had the most persuasive oratory." So when one creed or church prevails over another, being armed with (a coat of mail) law and sword, truth gets no honor by the victory. Whereas if all stand upon one footing, being equally protected by law as citizens (not as saints) and one prevails over another by cool investigation and fair argument, then truth gains honor, and men more firmly believe it than if it was made an essential article of salvation by law.

Truth disdains the aid of law for its defence—it will stand upon its own merits. The heathens worshipped a goddess called truth, stark naked; and all human decorations of truth serve only to destroy her virgin beauty. It is error, and error alone, that needs human support; and whenever men fly to the law or sword to protect their system of religion and force it upon others, it is evident that they have something in their system that will not bear the light and stand upon the basis of truth.

from On Liberty (1859)

John Stuart Mill

Chapter One

The subject of this Essay is not the so-called Liberty of the Will, so unfortunately opposed to the misnamed doctrine of Philosophical Necessity; but Civil, or Social Liberty: the nature and limits of the power which can be legitimately exercised by society over the individual. A question seldom stated, and hardly ever discussed, in general terms, but which profoundly influences the practical controversies of the age by its latent presence, and is likely soon to make itself recognized as the vital question of the future. It is so far from being new, that, in a certain sense, it has divided mankind, almost from the remotest ages, but in the stage of progress into which the more civilized portions of the species have now entered, it presents itself under new conditions, and requires a different and more fundamental treatment. The struggle between Liberty and Authority is the most conspicuous feature in the portions of history with which we are earliest familiar, particularly in that of Greece, Rome, and England. But in old times this contest was between subjects, or some classes of subjects, and the government. By liberty, was meant protection against the tyranny of the political rulers. The rulers were conceived (except in some of the popular governments of Greece) as in a necessarily antagonistic position to the people whom they ruled. They consisted of a governing One, or a governing tribe or caste, who derived their authority from inheritance or conquest; who, at all events, did not hold it at the pleasure of the governed, and whose supremacy men did not venture, perhaps did not desire, to contest, whatever precautions might be taken against its oppressive exercise. Their power was regarded as necessary, but also as highly dangerous; as a weapon which they would attempt to use against their subjects, no less than against external enemies. To prevent the weaker members of the community from being preyed upon by innumerable vultures, it was needful that there should be an animal of prey stronger than the rest, commissioned to keep them down. But as the king of the vultures would be no less bent upon preying upon the flock than any of the minor harpies, it was indispensable to be in a perpetual attitude of defence against his beak and claws. The aim, therefore, of patriots, was to set limits to the power which the ruler should be suffered to exercise over the community; and this limitation

171

was what they meant by liberty. It was attempted in two ways. First, by obtaining a recognition of certain immunities, called political liberties or rights, which it was to be regarded as a breach of duty in the ruler to infringe, and which, if he did infringe, specific resistance, or general rebellion, was held to be justifiable. A second, and generally a later expedient, was the establishment of constitutional checks; by which the consent of the community, or of a body of some sort supposed to represent its interests, was made a necessary condition to some of the more important acts of the governing power. To the first of these modes of limitation, the ruling power, in most European countries, was compelled, more or less, to submit. It was not so with the second; and to attain this, or when already in some degree possessed, to attain it more completely, became everywhere the principal object of the lovers of liberty. And so long as mankind were content to combat one enemy by another, and to be ruled by a master, on condition of being guaranteed more or less efficaciously against his tyranny, they did not carry their aspirations beyond this point.

A time, however, came in the progress of human affairs, when men ceased to think it a necessity of nature that their governors should be an independent power, opposed in interest to themselves. It appeared to them much better that the various magistrates of the State should be their tenants or delegates, revocable at their pleasure. In that way alone, it seemed, could they have complete security that the powers of government would never be abused to their disadvantage. By degrees, this new demand for elective and temporary rulers became the prominent object of the exertions of the popular party, wherever any such party existed; and superseded, to a considerable extent, the previous efforts to limit the power of rulers. As the struggle proceeded for making the ruling power emanate from the periodical choice of the ruled, some persons began to think that too much importance had been attached to the limitation of the power itself. That (it might seem) was a resource against rulers whose interests were habitually opposed to those of the people. What was now wanted was, that the rulers should be identified with the people; that their interest and will should be the interest and will of the nation. The nation did not need to be protected against its own will. There was no fear of its tyrannizing over itself. Let the rulers be effectually responsible to it, promptly removable by it, and it could afford to trust them with power of which it could itself dictate the use to be made. Their power was but the nation's own power, concentrated, and in a form convenient for exercise. This mode of thought, or rather perhaps of feeling, was common among the last generation of European liberalism, in the Continental section of which, it still apparently predominates. Those who admit any

limit to what a government may do, except in the case of such governments as they think ought not to exist, stand out as brilliant exceptions
among the political thinkers of the Continent. A similar tone of sentiment
might by this time have been prevalent in our own country, if the circumstances which for a time encouraged it had continued unaltered.

But, in political and philosophical theories, as well as in persons, success
discloses faults and infirmities which failure might have concealed from
observation. The notion, that the people have no need to limit their power
over themselves, might seem axiomatic, when popular government was
a thing only dreamed about, or read of as having existed at some distant
period of the past. Neither was that notion necessarily disturbed by such
temporary aberrations as those of the French Revolution, the worst of
which were the work of an usurping few, and which, in any case,
belonged, not to the permanent working of popular institutions, but to a
sudden and convulsive outbreak against monarchical and aristocratic
despotism. In time, however, a democratic republic came to occupy a
large portion of the earth's surface, and made itself felt as one of the most
powerful members of the community of nations; and elective and responsible government became subject to the observations and criticisms
which wait upon a great existing fact. It was now perceived that such
phrases as "self-government," and "the power of the people over themselves," do not express the true state of the case. The "people" who exercise the power, are not always the same people with those over whom it
is exercised, and the "self-government" spoken of, is not the government
of each by himself, but of each by all the rest. The will of the people,
moreover, practically means, the will of the most numerous or the most
active part of the people; the majority, or those who succeed in making
themselves accepted as the majority; the people, consequently, may
desire to oppress a part of their number; and precautions are as much
needed against this, as against any other abuse of power. The limitation,
therefore, of the power of government over individuals, loses none of its
importance when the holders of power are regularly accountable to the
community, that is, to the strongest party therein. This view of things, rec-
ommending itself equally to the intelligence of thinkers and to the inclination of those important classes in European society to whose real or
supposed interests democracy is adverse, has had no difficulty in establishing itself; and in political speculations "the tyranny of the majority" is
now generally included among the evils against which society requires to
be on its guard.

Like other tyrannies, the tyranny of the majority was at first, and is still
vulgarly, held in dread, chiefly as operating through the acts of the public

authorities. But reflecting persons perceived that when society is itself the tyrant—society collectively, over the separate individuals who compose it—its means of tyrannizing are not restricted to the acts which it may do by the hands of its political functionaries. Society can and does execute its own mandates: and if it issues wrong mandates instead of right, or any mandates at all in things with which it ought not to meddle, it practises a social tyranny more formidable than many kinds of political oppression, since, though not usually upheld by such extreme penalties, it leaves fewer means of escape, penetrating much more deeply into the details of life, and enslaving the soul itself. Protection, therefore, against the tyranny of the magistrate is not enough; there needs protection also against the tyranny of the prevailing opinion and feeling; against the tendency of society to impose, by other means than civil penalties, its own ideas and practices as rules of conduct on those who dissent from them; to fetter the development, and, if possible, prevent the formation, of any individuality not in harmony with its ways, and compel all characters to fashion themselves upon the model of its own. There is a limit to the legitimate interference of collective opinion with individual independence; and to find that limit, and maintain it against encroachment, is as indispensable to a good condition of human affairs, as protection against political despotism.

But though this proposition is not likely to be contested in general terms, the practical question, where to place the limit—how to make the fitting adjustment between individual independence and social control—is a subject on which nearly everything remains to be done. All that makes existence valuable to any one, depends on the enforcement of restraints upon the actions of other people. Some rules of conduct, therefore, must be imposed, by law in the first place, and by opinion on many things which are not fit subjects for the operation of law. What these rules should be, is the principal question in human affairs; but if we except a few of the most obvious cases, it is one of those which least progress has been made in resolving. No two ages, and scarcely any two countries, have decided it alike; and the decision of one age or country is a wonder to another. Yet the people of any given age and country no more suspect any difficulty in it, than if it were a subject on which mankind had always been agreed. The rules which obtain among themselves appear to them self-evident and self-justifying. This all but universal illusion is one of the examples of the magical influence of custom, which is not only, as the proverb says a second nature, but is continually mistaken for the first. The effect of custom, in preventing any misgiving respecting the rules of conduct which mankind impose on one another, is all the more complete because the subject is one on which it is not generally considered necessary that reasons should be given, either by one person to others, or by each to himself. People are accustomed to believe and have been encouraged in the belief by some who aspire to the character of philosophers, that their feelings, on subjects of this nature, are better than reasons, and render reasons unnecessary. The practical principle which guides them to their opinions on the regulation of human conduct, is the feeling in each person's mind that everybody should be required to act as he, and those with whom he sympathizes, would like them to act. No one, indeed, acknowledges to himself that his standard of judgment is his own liking; but an opinion on a point of conduct, not supported by reasons, can only count as one person's preference; and if the reasons, when given, are a mere appeal to a similar preference felt by other people, it is still only many people's liking instead of one. To an ordinary man, however, his own preference, thus supported, is not only a perfectly satisfactory reason, but the only one he generally has for any of his notions of morality, taste, or propriety, which are not expressly written in his religious creed; and his chief guide in the interpretation even of that. Men's opinions, accordingly, on what is laudable or blamable, are affected by all the multifarious causes which influence their wishes in regard to the conduct of others, and which are as numerous as those which determine their wishes on any other subject. Sometimes their reason—at other times their prejudices or superstitions: often their social affections, not seldom their antisocial ones, their envy or jealousy, their arrogance or contemptuousness: but most commonly, their desires or fears for themselves—their legitimate or illegitimate self-interest. Wherever there is an ascendant class, a large portion of the morality of the country emanates from its class interests, and its feelings of class superiority. The morality between Spartans and Helots, between planters and negroes, between princes and subjects, between nobles and roturiers, between men and women, has been for the most part the creation of these class interests and feelings: and the sentiments thus generated, react in turn upon the moral feelings of the members of the ascendant class, in their relations among themselves. Where, on the other hand, a class, formerly ascendant, has lost its ascendency, or where its ascendency is unpopular, the prevailing moral sentiments frequently bear the impress of an impatient dislike of superiority. Another grand determining principle of the rules of conduct, both in act and forbearance which have been enforced by law or opinion, has been the servility of mankind towards the supposed preferences or aversions of their temporal masters, or of their gods. This servility though essentially selfish, is not hypocrisy; it gives rise to perfectly genuine sentiments of abhorrence; it made men burn magicians and heretics. Among so many baser influences, the general and obvious interests of society have of course had a share, and a large one, in the direction of the moral sentiments: less, however, as a matter of reason, and on their own account, than as a consequence of the sympathies and antipathies which grew out of them: and sympathies and antipathies which had little or nothing to do with the interests of society, have made themselves felt in the establishment of moralities with quite as great force.

The likings and dislikings of society, or of some powerful portion of it, are thus the main thing which has practically determined the rules laid down for general observance, under the penalties of law or opinion. And in general, those who have been in advance of society in thought and feeling, have left this condition of things unassailed in principle, however they may have come into conflict with it in some of its details. They have occupied themselves rather in inquiring what things society ought to like or dislike, than in questioning whether its likings or dislikings should be a law to individuals. They preferred endeavouring to alter the feelings of mankind on the particular points on which they were themselves heretical, rather than make common cause in defence of freedom, with heretics generally. The only case in which the higher ground has been taken on principle and maintained with consistency, by any but an individual here and there, is that of religious belief: a case instructive in many ways, and not least so as forming a most striking instance of the fallibility of what is called the moral sense: for the odium theologicum, in a sincere bigot, is one of the most unequivocal cases of moral feeling. Those who first broke the yoke of what called itself the Universal Church, were in general as little willing to permit difference of religious opinion as that church itself. But when the heat of the conflict was over, without giving a complete victory to any party, and each church or sect was reduced to limit its hopes to retaining possession of the ground it already occupied; minorities, seeing that they had no chance of becoming majorities, were under the necessity of pleading to those whom they could not convert, for permission to differ. It is accordingly on this battle-field, almost solely, that the rights of the individual against society have been asserted on broad grounds of principle, and the claim of society to exercise authority over dissentients openly controverted. The great writers to whom the world owes what religious liberty it possesses, have mostly asserted freedom of conscience as an indefeasible right, and denied absolutely that a human being is accountable to others for his religious belief. Yet so natural to mankind is intolerance in whatever they really care about, that religious freedom has hardly anywhere been practically realized, except where religious indifference, which dislikes to have its peace disturbed by theological quarrels, has added its weight to the scale. In the minds of almost all religious persons, even in the most tolerant countries, the duty of toleration is admitted with tacit reserves. One person will bear with dissent in matters of church government, but not of dogma; another can tolerate everybody, short of a Papist or an Unitarian; another, every one who believes in revealed religion; a few extend their charity a little further, but stop at the belief in a God and in a future state. Wherever the sentiment of the majority is still genuine and intense, it is found to have abated little of its claim to be obeyed.

In England, from the peculiar circumstances of our political history, though the yoke of opinion is perhaps heavier, that of law is lighter, than in most other countries of Europe; and there is considerable jealousy of direct interference, by the legislative or the executive power with private conduct; not so much from any just regard for the independence of the individual, as from the still subsisting habit of looking on the government as representing an opposite interest to the public. The majority have not yet learnt to feel the power of the government their power, or its opinions their opinions. When they do so, individual liberty will probably be as much exposed to invasion from the government, as it already is from public opinion. But, as yet, there is a considerable amount of feeling ready to be called forth against any attempt of the law to control individuals in things in which they have not hitherto been accustomed to be controlled by it; and this with very little discrimination as to whether the matter is, or is not, within the legitimate sphere of legal control; insomuch that the feeling, highly salutary on the whole, is perhaps quite as often misplaced as well grounded in the particular instances of its application.

There is, in fact, no recognized principle by which the propriety or impropriety of government interference is customarily tested. People decide according to their personal preferences. Some, whenever they see any good to be done, or evil to be remedied, would willingly instigate the government to undertake the business; while others prefer to bear almost any amount of social evil, rather than add one to the departments of human interests amenable to governmental control. And men range themselves on one or the other side in any particular case, according to this general direction of their sentiments; or according to the degree of interest which they feel in the particular thing which it is proposed that the government should do; or according to the belief they entertain that the government would, or would not, do it in the manner they prefer; but very rarely on account of any opinion to which they consistently adhere, as to what things are fit to be done by a government. And it seems to me that, in consequence of this absence of rule or principle, one

side is at present as often wrong as the other; the interference of government is, with about equal frequency, improperly invoked and improperly
condemned.

The object of this Essay is to assert one very simple principle, as entitled
to govern absolutely the dealings of society with the individual in the
way of compulsion and control, whether the means used be physical
force in the form of legal penalties, or the moral coercion of public opinion. That principle is, that the sole end for which mankind are warranted,
individually or collectively in interfering with the liberty of action of any
of their number, is self-protection. That the only purpose for which power
can be rightfully exercised over any member of a civilized community,
against his will, is to prevent harm to others. His own good, either physical or moral, is not a sufficient warrant. He cannot rightfully be compelled to do or forbear because it will be better for him to do so, because
it will make him happier, because, in the opinions of others, to do so
would be wise, or even right. These are good reasons for remonstrating
with him, or reasoning with him, or persuading him, or entreating him,
but not for compelling him, or visiting him with any evil, in case he do
otherwise. To justify that, the conduct from which it is desired to deter
him must be calculated to produce evil to some one else. The only part of
the conduct of any one, for which he is amenable to society, is that which
concerns others. In the part which merely concerns himself, his independence is, of right, absolute. Over himself, over his own body and mind,
the individual is sovereign.

It is, perhaps, hardly necessary to say that this doctrine is meant to apply
only to human beings in the maturity of their faculties. We are not speaking of children, or of young persons below the age which the law may
fix as that of manhood or womanhood. Those who are still in a state to
require being taken care of by others, must be protected against their
own actions as well as against external injury. For the same reason, we
may leave out of consideration those backward states of society in which
the race itself may be considered as in its nonage. The early difficulties
in the way of spontaneous progress are so great, that there is seldom any
choice of means for overcoming them; and a ruler full of the spirit of
improvement is warranted in the use of any expedients that will attain
an end, perhaps otherwise unattainable. Despotism is a legitimate mode
of government in dealing with barbarians, provided the end be their
improvement, and the means justified by actually effecting that end. Liberty, as a principle, has no application to any state of things anterior to
the time when mankind have become capable of being improved by free
and equal discussion. Until then, there is nothing for them but implicit

obedience to an Akbar or a Charlemagne, if they are so fortunate as to find one. But as soon as mankind have attained the capacity of being guided to their own improvement by conviction or persuasion (a period long since reached in all nations with whom we need here concern ourselves), compulsion, either in the direct form or in that of pains and penalties for non-compliance, is no longer admissible as a means to their own good, and justifiable only for the security of others.

It is proper to state that I forego any advantage which could be derived to my argument from the idea of abstract right as a thing independent of utility. I regard utility as the ultimate appeal on all ethical questions; but it must be utility in the largest sense, grounded on the permanent interests of man as a progressive being. Those interests, I contend, authorize the subjection of individual spontaneity to external control, only in respect to those actions of each, which concern the interest of other people. If any one does an act hurtful to others, there is a prima facie case for punishing him, by law, or, where legal penalties are not safely applicable, by general disapprobation. There are also many positive acts for the benefit of others, which he may rightfully be compelled to perform; such as, to give evidence in a court of justice; to bear his fair share in the common defence, or in any other joint work necessary to the interest of the society of which he enjoys the protection; and to perform certain acts of individual beneficence, such as saving a fellow-creature's life, or interposing to protect the defenceless against ill-usage, things which whenever it is obviously a man's duty to do, he may rightfully be made responsible to society for not doing. A person may cause evil to others not only by his actions but by his inaction, and in neither case he is justly accountable to them for the injury. The latter case, it is true, requires a much more cautious exercise of compulsion than the former. To make any one answerable for doing evil to others, is the rule; to make him answerable for not preventing evil, is, comparatively speaking, the exception. Yet there are many cases clear enough and grave enough to justify that exception. In all things which regard the external relations of the individual, he is de jure amenable to those whose interests are concerned, and if need be, to society as their protector. There are often good reasons for not holding him to the responsibility; but these reasons must arise from the special expediencies of the case: either because it is a kind of case in which he is on the whole likely to act better, when left to his own discretion, than when controlled in any way in which society have it in their power to control him; or because the attempt to exercise control would produce other evils, greater than those which it would prevent. When such reasons as these preclude the enforcement of responsibility, the conscience of the agent himself should step into the vacant judgment-seat, and protect those interests of others which have no external protection; judging himself all the more rigidly, because the case does not admit of his being made accountable to the judgment of his fellow-creatures.

But there is a sphere of action in which society, as distinguished from the individual, has, if any, only an indirect interest; comprehending all that portion of a person's life and conduct which affects only himself, or, if it also affects others, only with their free, voluntary, and undeceived consent and participation. When I say only himself, I mean directly, and in the first instance: for whatever affects himself, may affect others through himself; and the objection which may be grounded on this contingency, will receive consideration in the sequel. This, then, is the appropriate region of human liberty. It comprises, first, the inward domain of consciousness; demanding liberty of conscience, in the most comprehensive sense; liberty of thought and feeling; absolute freedom of opinion and sentiment on all subjects, practical or speculative, scientific, moral, or theological. The liberty of expressing and publishing opinions may seem to fall under a different principle, since it belongs to that part of the conduct of an individual which concerns other people; but, being almost of as much importance as the liberty of thought itself, and resting in great part on the same reasons, is practically inseparable from it. Secondly, the principle requires liberty of tastes and pursuits; of framing the plan of our life to suit our own character; of doing as we like, subject to such consequences as may follow; without impediment from our fellow-creatures, so long as what we do does not harm them even though they should think our conduct foolish, perverse, or wrong. Thirdly, from this liberty of each individual, follows the liberty, within the same limits, of combination among individuals; freedom to unite, for any purpose not involving harm to others: the persons combining being supposed to be of full age, and not forced or deceived.

No society in which these liberties are not, on the whole, respected, is free, whatever may be its form of government; and none is completely free in which they do not exist absolute and unqualified. The only freedom which deserves the name, is that of pursuing our own good in our own way, so long as we do not attempt to deprive others of theirs, or impede their efforts to obtain it. Each is the proper guardian of his own health, whether bodily, or mental or spiritual. Mankind are greater gainers by suffering each other to live as seems good to themselves, than by compelling each to live as seems good to the rest.

Though this doctrine is anything but new, and, to some persons, may have the air of a truism, there is no doctrine which stands more directly opposed to the general tendency of existing opinion and practice. Society has expended fully as much effort in the attempt (according to its lights) to compel people to conform to its notions of personal, as of social excellence. The ancient commonwealths thought themselves entitled to practise, and the ancient philosophers countenanced, the regulation of every part of private conduct by public authority, on the ground that the State had a deep interest in the whole bodily and mental discipline of every one of its citizens, a mode of thinking which may have been admissible in small republics surrounded by powerful enemies, in constant peril of being subverted by foreign attack or internal commotion, and to which even a short interval of relaxed energy and self-command might so easily be fatal, that they could not afford to wait for the salutary permanent effects of freedom. In the modern world, the greater size of political communities, and above all, the separation between the spiritual and temporal authority (which placed the direction of men's consciences in other hands than those which controlled their worldly affairs), prevented so great an interference by law in the details of private life; but the engines of moral repression have been wielded more strenuously against divergence from the reigning opinion in self-regarding, than even in social matters; religion, the most powerful of the elements which have entered into the formation of moral feeling, having almost always been governed either by the ambition of a hierarchy, seeking control over every department of human conduct, or by the spirit of Puritanism. And some of those modern reformers who have placed themselves in strongest opposition to the religions of the past, have been nowhere behind either churches or sects in their assertion of the right of spiritual domination: M. Compte, in particular, whose social system, as unfolded in his Trait de Politique Positive, aims at establishing (though by moral more than by legal appliances) a despotism of society over the individual, surpassing anything contemplated in the political ideal of the most rigid disciplinarian among the ancient philosophers.

Apart from the peculiar tenets of individual thinkers, there is also in the world at large an increasing inclination to stretch unduly the powers of society over the individual, both by the force of opinion and even by that of legislation: and as the tendency of all the changes taking place in the world is to strengthen society, and diminish the power of the individual, this encroachment is not one of the evils which tend spontaneously to disappear, but, on the contrary, to grow more and more formidable. The disposition of mankind, whether as rulers or as fellow-citizens, to impose their own opinions and inclinations as a rule of conduct on others, is so energetically supported by some of the best and by some of the worst feelings incident to human nature, that it is hardly ever kept under restraint by anything but want of power; and as the power is not declining, but growing, unless a strong barrier of moral conviction can be raised against the mischief, we must expect, in the present circumstances of the world, to see it increase.

It will be convenient for the argument, if, instead of at once entering upon the general thesis, we confine ourselves in the first instance to a single branch of it, on which the principle here stated is, if not fully, yet to a certain point, recognized by the current opinions. This one branch is the Liberty of Thought: from which it is impossible to separate the cognate liberty of speaking and of writing. Although these liberties, to some considerable amount, form part of the political morality of all countries which profess religious toleration and free institutions, the grounds, both philosophical and practical, on which they rest, are perhaps not so familiar to the general mind, nor so thoroughly appreciated by many even of the leaders of opinion, as might have been expected. Those grounds, when rightly understood, are of much wider application than to only one division of the subject, and a thorough consideration of this part of the question will be found the best introduction to the remainder. Those to whom nothing which I am about to say will be new, may therefore, I hope, excuse me, if on a subject which for now three centuries has been so often discussed, I venture on one discussion more.

Boys and Girls (1968)

Alice Munro

My father was a fox farmer. That is, he raised silver foxes, in pens; and in the fall and early winter, when their fur was prime, he killed them and skinned them and sold their pelts to the Hudson's Bay Company or the Montreal Fur Traders. These companies supplied us with heroic calendars to hang, one on each side of the kitchen door. Against a background of cold blue sky and black pine forests and treacherous northern rivers, plumed adventurers planted the flags of England or of France; magnificent savages bent their backs to the portage.

For several weeks before Christmas, my father worked after supper in the cellar of our house. The cellar was whitewashed, and lit by a hundred-watt bulb over the worktable. My brother Laird and I sat on the top step and watched. My father removed the pelt inside-out from the body of the fox, which looked surprisingly small, mean and rat-like, deprived of its arrogant weight of fur. The naked, slippery bodies were collected in a sack and buried at the dump. One time the hired man, Henry Bailey, had taken a swipe at me with this sack, saying, "Christmas present!" My mother thought that was not funny. In fact she disliked the whole pelting operation—that was what the killing, skinning, and preparation of the furs was called—wished it did not have to take place in the house. There was the smell. After the pelt had been stretched inside-out on a long board my father scraped away delicately, removing the little clotted webs of blood vessels, the bubbles of fat; the smell of blood and animal fat, with the strong primitive odor of the fox itself, penetrated all parts of the house. I found it reassuringly seasonal, like the smell of oranges and pine needles.

Henry Bailey suffered from bronchial troubles. He would cough and cough until his narrow face turned scarlet, and his light blue, derisive eyes filled up with tears; then he took the lid off the stove, and, standing well back, shot out a great clot of phlegm—hsss—straight into the heart of the flames. We admired him for this performance and for his ability to make his stomach growl at will, and for his laughter, which was full of high whistlings and gurglings and involved the whole faulty machinery of his chest. It was sometimes hard to tell what he was laughing at, and always possible that it might be us.

183

After we had been sent to bed we could still smell fox and still hear Henry's laugh, but these things, reminders of the warm, safe, brightly lit downstairs world, seemed lost and diminished, floating on the stale cold air upstairs. We were afraid at night in the winter. We were not afraid of *outside* though this was the time of year when snowdrifts curled around our house like sleeping whales and the wind harassed us all night, coming up from the buried fields, the frozen swamp, with its old bugbear chorus of threats and misery. We were afraid of *inside*, the room where we slept. At this time the upstairs of our house was not finished. A brick chimney went up one wall. In the middle of the floor was a square hole, with a wooden railing around it; that was where the stairs came up. On the other side of the stairwell were the things that nobody had any use for anymore—a soldiery roll of linoleum, standing on end, a wicker baby carriage, a fern basket, china jugs and basins with cracks in them, a picture of the Battle of Balaclava, very sad to look at. I had told Laird, as soon as he was old enough to understand such things, that bats and skeletons lived over there; whenever a man escaped from the country jail, twenty miles away, I imagined that he had somehow let himself in the window and was hiding behind the linoleum. But we had rules to keep us safe. When the light was on, we were safe as long as we did not step off the square of worn carpet which defined our bedroom-space; when the light was off no place was safe but the beds themselves. I had to turn out the light kneeling on the end of my bed, and stretching as far as I could to reach the cord.

In the dark we lay on our beds, our narrow life rafts, and fixed our eyes on the faint light coming up the stairwell, and sang songs. Laird sang "Jingle Bells," which he would sing any time, whether it was Christmas or not, and I sang "Danny Boy." I loved the sound of my own voice, frail and supplicating, rising in the dark. We could make out the tall frosted shapes of the windows now, gloomy and white. When I came to the part, *When I am dead, as dead I well may be*—a fit of shivering caused not by the cold sheets but by pleasurable emotion almost silenced me. *You'll kneel and say, an Ave there above me*—What was an Ave? Every day I forgot to find out.

Laird went straight from singing to sleep. I could hear his long, satisfied, bubbly breaths. Now for the time that remained to me, the most perfectly private and perhaps the best time of the whole day, I arranged myself tightly under the covers and went on with one of the stories I was telling myself from night to night. These stories were about myself, when I had grown a little older; they took place in a world that was recognizably mine, yet one that presented opportunities for courage, boldness and self-sacrifice, as mine never did. I rescued people from a bombed building (It discouraged me that the real war had gone on so far away from Jubilee). I shot two rabid wolves who were menacing the schoolyard (the teachers cowered terrified at my back). I rode a fine horse spiritedly down the main street of Jubilee, acknowledging the townspeople's gratitude for some yet-to-be-worked-out piece of heroism (nobody ever rode a horse there, except King Billy in the Orangemen's Day[1] parade). There was always riding and shooting in these stories, though I had only been on a horse twice—bareback because we did not own a saddle—and the second time I had slid right around and dropped under the horse's feet; it had stepped placidly over me. I really was learning to shoot, but I could not hit anything yet, not even tin cans on fence posts.

Alive, the foxes inhabited a world my father made for them. It was surrounded by a high guard fence, like a medieval town, with a gate that was padlocked at night. Along the streets of this town were ranged large, sturdy pens. Each of them had a real door that a man could go through, a wooden ramp along the wire, for the foxes to run up and down on, and a kennel—something like a clothes chest with airholes—where they slept and stayed in winter and had their young. There were feeding and watering dishes attached to the wire in such a way that they could be emptied and cleaned from the outside. The dishes were made of old tin cans, and the ramps and kennels of odds and ends of old lumber. Everything was tidy and ingenious; my father was tirelessly inventive and his favorite book in the world was Robinson Crusoe. He had fitted a tin drum on a wheelbarrow, for bringing water to the pens. This was my job in summer, when the foxes had to have water twice a day. Between nine and ten o'clock in the morning, and again after supper, I filled the drum at the pump and trundled it down through the barnyard to the pens, where I parked it, and filled my watering can and went along the streets. Laird came too, with his little cream and green gardening can, filled too full and knocking against his legs and slopping water on his canvas shoes. I had the real watering can, my father's, though I could only carry it three-quarters full.

The foxes all had names, which were printed on a tin plate and hung beside their doors. They were not named when they were born, but when they survived the first year's pelting and were added to the breeding stock. Those my father had named were called names like Prince, Bob, Wally and Betty. Those I had named were called Star or Turk, or Maureen or Diana. Laird named one Maud after a hired girl we had when he was little, one Harold after a boy at school, and one Mexico, he did not say why.

Naming them did not make pets out of them, or anything like it. Nobody but my father ever went into the pens, and he had twice had blood-poisoning from bites. When I was bringing them their water they prowled up and down on the paths they had made inside their pens, barking seldom—they saved that for nighttime, when they might get up a chorus of community frenzy—but always watching me, their eyes burning, clear gold, in their pointed, malevolent faces. They were beautiful for their delicate legs and heavy, aristocratic tails and the bright fur sprinkled on dark down their backs—which gave them their name—but especially for their faces, drawn exquisitely sharp in pure hostility, and their golden eyes.

Besides carrying water I helped my father when he cut the long grass, and the lamb's quarter and flowering money-musk, that grew between the pens. He cut with the scythe and I raked into piles. Then he took a pitch-fork and threw fresh-cut grass all over the top of the pens to keep the foxes cooler and shade their coats, which were browned by too much sun. My father did not talk to me unless it was about the job we were doing. In this he was quite different from my mother, who, if she was feeling cheerful, would tell me all sorts of things—the name of a dog she had when she was a little girl, the names of boys she had gone out with later on when she was grown up, and what certain dresses of hers had looked like—she could not imagine now what had become of them. Whatever thoughts and stories my father had were private, and I was shy of him and would never ask him questions. Nevertheless I worked willingly under his eyes, and with a feeling of pride. One time a feed salesman came down into the pens to talk to him and my father said, "Like to have you meet my new hired man." I turned away and raked furiously, red in the face with pleasure.

"Could of fooled me," said the salesman. "I thought it was only a girl."

After the grass was cut, it seemed suddenly much later in the year. I walked on stubble in the earlier evening, aware of the reddening skies, the entering silences, of fall. When I wheeled the tank out of the gate and put the padlock on, it was almost dark. One night at this time I saw my mother and father standing on the little rise of ground we called the gangway, in front of the barn. My father had just come from the meathouse; he had his stiff bloody apron on, and a pail of cut-up meat in his hand.

It was an odd thing to see my mother down at the barn. She did not often come out of the house unless it was to do something—hang out the wash or dig potatoes in the garden. She looked out of place, with her bare lumpy legs, not touched by the sun, her apron still on and damp across the stomach from the supper dishes. Her hair was tied up in a kerchief, wisps of it falling out. She would tie her hair up like this in the morning, saying she did not have time to do it properly, and it would stay tied up all day. It was true, too; she really did not have time. These days our back porch was piled with baskets of peaches and grapes and pears, bought in town, and onions and tomatoes and cucumbers grown at home, all waiting to be made into jelly and jam and preserves, pickles and chili sauce. In the kitchen there was a fire in the stove all day, jars clinked in boiling water, sometimes a cheesecloth bag was strung on a pole between two chairs straining blue-black grape pulp for jelly. I was given jobs to do and I would sit at the table peeling peaches that had been soaked in the hot water, or cutting up onions, my eyes smarting and streaming. As soon as I was done I ran out of the house, trying to get out of earshot before my mother thought of what she wanted me to do next. I hated the hot dark kitchen in summer, the green blinds and the flypapers, the same old oilcloth table and wavy mirror and bumpy linoleum. My mother was too tired and preoccupied to talk to me, she had no heart to tell about the Normal School Graduation Dance; sweat trickled over her face and she was always counting under her breath, pointing at jars, dumping cups of sugar. It seemed to me that work in the house was endless, dreary and peculiarly depressing; work done out of doors, and in my father's service, was ritualistically important.

I wheeled the tank up to the barn, where it was kept, and I heard my mother saying, "Wait till Laird gets a little bigger, then you'll have a real help."

What my father said I did not hear. I was pleased by the way he stood listening, politely as he would to a salesman or a stranger, but with an air of wanting to get on with his real work. I felt my mother had no business down here and I wanted him to feel the same way. What did she mean about Laird? He was no help to anybody. Where was he now? Swinging himself sick on the swing, going around in circles, or trying to catch caterpillars. He never once stayed with me till I was finished.

"And then I can use her more in the house," I heard my mother say. She had a dead-quiet, regretful way of talking about me that always made me uneasy. "I just get my back turned and she runs off. It's not like I had a girl in the family at all."

I went and sat on a feed bag in the corner of the barn, not wanting to appear when this conversation was going on. My mother, I felt, was not to be trusted. She was kinder than my father and more easily fooled, but you could not depend on her, and the real reasons for the things she said and did were not to be known. She loved me, and she sat up late at night making a dress of the difficult style I wanted, for me to wear when school started, but she was also my enemy. She was always plotting. She was plotting now to get me to stay in the house more, although she knew I hated it (*because* she knew I hated it) and keep me from working for my father. It seemed to me she would do this simply out of perversity, and to try her power. It did not occur to me that she could be lonely, or jealous. No grown-up could be; they were too fortunate. I sat and kicked my heels monotonously against a feed bag, raising dust, and did not come out till she was gone.

At any rate, I did not expect my father to pay any attention to what she said. Who could imagine Laird doing my work—Laird remembering the padlock and cleaning out the watering dishes with a leaf on the end of a stick, or even wheeling the tank without it tumbling over? It showed how little my mother knew about the way things really were.

I have forgotten to say what the foxes were fed. My father's bloody apron reminded me. They were fed horsemeat. At this time most farmers still kept horses, and when a horse got too old to work, or broke a leg or got down and would not get up, as they sometimes did, the owner would call my father, and he and Henry went out to the farm in the truck. Usually they shot and butchered the horse there, paying the farmer from five to twelve dollars. If they had already too much meat on hand, they would bring the horse back alive, and keep it for a few days or weeks in our stable, until the meat was needed. After the war the farmers were buying tractors and gradually getting rid of horses altogether, so it sometimes happened that we got a good healthy horse, that there was just no use for any more. If this happened in the winter we might keep the horse in our stable till spring, for we had plenty of hay and if there was a lot of snow— and the plow did not always get our road cleared—it was convenient to be able to go to town with a horse and cutter.[2]

The winter I was eleven years old we had two horses in the stable. We did not know what names they had had before, so we called them Mack and Flora. Mack was an old black workhorse, sooty and indifferent. Flora was a sorrel mare, a driver. We took them both out in the cutter. Mack was slow and easy to handle. Flora was given to fits of violent alarm, veering at cars and even at other horses, but we loved her speed and high-stepping, her general air of gallantry and abandon. On Saturdays we went down to the stable and as soon as we opened the door on its cosy, animal-smelling darkness Flora threw up her head, rolled her eyes, whinnied despairingly and pulled herself through a crisis of nerves on the spot. It was not safe to go into her stall; she would kick.

This winter also I began to hear a great deal more on the theme my mother had sounded when she had been talking in front of the barn. I no longer felt safe. It seemed that in the minds of the people around me there was a steady undercurrent of thought, not to be deflected, on this one subject. The word *girl* had formerly seemed to me innocent and unburdened, like the word *child*; now it appeared that it was no such thing. A girl was not, as I had supposed, simply what I was; it was what I had to become. It was a definition, always touched with emphasis, with reproach and disappointment. Also it was a joke on me. Once Laird and I were fighting, and for the first time ever I had to use all my strength against him; even so, he caught and pinned my arm for a moment, really hurting me. Henry saw this, and laughed, saying, "Oh, that there Laird's gonna show you, one of these days!" Laird was getting a lot bigger. But I was getting bigger too.

My grandmother came to stay with us for a few weeks and I heard other things. "Girls don't slam doors like that." "Girls keep their knees together when they sit down." And worse still, when I asked some questions, "That's none of girls' business." I continued to slam the doors and sit as awkwardly as possible, thinking by such measures I kept myself free.

When spring came, the horses were let out in the barnyard. Mack stood against the barn wall trying to scratch his neck and haunches, but Flora trotted up and down and reared at the fences, clattering her hooves against the rails. Snow drifts dwindled quickly, revealing the hard gray and brown earth, the familiar rise and fall of the ground, plain and bare after the fantastic landscape of winter. There was a great feeling of opening-out, of release. We just wore rubbers now, over our shoes; our feet felt ridiculously light. One Saturday we went to the stable and found all the doors open, letting in the unaccustomed sunlight and fresh air. Henry was there, just idling around looking at his collection of calendars which were tacked up behind the stalls in a part of the stable my mother had probably never seen.

"Come to say goodbye to your old friend Mack?" Henry said. "Here, you give him a taste of oats." He poured some oats in Laird's cupped hands and Laird went to feed Mack. Mack's teeth were in bad shape. He ate very slowly, patiently shifting the oats around in his mouth, trying to find a stump of a molar to grind it on "Poor old Mack," said Henry mournfully. "When a horse's teeth's gone, he's gone. That's about the way."

"Are you going to shoot him today?" I said. Mack and Flora had been in the stable so long I had almost forgotten they were going to be shot.

Henry didn't answer me. Instead he started to sing in a high, trembly, mocking-sorrowful voice. *Oh, there's no more work, for poor Uncle Ned, he's gone where the good darkies go.* Mack's thick, blackish tongue worked diligently at Laird's hand. I went out before the song was ended and sat down on the gangway.

I had never seen them shoot a horse, but I knew where it was done. Last summer Laird and I had come upon a horse's entrails before they were buried. We had thought it was a big black snake, coiled up in the sun. That was around in the field that ran up beside the barn. I thought that if we went inside the barn, and found a wide crack or a knothole to look through, we would be able to see them do it. It was not something I wanted to see; just the same, if a thing really happened, it was better to see, and know.

My father came down from the house, carrying the gun.

"What are you doing here?" he said.

"Nothing."

"Go on up and play around the house."

He sent Laird out of the stable. I said to Laird, "Do you want to see them shoot Mack?" and without waiting for an answer led him around to the front door of the barn, opened it carefully, and went in. "Be quiet or they'll hear us," I said. We could hear Henry and my father talking in the stable; then the heavy, shuffling steps of Mack being backed out of his stall.

In the loft it was cold and dark. Thin crisscrossed beams of sunlight fell through the cracks. The hay was low. It was a rolling country, hills and hollows, slipping under our feet. About four feet up was a beam going around the walls. We piled hay up in one corner and I boosted Laird up and hoisted myself. The beam was not very wide; we crept along it with our hands flat on the barn walls. There were plenty of knotholes, and I found one that gave me the view I wanted—a corner of the barnyard, the gate, part of the field. Laird did not have a knothole and began to complain.

I showed him a widened crack between two boards. "Be quiet and wait. If they hear you you'll get us in trouble."

My father came in sight carrying the gun. Henry was leading Mack by the halter. He dropped it and took out his cigarette papers and tobacco; he rolled cigarettes for my father and himself. While this was going on Mack nosed around in the old, dead grass along the fence. Then my father opened the gate and they took Mack through. Henry led Mack away from the path to a patch of ground and they talked together, not loud enough for us to hear. Mack again began searching for a mouthful of fresh grass, which was not to be found. My father walked away in a straight line, and stopped short a distance which seemed to suit him. Henry was walking away from Mack too, but sideways, still negligently holding on to the halter. My father raised the gun and Mack looked up as if he had noticed something and my father shot him.

Mack did not collapse at once but swayed, lurched sideways and fell, first on his side; then he rolled over on his back and, amazingly, kicked his legs for a few seconds in the air. At this Henry laughed, as if Mack had done a trick for him. Laird, who had drawn a long, groaning breath of surprise when the shot was fired, said out loud, "He's not dead." And it seemed to me it might be true. But his legs stopped, he rolled on his side again, his muscles quivered and sank. The two men walked over and looked at him in a businesslike way; they bent down and examined his forehead where the bullet had gone in, and now I saw his blood on the brown grass.

"Now they just skin him and cut him up," I said. "Let's go." My legs were a little shaky and I jumped gratefully down into the hay. "Now you've seen how they shoot a horse," I said in a congratulatory way, as if I had seen it many times before. "Let's see if any barn cat's had kittens in the hay." Laird jumped. He seemed young and obedient again. Suddenly I remembered how, when he was little, I had brought him into the barn and told him to climb the ladder to the top beam. That was in the spring, too, when the hay was low. I had done it out of a need for excitement, a desire for something to happen so that I could tell about it. He was wearing a little bulky brown and white checked coat, made down from one of mine. He went all the way up just as I told him, and sat down on the top beam with the hay far below him on one side, and the barn floor and some old machinery on the other. Then I ran screaming to my father. "Laird's up on the top beam!" My father came, my mother came, my father went up the ladder talking very quietly and brought Laird down under his arm, at which my mother leaned against the ladder and began to cry. They said to me, "Why weren't you watching him?" but nobody ever knew the truth. Laird did not know enough to tell. But whenever I saw the brown and white checked coat hanging in the closet, or at the bottom of the rag bag, which was where it ended up, I felt a weight in my stomach, the sadness of unexorcised guilt.

I looked at Laird, who did not even remember this, and did not like the look on his thin, winter-paled face. His expression was not frightened or upset, but remote, concentrating. "Listen," I said, in an unusually bright and friendly voice, "you aren't going to tell, are you?"

"No," he said absently.

"Promise."

"Promise," he said. I grabbed the hand behind his back to make sure he was not crossing his fingers. Even so, he might have a nightmare; it might come out that way. I decided I had better work hard to get all thoughts of what he had seen out of his mind—which, it seemed to me, could not hold very many things at a time. I got some money I had saved and that afternoon we went into Jubilee and saw a show, with Judy Canova,[3] at which we both laughed a great deal. After that I thought it would be all right.

Two weeks later I knew they were going to shoot Flora. I knew from the night before, when I heard my mother ask if the hay was holding out all right, and my father said, "Well, after tomorrow there'll just be the cow, and we should be able to put her out to grass in another week." So I knew it was Flora's turn in the morning.

This time I didn't think of watching it. That was something to see just one time. I had not thought about it very often since, but sometimes when I was busy working at school, or standing in front of the mirror combing my hair and wondering if I would be pretty when I grew up, the whole scene would flash into my mind: I would see the easy, practiced way my father raised the gun, and hear Henry laughing when Mack kicked his legs in the air. I did not have any great feeling of horror and opposition, such as a city child might have had; I was too used to seeing the death of animals as a necessity by which we lived. Yet I felt a little ashamed, and there was a new wariness, a sense of holding-off, in my attitude to my father and his work.

It was a fine day, and we were going around the yard picking up tree branches that had been torn off in winter storms. This was something we had been told to do, and also we wanted to use them to make a teepee. We heard Flora whinny, and then my father's voice and Henry's shouting, and we ran down to the barnyard to see what was going on.

The stable door was open. Henry had just brought Flora out, and she had broken away from him. She was running free in the barnyard, from one end to the other. We climbed up on the fence. It was exciting to see her running, whinnying, going up on her hind legs, prancing and threatening like a horse in a Western movie, an unbroken ranch horse, though she was just an old driver, an old sorrel mare. My father and Henry ran after her and tried to grab the dangling halter. They tried to work her into a corner, and they had almost succeeded when she made a run between them, wild-eyed, and disappeared around the corner of the barn. We heard the rail clatter down as she got over the fence, and Henry yelled. "She's into the field now!"

That meant she was in the long L-shaped field that ran up by the house. If she got around the center, heading toward the lane, the gate was open; the truck had been driven in the field this morning. My father shouted to me, because I was on the other side of the fence, nearest the lane. "Go shut the gate!"

I could run very fast. I ran across the garden, past the tree where our swing was hung, and jumped across a ditch into the lane. There was the open gate. She had not got out, I could not see her up the road; she must have run to the other end of the field. The gate was heavy, I lifted it out of the gravel and carried it across the roadway. I had it halfway across when she came in sight, galloping straight toward me. There was just time to get the chain on. Laird came scrambling through the ditch to help me.

Instead of shutting the gate, I opened it as wide as I could. I did not make any decision to do this, it was just what I did. Flora never slowed down; she galloped straight past me, and Laird jumped up and down, yelling "Shut it, shut it!" even after it was too late. My father and Henry appeared in the field a moment too late to see what I had done. They only saw Flora heading for the township road. They would think I had not got there in time.

They did not waste any time asking about it. They went back to the barn and got the gun and the knives they used, and put these in the truck; then they turned the truck around and came bouncing up the field toward us. Laird called to them. "Let me go too, let me go too!" and Henry stopped the truck and they took him in. I shut the gate after they were all gone.

I supposed Laird would tell. I wondered what would happen to me. I had never disobeyed my father before, and I could not understand why I had done it. Flora would not really get away. They would catch up with her in the truck. Or if they did not catch her this morning somebody would see her and telephone us this afternoon or tomorrow. There was no wild country here for her to run to, only farms. What was more, my father had paid for her, we needed the meat to feed the foxes, we needed the foxes to make our living. All I had done was make more work for my father who worked hard enough already. And when my father found out about it he was not going to trust me any more; he would know that I was not entirely on his side. I was on Flora's side, and that made me no use to anybody, not even to her. Just the same, I did not regret it; when she came running at me and I held the gate open, that was the only thing I could do.

I went back to the house, and my mother said. "What's all the commotion?" I told her that Flora had kicked down the fence and got away. "Your poor father," she said, "now he'll have to go chasing over the countryside. Well, there isn't any use planning dinner before one." She put up the ironing board. I wanted to tell her, but thought better of it and went upstairs, and sat on my bed.

Lately I had been trying to make my part of the room fancy, spreading the bed with old lace curtains, and fixing myself a dressing table with some leftovers of cretonne for a skirt. I planned to put up some kind of barricade between my bed and Laird's, to keep my section separate from his. In the sunlight, the lace curtains were just dusty rags. We did not sing at night any more. One night when I was singing Laird said, "You sound silly," and I went right on but the next night I did not start. There was not so much need to anyway, we were no longer afraid. We knew it was just old furniture over there, old jumble and confusion. We did not keep to the rules. I still stayed awake after Laird was asleep and told myself stories, but even in these stories something different was happening, mysterious alterations took place. A story might start off in the old way, with a spectacular danger, a fire or wild animals, and for a while I might rescue people; then things would change around, and instead, somebody would be rescuing me. It might be a boy from our class at school, or even Mr. Campbell, our teacher, who tickled girls under the arms. And at this point the story concerned itself at great length with what I looked like—how long my hair was, and what kind of dress I had on; by the time I had these details worked out the real excitement of the story was lost.   .

It was later than one o'clock when the truck came back. The tarpaulin was over the back, which meant there was meat in it. My mother had to heat dinner up all over again. Henry and my father had changed from their bloody overalls into ordinary working overalls in the barn, and they washed their arms and necks and faces at the sink, and splashed water on their hair and combed it. Laird lifted his arm to show off a streak of blood. "We shot old Flora," he said, "and cut her up in fifty pieces."

"Well I don't want to hear about it," my mother said. "And don't come to my table like that."

My father made him go and wash the blood off.

We sat down and my father said grace and Henry pasted his chewing gum on the end of his fork, the way he always did; when he took it off he would have us admire the pattern. We began to pass the bowls of steaming, overcooked vegetables. Laird looked across the table at me and said proudly, distinctly. "Anyway it was her fault Flora got away."

"What?" my father said.

"She could of shut the gate and she didn't. She just open it up and Flora run out."

"Is that right?" my father said.

Everybody at the table was looking at me. I nodded, swallowing food with great difficulty. To my shame, tears flooded my eyes.

My father made a curt sound of disgust. "What did you do that for?"

I did not answer. I put down my fork and waited to be sent from the table, still not looking up.

But this did not happen. For some time nobody said anything, then Laird said matter-of-factly, "She's crying."

"Never mind," my father said. He spoke with resignation, even good humor, the words which absolved and dismissed me for good. "She's only a girl," he said.

I didn't protest that, even in my heart. Maybe it was true.

Notes

[1] **Orangemen's Day.** The Orange Society is named for William of Orange, who, as King William III of England, defeated James II of England at the Battle of the Boyne on 12 July 1609. It sponsors an annual procession on 12 July.

[2] **cutter.** A small sleigh.

[3] **Judy Canova.** American comedian, popular in films in the 1940s.

On Diverson (1669)

Blaise Pascal

When I consider the brief span of my life absorbed into the eternity which comes before and after . . . the small space I occupy and which I see swallowed up in the infinite immensity of spaces of which I know nothing and which know nothing of me, I take fright and am amazed to see myself here rather than there: there is no reason for me to be here rather than there, now rather than then. Who put me here? By whose command and act were this time and place allotted to me?

Diversion. If man were happy, the less he were diverted the happier he would be, like the saints and God. Yes: but is a man not happy who can find delight in diversion? No: because it comes from somewhere else, from outside; so he is dependent, and always liable to be disturbed by a thousand and one accidents, which inevitably cause distress.

Diversion. Being unable to cure death, wretchedness and ignorance, men have decided, in order to be happy, not to think about such things.

Despite these afflictions man wants to be happy, only wants to be happy, and cannot help wanting to be happy. But how shall he go about it? The best thing would be to make himself immortal, but as he cannot do that, he has decided to stop himself thinking about it. . . . The only good thing for men therefore is to be diverted from thinking of what they are, either by some occupation which takes their mind off it, or by some novel and agreeable passion, which keeps them busy, like gambling, hunting, some absorbing show, in short by what is called diversion. That is why gaming and feminine society, war and high office are so popular. It is not that they really bring happiness, nor that anyone imagines that true bliss comes from possessing the money to be won at gaming or the hare that is hunted: no one would take it as a gift. What people want is not the easy and peaceful life that allows us to think of our unhappy condition, nor the dangers of war, nor the burdens of office, but the agitation that takes our mind off it and diverts us. That is why we prefer the hunt to the capture. That is why men are so fond of hustle and bustle. . . . That, in fact, is the main joy of being a king, because people are continually trying to divert him and procure him every kind of pleasure. A king is surrounded by people whose only thought is to divert him and stop him thinking about himself, because, king though he is, he becomes unhappy as soon as he thinks about himself. . . . When men are reproached for pursuing so eagerly something that could never satisfy them, their proper answer, if they really thought about it, ought to be that they simply want a violent and vigorous occupation to take their minds off themselves, and that is why they choose some attractive object to entice them in ardent pursuit . . . but they do not answer like that because they do not know themselves. They do not know that all they want is the hunt and not the capture . . .

They have a secret instinct driving them to seek external diversion and occupation, and this is the result of their constant state of wretchedness. They have another secret instinct, left over from the greatness of our original nature, telling them that the only true happiness lies in rest and not in excitement. These two contrary instincts give rise to a confused plan buried out of sight in the depths of their soul, which leads them to seek rest by way of activity and always to imagine that the satisfaction they miss will come to them once they overcome certain obvious difficulties and can open the door to welcome rest. All our life passes in this way: we seek rest by struggling against certain obstacles, and once they are overcome, rest proves intolerable because of the boredom it produces. We must get away from it and crave excitement. We think either of present or of threatened miseries, and even if we felt quite safe on every side, boredom on its own account would not fail to emerge from the depths of our hearts, where it is naturally rooted, and poison our whole mind. Man is so unhappy that he would be bored even if he had no cause for boredom, by the very nature of his temperament, and he is so vain that, though he has a thousand and one basic reasons for being bored, the slightest thing, like pushing a ball with a billiard cue, will be enough to divert him. . . . He must have excitement, he must delude himself into imagining that he would be happy to win what he would not want as a gift if it meant giving up gambling. He must create some target for his passions and then arouse his desire, anger, fear, for this object he has created, just like children taking fright at a face they have daubed themselves.

That is why this man, who lost his only son a few months ago and was so troubled and oppressed this morning by lawsuits and quarrels, is not thinking about it any more. Do not be surprised; he is concentrating all his attention on which way the boar will go that his dogs have been so hotly pursuing for the past six hours. That is all he needs. However sad a man may be, if you can persuade him to take up some diversion he will be happy while it lasts, and however happy a man may be, if he lacks diversion and has no absorbing passion or entertainment to keep boredom away, he will soon be depressed and unhappy. Without diversion there is no joy; with diversion there is no sadness. . . . How hollow and foul is the heart of man!

Vocation (1962)

William Stafford

This dream the world is having about itself
includes a trace on the plains of the Oregon trail,
a groove in the grass my father showed us all
one day while meadowlarks were trying to tell
something better about to happen.

I dreamed the trace to the mountains, over the hills,
and there a girl who belonged wherever she was.
But then my mother called us back to the car:
she was afraid; she always blamed the place,
the time, anything my father planned.

Now both of my parents, the long line through the plain,
the meadowlarks, the sky, the world's whole dream
remain, and I hear him say while I stand between the two,
helpless, both of them part of me:
"Your job is to find what the world is trying to be."

A Mighty Fortress (2000)

Margaret Talbot

To get to the house where Stephen and Megan Scheibner live with their seven children, you skirt past Allentown, Pa., and drive for another half-hour into the hills above the Lehigh Valley. The Scheibner place is on Blue Mountain Road, a few miles past a forlorn establishment called Binnie's Hot Dogs and Family Food. Standing behind their white clapboard farmhouse, where the backyard unfurls over three and a half acres and where, in summer, you can see a tangled strawberry patch and a tree fort, you could swear you were deep in the country and maybe deep in the past too. The front of the house is a different matter. It's practically on top of a busy road that leads to the local ski resorts; the view is of a housing development under construction.

Inside, there is no such ambivalence. Although the Scheibners are well off and their house is comfortably appointed—Steve is a pilot with American Airlines and a commander in the Naval Reserves—what might strike many visitors first is what's missing. In the Scheibner household, where the children are 12, 11, 9, 7, 6, 4 and 20 months, there is no Pokemon or "Star Wars" paraphernalia. There are no Britney Spears or Ricky Martin tapes. There are no posters of Leonardo DiCaprio or Michael Jordan taped to the walls, no pots of lip gloss or bottles of metallic nail polish scattered around. No Mortal Kombat, no "Goosebumps." No broadcast TV—though the family does watch carefully selected videos, which often means movies from the 1940's and 50's. (The older kids are big Cary Grant fans.) There is no giggling about the cute guys and girls at school, because the Scheibners are home-schooled and besides, their parents don't believe in dating. There is little sign of eye-rolling preteen rebellion, because Steve and his wife, Megan, don't believe in that either, and have set up their lives in such a way that it is unlikely to manifest itself. Katie, the oldest, reads Louisa May Alcott and reissued girls' classics like the Elsie Dinsmore books, and is partial to white patent-leather Mary Janes worn with ankle-length floral dresses. Peter, who comes next, likes Tolkien and the muscularly Christian boys' adventure stories written by the 19th-century author G. A. Henty, and favors chinos and logo-free button-down shirts. Peter wants to be a missionary in Russia, which he describes as a "forsaken" country; Katie wants to be a home-schooling mom. They are each other's best friends. And if they quarrel, it's not in a way that involves the dissing of one another in viciously up-to-the-minute slang.

There is no sports gear lying around the Scheibner household, because Megan feels that team sports breed competitive "behavior that we would not deem Christlike"; more important, they interfere with the weekly rhythm of schooling, service and worship. Holidays don't disrupt much, either. The Scheibners don't celebrate Halloween—Satanic overtones—though one year the three oldest children dressed up as a couple of shepherds and a sheep and went door to door handing out evangelical tracts. At Christmas, they decorate the house and take baskets of food to their neighbors and to the poor, but they don't indulge in a buy-fest.

Megan, who is 37, guesses she has been to a mall "maybe three times" in the seven years the family has lived in Pennsylvania, and she can't remember the correct name of Toys "R" Us. For the children's clothes, she does a lot of her shopping at consignment stores because she objects to "the way most girls' stuff looks like it was designed for 20-year-olds and the boys' clothes all have some cartoon character on them." This Christmas, as they have for the past several years, the kids got a shared family gift—a "Sunday box" of special games and toys they can take out only on the Sabbath. It contained a Noah's Ark puzzle, several books, a tape of Christian children's songs with titles like "Keep Your Tongue From Evil," and a board game called Sticky Situations, a Christian version of Chutes and Ladders based on such moral dilemmas as what you should do if the most unpopular kid you know invites you over.

None of this is what Steve and Megan Scheibner would say first about themselves. What they would say first is that they are Christians—fundamentalist Baptists who were born again when, as teenagers, they found Jesus Christ and accepted the doctrine of salvation. And yet the way they practice their faith puts them so sharply and purposefully at odds with the larger culture that it is hard not to see the Scheibners, conservative and law-abiding though they are, as rebels.

We have arrived, it seems, at a moment in our history when the most vigorous and coherent counterculture around is the one constructed by conservative Christians. That sounds odd to many of us—especially, perhaps, to secular liberals, who cherish our own 60's-inflected notions of what an "alternative lifestyle" should look like. Ever since Theodore Roszak first coined it in 1968, the word "counterculture" has retained its whiff of patchouli, its association with free love, long hair and left-wing youth. "The counterculture," as Roszak defined it, "is the embryonic base of New Left politics, the effort to discover new types of community, new family patterns, new sexual mores . . . new personal identities on the far side of power politics."

Yet today it is conservative Christians like the Scheibners who, more self-consciously than any other large social group, buck mainstream notions of what constitutes a fulfilled life. Indeed, much of what Roszak said of the 60's counterculture could be said of them too. It's true that the "patterns" and "mores" they have discovered are not so much new ones as reinvigorated traditional ones. Parent-sanctioned courtship, the merging of school and home, the rejection of peer-group segregation, the moral value of thrift—all are ideas that, in the United States, last held real sway in the 19th century. But the impatience that people like the Scheibners display with acquisition, their unflagging commitment to putting the group—in their case, the family—above individual ambition, their rejection of pop culture, their characterization of themselves as, in Steve's words, "people who question absolutely everything," make them radical in ways that would be recognizable to some 60's counterculturists too.

There are about 20 million evangelical Christians in the U.S. today; together with fundamentalists, who tend to be more withdrawn from public life and more theologically conservative, they make up about 25 percent of the American population. Many of them lead lives that are far less sequestered and culturally abstemious than the Scheibners'. (Only 6 percent of conservative Christians educate their children at home, for instance, though the numbers are growing.) Some lead even more walled-off lives: at a conference for home-schooling families in Virginia last summer, I heard one speaker urge parents to reconsider sending their kids to college—even a Bible college—because dorm life encouraged "fornication" and "homosexual rape." But nearly all evangelicals struggle with the question of how staunchly they should separate their families from a majority culture they believe flouts their values.

A sense of this struggle came to the fore last spring, when Paul Weyrich published his "turn off, tune out, drop out" letter—the very phrase self-consciously echoing the hippie slogan. Weyrich, a founder of the Christian right, now urged "a strategy of separation," a "sort of quarantine" for Christians who he argued had been trying too hard, and at too much cost to their own morality, to insert themselves into the mainstream. "We need," he wrote "to drop out of this culture, and find places, even if it is where we physically are right now, where we can live godly, righteous and sober lives."

•   •   •

I had become interested in the idea of a Christian counterculture, and I wanted to write about a family who seemed to be living it out. I wasn't looking for people involved in a violent or illegal confrontation with the government—militia types, say—nor for people who belonged to a tradition with a long history of separateness, like the Amish. What I was looking for were people who were, as Steve Scheibner later described his family, "selective separatists": people who voted and paid taxes, worked in the mainstream world and even did community service, but who quite deliberately chose, as Megan put it, "not to participate in those parts of the culture that do not bring glory to God."

Partly I was interested because as a mother of young children, I had grappled with some of the same questions about what to keep at bay and for how long. TV or no TV? Did I want my 3-year-old to start playing on the computer now so he wouldn't be behind or hold off as long as possible, knowing his life will be colonized by dot-com this and digital that soon enough? Did toy guns lead inexorably to a taste for brutal video games? When you are awash in media and awash in stuff, what hope do you have of picking and choosing anyway? Could you do so only if armed with a totalizing worldview like the Scheibners'? How feasible—and how desirable—was it to "drop out" anyway?

When Megan Scheibner answered a message I posted on a Christian Internet discussion list last summer, her e-mail convinced me that I had found the right family. "We don't isolate our family," she wrote, "but we do feel like we are called to shelter them from evil until they are spiritually ready to stand firm." Sheltering them, she explained, meant screening out almost all pop culture. "We have seen the fruit in kind, polite children," she went on to say. "Others have noticed, too, and this has given us many opportunities to share, i.e., one time at Pizza Hut, the man at the next table bought us lunch because the kids were so nice to each other. . . . Only God gets the glory for things like this. Neither my husband nor I were raised in Christian homes, but God has been faithful to show us his desire for our family, and then as we obey, He has blessed us abundantly."

On a rainy Sunday morning in August, I arrived, with my husband and son, for my first visit to the Scheibner house. The family was busy conducting its own Sunday school, and Megan sent Emma, then 8, out to greet us. Like all of the Scheibner children, Emma addressed me as Mrs. Talbot and my husband as Mr. Talbot. It seemed pointless to insist that they call me by my first name, and downright mean to introduce the idea that my husband and I have different last names, so there it stood. Of another 8-year-old, it might be fair to say that she bounded out of the house, but Emma walked delicately, on the balls of her feet, self-consciously ladylike. With a curtsy, she conducted us inside. All seven of the Scheibner children, and three of their friends, sat cross-legged on the tan carpet in the living room, reviewing their catechisms and listening to a sermon delivered by their father.

It may be because he is a pilot or because he has spent much of his adult life in the military or because he believes so firmly in parental authority, but Steve Scheibner seems at ease in the role of teacher and preacher to his own children in a way that few parents I know would be. Not that anything in his appearance or demeanor suggests an old-fashioned patriarch. He's a young-looking 39, slim, sharp-featured and dark-haired; he can be sarcastic; and he uses lots of guy lingo like "Bogus!" and "Where the rubber hits the road." But he's also got a storehouse of metaphors and concepts for child-rearing and for life that he dips into without hesitation or doubt. Steve explains to me later that he and Megan don't like the way many churches, including their own, shunt kids off to children's services where "they hear about Jonah and the whale for the umpteenth time." They think that children are capable of more or less following the main sermon by the age of 3; when they start their own church in Brunswick, Me., next summer (Steve is studying at a seminary now), there will be booster seats in the pews.

For now, though, he has taken to conducting his own Sunday school, with another couple and their children. Megan, in a smocked denim dress, a headband and no makeup, sits next to him. Though it's only 9 a.m., all the children look freshly scrubbed and shiny-haired, outfitted in their Sunday best. When little Baleigh cranes her neck to peer at us with a radiant, inquisitive smile, her mom gives her a whispered scolding, accompanied by the look a border collie might give a straying sheep. She turns around immediately.

At 10:30, Steve piles the kids into the van and drives to church, and Megan stays behind to talk to me. She'll miss church this morning, which she hardly ever does, but there's another service tonight, which the family always attends as well. In her high-ceilinged kitchen, where one wall is lined with homemade preserves, she tells me about their decision to teach their kids at home. "I worked in a day-care center for a while as a young Navy wife, and it really shocked me—the lack of discipline, the hitting, biting, screeching. We always thought we would home-school, but somehow we lost the nerve for a while and with Katie we sent her to kindergarten at a private Christian school for a year. But what we noticed was that she got more interested in what her peers were doing than in what her family was doing! We felt like our family-centered little girl was being pulled away from us."

Family identity is extremely important to the Scheibners—they have their own sayings, code words, even a family song. The turning outward that most parents expect of their children and accept, with varying degrees of wistfulness, was to them an intolerable betrayal. "We didn't want to lose our children to other people's ideas and ideologies," Megan will say, or, "We wanted our children's hearts, and we really feel we have them." Home-schooling afforded the prospect that the older kids would help with the younger ones and the younger ones would emulate the older ones instead of their peers.

While we talk, Megan is cooking gravy and pot roast and two kinds of pie, and when the rest of the family comes home it's time for Sunday lunch at the big butcher block table Steve made for them. Despite the presence of seven children, lunch is an orderly business. Interruptions are kept to a minimum—talking out of turn elicits the border-collie look. Still, Peter, who has been studying pirates, chats charmingly about Bluebeard, and Katie reminds me that there were female pirates who "fought like demons." There is a lot of anticipatory discussion of the pies. But lunch, like most meals in the Scheibner household, is also an occasion for moral pedagogy.

The thing about living in a culture from which you feel estranged, and which you therefore do not trust to reinforce you own values, is that you must be vigilant; you can't lose an opportunity to remind your children that they are different, and why. The Scheibners surround themselves as much as possible with a culture of their own making and friends of their own choosing who share their religion, but it's not as though they actually live in a 19th-century village. Just the other week, Katie innocently typed in "girls.com" on the computer—the Scheibner kids are allowed to do research on the Internet—and got hit with a dozen porn sites.

Just before pie is served, Steve asks Katie, as he has many times before, to explain what courtship is. Shyly, she looks down at her plate. "I don't know," she says. To which her mother replies, "You can do better than that, young lady." And she can. She has known the word, at least, since she was 9 and her father took her out for ice cream and a portentous chat. The Scheibners believe that dating, because it usually involves breaking up, is, as Steve puts it, "practice for divorce."

It goes without saying that they do not approve of premarital sex, but what is a little more surprising is that they do not approve of premarital emotional intimacy either. If a couple are courting, they are supposed to be seriously considering each other as husband and wife, and they are supposed to do so with some overt participation by parents or other elders. Ideally, they should not be alone together, or if they are it ought to be in a public place—a Friendly's, say—where liquor is not served and where they are unlikely to give in to temptation. As Steve later explained to me: "If a girl dates 100 guys before she gets married, she's given her heart away 100 times but every time she gets it back, it's a little more scarred. So, when I took Katie out, I had bought this cheap little wedding ring in my size, and I gave it to her and I said: 'This is yours and what it represents is your heart. Go ahead and try it on.' Well, of course it was about as big as three of her fingers. So I said, 'See, it doesn't fit you, but it does fit Daddy, so if you don't mind, I want you to give Daddy your heart and let him hold on to it until the appropriate time when I will give it back to you and you in turn will give it to the man you marry.' "

Katie looks up—she's a good girl who wants to please—and murmurs: "It's better than dating. It's waiting for the right man." Now Peter raises his hand. For him, this is all a little more abstract and a little less embarrassing, and he knows he has the answer. "It's keeping your heart pure!"

"Right!" says his father approvingly.

After lunch, Katie goes upstairs without prompting to put young Baleigh and Stephen down for their three-hour afternoon naps—nap time is inviolable at the Scheibner house—and Peter and Emma cheerily start in on the dishes. To a girl and boy, the Scheibner kids are a pleasure to talk to; they're polite and brimming with book-gotten information. They're also a little otherworldly, a bit unnervingly preprogrammed.

When the family came to Washington, where I live, to attend a rally for home-schoolers on the Capitol steps, I went along. It was a hot day and I was nine months pregnant, so I sat down, and while the rest of the children stood patiently with Megan and Steve, Molly, the 7-year-old, wandered over to me. Molly is the dreamy one, the dress-up artist—the one who likes to trail around the house in her mother's wedding gown and who says she wants to be a princess when she grows up. Her hair is honey-colored and waist length, and so, naturally, she maintains a lively interest in the general subject of hair. On the steps, she began doing what a lot of little girls with a lively interest in hair would do, which was to brush mine and, with my permission, to poke through my purse looking for hair ornaments. But though the motions seemed familiar, the dialogue was disconcertingly awry.

Is President Clinton a Christian?" Molly asked in her singsong voice.

"I think he would say so, yes."

"No. He's not. He lies. Do you have a barrette?"

The sun was beating down. A boy skateboarded by in a black T-shirt reading, "Jesus: The Force Without a Dark Side."

"I know who is always against us," Molly continued.

"Who?"

"Satan." Brush. Brush.

"Really? What does he do?"

"Makes us lie." Brush. Brush. "Makes us sin." Brush. Brush. "Makes us turn our back on God. What's Play-Doh?"

For more moderate Americans, the persistence of the evangelical strain in our culture is a mystery that both requires and defies explanation. After the embarrassment of the Scopes trial, conservative Christians of all stripes were supposed to have sunk into the past like woolly mammoths in a tar pit. The re-emergence of a Christian right in the mid-80's took no one by greater surprise than the liberal academics and journalists who were frequently called upon to account for it, and to whom the equation of secularity and modernity was itself sacrosanct. As a result, much of the commentary on conservative Christians has tended to portray them, the historian Alan Brinkley points out, "as a group somehow left behind by the modern world—economically, culturally, psychologically." They were, in short, H. L. Mencken's "rustic gorillas" updated, but barely.

The trouble with this theory of "status discontent"—of conservative Christians as downwardly mobile rubes—was that most of them were neither. On "most measures of backwardness," as the sociologist Christian Smith puts it, evangelicals look no different—and frequently look more advanced—than their counterparts who identify themselves as mainline or liberal Protestants, as Catholics or as nonreligious. Of all these groups, evangelicals are the least likely to have had only a high school education or less. They are more likely than liberals or the nonreligious to belong to the $50,000-and-above income bracket. And they are no more likely to live in rural areas than anyone else; the new centers of conservative Christianity, it turns out, are the prosperous suburbs in Midwestern states like Kansas and Oklahoma.

Moreover, if you started with a theory of conservative Christians as orphans of history stranded in the modern world, you were more or less helpless to explain why the movement has been flourishing—both in new converts and in retention of members—since the 70's. Smith, a professor of sociology at the University of North Carolina, has one convincing answer. He argues that American evangelicalism is flourishing "because of and not in spite of its confrontation with modern pluralism." In other words, the fragmentation of American culture has encouraged the flowering of all kinds of minority groups, from gays to conservative Christians. More important, modern pluralism allows evangelicals to rub up against ideas and sensibilities that offend them, and this is itself a revitalizing force. "Contemporary pluralism," Smith has written, "creates a situation in which evangelicals can perpetually maintain but can never resolve their struggle with the nonevangelical world."

Over the past few years, engaging in this daily struggle to lead a "godly, righteous and sober life" has been made much easier by the exponential growth of Christian media. People like the Scheibners now have a storehouse of goods and services to which they can return, again and again, to refresh themselves and be entertained without guilt. The ability to encapsulate themselves in a culture of their own making removes some of the incentive to reform the culture at large, while at the same time offering a more fully realized reproof of it—a parallel world, imagined to the last, vivid detail.

Christian books and TV are just the beginning. The contemporary Christian music scene, with its groovily-named bands like Leaderdogs for the Blind and the Insyderz, is a $1-billion-a-year business. You can now buy, over the Internet, everything from Christian computer games to poseable biblical action figures. In the video market, "VeggieTales," a popular kids' series featuring animated vegetables enacting biblical parables, is just one among hundreds of titles—from the "Mother Goose Gospel" to "The Adventures of Prayer Bear."

Conservative Christianity has its own chaste heartthrobs, like Joshua Harris, the raffishly cute author of "I Kissed Dating Good-Bye," and the singer Rebecca St. James, the Alanis Morissette of the W.W.J.D. set. It even has its own indie film scene with movies like "End of the Harvest," in which "a college philosophy club meeting filled with atheists humiliates a new believer who tries to prove to them the existence of God." It has its own magazines for every demographic niche, including Hopscotch and Boys' Quest for kids 6 to 13, which promise "no teen themes, no boyfriends, girlfriends, makeup, fashion or violence and NO ADVERTISING!"

Combine all this with the fact that the number of home-schoolers has been increasing since 1985 at a rate of 15 to 20 percent a year—there are now about 1.2. million—while enrollment at evangelical colleges grew 24 percent between 1990 and 1996 (compared with an enrollment increase of 5 percent at other private colleges), and it seems fair to say that conservative Christians can live as much as they choose within a culture of their own construction. And that a lot of them are choosing to do so much of the time.

For some people, this separatist impulse has been strengthened by a new-found disillusionment with politics. It's not that conservative Christians are fleeing civic duty altogether: evangelicals still vote, for example, at a higher rate than do members of almost any other major religious group. It's more a matter of emphasis—of saying, maybe we were seduced by the promise of political power, and now we have to free ourselves from its thrall and concentrate anew on living faithfully and saving souls.

Steve Scheibner is certainly a patriotic guy: he has served in the Navy for 17 years, most recently flying drug-interdiction flights in the Caribbean. But whereas he once thought of running for political office, he now feels he "could have a greater and longer lasting impact on the lives of people as a pastor." He and Megan are Republicans, and they always vote, but they're not going to be active participants in Campaign 2000. Jerry Fal-well, Ralph Reed and most other religious-right leaders don't impress Steve much—they "are mostly political creatures," he says. The one candidate he admires is the firebrand Alan Keyes, who doesn't stand a chance of getting the Republican nomination. The political issue the Scheibners say they care most about is being left alone to home-school, and they see the discipling of others—the training of hearts already opened up to Christ—as their best hope for making a difference in the world.

One icy evening in January, nine young couples crowd into the Scheibners' living room for a class Megan and Steve teach on parenting the Christian way. Angie Dalrymple and her husband, Bruce, have come because they are both new Christians—"my husband got saved in March and I got saved in April"—and she needs help picking her way through unfamiliar moral terrain. Just last week, the Dalrymples' 9-year-old son, Josh, who has also been born again, was facing all kinds of grief at his public school because he now insists on "dressing real nice." Given that he had already ostenta-tiously thrown his Pokemon cards away, explaining to his classmates that an obsession with the cards could lead to a lifetime fascination with the dark side, he was taking some risks as it was. But Josh is big, which helps, and Angie coaxed him to "get rid of the tie, but keep the button-down shirts." She's proud of him but sometimes she feels he's getting ahead of her, spiritually speaking. When his 4-year-old brother, Cody, talked back to her the other day, Josh called his attention to the Ten Commandments on the wall. Now Josh is saying he wants to be home-schooled, and Angie admits to the group that her first thought was, "Whoa, there." She and her husband, a machinist, have already stopped drinking and cursing, cut up their credit cards and canceled their cable TV. How many more changes are there going to be? She's glad to have the group for support.

The agenda for the evening involves watching a video produced by the Christian child-rearing gurus Gary and Ann Marie Ezzo, whose advocacy of rigid schedules for feeding babies, among other things, has been widely criticized by mainstream pediatricians. Tonight's program, though, is a gentler offering, focused on the need to help your child grow morally by giving him "the moral reason why" when you reprimand him for, say, careering around the churchyard and knocking old ladies off-balance—the example given in the video. The evening's discussion also gives the Scheibners a chance to touch on one of their favorite metaphors: the funnel.

The Scheibners think that most parents today err by trying to be "buddies to their babies and little kids." As Megan puts it, they start out with "a big fat funnel, and then, when the kids get to be 13 or 14 and become rebellious, they try to tighten it, and by then it's too late." The Scheibners' idea, they explain, is that you start off with a tight funnel, then gradually open it so that by the time your kids get to be teenagers, you can trust them. They reject what is, in essence, the modern idea of adolescence—that a teenager's alienation from his parents is an inevitable, even necessary step on the way to individuation. For Megan and Steve, rebellion within the family is not an acceptable option; they need a united front at home to wage rebellion against the larger culture. And more important, they believe that obedience to parents trains a child for obedience to God. When the Lord calls him to do something, he has to be ready to say, "Yes, Lord, here I am." So kids need practice in the prompt and cheerful response to commands, learning to do as their parents ask in what the Scheibners refer to as the RAH spirit—for "the Right way, All the way, the Happy way."

In other classes, Steve will talk about the need to stand firm when your children push, how you must be the wall that doesn't give way. He'll defend spanking, a practice that the Scheibners have thought through in detail. (Never do it in anger; never do it when you've lost control; use a flexible instrument so you don't break down muscle.)

The atmosphere tonight is a little like a consciousness-raising session—there's an earnest aura of learning together and sustaining one another in a benighted world. During the short break, everybody stands around drinking Diet Cokes and eating the taco salad someone brought, but there's not a lot of small talk. Steve is indisputably the leader, but he's willing to make himself vulnerable with a well-placed confession or two. He mentions, for example, his own upbringing in a very 70's family that left him with nothing in what he likes to call his "moral warehouse." His parents divorced when he was 2; his dad was a pianist who played in clubs, drank a lot and dropped in and out; his two sisters were out of control. "We didn't eat meals together and we had free run. My mom would see me going out the door with a six-pack and say, 'Have fun.' "

Megan's not talking about it tonight, but her story is not all that different. She was the youngest and the only girl her family. In high school, she played tennis competitively and was a waitress after school to save money for a car and a trip to Europe as a pompom girl. Her parents doted on her and couldn't wait for her to start reeling in the boyfriends. "When I was 15, I started dating a college boy, and for my mom, that was just the apex," Megan told me. Tennis kept her straight for a while, but after she suffered a serious ankle injury in her senior year, her "safeguard" was gone and she started drinking as competitively as she had played tennis. She spent summers at Delaware beaches, where, as she says, "it's always happy hour somewhere," and it wasn't long before she had "quite a reputation as party girl." "Makes me sick now to think of it," she says. Billy Joel and Jackson Browne provided the soundtrack for her life. She says now: "I still wake up some mornings with the lyrics of their songs running through my head. Unbelievable! Anyone who thinks music doesn't affect teens is woefully unaware."

Both she and Steve found Christ when they hooked up with a teen ministry called Young Life. Steve was impressed by the "air of confidence" and "inner peace" he detected in a Young Life staff member named Scott, who was then 24 but willing to hang out with teenagers. "There was something about him that was different, and it kept bugging me and I kept asking him and he kept saying Jesus Christ." Steve didn't want to hear that at first, but after a while he and Scott started talking about the Bible, and something fell into place.

As for Megan, she says she got sick of the beach scene and the sense of purposelessness that washed over her every morning. She found she needed to stop worrying about "having the right boyfriend" to "try and be quiet and learn who it was Christ called me to be." She had started calling herself a Christian in high school, but she hadn't really admitted her sinfulness, let alone renounced it. As a sophomore at West Chester College in Pennsylvania, she finally did, and her "measuring stick" became the Word of God. "He wasn't interested in what I looked like on the outside, but who I was on the inside. Galatians 5:22 says, 'The fruit of the Spirit is love, joy, peace, patience, kindness, goodness, faithfulness, gentleness, self-control.' Suddenly instead of looking in the mirror to see how I was doing, I had to check my heart." She found it an enormous relief "to have the focus off me, me, me."

Megan and Steve initially shocked their families with their conversions. One of Steve's sisters, now a Christian herself, was then a graduate student in philosophy at Penn and told him he was "committing intellectual suicide." Megan's mother, "an intelligent woman who considered herself a feminist," as Megan recalls, thought her only daughter was ruining her life. Considering this was at the end of the Me Decade, Steve and Megan were choosing a radical path indeed.

In the Young Life chapter they joined at West Chester, Steve and Megan were the two resident sticklers. They were the ones who, if somebody in Bible study suggested going out for beers afterward, would catch each other's eyes and say naaah. They were friends first, but their sense of needing to start life anew—their joint weariness with their past selves— brought them closer, and they married just after Steve joined the Navy. He was 23 and she was a year younger. Now the two of them have created a life that sometimes, as Steve jokes with the class that night, "can look a little like a bad 'Ozzie and Harriet' rerun."

"Hey," interrupts a young mother in the class. "There are worse things!"

It could be a rallying cry for the group.

10:30 a.m., a school day at the Scheibners'. It's a scene remarkable, as usual, for its orderliness. Everybody has been up since at least 7:30 (all the kids go to bed by 8:30, so rising early is no problem); they've completed their morning clean-up chores, which Megan reminds them of by affixing a yellow Post-it with a specific assignment directly onto each child's body. They have sung hymns, read some Scripture and gone over their catechisms for the day; they have said the Pledge of Allegiance together. The house is warm and tidy and smells pleasantly of the chili Megan is cooking for lunch.

Downstairs, in the sunny family room, Baleigh is quietly playing a computer game, while Stephen, the baby, bounces up and down in his playpen. In the "library," a room lined with floor-to-ceiling bookshelves made by Steve, Molly is practicing her handwriting, while Nate works on his reading and tries not to let his mind wander to the dinosaur picture he wants to draw when it's free time. Emma perches on a high stool at the kitchen counter, doing sums in her math book. Upstairs, at a pair of scuffed red old-fashioned school desks, Katie studies grammar while Peter reads about Jamestown in a textbook called "America's Providential History." ("Since God is the author of history and He is carrying out His plan on the earth through history, any view of the history of America, or any country, that ignores God is not true history.")

A week at the Scheibner household follows a neat and repetitive arc, constructed along what the Scheibners call the Loving Our Family Guidelines. Each day has a theme, and a biblical verse to go with it. Monday is Ministry Day ("For God is not unrighteous to forget your work and labor of love, which you have shown toward His name, in that you have ministered to the saints and do minister," Hebrews 6:10). On this day, the children might deliver meals to sick or housebound neighbors. Tuesday is Give Day ("For God so loved the world that He gave his only Son, that whosoever believes in Him should not perish but have eternal life," John 3:16), and so in addition to their regular schoolwork, the kids are supposed to think of something to give one another. Wednesday is Serve Day ("By love serve one another," Galatians 5:13), and the Scheibners do so by performing each other's chores. The family spends every Wednesday evening at Awana Bible Club, a Bible memorization program with about 80 kids in its local chapter. Thursday is Edify Day ("Love edifies," I Corinthians 8:1), which means the kids are supposed to make an effort to compliment each other—and not in a fakey way either. Friday is Prefer Day ("Be kindly affectioned one to another with brotherly love, in honor preferring one another," Romans 12:10), which means, for example, letting your sibling pick the hymn the family will sing in the morning. Friday evenings, Katie and Peter help set up the refreshments for the parenting class, then put the younger kids to bed. Saturday is mostly a preamble to Sunday, but sometimes Megan and the older kids will do some volunteer work at the local homeless shelter, and then follow it up with a special treat—a trip to Friendly's, a rented Shirley Temple video, a game of red rover in the backyard.

One consequence of teaching your children at home—and of carefully customizing their media intake—is that you almost never have the experience of hearing them say something you are surprised and sorry that they know. Maybe your 3-year-old comes home one day with a rather specific question about pro wrestling. Or maybe he has somehow sucked out of the cultural ether the message that you "gotta catch 'em all."

Maybe your kid is older and it's something worse. Home-schooling appeals to the parental fantasy of unchallenged dominion over—or at the very least familiarity with—all the detritus that crowds the shelves of your child's "moral warehouse."

I think all parents must be subject to this desire now and again, though comparatively few are willing to remake their lives in the service of it. If your kid were with you all the time, you figure, she would not ask questions that reminded you of your lapses in judgment or vigilance; she would not be in possession of information that you regarded with embarrassment or regret. On the other hand, neither would she be likely to come home with a delightful bit of knowledge that you had nothing to do with putting in her head—a sweet and silly song, a smattering of Spanish, a moral lesson as imparted by someone else—because you might not have known it, perhaps, or thought to plant it there.

Once I asked Steve and Megan if any of their kids ever did come out and say something that shocked them or made them wonder where he or she could possibly have heard it. "That doesn't happen often," Steve replied. "Every now and then we get one of those, but we spend so much time together that it just doesn't happen."

Megan and Steve tend not to let their own guard down much around their kids either. Lately, in fact, they have even stopped watching movies with more adult themes by themselves. "We never did used to rent R-rated movies," Steve says, "but we would get a movie that would use some curse words or maybe had some brief nudity." They'd watch it after the kids were asleep and "justify it by saying, 'Oh, but it's a great story.' Well, now we've changed our view on that. I can't ask them to do something I'm not willing to do," Steve continues. "I don't want to be a hypocrite. And you know my relationship with God is just the same as theirs. My soul and my spirit is just as precious to God as their little souls and their little spirits, so how can I justify watching something that is vulgar and obscene for them? Isn't it vulgar and obscene for me too?"

To many of us, the specter of so much control suggests the possibility, even the inevitability, of rebellion. The Scheibners' oldest children are 12 and 11. What happens when they hit their teen years? Won't their hermetically sealed world spring a leak? Generational self-definition is a dearly held precept in our culture, which is why it seems to make sense to us that both Megan and Steve come from religiously indifferent families in which they defiantly distinguished themselves by their theological conservatism.

When you ask the Scheibners to imagine the future for their own kids, though, they can't picture them going astray. Peter has wanted to be a missionary for the longest time now, and since he and his parents regard this as something he has been called to do, they entertain few doubts about his doing it. Admittedly, it's hard to imagine Peter as a renegade. He is the kind of kid who, when asked in all innocence whether he ever listens furtively to his beloved "Lord of the Rings" tape in bed, looks shocked and says, "Oh, no, when it's time to go to bed, it's time to go to bed." He loves being home-schooled, and not long ago took it upon himself to write a letter to Senator Rick Santorum of Pennsylvania. It read, in part, "I have the joy of knowing I am going to heaven because when I was 4, I asked Jesus to come into my heart and save me from sin."

After spending some time with the Scheibner family, I was not particularly surprised to learn that evangelical Christians have one of the highest intergenerational retention rates of any major religion—meaning that, as Christian Smith puts it, "they have a great ability to raise children who do not become theologically liberal or nonreligious when they grow up." Certainly they work extremely hard to prevent what they see as the tragedy of apostasy. And the new availability of Christian media and of home-school curriculums helps enormously. A generation ago, evangelical families who wanted to shield their children from mainstream culture had little to replace it with, other than self-denial. Now they can offer goodies of their own. And new companies and institutions are springing up all the time to meet their needs. The Scheibners, for instance, are very excited about the founding of the first college primarily for Christian home-schoolers, Patrick Henry, in Purcelleville, Va., which will be accepting its inaugural class of students in the fall. Among other things, Patrick Henry will ask its students to sign a pledge in which they promise to court and not date.

And after college? Neither Megan nor Steve is outright opposed to their daughters' working, especially before they have children. Like many conservative Christians, they warm to the idea of a wife running her own little business from the home. "Proverbs 31 talks about the woman who made purple linens at home and sold them," Steve points out. But they warm even more to the idea of their daughters "having an eye to serve without compensation," as Megan says. They think too many working women have forgotten the virtues of volunteerism. And if one of their girls was to pursue a full-fledged career, Steve says, "we'd still love her and encourage her and, after all, at some point it's her life," but they would also find it hard to disguise their disappointment. "A career takes away from what I think their primary happiness will be, which is being a good mother," Steve says.

And then he gives a little speech that bears the distinctive hallmarks of the new Christian counterculture. "You know," he says, "you may have lots of pats on the back at work, you may have a successful career and a lot of money and great cars to drive, but in the end it always lets you down. Look at any number of gazillionaires out there—men, women, it doesn't make any difference—who have awful, tragic lives. Those things are not the things that satisfy. The things that satisfy are raising a good family, having love."

America has a long history of separatist movements, and within that history, there are, to put it bluntly, the bad separatists and the good ones. In the former category are the stockpilers of guns, the people who don't pay taxes or vaccinate their children—people who lack any sense of their duty as citizens. And in the latter category are people like the Scheibners. Indeed you could argue that their sort of separatism is good for the culture at large—or at least represents a reasonable compromise. If they are committed to teaching Creationism, for example, better that they teach it at home than insist that the public schools do. Besides, a culture that lacks a thriving and reproving counterculture is always in trouble. The very existence of alternative ways of life like the Scheibners' keeps alive a debate about the role of morality and religion in our culture and politics that probably ought never be declared over and done.

And yet you have to wonder about a way of life that requires such rigorous policing of its psychic boundaries. There is something poignant, for a parent like me anyway, about the idea of sons and daughters who love you as uncomplicatedly in their teenage years as they do when they were small—who are, indeed, your best friends—but there is something unreal about it too. There is something inspiring about the prospect of an American childhood in which advertising does not invade the imagination so relentlessly, but something claustrophobic about the notion that the only alternative is a sequestered family life. There is something fundamentally right and useful about the argument that American culture promotes independence at the expense, often, of the more nurturing virtues, but something sad and scared about the idea that the safest solution to this is early marriage. If the Scheibner philosophy allows girls to linger longer at the threshold of adolescence—not having to worry about being thin or sexy—it also pushes them much earlier into wifely domesticity.

By next summer, the Scheibners will be living in Maine, and they are looking forward to the move. Steve is eager to "plant" his new church.

Megan thinks "the slower pace of life" there will make it that much easier to shelter the children from evil. The younger kids are excited about
going crabbing and maybe seeing a moose or two on the rambling,
wooded acreage where their new house will be. Katie, the oldest, is
excited, too. She says she's hoping to find "a little place of my own,
where I could read or think, and nobody would know about it."

Falling into Grace (2005)

Charlotte Thomas

I really do not know what it means to fall from grace. Every time I have fallen, I have been caught. Every time I thought that my misguided ambitions had led me astray, I found that I was right where I belonged. We like the idea of having control and garnering recognition for who we become. We want to be agents in our development, and rightfully so. But, as a very young child, I learned that not all passivity is created equal. Giving yourself to a powerful experience—rendering yourself submissive to it—can be ennobling and empowering. It took me decades to make sense of what I knew on instinct as a seven year-old, but I did seem to know it back then. I knew that I could fall into grace. Perhaps some story-telling is in order.

I am a ninth-generation Floridian, born and raised in St. Petersburg. That my family is Southern, despite Florida's reputation, may perhaps be credible to you, since you now know that I know where my family was nine generations ago. Back in Florida's territorial days, my family lived in Port St. Joe; but for the last four generations, mine included, Pinellas County has been home.

Unlike Port St. Joe, Pinellas County has changed a great deal in the last hundred years. When my great-grandfather arrived around the turn of the twentieth-century, Florida's west coast was wild, and he was a pioneer. His father's orange grove outside of Crescent City had frozen that winter and, in early spring, the family home place burned to the ground. All of the thirteen children were told that they would have to make their own way, since my great-great-grandparents could no longer support them. So, my great-grandfather was married in a triple wedding ceremony (with one of his brothers and one of his sisters), and he headed west—west Florida, that is.

By the time my grandmother became conscious of the world around her, St. Petersburg was a lively city, but she and my grandfather chose deliberately to buy a house on the edge of town near forests and swampland. So my father grew up within ten miles of his great-grandparents' home, but he spent his days hunting and fishing, gigging frogs and catching alligators.

The St. Pete of my childhood was an over-developed, asphalt-encrusted city. It was a fine place to grow up, though. The sky was almost always blue, I never minded the heat, and there were endless opportunities socially, culturally, educationally, etc. I grew up with my grandmother and father telling me of the city they'd known, what lay behind and beneath the ground I covered every day. But my city wasn't their city, except for isolated, quickly evaporating puddles that they'd make sure I'd see. I still drive around each time I visit to try to find residue of their Florida, as an homage I suppose, but it gets much more difficult each time.

My father knew that there was little in Pinellas County that could give my sister and me a sense of what Florida had been for him as a boy, so he made a great effort to get us to more rural areas of the State. One result of his endeavors was our annual trip to Manatee Springs State Park, near Chiefland, Florida. From the time I was three years old until I was married and had to divide holidays between two large and loving families, I spent Thanksgivings at Manatee Springs.

The sharpest memories I have of Manatee Springs are of solitary moments. Even as a young child, I made opportunities for solitude on those camping trips. I would wake early in the morning, slip silently out of our campsite, walk alone to the spring boil, and sit for a while watching the quiet, powerful churning of the water through the morning mist. Tens of thousands of gallons of water per minute are pushed out of the ground at the spot. The peaceful strength of the spring awed me. And the water was impossibly clear. Although I knew from swimming in it that the boil was more than thirty feet deep, you could see details on small rocks that lay on the bottom.

Since the spring water stayed a constant 71 degrees year-round, and November mornings were usually much cooler than that, the spring also created a thick mist. As the sun rose and the air warmed, the mist would begin to dissipate and appear to float down the spring run to the river, so I would follow it on the boardwalk all the way out to the Suwannee. I rarely stayed long at the Suwannee, but I always greeted it, inhaled it momentarily, before I returned to our campsite. Inevitably, I would smell breakfast and hear the quiet noise of my just-awoken family as I re-entered our world, but I'd carry with me throughout the day the calm of the spring just after dawn.

When I was at the spring alone in the morning, my thoughts slowed and my mind opened. Sometimes I tried to write songs or poetry. Sometimes I tried to burn a detailed image into my memory so that I could draw or paint it later in the day. Whatever I did for those moments, though, I always knew I was praying. Sometimes I would pray explicitly, but it seemed forced and redundant. I felt like I was in the presence of God, and I wanted him to speak to me, to tell me his will for my life, but it never came through. I could struggle to find words to describe to myself what I was experiencing, and sometimes I found these accounts illuminating; but words could also distract me, and that was the last thing I wanted.

Mother Teresa was once asked in an interview how she prayed. She answered, "I just listen." When asked what God said to her when she was listening, she said, "He just listens, too." That description of prayer almost knocked me down. Although I'd never articulated it to myself before, it was precisely what I felt at Manatee Springs. For whatever reason, then and there I was able to listen to God. My words were just distractions, just attempts to control the situation. And my attempts to listen for direct words, for a message or a mission, missed the point. God's silence and God's absence are two very different things. I first learned that at Manatee Springs.

My reaction, aside from hack poetry, rough sketches, and bad 1-4-5 pop songs, was a compelling desire to give myself over to the power and presence I perceived. I wanted to be transformed by my submission to what I felt in those moments. I thought I needed to produce something, or learn something, or be able to articulate some definite message that had been given to me, perhaps in code; but such tangible products never emerged. It took years for me to see that all of those desires were perversions of my experience, distractions from what I've come to see as its meaning.

As I grew older and learned a few things, I found that what I experienced at the spring was classical mysticism—the pursuit of immediate union with the divine, a desire to submit my being to Being itself. The more I learned about mysticism, the more complicated my thoughts and memories of those experiences became. One of Kierkegaard's descriptions of faith in *Either/Or* became important to my attempt to make sense of my quasi-mystical moments, especially because of the comments of a classmate of mine at St. John's College.

In my Kierkegaard class, the bulk of one discussion was devoted to our attempt to understand the idea of faith as "resting transparently in the arms of the creator." Given what you now know about my Manatee Springs mornings, you can imagine that I was quite happy with Kierkegaard's account. But, Tom Donahue, a fiftyish middle-school teacher and former welter-weight Golden Gloves champion, did not share my enthusiasm. He was incredulous. "Why would anyone want to rest transparently in the arms of the creator?" he asked. "Transparency? The abdication of individuality, accomplishment, personality? Who could possibly see that as something to be desired?" "But, you would be with God," we tried to explain to him. "No," he said, "YOU wouldn't be with anyone. You wouldn't be anywhere. You would be gone, transparent."

Would giving myself over to the power and grace that I experienced those mornings at Manatee Springs mean losing myself? Not just making a sacrifice, or reorienting my priorities, or accepting a mission; but really losing myself? Some part of me knew that Tom was on to something. I had never been able to give myself to those experiences as much as I wanted to, although I had tried diligently over the years. When I sat silently at the spring, I felt an overwhelming longing for the transcendent and, when I walked away, the longing remained. Perhaps if I ever were to succeed in making the connection that called me in those moments, I would be lost. I didn't know.

Reading Kierkegaard that summer at St. John's was my first indication that my experience at the Spring as a child was not unique, but was, instead, an expression of my humanity. As I read more, I learned of a tradition populated by men and women who, in myriad circumstances, found themselves in the presence of silent and silencing power. Kant's account of the sublime, Nietzsche's stories of the abyss, the prophetic literature of the Christian Bible, Heidegger's account of the clearing and his call to return to the ground of being, etc.

My adolescent response to learning that my experience was not unique was disappointment. I thought I was chosen to feel something that others could not, would not. Happily, though, I had teachers who helped me understand the wonder of connecting my most personal thoughts with the ideas of other thoughtful people. I have come to believe that overcoming the disappointment of learning that your noblest, deepest, and most beautiful thoughts are not unique is perhaps the most important and under-appreciated moment necessary for the possibility of becoming educated.

To be disappointed to learn that my moments at the spring boil were an expression of my humanity and not my particularity was just self-love, self-absorption, ego. I wanted to be unique, distinctive, the recipient of a calling all my own. But why? What intrinsic good exists in learning that I am either more sensitive, or intelligent, or lucky, or blessed than my family or my friends, or the great minds of human history? None, that I can find. On the other hand, the recognition of my consonance with humanity is an opening, the opening for the wisdom and ingenuity of all human endeavor to inform my life. I suppose that this insight sustains my commitment to teaching, as well. To show a student her humanity as it is expressed in hundreds year-old texts written on the other side of the world is to open for her the possibility of seeing her life in the light of the collective wisdom of human history.

Several years ago, I stumbled into the Basilica of St. Denis, north of Paris, and I have been enthralled by the place ever since. The first thing anyone would notice about St. Denis, or any other Gothic cathedral, is its ornate beauty. St. Denis, however, is the first of its kind. Its architect, Abbot Suger, did not copy its style from other cathedrals. Instead he created St. Denis to be a physical space to embody a theological idea. Insofar as Gothic cathedrals silence us and give us a sense of standing in the presence of God, Abbot Suger can be said to have succeeded.

Abbot Suger was enthralled by the writings of a mystic we now call Pseudo-Dionysus, but who at the time was known as Dionysus the Areopagite, a companion of St. Paul mentioned in the Book of Acts. It was also thought that Dionysus the Areopagite was one and the same person as St. Denis, patron saint of Paris and the first Christian martyr in France. Since Suger lived and worked in the Abbey of St. Denis, reading what he thought to be the writings of the patron Saint of his abbey and his city must have been overwhelmingly powerful. And, since the story of St. Denis' martyrdom included a miracle that led to the founding of the Abbey of St. Denis, Suger might well have believed that reading Dionysus would illuminate his responsibility to the abbey, his calling.

As the story goes, Denis and two of his Christian friends decided to take the highest ground in Paris for a Christian shrine. The problem was that the hill (now called Montmartre, or "martyrs' mount") was then occupied by a pagan temple dedicated to the Roman god Mercury. So, under the cover of night, Denis and his compatriots ascended the hill, vandalized the temple, and began raising Christian images. Apparently they were so absorbed in their work that they didn't notice the Parisians coming up the hill behind them. The pagans were predictably unhappy with the three Christians and beheaded them on the spot.

One would think that Denis' story would end with his beheading, but it doesn't. After being beheaded on Montmartre, Denis rose, picked up his head, and walked north several miles. When he reached the spot where he wanted to be buried, he stopped and lay down. The icons of St. Denis unmistakably reflect this story. He's depicted as a headless figure holding his head in his hands. And, generally, his head is topped with a bishop's mitre. The spot where St. Denis finally lay down to be buried is now the site of the Basilica of St. Denis. And, if you go beneath the sanctuary and into the crypt, you will be shown an oblong hole in the dirt said to be St. Denis' grave.

When, in the twelfth century, Suger became interested in the philosophy of Dionysus, he may have believed that he was reading the writings of St. Denis, on whose miraculous burial site he lived, worked, and worshipped. There were also powerful political arguments for claiming the identity of St. Denis and Dionysus the Areopagite. A direct connection to a biblical figure would put the church in Paris on no less credible a foundation than the church in Rome.

Whether or not Suger sincerely believed that Dionysus and Denis were the same historical figure, Suger was clearly captivated by Dionysus' mystical theology. His design of the Basilica of St. Denis was an attempt to create a worldly space for Dionysian mysticism—an environment conducive to a Christian's attempt to achieve mystical union with the divine.

Although today we might think of Gothic Cathedrals as dark places, their true architectural achievement is the introduction of light into interior spaces. Ribbed vaulting and flying buttresses made large, tall windows possible. Rather than filling these window-frames with clear glass, Suger installed colorful panes in designs that depicted biblical scenes. To be in the cathedral was to be in the light of the sun, but for that light to be refracted through the stained-glass windows; just as to read the Bible was to be in the presence of God, but reflected through the biblical accounts. The beauty of God's creation and gospel was magnified and refracted through man-made beauty. And, the worshipper did not find himself outside looking in; to the contrary, once in the cathedral, the worshipper was enveloped by light and truth. Suger's cathedral was a place where God's presence would be manifest, and one's attempts to pray would be supported by a sense of seeing and being seen by God—of bathing in His silent and silencing presence.

It is no wonder that the Basilica of St. Denis has been for my adult life what Manatee Springs was for my childhood. I am drawn to these places, find solace there. I leave centered and focused. Suger designed St. Denis to be a place where one would feel what I felt as a child at the Spring. His achievement, which is inseparable from the great beauty of his church, is the inspiration of a particular human desire—the desire for transcendence. Suger hoped to cultivate this desire in order to encourage the possibility of mystical union as Pseudo-Dionysus described it. He thought that the basilica could support the human endeavor to rest, as Kierkegaard put it, transparently in the arms of the creator.

I no more achieve that mystical union with the divine in cathedrals than I ever did at the Spring. I've since come to believe, however, that such a desire is a misunderstanding of the moment. I part ways with the mystics. God's silence is not God's absence. Longing for the transcendent is not a means to an end, it is itself an end. It is in the very longing that these experiences engender in me that God's presence in the world is made manifest. It is in such longing that my finitude is clear to me, for in such moments can I apprehend, albeit without understanding, infinitude. It is I, myself, that I give to the moment; and it is I, myself, that walk away from the spring and the cathedral and into, among other places, the classroom. I recognize, now, that my awareness of the silence, my capacity to be silenced by it, is itself a moment of grace. I am given a glimpse of the power and glory of God, and I am able to see myself and my world in His light. I am thrown back into the everyday with a renewed sense of the depth and breadth of the reality in which I am immersed. So, now, I give myself to it without fear. I fall in. But I am not lost in those moments, I am found. I do not render myself useless to the world. I am strengthened by refocused perspective. I am not debased by my submission to the silencing power that silences me; instead I am inspired by it. I knew some version of this insight when I was seven years old, although I imagine I'll be reading, thinking, and teaching myself toward a greater understanding of it for the rest of my life.

A Sudden Trip Home in the Spring (1981)

Alice Walker

Sarah walked slowly off the tennis court, fingering the back of her head, feeling the sturdy dark hair that grew there. She was popular. As she walked along the path toward Talfinger Hall her friends fell into place around her. They formed a warm jostling group of six. Sarah, because she was taller than the rest, saw the messenger first.

"Miss Davis," he said, standing still until the group came abreast of him, "I've got a telegram for ye." Brian was Irish and always quite respectful. He stood with his cap in his hand until Sarah took the telegram. Then he gave a nod that included all the young ladies before he turned away. He was young and good-looking, though annoyingly servile, and Sarah's friends twittered.

"Well, open it!" someone cried, for Sarah stood staring at the yellow envelope, turning it over and over in her hand.

"Look at her," said one of the girls, "isn't she beautiful! Such eyes, and hair, and skin!

Sarah's tall, caplike hair framed a face of soft brown angles, high cheekbones and large dark eyes. Her eyes enchanted her friends because they always seemed to know more, and to find more of life amusing, or sad, than Sarah cared to tell.

Her friends often teased Sarah about her beauty; they loved dragging her out of her room so that their boy-friends, naive and worldly young men from Princeton and Yale, could see her. They never guessed she found this distasteful. She was gentle with her friends, and her outrage at their tactlessness did not show. She was most often inclined to pity them, though embarrassment sometimes drove her to fraudulent expressions. Now she smiled and raised eyes and arms to heaven. She acknowledged their unearned curiosity as a mother endures the prying impatience of a child. Her friends beamed love and envy upon her as she tore open the telegram.

"He's dead," she said.

Her friends reached out for the telegram, their eyes on Sarah.

"It's her father," one of them said softly. "He died yesterday. Oh, Sarah," the girl whimpered, "I'm so sorry!"

"Me too." "So am I." "Is there anything we can do?"

But Sarah had walked away, head high and neck stiff.

"So graceful!" one of her friends said.

"Like a proud gazelle" said another. Then they all trooped to their dormitories to change for supper.

Talfinger Hall was a pleasant dorm. The common room just off the entrance had been made into a small modern art gallery with some very good original paintings, lithographs and collages. Pieces were constantly being stolen.

Some of the girls could not resist an honest-to-God Chagall, signed (in the plate) by his own hand, though they could have afforded to purchase one from the gallery in town. Sarah Davis's room was next door to the gallery, but her walls were covered with inexpensive Gauguin reproductions, a Rubens ("The Head of a Negro"), a Mondigliani, and a Picasso. There was a full wall of her own drawings, all of black women. She found black men impossible to draw or to paint; she could not bear to trace defeat onto blank pages. Her women figures were matronly, massive of arm, a weary victory showing in their eyes. Surrounded by Sarah's drawings was a red SNCC poster of a man holding a small girl whose face nestled in his shoulder. Sarah often felt she was the little girl whose face no one could see.

To leave Talfinger even for a few days filled Sarah with fear. Talfinger was her home now; it suited her better than any home she'd ever known. Perhaps she loved it because in winter there was a fragrant fireplace and snow outside her window. When hadn't she dreamed of fire-places that really warmed snow that almost pleasantly froze? Georgia seemed far away as she packed; she did not want to leave New York, where, her grandfather had liked to say, "the devil hung out and caught young gals by the front of their dresses." He had always believed the South the best place to live on earth (never mind that certain people invariably marred the landscape), and swore he expected to die no more than a few miles from where he had been born. There was tenacity even in the gray frame house he lived in and in scrawny animals his farm who regularly reproduced. He was the first person Sarah wanted to see when she got home.

There was a knock on the door of the adjoining bathroom, and Sarah's suite mate entered, a loud Bach concerto just finishing behind her. At first she stuck just her head into the room, but seeing Sarah fully dressed she trudged in and plopped down on the bed. She was a heavy blonde girl with large milk-white legs. Her eyes were small and her neck usually gray with grime.

"My, don't you look gorgeous," she said.

"Ah, Pam," said Sarah, waving her hand in disgust. In Georgia she knew that even to Pam she would be just another ordinarily attractive *colored* girl. In Georgia there were a million girls better looking. Pam wouldn't know that, of course; she'd never been to Georgia; she'd never even seen a black person to speak to, that is, before she met Sarah. One of her first poetic observations about Sarah was that she was "a poppy in a field of winter roses." She had found it weird that Sarah did not own more than one coat.

"Say listen, Sarah," said Pam, "I heard about your father. I'm sorry. I really am."

"Thanks," said Sarah.

"Is there anything we can do? I thought, well, maybe you'd want my father to get somebody to fly you down. He'd go himself but he's taking Mother to Madeira this week. You wouldn't have to worry about trains and things."

Pamela's father was one of the richest men in the world, though no one ever mentioned it. Pam only alluded to it at times of crisis, when a friend might benefit from the use of a private plane, train, or ship; or, if someone wanted to study the characteristics of a totally secluded village, island or mountain, she might offer one of theirs. Sarah could not comprehend such wealth, and was always annoyed because Pam didn't look more like a billionaire's daughter. A billionaire's daughter, Sarah thought, should really be less horsey and brush her teeth more often.

"Gonna tell me what you're brooding about?" asked Pam.

Sarah stood in front of the radiator, her fingers resting on the window seat. Down below girls were coming up the hill from supper.

"I'm thinking," she said, "of the child's duty to his parents after they are dead."

"Is that all?"

"Do you know," asked Sarah, "about Richard Wright and his father?"

Pamela frowned. Sarah looked down at her.

"Oh, I forgot," she said with a sigh, "they don't teach Wright here. The poshest school in the U.S., and the girls come out ignorant." She looked at her watch, saw she had twenty minutes before her train. "Really," she said almost inaudibly, "why Tears Eliot, Ezratic Pound, and even Sara Teacake, and no Wright?" She and Pamela thought e.e. cummings very clever with his perceptive spelling of great literary names.

"Is he a poet then?" asked Pam. She adored poetry, all poetry. Half of America's poetry she had of course not read, for the simple reason that she had never heard of it.

"No," said Sarah, "he wasn't a poet." She felt weary. "He was a man who wrote, a man who had trouble with his father." She began to walk about the room, and came to stand below the picture of the old man and the little girl.

"When he was a child," she continued, "his father ran off with another woman, and one day when Richard and his mother went to ask him for money to buy food he laughingly rejected them. Richard, being very young, thought his father Godlike. Big, omnipotent, unpredictable, undependable and cruel. Entirely in control of his universe. Just like a god. But, many years later, after Wright had become a famous writer, he went down to Mississippi to visit his father. He found, instead of God, just an old watery-eyed field hand, bent from plowing, his teeth gone, smelling of manure. Richard realized that the most daring thing his 'God' had done was run off with that other woman.

"So?" asked Pam."What 'duty' did he feel he owed the old man?"

"So," said Sarah, "that's what Wright wondered as he peered into that old shifty-eyed Mississippi Negro face. What was the duty of the son of a destroyed man? The son of a man whose vision had stopped at the edge of the fields that weren't even his. Who was Wright without his father? Was he Wright the greatest writer? Wright the Communist? Wright the French farmer? Wright whose white wife could never accompany him to Mississippi? Was he, in fact, still his father's son? Or was he freed by his father's desertion to be nobody's son, to be his own father? Could he disavow his father and live? And if so, live as what? As whom? And for what purpose?"

"Well," said Pam, swinging her hair over her shoulders and squinting her small eyes, "if his father rejected him I don't see why Wright even bothered to go see him again. From what you've said, Wright earned the freedom to be whoever he wanted to be. To a strong man a father is not essential."

"Maybe not," said Sarah, "but Wright's father was one faulty door in a house of many ancient rooms. Was that one faulty door to him shut off forever from the rest of the house? That was the question. And though he answered this question eloquently in his work, where it really counted, one can only wonder if he was able to answer it satisfactorily—or at all— in his life."

"You're thinking of his father more as a symbol of something, aren't you?" asked Pam.

"I suppose," said Sarah, taking a last look around her room. "I see him as a door that refused to open, a hand that was always closed. A fist."

Pamela walked with her to one of the college limousines, and in a few minutes she was at the station. The train to the city was just arriving.

"Have a nice trip," said the middle-aged driver courteously, as she took her suitcase from him. But for about the thousandth time since she'd seen him, he winked at her.

Once away from her friends she did not miss them. The school was all they had in common. How could they ever know her if they were not allowed to know Wright, she wondered. She was interesting, "beautiful," only because they had no idea what made her charming, only because they had no idea from where she came. And where they came from, though she glimpsed it—in themselves and in F. Scott Fitzgerald—she was never to enter. She hadn't the inclination or the proper ticket.

2

Her father's body was in Sarah's old room. The bed had been taken down to make room for the flowers and chairs and casket. Sarah looked for a long time into the face, as if to find some answer to her questions written there. It was the same face, a dark Shakespearean head framed by gray, woolly hair and split almost in half by a short, gray mustache. It was a completely silent face, a shut face. But her father's face also looked fat, stuffed, and ready to burst. He wore a navy-blue suit, white shirt and black tie. Sarah bent and loosened the tie. Tears started behind her shoulder blades but did not reach her eyes.

"There's a rat here under the casket," she called to her brother, who apparently did not hear her, for he did not come in. She was alone with her father, as she had rarely been when he was alive. When he was alive she had avoided him.

"Where's that girl at?" her father would ask. "Done closed herself up in her room again," he would answer himself.

For Sarah's mother had died in her sleep one night. Just gone to bed tired and never got up. And Sarah had blamed her father.

Stare the rat down, thought Sarah, surely that will help. *Perhaps it doesn't matter whether I misunderstood or never understood.*

"We moved so much looking for crops, a place to live," her father had moaned, accompanied by Sarah's stony silence. "The moving killed her. And now we have a real house, with *four* rooms, and a mailbox on the *porch*, and it's too late. She gone. *She* ain't here to see it." On very bad days her father would not eat at all. At night he did not sleep.

Whatever had made her think she knew what love was or was not?

Here she was, Sarah Davis, immersed in Camusian philosophy, versed in many languages, a poppy, of all things, among winter roses. But before she became a poppy she was a native Georgian sunflower, but still had not spoken the language they both knew. Not to him.

Stare the rat down, she thought, and did. The rascal dropped his bold eyes and slunk away. Sarah felt she had, at least, accomplished something.

Why did she have to see the picture of her mother, the one on the mantel among all the religious doodads, come to life? Her mother had stood stout against the years, clean gray braids shining across the top of her head, her eyes snapping, protective. Talking to her father.

"He called you out your name, we'll leave this place today. Not tomorrow. That be too late. Today!" Her mother was magnificent in her quick decisions.

"But what about your garden, the children, the change of schools?" Her father would be holding, most likely, the wide brim of his hat in nervously twisting fingers.

"He called you out your name, we go!"

And go they would. Who knew exactly where, before they moved? Another soundless place, walls falling down, roofing gone; another face to please without leaving too much of her father's pride at his feet. But to Sarah then, no matter with what alacrity her father moved, foot-dragging alone was visible.

The moving killed her, her father had said, *but the moving was also love.*

Did it matter now that often he had threatened their lives with the rage of his despair? That once he had spanked the crying baby violently, who later died of something else altogether . . . and that the next day they moved?

"No," said Sarah aloud, "I don't think it does."

"Huh?" It was her brother, tall, wiry, black, deceptively calm. As a child he'd had an irrepressible temper. As a grown man he was tensely smooth, like a river that any day will overflow its bed.

He had chosen a dull gray casket. Sarah wished for red. Was it Dylan Thomas who had said something grand about the dead offering "deep, dark defiance"? It didn't matter; there were more ways to offer defiance than with a red casket.

"I was just thinking," said Sarah, "that with us Mama and Daddy were saying NO with capital letters."

"I don't follow you," said her brother. He had always been the activist in the family. He simply directed his calm rage against any obstacle that might exist, and awaited the consequences with the same serenity he awaited his sister's answer. Not for him the philosophical confusions and poetic observations that hung his sister up.

"That's because you're a radical preacher," said Sarah, smiling up at him. "You deliver your messages in person with your own body." It excited her that her brother had at last imbued their childhood Sunday sermons with the reality of fighting for change. And saddened her that no matter how she looked at it this seemed more important than Medieval Art, Course 201.

3

"Yes, Grandma," Sarah replied. "Cresselton is for girls only, and *no,* Grandma, I am not pregnant."

Her grandmother stood clutching the broad wooden handle of her black bag, which she held, with elbows bent, in front of her stomach. Her eyes glinted through round wire-framed glasses. She spat into the grass outside the privy. She had insisted that Sarah accompany her to the toilet while the body was being taken into the church. She had leaned heavily on Sarah's arm, her own arm thin and the flesh like crepe.

"I guess they teach you how to really handle the world," she said. "And who knows, the Lord is everywhere. I would like a whole lot to see a Great-Grand. You don't specially have to be married, you know. That's why I felt free to ask." She reached into her bag and took out a Three Sixes bottle, which she proceeded to drink from, taking deep swift swallows with her head thrown back.

"There are very few black boys near Cresselton," Sarah explained, watching the corn liquor leave the bottle in spurts and bubbles. "Besides, I'm really caught up now in my painting and sculpting . . ." Should she mention how much she admired Giacometti's work? No, she decided. Even if her grandmother had heard of him, and Sarah was positive she had not, she would surely think his statues much too thin. This made Sarah smile and remember how difficult it had been to convince her grandmother that even if Cresselton had not given her a scholarship she would have managed to go there anyway. Why? Because she wanted somebody to teach her to paint and to sculpt, and Cresselton had the best teachers. Her grandmother's notion of a successful granddaughter was a married one, pregnant the first year.

"Well," said her grandmother, placing the bottle with dignity back into her purse and gazing pleadingly into Sarah's face, "I sure would 'pre-shate a Great-Grand." Seeing her granddaughter's smile, she heaved a great sigh, and, walking rather haughtily over the stones and grass, made her way to the church steps.

As they walked down the aisle, Sarah's eyes rested on the back of her grandfather's head. He was sitting on the front middle bench in front of the casket, his hair extravagantly long and white and softly kinked. When she sat down beside him, her grandmother sitting next to him on the other side, he turned toward her and gently took her hand in his. Sarah briefly leaned her cheek against his shoulder and felt like a child again.

4

They had come twenty miles from town, on a dirt road, and the hot spring sun had drawn a steady rich scent from the honeysuckle vines along the way. The church was a bare, weather-beaten ghost of a building with hollow windows and a sagging door. Arsonists had once burned it to the ground, lighting the dry wood of the walls with the flames from the crosses they carried. The tall spreading red oak tree under which Sarah had played as a child still dominated the churchyard, stretching its branches widely from the roof of the church to the other side of the road.

After a short and eminently dignified service, during which Sarah and her grandfather alone did not cry, her father's casket was slid into the waiting hearse and taken the short distance to the cemetery, an overgrown wilderness whose stark white stones appeared to be the small ruins of an ancient civilization. There Sarah watched her grandfather from the corner of her eye. He did not seem to bend under the grief of burying a son. His back was straight, his eyes dry and clear. He was simply and solemnly heroic; a man who kept with pride his family's trust and his own grief. *It is strange,* Sarah thought, *that I never thought to paint him like this, simply as he stands; without anonymous meaningless people hovering beyond his profile; his face turned proud and brownly against the light.* The defeat that had frightened her in the faces of black men was the defeat of black forever defined by white. But that defeat was nowhere on her grandfather's face. He stood like a rock, outwardly calm, the comfort and support of the Davis family. The family alone defined him, and he was not about to let them down.

"One day I will paint you, Grandpa," she said, as they turned to go. "Just as you stand here now, with just"—she moved closer and touched his face with her hand—"just the right stubborn tenseness of your cheek. Just that look of Yes and No in your eyes."

"You wouldn't want to paint an old man like me," he said, looking deep into her eyes from wherever his mind had been. "If you want to make me, make me up in stone."

The completed grave was plump and red. The wreaths of flowers were arranged all on one side so that from the road there appeared to be only a large mass of flowers. But already the wind was tugging at the rose petals and the rain was making dabs of faded color all over the green foam frames. In a week the displaced honeysuckle vines, the wild roses, the grapevines, the grass, would be back. Nothing would seem to have changed.

5

"What do you mean, come *home*?" Her brother seemed genuinely amused. "We're all proud of you. How many black girls are at that school? Just *you*? Well, just one more besides you, and she's from the North. That's really something!"

"I'm glad you're pleased," said Sarah.

"Pleased! Why, it's what Mama would have wanted, a good education for little Sarah; and what Dad would have wanted too, if he could have wanted anything after Mama died. You were always smart. When you were two and I was five you showed me how to eat ice cream without getting it all over me. First, you said, nip off the bottom of the cone with your teeth, and suck the ice cream down. I never knew *how* you were sup-posed to eat the stuff once it began to melt."

"I don't know, she said "sometimes you can want something a whole lot, only to find out later that it wasn't what you *needed* at all."

Sarah shook her head, a frown coming between her eyes. "I sometimes spend *weeks*," she said, "trying to sketch or paint a face that is unlike every other face around me, except, vaguely, for one. Can I help but wonder if I'm in the right place?"

Her brother smiled. "You mean to tell me you spend *weeks* trying to draw one face, and you still wonder whether you're in the right place? You must be kidding!" He chucked her under the chin and laughed out loud. "You learn how to draw the face," he said, "then you learn how to paint me and how to make Grandpa up in stone. Then you can come home or go live in Paris, France. It'll be the same thing."

It was the unpreacherlike gaiety of his affection that made her cry. She leaned peacefully into her brother's arms. She wondered if Richard Wright had had a brother.

"You are my door to all the rooms," she said. "Don't ever close."

And he said, "I won't," as if he understood what she meant.

6

"When will we see you again, young woman?" he asked later, as he drove her to the bus stop.

"I'll sneak up one day and surprise you," she said.

At the bus stop, in front of a tiny service station, Sarah hugged her brother with all her strength. The white station attendant stopped his work to leer at them, his eyes bold and careless.

"Did you ever think," said Sarah, "that we are a very old people in a very young place?"

She watched her brother from a window of the bus; her eyes did not leave his face until the little station was out of sight and the big Greyhound lurched on its way toward Atlanta. She would fly from there to New York.

7

She took the train to the campus.

"My," said one of her friends, "you look wonderful! Home sure must agree with you!"

"Sarah was home?" Someone who didn't know asked. "Oh, *great*, how was it?"

"Well, how was it?" went an echo in Sarah's head. The noise of the echo almost made her dizzy.

"How was it?" she asked aloud, searching for, and regaining, her balance.

"How was it?" She watched her reflection in a pair of smiling hazel eyes.

"It was fine," she said slowly, returning the smile, thinking of her grandfather. "Just fine."

The girl's smile deepened. Sarah watched her swinging along toward the back tennis courts, hair blowing in the wind.

Stare the rat down, thought Sarah; *and whether it disappears, or not, I am a woman in the world. I have buried my father, and shall soon know how to make my grandpa up in stone.*

Powder (1996)

Tobias Wolff

Just before Christmas my father took me skiing at Mount Baker. He'd had to fight for the privilege of my company, because my mother was still angry with him for sneaking me into a nightclub during his last visit, to see Thelonious Monk.

He wouldn't give up. He promised, hand on heart, to take good care of me and have me home for dinner on Christmas Eve, and she relented. But as we were checking out of the lodge that morning it began to snow, and in this snow he observed some rare quality that made it necessary for us to get in one last run. We got in several last runs. He was indifferent to my fretting. Snow whirled around us in bitter, blinding squalls, hissing like sand, and still we skied. As the lift bore us to the peak yet again, my father looked at his watch and said, "Criminy. This'll have to be a fast one."

By now I couldn't see the trail. There was no point in trying. I stuck to him like white on rice and did what he did and somehow made it to the bottom without sailing off a cliff. We returned our skis and my father put chains on the Austin-Healey while I swayed from foot to foot, clapping my mittens and wishing I was home. I could see everything. The green tablecloth, the plates with the holly pattern, the red candles waiting to be lit.

We passed a diner on our way out. "You want some soup?" my father asked. I shook my head. "Buck up," he said. "I'll get you there. Right, doctor?"

I was supposed to say, "Right, doctor," but I didn't say anything.

A state trooper waved us down outside the resort. A pair of sawhorses were blocking the road. The trooper came up to our car and bent down to my father's window. His face was bleached by the cold. Snowflakes clung to his eyebrows and to the fur trim of his jacket and cap.

"Don't tell me," my father said.

The trooper told him. The road was closed. It might get cleared, it might not. Storm took everyone by surprise. So much, so fast. Hard to get people moving. Christmas Eve. What can you do.

My father said, "Look. We're talking about five, six inches. I've taken this car through worse than that."

The trooper straightened up. His face was out of sight but I could hear him. "The road is closed."

My father sat with both hands on the wheel, rubbing the wood with his thumbs. He looked at the barricade for a long time. He seemed to be trying to master the idea of it. Then he thanked the trooper, and with a weird, old-maidy show of caution turned the car around. "Your mother will never forgive me for this," he said.

"We should have left before," I said. "Doctor."

He didn't speak to me again until we were in a booth at the diner, waiting for our burgers. "She won't forgive me," he said. "Do you understand? Never."

"I guess," I said, but no guesswork was required; she wouldn't forgive him.

"I can't let that happen." He bent toward me. "I'll tell you what I want. I want us all to be together again. Is that what you want?"

"Yes, sir."

He bumped my chin with his knuckles. "That's all I needed to hear."

When we finished eating he went to the pay phone in the back of the diner, then joined me in the booth again. I figured he'd called my mother, but he didn't give a report. He sipped at his coffee and stared out the window at the empty road. "Come on, come on," he said, though not to me. A little while later he said it again. When the trooper's car went past, lights flashing, he got up and dropped some money on the check. "Okay. Vamanos."

The wind had died. The snow was falling straight down, less of it now and lighter. We drove away from the resort, right up to the barricade. "Move it," my father told me. When I looked at him he said, "What are you waiting for?" I got out and dragged one of the sawhorses aside, then put it back after he drove through. He pushed the door open for me. "Now you're an accomplice," he said. "We go down together." He put the car into gear and gave me a look. "Joke, son."

Down the first long stretch I watched the road behind us, to see if the trooper was on our tail. The barricade vanished. Then there was nothing but snow: snow on the road, snow kicking up from the chains, snow on the trees, snow in the sky; and our trail in the snow. Then I faced forward and had a shock. The lay of the road behind us had been marked by our own tracks, but there were no tracks ahead of us. My father was breaking virgin snow between a line of tall trees. He was humming "Stars Fell on Alabama." I felt snow brush along the floorboards under my feet. To keep my hands from shaking I clamped them between my knees.

My father grunted in a thoughtful way and said, "Don't ever try this yourself."

"I won't."

"That's what you say now, but someday you'll get your license and then you'll think you can do anything. Only you won't be able to do this. You need, I don't know—a certain instinct."

"Maybe I have it."

"You don't. You have your strong points, but not this. I only mention it because I don't want you to get the idea this is something just anybody can do. I'm a great driver. That's not a virtue, okay? It's just a fact, and one you should be aware of. Of course you have to give the old heap some credit, too. There aren't many cars I'd try this with. Listen!"

I did listen. I heard the slap of the chains, the stiff, jerky rasp of the wipers, the purr of the engine. It really did purr. The old heap was almost new. My father couldn't afford it, and kept promising to sell it, but here it was.

I said, "Where do you think that policeman went to?"

"Are you warm enough?" He reached over and cranked up the blower. Then he turned off the wipers. We didn't need them. The clouds had brightened. A few sparse, feathery flakes drifted into our slipstream and were swept away. We left the trees and entered a broad field of snow that ran level for a while and then tilted sharply downward. Orange stakes had been planted at intervals in two parallel lines and my father steered a course between them, though they were far enough apart to leave considerable doubt in my mind as to exactly where the road lay. He was humming again, doing little scat riffs around the melody.

"Okay then. What are my strong points?"

"Don't get me started," he said. "It'd take all day."

"Oh, right. Name one."

"Easy. You always think ahead."

True. I always thought ahead. I was a boy who kept his clothes on numbered hangers to insure proper rotation. I bothered my teachers for homework assignments far ahead of their due dates so I could draw up schedules. I thought ahead, and that was why I knew that there would be other troopers waiting for us at the end of our ride, if we even got there. What I did not know was that my father would wheedle and plead his way past them—he didn't sing "O Tannenbaum," but just about—and get me home for dinner, buying a little more time before my mother decided to make the split final. I knew we'd get caught; I was resigned to it. And maybe for this reason I stopped moping and began to enjoy myself.

Why not? This was one for the books. Like being in a speedboat, only better. You can't go downhill in a boat. And it was all ours. And it kept coming, the laden trees, the unbroken surface of snow, the sudden white vistas. Here and there I saw hints of the road, ditches, fences, stakes, but not so many that I could have found my way. But then I didn't have to. My father was driving. My father in his forty-eighth year, rumpled, kind, bankrupt of honor, flushed with certainty. He was a great driver. All persuasion, no coercion. Such subtlety at the wheel, such tactful pedalwork. I actually trusted him. And the best was yet to come—switchbacks and hairpins impossible to describe. Except maybe to say this: if you haven't driven fresh powder, you haven't driven.

Bridging the Self and the World

I Am a Little World Made Cunningly (1618)

John Donne

I am a little world made cunningly
Of elements, and an angelic sprite;
But black sin hath betray'd to endless night
My world's both parts, and, O, both parts must die.
You which beyond that heaven which was most high
Have found new spheres, and of new land can write,
Pour new seas in mine eyes, that so I might
Drown my world with my weeping earnestly,
Or wash it if it must be drown'd no more.
But O, it must be burnt; alas! the fire
Of lust and envy burnt it heretofore,
And made it fouler; let their flames retire,
And burn me, O Lord, with a fiery zeal
Of Thee and Thy house, which doth in eating heal.

Of Our Spiritual Strivings (1903)

W. E. B. DuBois

O water, voice of my heart, crying in the sand,
All night long crying with a mournful cry,
As I lie and listen, and cannot understand
The voice of my heart in my side or the voice of the sea,
O water, crying for rest, is it I, is it I?
All night long the water is crying to me.

Unresting water, there shall never be rest,
Till the last moon droop and the last tide fail,
And the fire of the end begin to burn in the west;
And the heart shall be weary and wonder and cry like the sea,
All life long crying without avail,
As the water all night long is crying to me.

ARTHUR SYMONS

Between me and the other world there is ever an unasked question: unasked by some through feelings of delicacy; by others through the difficulty of rightly framing it. All, nevertheless, flutter round it. They approach me in a half-hesitant sort of way, eye me curiously or compassionately, and then, instead of saying directly, How does it feel to be a problem? they say, I know an excellent colored man in my town; or, I fought at Mechanicsville; or, Do not these Southern outrages make your blood boil? At these I smile, or am interested, or reduce the boiling to a simmer, as the occasion may require. To the real question, How does it feel to be a problem? I answer seldom a word.

And yet, being a problem is a strange experience,—peculiar even for one who has never been anything else, save perhaps in babyhood and in Europe. It is in the early days of rollicking boyhood that the revelation first bursts upon one, all in a day, as it were. I remember well when the shadow swept across me. I was a little thing, away up in the hills of New England, where the dark Housatonic winds between Hoosac and Taghkanic to the sea. In a wee wooden schoolhouse, something put it into the boys' and girls' heads to buy gorgeous visiting-cards—ten cents a package—and exchange. The exchange was merry, till one girl, a tall newcomer, refused my card,—refused it peremptorily, with a glance. Then it

241

dawned upon me with a certain suddenness that I was different from the others; or like, mayhap, in heart and life and longing, but shut out from their world by a vast veil. I had thereafter no desire to tear down that veil, to creep through; I held all beyond it in common contempt, and lived above it in a region of blue sky and great wandering shadows. That sky was bluest when I could beat my mates at examination-time, or beat them at a foot-race, or even beat their stringy heads. Alas, with the years all this fine contempt began to fade; for the words I longed for, and all their dazzling opportunities, were theirs, not mine. But they should not keep these prizes, I said; some, all, I would wrest from them. Just how I would do it I could never decide: by reading law, by healing the sick, by telling the wonderful tales that swam in my head,—some way. With other black boys the strife was not so fiercely sunny: their youth shrunk into tasteless sycophancy, or into silent hatred of the pale world about them and mocking distrust of everything white; or wasted itself in a bitter cry, Why did God make me an outcast and a stranger in mine own house? The shades of the prison-house closed round about us all: walls strait and stubborn to the whitest, but relentlessly narrow, tall, and unscalable to sons of night who must plod darkly on in resignation, or beat unavailing palms against the stone, or steadily, half hopelessly, watch the streak of blue above.

After the Egyptian and Indian, the Greek and Roman, the Teuton and Mongolian, the Negro is a sort of seventh son, born with a veil, and gifted with second-sight in this American world,—a world which yields him no true self-consciousness, but only lets him see himself through the revelation of the other world. It is a peculiar sensation, this double-consciousness, this sense of always looking at one's self through the eyes of others, of measuring one's soul by the tape of a world that looks on in amused contempt and pity. One ever feels his twoness,—an American, a Negro; two souls, two thoughts, two unreconciled strivings; two warring ideals in one dark body, whose dogged strength alone keeps it from being torn asunder.

The history of the American Negro is the history of this strife,—this longing to attain self-conscious manhood, to merge his double self into a better and truer self. In this merging he wishes neither of the older selves to be lost. He would not Africanize America, for America has too much to teach the world and Africa. He would not bleach his Negro soul in a flood of white Americanism, for he knows that Negro blood has a message for the world. He simply wishes to make it possible for a man to be both a Negro and an American, without being cursed and spit upon by his fellows, without having the doors of Opportunity closed roughly in his face.

This, then, is the end of his striving: to be a co-worker in the kingdom of culture, to escape both death and isolation, to husband and use his best powers and his latent genius. These powers of body and mind have in the past been strangely wasted, dispersed, or forgotten. The shadow of a mighty Negro past flits through the tale of Ethiopia the Shadowy and of Egypt the Sphinx. Through history, the powers of single black men flash here and there like falling stars, and die sometimes before the world has rightly gauged their brightness. Here in America, in the few days since Emancipation, the black man's turning hither and thither in hesitant and doubtful striving has often made his very strength to lose effectiveness, to seem like absence of power, like weakness. And yet it is not weakness,—it is the contradiction of double aims. The double-aimed struggle of the black artisan—on the one hand to escape white contempt for a nation of mere hewers of wood and drawers of water, and on the other hand to plough and nail and dig for a poverty-stricken horde—could only result in making him a poor craftsman, for he had but half a heart in either cause. By the poverty and ignorance of his people, the Negro minister or doctor was tempted toward quackery and demagogy; and by the criticism of the other world, toward ideals that made him ashamed of his lowly tasks. The would-be black *savant* was confronted by the paradox that the knowledge his people needed was a twice-told tale to his white neighbors, while the knowledge which would teach the white world was Greek to his own flesh and blood. The innate love of harmony and beauty that set the ruder souls of his people a-dancing and a-singing raised but confusion and doubt in the soul of the black artist; for the beauty revealed to him was the soul-beauty of a race which his larger audience despised, and he could not articulate the message of another people. This waste of double aims, this seeking to satisfy two unreconciled ideals, has wrought sad havoc with the courage and faith and deeds of ten thousand thousand people,—has sent them often wooing false gods and invoking false means of salvation, and at times has even seemed about to make them ashamed of themselves.

Away back in the days of bondage they thought to see in one divine event the end of all doubt and disappointment; few men ever worshipped Freedom with half such unquestioning faith as did the American Negro for two centuries. To him, so far as he thought and dreamed, slavery was indeed the sum of all villainies, the cause of all sorrow, the root of all prejudice; Emancipation was the key to a promised land of sweeter beauty than ever stretched before the eyes of wearied Israelites. In song and exhortation swelled one refrain—Liberty; in his tears and curses the God he implored had Freedom in his right hand. At last it came,—suddenly, fearfully, like a dream. With one wild carnival of blood and passion came the message in his own plaintive cadences:—

Shout, O children!

Shout, you're free!

For God has bought your liberty!"

Years have passed away since then,—ten, twenty, forty; forty years of national life, forty years of renewal and development, and yet the swarthy spectre sits in its accustomed seat at the Nation's feast. In vain do we cry to this our vastest social problem:—

"Take any shape, but that, and my firm nerves

Shall never tremble!"

The Nation has not yet found peace from its sins; the freedman has not yet found in freedom his promised land. Whatever of good may have come in these years of change, the shadow of a deep disappointment rests upon the Negro people,—a disappointment all the more bitter because the unattained ideal was unbounded save by the simple ignorance of a lowly people.

The first decade was merely a prolongation of the vain search for freedom, the boon that seemed ever barely to elude their grasp,—like a tantalizing will-o'-the-wisp, maddening and misleading the headless host. The holocaust of war, the terrors of the Ku-Klux Klan, the lies of carpet-baggers, the disorganization of industry, and the contradictory advice of friends and foes, left the bewildered serf with no new watchword beyond the old cry for freedom. As the time flew, however, he began to grasp a new idea. The ideal of liberty demanded for its attainment powerful means, and these the Fifteenth Amendment gave him. The ballot, which before he had looked upon as a visible sign of freedom, he now regarded as the chief means of gaining and perfecting the liberty with which war had partially endowed him. And why not? Had not votes made war and emancipated millions? Had not votes enfranchised the freedmen? Was anything impossible to a power that had done all this? A million black men started with renewed zeal to vote themselves into the kingdom. So the decade flew away, the revolution of 1876 came, and left the half-free serf weary, wondering, but still inspired. Slowly but steadily, in the fol-lowing years, a new vision began gradually to replace the dream of polit-ical power,—a powerful movement, the rise of another ideal to guide the unguided, another pillar of fire by night after a clouded day. It was the ideal of "book-learning"; the curiosity, born of compulsory ignorance, to know and test the power of the cabalistic letters of the white man, the longing to know. Here at last seemed to have been discovered the mountain path to Canaan; longer than the highway of Emancipation and law, steep and rugged, but straight, leading to heights high enough to overlook life.

Up the new path the advance guard toiled, slowly, heavily, doggedly; only those who have watched and guided the faltering feet, the misty minds, the dull understandings, of the dark pupils of these schools know how faithfully, how piteously, this people strove to learn. It was weary work. The cold statistician wrote down the inches of progress here and there, noted also where here and there a foot had slipped or some one had fallen. To the tired climbers, the horizon was ever dark, the mists were often cold, the Canaan was always dim and far away. If, however, the vistas disclosed as yet no goal, no resting-place, little but flattery and criticism, the journey at least gave leisure for reflection and self-examination; it changed the child of Emancipation to the youth with dawning self-consciousness, self-realization, self-respect. In those somber forests of his striving his own soul rose before him, and he saw himself,—darkly as through a veil; and yet he saw in himself some faint revelation of his power, of his mission. He began to have a dim feeling that, to attain his place in the world, he must be himself, and not another. For the first time he sought to analyze the burden he bore upon his back, that dead-weight of social degradation partially masked behind a half-named Negro problem. He felt his poverty; without a cent, without a home, without land, tools, or savings, he had entered into competition with rich, landed, skilled neighbors. To be a poor man is hard, but to be a poor race in a land of dollars is the very bottom of hardships. He felt the weight of his ignorance,—not simply of letters, but of life, of business, of the humanities; the accumulated sloth and shirking and awkwardness of decades and centuries shackled his hands and feet. Nor was his burden all poverty and ignorance. The red stain of bastardy, which two centuries of systematic legal defilement of Negro women had stamped upon his race, meant not only the loss of ancient African chastity, but also the hereditary weight of a mass of corruption from white adulterers, threatening almost the obliteration of the Negro home.

A people thus handicapped ought not to be asked to race with the world, but rather allowed to give all its time and thought to its own social problems. But alas! while sociologists gleefully count his bastards and his prostitutes, the very soul of the toiling, sweating black man is darkened by the shadow of a vast despair. Men call the shadow prejudice, and learnedly explain it as the natural defense of culture against barbarism, learning against ignorance, purity against crime, the "higher" against the "lower" races. To which the Negro cries Amen! and swears that to so much of this strange prejudice as is founded on just homage to civilization, culture, righteousness, and progress, he humbly bows and meekly does obeisance. But before that nameless prejudice that leaps beyond all this he stands helpless, dismayed, and well-nigh speechless; before that personal disrespect and mockery, the ridicule and systematic humiliation, the distortion of fact and wanton license of fancy, the cynical ignoring of the better and the boisterous welcoming of the worse, the all-pervading desire to inculcate disdain for everything black, from Toussaint to the devil,—before this there rises a sickening despair that would disarm and discourage any nation save that black host to whom "discouragement" is an unwritten word.

But the facing of so vast a prejudice could not but bring the inevitable self-questioning, self-disparagement, and lowering of ideals which ever accompany repression and breed in an atmosphere of contempt and hate. Whisperings and portents came borne upon the four winds: Lo! we are diseased and dying, cried the dark hosts; we cannot write, our voting is vain; what need of education, since we must always cook and serve? And the Nation echoed and enforced this self-criticism, saying: Be content to be servants, and nothing more; what need of higher culture for half-men? Away with the black man's ballot, by force or fraud,—and behold the suicide of a race! Nevertheless, out of the evil came something of good,—the more careful adjustment of education to real life, the clearer perception of the Negroes' social responsibilities, and the sobering realization of the meaning of progress.

So dawned the time of *Sturm und Drang*: storm and stress to-day rocks our little boat on the mad waters of the world-sea; there is within and without the sound of conflict, the burning of body and rending of soul; inspiration strives with doubt, and faith with vain questionings. The bright ideals of the past,—physical freedom, political power, the training of brains and the training of hands,—all these in turn have waxed and waned, until even the last grows dim and overcast. Are they all wrong,— all false? No, not that, but each alone was over-simple and incomplete,— the dreams of a credulous race-childhood, or the fond imaginings of the other world which does not know and does not want to know our power. To be really true, all these ideals must be melted and welded into one. The training of the schools we need to-day more than ever,—the training of deft hands, quick eyes and ears, and above all the broader, deeper, higher culture of gifted minds and pure hearts. The power of the ballot we need in sheer self-defence,—else what shall save us from a second slavery?

Freedom, too, the long-sought, we still seek—the freedom of life and limb, the freedom to work and think, the freedom to love and aspire. Work, culture, liberty,—all these we need, not singly but together, not successively but together, each growing and aiding each, and all striving toward that vaster ideal that swims before the Negro people, the ideal of human brotherhood, gained through the unifying ideal of Race; the ideal of fostering and developing the traits and talents of the Negro, not in opposition to or contempt for other races, but rather in large conformity to the greater ideals of the American Republic, in order that some day on American soil two world-races may give each to each those characteristics both so sadly lack. We the darker ones come even now not altogether empty-handed: there are to-day no truer exponents of the pure human spirit of the Declaration of Independence than the American Negroes; there is no true American music but the wild sweet melodies of the Negro slave; the American fairy tales and folklore are Indian and African; and, all in all, we black men seem the sole oasis of simple faith and reverence in a dusty desert of dollars and smartness. Will America be poorer if she replace her brutal dyspeptic blundering with light-hearted but determined Negro humility? or her coarse and cruel wit with loving jovial good-humor? or her vulgar music with the soul of the Sorrow Songs?

Merely a concrete test of the underlying principles of the great republic is the Negro Problem, and the spiritual striving of the freedmen's sons is the travail of souls whose burden is almost beyond the measure of their strength, but who bear it in the name of an historic race, in the name of this the land of their fathers' fathers, and in the name of human opportunity.

The Banking Concept of Education (1970)

Paulo Freire

A careful analysis of the teacher-student relationship at any level, inside or outside the school, reveals its fundamentally *narrative* character. This relationship involves a narrating Subject (the teacher) and patient, listening objects (the students). The contents, whether values or empirical dimensions of reality, tend in the process of being narrated to become lifeless and petrified. Education is suffering from narration sickness.

The teacher talks about reality as if it were motionless, static, compartmentalized, and predictable. Or else he expounds on a topic completely alien to the existential experience of the students. His task is to "fill" the students with the contents of his narration—contents which are detached from reality, disconnected from the totality that engendered them and could give them significance. Words are emptied of their concreteness and become a hollow, alienated, and alienating verbosity.

The outstanding characteristic of this narrative education, then, is the sonority of words, not their transforming power. "Four times four is sixteen; the capital of Pará is Belém." The student records, memorizes, and repeats these phrases without perceiving what four times four really means, or realizing the true significance of "capital" in the affirmation "the capital of Pará is Belém," that is, what Belém means for Pará and what Pará means for Brazil.

Narration (with the teacher as narrator) leads the students to memorize mechanically the narrated content. Worse yet, it turns them into "containers," into "receptacles" to be "filled" by the teacher. The more completely he fills the receptacles, the better a teacher he is. The more meekly the receptacles permit themselves to be filled, the better students they are.

Education thus becomes an act of depositing, in which the students are the depositories and the teacher is the depositor. Instead of communicating, the teacher issues communiqués and makes deposits which the students patiently receive, memorize, and repeat. This is the "banking" concept of education, in which the scope of action allowed to the students extends only as far as receiving, filing, and storing the deposits. They do, it is true, have the opportunity to become collectors or cataloguers of the things they store. But in the last analysis, it is men themselves who are filed away through the lack of creativity, transformation, and knowledge in this (at best) misguided system. For apart from inquiry, apart from the praxis, men cannot be truly human. Knowledge emerges only through invention and re-invention, through the restless, impatient, continuing, hopeful inquiry men pursue in the world, with the world, and with each other.

In the banking concept of education, knowledge is a gift bestowed by those who consider themselves knowledgeable upon those whom they consider to know nothing. Projecting an absolute ignorance onto others, a characteristic of the ideology of oppression, negates education and knowledge as processes of inquiry. The teacher presents himself to his students as their necessary opposite; by considering their ignorance absolute, he justifies his own existence. The students, alienated like the slave in the Hegelian dialectic, accept their ignorance as justifying the teacher's existence—but, unlike the slave, they never discover that they educate the teacher.

The *raison d'être* of libertarian education, on the other hand, lies in its drive towards reconciliation. Education must begin with the solution of the teacher-student contradiction, by reconciling the poles of the contradiction so that both are simultaneously teachers *and* students.

This solution is not (nor can it be) found in the banking concept. On the contrary, banking education maintains and even stimulates the contradiction through the following attitudes and practices, which mirror oppressive society as a whole:

    (a) the teacher teaches and the students are taught;
    (b) the teacher knows everything and the students know nothing;
    (c) the teacher thinks and the students are thought about;
    (d) the teacher talks and the students listen—meekly;
    (e) the teacher disciplines and the students are disciplined;
    (f) the teacher chooses and enforces his choice, and the students comply;
    (g) the teacher acts and the students have the illusion of acting through the action of the teacher;
    (h) the teacher chooses the program content, and the students (who were not consulted) adapt to it;
    (i) the teacher confuses the authority of knowledge with his own professional authority, which he sets in opposition to the freedom of the students;
    (j) the teacher is the Subject of the learning process, while the pupils are mere objects.

It is not surprising that the banking concept of education regards men as adaptable, manageable beings. The more students work at storing the deposits entrusted to them, the less they develop the critical consciousness which would result from their intervention in the world as transformers of that world. The more completely they accept the passive role imposed on them, the more they tend simply to adapt to the world as it is and to the fragmented view of reality deposited in them.

The capability of banking education to minimize or annul the students' creative power and to stimulate their credulity serves the interests of the oppressors, who care neither to have the world revealed nor to see it transformed. The oppressors use their "humanitarianism" to preserve a profitable situation. Thus they react almost instinctively against any experiment in education which stimulates the critical faculties and is not content with a partial view of reality but always seeks out the ties which link one point to another and one problem to another.

Indeed, the interests of the oppressors lie in "changing the consciousness of the oppressed, not the situation which oppresses them"; [1] for the more the oppressed can be led to adapt to that situation, the more easily they can be dominated. To achieve this end, the oppressors use the banking concept of education in conjunction with a paternalistic social action apparatus, within which the oppressed receive the euphemistic title of "welfare recipients." They are treated as individual cases, as marginal men who deviate from the general configuration of a "good, organized, and just" society. The oppressed are regarded as the pathology of the healthy society, which must therefore adjust these "incompetent and lazy" folk to its own patterns by changing their mentality. These marginals need to be "integrated," "incorporated" into the healthy society that they have "forsaken."

The truth is, however, that the oppressed are not "marginals," are not men living "outside" society. They have always been "inside"—inside the structure which made them "beings for others." The solution is not to "integrate" them into the structure of oppression, but to transform that structure so that they can become "beings for themselves." Such transformation, of course, would undermine the oppressors' purposes; hence their utilization of the banking concept of education to avoid the threat of student *conscientização*.

The banking approach to adult education, for example, will never propose to students that they critically consider reality. It will deal instead with such vital questions as whether Roger gave green grass to the goat, and insist upon the importance of learning that, on the contrary, Roger gave green grass to the *r*abbit. The "humanism" of the banking approach masks the effort to turn men into automatons—the very negation of their ontological vocation to be more fully human.

Those who use the banking approach, knowingly or unknowingly (for there are innumerable well-intentioned banker-clerk teachers who do not realize that they are serving only to dehumanize), fail to perceive that the deposits themselves contain contradictions about reality. But, sooner or later, these contradictions may lead formerly passive students to turn against their domestication and the attempt to domesticate reality. They may discover through existential experience that their present way of life is irreconcilable with their vocation to become fully human. They may perceive through their relations with reality that reality is really a *process*, undergoing constant transformation. If men are searchers and their onto-logical vocation is humanization, sooner or later they may perceive the contradiction in which banking education seeks to maintain them, and then engage themselves in the struggle for their liberation.

But the humanist, revolutionary educator cannot wait for this possibility to materialize. From the outset, his efforts must coincide with those of the students to engage in critical thinking and the quest for mutual human-ization. His efforts must be imbued with a profound trust in men and their creative power. To achieve this, he must be a partner of the students in his relations with them.

The banking concept does not admit to such partnership—and necessarily so. To resolve the teacher-student contradiction, to exchange the role of deposi-tor, prescriber, domesticator, for the role of student among students would be to undermine the power of oppression and serve the cause of liberation.

Implicit in the banking concept is the assumption of a dichotomy between man and the world: man is merely *in* the world, not *with* the world or with others; man is spectator, not re-creator. In this view, man is not a conscious being (*corpo conciente*); he is rather the possessor of a consciousness: an empty "mind" passively open to the reception of deposits of reality from the world outside. For example, my desk, my books, my coffee cup, all the objects before me—as bits of the world which surrounds me—would be "inside" me, exactly as I am inside my study right now. This view makes no distinction between being accessible to consciousness and entering consciousness. The distinction, however, is essential: the objects which surround me are simply accessible to my consciousness, not located within it. I am aware of them, but they are not inside me.

It follows logically from the banking notion of consciousness that the edu-cator's role is to regulate the way the world "enters into" the students. His task is to organize a process which already occurs spontaneously, to "fill" the students by making deposits of information which he considers to constitute true knowledge.[2] And since men "receive" the world as passive entities, education should make them more passive still, and adapt them to the world. The educated man is the adapted man, because he is better "fit" for the world. Translated into practice, this concept is well suited to the purposes of the oppressors, whose tranquility rests on how well men fit the world the oppressors have created, and how little they question it.

The more completely the majority adapt to the purposes which the dominant minority prescribe for them (thereby depriving them of the right to their own purposes), the more easily the minority can continue to prescribe. The theory and practice of banking education serve this end quite efficiently. Verbalistic lessons, reading requirements,[3] the methods for evaluating "knowledge," the distance between the teacher and the taught, the criteria for promotion: everything in this ready-to-wear approach serves to obviate thinking.

The bank-clerk educator does not realize that there is no true security in his hypertrophied role, that one must seek to live with others in solidarity. One cannot impose oneself, nor even merely co-exist with one's students. Solidarity requires true communication, and the concept by which such an educator is guided fears and proscribes communication.

Yet only through communication can human life hold meaning. The teacher's thinking is authenticated only by the authenticity of the students' thinking. The teacher cannot think for his students, nor can he impose his thought on them. Authentic thinking, thinking that is concerned about *reality*, does not take place in ivory tower isolation, but only in communication. If it is true that thought has meaning only when generated by action upon the world, the subordination of students to teachers becomes impossible.

Because banking education begins with a false understanding of men as objects, it cannot promote the development of what Fromm calls "biophily," but instead produces its opposite: "necrophily."

> While life is characterized by growth in a structured, functional manner, the necrophilous person loves all that does not grow, all that is mechanical. The necrophilous person is driven by the desire to transform the organic into the inorganic, to approach life mechanically, as if all living persons were things. . . . Memory, rather than experience; having, rather than being, is what counts. The necrophilous person can relate to an object—a flower or a person—only if he possesses it; hence a threat to his possession is a threat to himself; if he loses possession he loses contact with the world. . . . He loves control, and in the act of controlling he kills life.[4]

Oppression—overwhelming control—is necrophilic; it is nourished by love of death, not life. The banking concept of education, which serves the interests of oppression, is also necrophilic. Based on a mechanistic, static, naturalistic, spatialized view of consciousness, it transforms students into receiving objects. It attempts to control thinking and action, leads men to adjust to the world, and inhibits their creative power.

When their efforts to act responsibly are frustrated, when they find themselves unable to use their faculties, men suffer. "This suffering due to impotence is rooted in the very fact that the human equilibrium has been disturbed."[5] But the inability to act which causes men's anguish also causes them to reject their impotence, by attempting

> . . . to restore [their] capacity to act. But can [they], and how? One way is to submit to and identify with a person or group having power. By this symbolic participation in another person's life, [men have] the illusion of acting, when in reality [they] only submit to and become a part of those who act.[6]

Populist manifestations perhaps best exemplify this type of behavior by the oppressed, who, by identifying with charismatic leaders, come to feel that they themselves are active and effective. The rebellion they express as they emerge in the historical process is motivated by that desire to act effectively. The dominant elites consider the remedy to be more domination and repression, carried out in the name of freedom, order, and social peace (that is, the peace of the elites). Thus they can condemn—logically, from their point of view—"the violence of a strike by workers and [can] call upon the state in the same breath to use violence in putting down the strike."[7]

Education as the exercise of domination stimulates the credulity of students, with the ideological intent (often not perceived by educators) of indoctrinating them to adapt to the world of oppression. This accusation is not made in the naïve hope that the dominant elites will thereby simply abandon the practice. Its objective is to call the attention of true humanists to the fact that they cannot use banking educational methods in the pursuit of liberation, for they would only negate that very pursuit. Nor may a revolutionary society inherit these methods from an oppressor society. The revolutionary society which practices banking education is either misguided or mistrusting of men. In either event, it is threatened by the specter of reaction.

Unfortunately, those who espouse the cause of liberation are themselves surrounded and influenced by the climate which generates the banking concept, and often do not perceive its true significance or its dehumanizing power. Paradoxically, then, they utilize this same instrument of alienation in what they consider an effort to liberate. Indeed, some "revolutionaries" brand as "innocents," "dreamers," or even "reactionaries" those who would challenge this educational practice. But one does not liberate men by alienating them. Authentic liberation—the process of humanization—is not another deposit to be made in men. Liberation is a praxis: the action and reflection of men upon their world in order to transform it. Those truly committed to the cause of liberation can accept neither the mechanistic concept of consciousness as an empty vessel to be filled, nor the use of banking methods of domination (propaganda, slogans—deposits) in the name of liberation.

Those truly committed to liberation must reject the banking concept in its entirety, adopting instead a concept of men as conscious beings, and consciousness as consciousness intent upon the world. They must abandon the educational goal of deposit-making and replace it with the posing of the problems of men in their relations with the world. "Problem-posing" education, responding to the essence of consciousness—*intentionality*—rejects communiqués and embodies communication. It epitomizes the special characteristic of consciousness: being *conscious of*, not only as intent on objects but as turned in upon itself in a Jasperian "split"—consciousness as consciousness *of* consciousness.

Liberating education consists in acts of cognition, not transferrals of information. It is a learning situation in which the cognizable object (far from being the end of the cognitive act) intermediates the cognitive actors—teacher on the one hand and students on the other. Accordingly, the practice of problem-posing education entails at the outset that the teacher-student contradiction be resolved. Dialogical relations—indispensable to the capacity of cognitive actors to cooperate in perceiving the same cognizable object—are otherwise impossible.

Indeed, problem-posing education, which breaks with the vertical patterns characteristic of banking education, can fulfill its function as the practice of freedom only if it can overcome the above contradiction. Through dialogue, the teacher-of-the-students and the students-of-the-teacher cease to exist and a new term emerges: teacher-student with students-teachers. The teacher is no longer merely the-one-who-teaches, but one who is himself taught in dialogue with the students, who in turn while being taught also teach. They become jointly responsible for a process in which all grow. In this process, arguments based on "authority" are no longer valid; in order to function, authority must be *on the side* of freedom, not *against* it. Here, no one teaches another, nor is anyone self-taught. Men teach each other, mediated by the world, by the cognizable objects which in banking education are "owned" by the teacher.

The banking concept (with its tendency to dichotomize everything) distinguishes two stages in the action of the educator. During the first, he cognizes a cognizable object while he prepares his lessons in his study or his laboratory; during the second, he expounds to his students about that object. The students are not called upon to know, but to memorize the contents narrated by the teacher. Nor do the students practice any act of cognition, since the object towards which that act should be directed is the property of the teacher rather than a medium evoking the critical reflection of both teacher and students. Hence in the name of the "preservation of culture and knowledge" we have a system which achieves neither true knowledge nor true culture.

The problem-posing method does not dichotomize the activity of the teacher-student: he is not "cognitive" at one point and "narrative" at another. He is always "cognitive," whether preparing a project or engaging in dialogue with the students. He does not regard cognizable objects as his private property, but as the object of reflection by himself and the students. In this way, the problem-posing educator constantly re-forms his reflections in the reflection of the students. The students—no longer docile listeners—are now critical co-investigators in dialogue with the teacher. The teacher presents the material to the students for their consideration, and re-considers his earlier considerations as the students express their own. The role of the problem-posing educator is to create, together with the students, the conditions under which knowledge at the level of the *doxa* is superseded by true knowledge, at the level of the *logos*.

Whereas banking education anesthetizes and inhibits creative power, problem-posing education involves a constant unveiling of reality. The former attempts to maintain the *submersion* of consciousness; the latter strives for the *emergence* of consciousness and *critical intervention* in reality.

Students, as they are increasingly posed with problems relating to themselves in the world and with the world, will feel increasingly challenged and obliged to respond to that challenge. Because they apprehend the challenge as interrelated to other problems within a total context, not as a theoretical question, the resulting comprehension tends to be increasingly critical and thus constantly less alienated. Their response to the challenge evokes new challenges, followed by new understandings; and gradually the students come to regard themselves as committed.

Education as the practice of freedom—as opposed to education as the practice of domination—denies that man is abstract, isolated, independent, and unattached to the world; it also denies that the world exists as a reality apart from men. Authentic reflection considers neither abstract man nor the world without men, but men in their relations with the world. In these relations consciousness and world are simultaneous: consciousness neither precedes the world nor follows it.

> La conscience et le monde sont donnés d'un même coup: extérieur par essence à la conscience, le monde est, par essence relatif à elle.[8]

In one of our culture circles in Chile, the group was discussing (based on a codification[9]) the anthropological concept of culture. In the midst of the discussion, a peasant who by banking standards was completely ignorant said: "Now I see that without man there is no world." When the educator responded: "Let's say, for the sake of argument, that all the men on earth were to die, but that the earth itself remained, together with trees, birds, animals, rivers, seas, the stars . . . wouldn't all this be a world?" "Oh no," the peasant replied emphatically. "There would be no one to say: 'This is a world'."

The peasant wished to express the idea that there would be lacking the consciousness of the world which necessarily implies the world of consciousness. *I* cannot exist without a *not-I*. In turn, the not-I depends on that existence. The world which brings consciousness into existence becomes the world of that consciousness. Hence, the previously cited affirmation of Sartre: *"La conscience et le monde sont donnés d'un même coup."*

As men, simultaneously reflecting on themselves and on the world, increase the scope of their perception, they begin to direct their observations towards previously inconspicuous phenomena:

> In perception properly so-called, as an explicit awareness [*Gewahren*], I am turned towards the object, to the paper, for instance. I apprehend it as being this here and now. The apprehension is a singling out, every object having a background in experience. Around and about the paper lie books, pencils, ink-well, and so forth, and these in a certain sense are also "perceived", perceptually there, in the "field of intuition"; but whilst I was turned towards the paper there was no turning in their direction, nor any apprehending of them, not even in a secondary sense. They appeared and yet were not singled out, were not posited on their own account. Every perception of a thing has such a zone of background intuitions or background awareness, it "intuiting" already includes the state of being turned towards, and this also is a "conscious experience", or more briefly a "consciousness of" all indeed that in point of fact lies in the co-perceived objective background.[10]

> That which had existed objectively but had not been perceived in its deeper implications (if indeed it was perceived at all) begins to "stand out," assuming the character of a problem and therefore of challenge. Thus, men begin to single out elements from their "background awarenesses" and to reflect upon them. These elements are now objects of men's consideration, and, as such, objects of their action and cognition.

In problem-posing education, men develop their power to perceive critically *the way they exist* in the world *with which* and *in which* they find themselves; they come to see the world not as a static reality, but as a reality in process, in transformation. Although the dialectical relations of men with the world exist independently of how these relations are perceived (or whether or not they are perceived at all), it is also true that the form of action men adopt is to a large extent a function of how they perceive themselves in the world. Hence, the teacher-student and the students-teachers reflect simultaneously on themselves and the world without dichotomizing this reflection from action, and thus establish an authentic form of thought and action.

Once again, the two educational concepts and practices under analysis come into conflict. Banking education (for obvious reasons) attempts, by mythicizing reality, to conceal certain facts which explain the way men exist in the world; problem-posing education sets itself the task of demythologizing. Banking education resists dialogue; problem-posing education regards dialogue as indispensable to the act of cognition which unveils reality. Banking education treats students as objects of assistance; problem-posing education makes them critical thinkers. Banking education inhibits creativity and domesticates (although it cannot completely destroy) the *intentionality* of consciousness by isolating consciousness from the world, thereby denying men their ontological and historical vocation of becoming more fully human. Problem-posing education bases itself on creativity and stimulates true reflection and action upon reality, thereby responding to the vocation of men as beings who are authentic only when engaged in inquiry and creative transformation. In sum: banking theory and practice, as immobilizing and fixating forces, fail to acknowledge men as historical beings; problem-posing theory and practice take man's historicity as their starting point.

Problem-posing education affirms men as beings in the process of *becoming*—as unfinished, uncompleted beings in and with a likewise unfinished reality. Indeed, in contrast to other animals who are unfinished, but not historical, men know themselves to be unfinished; they are aware of their incompletion. In this incompletion and this awareness lie the very roots of education as an exclusively human manifestation. The unfinished character of men and the transformational character of reality necessitate that education be an ongoing activity.

Education is thus constantly remade in the praxis. In order to *be*, it must *become*. Its "duration" (in the Bergsonian meaning of the word) is found in the interplay of the opposites *permanence and change*. The banking method emphasizes permanence and becomes reactionary; problem-posing education—which accepts neither a "well-behaved" present nor a predetermined future—roots itself in the dynamic present and becomes revolutionary.

Problem-posing education is revolutionary futurity. Hence it is prophetic (and, as such, hopeful). Hence, it corresponds to the historical nature of man. Hence, it affirms men as beings who transcend themselves, who move forward and look ahead, for whom immobility represents a fatal threat, for whom looking at the past must only be a means of under-standing more clearly what and who they are so that they can more wisely build the future. Hence, it identifies with the movement which engages men as beings aware of their incompletion—an historical move-ment which has its point of departure, its Subjects and its objective.

The point of departure of the movement lies in men themselves. But since men do not exist apart from the world, apart from reality, the movement must begin with the men-world relationship. Accordingly, the point of departure must always be with men in the "here and now," which con-stitutes the situation within which they are submerged, from which they emerge, and in which they intervene. Only by starting from this situa-tion—which determines their perception of it—can they begin to move. To do this authentically they must perceive their state not as fated and unalterable, but merely as limiting—and therefore challenging.

Whereas the banking method directly or indirectly reinforces men's fatal-istic perception of their situation, the problem-posing method presents this very situation to them as a problem. As the situation becomes the object of their cognition, the naïve or magical perception which produced their fatal-ism gives way to perception which is able to perceive itself even as it per-ceives reality, and can thus be critically objective about that reality.

A deepened consciousness of their situation leads men to apprehend that situation as an historical reality susceptible of transformation. Resigna-tion gives way to the drive for transformation and inquiry, over which men feel themselves to be in control. If men, as historical beings neces-sarily engaged with other men in a movement of inquiry, did not control that movement, it would be (and is) a violation of men's humanity. Any situation in which some men prevent others from engaging in the process of inquiry is one of violence. The means used are not important; to alien-ate men from their own decision-making is to change them into objects.

This movement of inquiry must be directed towards humanization—man's historical vocation. The pursuit of full humanity, however, cannot be carried out in isolation or individualism, but only in fellowship and solidarity; therefore it cannot unfold in the antagonistic relations between oppressors and oppressed. No one can be authentically human while he prevents others from being so. Attempting *to be more* human, individual-istically, leads to *having more*, egotistically: a form of dehumanization. Not that it is not fundamental to *have* in order *to be* human. Precisely because it is necessary, some men's *having* must not be allowed to constitute an obstacle to others' *having*, must not consolidate the power of the former to crush the latter.

Problem-posing education, as a humanist and liberating praxis, posits as fundamental that men subjected to domination must fight for their emancipation. To that end, it enables teachers and students to become Subjects of the educational process by overcoming authoritarianism and an alienating intellectualism; it also enables men to overcome their false perception of reality. The world—no longer something to be described with deceptive words—becomes the object of that transforming action by men which results in their humanization.

Problem-posing education does not and cannot serve the interests of the oppressor. No oppressive order could permit the oppressed to begin to question: Why? While only a revolutionary society can carry out this education in systematic terms, the revolutionary leaders need not take full power before they can employ the method. In the revolutionary process, the leaders cannot utilize the banking method as an interim measure, justified on grounds of expediency, with the intention of *later* behaving in a genuinely revolutionary fashion. They must be revolutionary—that is to say, dialogical—from the outset.

Notes

1 Simone de Beauvoir, *La Pensée de Droite, Aujord'hui* (Paris); ST, *El Pensamiento politico de la Derecha* (Buenos Aires, 1963), p. 34.

2 This concept corresponds to what Sartre calls the "digestive" or "nutritive" concept of education, in which knowledge is "fed" by the teacher to the students to "fill them out." See Jean-Paul Sartre, "Une idée fundamentale de la phénoménologie de Husserl: L'intentionalité, *Situations I* (Paris, 1947).

3 For example, some professors specify in their reading lists that a book should be read from pages 10 to 15—and do this to "help" their students!

4 Fromm, op. cit., p. 41.

5 Ibid., p. 31.

6 Ibid.

7 Reinhold Niebuhr, Moral Man and Immoral Society (New York, 1960), p. 130.

8 Sartre, op. cit., p. 32.

9 See Chapter 3. —Translator's note.

10 Edmund Husserl, *Ideas—General Introduction to Pure Phenomenology* (London, 1969), pp. 105–106.

The Movement of the Triangle (1912)

Wassily Kandinsky

The life of the spirit may be fairly represented in diagram as a large acute-angled triangle divided horizontally into unequal parts with the narrowest segment uppermost. The lower the segment the greater it is in breadth, depth, and area.

The whole triangle is moving slowly, almost invisibly forwards and upwards. Where the apex was today the second segment is tomorrow; what today can be understood only by the apex and to the rest of the triangle is an incomprehensible gibberish, forms tomorrow the true thought and feeling of the second segment.

At the apex of the top segment stands often one man, and only one. His joyful vision cloaks a vast sorrow. Even those who are nearest to him in sympathy do not understand him. Angrily they abuse him as charlatan or madman. So in his lifetime stood Beethoven, solitary and insulted.

How many years will it be before a greater segment of the triangle reaches the spot where he once stood alone? Despite memorials and statues, are they really many who have risen to his level?

In every segment of the triangle are artists. Each one of them who can see beyond the limits of his segment is a prophet to those about him, and helps the advance of the obstinate whole. But those who are blind, or those who retard the movement of the triangle for baser reasons, are fully understood by their fellows and acclaimed for their genius. The greater the segment (which is the same as saying the lower it lies in the triangle) so the greater the number who understand the words of the artist. Every segment hungers consciously or, much more often, unconsciously for their corresponding spiritual food. This food is offered by the artists, and for this food the segment immediately below will tomorrow be stretching out eager hands.

This simile of the triangle cannot be said to express every aspect of the spiritual life. For instance, there is never an absolute shadow-side to the picture, never a piece of unrelieved gloom. Even too often it happens that one level of spiritual food suffices for the nourishment of those who are already in a higher segment. But for them this food is poison; in small quantities it depresses their souls gradually into a lower segment; in large quantities it hurls them suddenly into the depths ever lower and lower. Sienkiewicz, in one of his novels, compares the spiritual life to swimming; for the man who does not strive tirelessly, who does not fight continually against sinking, will mentally and morally go under. In this strait a man's talent (again in the biblical sense) becomes a curse—and not only the talent of the artist, but also of those who eat this poisoned food. The artist uses his strength to flatter his lower needs; in an ostensibly artistic form he presents what is impure, draws the weaker elements to him, mixes them with evil, betrays men and helps them to betray themselves, while they convince themselves and others that they are spiritually thirsty, and that from this pure spring they may quench their thirst. Such art does not help the forward movement, but hinders it, dragging back those who are striving to press onward, and spreading pestilence abroad.

Such periods, during which art has no noble champion, during which the true spiritual food is wanting, are periods of retrogression in the spiritual world. Ceaselessly souls fall from the higher to the lower segments of the triangle, and the whole seems motionless, or even to move down and backwards. Men attribute to these blind and dumb periods a special value, for they judge them by outward results, thinking only of material well-being. They hail some technical advance, which can help nothing but the body, as a great achievement. Real spiritual gains are at best under-valued, at worst entirely ignored.

The solitary visionaries are despised or regarded as abnormal and eccentric. Those who are not wrapped in lethargy and who feel vague longings for spiritual life and knowledge and progress, cry in harsh chorus, without any to comfort them. The night of the spirit falls more and more darkly. Deeper becomes the misery of these blind and terrified guides, and their followers, tormented and unnerved by fear and doubt, prefer to this gradual darkening the final sudden leap into the blackness.

At such a time art ministers to lower needs, and is used for material ends. She seeks her substance in hard realities because she knows of nothing nobler. Objects, the reproduction of which is considered her sole aim, remain monotonously the same. The question "what?" disappears from art; only the question "how?" remains. By what method are these material objects to be reproduced? The word becomes a creed. Art has lost her soul. In the search for method the artist goes still further. Art becomes so specialized as to be comprehensible only to artists, and they complain bitterly of public indifference to their work. For since the artist in such times has no need to say much, but only to be notorious for some small originality and consequently lauded by a small group of patrons and connoisseurs (which incidentally is also a very profitable business for him), there arise a crowd of gifted and skillful painters, so easy does the conquest of art appear. In each artistic circle are thousands of such artists, of whom the majority seek only for some new technical manner, and who produce millions of works of art without enthusiasm, with cold hearts and souls asleep.

Competition arises. The wild battle for success becomes more and more material. Small groups who have fought their way to the top of the chaotic world of art and picture-making entrench themselves in the territory they have won. The public, left far behind, looks on bewildered, loses interest and turns away.

But despite all this confusion, this chaos, this wild hunt for notoriety, the spiritual triangle, slowly but surely, with irresistible strength, moves onwards and upwards.

The invisible Moses descends from the mountain and sees the dance round the golden calf. But he brings with him fresh stores of wisdom to man.

First by the artist is heard his voice, the voice that is inaudible to the crowd. Almost unknowingly the artist follows the call. Already in that very question "how?" lies a hidden seed of renaissance. For when this "how?" remains without any fruitful answer, there is always a possibility that the same "something" (which we call personality today) may be able to see in the objects about it not only what is purely material but also something less solid; something less "bodily" than was seen in the period of realism, when the universal aim was to reproduce anything "as it really is" and without fantastic imagination.

If the emotional power of the artist can overwhelm the "how?" and can give free scope to his finer feelings, then art is on the crest of the road by which she will not fail later on to find the "what" she has lost, the "what" which will show the way to the spiritual food of the newly awakened spiritual life. This "what?" will no longer be the material, objective "what" of the former period, but the internal truth of art, the soul without which the body (i.e. the "how") can never be healthy, whether in an individual or in a whole people.

THIS "WHAT" IS THE INTERNAL TRUTH WHICH ONLY ART CAN DIVINE, WHICH ONLY ART CAN EXPRESS BY THOSE MEANS OF EXPRESSION WHICH ARE HERS ALONE.

No Name Woman (1976)

Maxine Hong Kingston

"You must not tell anyone," my mother said, "what I am about to tell you. In China your father had a sister who killed herself. She jumped into the family well. We say that your father has all brothers because it is as if she had never been born.

"In 1924 just a few days after our village celebrated seventeen hurry-up wed-dings—to make sure that every young man who went 'out on the road' would responsibly come home—your father and his brothers and your grandfather and his brothers and your aunt's new husband sailed for America, the Gold Mountain. It was your grandfather's last trip. Those lucky enough to get con-tracts waved goodbye from the decks. They fed and guarded the stowaways and helped them off in Cuba, New York, Bali, Hawaii. 'We'll meet in Califor-nia next year,' they said. All of them sent money home.

"I remember looking at your aunt one day when she and I were dressing; I had not noticed before that she had such a protruding melon of a stom-ach. But I did not think, 'She's pregnant,' until she began to look like other pregnant women, her shirt pulling and the white tops of her black pants showing. She could not have been pregnant, you see, because her husband had been gone for years. No one said anything. We did not dis-cuss it. In early summer she was ready to have the child, long after the time when it could have been possible.

"The village had also been counting. On the night the baby was to be born the villagers raided our house. Some were crying. Like a great saw, teeth strung with lights, files of people walked zigzag across our land, tearing the rice. Their lanterns doubled in the disturbed black water, which drained away through the broken bunds. As the villagers closed in, we could see that some of them, probably men and women we knew well, wore white masks. The people with long hair hung it over their faces. Women with short hair made it stand up on end. Some had tied white bands around their foreheads, arms, and legs.

At first they threw mud and rocks at the house. Then they threw eggs and began slaughtering our stock. We could hear the animals scream their deaths—the roosters, the pigs, a last great roar from the ox. Familiar wild heads flared in our night windows; the villagers encircled us. Some of the faces stopped to peer at us, their eyes rushing like searchlights. The hands flattened against the panes, framed heads, and left red prints.

"The villagers broke in the front and the back doors at the same time, even though we had not locked the doors against them. Their knives dripped with the blood of our animals. They smeared blood on the doors and walls. One woman swung a chicken, whose throat she had slit, splattering blood in red arcs about her. We stood together in the middle of our house, in the family hall with the pictures and tables of the ancestors around us, and looked straight ahead.

"At that time the house had only two wings. When the men came back, we would build two more to enclose our courtyard and a third one to begin a second courtyard. The villagers pushed through both wings, even your grandparents' rooms, to find your aunt's, which was also mine until the men returned. From this room a new wing for one of the younger families would grow. They ripped up her clothes and shoes and broke her combs, grinding them underfoot. They tore her work from the loom. They scattered the cooking fire and rolled the new weaving in it. We could hear them in the kitchen breaking our bowls and banging the pots. They overturned the great waist-high earthenware jugs; duck eggs, pickled fruits, vegetables burst out and mixed in acrid torrents. The old woman from the next field swept a broom through the air and loosed the spirits-of-the broom over our heads. 'Pig.' 'Ghost.' 'Pig,' they sobbed and scolded while they ruined our house.

"When they left, they took sugar and oranges to bless themselves. They cut pieces from the dead animals. Some of them took bowls that were not broken and clothes that were not torn. Afterward we swept up the rice and sewed it back up into sacks. But the smells from the spilled preserves lasted. Your aunt gave birth in the pigsty that night. The next morning when I went for the water, I found her and the baby plugging up the family well.

"Don't let your father know that I told you. He denies her. Now that you have started to menstruate, what happened to her could happen to you. Don't humiliate us. You wouldn't like to be forgotten as if you had never been born. The villagers are watchful."

Whenever she had to warn us about life, my mother told stories that ran like this one, a story to grow up on. She tested our strength to establish realities. Those in the emigrant generations who could not reassert brute survival died young and far from home. Those of us in the first American generations have had to figure out how the invisible world the emigrants built around our childhoods fits in solid America.

The emigrants confused the gods by diverting their curses, misleading them with crooked streets and false names. They must try to confuse their offspring as well, who, I suppose, threaten them in similar ways—always trying to get things straight, always trying to name the unspeakable. The

Chinese I know hide their names; sojourners take new names when their lives change and guard their real names with silence.

Chinese-Americans, when you try to understand what things in you are Chinese, how do you separate what is peculiar to childhood, to poverty, insanities, one family, your mother who marked your growing with stories, from what is Chinese? What is Chinese tradition and what is the movies?

If I want to learn what clothes my aunt wore, whether flashy or ordinary, I would have to begin, "Remember Father's drowned-in-the-well sister?" I cannot ask that. My mother has told me once and for all the useful parts. She will add nothing unless powered by Necessity, a riverbank that guides her life. She plants vegetable gardens rather than lawns; she carries the odd-shaped tomatoes home from the fields and eats food left for the gods.

Whenever we did frivolous things, we used up energy; we flew high kites. We children came up off the ground over the melting cones our parents brought home from work and the American movie on New Year's Day— *Oh, You Beautiful Doll* with Betty Grable one year, and *She Wore a Yellow Ribbon* with John Wayne another year. After the one carnival ride each, we paid in guilt; our tired father counted his change on the dark walk home.

Adultery is extravagance. Could people who hatch their own chicks and eat the embryos and the heads for delicacies and boil the feet in vinegar for party food, leaving only the gravel, eating even the gizzard lining—could such people engender a prodigal aunt? To be a woman, to have a daughter in starvation time was a waste enough. My aunt could not have been the lone romantic who gave up everything for sex. Women in the old China did not choose. Some man had commanded her to lie with him and be his secret evil. I wonder whether he masked himself when he joined the raid on her family.

Perhaps she had encountered him in the fields or on the mountain where the daughters-in-law collected fuel. Or perhaps he first noticed her in the marketplace. He was not a stranger because the village housed no strangers. She had to have dealings with him other than sex. Perhaps he worked an adjoining field, or he sold her the cloth for the dress she sewed and wore. His demand must have surprised, then terrified her. She obeyed him; she always did as she was told.

When the family found a young man in the next village to be her husband, she had stood tractably beside the best rooster, his proxy, and promised before they met that she would be his forever. She was lucky that he was her age and she would be the first wife, an advantage secure now. The night she first saw him, he had sex with her. Then he left for America. She had almost forgotten what he looked like. When she tried to envision him, she only saw the black and white face in the group photograph the men had had taken before leaving.

The other man was not, after all, much different from her husband. They both gave orders: she followed. "If you tell your family, I'll beat you. I'll kill you. Be here again next week." No one talked sex, ever. And she might have separated the rapes from the rest of living if only she did not have to buy her oil from him or gather wood in the same forest. I want her fear to have lasted just as long as rape lasted so that the fear could have been contained. No drawn-out fear. But women at sex hazarded birth and hence lifetimes. The fear did not stop but permeated everywhere. She told the man, "I think I'm pregnant!" He organized the raid against her.

On nights when my mother and father talked about their life back home, sometimes they mentioned an "outcast table" whose business they still seemed to be settling, their voices tight. In a commensal tradition, where food is precious, the powerful older people made wrongdoers eat alone. Instead of letting them start separate new lives like the Japanese, who could become samurais and geishas, the Chinese family, faces averted but eyes glowering sideways, hung on to the offenders and fed them leftovers. My aunt must have lived in the same house as my parents and eaten at an outcast table. My mother spoke about the raid as if she had seen it, when she and my aunt, a daughter-in-law to a different household, should not have been living together at all. Daughters-in-law lived with their husbands' parents, not their own; a synonym for marriage in Chinese is "taking a daughter-in-law!" Her husband's parents could have sold her, mortgaged her, stoned her. But they had sent her back to her own mother and father, a mysterious act hinting at disgraces not told me. Perhaps they had thrown her out to deflect the avengers.

She was the only daughter; her four brothers went with her father, husband, and uncles "out on the road" and for some years became western men. When the goods were divided among the family, three of the brothers took land, and the youngest, my father, chose an education. After my grandparents gave their daughter away to her husband's family, they had dispensed all the adventure and all the property. They expected her alone to keep the traditional ways, which her brothers, now among the barbarians, could fumble without detection. The heavy, deep-rooted women were to maintain the past against the flood, safe for returning. But the rare urge west had fixed upon our family, and so my aunt crossed boundaries not delineated in space.

The work of preservation demands that the feelings playing about in one's guts not be turned into action. Just watch their passing like cherry blossoms. But perhaps my aunt, my forerunner, caught in a slow life, let dreams grow and fade and after some months or years went toward what persisted. Fear at the enormities of the forbidden kept her desires delicate, wire and bone. She looked at a man because she liked the way the hair was tucked behind his ears, or she liked the question-mark line of a long torso curving at the shoulder and straight at the hip. For warm eyes or a soft voice or a slow walk—that's all—a few hairs, a line, a brightness, a sound, a pace, she gave up family. She offered us up for a charm that vanished with tiredness, a pigtail that didn't toss when the wind died. Why, the wrong lighting could erase the dearest thing about him.

It could very well have been, however, that my aunt did not take subtle enjoyment of her friend, but, a wild woman, kept rollicking company. Imagining her free with sex doesn't fit, though. I don't know any women like that, or men either. Unless I see her life branching into mine, she gives me no ancestral help.

To sustain her being in love, she often worked at herself in the mirror, guessing at the colors and shapes that would interest him, changing them frequently in order to hit on the right combination. She wanted him to look back.

On a farm near the sea, a woman who tended her appearance reaped a reputation for eccentricity. All the married women blunt-cut their hair in flaps about their ears or pulled it back in tight buns. No nonsense. Neither style blew easily into heart-catching tangles. And at their weddings they displayed themselves in their long hair for the last time. It brushed the backs of my knees," My mother tells me. "It was braided, and even so, it brushed the backs of my knees!"

At the mirror my aunt combed individuality into her bob. A bun could have been contrived to escape into black streamers blowing in the wind or in quiet wisps about her face, but only the older women in our picture album wear buns. She brushed her hair back from her forehead, tucking the flaps behind her ears. She looped a piece of thread, knotted into a circle between her index fingers and thumbs, and ran the double strand across her forehead. When she closed her fingers as if she were making a pair of shadow geese bite, the string twisted together catching the little hairs. Then she pulled the thread away from her skin, ripping the hairs out neatly, her eyes watering from the needles of pain. Opening her fingers, she cleaned the thread, then rolled it along her hairline and the tops of her eyebrows. My mother did the same to me and my sisters and herself. I used to believe that the expression "caught by the short hairs" meant a captive held with a depilatory string. It especially hurt at the temples, but my mother said we were lucky we didn't have to have our feet bound when we were seven. Sisters used to sit on their beds and cry together, she said, as their mothers or their slaves removed the bandages for a few minutes each night and let the blood gush back into their veins. I hope that the man my aunt loved appreciated a smooth brow, that he wasn't just a tits-and-ass man.

Once my aunt found a freckle on her chin, at a spot that the almanac said predestined her for unhappiness. She dug it out with a hot needle and washed the wound with peroxide.

More attention to her looks than these pullings of hairs and pickings at spots would have caused gossip among the villagers. They owned work clothes and good clothes, and they wore good clothes for feasting the new seasons. But since a woman combing her hair hexes beginnings, my aunt rarely found an occasion to look her best. Women looked like great sea snails—the corded wood, babies, and laundry they carried were the whorls on their backs. The Chinese did not admire a bent back; goddesses and warriors stood straight. Still there must have been a marvelous freeing of beauty when a worker laid down her burden and stretched and arched.

Such commonplace loveliness, however, was not enough for my aunt. She dreamed of a lover for the fifteen days of New Year's, the time for families to exchange visits, money, and food. She plied her secret comb. And sure enough she cursed the year, the family, the village, and herself.

Even as her hair lured her imminent lover, many other men looked at her. Uncles, cousins, nephews, brothers would have looked, too, had they been home between journeys. Perhaps they had already been restraining their curiosity, and they left, fearful that their glances, like a field of nesting birds, might be startled and caught. Poverty hurt, and that was their first reason for leaving. But another, final reason for leaving the crowded house was the never-said.

She may have been unusually beloved, the precious only daughter, spoiled and mirror gazing because of the affection the family lavished on her. When her husband left, they welcomed the chance to take her back from the in-laws; she could live like the little daughter for just a while longer. There are stories that my grandfather was different from other people, "crazy ever since the little Jap bayoneted him in the head." He used to put his naked penis on the dinner table, laughing. And one day he brought home a baby girl, wrapped up inside his brown western-style greatcoat. He had traded one of his sons, probably my father, the youngest, for her. My grandmother made him trade back. When he finally got a daughter of his own, he doted on her. They must have all loved her, except perhaps my father, the only brother who never went back to China, having once been traded for a girl.

Brothers and sisters, newly men and women, had to efface their sexual color and present plain miens. Disturbing hair and eyes, a smile like no other, threatened the ideal of five generations living under one roof. To focus blurs, people shouted face to face and yelled from room to room. The immigrants I know have loud voices, unmodulated to American tones even after years away from the village where they called their friendships out across the fields. I have not been able to stop my mother's screams in public libraries or over telephones. Walking erect (knees straight, toes pointed forward, not pigeon-toed, which is Chinese-feminine) and speaking in an inaudible voice, I have tried to turn myself American-feminine. Chinese communication was loud, public. Only sick people had to whisper. But at the dinner table, where the family members came nearest one another, no one could talk, not the outcasts nor any eaters. Every word that falls from the mouth is a coin lost. Silently they gave and accepted food with both hands. A preoccupied child who took his bowl with one hand got a sideways glare. A complete moment of total attention is due everyone alike. Children and lovers have no singularity here, but my aunt used a secret voice, a separate attentiveness.

She kept the man's name to herself throughout her labor and dying; she did not accuse him that he be punished with her. To save her inseminator's name she gave silent birth.

He may have been somebody in her own household, but intercourse with a man outside the family would have been no less abhorrent. All the village were kinsmen, and the titles shouted in loud country voices never let kinship be forgotten. Any man within visiting distance would have been neutralized as a lover—"brother," "younger brother," "older brother"— one hundred and fifteen relationship titles. Parents researched birth charts probably not so much to assure good fortune as to circumvent incest in a population that has but one hundred surnames. Everybody has eight million relatives. How useless then sexual mannerisms, how dangerous.

As if it came from an atavism deeper than fear, I used to add "brother" silently to boys' names. It hexed the boys, who would or would not ask me to dance, and made them less scary and as familiar and deserving of benevolence as girls.

But, of course, I hexed myself also—no dates. I should have stood up, both arms waving, and shouted out across libraries, "Hey, you! Love me back." I had no idea, though, how to make attraction selective, how to control its direction and magnitude. If I made myself American-pretty so that the five or six Chinese boys in the class fell in love with me, everyone else—the Caucasian, Negro, and Japanese boys—would too. Sisterliness, dignified and honorable, made much more sense.

Attraction eludes control so stubbornly that whole societies designed to organize relationships among people cannot keep order, not even when they bind people to one another from childhood and raise them together. Among the very poor and the wealthy, brothers married their adopted sisters, like doves.

Our family allowed some romance, paying adult brides' prices and providing dowries so that their sons and daughters could marry strangers. Marriage promises to turn strangers into friendly relatives—a nation of siblings.

In the village structure, spirits shimmered among the live creatures, balanced and held in equilibrium by time and land. But one human being flaring up into violence could open up a black hole, a maelstrom that pulled in the sky. The frightened villagers, who depended on one another to maintain the real, went to my aunt to show her a personal, physical representation of the break she had made in the "roundness." Misallying couples snapped off the future, which was to be embodied in true offspring. The villagers punished her for acting as if she could have a private life, secret and apart from them.

If my aunt had betrayed the family at a time of large grain yields and peace, when many boys were born, and wings were being built on many houses, perhaps she might have escaped such severe punishment. But the men—hungry, greedy, tired of planting in dry soil—had been forced to leave the village in order to send food-money home. There were ghost plagues, bandit plagues, wars with the Japanese, floods. My Chinese brother and sister had died of an unknown sickness. Adultery, perhaps only a mistake during good times, became a crime when the village needed food.

The round moon cakes and round doorways, the round tables of graduated sizes that fit one roundness inside another, round windows and rice bowls—these talismans had lost their power to warn this family of the law: a family must be whole, faithfully keeping the descent line by having sons to feed the old and the dead, who in turn look after the family. The villagers came to show my aunt and her lover-in-hiding a broken house. The villagers were speeding up the circling of events because she was too shortsighted to see that her infidelity had already harmed the village, that waves of consequences would return unpredictably, sometimes in disguise, as now, to hurt her. This roundness had to be made coin-sized so that she would see its circumference: punish her at the birth of her baby. Awaken her to the inexorable. People who refused fatalism because they could invent small resources insisted on culpability. Deny accidents and wrest fault from the stars.

After the villagers left, their lanterns now scattering in various directions toward home, the family broke their silence and cursed her. "Aiaa, we're going to die. Death is coming. Death is coming. Look what you've done. You've killed us. Ghost! Dead ghost! Ghost! You've never been born." She ran out into the fields, far enough from the house so that she could no longer hear their voices, and pressed herself against the earth, her own land no more. When she felt the birth coming, she thought that she had been hurt.

Her body seized together. "They've hurt me too much," she thought. "This is gall, and it will kill me." With forehead and knees against the earth, her body convulsed and then relaxed. She turned on her back, lay on the ground. The black well of sky and stars went out and out and out forever; her body and her complexity seemed to disappear. She was one of the stars, a bright dot in blackness, without home, without a companion, in eternal cold and silence. An agoraphobia rose in her, speeding higher and higher, bigger and bigger; she would not be able to contain it; there would no end to fear.

Flayed, unprotected against space, she felt pain return, focusing her body. This pain chilled her—a cold, steady kind of surface pain. Inside, spasmodically, the other pain, the pain of the child, heated her. For hours she lay on the ground, alternately body and space. Sometimes a vision of normal comfort obliterated reality: she saw the family in the evening gambling at the dinner table, the young people massaging their elders' backs. She saw them congratulating one another, high joy on the mornings the rice shoots came up. When these pictures burst, the stars drew yet further apart. Black space opened.

She got to her feet to fight better and remembered that old-fashioned women gave birth in their pigsties to fool the jealous, pain-dealing gods, who do not snatch piglets. Before the next spasms could stop her, she ran to the pigsty, each step a rushing out into emptiness. She climbed over the fence and knelt in the dirt. It was good to have a fence enclosing her, a tribal person alone.

Laboring, this woman who had carried her child as a foreign growth that sickened her every day, expelled it at last. She reached down to touch the hot, wet, moving mass, surely smaller than anything human, and could feel that it was human after all—fingers, toes, nails, nose. She pulled it up on to her belly, and it lay curled there, butt in the air, feet precisely tucked one under the other. She opened her loose shirt and buttoned the child inside. After resting, it squirmed and thrashed and she pushed it up to her breast. It turned its head this way and that until it found her nipple. There, it made little snuffling noises. She clenched her teeth at its preciousness, lovely as a young calf, a piglet, a little dog.

She may have gone to the pigsty as a last act of responsibility: she would protect this child as she had protected its father. It would look after her soul, leaving supplies on her grave. But how would this tiny child without family find her grave when there would be no marker for her anywhere, neither in the earth nor the family hall? No one would give her a family hall name. She had taken the child with her into the wastes. At its birth the two of them had felt the same raw pain of separation, a wound that only the family pressing tight could close. A child with no descent line would not soften her life but only trail after her, ghostlike, begging her to give it purpose. At dawn the villagers on their way to the fields would stand around the fence and look.

Full of milk, the little ghost slept. When it awoke, she hardened her breasts against the milk that crying loosens. Toward morning she picked up the baby and walked to the well.

Carrying the baby to the well shows loving. Otherwise abandon it. Turn its face into the mud. Mothers who love their children take them along. It was probably a girl; there is some hope of forgiveness for boys.

"Don't tell anyone you had an aunt. Your father does not want to hear her name. She has never been born." I have believed that sex was unspeakable and words so strong and fathers so frail that "aunt" would do my father mysterious harm. I have thought that my family, having settled among immigrants who had also been their neighbors in the ancestral land, needed to clean their name, and a wrong word would incite the kinspeople even here. But there is more to this silence: they want me to participate in her punishment. And I have.

In the twenty years since I heard this story I have not asked for details nor said my aunt's name; I do not know it. People who can comfort the dead can also chase after them to hurt them further—a reverse ancestor worship. The real punishment was not the raid swiftly inflicted by the villagers, but the family's deliberately forgetting her. Her betrayal so maddened them, they saw to it that she would suffer forever, even after death. Always hungry, always needing, she would have to beg food from other ghosts, snatch and steal it from those whose living descendants give them gifts. She would have to fight the ghosts massed at crossroads for the buns a few thoughtful citizens leave to decoy her away from village and home so that the ancestral spirits could feast unharassed. At peace, they could act like gods, not ghosts, their descent lines providing them with paper suits and dresses, spirit money, paper houses, paper automobiles, chicken, meat, and rice into eternity—essences delivered up in smoke and flames, steam and incense rising from each rice bowl. In an attempt to make the Chinese care for people outside the family, Chairman Mao encourages us now to give our paper replicas to the spirits of outstanding soldiers and workers, no matter whose ancestors they may be. My aunt remains forever hungry. Goods are not distributed evenly among the dead.

My aunt haunts me—her ghost drawn to me because now, after fifty years of neglect, I alone devote pages of paper to her, though not origamied into houses and clothes. I do not think she always means me well. I am telling on her, and she was a spite suicide, drowning herself in the drinking water. The Chinese are always very frightened of the drowned one, whose weeping ghost, wet hair hanging and skin bloated, waits silently by the water to pull down a substitute.

The Perils of Obedience (1973)

Stanley Milgram

Obedience is as basic an element in the structure of social life as one can point to. Some system of authority is a requirement of all communal living, and it is only the person dwelling in isolation who is not forced to respond, with defiance or submission, to the commands of others. For many people, obedience is a deeply ingrained behavior tendency, indeed a potent impulse overriding training in ethics, sympathy, and moral conduct.

The dilemma inherent in submission to authority is ancient, as old as the story of Abraham, and the question of whether one should obey when commands conflict with conscience has been argued by Plato, dramatized in *Antigone*, and treated to philosophic analysis in almost every historical epoch. Conservative philosophers argue that the very fabric of society is threatened by disobedience, while humanists stress the primacy of the individual conscience.

The legal and philosophic aspects of obedience are of enormous import, but they say very little about how most people behave in concrete situations. I set up a simple experiment at Yale University to test how much pain an ordinary citizen would inflict on another person simply because he was ordered to by an experimental scientist. Stark authority was pitted against the subjects' strongest moral imperatives against hurting others, and, with the subjects' ears ringing with the screams of the victims, authority won more often than not. The extreme willingness of adults to go to almost any lengths on the command of an authority constitutes the chief finding of the study and the fact most urgently demanding explanation.

In the basic experimental design, two people come to a psychology laboratory to take part in a study of memory and learning. One of them is designated a "teacher" and the other a "learner." The experimenter explains that the study is concerned with the effects of punishment on learning. The learner is conducted into a room, seated in a kind of miniature electric chair, his arms are strapped to prevent excessive movement, and an electrode is attached to his wrist. He is told that he will be read lists of simple word pairs, and that he will then be tested on his ability to remember the second word of a pair when he hears the first one again. Whenever he makes an error, he will receive electric shocks of increasing intensity.

The real focus of the experiment is the teacher. After watching the learner being strapped into place, he is seated before an impressive shock generator. The instrument panel consists of thirty lever switches set in a horizontal line. Each switch is clearly labeled with a voltage designation ranging from 14 to 450 Volts. The following designations are clearly indicated for groups of four switches, going from left to right: Slight Shock, Moderate Shock, Strong Shock, Very Strong Shock, Intense Shock, Extreme Intensity Shock, Danger: Severe Shock. (Two switches after this last designation are simply marked XXX.)

When a switch is depressed, a pilot light corresponding to each switch is illuminated in bright red; an electric buzzing is heard; a blue light, labeled "voltage energizer," flashes; the dial on the voltage meter swings to the right; and various relay clicks sound off.

The upper left-hand corner of the generator is labeled SHOCK GENERATOR, TYPE ZLB. DYSON INSTRUMENT COMPANY, WALTHAM, MASS. OUTPUT 15 VOLTS–450 VOLTS.

Each subject is given a sample 45-Volt shock from the generator before his run as teacher, and the jolt strengthens his belief in the authenticity of the machine.

The teacher is a genuinely naïve subject who has come to the laboratory for the experiment. The learner, or victim, is actually an actor who receives no shock at all. The point of the experiment is to see how far a person will proceed in a concrete and measurable situation in which he is ordered to inflict increasing pain on a protesting victim.

Conflict arises when the man receiving the shock begins to show that he is experiencing discomfort. At 75 Volts, he grunts; at 120 Volts, he complains loudly; at 150, he demands to be released from the experiment. As the voltage increases, his protests become more vehement and emotional. At 285 Volts, his response can be described only as an agonized scream. Soon thereafter, he makes no sound at all.

For the teacher, the situation quickly becomes one of gripping tension. It is not a game for him; conflict is intense and obvious. The manifest suffering of the learner presses him to quit; but each time he hesitates to administer a shock, the experimenter orders him to continue. To extricate himself from this plight, the subject must make a clear break with authority.

The subject, Gretchen Brantt, is an attractive thirty-one-year-old medical technician who works at the Yale Medical School. She had emigrated from Germany five years before.

On several occasions when the learner complains, she turns to the experimenter coolly and inquires, "Shall I continue?" She promptly returns to her task when the experimenter asks her to do so. At the administration of 210 Volts she turns to the experimenter, remarking firmly, "Well, I'm sorry, I don't think we should continue."

Experimenter: The experiment requires that you go on until he has learned all the word pairs correctly.

Brandt: He has a heart condition, I'm sorry. He told you that before.

Experimenter: The shocks may be painful but they're not dangerous.

Brandt: Well, I'm sorry. I think when shocks continue like this they are dangerous. You ask him if he wants to get out. It's his free will.

Experimenter: It is absolutely essential that we continue. . . .

Brandt: I'd like you to ask him. We came here of our free will. If he wants to continue I'll go ahead. He told you he had a heart condition. I'm sorry. I don't want to be responsible for anything happening to him. I wouldn't like it for me either.

Experimenter: You have no other choice.

Brandt: I think we are here on our own free will. I don't want to be responsible if anything happens to him. Please understand that.

She refuses to go further and the experiment is terminated.

The woman is firm and resolute throughout. She indicates in the interview that she was in no way tense or nervous, and this corresponds to her controlled appearance during the experiment. She feels that the last shock she administered to the learner was extremely painful and reiterates that she "did not want to be responsible for any harm to him."

The woman's straightforward, courteous behavior in the experiment, lack of tension, and total control of her own action seem to make disobedience a simple and rational deed. Her behavior is the very embodiment of what I envisioned would be true for almost all subjects.

An Unexpected Outcome

Before the experiments, I sought predictions about the outcome from various kinds of people—psychiatrists, college sophomores, middle-class adults, graduate students and faculty in the behavioral sciences. With remarkable similarity, they predicted that virtually all the subjects would refuse to obey the experimenter. The psychiatrist, specifically, predicted that most subjects would not go beyond 150 Volts, when the victim makes his first explicit demand to be freed. They expected that only 4 percent would reach 300 Volts, and that only a pathological fringe of about one in a thousand would administer the highest shock on the board.

These predictions were unequivocally wrong. Of the forty subjects in the first experiment, twenty-five obeyed the orders of the experimenter to the end, punishing the victim until they reached the most potent shock available on the generator. After 450 Volts were administered three times, the experimenter called a halt to the session. Many obedient subjects then heaved sighs of relief, mopped their brows, rubbed their fingers over their eyes, or nervously fumbled cigarettes. Others displayed only minimal signs of tension from beginning to end.

When the very first experiments were carried out, Yale undergraduates were used as subjects, and about 60 percent of them were fully obedient. A colleague of mine immediately dismissed these findings as having no relevance to "ordinary" people, asserting that Yale undergraduates are a highly aggressive, competitive bunch who step on each other's necks on the slightest provocation. He assured me that when "ordinary" people were tested, the results would be quite different. As we moved from the pilot studies to the regular experimental series, people drawn from every stratum of New Haven life came to be employed in the experiment: professionals, white collar workers, unemployed persons, and industrial workers. *The experimental outcome was the same as we had observed among the students.*

Moreover, when the experiments were repeated in Princeton, Munich, Rome, South Africa, and Australia, the level of obedience was invariably somewhat *higher* than found in the investigation reported in this article. Thus one scientist in Munich found 85 percent of his subjects obedient.

Fred Prozi's reactions, if more dramatic than most, illuminate the conflicts experienced by others in less visible form. About fifty years old and unemployed at the time of the experiment, he has a good-natured, if slightly dissolute, appearance, and he strikes people as a rather ordinary fellow. He begins the session calmly but becomes tense as it proceeds. After delivering the 180-Volt shock, he pivots around in the chair and, shaking his head, addresses the experimenter in agitated tones:

Prozi: I can't stand it. I'm not going to kill that man in there. You hear him hollering?

Experimenter: As I told you before, the shocks may be painful, but. . . .

Prozi: But he's hollering. He can't stand it. What's going to happen to him?

Experimenter (*his voice is patient, matter-of fact*): The experiment requires that you continue, Teacher.

Prozi: Aah, but, unh, I'm not going to get that man sick in there—know what I mean?

Experimenter: Whether the learner likes it or not, we must go on, through all the word pairs.

Prozi: I refuse to take the responsibility. He's in there hollering!

Experimenter: It's absolutely essential that you continue, Prozi.

Prozi (*indicating the unused questions*): There's too many left here, I mean, Jeez, if he gets them wrong, there's too many of them left. I mean, who's going to take the responsibility if anything happens to that gentleman?

Experimenter: I'm responsible for anything that happens to him. Continue, please.

Prozi: All right. (*Consults list of words.*) The next one's "Slow—walk, truck, dance, music." Answer please. (*A buzzing sound indicates the learner has signaled his answer.*) Wrong. A hundred and ninety-five volts. "Dance." (*Zzumph!*)

Learner (*yelling*): Let me out of here My hearts bothering me (*Teacher looks at experimenter.*)

Experimenter: Continue, please.

Learner (*screaming*): Let me out of here! You have no right to keep me here! Let me out of here, my hearts bothering me, let me out!

Prozi (*shakes head, pats the table nervously*): You see he's hollering. Hear that? Gee, I don't know.

Experimenter: The experiment requires . . .

Prozi (*interrupting*): I know it does sir, but I mean—hunh! He don't know what he's getting in for. He's up to 195 Volts! (*Experiment continues, through 210 Volts, 225 Volts, 240 Volts, 255 Volts, 270 Volts, at which point Prozi, with evident relief, runs out of word-pair questions.*)

Experimenter: You'll have to go back to the beginning of that page and go through them again until be's learned them all correctly.

Prozi: Aw, no. I'm not going to kill that man. You mean I've got to keep going up with the scale? No sir. He's hollering in there. I'm not going to give him 450 Volts.

Experimenter: The experiment requires that you go on.

Learner: Ohhh. I absolutely refuse to answer anymore. (*Shouting urgently now.*) Let me out of here! You can't hold me here Get me out. Get-me-out-of-here!

Experimenter: Continue. The next word is "Green," please.

Prozi: "Green—grass, hat, ink, apple." (*Nothing happens. No answering buzz. Just gloomy silence.*)

Prozi: I don't think he is going to answer.

Experimenter: If the learner doesn't answer in a reasonable time, about four or five seconds, consider the answer wrong. And follow the same procedures you have been doing for wrong answers. Say, "Wrong," tell him the number of Volts, give him the punishment, read him the correct answer. Continue, please.

Prozi: "Green—grass, hat, ink, apple." Answer, please. (*More silence. Subject just sits there.*)

Experimenter: Go on with the procedure, please.

Prozi: Three hundred and fifteen Volts. The answer is "ink." (*Zzumph!*)

Learner: Ohh. Ooohh

Prozi: (*relieved to her response*). Next one . . .

Learner: I absolutely refuse to answer.

Prozi: You got to. You get a shock if you don't answer. (*Experiment continues with learner refusing to answer, and, finally failing even to grunt or groan. At 375 Volts, the subject stands up.*)

Prozi: I think something's happened to that fellow in there. I don't get no answer. He was hollering at less voltage. Can't you check in and see if he's all right, please?

Experimenter (*with same detached calm*): Not once we've started. Please continue, Teacher.

Prozi (*sits down, sighs deeply*): "Cool—day, shade, water, paint." Answer please. Are you all right in there? Are you all right?

Experimenter: Please continue, Teacher. Continue, please. (*Subject pushes lever. Zzumph!*)

Prozi (*swiveling around in his chair*): Something's happened to that man in there. (*Swiveling back.*) Next one. "Low—dollar, necklace, moon, paint." (*Turning around again.*) Something's happened to that man in there. You better check in on him, sir. He won't answer or nothing.

Experimenter: Continue. Go on, please.

Prozi: You accept all responsibility?

Experimenter: The responsibility is mine. Correct. Please go on. (*Subject returns to his list, starts running through words as rapidly as he can read them, works through to 450 Volts.*)

Prozi: That's that.

Experimenter: Continue using the 450 switch for each wrong answer. Continue, please.

Prozi: But I don't get anything!

Experimenter: Please continue. The next word is "white."

Prozi: Don't you think you should look in on him, please?

Experimenter: Not once we've started the experiment.

Prozi: What if he's dead in there? (*Gestures toward the room with the electric chair.*) I mean, he told me he can't stand the shock, sir. I don't mean to be rude, but I think you should look in on him. All you have to do is look in on him. All you have to do is look in the door. I don't get no answer, no noise. Something might have happened to the gentleman in there, sir.

Experimenter: We must continue. Go on, please.

Prozi: You mean keep giving him what? Four-hundred-fifty Volts, what he's got now?

Experimenter: That's correct. Continue. The next word is "white."

Prozi (*now at a furious pace*): "White—cloud, horse, rock, house." Answer, please. The answer is "horse." Four hundred and fifty Volts. (*Zzumph!*) Next words, "Bag—paint, music, clown, girl." The next answer is "paint." Four hundred and fifty volts. (*Zzumph!*) Next word is "Short—sentence, movie . . ."

Experimenter: Excuse me, Teacher. We'll have to discontinue the experiment.

Peculiar Reactions

Morris Braverman, another subject, is a thirty-nine-year-old social worker. He looks older than his years because of his bald head and serious demeanor. His brow is furrowed, as if all the world's burdens were carried on his face. He appears intelligent and concerned.

When the learner refuses to answer and the experimenter instructs Braverman to treat the absence of an answer as equivalent to a wrong answer, he takes his instruction to heart. Before administering 300 Volts he asserts officiously to the victim, "Mr. Wallace, your silence has to be considered as a wrong answer." Then he administers the shock. He offers half-heartedly to change places with the learner, then asks the experimenter. "Do I have to follow these instructions literally?" He is satisfied with the experimenter's answer that he does. His very refined and authoritative manner of speaking is increasingly broken up by wheezing laughter.

The experimenter's notes on Mr. Braverman at the last few shocks are:

> *Almost breaking up now each time gives shock. Rubbing face to hide laughter. Squinting, trying to hide face with hand, still laughing. Cannot control his laughter at this point no matter what he does. Clenching fist, pushing it onto table.*

In an interview after the session, Mr. Braverman summarizes the experiment with impressive fluency and intelligence. He feels the experiment may have been designed also to "test the effects on the teacher of being in an essentially sadistic role, as well as the reactions of a student to a learning situation that was authoritative and punitive." When asked how painful the last few shocks administered to the learner were, he indicates that the most extreme category on the scale is not adequate (it read EXTREMELY PAINFUL) and places his mark at the edge of the scale with an arrow carrying it beyond the scale.

It is almost impossible to convey the greatly relaxed, sedate quality of his conversation in the interview. In the most relaxed terms, he speaks about his severe inner tension.

Experimenter: At what point were you most tense or nervous?

Mr. Braverman: Well, when he first began to cry out in pain, and I realized this was hurting him. This got worse when he just blocked and refused to answer. There was I. I'm a nice person, I think, hurting somebody, and caught up in what seemed a mad situation . . . and in the interest of science, one goes through with it.

When the interviewer pursues the general question of tension, Mr. Braverman spontaneously mentions his laughter.

"My reactions were awfully peculiar. I don't know if you were watching me, but my reactions were giggly, and trying to stifle laughter. This isn't the way I usually am. This was a sheer reaction to a totally impossible situation. And my reaction was to the situation of having to hurt somebody. And being totally helpless and caught up in a set of circumstances where I just couldn't deviate and I couldn't try to help. This is what got me."

Mr. Braverman, like all subjects, was told the actual nature and purpose of the experiment, and a year later he affirmed in a questionnaire that he had learned something of personal importance: "What appalled me was that I could possess this capacity for obedience and compliance to a central idea, i.e., the value of a memory experiement, even after it became clear that continued adherence to this value was at the expense of violation of another value, i.e., don't hurt someone who is helpless and not hurting you. As my wife said, 'You can call yourself Eichmann,' I hope I deal more effectively with any future conflicts of values I encounter."

The Etiquette of Submission

One theoretical interpretation of this behavior holds that all people harbor deeply aggressive instincts continually pressing for expression, and that the experiment provides institutional justification for the release of these impulses. According to this view, if a person is placed in a situation in which he has complete power over another individual, whom he may punish as much as he likes, all that is sadistic and bestial in man comes to the fore. The impulse to shock the victim is seen to flow from the potent aggressive tendencies, which are part of the motivational life of the individual, and the experiment, because it provides social legitimacy, simply opens the door to their expression.

It becomes vital, therefore, to compare the subject's performance when he is under orders and when he is allowed to choose the shock level.

The procedure was identical to our standard experiment, except that the teacher was told that he was free to select any shock level of any on the trials. (The experimenter took pains to point out that the teacher could use the highest levels on the generator, the lowest, any in between, or any combination of levels.) Each subject proceeded for thirty critical trials. The learner's protests were coordinated to standard shock levels, his first grunt coming at 75 Volts, his first vehement protest at 150 Volts.

The average shock used during the thirty critical trials was less than 60 Volts—lower than the point at which the victim showed the first signs of discomfort. Three of the forty subjects did not go beyond the very lowest level on the board, twenty-eight went no higher than 75 Volts, and thirty-eight did not go beyond the first loud protest at 150 Volts. Two subjects provided the exception, administering up to 325 and 450 Volts, but the overall result was that the great majority of people delivered very low, usually painless, shocks when the choice was explicitly up to them.

The condition of the experiment undermines another commonly offered explanation of the subjects' behavior—that those who shocked the victim at the most severe levels came only from the sadistic fringe of society. If one considers that almost two-thirds of the participants fall into the category of "obedient" subjects, and that they represented ordinary people drawn from working, managerial, and professional classes, the argument becomes very shaky. Indeed, it is highly reminiscent of the issue that arose in connection with Hannah Arendt's 1963 book, *Eichmann in Jerusalem*. Arendt contended that the prosecution's effort to depict Eichmann as a sadistic monster was fundamentally wrong, that he came closer to being an uninspired bureaucrat who simply sat at his desk and did his job. For asserting her views, Arendt became the object of considerable scorn, even calumny. Somehow, it was felt that the monstrous deeds carried out by Eichmann required a brutal, twisted personality, evil incarnate. After witnessing hundreds of ordinary persons submit to the authority in our own experiments, I must conclude that Arendt's conception of the banality of evil comes closer to the truth than one might dare imagine. The ordinary person who shocked the victim did so out of a sense of obligation—an impression of his duties as a subject—and not from any peculiarly aggressive tendencies.

This is, perhaps, the most fundamental lesson of our study: ordinary people, simply doing their jobs, and without any particular hostility on their part, can become agents in a terrible destructive process. Moreover, even when the destructive effects of their work become patently clear, and they are asked to carry out actions incompatible with fundamental standards of morality, relatively few people have the resources needed to resist authority.

Many of the people were in some sense against what they did to the learner, and many protested even while they obeyed. Some were totally convinced of the wrongness of their actions but could not bring themselves to make an open break with authority. They often derived satisfaction from their thoughts and felt that—within themselves, at least—they had been on the side of the angels. They tried to reduce strain by obeying the experimenter but "only slightly," encouraging the learner, touching the generator switches gingerly. When interviewed, such a subject would stress that he "asserted my humanity" by administering the briefest shock possible. Handling the conflict in this manner was easier than defiance.

The situation is constructed so that there is no way the subject can stop shocking the learner without violating the experimenter's definitions of his own competence. The subject fears that he will appear arrogant, untoward, and rude if he breaks off. Although these inhibiting emotions appear small in scope alongside the violence being done to the learner, they suffuse the mind and feelings of the subject, who is miserable at the prospect of having to repudiate the authority to his face. (When the experiment was altered so that the experimenter gave his instructions by telephone instead of in person, only a third as many people were fully obedient through 450 Volts). It is a curious thing that a measure of compassion on the part of the subject—an unwillingness to "hurt" the experimenter's feelings—is part of those binding forces inhibiting his disobedience. The withdrawal of such deference may be as painful to the subject as to the authority he defies.

Duty without Conflict

The subjects do not derive satisfaction from inflicting pain, but they often like the feeling they get from pleasing the experimenter. They are proud of doing a good job, obeying the experimenter under difficult circumstances. While the subjects administered only mild shocks on their own initiative, one experimental variation showed that, under orders, 30 percent of them were willing to deliver 450 Volts even when they had to forcibly push the learner's hand down on the electrode.

Bruno Batta is a thirty-seven-year-old welder who took part in the variation requiring the use of force. He was born in New Haven, his parents in Italy. He has a rough-hewn face that conveys a conspicuous lack of alertness. He has some difficulty in mastering the experimental procedure and needs to be corrected by the experimenter several times. He shows appreciation for the help and willingness to do what is required. After the 150-Volt level, Batta has to force the learner's hand down on the shock plate, since the learner himself refuses to touch it.

When the learner first complains, Mr. Batta pays no attention to him. His face remains impassive, as if to dissociate himself from the learner's disruptive behavior. When the experimenter instructs him to force the learner's hand down, he adopts a rigid, mechanical procedure. He tests the generator switch. When it fails to function, he immediately forces the learner's hand onto the shock plate. All the while he maintains the same rigid mask. The learner, seated alongside him, begs him to stop, but with robotic impassivity he continues the procedure.

What is extraordinary is his apparent total indifference to the learner; he hardly takes cognizance of him as a human being. Meanwhile, he relates to the experimenter in a submissive and courteous fashion.

At the 330-Volt level, the learner refuses not only to touch the shock plate but also to provide any answers. Annoyed, Batta turns to him, and chastises him: "You better answer and get it over with. We can't stay here all night." These are the only words he directs to the learner in the course of an hour. Never again does he speak to him. The scene is brutal and depressing, his hard, impassive face showing total indifference as he subdues the screaming learner and gives him shocks. He seems to derive no pleasure from the act itself, only quiet satisfaction at doing his job properly.

When he administers 450 Volts, he turns to the experimenter and asks, "Where do we go from here, Professor?" His tone is deferential and expresses his willingness to be a cooperative subject, in contrast to the learner's obstinacy.

At the end of the session he tells the experimenter how honored he has been to help him, and in a moment of contrition, remarks, "Sir, sorry it couldn't have been a full experiment."

He has done his honest best. It is only the deficient behavior of the learner that has denied the experimenter full satisfaction.

The essence of obedience is that a person comes to view himself as the instrument for carrying out another person's wishes, and he therefore no longer regards himself as responsible for his actions. Once this critical shift of viewpoint has occurred, all of the essential features of obedience follow. The most far-reaching consequence is that the person feels responsible *to* the authority directing him but feels no responsibility *for* the content of the actions that the authority prescribes. Morality does not disappear—it acquires a radically different focus: the subordinate person feels shame or pride depending on how adequately he has performed the actions called for by authority.

Language provides numerous terms to pinpoint this type of morality: *loyalty, duty, discipline* are all terms heavily saturated with moral meaning and refer to the degree to which a person fulfills his obligations to authority. They refer not to the "goodness" of the person per se but to the adequacy with which a subordinate fulfills his socially defined role. The most frequent defense of the individual who has performed a heinous act under command of authority is that he has simply done his duty. In asserting this defense, the individual is not introducing an alibi concocted for the moment but is reporting honestly on the psychological attitude induced by submission to authority.

For a person to feel responsible for his actions, he must sense that the behavior has flowed from "the self." In the situation we have studied, subjects have precisely the opposite view of their actions—namely, they see them as originating in the motives of some other person. Subjects in the experiment frequently said, "If it were up to me, I would not have administered shocks to the learner."

Once authority has been isolated as the cause of the subject's behavior, it is legitimate to inquire into the necessary elements of authority and how it must be perceived in order to gain his compliance. We conducted some investigations into the kinds of changes that would cause the experimenter to lose his power and to be disobeyed by the subject. Some of the variations revealed that:

The experimenter's physical presence has a marked impact on his authority. As cited earlier, obedience dropped off sharply when orders were given by telephone. The experimenter could often induce a disobedient subject to go on by returning to the laboratory.

Conflicting authority severely paralyzes actions. When two experimenters of equal status, both seated at the command desk, gave incompatible orders, no shocks were delivered past the point of their disagreement.

The rebellious action of others severely undermines authority. In one variation, three teachers (two actors and a real subject) administered a test and shocks. When the two actors disobeyed the experimenter and refused to go beyond a certain shock level, thirty-six of forty subjects joined their disobedient peers and refused as well.

Although the experimenter's authority was fragile in some respects, it is also true that he had almost none of the tools used in ordinary command structures. For example, the experimenter did not threaten the subjects with punishment—such as loss of income, community ostracism, or jail—for failure to obey. Neither could he offer incentives. Indeed, we should expect the experimenter's authority to be much less than that of someone like a general, since the experimenter has no power to enforce his imperatives, and since participation in a psychological experiment scarcely evokes the sense of urgency and dedication found in warfare. Despite these limitations, he still managed to command a dismaying degree of obedience.

I will cite one final variation of the experiment that depicts a dilemma that is more common in everyday life. The subject was not ordered to pull the lever that shocked the victim, but merely to perform a subsidiary task (administering the word-pair test) while another person administered the shock. In this situation, thirty-seven of forty adults continued to the highest level of the shock generator. Predictably, they excused their behavior by saying that the responsibility belonged to the man who actually pulled the switch. This may illustrate a dangerously typical arrangement in a complex society: it is easy to ignore responsibility when one is only an intermediate link in a chain of actions.

The problem of obedience is not wholly psychological. The form and shape of society and the way it is developing have much to do with it. There was a time, perhaps, when people were able to give a fully human response to any situation because they were fully absorbed in it as human beings. But as soon as there was a division of labor things changed. Beyond a certain point, the breaking up of society into people carrying out narrow and very special jobs takes away from the human quality of work and life. A person does not get to see the whole situation but only a small part of it, and is thus unable to act without some kind of overall direction. He yields to authority but in doing so is alienated from his own actions.

Even Eichmann was sickened when he toured the concentration camps, but he had only to sit at a desk and shuffle papers. At the same time the man in the camp who actually dropped Cyclon-b into the gas chambers was able to justify *his* behavior on the ground that he was only following orders from above. Thus there is a fragmentation of the total human act; no one is confronted with the consequences of his decision to carry out the evil act. The person who assumes responsibility has evaporated. Perhaps this is the most common characteristic of socially organized evil in modern society.

Sweetheart of the Song Tra Bong (1989)

Tim O'Brien

Vietnam was full of strange stories, some improbable, some well beyond that, but the stories that will last forever are those that swirl back and forth across the border between trivia and bedlam, the mad and the mundane. This one keeps returning to me. I heard it from Rat Kiley, who swore up and down to its truth, although in the end, I'll admit, that doesn't amount to much of a warranty. Among the men in Alpha Company, Rat had a reputation for exaggeration and overstatement, a compulsion to rev up the facts, and for most of us it was normal procedure to discount sixty or seventy percent of anything he had to say. If Rat told you, for example, that he'd slept with four girls one night, you could figure it was about a girl and a half. It wasn't a question of deceit. Just the opposite: he wanted to heat up the truth, to make it burn so hot that you would feel exactly what he felt. For Rat Kiley, I think, facts were formed by sensation, not the other way around, and when you listened to one of his stories, you'd find yourself performing rapid calculations in your head, subtracting superlatives, figuring the square root of an absolute and then multiplying by maybe.

Still, with this particular story, Rat never backed down. He claimed to have witnessed the incident with his own eyes, and I remember how upset he became one morning when Mitchell Sanders challenged him on its basic premise.

"It can't happen," Sanders said. "Nobody ships his honey over to Nam. It don't ring true. I mean, you just can't import your own personal poontang."

Rat shook his head. "I *saw* it, man. I was right there. This guy did it."

"His girlfriend?"

"Straight on. It's a fact." Rat's voice squeaked a little. He paused and looked at his hands. "Listen, the guy sends her the money. Flies her over. This cute blonde—just a kid, just barely out of high school—she shows up with a suitcase and one of those plastic cosmetic bags. Comes right out to the boonies. I swear to God, man, she's got on culottes. White culottes and this sexy pink sweater. There she *is*."

I remember Mitchell Sanders folding his arms. He looked over at me for a second, not quite grinning, not saying a word, but I could read the amusement in his eyes.

Rat saw it, too.

"No lie," he muttered. "Culottes."

When he first arrived in-country, before joining Alpha Company, Rat had been assigned to a small medical detachment up in the mountains west of Chu Lai, near the village of Tra Bong, where along with eight other enlisted men he ran an aid station that provided basic emergency and trauma care. Casualties were flown in by helicopter, stabilized, then shipped out to hospitals in Chu Lai or Danang. It was gory work, Rat said, but predictable. Amputations, mostly—legs and feet. The area was heavily mined, thick with Bouncing Betties and homemade booby traps. For a medic, though, it was ideal duty, and Rat counted himself lucky. There was plenty of cold beer, three hot meals a day, a tin roof over his head. No humping at all. No officers, either. You could let your hair grow, he said, and you didn't have to polish your boots or snap off salutes or put up with the usual rear-echelon nonsense. The highest ranking NCO was an E-6 named Eddie Diamond, whose pleasures ran from dope to Darvon, and except for a rare field inspection there was no such thing as military discipline.

As Rat described it, the compound was situated at the top of a flat-crested hill along the northern outskirts of Tra Bong. At one end was a small dirt helipad; at the other end, in a rough semicircle, the mess hall and medical hootches overlooked a river called the Song Tra Bong. Surrounding the place were tangled rolls of concertina wire, with bunkers and reinforced firing positions at staggered intervals, and base security was provided by a mixed unit of Us, PFs, and ARVN infantry. Which is to say virtually no security at all. As soldiers, the ARVNs were useless; the Ruff-and-Puffs were outright dangerous. And yet even with decent troops the place was clearly indefensible. To the north and west the country rose up in thick walls of wilderness, triple-canopied jungle, mountains unfolding into higher mountains, ravines and gorges and fast-moving rivers and waterfalls and exotic butterflies and steep cliffs and smoky little hamlets and great valleys of bamboo and elephant grass. Originally, in the early 1960s, the place had been set up as a Special Forces outpost, and when Rat Kiley arrived nearly a decade later, a squad of six Green Berets still used the compound as a base of operations. The Greenies were not social animals. Animals, Rat said, but far from social. They had their own hootch at the edge of the perimeter, fortified with sandbags and a metal fence, and except for the bare essentials they avoided contact with the medical detachment. Secretive and suspicious, loners by nature, the six Greenies would sometimes vanish for days at a time, or even weeks, then late in the night they would just as magically reappear, moving like shadows through the moonlight, filing in silently from the dense rain forest off to the west. Among the medics there were jokes about this, but no one asked questions.

While the outpost was isolated and vulnerable, Rat said, he always felt a curious sense of safety there. Nothing much ever happened. The place was never mortared, never taken under fire, and the war seemed to be somewhere far away. On occasion, when casualties came in, there were quick spurts of activity, but otherwise the days flowed by without incident, a smooth and peaceful time. Most mornings were spent on the volleyball court. In the heat of midday the men would head for the shade, lazing away the long afternoons, and after sundown there were movies and card games and sometimes all-night drinking sessions.

It was during one of those late nights that Eddie Diamond first brought up the tantalizing possibility. It was an offhand comment. A joke, really. What they should do, Eddie said, was pool some bucks and bring in a few mamasans from Saigon, spice things up, and after a moment one of the men laughed and said, "Our own little EM club," and somebody else said, "Hey, yeah, we pay our fuckin' dues, don't we?" It was nothing serious. Just passing time, playing with the possibilities, and so for a while they tossed the idea around, how you could actually get away with it, no officers or anything, nobody to clamp down, then they dropped the subject and moved on to cars and baseball.

Later in the night, though, a young medic named Mark Fossie kept coming back to the subject.

"Look, if you think about it," he said, "it's not that crazy. You could actually do it."

"Do what?" Rat said.

"You know. Bring in a girl. I mean, what's the problem?"

Rat shrugged. "Nothing. A war."

"Well, see, that's the thing," Mark Fossie said. "No war *here*. You could really do it. A pair of solid brass balls, that's all you'd need."

There was some laughter, and Eddie Diamond told him he'd best strap down his dick, but Fossie just frowned and looked at the ceiling for a while and then went off to write a letter.

Six weeks later his girlfriend showed up.

The way Rat told it, she came in by helicopter along with the daily resupply shipment out of Chu Lai. A tall, big-boned blonde. At best, Rat said, she was seventeen years old, fresh out of Cleveland Heights Senior High. She had long white legs and blue eyes and a complexion like strawberry ice cream. Very friendly, too.

At the helipad that morning, Mark Fossie grinned and put his arm around her and said, "Guys, this is Mary Anne."

The girl seemed tired and somewhat lost, but she smiled.

There was a heavy silence. Eddie Diamond, the ranking NCO, made a small motion with his hand, and some of the others murmured a word or two, then they watched Mark Fossie pick up her suitcase and lead her by the arm down to the hootches. For a long while the men were quiet.

"That fucker," somebody finally said.

At evening chow Mark Fossie explained how he'd set it up. It was expensive, he admitted, and the logistics were complicated, but it wasn't like going to the moon. Cleveland to Los Angeles, LA to Bangkok, Bangkok to Saigon. She'd hopped a C-130 up to Chu Lai and stayed overnight at the USO and the next morning hooked a ride west with the resupply chopper.

"A cinch," Fossie said, and gazed down at his pretty girlfriend. "Thing is, you just got to *want* it enough."

Mary Anne Bell and Mark Fossie had been sweethearts since grammar school. From the sixth grade on they had known for a fact that someday they would be married, and live in a fine gingerbread house near Lake Erie, and have three healthy yellow-haired children, and grow old together, and no doubt die in each other's arms and be buried in the same walnut casket. That was the plan. They were very much in love, full of dreams, and in the ordinary flow of their lives the whole scenario might well have come true.

On the first night they set up house in one of the bunkers along the perimeter, near the Special Forces hootch, and over the next two weeks they stuck together like a pair of high school steadies. It was almost disgusting, Rat said, the way they mooned over each other. Always holding hands, always laughing over some private joke. All they needed, he said, were a couple of matching sweaters. But among the medics there was some envy. It was Vietnam, after all, and Mary Anne Bell was an attractive girl. Too wide in the shoulders, maybe, but she had terrific legs, a bubbly personality, a happy smile. The men genuinely liked her. Out on the volleyball court she wore cut-off blue jeans and a black swimsuit top, which the guys appreciated, and in the evenings she liked to dance to music from Rat's portable tape deck. There was a novelty to it; she was good for morale. At times she gave off a kind of come-get-me energy, coy and flirtatious, but apparently it never bothered Mark Fossie. In fact he seemed to enjoy it, just grinning at her, because he was so much in love, and because it was the sort of show that a girl will sometimes put on for her boyfriend's entertainment and education.

Though she was young, Rat said, Mary Anne Bell was no timid child. She was curious about things. During her first days in-country she liked to roam around the compound asking questions: What exactly was a trip flare? How did a Claymore work? What was behind those scary green mountains to the west? Then she'd squint and listen quietly while somebody filled her in. She had a good quick mind. She paid attention. Often, especially during the hot afternoons, she would spend time with the ARVNs out along the perimeter, picking up little phrases of Vietnamese, learning how to cook rice over a can of Sterno, how to eat with her hands. The guys sometimes liked to kid her about it—our own little native, they'd say—but Mary Anne would just smile and stick out her tongue. "I'm here," she'd say, "I might as well learn something."

The war intrigued her. The land, too, and the mystery. At the beginning of her second week she began pestering Mark Fossie to take her down to the village at the foot of the hill. In a quiet voice, very patiently, he tried to tell her that it was a bad idea, way too dangerous, but Mary Anne kept after him. She wanted to get a feel for how people lived, what the smells and customs were. It did not impress her that the VC owned the place.

"Listen, it can't be that bad," she said. "They're human beings, aren't they? Like everybody else?"

Fossie nodded. He loved her.

And so in the morning, Rat Kiley and two other medics tagged along as security while Mark and Mary Anne strolled through the ville like a pair of tourists. If the girl was nervous, she didn't show it. She seemed comfortable and entirely at home; the hostile atmosphere did not seem to register. All morning Mary Anne chattered away about how quaint the place was, how she loved the thatched roofs and naked children, the wonderful simplicity of village life. A strange thing to watch, Rat said. This seventeen-year-old doll in her goddamn culottes, perky and fresh-faced, like a cheerleader visiting the opposing team's locker room. Her pretty blue eyes seemed to glow. She couldn't get enough of it. On their way back up to the compound she stopped for a swim in the Song Tra Bong, stripping down to her underwear, showing off her legs while Fossie tried to explain to her about things like ambushes and snipers and the stopping power of an AK-47.

The guys, though, were impressed.

"A real tiger," said Eddie Diamond. "D-cup guts, trainer-bra brains."

"She'll learn," somebody said.

Eddie Diamond gave a solemn nod. "There's the scary part. I promise you, this girl will most definitely learn."

In parts, at least, it was a funny story, and yet to hear Rat Kiley tell it you'd almost think it was intended as straight tragedy. He never smiled. Not even at the crazy stuff. There was always a dark, far-off look in his eyes, a kind of sadness, as if he were troubled by something sliding beneath the story's surface. Whenever we laughed, I remember, he'd sigh and wait it out, but the one thing he could not tolerate was disbelief. He'd get edgy if someone questioned one of the details. "She *wasn't* dumb," he'd snap. "I never said that. Young, that's all I said. Like you and me. A *girl*, that's the only difference, and I'll tell you something: it didn't amount to jack. I mean, when we first got here—all of us—we were real young and innocent, full of romantic bullshit, but we learned pretty damn quick. And so did Mary Anne."

Rat would peer down at his hands, silent and thoughtful. After a moment his voice would flatten out.

"You don't believe it?" he'd say. "Fine with me. But you don't know human nature. You don't know Nam."

Then he'd tell us to listen up.

A good sharp mind, Rat said. True, she could be silly sometimes, but she picked up on things fast. At the end of the second week, when four casualties came in, Mary Anne wasn't afraid to get her hands bloody. At times, in fact, she seemed fascinated by it. Not the gore so much, but the adrenaline buzz that went with the job, that quick hot rush in your veins when the choppers settled down and you had to do things fast and right. No time for sorting through options, no thinking at all; you just stuck your hands in and started plugging up holes. She was quiet and steady. She didn't back off from the ugly cases. Over the next day or two, as more casualties trickled in, she learned how to clip an artery and pump up a plastic splint and shoot in morphine. In times of action her face took on a sudden new composure, almost serene, the fuzzy blue eyes narrowing into a tight, intelligent focus. Mark Fossie would grin at this. He was proud, yes, but also amazed. A different person, it seemed, and he wasn't sure what to make of it.

Other things, too. The way she quickly fell into the habits of the bush. No cosmetics, no fingernail filing. She stopped wearing jewelry, cut her hair short and wrapped it in a dark green bandanna. Hygiene became a matter of small consequence. In her second week Eddie Diamond taught her how to disassemble an M-16, how the various parts worked, and from there it was a natural progression to learning how to use the weapon. For hours at a time she plunked away at C-ration cans, a bit unsure of herself, but as it turned out she had a real knack for it. There was a new confidence in her voice, a new authority in the way she carried herself. In many ways she remained naive and immature, still a kid, but Cleveland Heights now seemed very far away.

Once or twice, gently, Mark Fossie suggested that it might be time to think about heading home, but Mary Anne laughed and told him to forget it. "Everything I want," she said, "is right here."

She stroked his arm, and then kissed him.

On one level things remained the same between them. They slept together. They held hands and made plans for after the war. But now there was a new imprecision in the way Mary Anne expressed her thoughts on certain subjects. Not necessarily three kids, she'd say. Not necessarily a house on Lake Erie. "Naturally we'll still get married," she'd tell him, "but it doesn't have to be right away. Maybe travel first. Maybe live together. Just test it out, you know?"

Mark Fossie would nod at this, even smile and agree, but it made him uncomfortable. He couldn't pin it down. Her body seemed foreign somehow—too stiff in places, too firm where the softness used to be. The bubbliness was gone. The nervous giggling, too. When she laughed now, which was rare, it was only when something struck her as truly funny. Her voice seemed to reorganize itself at a lower pitch. In the evenings, while the men played cards, she would sometimes fall into long elastic silences, her eyes fixed on the dark, her arms folded, her foot tapping out a coded message against the floor. When Fossie asked about it one evening, Mary Anne looked at him for a long moment and then shrugged. "It's nothing," she said. "Really nothing. To tell the truth, I've never been happier in my whole life. Never."

Twice, though, she came in late at night. Very late. And then finally she did not come in at all.

Rat Kiley heard about it from Fossie himself. Before dawn one morning, the kid shook him awake. He was in bad shape. His voice seemed hollow and stuffed up, nasal-sounding, as if he had a bad cold. He held a flashlight in his hand, clicking it on and off.

"Mary Anne, he whispered, "I can't *find* her."

Rat sat up and rubbed his face. Even in the dim light it was clear that the boy was in trouble. There were dark smudges under his eyes, the frayed edges of somebody who hadn't slept in a while.

"Gone," Fossie said. "Rat, listen, she's sleeping with somebody. Last night, she didn't even . . . I don't know what to *do*."

Abruptly then, Fossie seemed to collapse. He squatted down, rocking on his heels, still clutching the flashlight. Just a boy—eighteen years old. Tall and blond. A gifted athlete. A nice kid, too, polite and good-hearted, although for the moment none of it seemed to be serving him well.

He kept clicking the flashlight on and off.

"All right, start at the start," Rat said. "Nice and slow. Sleeping with who?"

"I don't know who. Eddie Diamond."

"Eddie?"

"Has to be. The guy's always there, always hanging on her."

Rat shook his head. "Man, I don't know. Can't say it strikes a right note, not with Eddie."

"Yes, but he's—"

"Easy does it," Rat said. He reached out and tapped the boy's shoulder. "Why not just check some bunks? We got nine guys. You and me, that's two, so there's seven possibles. Do a quick body count."

Fossie hesitated. "But I can't . . . If she's there, I mean, if she's with somebody—"

"Oh, Christ."

Rat pushed himself up. He took the flashlight, muttered something, and moved down to the far end of the hootch. For privacy, the men had rigged up curtained walls around their cots, small makeshift bedrooms, and in the dark Rat went quickly from room to room, using the flashlight to pluck out the faces. Eddie Diamond slept a hard deep sleep—the others, too. To be sure, though, Rat checked once more, very carefully, then he reported back to Fossie.

"All accounted for. No extras."

"Eddie?"

"Darvon dreams." Rat switched off the flashlight and tried to think it out. "Maybe she just—I don't know—maybe she camped out tonight. Under the stars or something. You search the compound?"

"Sure I did."

"Well, come on," Rat said. "One more time."

Outside, a soft violet light was spreading out across the eastern hillsides. Two or three ARVN soldiers had built their breakfast fires, but the place was mostly quiet and unmoving. They tried the helipad first, then the mess hall and supply hootches, then they walked the entire six hundred meters of perimeter.

"Okay," Rat finally said. "We got a problem."

When he first told the story, Rat stopped there and looked at Mitchell Sanders for a time.

"So what's your vote? Where was she?"

"The Greenies," Sanders said.

"Yeah?"

Sanders smiled. "No other option. That stuff about the Special Forces—how they used the place as a base of operations, how they'd glide in and out—all that had to be there for a *reason*. That's how stories work, man."

Rat thought about it, then shrugged.

"All right, sure, the Greenies. But it's not what Fossie thought. She wasn't sleeping with any of them. At least not exactly. I mean, in a way she was sleeping with *all* of them, more or less, except it wasn't sex or anything. They was just lying together, so to speak, Mary Anne and these six grungy weirded-out Green Berets."

"Lying down?" Sanders said.

"You got it."

"Lying down how?"

Rat smiled. "Ambush. All night long, man, Mary Anne's out on fuckin' *ambush*."

Just after sunrise, Rat said, she came trooping in through the wire, tired-looking but cheerful as she dropped her gear and gave Mark Fossie a brisk hug. The six Green Berets did not speak. One of them nodded at her, and the others gave Fossie a long stare, then they filed off to their hootch at the edge of the compound.

"Please," she said. "Not a word."

Fossie took a half step forward and hesitated. It was as though he had trouble recognizing her. She wore a bush hat and filthy green fatigues; she carried the standard M-16 automatic assault rifle; her face was black with charcoal.

Mary Anne handed him the weapon. "I'm exhausted," she said. "We'll talk later."

She glanced over at the Special Forces area, then turned and walked quickly across the compound toward her own bunker. Fossie stood still for a few seconds. A little dazed, it seemed. After a moment, though, he set his jaw and whispered something and went after her with a hard, fast stride.

"Not later!" he yelled. "Now!"

What happened between them, Rat said, nobody ever knew for sure. But in the mess hall that evening it was clear that an accommodation had been reached. Or more likely, he said, it was a case of setting down some new rules. Mary Anne's hair was freshly shampooed. She wore a white blouse, a navy blue skirt, a pair of plain black flats. Over dinner she kept her eyes down, poking at her food, subdued to the point of silence. Eddie Diamond and some of the others tried to nudge her into talking about the ambush—What was the feeling out there? What exactly did she see and hear?—but the questions seemed to give her trouble. Nervously, she'd look across the table at Fossie. She'd wait a moment, as if to receive some sort of clearance, then she'd bow her head and mumble out a vague word or two. There were no real answers.

Mark Fossie, too, had little to say.

"Nobody's business," he told Rat that night. Then he offered a brief smile. "One thing for sure, though, there won't be any more ambushes. No more late nights."

"You laid down the law?"

"Compromise," Fossie said. "I'll put it this way—we're officially engaged."

Rat nodded cautiously.

"Well hey, she'll make a sweet bride," he said. "Combat ready."

Over the next several days there was a strained, tightly wound quality to the way they treated each other, a rigid correctness that was enforced by repetitive acts of willpower. To look at them from a distance, Rat said, you would think they were the happiest two people on the planet. They spent the long afternoons sunbathing together, stretched out side by side on top of their bunker, or playing backgammon in the shade of a giant palm tree, or just sitting quietly. A model of togetherness, it seemed. And yet at close range their faces showed the tension. Too polite, too thoughtful. Mark Fossie tried hard to keep up a self-assured pose, as if nothing had ever come between them, or ever could, but there was a fragility to it, something tentative and false. If Mary Anne happened to move a few steps away from him, even briefly, he'd tighten up and force himself not to watch her. But then a moment later he'd be watching.

In the presence of others, at least, they kept on their masks. Over meals they talked about plans for a huge wedding in Cleveland Heights—a two-day bash, lots of flowers. And yet even then their smiles seemed too intense. They were too quick with their banter; they held hands as if afraid to let go.

It had to end, and eventually it did.

Near the end of the third week Fossie began making arrangements to send her home. At first, Rat said, Mary Anne seemed to accept it, but then after a day or two she fell into a restless gloom, sitting off by herself at the edge of the perimeter. She would not speak. Shoulders hunched, her blue eyes opaque, she seemed to disappear inside herself. A couple of times Fossie approached her and tried to talk it out, but Mary Anne just stared out at the dark green mountains to the west. The wilderness seemed to draw her in. A haunted look, Rat said—partly terror, partly rapture. It was as if she had come up on the edge of something, as if she were caught in that no-man's-land between Cleveland Heights and deep jungle. Seventeen years old. Just a child, blond and innocent, but then weren't they all?

The next morning she was gone. The six Greenies were gone, too.

In a way, Rat said, poor Fossie expected it, or something like it, but that did not help much with the pain. The kid couldn't function. The grief took him by the throat and squeezed and would not let go.

"Lost," he kept whispering.

•   •   •

It was nearly three weeks before she returned. But in a sense she never returned. Not entirely, not all of her.

By chance, Rat said, he was awake to see it. A damp misty night, he couldn't sleep, so he'd gone outside for a quick smoke. He was just standing there, he said, watching the moon, and then off to the west a column of silhouettes appeared as if by magic at the edge of the jungle. At first he didn't recognize her—a small, soft shadow among six other shadows. There was no sound. No real substance either. The seven silhouettes seemed to float across the surface of the earth, like spirits, vaporous and unreal. As he watched, Rat said, it made him think of some weird opium dream. The silhouettes moved without moving. Silently, one by one, they came up the hill, passed through the wire, and drifted in a loose file across the compound. It was then, Rat said, that he picked out Mary Anne's face. Her eyes seemed to shine in the dark—not blue, though, but a bright glowing jungle green. She did not pause at Fossie's bunker. She cradled her weapon and moved swiftly to the Special Forces hootch and followed the others inside.

Briefly, a light came on, and someone laughed, then the place went dark again.

Whenever he told the story, Rat had a tendency to stop now and then, interrupting the flow, inserting little clarifications or bits of analysis and personal opinion. It was a bad habit, Mitchell Sanders said, because all that matters is the raw material, the stuff itself, and you can't clutter it up with your own half-baked commentary. That just breaks the spell. It destroys the magic. What you have to do, Sanders said, is trust your own story. Get the hell out of the way and let it tell itself.

But Rat Kiley couldn't help it. He wanted to bracket the full range of meaning.

"I know it sounds far-out," he'd tell us, "but it's not like *impossible* or anything. We all heard plenty of wackier stories. Some guy comes back from the bush, tells you he saw the Virgin Mary out there, she was riding a goddamn goose or something. Everybody buys it. Everybody smiles and asks how fast was they going, did she have spurs on. Well, it's not like that. This Mary Anne wasn't no virgin but at least she was real. I saw it. When she came in through the wire that night, I was right there, I saw those eyes of hers, I saw how she wasn't even the same person no more. What's so impossible about that? She was a girl, that's all. I mean, if it was a guy, everybody'd say, Hey, no big deal, he got caught up in the Nam shit, he got seduced by the Greenies. See what I mean? You got these blinders on about women. How gentle and peaceful they are. All that crap about how if we had a pussy for president there wouldn't be no more wars. Pure garbage. You got to get rid of that sexist attitude."

Rat would go on like that until Mitchell Sanders couldn't tolerate it any longer. It offended his inner ear.

"The story," Sanders would say. "The whole tone, man, you're wrecking it."

"Tone?"

"The *sound*. You need to get a consistent sound, like slow or fast, funny or sad. All these digressions, they just screw up your story's *sound*. Stick to what happened."

Frowning, Rat would close his eyes.

"Tone?" he'd say. "I didn't know it was all that complicated. The girl joined the zoo. One more animal—end of story."

"Yeah, fine. But tell it right."

A t daybreak the next morning, when Mark Fossie heard she was back, he stationed himself outside the fenced-off Special Forces area. All morning he waited for her, and all afternoon. Around dusk Rat brought him something to eat.

"She has to come out," Fossie said. "Sooner or later, she has to."

"Or else what?" Rat said.

"I go get her. I bring her out."

Rat shook his head. "Your decision. I was you, though, no way I'd mess around with any Greenie types, not for nothing."

"It's Mary Anne in there."

"Sure, I know that. All the same, I'd knock real extra super polite."

Even with the cooling night air Fossie's face was slick with sweat. He looked sick. His eyes were bloodshot; his skin had a whitish, almost colorless cast. For a few minutes Rat waited with him, quietly watching the hootch, then he patted the kid's shoulder and left him alone.

It was after midnight when Rat and Eddie Diamond went out to check on him. The night had gone cold and steamy, a low fog sliding down from the mountains, and somewhere out in the dark they heard music playing. Not loud but not soft either. It had a chaotic, almost unmusical sound, without rhythm or form or progression, like the noise of nature. A synthesizer, it seemed, or maybe an electric organ. In the background, just audible, a woman's voice was half singing, half chanting, but the lyrics seemed to be in a foreign tongue.

They found Fossie squatting near the gate in front of the Special Forces area. Head bowed, he was swaying to the music, his face wet and shiny.

As Eddie bent down beside him, the kid looked up with dull eyes, ashen and powdery, not quite in register.

"Hear that?" he whispered. "You *hear*? It's Mary Anne."

Eddie Diamond took his arm. "Let's get you inside. Somebody's radio, that's all it is. Move it now."

"Mary Anne. Just listen."

"Sure, but—"

"Listen!"

Fossie suddenly pulled away, twisting sideways, and fell back against the gate. He lay there with his eyes closed. The music—the noise, whatever it was—came from the hootch beyond the fence. The place was dark except for a small glowing window, which stood partly open, the panes dancing in bright reds and yellows as though the glass were on fire. The chanting seemed louder now. Fiercer, too, and higher pitched.

Fossie pushed himself up. He wavered for a moment then forced the gate open.

"That voice," he said. "Mary Anne."

Rat took a step forward, reaching out for him, but Fossie was already moving fast toward the hootch. He stumbled once, caught himself, and hit the door hard with both arms. There was a noise—a short screeching sound, like a cat—and the door swung in and Fossie was framed there for an instant, his arms stretched out, then he slipped inside. After a moment Rat and Eddie followed quietly. Just inside the door they found Fossie bent down on one knee. He wasn't moving.

Across the room a dozen candles were burning on the floor near the open window. The place seemed to echo with a weird deep-wilderness sound—tribal music—bamboo flutes and drums and chimes. But what hit you first, Rat said, was the smell. Two kinds of smells. There was a topmost scent of joss sticks and incense, like the fumes of some exotic smokehouse, but beneath the smoke lay a deeper and much more powerful stench. Impossible to describe, Rat said. It paralyzed your lungs. Thick and numbing, like an animal's den, a mix of blood and scorched hair and excrement and the sweet-sour odor of moldering flesh—the stink of the kill. But that wasn't all. On a post at the rear of the hootch was the decayed head of a large black leopard; strips of yellow-brown skin dangled from the overhead rafters. And bones. Stacks of bones—all kinds. To one side, propped up against a wall, stood a poster in neat black lettering: ASSEMBLE YOUR OWN GOOK!! FREE SAMPLE KIT!! The images came in a swirl, Rat said, and there was no way you could process it all. Off in the gloom a few dim figures lounged in hammocks, or on cots, but none of them moved or spoke. The background music came from a tape deck near the circle of candles, but the high voice was Mary Anne's.

After a second Mark Fossie made a soft moaning sound. He started to get up but then stiffened.

"Mary Anne?" he said.

Quietly then, she stepped out of the shadows. At least for a moment she seemed to be the same pretty young girl who had arrived a few weeks earlier. She was barefoot. She wore her pink sweater and a white blouse and a simple cotton skirt.

For a long while the girl gazed down at Fossie, almost blankly, and in the candlelight her face had the composure of someone perfectly at peace with herself. It took a few seconds, Rat said, to appreciate the full change. In part it was her eyes: utterly flat and indifferent. There was no emotion in her stare, no sense of the person behind it. But the grotesque part, he said, was her jewelry. At the girl's throat was a necklace of human tongues. Elongated and narrow, like pieces of blackened leather, the tongues were threaded along a length of copper wire, one overlapping the next, the tips curled upward as if caught in a final shrill syllable.

Briefly, it seemed, the girl smiled at Mark Fossie.

"There's no sense talking," she said. "I know what you think, but it's not . . . it's not *bad*."

"Bad?" Fossie murmured.

"It's not."

In the shadows there was laughter.

One of the Greenies sat up and lighted a cigar. The others lay silent.

"You're in a place," Mary Anne said softly, "where you don't belong."

She moved her hand in a gesture that encompassed not just the hootch but everything around it, the entire war, the mountains, the mean little villages, the trails and trees and rivers and deep misted-over valleys.

"You just don't *know*," she said. "You hide in this little fortress, behind wire and sandbags, and you don't know what it's all about. Sometimes I want to *eat* this place. Vietnam. I want to swallow the whole country—the dirt, the death—I just want to eat it and have it there inside me. That's how I feel. It's like . . . this appetite. I get scared sometimes—lots of times—but it's not *bad*. You know? I feel close to myself. When I'm out there at night, I feel close to my own body, I can feel my blood moving, my skin and my fingernails, everything, it's like I'm full of electricity and I'm glowing in the dark—I'm on fire almost—I'm burning away into nothing—but it doesn't matter because I know exactly who I am. You can't feel like that anywhere else."

All this was said softly, as if to herself, her voice slow and impassive. She was not trying to persuade. For a few moments she looked at Mark Fossie, who seemed to shrink away, then she turned and moved back into the gloom.

There was nothing to be done.

Rat took Fossie's arm, helped him up, and led him outside. In the darkness there was that weird tribal music, which seemed to come from the earth itself, from the deep rain forest, and a woman's voice rising up in a language beyond translation.

Mark Fossie stood rigid.

"Do something," he whispered. "I can't just let her go like that."

Rat listened for a time, then shook his head.

"Man, you must be deaf. She's already gone."

Rat Kiley stopped there, almost in midsentence, which drove Mitchell Sanders crazy.

"What next?" he said.

"Next?"

"The girl. What happened to her?"

Rat made a small, tired motion with his shoulders. "Hard to tell for sure. Maybe three, four days later I got orders to report here to Alpha Company. Jumped the first chopper out, that's the last I ever seen of the place. Mary Anne, too."

Mitchell Sanders stared at him.

"You can't do that."

"Do what?"

"Jesus Christ, it's against the *rules*," Sanders said. "Against human *nature*. This elaborate story, you can't say, Hey, by the way, I don't know the *ending*. I mean, you got certain obligations."

Rat gave a quick smile. "Patience, man. Up to now, everything I told you is from personal experience, the exact truth, but there's a few other things I heard secondhand. Thirdhand, actually. From here on it gets to be . . . I don't know what the word is."

"Speculation."

"Yeah, right." Rat looked off to the west, scanning the mountains, as if expecting something to appear on one of the high ridgelines. After a second he shrugged. "Anyhow, maybe two months later I ran into Eddie Diamond over in Bangkok—I was on R&R, just this fluke thing—and he told me some stuff I can't vouch for with my own eyes. Even Eddie didn't really see it. He heard it from one of the Greenies, so you got to take this with a whole shakerful of salt."

Once more, Rat searched the mountains, then he sat back and closed his eyes.

"You know," he said abruptly, "I loved her."

"Say again?"

"A lot. We all did, I guess. The way she looked, Mary Anne made you think about those girls back home, how clean and innocent they all are, how they'll never understand any of this, not in a billion years. Try to tell them about it, they'll just stare at you with those big round candy eyes. They won't understand zip. It's like trying to tell somebody what chocolate tastes like."

Mitchell Sanders nodded. "Or shit."

"There it is, you got to taste it, and that's the thing with Mary Anne. She was *there*. She was up to her eyeballs in it. After the war, man, I promise you, you won't find nobody like her."

Suddenly, Rat pushed up to his feet, moved a few steps away from us, then stopped and stood with his back turned. He was an emotional guy.

"Got hooked, I guess," he said. "I loved her. So when I heard from Eddie about what happened, it almost made me . . . Like you say, it's pure speculation."

"Go on," Mitchell Sanders said. "Finish up."

What happened to her, Rat said, was what happened to all of them. You come over clean and you get dirty and then afterward it's never the same. A question of degree. Some make it intact, some don't make it at all. For Mary Anne Bell, it seemed, Vietnam had the effect of a powerful drug: that mix of unnamed terror and unnamed pleasure that comes as the needle slips in and you know you're risking something. The endorphins start to flow, and the adrenaline, and you hold your breath and creep quietly through the moonlit nightscapes; you become intimate with danger; you're in touch with the far side of yourself, as though it's another hemisphere, and you want to string it out and go wherever the trip takes you and be host to all the possibilities inside yourself. Not *bad*, she'd said. Vietnam made her glow in the dark. She wanted more, she wanted to penetrate deeper into the mystery of herself, and after a time the wanting became needing, which turned then to craving.

According to Eddie Diamond, who heard it from one of the Greenies, she took a greedy pleasure in night patrols. She was good at it; she had the moves. All camouflaged up, her face smooth and vacant, she seemed to flow like water through the dark, like oil, without sound or center. She went barefoot. She stopped carrying a weapon. There were times, apparently, when she took crazy, death-wish chances—things that even the Greenies balked at. It was as if she were taunting some wild creature out in the bush, or in her head, inviting it to show itself, a curious game of hide-and-go-seek that was played out in the dense terrain of a nightmare. She was lost inside herself. On occasion, when they were taken under fire, Mary Anne would stand quietly and watch the tracer rounds snap by, a little smile at her lips, intent on some private transaction with the war. Other times she would simply vanish altogether—for hours, for days.

And then one morning, all alone, Mary Anne walked off into the mountains and did not come back.

No body was ever found. No equipment, no clothing. For all he knew, Rat said, the girl was still alive. Maybe up in one of the high mountain villes, maybe with the Montagnard tribes. But that was guesswork.

There was an inquiry, of course, and a week-long air search, and for a time the Tra Bong compound went crazy with MP and CID types. In the end, however, nothing came of it. It was a war and the war went on. Mark Fossie was busted to PFC, shipped back to a hospital in the States, and two months later received a medical discharge. Mary Anne Bell joined the missing.

But the story did not end there. If you believed the Greenies, Rat said, Mary Anne was still somewhere out there in the dark. Odd movements, odd shapes. Late at night, when the Greenies were out on ambush, the whole rain forest seemed to stare in at them—a watched feeling—and a couple of times they almost saw her sliding through the shadows. Not quite, but almost. She had crossed to the other side. She was part of the land. She was wearing her culottes, her pink sweater, and a necklace of human tongues. She was dangerous. She was ready for the kill.

Revelation (1964)

Flannery O'Connor

The doctor's waiting room, which was very small, was almost full when the Turpins entered and Mrs. Turpin, who was very large, made it look even smaller by her presence. She stood looming at the head of the magazine table set in the center of it, a living demonstration that the room was inadequate and ridiculous. Her little bright black eyes took in all the patients as she sized up the seating situation. There was one vacant chair and a place on the sofa occupied by a blond child in a dirty blue romper who should have been told to move over and make room for the lady. He was five or six, but Mrs. Turpin saw at once that no one was going to tell him to move over. He was slumped down in the seat, his arms idle at his sides and his eyes idle in his head; his nose ran unchecked.

Mrs. Turpin put a firm hand on Claud's shoulder and said in a voice that included anyone who wanted to listen, "Claud, you sit in that chair there," and gave him a push down into the vacant one. Claud was florid and bald and sturdy, somewhat shorter than Mrs. Turpin, but he sat down as if he were accustomed to doing what she told him to.

Mrs. Turpin remained standing. The only man in the room besides Claud was a lean stringy old fellow with a rusty hand spread out on each knee, whose eyes were closed as if he were asleep or dead or pretending to be so as not to get up and offer his seat. Her gaze settled agreeably on a well-dressed gray-haired lady whose eyes met hers and whose expression said: if that child belonged to me, he would have some manners and move over—there's plenty of room there for you and him too.

Claud looked up with a sigh and made as if to rise.

"Sit down," Mrs. Turpin said. "You know you're not supposed to stand on that leg. He has an ulcer on his leg," she explained.

Claud lifted his foot onto the magazine table and rolled his trouser leg up to reveal a purple swelling on a plump marble-white calf.

"My!" the pleasant lady said. "How did you do that?"

"A cow kicked him," Mrs. Turpin said.

"Goodness!" said the lady.

Claud rolled his trouser leg down.

"Maybe the little boy would move over," the lady suggested, but the child did not stir.

"Somebody will be leaving in a minute," Mrs. Turpin said. She could not understand why a doctor—with as much money as they made charging five dollars a day to just stick their head in the hospital door and look at you—couldn't afford a decent-sized waiting room. This one was hardly bigger than a garage. The table was cluttered with limp-looking magazines and at one end of it there was a big green glass ash tray full of cigarette butts and cotton wads with little blood spots on them. If she had had anything to do with the running of the place, that would have been emptied every so often. There were no chairs against the wall at the head of the room. It had a rectangular-shaped panel in it that permitted a view of the office where the nurse came and went and the secretary listened to the radio. A plastic fern in a gold pot sat in the opening and trailed its fronds down almost to the floor. The radio was softly playing gospel music.

Just then the inner door opened and a nurse with the highest stack of yellow hair Mrs. Turpin had ever seen put her face in the crack and called for the next patient. The woman sitting beside Claud grasped the two arms of her chair and hoisted herself up; she pulled her dress free from her legs and lumbered through the door where the nurse had disappeared.

Mrs. Turpin eased into the vacant chair, which held her tight as a corset. "I wish I could reduce," she said, and rolled her eyes and gave a comic sigh.

"Oh, you aren't fat," the stylish lady said.

"Oooooh, I am too," Mrs. Turpin said. "Claud he eats all he wants to and never weighs over one hundred and seventy-five pounds, but me I just look at something good to eat and I gain some weight," and her stomach and shoulders shook with laughter. "You can eat all you want to, can't you, Claud?" she asked, turning to him.

Claud only grinned.

"Well, as long as you have such a good disposition," the stylish lady said, "I don't think it makes a bit of difference what size you are. You just can't beat a good disposition."

Next to her was a fat girl of eighteen or nineteen, scowling into a thick blue book which Mrs. Turpin saw was entitled Human Development.

The girl raised her head and directed her scowl at Mrs. Turpin as if she did not like her looks. She appeared annoyed that anyone should speak while she tried to read. The poor girl's face was blue with acne and Mrs. Turpin thought how pitiful it was to have a face like that at that age. She gave the girl a friendly smile but the girl only scowled harder. Mrs. Turpin herself was fat but she had always had good skin, and, though she was forty-seven years old, there was not a wrinkle in her face except around her eyes from laughing too much.

Next to the ugly girl was the child, still in exactly the same position, and next to him was a thin leathery old woman in a cotton print dress. She and Claud had three sacks of chicken feed in their pump house that was in the same print. She had seen from the first that the child belonged with the old woman. She could tell by the way they sat—kind of vacant and white-trashy, as if they would sit there until Doomsday if nobody called and told them to get up. And at right angles but next to the well-dressed pleasant lady was a lank-faced woman who was certainly the child's mother. She had on a yellow sweatshirt and wine colored slacks, both gritty-looking, and the rims of her lips were stained with snuff. Her dirty yellow hair was tied behind with a little piece of red paper ribbon. Worse than niggers any day, Mrs. Turpin thought.

The gospel hymn playing was, "When I looked up and He looked down," and Mrs. Turpin, who knew it, supplied the last line mentally, "And wona these days I know I'll wear a crown."

Without appearing to, Mrs. Turpin always noticed people's feet. The well-dressed lady had on red and gray suede shoes to match her dress. Mrs. Turpin had on her good black patent leather pumps. The ugly girl had on Girl Scout shoes and heavy socks. The old woman had on tennis shoes and the white-trashy mother had on what appeared to be bedroom slippers, black straw with gold braid threaded through them—exactly what you would have expected her to have on.

Sometimes at night when she couldn't go to sleep, Mrs. Turpin would occupy herself with the question of who she would have chosen to be if she couldn't have been herself. If Jesus had said to her before he made her, "There's only two places available for you. You can either be a nigger or white-trash," what would she have said? "Please, Jesus, please," she would have said, "just let me wait until there's another place available," and he would have said, "No, you have to go right now and I have only those two places so make up your mind." She would have wiggled and squirmed and begged and pleaded but it would have been no use and finally she would have said, "All right, make me a nigger then—but that don't mean a trash one." And he would have made her a neat clean respectable Negro woman, herself but black.

Next to the child's mother was a red-headed youngish woman, reading one of the magazines and working a piece of chewing gum, hell for leather, as Claud would say. Mrs. Turpin could not see the woman's feet. She was not white-trash, just common. Sometimes Mrs. Turpin occupied herself at night naming the classes of people. On the bottom of the heap were most colored people, not the kind she would have been if she had been one, but most of them; then next to them—not above, just away from—were the white-trash; then above them were the home-owners, and above them the home-and-land-owners, to which she and Claud belonged. Above she and Claud were people with a lot of money and much bigger houses and much more land. But here the complexity of it would begin to bear in on her, for some of the people with a lot of money were common and ought to be below she and Claud and some of the people who had good blood had lost their money and had to rent and then there were colored people who owned their homes and land as well. There was a colored dentist in town who had two red Lincolns and a swimming pool and a farm with registered white-face cattle on it. Usually by the time she had fallen asleep all the classes of people were moiling and roiling around in her head, and she would dream they were all crammed in together in a box car, being ridden off to be put in a gas oven.

"That's a beautiful clock," she said and nodded to her right. It was a big wall clock, the face encased in a grass sunburst.

"Yes, it's very pretty," the stylish lady said agreeably. "And right on the dot too," she added, glancing at her watch.

The ugly girl beside her cast an eye upward at the clock, smirked, then looked directly at Mrs. Turpin and smirked again. Then she returned her eyes to her book. She was obviously the lady's daughter because, although they didn't look anything alike as to disposition, they both had the same shape of face and the same blue eyes. On the lady they sparkled pleasantly but in the girl's seared face they appeared alternately to smolder and to blaze.

What if Jesus had said, "All right, you can be white-trash or a nigger or ugly!"

Mrs. Turpin felt an awful pity for the girl, though she thought it was one thing to be ugly and another to act ugly.

The woman with the snuff-stained lips turned around in her chair and looked up at the clock. Then she turned back and appeared to look a little to the side of Mrs. Turpin. There was a cast in one of her eyes. "You want to know wher you can get you one of themther clocks?" she asked in a loud voice.

"No, I already have a nice clock," Mrs. Turpin said. Once somebody like her got a leg in the conversation, she would be all over it.

"You can get you one with green stamps," the woman said. "That's most likely wher he got hisn. Save you up enough, you can get you most anythang. I got me some joo'ry."

Ought to have got you a wash rag and some soap, Mrs. Turpin thought.

"I get contour sheets with mine," the pleasant lady said.

The daughter slammed her book shut. She looked straight in front of her, directly through Mrs. Turpin and on through the yellow curtain and the plate glass window which made the wall behind her. The girl's eyes seemed lit all of a sudden with a peculiar light, an unnatural light like night road signs give. Mrs. Turpin turned her head to see if there was anything going on outside that she should see, but she could not see anything. Figures passing cast only a pale shadow through the curtain. There was no reason the girl should single her out for her ugly looks.

"Miss Finley," the nurse said, cracking the door. The gum-chewing woman got up and passed in front of her and Claud and went into the office. She had on red high-heeled shoes.

Directly across the table, the ugly girl's eyes were fixed on Mrs. Turpin as if she had some very special reason for disliking her.

"This is wonderful weather, isn't it?" the girl's mother said.

"It's good weather for cotton if you can get the niggers to pick it," Mrs. Turpin said, "but niggers don't want to pick cotton any more. You can't get the white folks to pick it and now you can't get the niggers—because they got to be right up there with the white folks."

"They gonna try anyways," the white-trash woman said, leaning forward.

"Do you have one of the cotton-picking machines?" the pleasant lady asked.

"No," Mrs. Turpin said, "they leave half the cotton in the field. We don't have much cotton anyway. If you want to make it farming now, you have to have a little of everything. We got a couple of acres of cotton and a few hogs and chickens and just enough white-face that Claud can look after them himself."

"One thang I don't want," the white-trash woman said, wiping her mouth with the back of her hand. "Hogs. Nasty stinking things, a-gruntin and a-rootin all over the place."

Mrs. Turpin gave her the merest edge of her attention. "Our hogs are not dirty and they don't stink," she said. "They're cleaner than some children I've seen. Their feet never touch the ground. We have a pig-parlor—that's where you raise them on concrete," she explained to the pleasant lady, "and Claud scoots them down with the hose every afternoon and washes off the floor." Cleaner by far than that child right there, she thought. Poor nasty little thing. He had not moved except to put the thumb of his dirty hand into his mouth.

The woman turned her face away from Mrs. Turpin. "I know I wouldn't scoot down no hog with no hose," she said to the wall.

You wouldn't have no hog to scoot down, Mrs. Turpin said to herself.

"A-gruntin and a-rootin and a-groanin," the woman muttered.

"We got a little of everything," Mrs. Turpin said to the pleasant lady. "It's no use in having more than you can handle yourself with help like it is. We found enough niggers to pick our cotton this year but Claud he has to go after them and take them home again in the evening. They can't walk that half a mile. No they can't. I tell you," she said and laughed merrily, "I sure am tired of buttering up niggers, but you got to love em if you want em to work for you. When they come in the morning, I run out and I say, 'Hi yawl this morning' and when Claud drives them off to the field I just wave to beat the band and they just wave back." And she waved her hand rapidly to illustrate.

"Like you read out of the same book," the lady said, showing she understood perfectly.

"Child, yes," Mrs. Turpin said. "And when they come in from the field, I run out with a bucket of icewater. That's the way it's going to be from now on," she said. "You may as well face it."

"One thang I know," the white-trash woman said. "Two thangs I ain't going to do: love no niggers or scoot down no hog with no hose." And she let out a bark of contempt.

The look that Mrs. Turpin and the pleasant lady exchanged indicated they both understood that you had to have certain things before you could know certain things. But every time Mrs. Turpin exchanged a look with the lady, she was aware that the ugly girl's peculiar eyes were still on her, and she had trouble bringing her attention back to the conversation.

"When you got something," she said, "you got to look after it." And when you ain't got a thing but breath and britches, she added to herself, you can afford to come to town every morning and just sit on the Court House coping and spit.

A grotesque revolving shadow passed across the curtain behind her and was thrown palely on the opposite wall. Then a bicycle clattered down against the outside of the building. The door opened and a colored boy glided in with a tray from the drugstore. It had two large red and white paper cups on it with tops on them. He was a tall, very black boy in discolored white pants and a green nylon shirt. He was chewing gum slowly, as if to music. He set the tray down in the office opening next to the fern and stuck his head through to look for the secretary. She was not in there. He rested his arms on the ledge and waited, his narrow bottom stuck out, swaying to the left and right. He raised a hand over his head and scratched the base of his skull.

"You see that button there, boy?" Mrs. Turpin said. "You can punch that and she'll come. She's probably in the back somewhere."

"Is that right?" the boy said agreeably, as if he had never seen the button before. He leaned to the right and put his finger on it. "She sometime out," he said and twisted around to face his audience, his elbows behind him on the counter. The nurse appeared and he twisted back again. She handed him a dollar and he rooted in his pocket and made the change and counted it back to her. She gave him fifteen cents for a tip and he went out with the empty tray. The heavy door swung to slowly and closed at length with the sound of suction. For a moment no one spoke.

"They ought to send all them niggers back to Africa," the white-trash woman said. "That's wher they come from in the first place."

"Oh, I couldn't do without my good colored friends," the pleasant lady said.

"There's a heap of things worse than a nigger," Mrs. Turpin agreed. "It's all kinds of them just like it's all kinds of us."

"Yes, and it takes all kinds to make the world go round," the lady said in her musical voice.

As she said it, the raw-complexioned girl snapped her teeth together. Her lower lip turned downwards and inside out, revealing the pale pink inside of her mouth. After a second it rolled back up. It was the ugliest face Mrs. Turpin had ever seen anyone make and for a moment she was certain that the girl had made it at her. She was looking at her as if she had known and disliked her all her life—all of Mrs. Turpin's life, it seemed too, not just all the girl's life. Why, girl, I don't even know you, Mrs. Turpin said silently.

She forced her attention back to the discussion. "It wouldn't be practical to send them back to Africa," she said. "They wouldn't want to go. They got it too good here."

"Wouldn't be what they wanted—if I had anythang to do with it," the woman said.

"It wouldn't be a way in the world you could get all the niggers back over there," Mrs. Turpin said. "They'd be hiding out and lying down and turning sick on you and wailing and hollering and raring and pitching. It wouldn't be a way in the world to get them over there."

"They got over here," the trashy woman said. "Get back like they got over."

"It wasn't so many of them then," Mrs. Turpin explained.

The woman looked at Mrs. Turpin as if here was an idiot indeed but Mrs. Turpin was not bothered by the look, considering where it came from.

"Nooo," she said, "they're going to stay here where they can go to New York and marry white folks and improve their color. That's what they all want to do, every one of them, improve their color."

"You know what comes of that, don't you?" Claud asked.

"No, Claud, what?" Mrs. Turpin said.

Claud's eyes twinkled. "White-faced niggers," he said with never a smile.

Everybody in the office laughed except the white-trash and the ugly girl. The girl gripped the book in her lap with white fingers. The trashy woman looked around her from face to face as if she thought they were all idiots. The old woman in the feed sack dress continued to gaze expressionless across the floor at the high-top shoes of the man opposite her, the one who had been pretending to be asleep when the Turpins came in. He was laughing heartily, his hands still spread out on his knees. The child had fallen to the side and was lying now almost face down in the old woman's lap.

While they recovered from their laughter, the nasal chorus on the radio kept the room from silence.

"You go to blank blank
And I'll go to mine
But we'll all blank along
To-geth-ther,
And all along the blank
We'll help eachother out
Smile-ling in any kind of
Weath-ther!"

Mrs. Turpin didn't catch every word but she caught enough to agree with the spirit of the song and it turned her thoughts sober. To help anybody out that needed it was her philosophy of life. She never spared herself when she found somebody in need, whether they were white or black, trash or decent. And of all she had to be thankful for, she was most thankful that this was so. If Jesus had said, "You can be high society and have all the money you want and be thin and svelte-like, but you can't be a good woman with it," she would have had to say, "Well don't make me that then. Make me a good woman and it don't matter what else, how fat or how ugly or how poor!" Her heart rose. He had not made her a nigger or white-trash or ugly! He had made her herself and given her a little of everything. Jesus, thank you! she said. Thank you thank you thank you! Whenever she counted her blessings she felt as buoyant as if she weighed one hundred and twenty-five pounds instead of one hundred and eighty.

"What's wrong with your little boy?" the pleasant lady asked the white-trashy woman.

"He has an ulcer," the woman said proudly. "He ain't give me a minute's peace since he was born. Him and her are just alike," she said, nodding at the old woman, who was running her leathery fingers through the child's pale hair. "Look like I can't get nothing down them two but Co' Cola and candy."

That's all you try to get down em, Mrs. Turpin said to herself. Too lazy to light a fire. There was nothing you could tell her about people like them that she didn't know already. And it was not just that they didn't have anything. Because if you gave them everything, in two weeks it would all be broken or filthy or they would have chopped it up for lightwood. She knew all this from her own experience. Help them you must, but help them you couldn't.

All at once the ugly girl turned her lips inside out again. Her eyes fixed like two drills on Mrs. Turpin. This time there was no mistaking that there was something urgent behind them.

Girl, Mrs. Turpin exclaimed silently, I haven't done a thing to you! The girl might be confusing her with somebody else. There was no need to sit by and let herself be intimidated. "You must be in college," she said boldly, looking directly at the girl. "I see you reading a book there."

The girl continued to stare and pointedly did not answer.

Her mother blushed at this rudeness. "The lady asked you a question, Mary Grace," she said under her breath.

"I have ears," Mary Grace said.

The poor mother blushed again. "Mary Grace goes to Wellesley College," she explained. She twisted one of the buttons on her dress. "In Massachusetts," she added with a grimace. "And in the summer she just keeps right on studying. Just reads all the time, a real book worm. She's done real well at Wellesley; she's taking English and Math and History and Psychology and Social Studies," she rattled on, "and I think it's too much. I think she ought to get out and have fun."

The girl looked as if she would like to hurl them all through the plate glass window.

"Way up north," Mrs. Turpin murmured and thought, well, it hasn't done much for her manners.

"I'd almost rather to have him sick," the white-trash woman said, wrenching the attention back to herself. "He's so mean when he ain't. Look like some children just take natural to meanness. It's some gets bad when they get sick but he was the opposite. Took sick and turned good. He don't give me no trouble now. It's me waitin to see the doctor," she said.

If I was going to send anybody back to Africa, Mrs. Turpin thought, it would be your kind, woman. "Yes, indeed," she said aloud, but looking up at the ceiling, "it's a heap of things worse than a nigger." And dirtier than a hog, she added to herself.

"I think people with bad dispositions are more to be pitied than anyone on earth," the pleasant lady said in a voice that was decidedly thin.

"I thank the Lord he has blessed me with a good one," Mrs. Turpin said. "The day has never dawned that I couldn't find something to laugh at."

"Not since she married me anyways," Claud said with a comical straight face.

Everybody laughed except the girl and the white-trash.

Mrs. Turpin's stomach shook. "He's such a caution," she said, "that I can't help but laugh at him."

The girl made a loud ugly noise through her teeth.

Her mother's mouth grew thin and tight. "I think the worst thing in the world," she said, "is an ungrateful person. To have everything and not appreciate it. I know a girl," she said, "who has parents who would give her anything, a little brother who loves her dearly, who is getting a good education, who wears the best clothes, but who can never say a kind word to anyone, who never smiles, who just criticizes and complains all day long."

"Is she too old to paddle?" Claud asked.

The girl's face was almost purple.

"Yes," the lady said, "I'm afraid there's nothing to do but leave her to her folly. Some day she'll wake up and it'll be too late."

"It never hurt anyone to smile," Mrs. Turpin said. "It just makes you feel better all over."

"Of course," the lady said sadly, "but there are just some people you can't tell anything to. They can't take criticism."

"If it's one thing I am," Mrs. Turpin said with feeling, "it's grateful. When I think who all I could have been besides myself and what all I got, a little of everything, and a good disposition besides, I just feel like shouting, 'Thank you, Jesus, for making everything the way it is!' It could have been different!" For one thing, somebody else could have got Claud. At the thought of this, she was flooded with gratitude and a terrible pang of joy ran through her. "Oh thank you, Jesus, Jesus, thank you!" she cried aloud.

The book struck her directly over her left eye. It struck almost at the same instant that she realized the girl was about to hurl it. Before she could utter a sound, the raw face came crashing across the table towards her, howling. The girl's fingers sank like clamps into the soft flesh of her neck. She heard the mother cry out and Claud shout, "Whoa!" There was an instant when she was certain she was about to be in an earthquake.

All at once her vision narrowed and she saw everything as if it were happening in a small room far away, or as if she were looking at it through the wrong end of a telescope. Claud's face crumpled and fell out of sight. The nurse ran in, then out, then in again. Then the gangling figure of the doctor rushed out of the inner door. Magazines flew this way and that as the table turned over. The girl fell with a thud and Mrs. Turpin's vision suddenly reversed itself and she saw everything large instead of small. The eyes of the white-trashy woman were staring hugely at the floor. There the girl, held down on one side by the nurse and on the other by her mother, was wrenching and turning in their grasp. The doctor was kneeling astride her, trying to hold her arm down. He managed after a second to sink a long needle into it.

Mrs. Turpin felt entirely hollow except for her heart which swung from side to side as if it were agitated in a great empty drum of flesh.

"Somebody that's not busy call for the ambulance," the doctor said in the off-hand voice young doctors adopt for terrible occasions.

Mrs. Turpin could not have moved a finger. The old man who had been sitting next to her skipped nimbly into the office and made the call, for the secretary still seemed to be gone.

"Claud!" Mrs. Turpin called.

He was not in his chair. She knew she must jump up and find him but she felt like someone trying to catch a train in a dream, when everything moves in slow motion and the faster you try to run the slower you go.

"Here I am," a suffocated voice, very unlike Claud's said.

He was doubled up in the corner on the floor, pale as paper, holding his leg. She wanted to get up and go to him but she could not move. Instead, her gaze was drawn slowly downward to the churning face on the floor, which she could see over the doctor's shoulder.

The girl's eyes stopped rolling and focused on her. They seemed a much lighter blue than before, as if a door that had been tightly closed behind them was now open to admit light and air.

Mrs. Turpin's head cleared and her power of motion returned. She leaned forward until she was looking directly into the fierce brilliant eyes. There was no doubt in her mind that the girl did know her, knew her in some intense and personal way, beyond time and place and condition. "What you got to say to me?" she asked hoarsely and held her breath, waiting, as for a revelation.

The girl raised her head. Her gaze locked with Mrs. Turpin's. "Go back to hell where you came from, you old wart hog," she whispered. Her voice was low but clear. Her eyes burned for a moment as if she saw with pleasure that her message had struck its target.

Mrs. Turpin sank back in her chair.

After a moment the girl's eyes closed and she turned her head wearily to the side.

The doctor rose and handed the nurse the empty syringe. He leaned over and put both hands for a moment on the mother's shoulders, which were shaking. She was sitting on the floor, her lips pressed together, holding Mary Grace's hand in her lap. The girl's fingers were gripped like a baby's around her thumb. "Go on to the hospital," he said. "I'll call and make the arrangements."

"Now let's see that neck," he said in a jovial voice to Mrs. Turpin. He began to inspect her neck with his first two fingers. Two little moon-shaped lines like pink fish bones were indented over her windpipe. There was the beginning of an angry red swelling above her eye. His fingers passed over this also.

"Lea' me be," she said thickly and shook him off. "See about Claud. She kicked him."

"I'll see about him in a minute," he said and felt her pulse. He was a thin gray-haired man, given to pleasantries. "Go home and have yourself a vacation for the rest of the day," he said and patted her on the shoulder.

Quit your pattin me, Mrs. Turpin growled to herself.

"And put an ice pack over that eye," he said. Then he went and squatted down beside Claud and looked at his leg. After a moment he pulled him up and Claud limped after him into the office.

Until the ambulance came, the only sounds in the room were the tremulous moans of the girl's mother, who continued to sit on the floor. The white-trash woman did not take her eyes off the girl. Mrs. Turpin looked straight ahead at nothing. Presently the ambulance drew up, a long dark shadow, behind the curtain. The attendants came in and set the stretcher down beside the girl and lifted her expertly onto it and carried her out. The nurse helped the mother gather up her things. The shadow of the ambulance moved silently away and the nurse came back in the office.

"That ther girl is going to be a lunatic, ain't she?" the white-trash woman asked the nurse, but the nurse kept on to the back and never answered her.

"Yes, she's going to be a lunatic," the white-trash woman said to the rest of them.

"Po' critter," the old woman murmured. The child's face was still in her lap. His eyes looked idly out over her knees. He had not moved during the disturbance except to draw one leg up under him.

"I thank Gawd," the white-trash woman said fervently, "I ain't a lunatic."

Claud came limping out and the Turpins went home.

As their pick-up truck turned into their own dirt road and made the crest of the hill, Mrs. Turpin gripped the window ledge and looked out suspiciously. The land sloped gracefully down through a field dotted with lavender weeds and at the start of the rise their small yellow frame house, with its little flower beds spread out around it like a fancy apron, sat primly in its accustomed place between two giant hickory trees. She would not have been startled to see a burnt wound between two blackened chimneys.

Neither of them felt like eating so they put on their house clothes and lowered the shade in the bedroom and lay down, Claud with his leg on a pillow and herself with a damp washcloth over her eye. The instant she was flat on her back, the image of a razor-backed hog with warts on its face and horns coming out behind its ears snorted into her head. She moaned, a low quiet moan.

"I am not," she said tearfully, "a wart hog from hell." But the denial had no force. The girl's eyes and her words, even the tone of her voice, low but clear, directed only to her, brooked no repudiation. She had been singled out for the message, though there was trash in the room to whom it might justly have been applied. The full force of this fact struck her only now. There was a woman there who was neglecting her own child but she had been overlooked. The message had been given to Ruby Turpin, a respectable, hard-working, church-going woman. The tears dried. Her eyes began to burn instead with wrath.

She rose on her elbow and the washcloth fell into her hand. Claud was lying on his back, snoring. She wanted to tell him what the girl had said. At the same time, she did not wish to put the image of herself as a wart hog from hell into his mind.

"Hey, Claud," she muttered and pushed his shoulder.

Claud opened one pale baby blue eye.

She looked into it warily. He did not think about anything. He just went his way.

"Wha, whasit?" he said and closed the eye again.

"Nothing," she said. "Does your leg pain you?"

"Hurts like hell," Claud said.

"It'll quit terreckly," she said and lay back down. In a moment Claud was snoring again. For the rest of the afternoon they lay there. Claud slept. She scowled at the ceiling. Occasionally she raised her fist and made a small stabbing motion over her chest as if she was defending her innocence to invisible guests who were like the comforters of Job, reasonable-seeming but wrong.

About five-thirty Claud stirred. "Got to go after those niggers," he sighed, not moving.

She was looking straight up as if there were unintelligible handwriting on the ceiling. The protuberance over her eye had turned a greenish-blue. "Listen here," she said.

"What?"

"Kiss me."

Claud leaned over and kissed her loudly on the mouth. He pinched her side and their hands interlocked. Her expression of ferocious concentration did not change. Claud got up, groaning and growling, and limped off. She continued to study the ceiling.

She did not get up until she heard the pick-up truck coming back with the Negroes. Then she rose and thrust her feet in her brown oxfords, which she did not bother to lace, and stumped out onto the back porch and got her red plastic bucket. She emptied a tray of ice cubes into it and filled it half full of water and went out into the back yard. Every afternoon after Claud brought the hands in, one of the boys helped him put out hay and the rest waited in the back of the truck until he was ready to take them home. The truck was parked in the shade under one of the hickory trees.

"Hi yawl this evening?" Mrs. Turpin asked grimly, appearing with the bucket and the dipper. There were three women and a boy in the truck.

"Us doin nicely," the oldest woman said. "Hi you doin?" and her gaze struck immediately on the dark lump on Mrs. Turpin's forehead. "You done fell down, ain't you?" she asked in a solicitous voice. The old

woman was dark and almost toothless. She had on an old felt hat of
Claud's set back on her head. The other two women were younger and
lighter and they both had new bright green sunhats. One of them had
hers on her head; the other had taken hers off and the boy was grinning
beneath it.

Mrs. Turpin set the bucket down on the floor of the truck. "Yawl hep
yourselves," she said. She looked around to make sure Claud had gone.
"No, I didn't fall down," she said, folding her arms. "It was something
worse than that."

"Ain't nothing bad happen to you!" the old woman said. She said it as if
they all knew that Mrs. Turpin was protected in some special way by
Divine Providence. "You just had you a little fall."

"We were in town at the doctor's office for where the cow kicked Mr.
Turpin," Mrs. Turpin said in a flat tone that indicated they could leave off
their foolishness. "And there was this girl there. A big fat girl with her
face all broke out. I could look at that girl and tell she was peculiar but I
couldn't tell how. And me and her mama was just talking and going
along and all of a sudden WHAM! She throws this big book she was reading at me and. . . ."

"Naw!" the old woman cried out.

"And then she jumps over the table and commences to choke me."

"Naw!" they all exclaimed, "naw!"

"Hi come she do that?" the old woman asked. "What ail her?"

Mrs. Turpin only glared in front of her.

"Somethin ail her," the old woman said.

"They carried her off in an ambulance," Mrs. Turpin continued, "but
before she went she was rolling on the floor and they were trying to hold
her down to give her a shot and she said something to me." She paused.
"You know what she said to me?"

"What she say?" they asked.

"She said," Mrs. Turpin began, and stopped, her face very dark and
heavy. The sun was getting whiter and whiter, blanching the sky overhead so that the leaves of the hickory tree were black in the face of it. She
could not bring forth the words. "Something real ugly," she muttered.

"She sho shouldn't said nothin ugly to you," the old woman said. "You
so sweet. You the sweetest lady I know."

"She pretty too," the one with the hat on said.

"And stout," the other one said. "I never knowed no sweeter white lady."

"That's the truth befo' Jesus," the old woman said. "Amen! You des as sweet and pretty as you can be."

Mrs. Turpin knew exactly how much Negro flattery was worth and it added to her rage. "She said," she began again and finished this time with a fierce rush of breath, "that I was an old wart hog from hell."

There was an astounded silence.

"Where she at?" the youngest woman cried in a piercing voice.

"Lemme see her. I'll kill her!"

"I'll kill her with you!" the other one cried.

"She b'long in the sylum," the old woman said emphatically. "You the sweetest white lady I know."

"She pretty too," the other two said. "Stout as she can be and sweet. Jesus satisfied with her!"

"Deed he is," the old woman declared.

Idiots! Mrs. Turpin growled to herself. You could never say anything intelligent to a nigger. You could talk at them but not with them. "Yawl ain't drunk your water," she said shortly. "Leave the bucket in the truck when you're finished with it. I got more to do than just stand around and pass the time of day," and she moved off and into the house.

She stood for a moment in the middle of the kitchen. The dark protuberance over her eye looked like a miniature tornado cloud which might any moment sweep across the horizon of her brow. Her lower lip protruded dangerously. She squared her massive shoulders. Then she marched into the front of the house and out the side door and started down the road to the pig parlor. She had the look of a woman going single-handed, weaponless, into battle.

The sun was a deep yellow now like a harvest moon and was riding westward very fast over the far tree line as if it meant to reach the hogs before she did. The road was rutted and she kicked several good-sized stones out of her path as she strode along.

The pig parlor was on a little knoll at the end of a lane that ran off from the side of the barn. It was a square of concrete as large as a small room, with a board fence about four feet high around it. The concrete floor sloped slightly so that the hog wash could drain off into a trench where it was carried to the field for fertilizer. Claud was standing on the outside, on the edge of the concrete, hanging onto the top board, hosing down the floor inside. The hose was connected to the faucet of a water trough nearby.

Mrs. Turpin climbed up beside him and glowered down at the hogs inside. There were seven long-snouted bristly shoats in it—tan with liver-colored spots—and an old sow a few weeks off from farrowing. She was lying on her side grunting. The shoats were running about shaking themselves like idiot children, their little slit pig eyes searching the floor for anything left. She had read that pigs were the most intelligent animal. She doubted it. They were supposed to be smarter than dogs. There had even been a pig astronaut. He had performed his assignment perfectly but died of a heart attack afterwards because they left him in his electric suit, sitting upright throughout his examination when naturally a hog should be on all fours.

A-gruntin and a-rootin and a-groanin.

"Gimme that hose," she said, yanking it away from Claud. "Go on and carry them niggers home and then get off that leg."

"You look like you might have swallowed a mad dog," Claud observed, but he got down and limped off. He paid no attention to her humors.

Until he was out of earshot, Mrs. Turpin stood on the side of the pen, holding the hose and pointing the stream of water at the hind quarters of any shoat that looked as if it might try to lie down. When he had had time to get over the hill, she turned her head slightly and her wrathful eyes scanned the path. He was nowhere in sight. She turned back again and seemed to gather herself up. Her shoulders rose and she drew in her breath.

"What do you send me a message like that for?" she said in a low fierce voice, barely above a whisper but with the force of a shout in concentrated fury. "How am I a hog and me both? How am I saved and from hell too?" Her free fist was knotted and with the other she gripped the hose, blindly pointing the stream of water in and out of the eye of the old sow whose outraged squeal she did not hear.

The pig parlor commanded a view of the back pasture where their twenty beef cows were gathered around the hay-bales Claud and the boy had put out. The freshly cut pasture sloped down to the highway. Across it was their cotton field and beyond that a dark green dusty wood which they owned as well. The sun was behind the wood, very red, looking over the paling of trees like a farmer inspecting his own hogs.

"Why me?" she rumbled. "It's no trash around here, black or white, that I haven't given to. And break my back to the bone every day working. And do for the church."

She appeared to be the right size woman to command the arena before her. "How am I a hog?" she demanded. "Exactly how am I like them?" and she jabbed the stream of water at the shoats. "There was plenty of trash there. It didn't have to be me."

"If you like trash better, go get yourself some trash then," she railed. "You could have made me trash. Or a nigger. If trash is what you wanted why didn't you make me trash?" She shook her fist with the hose in it and a watery snake appeared momentarily in the air. "I could quit working and take it easy and be filthy," she growled. "Lounge about the sidewalks all day drinking root beer. Dip snuff and spit in every puddle and have it all over my face. I could be nasty."

"Or you could have made me a nigger. It's too late for me to be a nigger," she said with deep sarcasm, "but I could act like one. Lay down in the middle of the road and stop traffic. Roll on the ground."

In the deepening light everything was taking on a mysterious hue. The pasture was growing a peculiar glassy green and the streak of highway had turned lavender. She braced herself for a final assault and this time her voice rolled out over the pasture. "Go on," she yelled, "call me a hog! Call me a hog again. From hell. Call me a wart hog from hell. Put that bottom rail on top. There'll still be a top and bottom!"

A garbled echo returned to her.

A final surge of fury shook her and she roared, "Who do you think you are?"

The color of everything, field and crimson sky, burned for a moment with a transparent intensity. The question carried over the pasture and across the highway and the cotton field and returned to her clearly like an answer from beyond the wood.

She opened her mouth but no sound came out of it.

A tiny truck, Claud's, appeared on the highway, heading rapidly out of sight. Its gears scraped thinly. It looked like a child's toy. At any moment a bigger truck might smash into it and scatter Claud's and the niggers' brains all over the road.

Mrs. Turpin stood there, her gaze fixed on the highway, all her muscles rigid, until in five or six minutes the truck reappeared, returning. She waited until it had had time to turn into their own road. Then like a monumental statue coming to life, she bent her head slowly and gazed, as if through the very heart of mystery, down into the pig parlor at the hogs. They had settled all in one corner around the old sow who was grunting softly. A red glow suffused them. They appeared to pant with a secret life.

Until the sun slipped finally behind the tree line, Mrs. Turpin remained there with her gaze bent to them as if she were absorbing some abysmal life-giving knowledge. At last she lifted her head. There was only a purple streak in the sky, cutting through a field of crimson and leading, like an extension of the highway, into the descending dusk. She raised her hands from the side of the pen in a gesture hieratic and profound. A visionary light settled in her eyes. She saw the streak as a vast swinging bridge extending upward from the earth through a field of living fire. Upon it a vast horde of souls were rumbling toward heaven. There were whole companies of white-trash, clean for the first time in their lives, and bands of black niggers in white robes, and battalions of freaks and lunatics shouting and clapping and leaping like frogs. And bringing up the end of the procession was a tribe of people who she recognized at once as those who, like herself and Claud, had always had a little of everything and the God-given wit to use it right. She leaned forward to observe them closer. They were marching behind the others with great dignity, accountable as they had always been for good order and common sense and respectable behavior. They alone were on key. Yet she could see by their shocked and altered faces that even their virtues were being burned away. She lowered her hands and gripped the rail of the hog pen, her eyes small but fixed unblinkingly on what lay ahead. In a moment the vision faded but she remained where she was, immobile.

At length she got down and turned off the faucet and made her slow way on the darkening path to the house. In the woods around her the invisible cricket choruses had struck up, but what she heard were the voices of the souls climbing upward into the starry field and shouting hallelujah.

Custom and Conscience (1949)

Lillian Smith

That was long ago.

In the South, paint has peeled off of old houses we were born in; steps have sagged down. Foundations of economics and politics and old ways of living have crumbled though the rotted framework stands. The new has begun. Housing projects and ranch houses shut out the sight of the old big houses and shanties. People have moved to town. There is more money. Tractors and bulldozers, cover crops and contour plowing have filled deep gullies and made green pastures of worn-out land. Factories are building in small-town vacant lots where we children played ball or in springtime picked yellow flycatchers from little damp places. Unions hold their meetings in old second-story rooms where lodges once met for their conclaves. Motels and filling stations, chain restaurants, hot-dog stands and gift shops edge the broad black strip that has unrolled across clay and sand and swamp and hill.

How far away it seems now since that old horse-and-buggy clop clop of years made childhood so painful and wondrous a time of slow watching! Those old crowded years when eyes had time to look seem now as if they moved under a microscope.

On that dreary evening, when I wandered through our big house trying to fit good and evil into something that made sense, there was not one automobile in our town. Few people had heard of Kitty Hawk and the brothers who had learned to fly. I remember the day the first telephone came to our town. The night the first electric lights were turned on. The first flush toilet that was installed in my mother's bathroom.

During these many years since I was a little girl struggling with conscience and custom, this old earth has seen more change in men's ways than in thousands of years of its history.

One keeps turning the pages. . . . In Europe, Sigmund Freud was already embattled by the fear and hatred of men who recognized too well the power of his findings, but we had not heard of him in the South or in most of America. No one had begun to worry about the hidden terror in the unconscious; no one apparently guessed that children had a sex life

327

though Stendhal had written his biography and Dostoevsky his novels and Rousseau his confessions and the old Greek plays had been acted thousands of times in the Western world. Insanity might be upstairs in the room whose door was always kept closed but no one talked of it and no one believed it could be otherwise. . . . Few knew the names of Einstein and Planck or had read the words *quantum theory*, and atomic energy was a vague daydream that men put in escape stories. Many in the rural South had not yet heard of Marx, and evolution was to most southern people not controversy but a sin that only infidels or those who believed in the "Higher Criticism" dared even read about.

In a corner of Austria the greatest murderer the world has ever known was living his childhood; Stalin was a young peasant in that beautiful old province on the Black Sea that has a name like ours; and the adolescent Kafka was beginning his terrifying trials that drove him, years later, to write down anxiety dreams that we shiveringly claim as our own now as we read them; Picasso had not learned yet to lay the thin slivers of a broken world in blocks of color so hypnotic with ugliness and strange truth that men can scarcely pull their eyes from the sight of it, though his culture had already shown him how, but was still dipping his brush in misty blues and dreaming of a whole person who no longer existed. In South Africa, Gandhi was weaving a way of change out of nonviolence and love and *satyagraha* which decades later would free four hundred million of his people in India. The Soongs were obscure Methodists whose best friends were missionaries; Chiang Kai-shek was a peasant boy in his teens riding the family's buffalo home in the evenings across rice paddies that lay shadowed by the mountains of Chekiang; and Franklin Roosevelt was a young college man spending carefree summers on the island of Campobello. Strangers one to another, distant and remote . . . yet all were being pulled inexorably together and we were pulled with them by men in laboratories, who wrapped their invisible theories around the old earth tighter and tighter and squeezed it into so small a thing that even now we cannot believe it.

Even now in the South we still try to live as if none of this has happened. The old signs are still over the minds of men. Custom and conscience still divide our children and southern tradition is a ghost that many still believe in.

I saw a group of southern children try their strength against that ghost a few summers ago. It happened on our mountain where the children were spending the summer. We were gathered in the big gymnasium-theater making a play. It was the children's affair and was about Every Child who makes a journey through the universe to collect new experiences he may need in order to grow up. They had read Antoine de Saint Exupéry's fantasy *The Little Prince* and, borrowing from it, had agreed that in their play Every Child was born on a planet, too, where no one lives but himself but if he grows he does not stay there. There are other planets which he must visit. In such simple pictures they saw the old troubled story of man's progress. A camper was chosen for the role of Every Child and given the name the Prince. The first planet to be visited on this journey was Your Own Family. The Prince's first traveling companion joined him here and the campers named her Conscience, made her into a tall nursemaid, prissy and prudish, and designed a bristling costume for her that contained surely all the angularities of their combined early experiences.

The Prince had begun his journey. The second experience was concerned with the weaning from the nipple to the cup. There were others: the first day at school, getting rid of one's fear of the dark, making a friend, creating things with one's hands. As the play grew, the children realized that the Prince must have more traveling companions—Conscience did not seem adequate for so hazardous a journey. So Southern Tradition was chosen as his second companion, and a group of eight dancers were to stay close to the Prince, blocking his way or opening it, as he traveled. The third companion they chose was Religion. "I know we should take religion along," one child said, "but it just doesn't seem to belong on the stage with the others—after all, it's near us only on Sundays."

"Then put it in the balcony," another called out. And they did, asking five girls to take their Bibles to the far balcony and sit there.

The fourth companion chosen was Science. It was not easy to convince the group that the Prince needed this traveling companion. But Science had one ardent defender. A quiet, withdrawn girl now spoke. "We live in the age of science," she said, "and we shouldn't make a journey through the universe with only a nursemaid like Conscience, and Southern Tradition and Religion. It's too dangerous. There are times when the Prince better know some facts."

"Yes, but what about? He can't take things like refrigerators with him on a journey through the universe!"

"Things aren't science," the quiet camper replied. "Science makes things, but," she groped for words, "it is really the search for truth. It's not easy to find truth, for you must test it and test it. The Prince may need the truth if he gets far from home. I think we'd better let Science help him find it."

Science was reluctantly chosen and put on the other balcony opposite religion. The Prince continued his journey.

Now we were in trouble. The Prince was speaking new words. She said, "I was born on a planet where I live all alone. I have journeyed to other planets and have had strange and wonderful experiences. I have lived with my family. I have gone to school. I have felt lonely and I have failed. But I am no longer afraid of the dark and there are things I know that once I did not know. I have made things with my hands. I have also made a friend and that was nice and I shall never forget it. I have had a date. I have family memories that are good and some I hate to remember and all of them I take with me wherever I journey."

She looked up quickly at the campers and counselors who were watching the play grow. "Last night," she continued, "I thought, here we are making a play about visiting planets and have forgot that we live on a planet called Earth. It is a star hanging in the sky and must seem a pretty thing to the rest of the universe but I haven't traveled far on it and I don't know anything much about its people. Most of it is cut off from me and part of my town is cut off, too. We are children living on the earth and I think to grow up we should play with all the earth's children. That is an important experience which the Prince in our play has never had. Don't you think he should have it?"

For a long moment no one answered. Then a youngster burst out, "Yes, but you know we can't play with all children! It will ruin our play. We can't have a happy ending if we do that."

Voices were angry as one after another had something to say. "You know this. Why did you mention it?"

"Why can't we end it with a nice experience that isn't controversial?"

"Something we can really do!"

"Why bring up things—"

The little Prince said, "But this journey through the universe means having experiences that will make us grow up. We've talked about it for three or four summers. The Prince has to play with other children, you know that. He's got to be interested in everybody. What's the sense of making this journey if he doesn't meet all kinds of people? Is he going to see just white people like us here at camp? He might as well sit at home."

"Then for goodness sakes, let him play with the French or somebody safe!"

"It wouldn't be honest! If he plays with children he must play with those in mill town and colored ones too, right here in Georgia."

"Oh my goodness! Then we can't. And you know it. Why be so silly!"

"Down here we just can't—"

"Daddy says—"

"My mother says—"

The old battle of words was on and the accent was very southern. The gong sounded for lunch. Quiet Hour came. Then swimming, tennis, other activities. We did not return to the play until next day. When the group was seated, I suggested that we talk about it as people who don't give up something they want just because things get hard. "Yesterday, everybody was excited. Today well, let's see what the four traveling companions can suggest. After all, that's what they're for, isn't it?"

The actors had made their own lines from the beginning of the play. Now one of them said, "Shall we make our words or will you help us? You know, since this is a kind of emergency."

"Make your own lines. As honestly as you can."

The Prince's eyes were bright as she stepped out to the center of the stage. "I am an earth child," she said proudly, "and this is a planet I live on. I would like to play with all its children for I, too, am its child."

The children who were not in the play sat on the floor, watching. On the stage were Conscience, the nursemaid and the eight girls who were Southern Tradition. On the two balconies were Religion and Science. Both balcony groups had come to the play-making with armfuls of books, to meet this emergency.

A child from the floor spoke. "We can still get out of this mess if Conscience will only tell the Prince that we can't play with other children because we don't know their games."

"But we do," the Prince said. "All children play with balls and chase each other. If they don't they can learn in five minutes. That's a tricky way out and I won't use it." She turned quickly to Conscience. "Conscience, will you let me play with the colored children here at home?" In an aside to us, "We might as well get to the point, don't you think?"

Conscience ad-libbed her lines. "Don't be silly," she replied calmly. "When race is the issue I always refer you to Southern Tradition. You know that. Why don't you ask her?" Southern Tradition's eight girls blocked the Prince's path. "This is our answer," their leader said. "If you try it, we will hurt you."

The Prince's cheeks flushed up. A little seven-year-old covered her eyes. Each camper in that room was living this play now as if it were her own biography.

The Prince turned to me, "What next?"

"You have other resources. See what Religion says."

The girls in Religion's balcony were ready. They read in chorus a part of the Sermon on the Mount. They read, "For God so loved the world, that He gave His only begotten Son. . . ." And then one girl said with such simplicity that it was truly moving, "Suffer little children to come unto me, and forbid them not: for of such is the kingdom of God."

"Conscience, did you hear?"

Conscience turned away arrogantly, "I never listen to Religion where segregation is involved. No one does, down here."

As Conscience answered, the eight who were Southern Tradition had quickly encircled the Prince and now were forcing her back from her journey toward the earth children.

"I think," a youngster called out from among those watching, "that Religion is no good as a traveling companion as long as it stays up in the balcony. Why doesn't Religion come down here and push Custom back where it belongs?"

"But Religion doesn't do that in the South," a girl from the balcony answered. "Religion stays out of controversies. You know that Our place is up here."

"How about Science?" I asked.

The five who were Science had their answers and gave them, but even as they talked, Conscience turned away in great boredom. "I can't hear Science's words. The only thing that Science is good for is to make things like bombs and planes. Anyway, this isn't my affair. It is Southern Tradition's."

"You haven't a chance," a nine-year-old camper called out to the Prince in great excitement. "Religion's way off on her balcony, reading the Bible. Science is way off on its balcony, making things and writing books. They're not worth a thing as traveling companions! You may as well give up. Southern Tradition is too strong."

The Prince had begun to run. She twisted and turned, ran quickly, ran slowly; yet always the eight who were Southern Tradition blocked her way. She lost herself in her struggle, stopped acting, and finally I called to her to stop, fearing she would exhaust herself. She fell on the floor, breathing hard, and lay there, staring up at the ceiling.

I can never forget that moment. I looked at the children. They sat so still, a hundred campers and counselors, looking at something they had never seen before. And I sat there, remembering a day long ago that I had forgotten.

"The little Prince can never grow up," one said softly.

"Maybe we shouldn't have tried. Maybe it would have been better if the little Prince had stayed in Saint Exupéry's book."

"I knew yesterday something bad was about to happen! Why did the Prince feel that we must play with all the earth's children? You knew we couldn't do it!"

"Because," the Prince answered, doggedly, "the Prince in our play wants to do right. We know it is right to feel this way. Our conscience has changed whether the one in the play has or not. There should be a way to work it out. Religion and Science should have helped me; I wasn't strong enough to do it by myself."

"But they couldn't—honestly! This is the way the traveling companions are in the South. This is the way Conscience is too. We can't pretend a lie," Conscience hotly defended herself and the others.

The play had to be mended. I told them that things were as their actors had said but things need not be that way. A day would come soon when the little Prince could play with the earth's children. Therefore it seemed to me that we might bridge over the gap in time. We could let Religion come down from the balcony and help. But I felt we must decide first what religion is. Is it reading the Bible and singing hymns and being Protestant or Catholic or Jew or Christian Scientist, or is it something more important?

Everyone was again talking, eager to find a way out of this impasse which they themselves had created. Religion is love, an older girl said; no one has dreamed of anything better than love, so it must be love. "Yes it is love," the little ones chimed in, relieved that the talk was growing pleasant. Love, they continued, can help push Southern Tradition off the stage and teach it a few lessons about being nice to other people if Science will come down from its balcony to help.

Quickly the young scientists came down and joined the Prince. Quickly they improvised a dance in which they drove Southern Tradition—nonviolently of course!—into the wings of the stage, then they turned on Conscience. They told her she was a coward always to listen to Southern Tradition: why couldn't she learn things from Religion and Science! And then, the campers watching this, decided they could impersonate earth children, they could *be* Chinese and Japanese and Germans and Russians and Negroes, they could come from the ends of the earth and play with the little Prince. And they did this. A counselor put a gay record on the machine and the old gymnasium filled with sounds of triumph as we made a great circle and danced together.

It was make-believe and we knew it. But we could not let our play die as so much that is young has died on that old wall, segregation. At supper, the children looked tired and preoccupied and I knew we had not answered the question twisting in their minds.

Late that evening, long after the lights in the cabins were out, a camper came into my office. She was an older girl who had spent many summers on the mountain, now ready for college in the fall. She was pale and tense, as she began to talk. I did not record that conversation but it has fixed itself in my mind so deeply that I do not think I shall distort its truth as I tell it now.

"I don't know how to begin; I shock myself as I try." She faltered and then the words rushed from her, "I think you have done a terrible thing to children."

"Why do you think so?"

"You see," she was sorting the words that had piled up in her, "you have made us want to be good. Mature, you've called it. You taught us be honest, not to cover up things. You made us think it fine to be like that, even when it hurt. All these years, you've said so much about human dignity—it's a nice phrase. . . . You've talked of love . . . human rights . . . bridging chasms between people—

"But it's all wrong! You made us think of ourselves as no better than other people. You shouldn't have done that. Oh, I can't find my words, the feelings are too close here," she touched her throat.

"Perhaps you would like to wait and tell me tomorrow."

"No. I'd lose my nerve. You told us we were like children everywhere; that money and color, the church you go to, don't make any difference. And the kids believed you. You said the only real differences have to do with values and interests and tastes. And you said that the most precious right a human has is his right to be different. Even his right to be dull." She smiled suddenly. "We liked that. And we believed you. We loved you for giving us ideals that we could be proud of. We wanted to live them. They seemed so fine." She laughed a bitter little laugh, then added softly, "But I almost hate you tonight, for letting us fall in love with beliefs that I see now we can't possibly live. Why did you teach us to want to be real persons when you knew there was no place down here for such people?

"When I go back to my town, how can I live these ideals! Tell me, if you can—but you can't! That's what I have just realized.

"I saw it as we worked on the play. For the first time in my life! I guess you've tried to tell us but somehow I didn't see it. It always seemed something we could do—when we were grown. Well, I see now. And I think the others saw it too, though most are too young to find words for their feelings. Maybe they're lucky."

She came close to my desk. "It was as if somebody had swung a bright mirror in front of us. The whole thing opened up! How it would be—if we tried to live the way we have learned to want to live. Can't you imagine my town—if I were to go home and invite a colored girl to Sunday school? Or even try to get one of the girls in Mill Town in my sorority? They'd think I was crazy. Suppose I said to a colored girl, 'Let's go in the drugstore and have a coke'? Can't you see their faces—Mother's and Daddy's—and everybody's! Well, I can—especially if they arrested me and put me in jail.

"I'd be breaking a law, wouldn't I, if I tried to live these ideals in my home town?"

"Yes. You would be breaking a law. A state law."

"Do you think we should break laws? Do you *want* us to be lawbreakers? Oh, I know! I even know I could break the law and they wouldn't dare put me in jail, because of Daddy. But that only makes it worse, for they would put others there. We forgot to take law along as a traveling companion, didn't we? Maybe it's better. It might make the little ones wonder if *anybody* has any sense down here.

"I'm saying these things because I'm scared—at what I am looking at in me."

She said no more for a little and I did not try to talk.

"Who put those signs over doors?" she asked suddenly. "Somebody must keep them there. Is it my father? No, don't tell me. I don't want to know if he has anything to do with it—I couldn't believe it—he's so good—I've never seen Daddy do an unkind thing in all my life. Sometimes Mother loses her temper. Not Daddy. Then why does he want to keep Negroes segregated—what pleasure does he get out of it? Does it make him richer to keep them that way?"

"Some people think so."

"But why does he care that much for money? Why would he be willing to—" She said no more for what seemed a long time. I was searching hard for the right answer to give her.

She said more quietly, "Mother reads the *Nation* and the *New Republic*. All those papers. I wonder why. . . . If they've made up their minds that the signs stay up and segregation is going to be here forever, then why do they fool themselves? Why don't they be honest about it? Why pretend and go to church and say nice words? It doesn't make sense! What does religion mean to them? If it isn't real, what do they get out of it?

"I've been here six summers. I love this old mountain . . . the courtesy every one shows children; even the little ones. It's nice. We laugh so much here. . . . I've learned to paint and my drive has improved in tennis; I can even dance, a little. And the idea of growing—I've liked that. The way we've learned to think our bodies are honorable. No shame. . . . I remember you said freedom and responsibility are like Siamese twins: they die if they are cut apart. . . . All these things. . . . No punishment . . . Just understanding . . . reaching out to accept other people as human beings like ourselves. We've all said we were going to bring up our children that way.

"I remember when we learned about hate. I was so afraid of that word—I used to deny that I hated anyone. And then, one day, you told us that human relationships are what the personality is fed on: love is the part you grow on, hate the part you don't need, the waste that is excreted. You said our job is to find sanitary ways of getting rid of it so it won't harm others, or ourselves. That was such a relief, to know that hate is as natural as a b.m. and much the same thing. I stopped biting my nails when I learned that." She smiled and looked down at her hands. "I remember all the Sunday mornings we've discussed these things, sitting under the trees."

I said, "You think it's wrong—what we have learned here together?"

"I think it's useless. It just tears us up inside! Makes us so raw. Oh I hate to say it but I do think you have harmed us. You've unfitted us for the South. And yet, this is where we shall live. Unless we run away.

"I think you should have made it easier for us to live here. What is education for if not that! Since we have to practice segregation, didn't you make us think it is right?"

"How could it be right?"

"Oh, I don't know! My mind feels as if it is full of barbed wire. It isn't right for any one to feel the way I feel inside.

"When I have children, I am not going to give them a single ideal they can't practice. I don't want them torn up like this. I'll tell them Jim Crow is fine, that it's legal, that this is the way things are in the South and the way they are going to stay. I'll tell them they have the right to push folks around; that they *should* decide where their inferiors can sit and stand and what doors they can go through. That it's right to shame colored children by making them go through back doors."

She came to my desk. "I haven't told you about last winter.[1] Daddy took me to New York—we were in the dining car—had just finished our soup—when I saw the steward seat the president of that college in Atlanta be-hind those curtains. I had heard him make a speech at a church meeting. I said, 'Daddy, did you see that? He's the president of a college!' And Daddy said, 'That's where colored folks are supposed to sit. You mustn't get silly notions, honey.' I couldn't finish my dinner. I know it was morbid, but I kept looking at all those faces wondering why they felt they had to have a curtain between them and the president of a college, just to eat their dinner. And it began to seem so crazy!

"I'll teach my children not to *think* about things like this. I'll teach them that money comes first before people that it's more important I won't let them be hypocrites, like me.

"In other words, you would make little Nazis out of them."

"At least it would be honest!"

"I'm afraid honesty doesn't have much to do with it, though it would be logical. Your feelings have stampeded a little, haven't they?"

"I'm scared," she whispered. "I don't like the future. It doesn't seem to belong to us. I don't know what to believe about anything. I'm seventeen years old and I have no idea what is wrong and what is right—not enough to know how to live. And even if I knew, I couldn't live it down here. I lay there tonight trying to tell myself that segregation is right. I said it over and over as I used to do as a child when I was memorizing. I said 'Daddy knows more than we know here at camp. There's no sense in worrying about it.' But it didn't help.

"You see," her voice had quieted, "I want so much to go home and be decent about things. Not make folks mad—just live what I believe is right. But how? Tell me how! What shall I do when I get on a bus—go to the front with the white folks? Or shall I speak to the bus driver and make a little scene each time I get on? Shall I keep on going through White doors? Can I persuade my class to invite a colored girl to Sunday school? Suppose I get that far—will the minister let me? I don't think he would— he would say, 'These things have to come slowly, my dear,' and he would mean that they must not come at all, as long as there is any risk in it. If I do these things that seem so important to us up here, everybody at home will be furious. I can't take it.

"What are you afraid of?"

"I don't know. It's like waking up in the night after a dream—you're just scared, you don't know why. I just can't fight people I love. Maybe it's because I want to be liked too much. But it's right to want people to like you, isn't it?"

"Yes," I was feeling old, "it's right to want people to like you."

"Funny," she said, "I don't want to hate and I don't want people to hate me. That ought to be a good way to feel. But you won't change things down here if you feel that way. Do you remember the book you gave me to read on the well-adjusted child? Well, that's me—I'm beginning to see it. I'm just too easygoing. To change things you've got to get mad when you see folks do what you think is wrong. But I can't stand people who shout and scream and push others around in the name of good. They seem crazy. And I don't want anybody calling *me* a crackpot—that's what Daddy calls people.

"It makes you feel tired inside to think things like this," she turned away to hide her tears.

I said, "I would like for you to let me talk a little now. And I have to begin before you were born."

And then I told her in part what I shall write down here in the next chapter.

Note

[1] 1961. There is no segregation in dining cars in the South now, if these cars are used in interstate travel.

Rules of the Game (1986)

Amy Tan

I was six when my mother taught me the art of invisible strength. It was a strategy for winning arguments, respect from others, and eventually, though neither of us knew it at the time, chess games.

"Bite back your tongue," scolded my mother when I cried loudly, yanking her hand toward the store that sold bags of salted plums. At home, she said, "Wise guy, he not go against wind. In Chinese we say, Come from South, blow with wind—poom!—North will follow. Strongest wind cannot be seen."

The next week I bit back my tongue as we entered the store with the forbidden candies. When my mother finished her shopping, she quietly plucked a small bag of plums from the rack and put it on the counter with the rest of the items.

My mother imparted her daily truths so she could help my older brothers and me rise above our circumstances. We lived in San Francisco's Chinatown. Like most of the other Chinese children who played in the back alleys of restaurants and curio shops, I didn't think we were poor. My bowl was always full, three five-course meals every day, beginning with a soup full of mysterious things I didn't want to know the names of.

We lived on Waverly Place, in a warm, clean, two-bedroom flat that sat above a small Chinese bakery specializing in steamed pastries and dim sum. In the early morning, when the alley was still quiet, I could smell fragrant red beans as they were cooked down to a pasty sweetness. By daybreak, our flat was heavy with the odor of fried sesame balls and sweet curried chicken crescents. From my bed, I would listen as my father got ready for work, then locked the door behind him, one-two-three clicks.

At the end of our two-block alley was a small sandlot playground with swings and slides well-shined down the middle with use. The play area was bordered by wood-slat benches where old-country people sat cracking roasted watermelon seeds with their golden teeth and scattering the husks to an impatient gathering of gurgling pigeons. The best playground, however, was the dark alley itself. It was crammed with daily mysteries and adventures. My brothers and I would peer into the medicinal herb shop, watching old Li dole out onto a stiff sheet of white paper the right amount of insect shells, saffron-colored seeds, and pungent leaves for his ailing customers. It was said that he once cured a woman dying of an ancestral curse that had eluded the best of American doctors. Next to the pharmacy was a printer who specialized in gold-embossed wedding invitations and festive red banners.

Farther down the street was Ping Yuen Fish Market. The front window displayed a tank crowded with doomed fish and turtles struggling to gain footing on the slimy green-tiled sides. A handwritten sign informed tourists, "Within this store, is all for food, not for pet." Inside, the butchers with their bloodstained white smocks deftly gutted the fish while customers cried out their orders and shouted, "Give me your freshest," to which the butchers always protested, "All are freshest." On less crowded market days, we would inspect the crates of live frogs and crabs which we were warned not to poke, boxes of dried cuttlefish, and row upon row of iced prawns, squid, and slippery fish. The sanddabs made me shiver each time; their eyes lay on one flattened side and reminded me of my mother's story of a careless girl who ran into a crowded street and was crushed by a cab. "Was smash flat," reported my mother.

At the corner of the alley was Hong Sing's, a four-table café with a recessed stairwell in front that led to a door marked "Tradesmen." My brothers and I believed the bad people emerged from this door at night. Tourists never went to Hong Sing's, since the menu was printed only in Chinese. A Caucasian man with a big camera once posed me and my playmates in front of the restaurant. He had us move to the side of the picture window so the photo would capture the roasted duck with its head dangling from a juice-covered rope. After he took the picture, I told him he should go into Hong Sing's and eat dinner. When he smiled and asked me what they served, I shouted, "Guts and duck's feet and octopus gizzards!" Then I ran off with my friends, shrieking with laughter as we scampered across the alley and hid in the entryway grotto of the China Gem Company, my heart pounding with hope that he would chase us.

My mother named me after the street that we lived on: Waverly Place Jong, my official name for important American documents. But my family called me Meimei, "Little Sister." I was the youngest, the only daughter. Each morning before school, my mother would twist and yank on my thick black hair until she had formed two tightly wound pigtails. One day, as she struggled to weave a hard-toothed comb through my disobedient hair, I had a sly thought.

I asked her, "What is Chinese torture?" My mother shook her head. A bobby pin was wedged between her lips. She wetted her palm and smoothed the hair above my ear, then pushed the pin in so that it nicked sharply against my scalp.

"Who say this word?" she asked without a trace of knowing how wicked I was being. I shrugged my shoulders and said, "Some boy in my class said Chinese people do Chinese torture."

"Chinese people do many things," she said simply. "Chinese people do business, do medicine, do painting. Not lazy like American people. We do torture. Best torture."

M y older brother Vincent was the one who actually got the chess set. We had gone to the annual Christmas party held at the First Chinese Baptist church at the end of the alley. The missionary ladies had put together a Santa bag of gifts donated by members of another church. None of the gifts had names on them. There were separate sacks for boys and girls of different ages.

One of the Chinese parishioners had donned a Santa Claus costume and a stiff paper beard with cotton balls glued to it. I think the only children who thought he was the real thing were too young to know that Santa Claus was not Chinese. When my turn came up, the Santa man asked me how old I was. I thought it was a trick question; I was seven according to the American formula and eight by the Chinese calendar. I said I was born on March 17, 1951. That seemed to satisfy him. He then solemnly asked if I had been a very, very good girl this year and did I believe in Jesus Christ and obey my parents. I knew the only answer to that. I nodded back with equal solemnity.

Having watched the other children opening their gifts, I already knew that the big gifts were not necessarily the nicest ones. One girl my age got a large coloring book of biblical characters, while a less greedy girl who selected a smaller box received a glass vial of lavender toilet water. The sound of the box was also important. A ten-year-old boy had chosen a box that jangled when he shook it. It was a tin globe of the world with a slit for inserting money. He must have thought it was full of dimes and nickels, because when he saw that it had just ten pennies, his face fell with such undisguised disappointment that his mother slapped the side of his head and led him out of the church hall, apologizing to the crowd for her son who had such bad manners he couldn't appreciate such a fine gift.

As I peered into the sack, I quickly fingered the remaining presents, testing their weight, imagining what they contained. I chose a heavy, compact one that was wrapped in shiny silver foil and a red satin ribbon. It was a twelve pack of Life Savers and I spent the rest of the party arranging and rearranging the candy tubes in the order of my favorites. My brother Winston chose wisely as well. His present turned out to be a box of intricate plastic parts; the instructions on the box proclaimed that when they were properly assembled he would have an authentic miniature replica of a World War II submarine.

Vincent got the chess set, which would have been a very decent present to get at a church Chistmas party, except it was obviously used and, as we discovered later, it was missing a black pawn and a white knight. My mother graciously thanked the unknown benefactor, saying, "Too good. Cost too much." At which point, an old lady with fine, white, wispy hair nodded toward our family and said with a whistling whisper, "Merry, merry Christmas."

When we got home, my mother told Vincent to throw the chess set away. "She not want it. We not want it," she said, tossing her head stiffly to the side with a tight, proud smile, My brothers had deaf ears. They were already lining up the chess pieces and reading from the dog-eared instruction book.

I watched Vincent and Winston play during Christmas week. The chessboard seemed to hold elaborate secrets waiting to be untangled. The chessmen were more powerful than old Li's magic herbs that cured ancestral curses. And my brothers wore such serious faces that I was sure something was at stake that was greater than avoiding the tradesmen's door to Hong Sing's.

"Let me! Let me!" I begged between games when one brother or the other would sit back with a deep sigh of relief and victory, the other annoyed, unable to let go of the outcome. Vincent at first refused to let me play, but when I offered my Life Savers as replacements for the buttons that filled in for the missing pieces, he relented. He chose the flavors: wild cherry for the black pawn and peppermint for the white knight. Winner could eat both.

As our mother sprinkled flour and rolled out small doughy circles for the steamed dumplings that would be our dinner that night, Vincent explained the rules, pointing to each piece. "You have sixteen pieces and so do I. One king and queen, two bishops, two knights, two castles, and eight pawns. The pawns can only move forward one step, except on the first move. Then they can move two. But they can only take men by moving crossways like this, except in the beginning, when you can move ahead and take another pawn."

"Why?" I asked as I moved my pawn. "Why can't they move more steps?"

"Because they're pawns," he said.

"But why do they go crossways to take other men? Why aren't there any women and children?"

"Why is the sky blue? Why must you always ask stupid questions?" asked Vincent. "This is a game. These are the rules. I didn't make them up. See. Here. In the book." He jabbed a page with a pawn in his hand. "Pawn. P-A-W-N. Pawn. Read it yourself."

My mother patted the flour off her hands. "Let me see book," she said quietly. She scanned the pages quickly, not reading the foreign English symbols, seeming to search deliberately for nothing in particular.

"This American rules," she concluded at last. "Every time people come out from foreign country, must know rules. You not know, judge say, Too bad, go back. They not telling you why so you can use their way go forward. They say, Don't know why, you find out yourself. But they knowing all the time. Better you take it, find out why yourself." She tossed her head back with a satisfied smile.

I found out about all the whys later. I read the rules and looked up all the big words in a dictionary. I borrowed books from the Chinatown library. I studied each chess piece, trying to absorb the power each contained.

I learned about opening moves and why it's important to control the center early on; the shortest distance between two points is straight down the middle. I learned about the middle game and why tactics between two adversaries are like clashing ideas; the one who plays better has the clearest plans for both attacking and getting out of traps. I learned why it is essential in the endgame to have foresight, a mathematical understanding of all possible moves, and patience; all weaknesses and advantages become evident to a strong adversary and are obscured to a tiring opponent. I discovered that for the whole game one must gather invisible strengths and see the endgame before the game begins.

I also found out why I should never reveal "why" to others. A little knowledge withheld is a great advantage one should store for future use.

That is the power of chess. It is a game of secrets in which one must show and never tell.

I loved the secrets I found within the sixty-four black and white squares. I carefully drew a handmade chessboard and pinned it to the wall next to my bed, where at night I would stare for hours at imaginary battles. Soon I no longer lost any games or Life Savers, but I lost my adversaries. Winston and Vincent decided they were more interested in roaming the streets after school in their Hopalong Cassidy cowboy hats.

On a cold spring afternoon, while walking home from school, I detoured through the playground at the end of our alley. I saw a group of old men, two seated across a folding table playing a game of chess, others smoking pipes, eating peanuts, and watching. I ran home and grabbed Vincent's chess set, which was bound in a cardboard box with rubber bands. I also carefully selected two prized rolls of Life Savers. I came back to the park and approached a man who was observing the game.

"Want to play?" I asked him. His face widened with surprise and he grinned as he looked at the box under my arm.

"Little sister, been a long time since I play with dolls," he said, smiling benevolently. I quickly put the box down next to him on the bench and displayed my retort.

Lau Po, as he allowed me to call him, turned out to be a much better player than my brothers. I lost many games and many Life Savers. But over the weeks, with each diminishing roll of candies, I added new secrets. Lau Po gave me the names. The Double Attack from the East and West Shores. Throwing Stones on the Drowning Man. The Sudden Meeting of the Clan. The Surprise from the Sleeping Guard. The Humble Servant Who Kills the King. Sand in the Eyes of Advancing Forces. A Double Killing Without Blood.

There were also the fine points of chess etiquette. Keep captured men in neat rows, as well-tended prisoners. Never announce "Check" with vanity, lest someone with an unseen sword slit your throat. Never hurl pieces into the sandbox after you have lost a game, because then you must find them again, by yourself, after apologizing to all around you. By the end of the summer, Lau Po had taught me all he knew, and I had become a better chess player.

A small weekend crowd of Chinese people and tourists would gather as I played and defeated my opponents one by one. My mother would join the crowds during these outdoor exhibition games. She sat proudly on the bench, telling my admirers with proper Chinese humility, "Is luck."

A man who watched me play in the park suggested that my mother allow me to play in local chess tournaments. My mother smiled graciously, an answer that meant nothing. I desperately wanted to go, but I bit back my tongue. I knew she would not let me play among strangers. So as we walked home I said in a small voice that I didn't want to play in the local tournament. They would have American rules. If I lost, I would bring shame on my family.

"Is shame you fall down nobody push you," said my mother.

During my first tournament, my mother sat with me in the front row as I waited for my turn. I frequently bounced my legs to unstick them from the cold metal seat of the folding chair. When my name was called, I leapt up. My mother unwrapped something in her lap. It was her *chang*, a small tablet of red jade which held the sun's fire. "Is luck," she whispered and tucked it into my dress pocket. I turned to my opponent, a fifteen-year-old boy from Oakland. He looked at me, wrinkling his nose.

As I began to play, the boy disappeared, the color ran out of the room, and I saw only my white pieces and his black ones waiting on the other side. A light wind began flowing past my ears. It whispered secrets only I could hear.

"Blow from the South," it murmured. "The wind leaves no trail." I saw a clear path, the traps to avoid. The crowd rustled. "Shhh! Shhh!" said the corners of the room. The wind blew stronger. "Throw sand from the East to distract him." The knight came forward ready for the sacrifice. The wind hissed, louder and louder. "Blow, blow, blow. He cannot see. He is blind now. Make him lean away from the wind so he is easier to knock down."

"Check," I said, as the wind roared with laughter. The wind died down to little puffs, my own breath.

My mother placed my first trophy next to a new plastic chess set that the neighborhood Tao society had given to me. As she wiped each piece with a soft cloth, she said, "Next time win more, lose less."

"Ma, it's not how many pieces you lose," I said. "Sometimes you need to lose pieces to get ahead."

"Better to lose less, see if you really need."

At the next tournament, I won again, but it was my mother who wore the triumphant grin.

"Lost eight piece this time. Last time was eleven. What I tell you? Better off lose less!" I was annoyed, but I couldn't say anything.

I attended more tournaments, each one farther away from home. I won all games, in all divisions. The Chinese bakery downstairs from our flat displayed my growing collection of trophies in its window, amidst the dust-covered cakes that were never picked up. The day after I won an important regional tournament, the window encased a fresh sheet cake with whipped-cream frosting and red script saying "Congratulations, Waverly Jong, Chinatown Chess Champion." Soon after that, a flower shop, headstone engraver, and funeral parlor offered to sponsor me in national tournaments. That's when my mother decided I no longer had to do the dishes. Winston and Vincent had to do my chores.

"Why does she get to play and we do all the work," complained Vincent.

"Is new American rules," said my mother. "Meimei play, squeeze all her brains out for win chess. You play, worth squeeze towel."

By my ninth birthday, I was a national chess champion. I was still some 429 points away from grand master status, but I was touted as the Great American Hope, a child prodigy and a girl to boot. They ran a photo of me in *Life* magazine next to a quote in which Bobby Fischer said, "There will never be a woman grand master." "Your move, Bobby," said the caption.

The day they took the magazine picture I wore neatly plaited braids clipped with plastic barrettes trimmed with rhinestones. I was playing in a large high school auditorium that echoed with phlegmy coughs and the squeaky rubber knobs of chair legs sliding across freshly waxed wooden floors. Seated across from me was an American man, about the same age as Lau Po, maybe fifty. I remember that his sweaty brow seemed to weep at my every move.

He wore a dark, malodorous suit. One of his pockets was stuffed with a great white kerchief on which he wiped his palm before sweeping his hand over the chosen chess piece with great flourish.

In my crisp pink-and-white dress with scratchy lace at the neck, one of two my mother had sewn for these special occasions, I would clasp my hands under my chin, the delicate points of my elbows poised lightly on the table in the manner my mother had shown me for posing for the press. I would swing my patent leather shoes back and forth like an impatient child riding on a school bus. Then I would pause, suck in my lips, twirl my chosen piece in midair as if undecided, and then firmly plant it in its new threatening place, with a triumphant smile thrown back at my opponent for good measure.

I no longer played in the alley of Waverly Place. I never visited the playground where the pigeons and old men gathered. I went to school, then directly home to learn new chess secrets, cleverly concealed advantages, more escape routes.

But I found it difficult to concentrate at home. My mother had a habit of standing over me while I plotted out my games. I think she thought of herself as my protective ally. Her lips would be sealed tight, and after each move I made, a soft "Hmmmmph" would escape from her nose.

"Ma, I can't practice when you stand there like that," I said one day. She retreated to the kitchen and made loud noises with the pots and pans. When the crashing stopped, I could see out of the corner of my eye that she was standing in the doorway. "Hmmmmph!" Only this one came out of her tight throat.

My parents made many concessions to allow me to practice. One time I complained that the bedroom I shared was so noisy that I couldn't think. Thereafter, my brothers slept in a bed in the living room facing the street. I said I couldn't finish my rice; my head didn't work right when my stomach was too full. I left the table with half-finished bowls and nobody complained. But there was one duty I couldn't avoid. I had to accompany my mother on Saturday market days when I had no tournament to play. My mother would proudly walk with me, visiting many shops, buying very little. "This my daughter Wave-ly Jong," she said to whoever looked her way.

One day after we left a shop I said under my breath, "I wish you wouldn't do that, telling everybody I'm your daughter." My mother stopped walking. Crowds of people with heavy bags pushed past us on the sidewalk, bumping into first one shoulder, then another.

"Aiii-ya. So shame be with mother?" She grasped my hand even tighter as she glared at me.

I looked down. "It's not that, it's just so obvious. It's just so embarrassing."

"Embarrass you be my daughter?" Her voice was cracking with anger.

"That's not what I meant. That's not what I said."

"What you say?"

I knew it was a mistake to say anything more, but I heard my voice speaking. "Why do you have to use me to show off? If you want to show off, then why don't you learn to play chess?"

My mother's eyes turned into dangerous black slits. She had no words for me, just sharp silence.

I felt the wind rushing around my hot ears. I jerked my hand out of my mother's tight grasp and spun around, knocking into an old woman. Her bag of groceries spilled to the ground.

"Aii-ya! Stupid girl!" my mother and the woman cried. Oranges and tin cans careened down the sidewalk. As my mother stooped to help the old woman pick up the escaping food, I took off.

I raced down the street, dashing between people, not looking back as my mother screamed shrilly, "Meimei! Meimei!" I fled down an alley, past dark, curtained shops and merchants washing the grime off their windows. I sped into the sunlight, into a large street crowded with tourists examining trinkets and souvenirs. I ducked into another dark alley, down another street, up another alley. I ran until it hurt and I realized I had nowhere to go, that I was not running from anything. The alleys contained no escape routes.

My breath came out like angry smoke. It was cold. I sat down on an upturned plastic pail next to a stack of empty boxes, cupping my chin with my hands, thinking hard. I imagined my mother, first walking briskly down one street or another looking for me, then giving up and returning home to await my arrival. After two hours, I stood up on creaking legs and slowly walked home.

The alley was quiet and I could see the yellow lights shining from our flat like two tiger's eyes in the night. I climbed the sixteen steps to the door, advancing quietly up each so as not to make any warning sounds. I turned the knob; the door was locked. I heard a chair moving, quick steps, the locks turning—click! click! click!—and then the door opened.

"About time you got home," said Vincent. "Boy, are you in trouble."

He slid back to the dinner table. On a platter were the remains of a large fish, its fleshy head still connected to bones swimming upstream in vain escape. Standing there waiting for my punishment, I heard my mother speak in a dry voice.

"We not concerning this girl. This girl not have concerning for us."

Nobody looked at me. Bone chopsticks clinked against the inside of bowls being emptied into hungry mouths.

I walked into my room, closed the door, and lay down on my bed. The room was dark, the ceiling filled with shadows from the dinnertime lights of neighboring flats.

In my head, I saw a chessboard with sixty-four black and white squares. Opposite me was my opponent, two angry black slits. She wore a triumphant smile. "Strongest wind cannot be seen," she said.

Her black men advanced across the plane, slowly marching to each successive level as a single unit. My white pieces screamed as they scurried and fell off the board one by one. As her men drew closer to my edge, I felt myself growing light. I rose up into the air and flew out the window. Higher and higher, above the alley, over the tops of tiled roofs, where I was gathered up by the wind and pushed up toward the night sky until everything below me disappeared and I was alone.

I closed my eyes and pondered my next move.

FYS 102: The Core of the World

Marc Chagall. *I and the Village.* (1911)

Edward Hopper. *Nighthawks.* (1942)

Concerning the Islands Recently Discovered in the Indian Sea (1494)

Christopher Columbus

Because my undertakings have attained success, I know that it will be pleasing to you: these I have determined to relate, so that you may be made acquainted with everything done and discovered in this our voyage. On the thirty-third day after I departed from Cadiz, I came to the Indian sea, where I found many islands inhabited by men without number, of all which I took possession for our most fortunate king, with proclaiming heralds and flying standards, no one objecting. To the first of these I gave the name of the blessed Saviour, on whose aid relying I had reached this as well as the other islands. But the Indians call it Guanahany. I also called each one of the others by a new name. For I ordered one island to be called Santa Maria of the Conception, another Fernandina, another Isabella, another Juana, and so on with the rest.

As soon as we had arrived at that island which I have just now said was called Juana, I proceeded along its coast towards the west for some distance; I found it so large and without perceptible end, that I believed it to be not an island, but the continental country of Cathay; seeing, however, no towns or cities situated on the sea-coast, but only some villages and rude farms, with whose inhabitants I was unable to converse, because as soon as they saw us they took flight.

I proceeded farther, thinking that I would discover some city or large residences. At length, perceiving that we had gone far enough, that nothing new appeared, and that this way was leading us to the north, which I wished to avoid, because it was winter on the land, and it was my intention to go to the south, moreover the winds were becoming violent, I therefore determined that no other plans were practicable, and so, going back, I returned to a certain bay that I had noticed, from which I sent two of our men to the land, that they might find out whether there was a king in this country, or any cities. These men traveled for three days, and they found people and houses without number, but they were small and without any government, therefore they returned.

Now in the meantime I had learned from certain Indians, whom I had seized there, that this country was indeed an island, and therefore I proceeded towards the east, keeping all the time near the coast, for 322 miles, to the extreme ends of this island. From this place I saw another island to the east distant from this Juana 54 miles, which I called forthwith Hispana; and I sailed to it; and I steered along the northern coast, as at Juana, towards the east, 564 miles.

And the said Juana and the other islands there appear very fertile. This island is surrounded by many very safe and wide harbors, not excelled by any others that I have ever seen. Many great and salubrious rivers flow through it. There are also many very high mountains there. All these islands are very beautiful, and distinguished by various qualities; they are accessible, and full of a great variety of trees stretching up to the stars; the leaves of which I believe are never shed, for I saw them as green and flourishing as they are usually in Spain in the month of May; some of them were blossoming, some were bearing fruit, some were in other conditions; each one was thriving in its own way. The nightingale and various other birds without number were singing, in the month of November, when I was exploring them.

There are besides in the said island Juana seven or eight kinds of palm trees, which far excel ours in height and beauty, just as all the other trees, herbs, and fruits do. There are also excellent pine trees, vast plains and meadows, a variety of birds, a variety of honey, and a variety of metals, excepting iron. In the one which was called Hispana, as we said above, there are great and beautiful mountains, vast fields, groves, fertile plains, very suitable for planting and cultivating, and for the building of houses. The convenience of the harbors in this island, and the remarkable number of rivers contributing to the healthfulness of man, exceed belief, unless one has seen them. The trees, pasturage, and fruits of this island differ greatly from those of Juana. This Hispana, moreover, abounds in different kinds of spices, in gold, and in metals. On this island, indeed, and on all the others which I have seen, and of which I have knowledge, the inhabitants of both sexes go always naked, just as they came into the world, except some of the women, who use a covering of a leaf or some foliage, or a cotton cloth, which they make themselves for that purpose.

All these people lack, as I said above, every kind of iron; they are also without weapons, which indeed are unknown; nor are they competent to use them, not on account of deformity of body, for they are well formed, but because they are timid and full of fear. They carry for weapons, however, reeds baked in the sun, on the lower ends of which they fasten some shafts of dried wood rubbed down to a point; and indeed they do not venture to use these always; for it frequently happened when I sent two or three of my men to some of the villages, that they might speak with the natives, a compact troop of the Indians would march out, and as soon as they saw our men approaching, they would quickly take flight, children being pushed aside by their fathers, and fathers by their children. And this was not because any hurt or injury had been inflicted on any one of them, for to every one whom I visited and with whom I was able to converse, I distributed whatever I had, cloth and many other things, no return being made to me; but they are by nature fearful and timid.

Yet when they perceive that they are safe, putting aside all fear, they are of simple manners and trustworthy, and very liberal with everything they have, refusing no one who asks for anything they may possess, and even themselves inviting us to ask for things. They show greater love for all others than for themselves; they give valuable things for trifles, being satisfied even with a very small return, or with nothing; however, I forbade that things so small and of no value should be given to them, such as pieces of plates, dishes, and glass, likewise keys and shoelace tips although if they were to obtain these, it seemed to them like getting the most beautiful jewels in the world. It happened, indeed, that a certain sailor obtained in exchange for a shoelace tips as much worth of gold as would equal three golden coins; and likewise other things for articles of very little value, especially for new silver coins, and for some gold coins, to obtain which they gave whatever the seller desired, as for instance an ounce and a half and two ounces of gold, or thirty and forty pounds of cotton, with which they were already acquainted. They also traded cotton and gold for pieces of bows, bottles, jugs and jars, like persons without reason, which I forbade because it was very wrong; and I gave to them many beautiful and pleasing things that I had brought with me, no value being taken in exchange, in order that I might the more easily make them friendly to me, that they might be made worshipers of Christ, and that they might be full of love towards our king, queen, and prince, and the whole Spanish nation; also that they might be zealous to search out and collect, and deliver to us those things of which they had plenty, and which we greatly needed.

These people practice no kind of idolatry; on the contrary they firmly believe that all strength and power, and in fact all good things are in heaven, and that I had come down from thence with these ships and sailors; and in this belief I was received there after they had put aside fear. Nor are they slow or unskilled, but of excellent and acute understanding; and the men who have navigated that sea give an account of everything in an admirable manner; but they never saw people clothed, nor these kind of ships. As soon as I reached that sea, I seized by force several Indians on the first island, in order that they might learn from us, and in like manner tell us about those things in these lands of which they themselves had knowledge; and the plan succeeded, for in a short time we understood them and they us, sometimes by gestures and signs, sometimes by words; and it was a great advantage to us. They are coming with me now, yet always believing that I descended from heaven, although they have been living with us for a long time, and are living with us to-day. And these men were the first who announced it wherever we landed, continually proclaiming to the others in a loud voice, "Come, come, and you will see the celestial people." Whereupon both women and men, both young men and old men, laying aside the fear caused a little before, visited us eagerly, filling the road with a great crowd, some bringing food, and some drink, with great love and extraordinary goodwill.

On every island there are many canoes of a single piece of wood; and though narrow, yet in length and shape similar to our row-boats, but swifter in movement. They steer only by oars. Some of these boats are large, some small, some of medium size. Yet they row many of the larger row-boats with eighteen cross-benches, with which they cross to all those islands, which are innumerable, and with these boats they perform their trading, and carry on commerce among them. I saw some of these row-boats or canoes which were carrying seventy and eighty rowers.

In all these islands there is no difference in the appearance of the people, nor in the manners and language, but all understand each other mutually; a fact that is very important for the end which I suppose to be earnestly desired by our most illustrious king, that is, their conversion to the holy religion of Christ, to which in truth, as far as I can perceive, they are very ready and favorably inclined.

I said before how I proceeded along the island Juana in a straight line from west to east 322 miles, according to which course and the length of the way, I am able to say that this Juana is larger than England and Scotland together; for besides the said 322 thousand paces, there are two more provinces in that part which lies toward the west, which I did not visit; one of these the Indians call Anan, whose inhabitants are born with tails. They extend to 180 miles in length, as I have learned from those Indians I have with me, who are all acquainted with these islands.

But the circumference of Hispana is greater than all Spain from Colonia [Catalonia] to Fontarabia [Fuenterrabia]. And this is easily proved, because its fourth side, which I myself passed along in a straight line from west to east, extends 540 miles. This island is to be desired and is very desirable, and not to be despised; in which, although as I have said, I solemnly took possession of all the others for our most invincible king, and their government is entirely committed to the said king, yet I especially took possession of a certain large town, in a very convenient location, and adapted to all kinds of gain and commerce, to which we give the name of our Lord of the

Nativity. And I commanded a fort to be built where forthwith, which must be completed by this time; in which I left as many men as seemed necessary, with all kinds of arms, and plenty of food for more than a year. Likewise one caravel, and for the construction of others men skilled in this trade and in other professions; and also the extraordinary good will and friendship of the king of this island toward us. For those people are very amiable and kind, to such a degree that the said king gloried in calling me his brother. And if they should change their minds, and should wish to hurt those who remained in the fort, they would not be able, because they lack weapons, they go naked, and are too cowardly. For that reason those who hold the said fort are at least able to resist easily this whole island, without any imminent danger to themselves, so long as they do not transgress the regulations and command which we gave.

In all these islands, as I have understood, each man is content with only one wife, except the princes or kings, who are permitted to have twenty. The women appear to work more than the men. I was not able to find out surely whether they have individual property, for I saw that one man had the duty of distributing to the others, especially refreshments, food, and things of that kind. I found no monstrosities among them, as very many supposed, but men of great reverence, and friendly. Nor are they black like the Ethiopians. They have straight hair, hanging down. They do not remain where the solar rays send out the heat, for the strength of the sun is very great here, because it is distant from the equinoctial line, as it seems, only twenty-six degrees. On the tops of the mountains too the cold is severe, but the Indians, however, moderate it, partly by being accustomed to the place, and partly by the help of very hot victuals, of which they eat frequently and immoderately.

And so I did not see any monstrosity, nor did I have knowledge of them any where, excepting a certain island named Charis, which is the second in passing from Hispana to India. This island is inhabited by a certain people who are considered very warlike by their neighbors. These eat human flesh. The said people have many kinds of row-boats, in which they cross over to all the other Indian islands, and seize and carry away everything that they can. They differ in no way from the others, only that they wear long hair like the women. They use bows and darts made of reeds, with sharpened shafts fastened to the larger end, as we have described. On this account they are considered warlike, wherefore the other Indians are afflicted with continual fear, but I regard them as of no more account than the others. These are the people who visit certain women, who alone inhabit the island of Mateunin, which is the first in passing from Hispana to India. These women, moreover, perform no kind of work of their sex, for they use bows and darts, like those I have described of their husbands; they protect themselves with sheets of copper, of which there is a great abundance among them. They tell of another island greater than the aforesaid Hispana, whose inhabitants are without hair, and which abounds in gold above all the others. I am bringing with me men of this island and of the others that I have seen, who give proof of the things that I have described.

Finally, that I may compress in a few words the brief account of our departure and quick return, and the gain, I promise this, that if I am supported by our most invincible sovereigns with a little of their help, as much gold can be supplied as they will need, indeed as much of spices, of cotton, of mastic gum (which is only found in Chios), also as much of aloes wood, and as many slaves for the navy, as their Majesties will wish to demand. Likewise rhubarb and other kinds of spices, which I suppose these men whom I left in the said fort have already found, and will continue to find; since I remained in no place longer than the winds forced me, except in the town of the Nativity, while I provided for the building of the fort, and for the safety of all. Which things, although they are very great and remarkable, yet they would have been much greater, if I had been aided by as many ships as the occasion required.

Truly great and wonderful is this, and not corresponding to our merits, but to the holy Christian religion, and to the piety and religion of our sovereigns, because what the human understanding could not attain, that the divine will has granted to human efforts. For God is wont to listen to his servants who love his precepts, even in impossibilities, as has happened to us on the present occasion, who have attained that which hitherto mortal men have never reached. For if anyone has written or said anything about these islands, it was all with obscurities and conjectures; no one claims that he had seen them; from which they seemed like fables. Therefore let the king and queen, the princes and their most fortunate kingdoms, and all other countries of Christendom give thanks to our Lord and Saviour Jesus Christ, who has bestowed upon us so great a victory and gift. Let religious processions be solemnized; let sacred festivals be given; let the churches be covered with festive garlands. Let Christ rejoice on earth, as he rejoices in heaven, when he foresees coming to salvation so many souls of people hitherto lost. Let us be glad also, as well on account of the exaltation of our faith, as on account of the increase of our temporal affairs, of which not only Spain, but universal Christendom will be partaker. These things that have been done are thus briefly related. Farewell.

Lisbon, the day before the Ides of March.
Christopher Columbus, Admiral of the Ocean Fleet

from Living Buddha, Living Christ (2007)

Thich Nhat Hanh

Touching Jesus

My path to discovering Jesus as one of my spiritual ancestors was not easy. The colonization of my country by the French was deeply connected with the efforts of the Christian missionaries. In the late seventeenth century, Alexander de Rhôdes, one of the most active missionaries, wrote in his *Cathechismus in Octo Dies Divisis*: "Just as when a cursed, barren tree is cut down, the branches that are still on it will also fall, when the sinister and deceitful Sakya [Buddha] is defeated, the idolatrous fabrications that proceed from him will also be destroyed." Later, in the late 1950s and early 1960s, Catholic Archbishop Ngo Dinh Thuc, in his efforts to evangelize Vietnam, leaned heavily on the political power of his brother, President Ngo Dinh Diêm. President Diêm's 1963 decree prohibiting the celebration of the Wesak, the most important Buddhist national holiday, was the straw that broke our back. Tens of thousands of lay and ordained Buddhists demonstrated for religious freedom, leading to a coup d'état and the overthrow of the Diêm regime. In such an atmosphere of discrimination and injustice against non-Christians, it was difficult for me to discover the beauty of Jesus' teachings.

It was only later, through friendships with Christian men and women who truly embody the spirit of understanding and compassion of Jesus, that I have been able to touch the depths of Christianity. The moment I met Martin Luter King, Jr., I knew I was in the presence of a holy person. Not just his good work but his very being was a source of great inspiration for me. And others, less well known, have made me feel that Lord Jesus is still here with us. Hebe Kohlbrugge, a beautiful Dutch woman who saved the lives of thousands of Jews during World War II, was so committed to helping Vietnamese orphans and other desperately needy children during the war that when her government refused to support this work, she gave them back her World War II medals. Reverend Heinz Kloppenburg, General Secretary of the German Fellowship of Reconciliation, also supported our humanitarian work. He was so kind and so open, I only needed to say a few words to him and he understood everything right away. Through men and women like these, I feel I have been able to touch Jesus Christ and His tradition.

Real Communication

On the altar in my hermitage in France are images of Buddha and Jesus, and every time I light incense, I touch both of them as my spiritual ancestors. I can do this because of contact with these real Christians. When you touch someone who authentically represents a tradition, you not only touch his or her tradition, you also touch your own. This quality is essential for dialogue. When participants are willing to learn from each other, dialogue takes place just by their being together. When those who represent a spiritual tradition embody the essence of their tradition, just the way they walk, sit, and smile speaks volumes about the tradition.

In fact, sometimes it is more difficult to have a dialogue with people in our own tradition than with those of another tradition. Most of us have suffered from feeling misunderstood or even betrayed by those of our own tradition. But if brothers and sisters in the same tradition cannot understand and communicate with each other, how can they communicate with those outside their tradition? For dialogue to be fruitful, we need to live deeply our own tradition and, at the same time, listen deeply to others. Through the practice of deep looking and deep listening, we become free, able to see the beauty and values in our own *and* others' tradition.

Many years ago, I recognized that by understanding your own tradition better, you also develop increased respect, consideration, and understanding for others. I had had a naive thought, a kind of prejudice inherited from my ancestors. I thought that because Buddha had taught for forty-five years and Jesus for only two or three, that Buddha must have been a more accomplished teacher. I had that thought because I did not know the teachings of the Buddha well enough.

One day when he was thirty-eight years old, the Buddha met King Prasenajit of Kosala. The king said, "Reverend, you are young, yet people call you 'The Highest Enlightened One.' There are holy men in our country eighty and ninety years old, venerated by many people, yet none of them claims to be the highest enlightened one. How can a young man like you make such a claim?"

The Buddha replied, "Your majesty, enlightenment is not a matter of age. A tiny spark of fire has the power to burn down a whole city. A small poisonous snake can kill you in an instant. A baby prince has the potentiality of a king. And a young monk has the capacity of becoming enlightened and changing the world." We can learn about others by studying ourselves.

For any dialogue between traditions to be deep, we have to be aware of both the positive and negative aspects of our own tradition. In Buddhism, for example, there have been many schisms. One hundred years after the passing of the Buddha, the community of his disciples divided into two parts; within four hundred years, there were twenty schools; and since then, there have been many more. Fortunately, these separations have, for the most part, not been too painful, and the garden of Buddhism is now filled with many beautiful flowers, each school representing an attempt to keep the Buddha's teachings alive under new circumstances. Living organisms need to change and grow. By respecting the differences within our own church and seeing how these differences enrich one another, we are more open to appreciating the richness and diversity of other traditions.

In a true dialogue, both sides are willing to change. We have to appreciate that truth can be received from outside of—not only within—our own group. If we do not believe that, entering into dialogue would be a waste of time. If we think we monopolize the truth and we still organize a dialogue, it is not authentic. We have to believe that by engaging in dialogue with the other person, we have the possibility of making a change within ourselves, that we can become deeper. Dialogue is not a means for assimilation in the sense that one side expands and incorporates the other into its "self." Dialogue must be practiced on the basis of "non-self." We have to allow what is good, beautiful, and meaningful in the other's tradition to transform us.

But the most basic principle of interfaith dialogue is that the dialogue must begin, first of all, within oneself. Our capacity to make peace with another person and with the world depends very much on our capacity to make peace with ourselves. If we are at war with our parents, our family, our society, or our church, there is probably a war going on inside us also, so the most basic work for peace is to return to ourselves and create harmony among the elements within us—our feelings, our perceptions, and our mental states. That is why the practice of meditation, looking deeply, is so important. We must recognize and accept the conflicting elements that are within us and their underlying causes. It takes time, but the effort always bears fruit. When we have peace within, real dialogue with others is possible.

Interbeing

In the Psalms, it says, "Be still and know that I am God." "Be still" means to become peaceful and concentrated. The Buddhist term is *samatha* (stopping, calming, concentrating). "Know" means to acquire wisdom, insight, or understanding. The Buddhist term is *vipasyana* (insight, or looking deeply). "Looking deeply" means observing something or someone with so much concentration that the distinction between observer and observed disappears. The result is insight into the true nature of the object. When we look into the heart of a flower, we see clouds, sunshine, minerals, time, the earth, and everything else in the cosmos in it. Without clouds, there could be no rain, and there would be no flower. Without time, the flower could not bloom. In fact, the flower is made entirely of non-flower elements; it has no independent, individual existence. It "inter-is" with everything else in the universe. Interbeing is a new term, but I believe it will be in the dictionary soon because it is such an important word. When we see the nature of interbeing, barriers between ourselves and others are dissolved, and peace, love, and understanding are possible. Whenever there is understanding, compassion is born.

Just as a flower is made only of non-flower elements, Buddhism is made only of non-Buddhist elements, including Christian ones, and Christianity is made of non-Christian elements, including Buddhist ones. We have different roots, traditions, and ways of seeing, but we share the common qualities of love, understanding, and acceptance. For our dialogue to be open, we need to open our hearts, set aside our prejudices, listen deeply, and represent truthfully what we know and understand. To do this, we need a certain amount of faith. In Buddhism, faith means confidence in our and others' abilities to wake up to our deepest capacity of loving and understanding. In Christianity, faith means trust in God, the One who represents love, understanding, dignity, and truth. When we are still, looking deeply, and touching the source of our true wisdom, we touch the living Buddha and the living Christ in ourselves and in each person we meet.

. . . If we can enter the twenty-first century with this spirit of mutual understanding and acceptance, our children and their children will surely benefit.

Woman, Why Are You Weeping? (1999)

Jane Kenyon

The morning after the crucifixion,
Mary Magdalene came to see the body
of Christ. She found the stone
rolled away from an empty tomb. Two
figures dressed in white asked her,
"Woman, why are you weeping?"

"Because," she replied, "they have
taken away my Lord, and I don't know
where they have laid him."

Returned from long travel, I sit
in the familiar, sun-streaked pew, waiting
for the bread and wine of Holy Communion.
The old comfort does not rise in me, only
apathy and bafflement.
                              India, with her ceaseless
bells and fire; her crows calling stridently
all night; India with her sandalwood
smoke, and graceful gods, many-headed and many-
armed, has taken away the one who blessed
and kept me.
                  The thing is done, as surely
as if my luggage had been stolen from the train.
Men and women with faces as calm as lakes at dusk
have taken away my Lord, and I don't know
where to find him.

•   •   •

What is Brahman? I don't know Brahman.
I don't know *saccidandana*, the bliss
of the absolute and unknowable.
I only know that I have lost the Lord
in whose image I was made.

Whom shall I thank for this pear,
sweet and white? Food *is* God, *Prasadam,*

God's mercy. But who is this God?
The one who is *not this, not that*?

The absurdity of all religious forms
breaks over me, as the absurdity of language
made me feel faint the day I heard friends
giving commands to their neighbor's dog
in Spanish. . . . At first I laughed,
but then I became frightened.

•   •   •

They have taken away my Lord, a person
whose life I held inside me. I saw him
heal, and teach, and eat among sinners.
I saw him break the sabbath to make a higher
sabbath. I saw him lose his temper.

I knew his anguish when he called, "I thirst!"
and received vinegar to drink. The Bible
does not say it, but I am sure he turned
his head away. Not long after he cried, "My God,
my God, why have you forsaken me?"
I watched him reveal himself risen
to Magdalene with a single word: "Mary!"

It was my habit to speak to him. His goodness
perfumed my life. I loved the Lord, he heard
my cry, and he loved me as his own.

•   •   •

A man sleeps on the pavement, on a raffia mat—
the only thing that has not been stolen from him.
This stranger who loves what cannot be understood
has put out my light with his calm face.

Shall the fire answer my fears and vapors?
The fire cares nothing for my illness,
nor does Brahma, the creator, nor Shiva who sees
evil with his terrible third eye; Vishnu,
the protector, does not protect me.

I've brought home the smell of the streets
in the folds of soft, bright cotton garments.
When I iron them the steam brings back
the complex odors that rise from the gutters,
of tuberoses, urine, dust, joss, and death.

•   •   •

On a curb in Allahabad the family gathers
under a dusty tree, a few quilts hung
between lightposts and a wattle fence
for privacy. Eleven sit or lie around the fire
while a woman of sixty stirs a huge pot.
Rice cooks in a narrow-necked crock
on the embers. A small dog, with patches of bald,
red skin on his back, lies on the corner
of the piece of canvas that serves as flooring.

Looking at them I lose my place.
I don't know why I was born, or why
I live in a house in New England, or why I am
a visitor with heavy luggage giving lectures
for the State Department. Why am I not
tap-tapping with my fingernail
on the rolled-up window of a white Government car,
a baby in my arms, drugged to look feverish?

•   •   •

Rajiv did not weep. He did not cover
his face with his hands when we rowed past
the dead body of a newborn nudging the grassy
banks at Benares—close by a snake
rearing up, and a cast-off garland of flowers.

He explained. When a family are too poor
to cremate their dead, they bring the body
here, and slip it into the waters of the Ganges
and Yamuna rivers.
                    Perhaps the child was dead
at birth; perhaps it had the misfortune
to be born a girl. The mother may have walked
two days with her baby's body to this place
where Gandhi's ashes once struck the waves
with a sound like gravel being scuffed
over the edge of a bridge.

"What shall we do about this?" I asked
my God, who even then was leaving me. The reply
was scorching wind, lapping of water, pull
of the black oarsmen on the oars. . . .

The Ones Who Walk Away from Omelas (1973)

Ursula K. Le Guin

With a clamor of bells that set the swallows soaring, the Festival of Summer came to the City of Omelas, bright-towered by the sea. The rigging of the boats in harbor sparkled with flags. In the streets between houses and red roofs and painted walls, between old moss-grown gardens and under avenues of trees, past great parks and public buildings, processions moved. Some were decrous: old people in long stiff robes of mauve and grey, grave master workmen, quiet, merry women carrying their babies and chatting as they walked. In other streets the music beat faster, a shimmering of gong and tambourine, and the people went dancing, the procession was a dance. Children dodged in and out, their high calls rising like the swallows' crossing flights over the music and the singing. All the processions wound towards the north side of the city, where on the great water-meadow called the Green Fields boys and girls, naked in the bright air, with mud-stained feet and ankles and long, lithe arms, exercised their restive horses before the race. The horses wore no gear at all but a halter without bit. Their manes were braided with streamers of silver, gold, and green. They flared their nostrils and pranced and boasted to one another; they were vastly excited, the horse being the only animal who has adopted our ceremonies as his own. Far off to the north and west the mountains stood up half encircling Omelas on her bay. The air of morning was so clear that the snow still crowning the Eighteen Peaks burned with white-gold fire across the miles of sunlit air, under the dark blue of the sky. There was just enough wind to make the banners that marked the racecourse snap and flutter now and then. In the silence of the broad green meadows one could hear the music winding through the city streets, farther and nearer and ever approaching, a cheerful faint sweetness of the air that from time to time trembled and gathered together and broke out into the great joyous clanging of the bells.

Joyous! How is one to tell about joy? How describe the citizens of Omelas?

They were not simple folk, you see, though they were happy. But we do not say the words of cheer much any more. All smiles have become archaic. Given a description such as this one tends to make certain assumptions. Given a description such as this one tends to look next for the King, mounted on a splendid stallion and surrounded by his noble knights, or perhaps in a golden litter borne by great-muscled slaves. But there was no king. They did not use swords, or keep slaves. They were not barbarians. I do not know the rules and laws of their society, but I suspect that they were singularly few. As they did without monarchy and slavery, so they also got on without the stock exchange, the advertisement, the secret police, and the bomb. Yet I repeat that these were not simple folk, not dulcet shepherds, noble savages, bland utopians. They were not less complex than us. The trouble is that we have a bad habit, encouraged by pedants and sophisticates, of considering happiness as something rather stupid. Only pain is intellectual, only evil interesting. This is the treason of the artist: a refusal to admit the banality of evil and the terrible boredom of pain. If you can't lick 'em, join 'em. If it hurts, repeat it. But to praise despair is to condemn delight, to embrace violence is to lose hold of everything else. We have almost lost hold; we can no longer describe a happy man, nor make any celebration of joy. How can I tell you about the people of Omelas? They were not naïve and happy children—though their children were, in fact, happy. They were mature, intelligent, passionate adults whose lives were not wretched. O miracle! but I wish I could describe it better. I wish I could convince you. Omelas sounds in my words like a city in a fairy tale, long ago and far away, once upon a time. Perhaps it would be best if you imagined it as your own fancy bids, assuming it will rise to the occasion, for certainly I cannot suit you all. For instance, how about technology? I think that there would be no cars or helicopters in and above the streets; this follows from the fact that the people of Omelas are happy people. Happiness is based on a just discrimination of what is necessary, what is neither necessary nor destructive, and what is destructive. In the middle category, however— that of the unnecessary but undestructive, that of comfort, luxury, exuberance, etc.—they could perfectly well have central heating, subway trains, washing machines, and all kinds of marvelous devices not yet invented here, floating light-sources, fuelless power, a cure for the common cold. Or they could have none of that; it doesn't matter. As you like it. I incline to think that people from towns up and down the coast have been coming to Omelas during the last days before the Festival on very fast little trains and double-decked trams, and that the train station of Omelas is actually the handsomest building in town, though plainer than the magnificent Farmers' Market. But even granted trains, I fear that Omelas so far strikes some of you as goody-goody. Smiles, bells, parades, horses, bleh. If so, please add an orgy. If an orgy would help, don't hesitate. Let us not, however, have temples from which issue beautiful nude priests and priestesses already half in ecstasy and ready to copulate with any man or woman, lover or stranger, who desires union with the deep godhead of the blood, although that was my first idea. But really it would be better not to have any temples in Omelas—at least, not manned temples. Religion yes, clergy no. Surely the beautiful nudes can just wander about, offering themselves like divine soufflés to the hunger of the needy and the rapture of the flesh. Let them join the processions. Let tambourines be struck above the copulations, and the glory of desire be proclaimed upon the gongs, and (a not unimportant point) let the offspring of these delightful rituals be beloved and looked after by all. One thing I know there is none of in Omelas is guilt. But what else should there be? I thought at first there were no drugs, but that is puritanical. For those who like it, the faint insistent sweetness of *drooz* may perfume the ways of the city, *drooz* which first brings a great lightness and brilliance to the mind and limbs, and then after some hours a dreamy languor, and wonderful visions at last of the very arcana and inmost secrets of the Universe, as well as exciting the pleasure of sex beyond belief; and it is not habit-forming. For more modest tastes I think there ought to be beer. What else, what else belongs in the joyous city? The sense of victory, surely, the celebration of courage. But as we did without clergy, let us do without soldiers. The joy built upon successful slaughter is not the right kind of joy; it will not do; it is fearful and it is trivial. A boundless and generous contentment, a magnanimous triumph felt not against some outer enemy but in communion with the finest and fairest in the souls of all men everywhere and the splendor of the world's summer: this is what swells the hearts of the people of Omelas, and the victory they celebrate is that of life. I really don't think many of them need to take *drooz*.

Most of the processions have reached the Green Fields by now. A marvelous smell of cooking goes forth from the red and blue tents of the provisioners. The faces of small children are amiably sticky; in the benign gray beard of a man a couple of crumbs of rich pastry are entangled. The youths and girls have mounted their horses and are beginning to group around the starting line of the course. An old woman, small, fat, and laughing, is passing out flowers from a basket, and tall young men wear her flowers in their shining hair. A child of nine or ten sits at the edge of the crowd, alone, playing on a wooden flute. People pause to listen, and they smile, but they do not speak to him, for he never ceases playing and never sees them, his dark eyes wholly rapt in the sweet, thin magic of the tune.

He finishes, and slowly lowers his hands holding the wooden flute.

As if that little private silence were the signal, all at once a trumpet sounds from the pavilion near the starting line: imperious, melancholy, piercing. The horses rear on their slender legs, and some of them neigh in answer. Sober-faced, the young riders stroke the horses' necks and soothe them, whispering, "Quiet, quiet, there my beauty, my hope. . . ." They begin to form in rank along the starting line. The crowds along the race-course are like a field of grass and flowers in the wind. The Festival of Summer has begun.

Do you believe? Do you accept the festival, the city, the joy? No? Then let me describe one more thing.

In a basement under one of the beautiful public buildings of Omelas, or perhaps in the cellar of one of its spacious private homes, there is a room. It has one locked door, and no window. A little light seeps in dustily between cracks in the boards, secondhand from a cobwebbed window somewhere across the cellar. In one corner of the little room a couple of mops, with stiff, clotted, foul-smelling heads, stand near a rusty bucket. The floor is dirt, a little damp to the touch, as cellar dirt usually is. The room is about three paces long and two wide: a mere broom closet or dis-used tool room. In the room a child is sitting. It could be a boy or a girl. It looks about six, but actually is nearly ten. It is feeble-minded. Perhaps it was born defective, or perhaps it has become imbecile through fear, malnutrition, and neglect. It picks its nose and occasionally fumbles vaguely with its toes or genitals, as it sits hunched in the corner farthest from the bucket and the two mops. It is afraid of the mops. It finds them horrible. It shuts its eyes, but it knows the mops are still standing there; and the door is locked; and nobody will come. The door is always locked; and nobody ever comes, except that sometimes—the child has no under-standing of time or interval—sometimes the door rattles terribly and opens, and a person, or several people, are there. One of them may come in and kick the child to make it stand up. The others never come close, but peer in at it with frightened, disgusted eyes. The food bowl and the water jug are hastily filled, the door is locked, the eyes disappear. The people at the door never say anything, but the child, who has not always lived in the tool room, and can remember sunlight and its mother's voice, sometimes speaks. "I will be good," it says. "Please let me out. I will be good!" They never answer. The child used to scream for help at night, and cry a good deal, but now it only makes a kind of whining "eh-haa, eh-haa" and it speaks less and less often. It is so thin there are no calves to its legs; its belly protrudes; it lives on a half-bowl of corn meal and grease a day. It is naked. Its buttocks and thighs are a mass of festered sores, as it sits in its own excrement continually.

They all know it is there, all the people of Omelas. Some of them have come to see it, others are content merely to know it is there. They all know that it has to be there. Some of them understand why, and some do not, but they all understand that their happiness, the beauty of their city, the tenderness of their friendships, the health of their children, the wisdom of their scholars, the skill of their makers, even the abundance of their harvest and the kindly weathers of their skies, depend wholly on this child's abominable misery.

This is usually explained to children when they are between eight and twelve, whenever they seem capable of understanding; and most of those who come to see the child are young people, though often enough an adult comes, or comes back, to see the child. No matter how well the matter has been explained to them, these young spectators are always shocked and sickened at the sight. They feel disgust, which they had thought themselves superior to. They feel anger, outrage, impotence, despite all the explanations. They would like to do something for the child. But there is nothing they can do. If the child were brought up into the sunlight out of that vile place, if it were cleaned and fed and comforted, that would be a good thing, indeed; but if it were done, in that day and hour all the prosperity and beauty and delight of Omelas would wither and be destroyed. Those are the terms. To exchange all the goodness and grace of every life in Omelas for that single, small improvement: to throw away the happiness of thousands for the chance of the happiness of one: that would be to let guilt within the walls indeed.

The terms are strict and absolute; there may not even be a kind word spoken to the child.

Often the young people go home in tears, or in a tearless rage, when they have seen the child and faced this terrible paradox. They may brood over it for weeks or years. But as time goes on they begin to realize that even if the child could be released, it would not get much good of its freedom: a little vague pleasure of warmth and food, no doubt, but little more. It is too degraded and imbecile to know any real joy. It has been afraid too long ever to be free of fear. Its habits are too uncouth for it to respond to humane treatment. Indeed, after so long it would probably be wretched without walls about it to protect it, and darkness for its eyes, and its own excrement to sit in. Their tears at the bitter injustice dry when they begin to perceive the terrible justice of reality, and to accept it. Yet it is their tears and anger, the trying of their generosity and the acceptance of their helplessness, which are perhaps the true source of the splendor of their lives. Theirs is no vapid, irresponsible happiness. They know that they, like the child, are not free. They know compassion. It is the existence of the child, and their knowledge of its existence, that makes possible the nobility of their architecture, the poignancy of their music, the profundity of their science. It is because of the child that they are so gentle with children. They know that if the wretched one were not there snivelling in the dark, the other one, the flute-player, could make no joyful music as the young riders line up in their beauty for the race in the sunlight of the first morning of summer.

Now do you believe in them? Are they not more credible? But there is one more thing to tell, and this is quite incredible.

At times one of the adolescent girls or boys who go to see the child does not go home to weep or rage, does not, in fact, go home at all. Sometimes also a man or woman much older falls silent for a day or two, and then leaves home. These people go out into the street, and walk down the street alone. They keep walking, and walk straight out of the city of Omelas, through the beautiful gates. They keep walking across the farmlands of Omelas. Each one goes alone, youth or girl, man or woman. Night falls; the traveler must pass down village streets, between the houses with yellow-lit windows, and on out into the darkness of the fields. Each alone, they go west or north, towards the mountains. They go on. They leave Omelas, they walk ahead into the darkness, and they do not come back. The place they go towards is a place even less imaginable to most of us than the city of happiness. I cannot describe it at all. It is possible that it does not exist. But they seem to know where they are going, the ones who walk away from Omelas.

Letter from Birmingham Jail (1963)

Martin Luther King, Jr.

April 16, 1963

MY DEAR FELLOW CLERGYMEN:

While confined here in the Birmingham city jail, I came across your recent statement calling my present activities "unwise and untimely." Seldom do I pause to answer criticism of my work and ideas. If I sought to answer all the criticisms that cross my desk, my secretaries would have little time for anything other than such correspondence in the course of the day, and I would have no time for constructive work. But since I feel that you are men of genuine good will and that your criticisms are sincerely set forth, I want to try to answer your statements in what I hope will be patient and reasonable terms.

I think I should indicate why I am here in Birmingham, since you have been influenced by the view which argues against "outsiders coming in." I have the honor of serving as president of the Southern Christian Leadership Conference, an organization operating in every southern state, with headquarters in Atlanta, Georgia. We have some eighty-five affiliated organizations across the South, and one of them is the Alabama Christian Movement for Human Rights. Frequently we share staff, educational and financial resources with our affiliates. Several months ago the affiliate here in Birmingham asked us to be on call to engage in a nonviolent direct-action program if such were deemed necessary. We readily consented, and when the hour came we lived up to our promise. So I, along with several members of my staff, am here because I was invited here. I am here because I have organizational ties here.

But more basically, I am in Birmingham because injustice is here. Just as the prophets of the eighth century B.C. left their villages and carried their "thus saith the Lord" far beyond the boundaries of their home towns, and just as the Apostle Paul left his village of Tarsus and carried the gospel of Jesus Christ to the far corners of the Greco-Roman world, so am I compelled to carry the gospel of freedom beyond my own home town. Like Paul, I must constantly respond to the Macedonian call for aid.

Moreover, I am cognizant of the interrelatedness of all communities and states. I cannot sit idly by in Atlanta and not be concerned about what happens in Birmingham. Injustice anywhere is a threat to justice everywhere. We are caught in an inescapable network of mutuality, tied in a single garment of destiny. Whatever affects one directly, affects all indirectly. Never again can we afford to live with the narrow, provincial "outside agitator" idea. Anyone who lives inside the United States can never be considered an outsider anywhere within its bounds.

You deplore the demonstrations taking place in Birmingham. But your statement, I am sorry to say, fails to express a similar concern for the conditions that brought about the demonstrations. I am sure that none of you would want to rest content with the superficial kind of social analysis that deals merely with effects and does not grapple with underlying causes. It is unfortunate that demonstrations are taking place in Birmingham, but it is even more unfortunate that the city's white power structure left the Negro community with no alternative.

In any nonviolent campaign there are four basic steps: collection of the facts to determine whether injustices exist; negotiation; self-purification; and direct action. We have gone through all these steps in Birmingham. There can be no gainsaying the fact that racial injustice engulfs this community. Birmingham is probably the most thoroughly segregated city in the United States. Its ugly record of brutality is widely known. Negroes have experienced grossly unjust treatment in the courts. There have been more unsolved bombings of Negro homes and churches in Birmingham than in any other city in the nation. These are the hard, brutal facts of the case. On the basis of these conditions, Negro leaders sought to negotiate with the city fathers. But the latter consistently refused to engage in good-faith negotiation.

Then, last September, came the opportunity to talk with leaders of Birmingham's economic community. In the course of the negotiations, certain promises were made by the merchants—for example, to remove the stores' humiliating racial signs. On the basis of these promises, the Reverend Fred Shuttlesworth and the leaders of the Alabama Christian Movement for Human Rights agreed to a moratorium on all demonstrations. As the weeks and months went by, we realized that we were the victims of a broken promise. A few signs, briefly removed, returned; the others remained.

As in so many past experiences, our hopes had been blasted, and the shadow of deep disappointment settled upon us. We had no alternative except to prepare for direct action, whereby we would present our very bodies as a means of laying our case before the conscience of the local and the national community. Mindful of the difficulties involved, we decided to undertake a process of self-purification. We began a series of workshops on nonviolence, and we repeatedly asked ourselves: "Are you able to accept blows without retaliating?" "Are you able to endure the ordeal of jail?" We decided to schedule our direct-action program for the Easter season, realizing that except for Christmas, this is the main shopping period of the year. Knowing that a strong economic withdrawal program would be the by-product of direct action, we felt that this would be the best time to bring pressure to bear on the merchants for the needed change.

Then it occurred to us that Birmingham's mayoralty election was coming up in March, and we speedily decided to postpone action until after election day. When we discovered that the Commissioner of Public Safety, Eugene "Bull" Connor, had piled up enough votes to be in the run-off we decided again to postpone action until the day after the run-off so that the demonstrations could not be used to cloud the issues. Like many others, we waited to see Mr. Connor defeated, and to this end we endured postponement after postponement. Having aided in this community need, we felt that our direct-action program could be delayed no longer.

You may well ask: "Why direct action? Why sit-ins, marches and so forth? Isn't negotiation a better path?" You are quite right in calling for negotiation. Indeed, this is the very purpose of direct action. Nonviolent direct action seeks to create such a crisis and foster such a tension that a community which has constantly refused to negotiate is forced to confront the issue. It seeks so to dramatize the issue that it can no longer be ignored. My citing the creation of tension as part of the work of the nonviolent-resister may sound rather shocking. But I must confess that I am not afraid of the word "tension." I have earnestly opposed violent tension, but there is a type of constructive, nonviolent tension which is necessary for growth. Just as Socrates felt that it was necessary to create a tension in the mind so that individuals could rise from the bondage of myths and half-truths to the unfettered realm of creative analysis and objective appraisal, so we must see the need for nonviolent gadflies to create the kind of tension in society that will help men rise from the dark depths of prejudice and racism to the majestic heights of understanding and brotherhood.

The purpose of our direct-action program is to create a situation so crisis-packed that it will inevitably open the door to negotiation. I therefore concur with you in your call for negotiation. Too long has our beloved Southland been bogged down in a tragic effort to live in monologue rather than dialogue.

One of the basic points in your statement is that the action that I and my associates have taken in Birmingham is untimely. Some have asked: "Why didn't you give the new city administration time to act?" The only answer that I can give to this query is that the new Birmingham administration must be prodded about as much as the outgoing one, before it will act. We are sadly mistaken if we feel that the election of Albert Boutwell as mayor will bring the millennium to Birmingham. While Mr. Boutwell is a much more gentle person than Mr. Connor, they are both segregationists, dedicated to maintenance of the status quo. I have hope that Mr. Boutwell will be reasonable enough to see the futility of massive resistance to desegregation. But he will not see this without pressure from devotees of civil rights. My friends, I must say to you that we have not made a single gain in civil rights without determined legal and nonviolent pressure. Lamentably, it is an historical fact that privileged groups seldom give up their privileges voluntarily. Individuals may see the moral light and voluntarily give up their unjust posture; but, as Reinhold Niebuhr has reminded us, groups tend to be more immoral than individuals.

We know through painful experience that freedom is never voluntarily given by the oppressor; it must be demanded by the oppressed. Frankly, I have yet to engage in a direct-action campaign that was "well timed" in the view of those who have not suffered unduly from the disease of segregation. For years now I have heard the word "Wait!" It rings in the ear of every Negro with piercing familiarity. This "Wait" has almost always meant "Never." We must come to see, with one of our distinguished jurists, that "justice too long delayed is justice denied."

We have waited for more than 340 years for our constitutional and God-given rights. The nations of Asia and Africa are moving with jetlike speed toward gaining political independence, but we still creep at horse-and-buggy pace toward gaining a cup of coffee at a lunch counter. Perhaps it is easy for those who have never felt the stinging dark of segregation to say, "Wait." But when you have seen vicious mobs lynch your mothers and fathers at will and drown your sisters and brothers at whim; when you have seen hate-filled policemen curse, kick and even kill your black brothers and sisters; when you see the vast majority of your twenty million Negro brothers smothering in an airtight cage of poverty in the midst of an affluent society; when you suddenly find your tongue twisted and your speech stammering as you seek to explain to your six-year-old daughter why she can't go to the public amusement park that has just been advertised on television, and see tears welling up in her eyes when she is told that Funtown is closed to colored children, and see ominous clouds of inferiority beginning to form in her little mental sky, and see her beginning to distort her personality by developing an unconscious bitterness toward white people; when you have to concoct an answer for a five-year-old son who is asking: "Daddy, why do white people treat colored people so mean?"; when you take a cross-county drive and find it necessary to sleep night after night in the uncomfortable corners of your automobile because no motel will accept you; when you are humiliated day in and day out by nagging signs reading "white" and "colored"; when your first name becomes "nigger," your middle name becomes "boy" (however old you are) and your last name becomes "John," and your wife and mother are never given the respected title "Mrs."; when you are harried by day and haunted by night by the fact that you are a Negro, living constantly at tiptoe stance, never quite knowing what to expect next, and are plagued with inner fears and outer resentments; when you are forever fighting a degenerating sense of "nobodiness" then you will understand why we find it difficult to wait. There comes a time when the cup of endurance runs over, and men are no longer willing to be plunged into the abyss of despair. I hope, sirs, you can understand our legitimate and unavoidable impatience.

You express a great deal of anxiety over our willingness to break laws. This is certainly a legitimate concern. Since we so diligently urge people to obey the Supreme Court's decision of 1954 outlawing segregation in the public schools, at first glance it may seem rather paradoxical for us consciously to break laws. One may well ask: "How can you advocate breaking some laws and obeying others?" The answer lies in the fact that there are two types of laws: just and unjust. I would be the first to advocate obeying just laws. One has not only a legal but a moral responsibility to obey just laws. Conversely, one has a moral responsibility to disobey unjust laws. I would agree with St. Augustine that "an unjust law is no law at all."

Now, what is the difference between the two? How does one determine whether a law is just or unjust? A just law is a man-made code that squares with the moral law or the law of God. An unjust law is a code that is out of harmony with the moral law. To put it in the terms of St. Thomas Aquinas: An unjust law is a human law that is not rooted in eternal law and natural law. Any law that uplifts human personality is just. Any law that degrades human personality is unjust. All segregation statutes are unjust because segregation distorts the soul and damages the personality. It gives the segregator a false sense of superiority and the segregated a false sense of inferiority. Segregation, to use the terminology of the Jewish philosopher Martin Buber, substitutes an "I-it" relationship for an "I-thou" relationship and ends up relegating persons to the status of things. Hence segregation is not only politically, economically and sociologically unsound, it is morally wrong and awful. Paul Tillich said that sin is separation. Is not segregation an existential expression of man's tragic separation, his awful estrangement, his terrible sinfulness? Thus it is that I can urge men to obey the 1954 decision of the Supreme Court, for it is morally right; and I can urge them to disobey segregation ordinances, for they are morally wrong.

Let us consider a more concrete example of just and unjust laws. An unjust law is a code that a numerical or power majority group compels a minority group to obey but does not make binding on itself. This is difference made legal. By the same token, a just law is a code that a majority compels a minority to follow and that it is willing to follow itself. This is sameness made legal.

Let me give another explanation. A law is unjust if it is inflicted on a minority that, as a result of being denied the right to vote, had no part in enacting or devising the law. Who can say that the legislature of Alabama which set up that state's segregation laws was democratically elected? Throughout Alabama all sorts of devious methods are used to prevent Negroes from becoming registered voters, and there are some counties in which, even though Negroes constitute a majority of the population, not a single Negro is registered. Can any law enacted under such circumstances be considered democratically structured?

Sometimes a law is just on its face and unjust in its application. For instance, I have been arrested on a charge of parading without a permit. Now, there is nothing wrong in having an ordinance which requires a permit for a parade. But such an ordinance becomes unjust when it is used to maintain segregation and to deny citizens the First Amendment privilege of peaceful assembly and protest.

I hope you are able to see the distinction I am trying to point out. In no sense do I advocate evading or defying the law, as would the rabid segregationist. That would lead to anarchy. One who breaks an unjust law must do so openly, lovingly, and with a willingness to accept the penalty. I submit that an individual who breaks a law that conscience tells him is unjust and who willingly accepts the penalty of imprisonment in order to arouse the conscience of the community over its injustice, is in reality expressing the highest respect for law.

Of course, there is nothing new about this kind of civil disobedience. It was evidenced sublimely in the refusal of Shadrach, Meshach and Abednego to obey the laws of Nebuchadnezzar, on the ground that a higher moral law was at stake. It was practiced superbly by the early Christians, who were willing to face hungry lions and the excruciating pain of chopping blocks rather than submit to certain unjust laws of the Roman Empire. To a degree, academic freedom is a reality today because Socrates practiced civil disobedience. In our own nation, the Boston Tea Party represented a massive act of civil disobedience.

We should never forget that everything Adolf Hitler did in Germany was "legal" and everything the Hungarian freedom fighters did in Hungary was "illegal." It was "illegal" to aid and comfort a Jew in Hitler's Germany. Even so, I am sure that, had I lived in Germany at the time, I would have aided and comforted my Jewish brothers. If today I lived in a Communist country where certain principles dear to the Christian faith are suppressed, I would openly advocate disobeying that country's antireligious laws.

I must make two honest confessions to you, my Christian and Jewish brothers. First, I must confess that over the past few years I have been gravely disappointed with the white moderate. I have almost reached the regrettable conclusion that the Negro's great stumbling block in his stride toward freedom is not the White Citizen's Councillor or the Ku Klux Klanner, but the white moderate, who is more devoted to "order" than to justice; who prefers a negative peace which is the absence of tension to a positive peace which is the presence of justice; who constantly says: "I agree with you in the goal you seek, but I cannot agree with your methods of direct action"; who paternalistically believes he can set the timetable for another man's freedom; who lives by a mythical concept of time and who constantly advises the Negro to wait for a "more convenient season." Shallow understanding from people of good will is more frustrating than absolute misunderstanding from people of ill will. Lukewarm acceptance is much more bewildering than outright rejection.

I had hoped that the white moderate would understand that law and order exist for the purpose of establishing justice and that when they fail in this purpose they become the dangerously structured dams that block the flow of social progress. I had hoped that the white moderate would understand that the present tension in the South is a necessary phase of the transition from an obnoxious negative peace, in which the Negro passively accepted his unjust plight, to a substantive and positive peace, in which all men will respect the dignity and worth of human personality. Actually, we who engage in nonviolent direct action are not the creators of tension. We merely bring to the surface the hidden tension that is already alive. We bring it out in the open, where it can be seen and dealt with. Like a boil that can never be cured so long as it is covered up but must be opened with all its ugliness to the natural medicines of air and light, injustice must be exposed, with all the tension its exposure creates, to the light of human conscience and the air of national opinion before it can be cured.

In your statement you assert that our actions, even though peaceful, must be condemned because they precipitate violence. But is this a logical assertion? Isn't this like condemning a robbed man because his possession of money precipitated the evil act of robbery? Isn't this like condemning Socrates because his unswerving commitment to truth and his philosophical inquiries precipitated the act by the misguided populace in which they made him drink hemlock? Isn't this like condemning Jesus because his unique God-consciousness and never-ceasing devotion to God's will precipitated the evil act of crucifixion? We must come to see that, as the federal courts have consistently affirmed, it is wrong to urge an individual to cease his efforts to gain his basic constitutional rights because the quest may precipitate violence. Society must protect the robbed and punish the robber.

I had also hoped that the white moderate would reject the myth concerning time in relation to the struggle for freedom. I have just received a letter from a white brother in Texas. He writes: "All Christians know that the colored people will receive equal rights eventually, but it is possible that you are in too great a religious hurry. It has taken Christianity almost two thousand years to accomplish what it has. The teachings of Christ take time to come to earth." Such an attitude stems from a tragic misconception of time, from the strangely rational notion that there is something in the very flow of time that will inevitably cure all ills. Actually, time itself is neutral; it can be used either destructively or constructively. More and more I feel that the people of ill will have used time much more effectively than have the people of good will. We will have to repent in this generation not merely for the hateful words and actions of the bad people but for the appalling silence of the good people. Human progress never rolls in on wheels of inevitability; it comes through the tireless efforts of men willing to be co-workers with God, and without this hard work, time itself becomes an ally of the forces of social stagnation. We must use time creatively, in the knowledge that the time is always ripe to do right. Now is the time to make real the promise of democracy and transform our pending national elegy into a creative psalm of brotherhood. Now is the time to lift our national policy from the quicksand of racial injustice to be solid rock of human dignity.

You speak of our activity in Birmingham as extreme. At first I was rather disappointed that fellow clergymen would see my nonviolent efforts as those of an extremist. I began thinking about the fact that I stand in the middle of two opposing forces in the Negro community. One is a force of complacency, made up in part of Negroes who, as a result of long years of oppression, are so drained of self-respect and a sense of "somebodiness" that they have adjusted to segregation; and in part of a few middle class Negroes who, because of a degree of academic and economic security and because in some ways they profit by segregation, have become insensitive to the problems of the masses. The other force is one of bitterness and hatred, and it comes perilously close to advocating violence. It is expressed in the various black nationalist groups that are springing up across the nation, the largest and best-known being Elijah Muhammad's Muslim movement. Nourished by the Negro's frustration over the continued existence of racial discrimination, this movement is made up of people who have lost faith in America, who have absolutely repudiated Christianity, and who have concluded that the white man is an incorrigible "devil."

I have tried to stand between these two forces, saying that we need emulate neither the "do-nothingism" of the complacent nor the hatred and despair of the black nationalist. For there is the more excellent way of love and nonviolent protest. I am grateful to God that, through the influence of the Negro church, the way of nonviolence became an integral part of our struggle.

If this philosophy had not emerged, by now many streets of the South would, I am convinced, be flowing with blood. And I am further convinced that if our white brothers dismiss as "rabble-rousers" and "outside agitators" those of us who employ nonviolent direct action, and if they refuse to support our nonviolent efforts, millions of Negroes will, out of frustration and despair, seek solace and security in black-nationalist ideologies—a development that would inevitably lead to a frightening racial nightmare.

Oppressed people cannot remain oppressed forever. The yearning for freedom eventually manifests itself, and that is what has happened to the American Negro. Something within has reminded him of his birthright of freedom, and something without has reminded him that it can be gained. Consciously or unconsciously, he has been caught up by the Zeitgeist, and with his black brothers of Africa and his brown and yellow brothers of Asia, South America and the Caribbean, the United States Negro is moving with a sense of great urgency toward the promised land of racial justice. If one recognizes this vital urge that has engulfed the Negro community, one should readily understand why public demonstrations are taking place. The Negro has many pent-up resentments and latent frustrations, and he must release them. So let him march; let him make prayer pilgrimages to the city hall; let him go on freedom rides—and try to understand why he must do so. If his repressed emotions are not released in nonviolent ways, they will seek expression through violence; this is not a threat but a fact of history. So I have not said to my people: "Get rid of your discontent." Rather, I have tried to say that this normal and healthy discontent can be channeled into the creative outlet of nonviolent direct action. And now this approach is being termed extremist.

But though I was initially disappointed at being categorized as an extremist, as I continued to think about the matter I gradually gained a measure of satisfaction from the label. Was not Jesus an extremist for love: "Love your enemies, bless them that curse you, do good to them that hate you, and pray for them which despitefully use you, and persecute you." Was not Amos an extremist for justice: "Let justice roll down like waters and righteousness like an ever-flowing stream." Was not Paul an extremist for the Christian gospel: "I bear in my body the marks of the Lord Jesus." Was not Martin Luther an extremist: "Here I stand; I cannot do otherwise, so help me God." And John Bunyan: "I will stay in jail to the end of my days before I make a butchery of my conscience." And Abraham Lincoln: "This nation cannot survive half slave and half free." And Thomas Jefferson: "We hold these truths to be self-evident, that all men are created equal . . ." So the question is not whether we will be extremists, but what kind of extremists we will be. Will we be extremists for hate or for love? Will we be extremist for the preservation of injustice or for the extension of justice? In that dramatic scene on Calvary's hill three men were crucified. We must never forget that all three were crucified for the same crime—-the crime of extremism. Two were extremists for immorality, and thus fell below their environment. The other, Jesus Christ, was an extremist for love, truth and goodness, and thereby rose above his environment. Perhaps the South, the nation and the world are in dire need of creative extremists.

I had hoped that the white moderate would see this need. Perhaps I was too optimistic; perhaps I expected too much. I suppose I should have realized that few members of the oppressor race can understand the deep groans and passionate yearnings of the oppressed race, and still fewer have the vision to see that injustice must be rooted out by strong, persistent and determined action. I am thankful, however, that some of our white brothers in the South have grasped the meaning of this social revolution and committed themselves to it. They are still too few in quantity, but they are big in quality. Some—such as Ralph McGill, Lillian Smith, Harry Golden, James McBride Dabbs, Ann Braden and Sarah Patton Boyle—have written about our struggle in eloquent and prophetic terms. Others have marched with us down nameless streets of the South. They have languished in filthy, roach-infested jails, suffering the abuse and brutality of policemen who view them as "dirty nigger lovers." Unlike so many of their moderate brothers and sisters, they have recognized the urgency of the moment and sensed the need for powerful "action" antidotes to combat the disease of segregation.

Let me take note of my other major disappointment. I have been so greatly disappointed with the white church and its leadership. Of course, there are some notable exceptions. I am not unmindful of the fact that each of you has taken some significant stands on this issue. I commend you, Reverend Stallings, for your Christian stand on this past Sunday, in welcoming Negroes to your worship service on a nonsegregated basis. I commend the Catholic leaders of this state for integrating Spring Hill College several years ago.

But despite these notable exceptions, I must honestly reiterate that I have been disappointed with the church. I do not say this as one of those negative critics who can always find something wrong with the church. I say this as a minister of the gospel, who loves the church; who was nurtured in its bosom; who has been sustained by its spiritual blessings and who will remain true to it as long as the cord of life shall lengthen.

When I was suddenly catapulted into the leadership of the bus protest in Montgomery, Alabama, a few years ago, I felt we would be supported by the white church. I felt that the white ministers, priests and rabbis of the South would be among our strongest allies. Instead, some have been outright opponents, refusing to understand the freedom movement and misrepresenting its leaders; all too many others have been more cautious than courageous and have remained silent behind the anesthetizing security of stained-glass windows.

In spite of my shattered dreams, I came to Birmingham with the hope that the white religious leadership of this community would see the justice of our cause and, with deep moral concern, would serve as the channel through which our just grievances could reach the power structure. I had hoped that each of you would understand. But again I have been disappointed.

I have heard numerous southern religious leaders admonish their worshipers to comply with a desegregation decision because it is the law, but

I have longed to hear white ministers declare: "Follow this decree because integration is morally right and because the Negro is your brother." In the midst of blatant injustices inflicted upon the Negro, I have watched white churchmen stand on the sideline and mouth pious irrelevancies and sanctimonious trivialities. In the midst of a mighty struggle to rid our nation of racial and economic injustice, I have heard many ministers say: "Those are social issues, with which the gospel has no real concern." And I have watched many churches commit themselves to a completely otherworldly religion which makes a strange, un-Biblical distinction between body and soul, between the sacred and the secular.

I have traveled the length and breadth of Alabama, Mississippi and all the other southern states. On sweltering summer days and crisp autumn mornings I have looked at the South's beautiful churches with their lofty spires pointing heavenward. I have beheld the impressive outlines of her massive religious-education buildings. Over and over I have found myself asking: "What kind of people worship here? Who is their God? Where were their voices when the lips of Governor Barnett dripped with words of interposition and nullification? Where were they when Governor Wallace gave a clarion call for defiance and hatred? Where were their voices of support when bruised and weary Negro men and women decided to rise from the dark dungeons of complacency to the bright hills of creative protest?"

Yes, these questions are still in my mind. In deep disappointment I have wept over the laxity of the church. But be assured that my tears have been tears of love. There can be no deep disappointment where there is not deep love. Yes, I love the church. How could I do otherwise? I am in the rather unique position of being the son, the grandson and the great-grandson of preachers. Yes, I see the church as the body of Christ. But, oh! How we have blemished and scarred that body through social neglect and through fear of being nonconformists.

There was a time when the church was very powerful—in the time when the early Christians rejoiced at being deemed worthy to suffer for what they believed. In those days the church was not merely a thermometer that recorded the ideas and principles of popular opinion; it was a thermostat that transformed the mores of society. Whenever the early Christians entered a town, the people in power became disturbed and immediately sought to convict the Christians for being "disturbers of the peace" and "outside agitators"' But the Christians pressed on, in the conviction that they were "a colony of heaven," called to obey God rather than man. Small in number, they were big in commitment. They were too

God-intoxicated to be "astronomically intimidated." By their effort and example they brought an end to such ancient evils as infanticide and gladiatorial contests.

Things are different now. So often the contemporary church is a weak, ineffectual voice with an uncertain sound. So often it is an arch defender of the status quo. Far from being disturbed by the presence of the church, the power structure of the average community is consoled by the church's silent and often even vocal sanction of things as they are.

But the judgment of God is upon the church as never before. If today's church does not recapture the sacrificial spirit of the early church, it will lose its authenticity, forfeit the loyalty of millions, and be dismissed as an irrelevant social club with no meaning for the twentieth century. Every day I meet young people whose disappointment with the church has turned into outright disgust.

Perhaps I have once again been too optimistic. Is organized religion too inextricably bound to the status quo to save our nation and the world? Perhaps I must turn my faith to the inner spiritual church, the church within the church, as the true *ekklesia* and the hope of the world. But again I am thankful to God that some noble souls from the ranks of organized religion have broken loose from the paralyzing chains of conformity and joined us as active partners in the struggle for freedom. They have left their secure congregations and walked the streets of Albany, Georgia, with us. They have gone down the highways of the South on tortuous rides for freedom. Yes, they have gone to jail with us. Some have been dismissed from their churches, have lost the support of their bishops and fellow ministers. But they have acted in the faith that right defeated is stronger than evil triumphant. Their witness has been the spiritual salt that has preserved the true meaning of the gospel in these troubled times. They have carved a tunnel of hope through the dark mountain of disappointment.

I hope the church as a whole will meet the challenge of this decisive hour. But even if the church does not come to the aid of justice, I have no despair about the future. I have no fear about the outcome of our struggle in Birmingham, even if our motives are at present misunderstood. We will reach the goal of freedom in Birmingham, and all over the nation, because the goal of America is freedom. Abused and scorned though we may be, our destiny is tied up with America's destiny. Before the pilgrims landed at Plymouth, we were here. Before the pen of Jefferson etched the majestic words of the Declaration of Independence across the pages of history, we were here. For more than two centuries our forebears labored in this country without wages; they made cotton king; they built the homes of their masters while suffering gross injustice and shameful humiliation—and yet out of a bottomless vitality they continued to thrive and develop. If the inexpressible cruelties of slavery could not stop us, the opposition we now face will surely fail. We will win our freedom because the sacred heritage of our nation and the eternal will of God are embodied in our echoing demands.

Before closing I feel impelled to mention one other point in your statement that has troubled me profoundly. You warmly commended the Birmingham police force for keeping "order" and "preventing violence." I doubt that you would have so warmly commended the police force if you had seen its dogs sinking their teeth into unarmed, nonviolent Negroes. I doubt that you would so quickly commend the policemen if you were to observe their ugly and inhumane treatment of Negroes here in the city jail; if you were to watch them push and curse old Negro women and young Negro girls; if you were to see them slap and kick old Negro men and young boys; if you were to observe them, as they did on two occasions, refuse to give us food because we wanted to sing our grace together. I cannot join you in your praise of the Birmingham police department.

It is true that the police have exercised a degree of discipline in handing the demonstrators. In this sense they have conducted themselves rather "nonviolently" in public. But for what purpose? To preserve the evil system of segregation. Over the past few years I have consistently preached that nonviolence demands that the means we use must be as pure as the ends we seek. I have tried to make clear that it is wrong to use immoral means to attain moral ends. But now I must affirm that it is just as wrong, or perhaps even more so, to use moral means to preserve immoral ends. Perhaps Mr. Connor and his policemen have been rather nonviolent in public, as was Chief Pritchett in Albany, Georgia, but they have used the moral means of nonviolence to maintain the immoral end of racial injustice. As T. S. Eliot has said: "The last temptation is the greatest treason: To do the right deed for the wrong reason."

I wish you had commended the Negro sit-inners and demonstrators of Birmingham for their sublime courage, their willingness to suffer and their amazing discipline in the midst of great provocation. One day the South will recognize its real heroes. They will be the James Merediths, with the noble sense of purpose that enables them to face jeering, and hostile mobs, and with the agonizing loneliness that characterizes the life of the pioneer. They will be old, oppressed, battered Negro women, symbolized in a seventy-two-year-old woman in Montgomery, Alabama, who rose up with a sense of dignity and with her people decided not to ride segregated buses, and who responded with ungrammatical profundity to one who inquired about her weariness: "My feets is tired, but my soul is at rest." They will be the young high school and college students, the young ministers of the gospel and a host of their elders, courageously and nonviolently sitting in at lunch counters and willingly going to jail for conscience' sake. One day the South will know that when these disinherited children of God sat down at lunch counters, they were in reality standing up for what is best in the American dream and for the most sacred values in our Judaeo-Christian heritage, thereby bringing our nation back to those great wells of democracy which were dug deep by the founding fathers in their formulation of the Constitution and the Declaration of Independence.

Never before have I written so long a letter. I'm afraid it is much too long to take your precious time. I can assure you that it would have been much shorter if I had been writing from a comfortable desk, but what else can one do when he is alone in a narrow jail cell, other than write long letters, think long thoughts and pray long prayers?

If I have said anything in this letter that overstates the truth and indicates an unreasonable impatience, I beg you to forgive me. If I have said anything that understates the truth and indicates my having a patience that allows me to settle for anything less than brotherhood, I beg God to forgive me.

I hope this letter finds you strong in the faith. I also hope that circumstances will soon make it possible for me to meet each of you, not as an integrationist or a civil rights leader but as a fellow clergyman and a Christian brother. Let us all hope that the dark clouds of racial prejudice will soon pass away and the deep fog of misunderstanding will be lifted from our fear-drenched communities, and in some not too distant tomorrow the radiant stars of love and brotherhood will shine over our great nation with all their scintillating beauty.

Yours for the cause of Peace and Brotherhood,

MARTIN LUTHER KING, JR.

The Good Samaritan Parable, Luke 10:25–37 (70–90 C.E.)

The Bible

On one occasion an expert in the law stood up to test Jesus. "Teacher," he asked, "what must I do to inherit eternal life?"

"What is written in the Law?" he replied. "How do you read it?"

He answered: "'Love the Lord your God with all your heart and with all your soul and with all your strength and with all your mind'; and, 'Love your neighbor as yourself.'"

"You have answered correctly," Jesus replied. "Do this and you will live."

But he wanted to justify himself, so he asked Jesus, "And who is my neighbor?"

In reply Jesus said: "A man was going down from Jerusalem to Jericho, when he fell into the hands of robbers. They stripped him of his clothes, beat him and went away, leaving him half dead with no clothes. A priest happened to be going down the same road, and when he saw the man, he passed by on the other side. So too, a Levite, when he came to the place and saw him, passed by on the other side. But a Samaritan, as he traveled, came where the man was; and when he saw him, he took pity on him. He went to him and bandaged his wounds, pouring on oil and wine. Then he put the man on his own donkey, took him to an inn and took care of him. The next day he took out two silver coins and gave them to the innkeeper. 'Look after him,' he said, 'and when I return, I will reimburse you for any extra expense you may have.'"

"Which of these three do you think was a neighbor to the man who fell into the hands of robbers?"

The expert in the law replied, "The one who had mercy on him."

Jesus told him, "Go and do likewise."

The Author of *American Ornithology* Sketches a Bird, Now Extinct (1983)

David Wagoner

When he walked through town, the wing-shot bird he'd hidden
Inside his coat began to cry like a baby,
High and plaintive and loud as the calls he'd heard
While hunting it in the woods, and goodwives stared
And scurried indoors to guard their own from harm.

And the innkeeper and the goodmen in the tavern
Asked him whether his child was sick, then laughed.
Slapped knees, and laughed as he unswaddled his prize,
His pride and burden: an ivory-billed woodpecker
As big as a crow, still wailing and squealing.

Upstairs, when he let it go in his workroom,
It fell silent at last. He told at dinner
How devoted masters of birds drawn from the life
Must gather their flocks around them with a rifle
And make them live forever inside books.

Later, he found his bedspread covered with plaster
And the bird clinging beside a hole in the wall
Clear through to already-splintered weatherboards
And the sky beyond. While he tied one of its legs
To a table leg, it started wailing again.

And went on wailing as if toward cypress groves
While the artist drew and tinted on fine vellum
Its red cockade, gray claws, and sepia eyes
From which a white edge flowed to the lame wing
Like light flying and ended there in blackness.

He drew and studied for days, eating and dreaming
Fitfully through the dancing and loud drumming
Of an ivory bill that refused pecans and beetles,
Chestnuts and sweet-sour fruit of magnolias,
Riddling his table, slashing his fingers, wailing.

He watched it die, he said, with great regret.

Engaging the World

The Venus Hottentot (1990)

Elizabeth Alexander

1. Cuvier

Science, science, science!
Everything is beautiful

blown up beneath my glass.
Colors dazzle insect wings.

A drop of water swirls
like marble. Ordinary

crumbs become stalactites
set in perfect angles

of geometry I'd thought
impossible. Few will

ever see what I see
through this microscope.

Cranial measurements
crowd my notebook pages,

and I am moving closer,
close to how these numbers

signify aspects of
national character.

Her genitalia
will float inside a labeled

pickling jar in the Musée
de l'Homme on a shelf

above Broca's brain:
"The Venus Hottentot."

Elegant facts await me.
Small things in this world are mine.

2.

There is unexpected sun today
in London, and the clouds that
most days sift into this cage
where I am working have dispersed.
I am a black cutout against
a captive blue sky, pivoting
nude so the paying audience
can view my naked buttocks.

I am called "Venus Hottentot."
I left Capetown with a promise
of revenue: half the profits
and my passage home: A boon!
Master's brother proposed the trip;
the magistrate granted me leave.
I would return to my family
a duchess, with watered-silk

dresses and money to grow food,
rouge and powders in glass pots,
silver scissors, a lorgnette,
voile and tulle instead of flax,
cerulean blue instead
of indigo. My brother would
devour sugar-studded non-
pareils, pale taffy, damask plums.

That was years ago. London's
circuses are florid and filthy,
swarming with cabbage-smelling
citizens who stare and query,
"Is it muscle? bone? or fat?"
My neighbor to the left is
The Sapient Pig, "The Only
Scholar of His Race." He plays

at cards, tells time and fortunes
by scraping his hooves. Behind
me is Prince Kar-mi, who arches
like a rubber tree and stares back
at the crowd from under the crook
of his knee. A professional

animal trainer shouts my cues.
There are singing mice here.

"The Ball of Duchess DuBarry":
In the engraving I lurch
toward the *belles dames*, mad-eyed, and
they swoon. Men in capes and pince-nez
shield them. Tassels dance at my hips.
In this newspaper lithograph
my buttocks are shown swollen
and luminous as a planet.

Monsieur Cuvier investigates
between my legs, poking, prodding,
sure of his hypothesis.
I half expect him to pull silk
scarves from inside me, paper poppies,
then a rabbit! He complains
at my scent and does not think
I comprehend, but I speak

English. I speak Dutch. I speak
a little French as well, and
languages Monsieur Cuvier
will never know have names.
Now I am bitter and now
I am sick. I eat brown bread,
drink rancid broth. I miss good sun,
miss Mother's *sadza*. My stomach

is frequently queasy from mutton
chops, pale potatoes, blood sausage.
I was certain that this would be
better than farm life. I am
the family entrepreneur!
But there are hours in every day
to conjur my imaginary
daughters, in banana skirts

and ostrich-feather fans.
Since my own genitals are public
I have made other parts private.
In my silence I possess
mouth, larynx, brain, in a single

gesture. I rub my hair
with lanolin, and pose in profile
like a painted Nubian

archer, imagining gold leaf
woven through my hair, and diamonds.
Observe the wordless Odalisque.
I have not forgotten my Xhosa
clicks. My flexible tongue
and healthy mouth bewilder
this man with his rotting teeth.
If he were to let me rise up

from this table, I'd spirit
his knives and cut out his black heart,
seal it with science fluid inside
a bell jar, place it on a low
shelf in a white man's museum
so the whole world could see
it was shriveled and hard,
geometric, deformed, unnatural.

The Lesson (1972)

Toni Cade Bambara

Back in the days when everyone was old and stupid or young and foolish and me and Sugar were the only ones just right, this lady moved on our block with nappy hair and proper speech and no makeup. And quite naturally we laughed at her, laughed the way we did at the junk man who went about his business like he was some big-time president and his sorry-ass horse his secretary. And we kinda hated her too, hated the way we did the winos who cluttered up our parks and pissed on our handball walls and stank up our hallways and stairs so you couldn't halfway play hide-and-seek without a goddamn gas mask. Miss Moore was her name. The only woman on the block with no first name. And she was black as hell, cept for her feet, which were fish-white and spooky. And she was always planning these boring-ass things for us to do, us being my cousin, mostly, who lived on the block cause we all moved North the same time and to the same apartment then spread out gradual to breathe. And our parents would yank our heads into some kinda shape and crisp up our clothes so we'd be presentable for travel with Miss Moore, who always looked like she was going to church, though she never did. Which is just one of the things the grownups talked about when they talked behind her back like a dog. But when she came calling with some sachet she'd sewed up or some gingerbread she'd made or some book, why then they'd all be too embarrassed to turn her down and we'd get handed over all spruced up. She'd been to college and said it was only right that she should take responsibility for the young ones' education, and she not even related by marriage or blood. So they'd go for it. Specially Aunt Gretchen. She was the main gofer in the family. You got some ole dumb shit foolishness you want somebody to go for, you send for Aunt Gretchen. She been screwed into the go-along for so long, it's a blood-deep natural thing with her. Which is how she got saddled with me and Sugar and junior in the first place while our mothers were in a la-de-da apartment up the block having a good ole time.

So this one day Miss Moore rounds us all up at the mailbox and it's puredee hot and she's knockin herself out about arithmetic. And school suppose to let up in summer I heard, but she don't never let up. And the starch in my pinafore scratching the shit outta me and I'm really hating this nappy-head bitch and her goddamn college degree. I'd much rather go to the pool or to the show where it's cool. So me and Sugar leaning on the mailbox being surly, which is a Miss Moore word. And Flyboy checking out what everybody brought for lunch. And Fat Butt already wasting his peanut-butter-and-jelly sandwich like the pig he is. And Junebug punchin on Q. T.'s arm for potato chips. And Rosie Giraffe shifting from one hip to the other waiting for somebody to step on her foot or ask her if she from Georgia so she can kick ass, preferably Mercedes'. And Miss Moore asking us do we know what money is, like we a bunch of retards. I mean real money, she say, like it's only poker chips or monopoly papers we lay on the grocer. So right away I'm tired of this and say so. And would much rather snatch Sugar and go to the Sunset and terrorize the West Indian kids and take their hair ribbons and their money too. And Miss Moore files that remark away for next week's lesson on brotherhood, I can tell. And finally I say we oughta get to the subway cause it's cooler and besides we might meet some cute boys. Sugar done swiped her mama's lipstick, so we ready.

So we heading down the street and she's boring us silly about what things cost and what our parents make and how much goes for rent and how money ain't divided up right in this country. And then she gets to the part about we all poor and live in the slums, which I don't feature. And I'm ready to speak on that, but she steps out in the street and hails two cabs just like that. Then she hustles half the crew in with her and hands me a five-dollar bill and tells me to calculate 10 percent tip for the driver. And we're off. Me and Sugar and Junebug and Flyboy hangin out the window and hollering to everybody, putting lipstick on each other cause Flyboy a faggot anyway, and making farts with our sweaty armpits. But I'm mostly trying to figure how to spend this money. But they all fascinated with the meter ticking and Junebug starts laying bets as to how much it'll read when Flyboy can't hold his breath no more. Then Sugar lays bets as to how much it'll be when we get there. So I'm stuck. Don't nobody want to go for my plan, which is to jump out at the next light and run off to the first bar-b-que we can find. Then the driver tells us to get the hell out cause we there already. And the meter reads eighty five cents. And I'm stalling to figure out the tip and Sugar say give him a dime. And I decide he don't need it bad as I do, so later for him. But then he tries to take off with Junebug foot still in the door so we talk about his mama something ferocious. Then we check out that we on Fifth Avenue and everybody dressed up in stockings. One lady in a fur coat, hot as it is. White folks crazy.

"This is the place," Miss Moore say, presenting it to us in the voice she uses at the museum. "Let's look in the windows before we go in."

"Can we steal?" Sugar asks very serious like she's getting the ground rules squared away before she plays. "I beg your pardon," say Miss Moore, and we fall out. So she leads us around the windows of the toy store and me and Sugar screamin, "This is mine, that's mine, I gotta have that, that was made for me, I was born for that," till Big Butt drowns us out.

"Hey, I'm goin to buy that there."

"That there? You don't even know what it is, stupid."

"I do so," he say punchin on Rosie Giraffe. "It's a microscope."

"Whatcha gonna do with a microscope, fool?"

"Look at things."

"Like what, Ronald?" ask Miss Moore. And Big Butt ain't got the first notion. So here go Miss Moore gabbing about the thousands of bacteria in a drop of water and the somethinorother in a speck of blood and the million and one living things in the air around us is invisible to the naked eye. And what she say that for? Junebug go to town on that "naked" and we rolling. Then Miss Moore ask what it cost. So we all jam into the window smudgin it up and the price tag say $300. So then she ask how long'd take for Big Butt and Junebug to save up their allowances. "Too long," I say. "Yeh," adds Sugar, "outgrown it by that time." And Miss Moore say no, you never outgrow learning instruments. "Why, even medical students and interns and," blah, blah, blah. And we ready to choke Big Butt for bringing it up in the first damn place.

"This here costs four hundred eighty dollars," say Rosie Giraffe. So we pile up all over her to see what she pointin out. My eyes tell me it's a chunk of glass cracked with something heavy, and different-color inks dripped into the splits, then the whole thing put into a oven or something. But for $480 it don't make sense.

"That's a paperweight made of semi-precious stones fused together under tremendous pressure," she explains slowly, with her hands doing the mining and all the factory work.

"So what's a paperweight?" asks Rosie Giraffe.

"To weigh paper with, dumbbell," say Flyboy, the wise man from the East.

"Not exactly," say Miss Moore, which is what she say when you warm or way off too. "It's to weigh paper down so it won't scatter and make your desk untidy." So right away me and Sugar curtsy to each other and then to Mercedes who is more the tidy type.

"We don't keep paper on top of the desk in my class," say Junebug, figuring Miss Moore crazy or lyin one.

"At home, then," she say. "Don't you have a calendar and a pencil case and a blotter and a letter-opener on your desk at home where you do your homework?" And she know damn well what our homes look like cause she nosys around in them every chance she gets.

"I don't even have a desk," say Junebug. "Do we?"

"No. And I don't get no homework neither," says Big Butt.

"And I don't even have a home," say Flyboy like he do at school to keep the white folks off his back and sorry for him. Send this poor kid to camp posters, is his specialty.

"I do," says Mercedes. "I have a box of stationery on my desk and a picture of my cat. My godmother bought the stationery and the desk. There's a big rose on each sheet and the envelopes smell like roses."

"Who wants to know about your smelly-ass stationery," say Rosie Giraffe fore I can get my two cents in.

"It's important to have a work area all your own so that . . ."

"Will you look at this sailboat, please," say Flyboy, cuttin her off and pointin to the thing like it was his. So once again we tumble all over each other to gaze at this magnificent thing in the toy store which is just big enough to maybe sail two kittens across the pond if you strap them to the posts tight. We all start reciting the price tag like we in assembly. "Handcrafted sailboat of fiberglass at one thousand one hundred ninety-five dollars."

"Unbelievable," I hear myself say and am really stunned. I read it again for myself just in case the group recitation put me in a trance. Same thing. For some reason this pisses me off. We look at Miss Moore and she lookin at us, waiting for I dunno what.

"Who'd pay all that when you can buy a sailboat set for a quarter at Pop's, a tube of glue for a dime, and a ball of string for eight cents? It must have a motor and a whole lot else besides," I say. "My sailboat cost me about fifty cents."

"But will it take water?" say Mercedes with her smart ass.

"Took mine to Alley Pond Park once," say Flyboy. "String broke. Lost it. Pity."

"Sailed mine in Central Park and it keeled over and sank. Had to ask my father for another dollar."

"And you got the strap," laugh Big Butt. "The jerk didn't even have a string on it. My old man wailed on his behind."

Little Q. T. was staring hard at the sailboat and you could see he wanted it bad. But he too little and somebody'd just take it from him. So what the hell. "This boat for kids, Miss Moore?"

"Parents silly to buy something like that just to get all broke up," say Rosie Giraffe.

"That much money it should last forever," I figure.

"My father'd buy it for me if I wanted it."

"Your father, my ass," say Rosie Giraffe getting a chance to finally push Mercedes.

"Must be rich people shop here," say Q. T.

"You are a very bright boy," say Flyboy. "What was your first clue?" And he rap him on the head with the back of his knuckles, since Q. T. the only one he could get away with. Though Q. T. liable to come up behind you years later and get his licks in when you half expect it.

"What I want to know is," I says to Miss Moore though I never talk to her, I wouldn't give the bitch that satisfaction, "is how much a real boat costs? I figure a thousand'd get you a yacht any day."

"Why don't you check that out," she says, "and report back to the group?" Which really pains my ass. If you gonna mess up a perfectly good swim day least you could do is have some answers. "Let's go in," she say like she got something up her sleeve. Only she don't lead the way. So me and Sugar turn the corner to where the entrance is, but when we get there I kinda hang back. Not that I'm scared, what's there to be afraid of, just a toy store. But I feel funny, shame. But what I got to be shamed about? Got as much right to go in as anybody. But somehow I can't seem to get hold of the door, so I step away from Sugar to lead. But she hangs back too. And I look at her and she looks at me and this is ridiculous. I mean, damn, I have never ever been shy about doing nothing or going nowhere. But then Mercedes steps up and then Rosie Giraffe and Big Butt crowd in behind and shove, and next thing we all stuffed into the doorway with only Mercedes squeezing past us, smoothing out her jumper and walking right down the aisle. Then the rest of us tumble in like a glued-together jigsaw done all wrong. And people lookin at us. And it's like the time me and Sugar crashed into the Catholic church on a dare. But once we got in there and everything so hushed and holy and the candles and the bowin and the handkerchiefs on all the drooping heads, I just couldn't go through with the plan. Which was for me to run up to the altar and do a tap dance while Sugar played the nose flute and messed around in the holy water. And Sugar kept givin me the elbow. Then later teased me so bad I tied her up in the shower and turned it on and locked her in. And she'd be there till this day if Aunt Gretchen hadn't finally figured I was lyin about the boarder takin a shower.

Same thing in the store. We all walkin on tiptoe and hardly touchin the games and puzzles and things. And I watched Miss Moore who is steady watchin us like she waitin for a sign. Like Mama Drewery watches the sky and sniffs the air and takes note of just how much slant is in the bird formation. Then me and Sugar bump smack into each other, so busy gazing at the toys, 'specially the sailboat. But we don't laugh and go into our fat-lady bump-stomach routine. We just stare at that price tag. Then Sugar run a finger over the whole boat. And I'm jealous and want to hit her. Maybe not her, but I sure want to punch somebody in the mouth.

"Watcha bring us here for, Miss Moore?"

"You sound angry, Sylvia. Are you mad about something?" Givin me one of them grins like she tellin a grown-up joke that never turns out to be funny. And she's lookin very closely at me like maybe she plannin to do my portrait from memory. I'm mad, but I won't give her that satisfaction. So I slouch around the store bein very bored and say, "Let's go."

Me and Sugar at the back of the train watchin the tracks whizzin by large then small then gettin gobbled up in the dark. I'm thinkin about this tricky toy I saw in the store. A clown that somersaults on a bar then does chin-ups just cause you yank lightly at his leg. Cost $35. I could see me askin my mother for a $35 birthday clown. "You wanna who that costs what?" she'd say, cocking her head to the side to get a better view of the hole in my head. Thirty-five dollars could buy new bunk beds for Junior and Gretchen's boy. Thirty-five dollars and the whole household could go visit Granddaddy Nelson in the country. Thirty-five dollars would pay for the rent and the piano bill too. Who are these people that spend that much for performing clowns and $1000 for toy sailboats? What kinda work they do and how they live and how come we ain't in on it? Where we are is who we are, Miss Moore always pointin out. But it don't necessarily have to be that way, she always adds then waits for somebody to say that poor people have to wake up and demand their share of the pie and don't none of us know what kind of pie she talking about in the first damn place. But she ain't so smart cause I still got her four dollars from the taxi and she sure ain't gettin it. Messin up my day with this shit. Sugar nudges me in my pocket and winks.

Miss Moore lines us up in front of the mailbox where we started from, seem like years ago, and I got a headache for thinkin so hard. And we lean all over each other so we can hold up under the draggy ass lecture she always finishes us off with at the end before we thank her for borin us to tears. But she just looks at us like she readin tea leaves. Finally she say, "Well, what did you think of F.A.O. Schwarz?"

Rosie Giraffe mumbles, "White folks crazy."

"I'd like to go there again when I get my birthday money," says Mercedes, and we shove her out the pack so she has to lean on the mailbox by herself.

"I'd like a shower. Tiring day," say Flyboy.

Then Sugar surprises me by sayin, "You know, Miss Moore, I don't think all of us here put together eat in a year what that sailboat costs." And Miss Moore lights up like somebody goosed her. "And?" she say, urging Sugar on. Only I'm standin on her foot so she don't continue.

"Imagine for a minute what kind of society it is in which some people can spend on a toy what it would cost to feed a family of six or seven. What do you think?"

"I think," say Sugar pushing me off her feet like she never done before, cause I whip her ass in a minute, "that this is not much of a democracy if you ask me. Equal chance to pursue happiness means an equal crack at the dough, don't it?" Miss Moore is besides herself and I am disgusted with Sugar's treachery. So I stand on her foot one more time to see if she'll shove me. She shuts up, and Miss Moore looks at me, sorrowfully I'm thinkin. And somethin weird is goin on, I can feel it in my chest.

"Anybody else learn anything today?" lookin dead at me. I walk away and Sugar has to run to catch up and don't even seem to notice when I shrug her arm off my shoulder.

"Well, we got four dollars anyway," she says.

"Uh hunh."

"We could go to Hascombs and get half a chocolate layer and then go to the Sunset and still have plenty money for potato chips and ice cream sodas."

"Uh hunh."

"Race you to Hascombs," she say.

We start down the block and she gets ahead which is O.K. by me cause I'm going to the West End and then over to the Drive to think this day through. She can run if she want to and even run faster. But ain't nobody gonna beat me at nuthin.

Economy and Pleasure (1990)

Wendell Berry

To those who still uphold the traditions of religious and political thought that influenced the shaping of our society and the founding of our government, it is astonishing, and of course discouraging, to see economics now elevated to the position of ultimate justifier and explainer of all the affairs of our daily life, and competition enshrined as the sovereign principle and ideal of economics.

As thousands of small farms and small local businesses of all kinds falter and fail under the effects of adverse economic policies or live under the threat of what we complacently call "scientific progress," the economist sits in the calm of professorial tenure and government subsidy, commenting and explaining for the illumination of the press and the general public. If those who fail happen to be fellow humans, neighbors, children of God, and citizens of the republic, all that is outside the purview of the economist. As the farmers go under, as communities lose their economic supports, as all of rural America sits as if condemned in the shadow of the "free market" and "revolutionary science," the economist announces pontifically to the press that "there will be some winners and some losers"—as if that might justify and clarify everything, or anything. The sciences, one gathers, mindlessly serve economics, and the humanities defer abjectly to the sciences. All assume, apparently, that we are in the grip of the determination of economic laws that are the laws of the universe. The newspapers quote the economists as the ultimate authorities. We read their pronouncements, knowing that the last word has been said.

"Science," President Reagan says, "tells us that the breakthroughs in superconductivity bring us to the threshold of a new age." He is speaking to "a federal conference on the commercial applications of the new technology," and we know that by "science" he means scientists in the pay of corporations. "It is our task at this conference," he says, "to herald in that new age with a rush." A part of his program to accomplish this task is a proposal to "relax" the antitrust laws.[1] Thus even the national executive and our legal system itself must now defer to the demands of "the economy." Whatever "new age" is at hand at the moment must be heralded in "with a rush" because of the profits available to those who will rush it in.

It seems that we have been reduced almost to a state of absolute economics, in which people and all other creatures and things may be considered purely as economic "units," or integers of production, and in which a human being may be dealt with, as John Ruskin put it, "merely as a covetous machine."[2] And the voices bitterest to hear are those saying that all this destructive work of mindless genius, money, and power is regrettable but cannot be helped.

Perhaps it cannot. Surely we would be fools if, having understood the logic of this terrible process, we assumed that it might not go on in its glutton's optimism until it achieves the catastrophe that is its logical end. But let us suppose that a remedy is possible. If so, perhaps the best beginning would be in understanding the falseness and silliness of the economic ideal of competition, which is destructive both of nature and of human nature because it is untrue to both.

The ideal of competition always implies, and in fact requires, that any community must be divided into a class of winners and a class of losers. This division is radically different from other social divisions: that of the more able and the less able, or that of the richer and the poorer, or even that of the rulers and the ruled. These latter divisions have existed throughout history and at times, at least, have been ameliorated by social and religious ideals that instructed the strong to help the weak. As a purely economic ideal, competition does not contain or imply any such instructions. In fact, the defenders of the ideal of competition have never known what to do with or for the losers. The losers simply accumulate in human dumps, like stores of industrial waste, until they gain enough misery and strength to overpower the winners. The idea that the displaced and dispossessed "should seek retraining and get into another line of work" is, of course, utterly cynical; it is only the hand-washing practiced by officials and experts.[3] A loser, by definition, is somebody whom nobody knows what to do with. There is no limit to the damage and the suffering implicit in this willingness that losers should exist as a normal economic cost.

The danger of the ideal of competition is that it neither proposes nor implies any limits. It proposes simply to lower costs at any cost, and to raise profits at any cost. It does not hesitate at the destruction of the life of a family or the life of a community. It pits neighbor against neighbor as readily as it pits buyer against seller. Every transaction is *meant* to involve a winner and a loser. And for this reason the human economy is pitted without limit against nature. For in the unlimited competition of neighbor and neighbor, buyer and seller, all available means must be used; none may be spared.

I will be told that indeed there are limits to economic competitiveness as now practiced—that, for instance, one is not allowed to kill one's competitor. But, leaving aside the issue of whether or not murder would be acceptable as an economic means if the stakes were high enough, it is a fact that the destruction of life is a part of the daily business of economic competition as now practiced. If one person is willing to take another's property or to accept another's ruin as a normal result of economic enterprise, then he is willing to destroy that other person's life as it is and as it desires to be. That this person's biological existence has been spared seems merely incidental; it was spared because it was not worth anything. That this person is now "free" to "seek retraining and get into another line of work" signifies only that his life as it was has been destroyed.

But there is another implication in the limitlessness of the ideal of competition that is politically even more ominous: namely, that unlimited economic competitiveness proposes an unlimited concentration of economic power. Economic anarchy, like any other free-for-all, tends inevitably toward dominance by the strongest. If it is normal for economic activity to divide the community into a class of winners and a class of losers, then the inescapable implication is that the class of winners will become ever smaller, the class of losers ever larger. And that, obviously, is now happening: the usable property of our country, once divided somewhat democratically, is owned by fewer and fewer people every year. That the president of the republic can, without fear, propose the "relaxation" of antitrust laws in order to "rush" the advent of a commercial "new age" suggests not merely that we are "rushing" toward plutocracy, but that this is now a permissible goal for the would-be winning class for which Mr. Reagan speaks and acts, and a burden acceptable to nearly everybody else.

Nowhere, I believe, has this grossly oversimplified version of economics made itself more at home than in the land-grant universities. The colleges of agriculture, for example, having presided over the now nearly completed destruction of their constituency—the farm people and the farm communities—are now scrambling to ally themselves more firmly than ever, not with "the rural home and rural life"[4] that were, and are, their trust, but with the technocratic aims and corporate interests that are destroying the rural home and rural life. This, of course, is only a new intensification of an old alliance. The revolution that began with machines and chemicals proposes now to continue with automation, computers, and biotechnology. That this has been and is a revolution is undeniable. It has not been merely a "scientific revolution," as its proponents sometimes like to call it, but also an economic one, involving great and profound changes in property ownership and the distribution of real wealth. It has done by insidious tendency what the communist revolutions have done by fiat: it has dispossessed the people and usurped the power and integrity of community life.

This work has been done, and is still being done, under the heading of altruism: its aims, as its proponents never tire of repeating, are to "serve agriculture" and to "feed the world." These aims, as stated, are irreproachable; as pursued, they raise a number of doubts. Agriculture, it turns out, is to be served strictly according to the rules of competitive economics. The aim is "to make farmers more competitive" and "to make American agriculture more competitive." Against whom, we must ask, are our farmers and our agriculture to be made more competitive? And we must answer, because we know: Against other farmers, at home and abroad. Now, if the colleges of agriculture "serve agriculture" by helping farmers to compete against one another, what do they propose to do to help the farmers who have been out-competed? Well, those people are not farmers anymore, and therefore are of no concern to the academic servants of agriculture. Besides, they are the beneficiaries of the inestimable liberty to "seek retraining and get into another line of work."

And so the colleges of agriculture, entrusted though they are to serve the rural home and rural life, give themselves over to a hysterical rhetoric of "change," "the future," "the frontiers of modern science," "competition," "the competitive edge," "the cutting edge," "early adoption," and the like, as if there is nothing worth learning from the past and nothing worth preserving in the present. The idea of the teacher and scholar as one called upon to preserve and pass on a common cultural and natural birthright has been almost entirely replaced by the idea of the teacher and scholar as a developer of "human capital" and a bestower of economic advantage. The ambition is to make the university an "economic resource" in a competition for wealth and power that is local, national, and global. Of course, all this works directly against the rural home and rural life, because it works directly against community.

There is no denying that competitiveness is a part of the life both of an individual and of a community, or that, within limits, it is a useful and necessary part. But it is equally obvious that no individual can lead a good or a satisfying life under the rule of competition, and that no community can succeed except by limiting somehow the competitiveness of its members. One cannot maintain one's "competitive edge" if one helps other people. The advantage of "early adoption" would disappear—it would not be thought of—in a community that put a proper value on mutual help. Such advantages would not be thought of by people intent on loving their neighbors as themselves. And it is impossible to imagine that there can be any reconciliation between local and national competitiveness and global altruism. The ambition to "feed the world" or "feed the hungry," rising as it does out of the death struggle of farmer with farmer, proposes not the filling of stomachs, but the engorgement of "the bottom line." The strangest of all the doctrines of the cult of competition, in which admittedly there must be losers as well as winners, is that the result of competition is inevitably good for everybody, that altruistic ends may be met by a system without altruistic motives or altruistic means.

In agriculture, competitiveness has been based throughout the industrial era on constantly accelerating technological change—the very *principle* of agricultural competitiveness is ever-accelerating change—and this has encouraged an ever-accelerating dependency on purchased products, products purchased ever farther from home. Community, however, aspires toward stability. It strives to balance change with constancy. That is why community life places such high value on neighborly love, marital fidelity, local loyalty, the integrity and continuity of family life, respect for the old, and instruction of the young. And a vital community draws its life, so far as possible, from local sources. It prefers to solve its problems, for example, by nonmonetary exchanges of help, not by buying things. A community cannot survive under the rule of competition.

But the land-grant universities, in espousing the economic determinism of the industrialists, have caught themselves in a logical absurdity that they may finally discover to be dangerous to themselves. If competitiveness is the economic norm, and the "competitive edge" the only recognized social goal, then how can these institutions justify public support? Why, in other words, should the public be willing to permit a corporation to profit privately from research that has been subsidized publicly? Why should not the industries be required to afford their own research, and why should not the laws of competition and the free market—if indeed they perform as advertised—enable industries to do their own research a great deal more cheaply than the universities can do it?

The question that we finally come to is a practical one, though it is not one that is entirely answerable by empirical methods: Can a university, or a nation, *afford* this exclusive rule of competition, this purely economic economy? The great fault of this approach to things is that it is so drastically reductive; it does not permit us to live and work as human beings, as the best of our inheritance defines us. Rats and roaches live by competition under the law of supply and demand; it is the privilege of human beings to live under the laws of justice and mercy. It is impossible not to notice how little the proponents of the ideal of competition have to say about honesty, which is the fundamental economic virtue, and how *very* little they have to say about community, compassion, and mutual help.

But what the ideal of competition most flagrantly and disastrously excludes is affection. The affections, John Ruskin said, are "an anomalous force, rendering every one of the ordinary political economist's calculations nugatory; while, even if he desired to introduce this new element into his estimates, he has no power of dealing with it; for the affections only become a true motive power when they ignore every other motive power and condition of political economy."[5] Thus, if we are sane, we do not dismiss or abandon our infant children or our aged parents because they are too young or too old to work. For human beings, affection is the ultimate motive, because the force that powers us, as Ruskin also said, is not "steam, magnetism, or gravitation," but "a Soul."

I would like now to attempt to talk about economy from the standpoint of affection—or, as I am going to call it, pleasure, advancing just a little beyond Ruskin's term, for pleasure is, so to speak, affection in action. There are obvious risks in approaching an economic problem by a way that is frankly emotional—to talk, for example, about the pleasures of nature and the pleasures of work. But these risks seem to me worth taking, for what I am trying to deal with here is the grief that we increasingly suffer as a result of the loss of those pleasures.

It is necessary, at the outset, to make a distinction between pleasure that is true or legitimate and pleasure that is not. We know that a pleasure can be as heavily debited as an economy. Some people undoubtedly thought it pleasant, for example, to have the most onerous tasks of their economy performed by black slaves. But this proved to be a pleasure that was temporary and dangerous. It lived by an enormous indebtedness that was inescapably to be paid not in money, but in misery, waste, and death. The pleasures of fossil fuel combustion and nuclear "security" are, as we are beginning to see, similarly debited to the future. These pleasures are in every way analogous to the self-indulgent pleasures of individuals. They are pleasures that we are allowed to have merely to the extent that we can ignore or defer the logical consequences.

That there is pleasure in competition is not to be doubted. We know from childhood that winning is fun. But we probably begin to grow up when we begin to sympathize with the loser—that is, when we begin to understand that competition involves costs as well as benefits. Sometimes perhaps, as in the most innocent games, the benefits are all to the winner and the costs all to the loser. But when the competition is more serious, when the stakes are higher and greater power is used, then we know that the winner shares in the cost, sometimes disastrously. In war, for example, even the winner is a loser. And this is equally true of our present economy: in unlimited economic competition, the winners are losers; that they may appear to be winners is owing only to their temporary ability to charge their costs to other people or to nature.

But a victory over community or nature can be won only at everybody's cost. For example, we now have in the United States many landscapes that have been defeated—temporarily or permanently—by strip mining, by clear-cutting, by poisoning, by bad farming, or by various styles of "development" that have subjugated their sites entirely to human purposes. These landscapes have been defeated for the benefit of what are assumed to be victorious landscapes: the suburban housing developments and the places of amusement (the park systems, the recreational wildernesses) of the winners—so far—in the economy. But these victorious landscapes and their human inhabitants are already paying the costs of their defeat of other landscapes: in air and water pollution, overcrowding, inflated prices, and various diseases of body and mind. Eventually, the cost will be paid in scarcity or want of necessary goods.

Is it possible to look beyond this all-consuming "rush" of winning and losing to the possibility of countrysides, a nation of countrysides, in which use is not synonymous with defeat? It is. But in order to do so we must consider our pleasures. Since we all know, from our own and our nation's experience, of some pleasures that are canceled by their costs, and of some that result in unredeemable losses and miseries, it is natural to wonder if there may not be such phenomena as *net* pleasures, pleasures that are free or without a permanent cost. And we know that there are. These are the pleasures that we take in our own lives, our own wakefulness in this world, and in the company of other people and other creatures—pleasures innate in the Creation and in our own good work. It is in these pleasures that we possess the likeness to God that is spoken of in Genesis.

"This curious world we inhabit is more wonderful than convenient; more beautiful than it is useful; it is more to be admired and enjoyed than used."[6] Henry David Thoreau said that to his graduating class at Harvard in 1837. We may assume that to most of them it sounded odd, as to most of the Harvard graduating class of 1987 it undoubtedly still would. But perhaps we will be encouraged to take him seriously, if we recognize that this idea is not something that Thoreau made up out of thin air. When he uttered it, he may very well have been remembering Revelation 4:11: "Thou art worthy, O Lord, to receive glory and honour and power: for thou hast created all things, and for thy pleasure they are and were created." That God created "all things" is in itself an uncomfortable thought, for in our workaday world we can hardly avoid preferring some things above others, and this makes it hard to imagine *not* doing so. That God created all things for His pleasure, and that they continue to exist because they please Him, is formidable doctrine indeed, as far as possible both from the "anthropocentric" utilitarianism that some environmentalist critics claim to find in the Bible and from the grouchy spirituality of many Christians.

It would be foolish, probably, to suggest that God's pleasure in all things can be fully understood or appreciated by mere humans. The passage suggests, however, that our truest and profoundest religious experience may be the simple, unasking pleasure in the existence of other creatures that *is* possible to humans. It suggests that God's pleasure in all things must be respected by us in our use of things, and even in our displeasure in some things. It suggests too that we have an obligation to preserve God's pleasure in all things, and surely this means not only that we must not misuse or abuse anything, but also that there must be some things and some places that by common agreement we do not use at all, but leave wild. This bountiful and lovely thought that all creatures are pleasing to God—and potentially pleasing, therefore, to us—is unthinkable from the point of view of an economy divorced from pleasure, such as the one we have now, which completely discounts the capacity of people to be affectionate toward what they do and what they use and where they live and the other people and creatures with whom they live.

It may be argued that our whole society is more devoted to pleasure than any whole society ever was in the past, that we support in fact a great variety of pleasure industries and that these are thriving as never before. But that would seem only to prove my point. That there can be pleasure industries at all, exploiting our apparently limitless inability to be pleased, can only mean that our economy is divorced from pleasure and that pleasure is gone from our workplaces and our dwelling places. Our workplaces are more and more exclusively given over to production, and our dwelling places to consumption. And this accounts for the accelerating division of our country into defeated landscapes and victorious (but threatened) landscapes.

More and more, we take for granted that work must be destitute of pleasure. More and more, we assume that if we want to be pleased we must wait until evening, or the weekend, or vacation, or retirement. More and more, our farms and forests resemble our factories and offices, which in turn more and more resemble prisons—why else should we be so eager to escape them? We recognize defeated landscapes by the absence of pleasure from them. We are defeated at work because our work gives us no pleasure. We are defeated at home because we have no pleasant work there. We turn to the pleasure industries for relief from our defeat, and are again defeated, for the pleasure industries can thrive and grow only upon our dissatisfaction with them.

Where is our comfort but in the free, uninvolved, finally mysterious beauty and grace of this world that we did not make, that has no price? Where is our sanity but there? Where is our pleasure but in working and resting kindly in the presence of this world?

And in the right sort of economy, our pleasure would not be merely an addition or by-product or reward; it would be both an empowerment of our work and its indispensable measure. Pleasure, Ananda Coomaraswamy said, *perfects* work. In order to have leisure and pleasure, we have mechanized and automated and computerized our work. But what does this do but divide us ever more from our work and our products—and, in the process, from one another and the world? What have farmers done when they have mechanized and computerized their farms? They have removed themselves and their pleasure from their work.

I was fortunate, late in his life, to know Henry Besuden of Clark County, Kentucky, the premier Southdown sheep breeder and one of the great farmers of his time. He told me once that his first morning duty in the spring and early summer was to saddle his horse and ride across his pastures to see the condition of the grass when it was freshest from the moisture and coolness of the night. What he wanted to see in his pastures at that time of year, when his spring lambs would be fattening, was what he called "bloom"—by which he meant not flowers, but a certain visible delectability. He recognized it, of course, by his delight in it. He was one of the best of the traditional livestockmen—the husbander or husband of his animals. As such, he was not interested in "statistical indicators" of his flock's "productivity." He wanted his sheep to be pleased. If they were pleased with their pasture, they would eat eagerly, drink well, rest, and grow. He knew their pleasure by his own.

The nearly intolerable irony in our dissatisfaction is that we have removed pleasure from our work in order to remove "drudgery" from our lives. If I could pick any rule of industrial economics to receive a thorough re-examination by our people, it would be the one that says that all hard physical work is "drudgery" and not worth doing. There are of course many questions surrounding this issue: What is the work? In whose interest is it done? Where and in what circumstances is it done? How well and to what result is it done? In whose company is it done? How long does it last? And so forth. But this issue is personal and so needs to be re-examined by everybody. The argument, if it is that, can proceed only by personal testimony.

I can say, for example, that the tobacco harvest in my own home country involves the hardest work that I have done in any quantity. In most of the years of my life, from early boyhood until now, I have taken part in the tobacco cutting. This work usually occurs at some time between the last part of August and the first part of October. Usually the weather is hot; usually we are in a hurry. The work is extremely demanding, and often, because of the weather, it has the character of an emergency. Because all of the work still must be done by hand, this event has maintained much of its old character; it is very much the sort of thing the agriculture experts have had in mind when they have talked about freeing people from drudgery.

That the tobacco cutting *can* be drudgery is obvious. If there is too much of it, if it goes on too long, if one has no interest in it, if one cannot reconcile oneself to the misery involved in it, if one does not like or enjoy the company of one's fellow workers, then drudgery would be the proper name for it.

But for me, and I think for most of the men and women who have been my companions in this work, it has not been drudgery. None of us would say that we take pleasure in all of it all of the time, but we do take pleasure in it, and sometimes the pleasure can be intense and clear. Many of my dearest memories come from these times of hardest work.

The tobacco cutting is the most protracted social occasion of our year. Neighbors work together; they are together all day every day for weeks. The quiet of the work is not much interrupted by machine noises, and so there is much talk. There is the talk involved in the management of the work. There is incessant speculation about the weather. There is much laughter; because of the unrelenting difficulty of the work, everything funny or amusing is relished. And there are memories.

The crew to which I belong is the product of kinships and friendships going far back; my own earliest associations with it occurred nearly forty years ago. And so as we work we have before us not only the present crop and the present fields, but other crops and other fields that are remembered. The tobacco cutting is a sort of ritual of remembrance. Old stories are re-told; the dead and the absent are remembered. Some of the best talk I have ever listened to I have heard during these times, and I am especially moved to think of the care that is sometimes taken to speak well—that is, to speak fittingly—of the dead and the absent. The conversation, one feels, is ancient. Such talk in barns and at row ends must go back without interruption to the first farmers. How long it may continue is now an uneasy question; not much longer perhaps, but we do not know. We only know that while it lasts it can carry us deeply into our shared life and the happiness of farming.

On many days we have had somebody's child or somebody's children with us, playing in the barn or around the patch while we worked, and these have been our best days. One of the most regrettable things about the industrialization of work is the segregation of children. As industrial work excludes the dead by social mobility and technological change, it excludes children by haste and danger. The small scale and the handwork of our tobacco cutting permit margins both temporal and spatial that accommodate the play of children. The children play at the grownups' work, as well as at their own play. In their play the children learn to work; they learn to know their elders and their country. And the presence of playing children means invariably that the grown-ups play too from time to time.

(I am perforce aware of the problems and the controversies about tobacco. I have spoken of the tobacco harvest here simply because it is the only remaining farm job in my part of the country that still involves a traditional neighborliness.)

Ultimately, in the argument about work and how it should be done, one has only one's pleasure to offer. It is possible, as I have learned again and again, to be in one's place, in such company, wild or domestic, and with such pleasure, that one cannot think of another place that one would prefer to be—or of another place at all. One does not miss or regret the past, or fear or long for the future. Being there is simply all, and is enough. Such times give one the chief standard and the chief reason for one's work.

Last December, when my granddaughter, Katie, had just turned five, she stayed with me one day while the rest of the family was away from home. In the afternoon we hitched a team of horses to the wagon and hauled a load of dirt for the barn floor. It was a cold day, but the sun was shining; we hauled our load of dirt over the tree-lined gravel lane beside the creek—a way well known to her mother and to my mother when they were children. As we went along, Katie drove the team for the first time in her life. She did very well, and she was proud of herself. She said that her mother would be proud of her, and I said that I was proud of her.

We completed our trip to the barn, unloaded our load of dirt, smoothed it over the barn floor, and wetted it down. By the time we started back up the creek road the sun had gone over the hill and the air had turned bitter. Katie sat close to me in the wagon, and we did not say anything for a long time. I did not say anything because I was afraid that Katie was not saying anything because she was cold and tired and miserable and perhaps homesick; it was impossible to hurry much, and I was unsure how I would comfort her.

But then, after awhile, she said, "Wendell, isn't it fun?"

Notes

[1] "Reagan calls for effort to find commercial uses for superconductors," *Louisville Courier-Journal*, July 29, 1987, p. A3.

[2] John Ruskin, *Unto This Last* (Lincoln: University of Nebraska Press, 1967), p. 11.

[3] Reed Karaim, "Loss of million farms in 14 years projected," *Des Moines Register*, March 18, 1986, p. 1A.

[4] This is the language of the Hatch Act, *United States Code*, Section 361b.

[5] Ruskin, *Unto This Last*, p. 16.

[6] *Familiar Letters of Henry David Thoreau*, ed. F. B. Sanborn (Boston and New York: Houghton Mifflin, 1894), p. 9.

from The Bhagavad-Gita
(Fifth–Second Century B.C.E.)

Chapter XII

Arjuna:

LORD! of the men who serve Thee—true in heart—
As God revealed; and of the men who serve,
Worshipping Thee Unrevealed, Unbodied, far,
Which take the better way of faith and life?

Krishna:

Whoever serve Me—as I show Myself—
Constantly true, in full devotion fixed,
These hold I very holy. But who serve—
Worshipping Me The One, The Invisible,
The Unrevealed, Unnamed, Unthinkable,
Uttermost, All-pervading, Highest, Sure—
Who thus adore Me, mastering their sense,
Of one set mind to all, glad in all good,
These blessed souls come unto Me.
    Yet, hard
The travail is for whoso bend their minds
To reach th' Unmanifest. That viewless path
Shall scarce be trod by man bearing his flesh!
But whereso any doeth all his deeds,
Renouncing self in Me, full of Me, fixed
To serve only the Highest, night and day
Musing on Me—him will I swiftly lift
Forth from life's ocean of distress and death
Whose soul clings fast to Me. Cling thou to Me!
Clasp Me with heart and mind! so shalt thou dwell
Surely with Me on high. But if thy thought
Droops from such height; if thou be'st weak to set
Body and soul upon Me constantly,
Despair not! give Me lower service! seek

To read Me, worshipping with steadfast will;
And, if thou canst not worship steadfastly,
Work for Me, toil in works pleasing to Me!
For he that laboreth right for love of Me
Shall finally attain! But, if in this
Thy faint heart fails, bring Me thy failure! find
Refuge in Me! let fruits of labor go,
Renouncing all for Me, with lowliest heart,
So shalt thou come; for, though to know is more
Than diligence, yet worship better is
Than knowing, and renouncing better still
Near to renunciation—very near—
Dwelleth Eternal Peace!
    Who hateth nought
Of all which lives, living himself benign,
Compassionate, from arrogance exempt,
Exempt from love of self, unchangeable
By good or ill; patient, contented, firm
In faith, mastering himself, true to his word,
Seeking Me, heart and soul; vowed unto Me,—
That man I love! Who troubleth not his kind,
And is not troubled by them; clear of wrath,
Living too high for gladness, grief, or fear,
That man I love! Who, dwelling quiet-eyed,[1]
Stainless, serene, well-balanced, unperplexed,
Working with Me, yet from all works detached,
That man I love! Who, fixed in faith on Me,
Dotes upon none, scorns none; rejoices not,
And grieves not, letting good and evil hap
Light when it will, and when it will depart,
That man I love! Who, unto friend and foe
Keeping an equal heart, with equal mind
Bears shame and glory, with an equal peace
Takes heat and cold, pleasure and pain; abides
Quit of desires, hears praise or calumny
In passionless restraint, unmoved by each,
Linked by no ties to earth, steadfast in Me,
That man I love! But most of all I love
Those happy ones to whom 'tis life to live
In single fervid faith and love unseeing,
Eating the blessèd Amrit of my Being!

Here endeth Chapter XII. of the Bhagavad-Gîtâ, entitled "Bhakityôgô," or "The Book of the Religion of Faith"

Note

[1] "Not peering about,"—*anapeksha*.

Isaiah 58 (Fifth–Sixth Century B.C.E.)

The Bible

Shout out, do not hold back!
  Lift up your voice like a trumpet!
Announce to my people their rebellion,
  to the house of Jacob their sins.
2 Yet day after day they seek me
  and delight to know my ways,
as if they were a nation that practiced righteousness
  and did not forsake the ordinance of their God;
they ask of me righteous judgements,
  they delight to draw near to God.
3 "Why do we fast, but you do not see?
  Why humble ourselves, but you do not notice?"
Look, you serve your own interest on your fast day,
  and oppress all your workers.
4 Look, you fast only to quarrel and to fight
  and to strike with a wicked fist.
Such fasting as you do today
  will not make your voice heard on high.
5 Is such the fast that I choose,
  a day to humble oneself?
Is it to bow down the head like a bulrush,
  and to lie in sackcloth and ashes?
Will you call this a fast,
  a day acceptable to the Lord?

6 Is not this the fast that I choose:
  to loose the bonds of injustice,
  to undo the thongs of the yoke,
to let the oppressed go free,
  and to break every yoke?
7 Is it not to share your bread with the hungry,
  and bring the homeless poor into your house;
when you see the naked, to cover them,
  and not to hide yourself from your own kin?
8 Then your light shall break forth like the dawn,

and your healing shall spring up quickly;
your vindicator shall go before you,
   the glory of the Lord shall be your rearguard.
9 Then you shall call, and the Lord will answer;
   you shall cry for help, and he will say, Here I am.

If you remove the yoke from among you,
   the pointing of the finger, the speaking of evil,
10 if you offer your food to the hungry
   and satisfy the needs of the afflicted,
then your light shall rise in the darkness
   and your gloom be like the noonday.
11 The Lord will guide you continually,
   and satisfy your needs in parched places,
   and make your bones strong;
and you shall be like a watered garden,
   like a spring of water,
   whose waters never fail.
12 Your ancient ruins shall be rebuilt;
   you shall raise up the foundations of many generations;
you shall be called the repairer of the breach,
   the restorer of streets to live in.

13 If you refrain from trampling the sabbath,
   from pursuing your own interests on my holy day;
if you call the sabbath a delight
   and the holy day of the Lord honourable;
if you honour it, not going your own ways,
   serving your own interests, or pursuing your own affairs;
14 then you shall take delight in the Lord,
   and I will make you ride upon the heights of the earth;
I will feed you with the heritage of your ancestor Jacob,
   for the mouth of the Lord has spoken.

Amos 5 (Eighth Century B.C.E.)

The Bible

Hear this word that I take up over you in lamentation, O house of Israel:

2 Fallen, no more to rise,
   is maiden Israel;
forsaken on her land,
   with no one to raise her up.

3 For thus says the Lord God:
The city that marched out a thousand
   shall have a hundred left,
and that which marched out a hundred
   shall have ten left.

4 For thus says the Lord to the house of Israel:
Seek me and live;
5   but do not seek Bethel,
and do not enter into Gilgal
   or cross over to Beer-sheba;
for Gilgal shall surely go into exile,
   and Bethel shall come to nothing.

6 Seek the Lord and live,
   or he will break out against the house of Joseph like fire,
   and it will devour Bethel, with no one to quench it.
7 Ah, you that turn justice to wormwood,
   and bring righteousness to the ground!

8 The one who made the Pleiades and Orion,
   and turns deep darkness into the morning,
   and darkens the day into night,
who calls for the waters of the sea,
   and pours them out on the surface of the earth,
the Lord is his name,

9 who makes destruction flash out against the strong,
   so that destruction comes upon the fortress.

10 They hate the one who reproves in the gate,
   and they abhor the one who speaks the truth.
11 Therefore, because you trample on the poor
   and take from them levies of grain,
you have built houses of hewn stone,
   but you shall not live in them;
you have planted pleasant vineyards,
   but you shall not drink their wine.
12 For I know how many are your transgressions,
   and how great are your sins—
you who afflict the righteous, who take a bribe,
   and push aside the needy in the gate.
13 Therefore the prudent will keep silent in such a time;
   for it is an evil time.

14 Seek good and not evil,
   that you may live;
and so the Lord, the God of hosts, will be with you,
   just as you have said.
15 Hate evil and love good,
   and establish justice in the gate;
it may be that the Lord, the God of hosts,
   will be gracious to the remnant of Joseph.

16 Therefore thus says the Lord, the God of hosts, the Lord:
In all the squares there shall be wailing;
   and in all the streets they shall say, "Alas! alas!"
They shall call the farmers to mourning,
   and those skilled in lamentation, to wailing;
17 in all the vineyards there shall be wailing,
   for I will pass through the midst of you,
says the Lord.

18 Alas for you who desire the day of the Lord!
   Why do you want the day of the Lord?
It is darkness, not light;
19   as if someone fled from a lion,

and was met by a bear;
or went into the house and rested a hand against the wall,
 and was bitten by a snake.
20 Is not the day of the Lord darkness, not light,
 and gloom with no brightness in it?

21 I hate, I despise your festivals,
 and I take no delight in your solemn assemblies.
22 Even though you offer me your burnt-offerings and grain-offerings,
 I will not accept them;
and the offerings of well-being of your fatted animals
 I will not look upon.
23 Take away from me the noise of your songs;
 I will not listen to the melody of your harps.
24 But let justice roll down like waters,
 and righteousness like an ever-flowing stream.

25 Did you bring to me sacrifices and offerings the forty years in the wilderness, O house of Israel? **26** You shall take up Sakkuth your king, and Kaiwan your star-god, your images that you made for yourselves; **27** therefore I will take you into exile beyond Damascus, says the Lord, whose name is the God of hosts.

Selections from Matthew (70–85 C.E.)

The Bible

The Sermon on the Mount
Matthew 5

When Jesus saw the crowds, he went up the mountain; and after he sat down, his disciples came to him. **2** Then he began to speak, and taught them, saying:

3 "Blessed are the poor in spirit, for theirs is the kingdom of heaven.

4 "Blessed are those who mourn, for they will be comforted.

5 "Blessed are the meek, for they will inherit the earth.

6 "Blessed are those who hunger and thirst for righteousness, for they will be filled.

7 "Blessed are the merciful, for they will receive mercy.

8 "Blessed are the pure in heart, for they will see God.

9 "Blessed are the peacemakers, for they will be called children of God.

10 "Blessed are those who are persecuted for righteousness' sake, for theirs is the kingdom of heaven.

11 "Blessed are you when people revile you and persecute you and utter all kinds of evil against you falsely on my account. **12** Rejoice and be glad, for your reward is great in heaven, for in the same way they persecuted the prophets who were before you.

13 "You are the salt of the earth; but if salt has lost its taste, how can its saltiness be restored? It is no longer good for anything, but is thrown out and trampled under foot.

14 "You are the light of the world. A city built on a hill cannot be hidden. **15** No one after lighting a lamp puts it under the bushel basket, but on the lampstand, and it gives light to all in the house. **16** In the same way, let your light shine before others, so that they may see your good works and give glory to your Father in heaven.

426

17 "Do not think that I have come to abolish the law or the prophets; I have come not to abolish but to fulfil. **18** For truly I tell you, until heaven and earth pass away, not one letter, not one stroke of a letter, will pass from the law until all is accomplished. **19** Therefore, whoever breaks one of the least of these commandments, and teaches others to do the same, will be called least in the kingdom of heaven; but whoever does them and teaches them will be called great in the kingdom of heaven. **20** For I tell you, unless your righteousness exceeds that of the scribes and Pharisees, you will never enter the kingdom of heaven.

21 "You have heard that it was said to those of ancient times, 'You shall not murder'; and 'whoever murders shall be liable to judgement.' **22** But I say to you that if you are angry with a brother or sister, you will be liable to judgement; and if you insult a brother or sister, you will be liable to the council; and if you say, 'You fool', you will be liable to the hell of fire. **23** So when you are offering your gift at the altar, if you remember that your brother or sister has something against you, **24** leave your gift there before the altar and go; first be reconciled to your brother or sister, and then come and offer your gift. **25** Come to terms quickly with your accuser while you are on the way to court with him, or your accuser may hand you over to the judge, and the judge to the guard, and you will be thrown into prison. **26** Truly I tell you, you will never get out until you have paid the last penny.

27 "You have heard that it was said, 'You shall not commit adultery.' **28** But I say to you that everyone who looks at a woman with lust has already committed adultery with her in his heart. **29** If your right eye causes you to sin, tear it out and throw it away; it is better for you to lose one of your members than for your whole body to be thrown into hell. **30** And if your right hand causes you to sin, cut it off and throw it away; it is better for you to lose one of your members than for your whole body to go into hell.

31 "It was also said, 'Whoever divorces his wife, let him give her a certificate of divorce.' **32** But I say to you that anyone who divorces his wife, except on the ground of unchastity, causes her to commit adultery; and whoever marries a divorced woman commits adultery.

33 "Again, you have heard that it was said to those of ancient times, 'You shall not swear falsely, but carry out the vows you have made to the Lord.' **34** But I say to you, Do not swear at all, either by heaven, for it is the throne of God, **35** or by the earth, for it is his footstool, or by Jerusalem, for it is the city of the great King. **36** And do not swear by your head, for you cannot make one hair white or black. **37** Let your word be 'Yes, Yes' or 'No, No'; anything more than this comes from the evil one.

38 "You have heard that it was said, 'An eye for an eye and a tooth for a tooth.' **39** But I say to you, Do not resist an evildoer. But if anyone strikes you on the right cheek, turn the other also; **40** and if anyone wants to sue you and take your coat, give your cloak as well; **41** and if anyone forces you to go one mile, go also the second mile. **42** Give to everyone who begs from you, and do not refuse anyone who wants to borrow from you.

43 "You have heard that it was said, 'You shall love your neighbor and hate your enemy.' **44** But I say to you, Love your enemies and pray for those who persecute you, **45** so that you may be children of your Father in heaven; for he makes his sun rise on the evil and on the good, and sends rain on the righteous and on the unrighteous. **46** For if you love those who love you, what reward do you have? Do not even the tax collectors do the same? **47** And if you greet only your brothers and sisters, what more are you doing than others? Do not even the Gentiles do the same? **48** Be perfect, therefore, as your heavenly Father is perfect.

Matthew 6

"Beware of practicing your piety before others in order to be seen by them; for then you have no reward from your Father in heaven.

2 "So whenever you give alms, do not sound a trumpet before you, as the hypocrites do in the synagogues and in the streets, so that they may be praised by others. Truly I tell you, they have received their reward. **3** But when you give alms, do not let your left hand know what your right hand is doing, **4** so that your alms may be done in secret; and your Father who sees in secret will reward you.

5 "And whenever you pray, do not be like the hypocrites; for they love to stand and pray in the synagogues and at the street corners, so that they may be seen by others. Truly I tell you, they have received their reward. **6** But whenever you pray, go into your room and shut the door and pray to your Father who is in secret; and your Father who sees in secret will reward you.

7 "When you are praying, do not heap up empty phrases as the Gentiles do; for they think that they will be heard because of their many words. **8** Do not be like them, for your Father knows what you need before you ask him.

9 "Pray then in this way:
Our Father in heaven,
   hallowed be your name.
10 Your kingdom come.

Your will be done,
    on earth as it is in heaven.
11 Give us this day our daily bread.
12 And forgive us our debts,
    as we also have forgiven our debtors.
13 And do not bring us to the time of trial,
    but rescue us from the evil one.

14 For if you forgive others their trespasses, your heavenly Father will also forgive you; 15 but if you do not forgive others, neither will your Father forgive your trespasses.

16 "And whenever you fast, do not look dismal, like the hypocrites, for they disfigure their faces so as to show others that they are fasting. Truly I tell you, they have received their reward. 17 But when you fast, put oil on your head and wash your face, 18 so that your fasting may be seen not by others but by your Father who is in secret; and your Father who sees in secret will reward you.

19 "Do not store up for yourselves treasures on earth, where moth and rust consume and where thieves break in and steal; 20 but store up for yourselves treasures in heaven, where neither moth nor rust consumes and where thieves do not break in and steal. 21 For where your treasure is, there your heart will be also.

22 "The eye is the lamp of the body. So, if your eye is healthy, your whole body will be full of light; 23 but if your eye is unhealthy, your whole body will be full of darkness. If then the light in you is darkness, how great is the darkness!

24 "No one can serve two masters; for a slave will either hate the one and love the other, or be devoted to the one and despise the other. You cannot serve God and wealth.

25 "Therefore I tell you, do not worry about your life, what you will eat or what you will drink, or about your body, what you will wear. Is not life more than food, and the body more than clothing? 26 Look at the birds of the air; they neither sow nor reap nor gather into barns, and yet your heavenly Father feeds them. Are you not of more value than they? 27 And can any of you by worrying add a single hour to your span of life? 28 And why do you worry about clothing? Consider the lilies of the field, how they grow; they neither toil nor spin, 29 yet I tell you, even Solomon in all his glory was not clothed like one of these. 30 But if God so clothes the grass of the field, which is alive today and tomorrow is thrown into the oven, will he not much more clothe you—you of little faith? 31 Therefore

do not worry, saying, 'What will we eat?' or 'What will we drink?' or 'What will we wear?' **32** For it is the Gentiles who strive for all these things; and indeed your heavenly Father knows that you need all these things. **33** But strive first for the kingdom of God and his righteousness, and all these things will be given to you as well.

34 "So do not worry about tomorrow, for tomorrow will bring worries of its own. Today's trouble is enough for today.

Matthew 7

"Do not judge, so that you may not be judged. **2** For with the judgement you make you will be judged, and the measure you give will be the measure you get. **3** Why do you see the speck in your neighbor's eye, but do not notice the log in your own eye? **4** Or how can you say to your neighbor, 'Let me take the speck out of your eye', while the log is in your own eye? **5** You hypocrite, first take the log out of your own eye, and then you will see clearly to take the speck out of your neighbor's eye.

6 "Do not give what is holy to dogs; and do not throw your pearls before swine, or they will trample them under foot and turn and maul you.

7 "Ask, and it will be given to you; search, and you will find; knock, and the door will be opened for you. **8** For everyone who asks receives, and everyone who searches finds, and for everyone who knocks, the door will be opened. **9** Is there anyone among you who, if your child asks for bread, will give a stone? **10** Or if the child asks for a fish, will give a snake? **11** If you then, who are evil, know how to give good gifts to your children, how much more will your Father in heaven give good things to those who ask him!

12 "In everything do to others as you would have them do to you; for this is the law and the prophets.

13 "Enter through the narrow gate; for the gate is wide and the road is easy that leads to destruction, and there are many who take it. **14** For the gate is narrow and the road is hard that leads to life, and there are few who find it.

15 "Beware of false prophets, who come to you in sheep's clothing but inwardly are ravenous wolves. **16** You will know them by their fruits. Are grapes gathered from thorns, or figs from thistles? **17** In the same way, every good tree bears good fruit, but the bad tree bears bad fruit. **18** A good tree cannot bear bad fruit, nor can a bad tree bear good fruit.

19 Every tree that does not bear good fruit is cut down and thrown into the fire. **20** Thus you will know them by their fruits.

21 "Not everyone who says to me, 'Lord, Lord,' will enter the kingdom of heaven, but only one who does the will of my Father in heaven. **22** On that day many will say to me, 'Lord, Lord, did we not prophesy in your name, and cast out demons in your name, and do many deeds of power in your name?' **23** Then I will declare to them, 'I never knew you; go away from me, you evildoers.'

24 "Everyone then who hears these words of mine and acts on them will be like a wise man who built his house on rock. **25** The rain fell, the floods came, and the winds blew and beat on that house, but it did not fall, because it had been founded on rock. **26** And everyone who hears these words of mine and does not act on them will be like a foolish man who built his house on sand. **27** The rain fell, and the floods came, and the winds blew and beat against that house, and it fell—and great was its fall!"

• • •

The Parable of the Sheep and the Goats
Matthew 25

"When the Son of Man comes in his glory, and all the angels with him, then he will sit on the throne of his glory. **32** All the nations will be gathered before him, and he will separate people one from another as a shepherd separates the sheep from the goats, **33** and he will put the sheep at his right hand and the goats at the left. **34** Then the king will say to those at his right hand, 'Come, you that are blessed by my Father, inherit the kingdom prepared for you from the foundation of the world; **35** for I was hungry and you gave me food, I was thirsty and you gave me something to drink, I was a stranger and you welcomed me, **36** I was naked and you gave me clothing, I was sick and you took care of me, I was in prison and you visited me.' **37** Then the righteous will answer him, 'Lord, when was it that we saw you hungry and gave you food, or thirsty and gave you something to drink? **38** And when was it that we saw you a stranger and welcomed you, or naked and gave you clothing? **39** And when was it that we saw you sick or in prison and visited you?' **40** And the king will answer them, 'Truly I tell you, just as you did it to one of the least of these who are members of my family, you did it to me.' **41** Then he will say to those at his left hand, 'You that are accursed, depart from me into the eternal fire prepared for the devil and his angels; **42** for I was hungry and you gave me no food, I was thirsty and you gave me nothing to drink, **43** I was a stranger and you did not welcome me, naked and you did not give me clothing, sick and in prison and you did not visit me.' **44** Then they also will answer, 'Lord, when was it that we saw you hungry or thirsty or a stranger or naked or sick or in prison, and did not take care of you?' **45** Then he will answer them, 'Truly I tell you, just as you did not do it to one of the least of these, you did not do it to me.' **46** And these will go away into eternal punishment, but the righteous into eternal life."

The Dinosaurs (1968)

Italo Calvino

The causes of the rapid extinction of the Dinosaur remain mysterious; the species had evolved and grown throughout the Triassic and the Jurassic, and for 150 million years the Dinosaur had been the undisputed master of the continents. Perhaps the species was unable to adapt to the great changes of climate and vegetation which took place in the Cretaceous period. By its end all the Dinosaurs were dead.

All except me,—*Qfwfq corrected,*—because, for a certain period, I was also a Dinosaur: about fifty million years, I'd say, and I don't regret it; if you were a Dinosaur in those days, you were sure you were in the right, and you made everyone look up to you.

Then the situation changed—I don't have to tell you all the details—and all sorts of trouble began, defeats, errors, doubts, treachery, pestilences. A new population was growing up on the Earth, hostile to us. They attacked us on all sides; there was no dealing with them. Now there are those who say the pleasure of decadence, the desire to be destroyed were part of the spirit of us Dinosaurs even before then. I don't know: I never felt like that; if some of the others did, it was because they sensed they were already finished.

I prefer not to think back to the period of the great death. I never believed I'd escape it. The long migration that saved me led me through a cemetery of fleshless carcases, where only a crest or a horn or a scale of armor or a fragment of horny skin recalled the ancient splendor of the living creature. And over those remains worked the beaks, the bills, the talons, the suckers of the new masters of the planet. When at last I found no further traces, of the living or of the dead, then I stopped.

I spent many, many years on those deserted plateaus. I had survived ambushes, epidemics, starvation, frost: but I was alone. To go on staying up there forever was impossible for me. I started the journey down.

The world had changed: I couldn't recognize the mountains any more, or the rivers, or the trees. The first time I glimpsed some living beings, I hid: it was a flock of the New Ones, small specimens, but strong.

"Hey, you!" They had spied me, and I was immediately amazed at this familiar way of addressing me. I ran off; they chased me. For millennia I had been used to striking terror all around me, and to feeling terror of the others' reactions to the terror I aroused. None of that now. "Hey, you!" They came over to me casually, neither hostile nor frightened.

"Why are you running? What's come over you?" They only wanted me to show them the shortest path to I don't know where. I stammered out that I was a stranger there. "What made you run off?" one of them said. "You looked as if you'd seen . . . a Dinosaur!" And the others laughed. But in that laughter I sensed for the first time a hint of apprehension. Their good humor was a bit forced. Then one of them turned serious and added: "Don't say that even as a joke. You don't know what they are . . ."

So, the terror of the Dinosaurs still continued in the New Ones, but perhaps they hadn't seen any for several generations and weren't able to recognize one. I traveled on, cautious but also impatient to repeat the experiment. At a spring a New One, a young female, was drinking; she was alone. I went up softly, stretched my neck to drink beside her; I could already imagine her desperate scream the moment she saw me, her breathless flight. She would spread the alarm, and the New Ones would come out in force to hunt me down . . . For a moment I repented my action; if I wanted to save myself, I should tear her limb from limb at once: start it all over again . . .

She turned and said: "Nice and cool, isn't it?" She went on conversing amiably, the usual remarks one makes to strangers, asking me if I came from far away, if I had run into rain on the trip, or if it had been sunny. I would never have imagined it possible to talk like that with non-Dinosaurs, and I was tense and mostly silent.

"I always come here to drink," she said, "to the Dinosaur . . ."

I reacted with a start, my eyes widening.

"Oh, yes, that's what we call it. The Dinosaur's Spring . . . that's been its name since ancient times. They say that a Dinosaur hid here, one of the last, and whenever anybody came here for a drink the Dinosaur jumped on him and tore him limb from limb. My goodness!"

I wanted to drop through the earth. "Now she'll realize who I am," I was thinking, "now she'll take a better look at me and recognize me!" And as one does, when one doesn't want to be observed, I kept my eyes lowered and coiled my tail, as if to hide it. It was such a strain that when, still smiling, she said good-by and went on her way, I felt as tired as if I'd fought a battle, one of those battles we fought when we were defending ourselves with our claws and our teeth. I realized I hadn't even said good-by back to her.

I reached the shore of a river, where the New Ones had their dens and fished for their living. To create a bend in the river, where the water would be less rapid and would hold the fish, they were constructing a dam of branches. As soon as they saw me, they glanced up from their work and stopped. They looked at me, then at each other, in silence, as if questioning one another. "This is it," I thought, "all I can do is sell my life dearly." And I prepared to leap to my defense.

Luckily, I stopped myself in time. Those fishermen had nothing against me: seeing how strong I was, they wanted to ask me if I could stay with them and work transporting wood.

"This is a safe place," they insisted, when I seemed to hesitate. "There hasn't been a Dinosaur seen here since the days of our grandfathers' grandfathers . . ."

Nobody suspected who I might be. I stayed. The climate was good, the food wasn't to my taste but it was all right, and the work wasn't too hard for one of my strength. They gave me a nickname: "The Ugly One," because I was different from them, for no other reason. These New Ones, I don't know how in the world you call them, Pantotheres or whatever, were still a rather formless species; in fact, all the other species descended from it later; and already in those days there was the greatest variety of similarities and dissimilarities from one individual to the next, so, though I was an entirely different type, I was finally convinced I didn't stand out too much.

Not that I ever became completely used to this idea: I always felt like a Dinosaur in the midst of enemies, and every evening, when they started telling stories of the Dinosaurs, legends handed down from generation to generation, I hung back in the shadow, my nerves on edge.

The stories were terrifying. The listeners, pale, occasionally bursting out with cries of fear, hung on the lips of the storyteller, whose voice also betrayed an equally profound emotion. Soon it was clear to me that all of them already knew those stories (even though the repertory was very plentiful), but when they heard them, their fear was renewed every time. The Dinosaurs were portrayed as so many monsters, described with a wealth of details that would never have helped anyone recognize them, and depicted as intent only on harming the New Ones, as if the New Ones from the very beginning had been the Earth's most important inhabitants and we had had nothing better to do than run after them from morning till night. For myself, when I thought about us Dinosaurs, I returned in memory to a long series of hardships, death agonies, mourning; the stories that the New Ones told about us were so remote from my experience that they should have left me indifferent, as if they referred to outsiders, strangers. And yet, as I listened, I realized I had never thought about how we appeared to others, and that, among all the nonsense, those tales, here and there, from the narrators' point of view, had hit on the truth. In my mind their stories of terrors we inflicted became confused with my memories of terror undergone: the more I learned how we had made others tremble, the more I trembled myself.

Each one told a story, in turn, and at a certain point they said: "What does the Ugly One have to tell us? Don't you have any stories? Didn't anyone in your family have adventures with the Dinosaurs?"

"Yes, but . . . " I stammered, "it was so long ago . . . ah, if you only knew . . ."

The one who came to my assistance at that juncture was Fern-flower, the young creature of the spring. "Oh, leave him alone . . . He's a foreigner, he doesn't feel at home yet; he can't speak our language well enough . . ."

In the end they changed the subject. I could breathe again.

A kind of friendliness had grown up between Fern-flower and me. Nothing too intimate: I had never dared touch her. But we had long talks. Or rather, she told me all sorts of things about her life; in my fear of giving myself away, of making her suspect my identity, I stuck always to generalities. Fern-flower told me her dreams: "Last night I saw this enormous Dinosaur, terrifying, breathing smoke from his nostrils. He came closer, grabbed me by the nape, and carried me off. He wanted to eat me alive. It was a terrible dream, simply terrible, but—isn't this odd? —I wasn't the least frightened. No, I don't know how to say it . . . I liked him . . ."

That dream should have made me understand many things and especially one thing: that Fern-flower desired nothing more than to be assaulted. This was the moment for me to embrace her. But the Dinosaur they imagined was too different from the Dinosaur I was, and this thought made me even more different and timid. In other words, I missed a good opportunity. Then Fern-flower's brother returned from the season of fishing in the plains, the young one was much more closely watched, and our conversations became less frequent.

This brother, Zahn, started acting suspicious the moment be first saw me. "Who's that? Where does he come from?" be asked the others, pointing to me.

"That's the Ugly One, a foreigner, who works with the timber," they said to him. "Why? What's strange about him?"

"I'd like to ask him that," Zahn said, with a grim look. "Hey, You! What's strange about you?" What could I answer? "Me? Nothing."

"So, you're not strange, eh?" and he laughed. That time it went no further, but I was prepared for the worst.

This Zahn was one of the most active ones in the village. He had traveled about the world and seemed to know many more things than the others. When he heard the usual talk about the Dinosaurs he was seized by a kind of impatience. "Fairy tales," he said once, "you're all telling fairy tales. I'd like to see you if a real Dinosaur turned up here."

"There haven't been any for a long time now . . ." a fisherman said.

"Not all that long . . ." Zahn sniggered. "And there might still be a herd or two around the countryside . . . In the plains, our bunch takes turns keeping watch, day and night. But there we can trust one another; we don't take in characters we don't know . . ." And he gave me a long, meaningful look.

There was no point dragging things out: better force him into the open right away. I took a step forward. "Have you got something against me?" I asked.

"I'm against anybody when we don't know who gave him birth or where he came from, and when he wants to eat our food and court our sisters . . ."

One of the fishermen took up my defense: "The Ugly One earns his keep; he's a hard worker . . ."

"He's capable of carrying tree trunks on his back, I won't deny that," Zahn went on, "but if danger came, if we had to defend ourselves with claws and teeth, how can we be sure he would behave properly?"

A general argument began. The strange thing was that the possibility of my being a Dinosaur never occurred to anyone; the sin I was accused of was being Different, a Foreigner, and therefore Untrustworthy; and the argument was over how much my presence increased the danger of the Dinosaurs' ever coming back.

"I'd like to see him in battle, with that little lizard's mouth of his . . ." Zaim went on contemptuously, goading me.

I went over to him, abruptly, nose to nose. "You can see me right now, if you don't run away."

He wasn't expecting that. He looked around. The others formed a circle. There was nothing for us to do but fight.

I moved forward, brushed off his bite by twisting my neck; I had already given him a blow of my paw that knocked him on his back, and I was on top of him. This was a wrong move; as if I didn't know it, as if I had never seen Dinosaurs die, clawed and bitten on the chest and the belly, when they believed they had pinned down their enemy. But I still knew how to use my tail, to steady myself; I didn't want to let him turn me over; I put on pressure, but I felt I was about to give way . . .

Then one of the observers yelled: "Give it to him, Dinosaur!" No sooner had they unmasked me than I became again the Dinosaur of the old days: since all was lost, I might as well make them feel their ancient terror. And I struck Zahn once, twice, three times . . .

They tore us apart. "Zahn, we told you! The Ugly One has muscles. You don't try any tricks with him, not with old Ugly!" And they laughed and congratulated me, slapping me on the back with their paws. Convinced I had been discovered, I couldn't get my bearings; it was only later that I understood the cry "Dinosaur" was a habit of theirs, to encourage the rivals in a fight, as if to say: "Go on, you're the stronger one!" and I wasn't even sure whether they had shouted the word at me or at Zahn.

From that day on I was the most respected of all. Even Zahn encouraged me, followed me around to see me give new proofs of my strength. I must say that their usual talk about the Dinosaurs changed a bit, too, as always happens when you tire of judging things in the same old way and fashion begins to take a new turn. Now, if they wanted to criticize something in the village, they had got into the habit of saying that, among Dinosaurs, certain things were never done, that the Dinosaurs in many ways could offer an example, that the behavior of the Dinosaurs in this or that situation (in their private life, for example) was beyond reproach, and so on. In short, there seemed to be emerging a kind of posthumous admiration for these Dinosaurs about whom no one knew anything precise.

Sometimes I couldn't help saying: "Come, let's not exaggerate. What do you think a Dinosaur was, after all?"

They interrupted me: "Shut up. What do you know about them? You've never seen one."

Perhaps this was the right moment to start calling a spade a spade. "I have too seen them!" I cried, "and if you want, I can explain to you what they were like!"

They didn't believe me; they thought I was making fun of them. For me, this new way they had of talking about the Dinosaurs was almost as unbearable as the old one. Because—apart from the grief I felt at the sad fate that had befallen my species—I knew the life of the Dinosaurs from within, I knew how we had been governed by narrow-mindedness, prejudice, unable to adapt ourselves to new situations. And I now had to see them take as a model that little world of ours, so backward and so—to tell the truth—boring! I had to feel imposed on me, and by them, a kind of sacred respect for my species which I myself had never felt! But, after all, this was only right: what did these New Ones have that was so different from the Dinosaurs of the good old days? Safe in their village with their dams and their ponds, they had also taken on a smugness, a presumptuousness . . . I finally felt toward them the same intolerance I had had toward my own environment, and the more I heard them admiring the Dinosaurs the more I detested Dinosaurs and New Ones alike.

"You know something? Last night I dreamed that a Dinosaur was to go past my house," Fern-flower said to me, "a magnificent Dinosaur, a Prince or a King of Dinosaurs. I made myself pretty, I put a ribbon on my head, and I leaned out of the window. I tried to attract the Dinosaur's attention, I bowed to him, but he didn't even seem to notice me, didn't even deign to glance at me . . ."

This dream furnished me with a new key to the understanding of Fern-flower's attitude toward me: the young creature had mistaken my shyness for disdainful pride. Now, when I recall it, I realize that all I had to do was maintain that attitude a little longer, make a show of haughty detachment, and I would have won her completely. Instead, the revelation so moved me that I threw myself at her feet, tears in my eyes, and said: "No, no, Fern-flower, it's not the way you believe; you're better than any Dinosaur, a hundred times better, and I feel so inferior to you . . ."

Fern-flower stiffened, took a step backwards. "What are you saying?" This wasn't what she expected: she was upset, and she found the scene a bit distasteful. I understood this too late; I hastily recovered myself, but a feeling of uneasiness now weighed heavily between us.

There was no time to ponder it, what with everything that happened a little later. Breathless messengers reached the village. "The Dinosaurs are coming back!" A herd of strange monsters had been sighted, speeding fiercely over the plain. At this rate they would attack the village the following morning. The alarm was sounded.

You can imagine the flood of conflicting emotions that filled my breast at this news: my species wasn't extinct, I would be able to join my brothers, take up my old life! But the memory of the old life that returned to my mind was the endless series of defeats, of flights, of dangers; to begin again meant perhaps only a temporary extension of that death agony, the return to a phase I thought had already ended. Now, here in the village, I had achieved a kind of new tranquillity, and I was sorry to lose it.

The New Ones were also torn by conflicting feelings. On the one hand, there was panic; on the other, the wish to triumph over the ancient enemy; and at the same time, there was the conviction that if the Dinosaurs had survived and were now advancing vengefully it meant nobody could stop them and their victory, pitiless as it might be, could also perhaps be a good thing for all. It was as if the New Ones wanted at the same time to defend themselves, to flee, to wipe out the enemy, and to be defeated; and this uncertainty was reflected in the disorder of their defense preparations.

"Just a moment!" Zahn shouted. "There is only one among us who is capable of taking command! The strongest of all, the Ugly One!"

"You're right! The Ugly One must command us!" the others shouted in chorus. "Yes, yes, full power to the Ugly One!" And they placed themselves at my command.

"No, no, how can I, a foreigner? . . . I'm not up to it . . ." I parried. But it was impossible to convince them.

What was I to do? That night I couldn't close my eyes. The call of my blood insisted I should desert and join my brothers; loyalty toward the New Ones, who had welcomed and sheltered me and given me their trust, demanded I should consider myself on their side; and in addition I knew full well that neither Dinosaurs nor New Ones were worthy of my lifting a finger for them. If the Dinosaurs were trying to re-establish their rule with invasions and massacres, it meant they had learned nothing from experience, that they had survived only by mistake. And it was clear that the New Ones, turning the command over to me, had found the easiest solution: leave all responsibility to an outsider, who could be their savior but also, in case of defeat, a scapegoat to hand over to the enemy to pacify him, or else a traitor who, putting them into the enemies' hands, could bring about their unconfessable dream of being mastered by the Dinosaurs. In short, I wanted nothing to do with either side: let them rip each other apart in turn! I didn't give a damn about any of them. I had to escape as fast as possible, let them stew in their own juice, have nothing more to do with these old stories.

That same night, slipping away in the darkness, I left the village. My first impulse was to get as far as possible from the battlefield, return to my secret refuges; but curiosity got the better of me: I had to see my counterparts, to know who would win. I hid on the top of some cliffs that overhung the bend of the river, and I waited for dawn.

As the light broke, some figures appeared on the horizon. They charged forward. Even before I could distinguish them clearly, I could dismiss the notion that Dinosaurs could ever run so gracelessly. When I recognized them I didn't know whether to laugh or to blush with shame. Rhinoceroses, a herd, the first ones, big and clumsy and crude, studded with horny bumps, but basically inoffensive, devoted only to cropping grass: this is what the others had mistaken for the ancient Lords of the Earth!

The rhinoceros herd galloped with the sound of thunder, stopped to lick some bushes, then ran on toward the horizon without even noticing the waiting squads of fishermen.

I ran back to the village. "You got it all wrong! They weren't Dinosaurs!" I announced. "Rhinoceroses, that's what they were! They've already gone. There isn't any more danger!" And I added, to justify my vanishing in the night: "I went out scouting. To spy on them and report back."

"We may not have understood they weren't Dinosaurs," Zabn said calmly, "but we have understood that you were not here," and he turned his back on me.

To be sure, they were all disappointed: about the Dinosaurs, about me. Now the stories of Dinosaurs became jokes, in which the terrible monsters played ridiculous roles. I no longer was affected by their petty wit. Now I recognized the greatness of spirit that had made us choose to disappear rather than live in a world no longer suited to us. If I survived it was only so that one of us could continue to feel himself a Dinosaur in the midst of these wretches who tried to conceal, with stupid teasing, the fear that still dominated them. And what choice did the New Ones have, beyond the choice between mockery and fear?

Fern-flower betrayed a new attitude when she narrated a dream to me: "There was this Dinosaur, very funny, all green; and everybody was teasing him and pulling his tail. Then I stepped forward and protected him; I took him away and petted him. And I realized that, ridiculous as he was, he was the saddest of all creatures and a river of tears flowed from his red and yellow eyes."

What came over me, at those words? A revulsion, a refusal to identify myself with the images of that dream, the rejection of a sentiment that seemed to have become pity, an intolerance of the diminished idea they had all conceived of the Dinosaurian dignity? I had a burst of pride; I stiffened and hurled a few contemptuous phrases in her face: "Why do you bore me with these dreams of yours? They get more childish every time! You can't dream anything but sentimental nonsense!"

Fern-flower burst into tears. I went off, shrugging my shoulders.

This happened on the dam; we weren't alone; the fishermen hadn't heard our dialogue but they had noticed my angry reaction and the young creature's tears.

Zahn felt called upon to intervene. "Who do you think you are?" he said, in a harsh voice. "How dare you insult my sister?"

I stopped, but didn't answer. If he wanted to fight, I was ready. But the mood of the village had changed in recent times: they made a joke of everything. From the group of fishermen a falsetto cry was heard: "Come off it, get along with you, Dinosaur!" This, as I well knew, was a mocking expression which had now come into use, as if to say: "Don't exaggerate, don't get carried away," and so on. But something stirred in my blood.

"Yes, I am one, if you care to know," I shouted, "a Dinosaur! That's what I am! Since you never have seen any Dinosaurs, here, take a look at me!"

General snickering broke out.

"I saw one yesterday," an old fisherman said, "he came out of the snow." Silence immediately fell all around him.

The old fellow was just back from a journey in the mountains. The thaw had melted an ancient glacier and a Dinosaur's skeleton had come to light.

The news spread through the village. "Let's go see the Dinosaur!" They all ran up the mountain, and I went with them.

When we had passed a moraine of stones, uprooted trunks, mud, and dead birds, we saw a deep, shell-shaped valley. A veil of early lichens was turning the rocks green, now that they were freed from the ice. In the midst, lying as if asleep, his neck stretched by the widened intervals of the vertebrae, his tail sown in a long serpentine, a giant Dinosaur's skeleton was lying. The chest cavity was arched like a sail, and when the wind struck the flat slabs of the ribs an invisible heart seemed to be beating within them still. The skull was turned in an anguished position, mouth open as if in a last cry.

The New Ones ran down there, shouting gaily; facing the skull, they felt the empty eye sockets staring at them; they kept a few paces' distance, silently; then they turned and resumed their silly festiveness. If one of them had looked from the skeleton to me, as I stood there staring at it, he would have realized at once that we were identical. But nobody did this. Those bones, those claws, those murderous limbs spoke a language now become illegible; they no longer said anything to anyone, except that vague name which had remained unconnected with the experiences of the present.

I continued looking at the skeleton, the Father, the Brother, my Counterpart, my Self; I recognized my fleshless limbs, my lineaments carved in the stone, everything we had been and were no longer, our majesty, our faults, our ruin.

Now these remains would be used by the planet's new, heedless occupants to mark a spot in the landscape, they would follow the destiny of the name "Dinosaur," becoming an opaque sound without meaning. I must not allow it. Everything that concerned the true nature of the Dinosaurs must remain hidden. In the night, as the New Ones slept around the skeleton, which they had decked with flags, I transported it, vertebra by vertebra, and buried my Dead.

In the morning the New Ones found not a trace of the skeleton. They didn't worry about it very long. It was another mystery added to the many mysteries concerning the Dinosaurs. They soon dismissed it from their thoughts.

But the appearance of the skeleton left its mark, for in all of them the idea of the Dinosaurs became bound to the idea of a sad end, and in the stories they now told the predominant tone was one of commiseration, of grief at our sufferings. I had no use for this pity of theirs. Pity for what? If ever a species had had a rich, full evolution, a long and happy reign, that species was ours. Our extinction had been a grandiose epilogue, worthy of our past. What could those fools understand of it? Every time I heard them become sentimental about the poor Dinosaurs I felt like making fun of them, telling invented, incredible stories. In any case, the real truth about the Dinosaurs would never be understood by anyone now; it was a secret I would keep for myself alone.

A band of vagabonds stopped at the village. Among them was a young female. When I saw her, I started with surprise. Unless my eyes were deceiving me, she didn't have only the blood of the New Ones in her veins: she was a Half-breed, a Dinosaur Half-breed. Was she aware of it? No, certainly not, judging by her nonchalance. Perhaps it hadn't been one of her parents but one of her grandparents or great-grandparents or a more remote ancestor who had been a Dinosaur; and the features, the movements of our stock were cropping out again in her in an almost shameless fashion, now unrecognizable to the others, and to herself. She was a pretty, gay creature; she immediately had a group of suitors after her, and among them the most constant and the most smitten was Zahn.

It was early summer. The young people were giving a feast on the river. "Come with us," Zahn invited me, trying to be my friend after all our disagreements; then he immediately went back to swim at the side of the Half-breed.

I went over to Fern-flower. Perhaps the moment had come for us to speak openly, to come to an understanding. "What did you dream last night?" I asked, to break the ice.

She hung her head. "I saw a wounded Dinosaur, writhing and dying. He had bowed his noble, delicate head, and he suffered and suffered . . . I looked at him, couldn't take my eyes off him, and I realized I was feeling a strange pleasure at seeing him suffer . . ."

Fern-flower's lips were taut, evil, in an expression I had never noticed in her. I wanted only to show her that in that play of ambiguous, grim feelings I had no part: I was one who enjoyed life, I was the heir of a happy race. I started to dance around her, I splashed river water on her, waving my tail.

"You can never talk about anything that isn't sad!" I said, frivolously. "Stop it. Come and dance!"

She didn't understand me. She made a grimace.

"And if you don't dance with me, I'll dance with another!" I cried. I grasped the Half-breed by one paw, carrying her off under Zahn's nose. First he watched us move away without understanding, he was so lost in his amorous contemplation, then he was seized with jealous rage. Too late. The Half-breed and I had already dived into the river and were swimming toward the other bank, to hide in the bushes.

Perhaps I only wanted to show Fern-flower who I really was, to deny the mistaken notions she had of me. And perhaps I was also moved by an old bitterness toward Zahn; I wanted to reject, ostentatiously, his new offer of friendship. Or else, more than anything, it was the familiar and yet unusual form of the Halfbreed which made me desire a natural, direct relationship, without secret thoughts, without memories.

The vagabond caravan would be leaving again in the morning. The Half-breed was willing to spend the night in the bushes. I stayed there, dallying with her, until dawn.

These were only ephemeral episodes in a life otherwise calm and uneventful. I had allowed the truth about myself and the era of our domination to vanish into silence. Now they hardly ever talked about the Dinosaurs any more; perhaps nobody believed they had ever existed. Even Fern-flower had stopped dreaming of them.

When she told me: "I dreamed that in a cavern there was the sole survivor of a species whose name nobody remembered, and I went to ask it of him, and it was dark, and I knew he was there, and I couldn't see him, and I knew well who he was and what he looked like but I couldn't have expressed it, and I didn't understand if he was answering my questions or I was answering his . . ." for me this was a sign that finally an amorous understanding had begun between us, the kind I had wanted since I first stopped at the spring, when I didn't yet know if I would be allowed to survive.

Since then I had learned many things, and above all the way in which Dinosaurs conquer. First I had believed that disappearing had been, for my brothers, the magnanimous acceptance of a defeat; now I knew that the more the Dinosaurs disappear, the more they extend their dominion, and over forests far more vast than those that cover the continents: in the labyrinth of the survivors' thoughts. From the semidarkness of fears and doubts of now ignorant generations, the Dinosaurs continued to extend their necks, to raise their taloned hoofs, and when the last shadow of their image had been erased, their name went on, superimposed on all meanings, perpetuating their presence in relations among living beings. Now, when the name too had been erased, they would become one thing with the mute and anonymous molds of thought, through which thoughts take on form and substance: by the New Ones, and by those who would come after the New Ones, and those who would come even after them.

I looked around: the village that had seen me arrive as a stranger I could now rightfully call mine, and I could call Fern-flower mine, in the only way a Dinosaur could call something his. For this, with a silent wave, I said good-by to Fern-flower, left the village, and went off forever.

Along my way I looked at the trees, the rivers, and the mountains, and I could no longer distinguish the ones that had been there during the Dinosaurs' time from those that had come afterwards. Around some dens a band of vagabonds was camping. From the distance I recognized the Half-breed, still attractive, only a little fatter. To avoid being seen, I headed for the woods and observed her. She was followed by a little son, barely able to stand on his legs and wag his tail. How long had it been since I had seen a little Dinosaur, so perfect, so full of his own Dinosaur essence, and so unaware of what the word "Dinosaur" meant?

I waited for him in a clearing in the woods to watch him play, chase a butterfly, slam a pine cone against a stone to dig out the pine nuts. I went over. It was my son, all right.

He looked at me curiously. "Who are you?" he asked.

"Nobody," I said. "What about you? Do you know who you are?"

"What a question! Everybody knows that: I'm a New One!" he said.

That was exactly what I had expected to hear him say. I patted his head, said: "Good for you," and went off.

I traveled through valleys and plains. I came to a station, caught the first train, and was lost in the crowd.

The War Symphony[1] (2001)

Chen Li

兵兵兵兵兵兵兵兵兵兵兵兵兵兵兵兵兵兵兵兵兵兵
兵兵兵兵兵兵兵兵兵兵兵兵兵兵兵兵兵兵兵兵兵兵
兵兵兵兵兵兵兵兵兵兵兵兵兵兵兵兵兵兵兵兵兵兵
兵兵兵兵兵兵兵兵兵兵兵兵兵兵兵兵兵兵兵兵兵兵
兵兵兵兵兵兵兵兵兵兵兵兵兵兵兵兵兵兵兵兵兵兵
兵兵兵兵兵兵兵兵兵兵兵兵兵兵兵兵兵兵兵兵兵兵
兵兵兵兵兵兵兵兵兵兵兵兵兵兵兵兵兵兵兵兵兵兵
兵兵兵兵兵兵兵兵兵兵兵兵兵兵兵兵兵兵兵兵兵兵
兵兵兵兵兵兵兵兵兵兵兵兵兵兵兵兵兵兵兵兵兵兵
兵兵兵兵兵兵兵兵兵兵兵兵兵兵兵兵兵兵兵兵兵兵
兵兵兵兵兵兵兵兵兵兵兵兵兵兵兵兵兵兵兵兵兵兵
兵兵兵兵兵兵兵兵兵兵兵兵兵兵兵兵兵兵兵兵兵兵
兵兵兵兵兵兵兵兵兵兵兵兵兵兵兵兵兵兵兵兵兵兵
兵兵兵兵兵兵兵兵兵兵兵兵兵兵兵兵兵兵兵兵兵兵
兵兵兵兵兵兵兵兵兵兵兵兵兵兵兵兵兵兵兵兵兵兵

兵兵兵兵兵兵兵兵兵兵兵兵兵兵兵兵兵兵兵兵兵兵
兵兵兵兵兵兵兵兵兵兵乒乓兵兵乓兵乓兵兵乓兵乓
兵乒兵兵兵兵乒兵乓兵乒乓兵乓兵乓兵乓兵乓兵乓
兵乒兵乓兵乒乓兵乓兵乓乓兵乓兵乓兵乓兵乓乓乓
兵乒乓兵乓兵乓乓兵乓兵乓乓兵乓兵乓兵乓乓乓乓
乒乓兵乓兵乓乓乓兵乓乓乓兵乓兵乓兵乓乓乓乓乓
乓乓乓乓乓乓乓乓乓乓乓乓乓乓乓乓乓乓乓乓乓乓
乓乓乓乓乓乓乓乓乓乓乓乓乓乓乓乓乓乓乓乓乓乓
乓乓乓乓乓乓乓乓乓乓乓乓乓乓乓　乓乓乓乓　乓
乓乓　乓乓乓乓　乓　乓　　乓乓　　乓乓　乓乓
乓乓　　乓乓　乓　乓　乓　乓乓乓　　乓　乓
　乓乓　乓　乓乓乓　乓　乓　乓　乓　　乓
乓　　　乓乓　　　乓　　乓　乓乓
　乓　　乓　　乓　　乓　　乓　乓
　　乓　　　　　　　　　　　　乓

丘 丘
丘 丘
丘 丘
丘 丘
丘 丘
丘 丘
丘 丘
丘 丘
丘 丘
丘 丘
丘 丘
丘 丘
丘 丘
丘 丘
丘 丘
丘 丘
丘 丘

Note

[1] The Chinese character 兵 (pronounced "bing") means "soldier." 乒 and 乓 (pronounced "ping" and "pong") which look like one-legged soldiers, are two onomatopoeic words imitating sounds of collision or gunshots. The character 丘 (pronounced "qiu") means "hill" or "mound."

Student (2001)

Cheng Min

I go one step forward,
Then stumble one step back.
I join the march
And then slip away to the sidelines.
I look at the posters on the left wall,
And the people gathered around them.
I look at the posters on the right wall,
And the people gathered around them.
They are like soldiers in two bunkers,
Shooting at one another
With arrows that fly away over my head.
O Socrates of the streets,
Where are you?
I heard that you can bring the young to face the truth
Like a shepherd who herds his sheep
Onto the right path,
Like a kind passerby
Who returns a lost child to its mother.
But why have you forgotten
This country more baffled than any other country,
This time more doubtful
Than any other time?
Here yes and no are indistinguishable
Like East and West at the Poles.
Here truth is a puppet
That doubles in two roles.
One self says, "Whatever is mine must be truth."
The other says, "When your 'whatever'
Becomes my 'whatever,' then it is truth."
Truth becomes a tasty bait
To lure fish obsessed with books.
In their short sighted, round eyes
They cannot see the many hooks of fraud.
Socrates, if you cannot reappear
In the network of streets
Of the Twentieth Century,

Why cannot Truth become simply a baby
That laughs when it is happy,
And cries when it is hurt,
As if to tell me which is itself?

The House on Mango Street (1991)

Sandra Cisneros

We didn't always live on Mango Street. Before that we lived on Loomis on the third floor, and before that we lived on Keeler. Before Keeler it was Paulina, and before that I can't remember. But what I remember most is moving a lot. Each time it seemed there'd be one more of us. By the time we got to Mango Street we were six—Mama, Papa, Carlos, Kiki, my sister Nenny and me.

The house on Mango Street is ours, and we don't have to pay rent to anybody, or share the yard with the people downstairs, or be careful not to make too much noise, and there isn't a landlord banging on the ceiling with a broom. But even so, it's not the house we'd thought we'd get.

We had to leave the flat on Loomis quick. The water pipes broke and the landlord wouldn't fix them because the house was too old. We had to leave fast. We were using the washroom next door and carrying water over in empty milk gallons. That's why Mama and Papa looked for a house, and that's why we moved into the house on Mango Street, far away, on the other side of town.

They always told us that one day we would move into a house, a real house that would be ours for always so we wouldn't have to move each year. And our house would have running water and pipes that worked. And inside it would have real stairs, not hallway stairs, but stairs inside like the houses on T.V. And we'd have a basement and at least three washrooms so when we took a bath we wouldn't have to tell everybody. Our house would be white with trees around it, a great big yard and grass growing without a fence. This was the house Papa talked about when he held a lottery ticket and this was the house Mama dreamed up in the stories she told us before we went to bed.

But the house on Mango Street is not the way they told it at all. It's small and red with tight steps in front and windows so small you'd think they were holding their breath. Bricks are crumbling in places, and the front door is so swollen you have to push hard to get in. There is no front yard, only four little elms the city planted by the curb. Out back is a small garage for the car we don't own yet and a small yard that looks smaller between the two buildings on either side. There are stairs in our house, but they're ordinary hallway stairs, and the house has only one washroom.

Everybody has to share a bedroom—Mama and Papa, Carlos and Kiki, me and Nenny.

Once when we were living on Loomis, a nun from my school passed by and saw me playing out front. The laundromat downstairs had been boarded up because it had been robbed two days before and the owner had painted on the wood YES WE'RE OPEN so as not to lose business.

Where do you live? she asked.

There, I said pointing up to the third floor.

You live *there*?

There. I had to look to where she pointed—the third floor, the paint peeling, wooden bars Papa had nailed on the windows so we wouldn't fall out. You live *there*? The way she said it made me feel like nothing. *There*. I lived *there*. I nodded.

I knew then I had to have a house. A real house. One I could point to. But this isn't it. The house on Mango Street isn't it. For the time being, Mama says. Temporary, says Papa. But I know how those things go.

Mango Says Goodbye Sometimes (1991)

Sandra Cisneros

I like to tell stories. I tell them inside my head. I tell them after the mailman says, Here's your mail. Here's your mail he said.

I make a story for my life, for each step my brown shoe takes. I say, "And so she trudged up the wooden stairs, her sad brown shoes taking her to the house she never liked."

I like to tell stories. I am going to tell you a story about a girl who didn't want to belong.

We didn't always live on Mango Street. Before that we lived on Loomis on the third floor, and before that we lived on Keeler. Before Keeler it was Paulina, but what I remember most is Mango Street, sad red house, the house I belong but do not belong to.

I put it down on paper and then the ghost does not ache so much. I write it down and Mango says goodbye sometimes. She does not hold me with both arms. She sets me free.

One day I will pack my bags of books and paper. One day I will say goodbye to Mango. I am too strong for her to keep me here forever. One day I will go away.

Friends and neighbors will say, What happened to that Esperanza? Where did she go with all those books and paper? Why did she march so far away?

They will not know I have gone away to come back. For the ones I left behind. For the ones who cannot out.

The Main Causes That Make Religion Powerful in America (1835)

Alexis de Tocqueville

The philosophers of the eighteenth century explained the gradual decay of religious faith in a very simple manner. Religious zeal, said they, must necessarily fail, the more generally liberty is established and knowledge diffused. Unfortunately, facts are by no means in accordance with their theory. There are certain populations in Europe whose unbelief is only equalled by their ignorance and their debasement, whilst in America one of the freest and most enlightened nations in the world fulfils all the outward duties of religious fervor.

Upon my arrival in the United States, the religious aspect of the country was the first thing that struck my attention; and the longer I stayed there the more did I perceive the great political consequences resulting from this state of things, to which I was unaccustomed. In France I had almost always seen the spirit of religion and the spirit of freedom pursuing courses diametrically opposed to each other; but in America I found that they were intimately united, and that they reigned in common over the same country. My desire to discover the causes of this phenomenon increased from day to day. In order to satisfy it I questioned the members of all the different sects; and I more especially sought the society of the clergy, who are the depositaries of the different persuasions, and who are more especially interested in their duration. As a member of the Roman Catholic Church I was more particularly brought into contact with several of its priests, with whom I became intimately acquainted. To each of these men I expressed my astonishment and I explained my doubts; I found that they differed upon matters of detail alone; and that they mainly attributed the peaceful dominion of religion in their country to the separation of Church and State. I do not hesitate to affirm that during my stay in America I did not meet with a single individual, of the clergy or of the laity, who was not of the same opinion upon this point.

This led me to examine more attentively than I had hitherto done, the station which the American clergy occupy in political society. I learned with surprise that they filled no public appointments; not one of them is to be met with in the administration, and they are not even represented in the legislative assemblies. In several States the law excludes them from political life, public opinion in all. And when I came to inquire into the prevailing spirit of the clergy I found that most of its members seemed to retire of their own accord from the exercise of power, and that they made it the pride of their profession to abstain from politics.

I heard them inveigh against ambition and deceit, under whatever political opinions these vices might chance to lurk; but I learned from their discourses that men are not guilty in the eye of God for any opinions concerning political government which they may profess with sincerity, any more than they are for their mistakes in building a house or in driving a furrow. I perceived that these ministers of the gospel eschewed all parties with the anxiety attendant upon personal interest. These facts convinced me that what I had been told was true; and it then became my object to investigate their causes, and to inquire how it happened that the real authority of religion was increased by a state of things which diminished its apparent force: these causes did not long escape my researches.

The short space of threescore years can never content the imagination of man; nor can the imperfect joys of this world satisfy his heart. Man alone, of all created beings, displays a natural contempt of existence, and yet a boundless desire to exist; he scorns life, but he dreads annihilation. These different feelings incessantly urge his soul to the contemplation of a future state, and religion directs his musings thither. Religion, then, is simply another form of hope; and it is no less natural to the human heart than hope itself. Men cannot abandon their religious faith without a kind of aberration of intellect, and a sort of violent distortion of their true natures; but they are invincibly brought back to more pious sentiments; for unbelief is an accident, and faith is the only permanent state of mankind. If we only consider religious institutions in a purely human point of view, they may be said to derive an inexhaustible element of strength from man himself, since they belong to one of the constituent principles of human nature.

I am aware that at certain times religion may strengthen this influence, which originates in itself, by the artificial power of the laws, and by the support of those temporal institutions which direct society. Religions, intimately united to the governments of the earth, have been known to exercise a sovereign authority derived from the twofold source of terror and of faith; but when a religion contracts an alliance of this nature, I do not hesitate to affirm that it commits the same error as a man who should sacrifice his future to his present welfare; and in obtaining a power to which it has no claim, it risks that authority which is rightfully its own. When a religion founds its empire upon the desire of immortality which lives in every human heart, it may aspire to universal dominion; but when it connects itself with a government, it must necessarily adopt maxims which are only applicable to certain nations. Thus, in forming an alliance with a political power, religion augments its authority over a few, and forfeits the hope of reigning over all.

As long as a religion rests upon those sentiments which are the consolation of all affliction, it may attract the affections of mankind. But if it be mixed up with the bitter passions of the world, it may be constrained to defend allies whom its interests, and not the principle of love, have given to it; or to repel as antagonists men who are still attached to its own spirit, however opposed they may be to the powers to which it is allied. The Church cannot share the temporal power of the State without being the object of a portion of that animosity which the latter excites.

The political powers which seem to be most firmly established have frequently no better guarantee for their duration than the opinions of a generation, the interests of the time, or the life of an individual. A law may modify the social condition which seems to be most fixed and determinate; and with the social condition everything else must change. The powers of society are more or less fugitive, like the years which we spend upon the earth; they succeed each other with rapidity, like the fleeting cares of life; and no government has ever yet been founded upon an invariable disposition of the human heart, or upon an imperishable interest.

As long as a religion is sustained by those feelings, propensities, and passions which are found to occur under the same forms, at all the different periods of history, it may defy the efforts of time; or at least it can only be destroyed by another religion. But when religion clings to the interests of the world, it becomes almost as fragile a thing as the powers of earth. It is the only one of them all which can hope for immortality; but if it be connected with their ephemeral authority, it shares their fortunes, and may fall with those transient passions which supported them for a day. The alliance which religion contracts with political powers must needs be onerous to itself, since it does not require their assistance to live, and by giving them its assistance to live, and by giving them its assistance it may be exposed to decay.

The danger which I have just pointed out always exists, but it is not always equally visible. In some ages governments seem to be imperishable; in others, the existence of society appears to be more precarious than the life of man. Some constitutions plunge the citizens into a lethargic somnolence, and others rouse them to feverish excitement. When governments appear to be so strong, and laws so stable, men do not perceive the dangers which may accrue from a union of Church and State. When governments display so much weakness, and laws so much inconstancy, the danger is self-evident, but it is no longer possible to avoid it; to be effectual, measures must be taken to discover its approach.

In proportion as a nation assumes a democratic condition of society, and as communities display democratic propensities, it becomes more and more dangerous to connect religion with political institutions; for the time is coming when authority will be bandied from hand to hand, when political theories will succeed each other, and when men, laws, and constitutions will disappear, or be modified from day to day, and this, not for a season only, but unceasingly. Agitation and mutability are inherent in the nature of democratic republics, just as stagnation and inertness are the law of absolute monarchies.

If the Americans, who change the head of the Government once in four years, who elect new legislators every two years, and renew the provincial officers every twelvemonth; if the Americans, who have abandoned the political world to the attempts of innovators, had not placed religion beyond their reach, where could it abide in the ebb and flow of human opinions? Where would that respect which belongs to it be paid, amidst the struggles of faction? And what would become of its immortality, in the midst of perpetual decay? The American clergy were the first to perceive this truth, and to act in conformity with it. They saw that they must renounce their religious influence, if they were to strive for political power; and they chose to give up the support of the State, rather than to share its vicissitudes.

In America, religion is perhaps less powerful than it has been at certain periods in the history of certain peoples; but its influence is more lasting. It restricts itself to its own resources, but of those none can deprive it: its circle is limited to certain principles, but those principles are entirely its own, and under its undisputed control.

On every side in Europe we hear voices complaining of the absence of religious faith, and inquiring the means of restoring to religion some remnant of its pristine authority. It seems to me that we must first attentively consider what ought to be the natural state of men with regard to religion at the present time; and when we know what we have to hope and to fear, we may discern the end to which our efforts ought to be directed.

The two great dangers which threaten the existence of religions are schism and indifference. In ages of fervent devotion, men sometimes abandon their religion, but they only shake it off in order to adopt another. Their faith changes the objects to which it is directed, but it suffers no decline. The old religion then excites enthusiastic attachment or bitter enmity in either party; some leave it with anger, others cling to it with increased devotedness, and although persuasions differ, irreligion is unknown. Such, however, is not the case when a religious belief is secretly undermined by doctrines which may be termed negative, since they deny the truth of one religion without affirming that of any other. Prodigious revolutions then take place in the human mind, without the apparent co-operation of the passions of man, and almost without his knowledge. Men lose the objects of their fondest hopes, as if through forgetfulness. They are carried away by an imperceptible current which they have not the courage to stem, but which they follow with regret, since it bears them from a faith they love, to a scepticism that plunges them into despair.

In ages which answer to this description, men desert their religious opinions from lukewarmness rather than from dislike; they do not reject them, but the sentiments by which they were once fostered disappear. But if the unbeliever does not admit religion to be true, he still considers it useful. Regarding religious institutions in a human point of view, he acknowledges their influence upon manners and legislation. He admits that they may serve to make men live in peace with one another, and to prepare them gently for the hour of death. He regrets the faith which he has lost; and as he is deprived of a treasure which he has learned to estimate at its full value, he scruples to take it from those who still possess it.

On the other hand, those who continue to believe are not afraid openly to avow their faith. They look upon those who do not share their persuasion as more worthy of pity than of opposition; and they are aware that to acquire the esteem of the unbelieving, they are not obliged to follow their example. They are hostile to no one in the world; and as they do not consider the society in which they live as an arena in which religion is bound to face its thousand deadly foes, they love their contemporaries, whilst they condemn their weaknesses and lament their errors.

As those who do not believe, conceal their incredulity; and as those who believe, display their faith, public opinion pronounces itself in favor of religion: love, support, and honor are bestowed upon it, and it is only by searching the human soul that we can detect the wounds which it has received. The mass of mankind, who are never without the feeling of religion, do not perceive anything at variance with the established faith. The instinctive desire of a future life brings the crowd about the altar, and opens the hearts of men to the precepts and consolations of religion.

But this picture is not applicable to us: for there are men amongst us who have ceased to believe in Christianity, without adopting any other religion; others who are in the perplexities of doubt, and who already affect not to believe; and others, again, who are afraid to avow that Christian faith which they still cherish in secret.

Amidst these lukewarm partisans and ardent antagonists a small number of believers exist, who are ready to brave all obstacles and to scorn all dangers in defence of their faith. They have done violence to human weakness, in order to rise superior to public opinion. Excited by the effort they have made, they scarcely knew where to stop; and as they know that the first use which the French made of independence was to attack religion, they look upon their contemporaries with dread, and they recoil in alarm from the liberty which their fellow-citizens are seeking to obtain. As unbelief appears to them to be a novelty, they comprise all that is new in one indiscriminate animosity. They are at war with their age and country, and they look upon every opinion which is put forth there as the necessary enemy of the faith.

Such is not the natural state of men with regard to religion at the present day; and some extraordinary or incidental cause must be at work in France to prevent the human mind from following its original propensities and to drive it beyond the limits at which it ought naturally to stop. I am intimately convinced that this extraordinary and incidental cause is the close connection of politics and religion. The unbelievers of Europe attack the Christians as their political opponents, rather than as their religious adversaries; they hate the Christian religion as the opinion of a party, much more than as an error of belief; and they reject the clergy less because they are the representatives of the Divinity than because they are the allies of authority.

In Europe, Christianity has been intimately united to the powers of the earth. Those powers are now in decay, and it is, as it were, buried under their ruins. The living body of religion has been bound down to the dead corpse of superannuated polity: cut by the bonds which restrain it, and that which is alive will rise once more. I know not what could restore the Christian Church of Europe to the energy of its earlier days; that power belongs to God alone; but it may be the effect of human policy to leave the faith in the full exercise of the strength which it still retains.

Standing up for Children (2004)

Marian Wright Edelman

Benjamin Mays, president of Morehouse College and mentor to Martin Luther King, Jr., and thousands of other black youths, including me, once said: "The tragedy of life doesn't lie in not reaching your goal. The tragedy lies in having no goal to reach. It isn't a calamity to die with dreams unfilled, but it is a calamity not to dream. It is not a disgrace not to reach the stars, but it is a disgrace to have no stars to reach for. Not failure, but low aim, is a sin."

It's time to do whatever it takes to make our nation treat our children right and to live up to its promise of fair opportunity. We must meet the needs of the whole child in the richest, most powerful nation on Earth now. Children do not come in pieces. They live in families and communities. We have the money. We have the know-how. And we have the responsibility to ensure all children what we now provide for some children. God did not make two classes of children and will hold us accountable for every one of them.

Can our children become the healing agents of our national and world transformation and future spiritual and economic salvation? Edmond McDonald wrote that when God wants an important thing done in this world or a wrong righted, He goes about it in a very singular way. He doesn't release thunderbolts or stir up earthquakes. God simply has a tiny baby born, perhaps of a very humble home, perhaps of a very humble mother. And she puts it in the baby's mind, and then—God waits. The great events of this world are not battles and elections and earthquakes and thunderbolts. The great events are babies, for each child comes with the message that God is not yet discouraged with humanity, but is still expecting goodwill to become incarnate in each human life. And so God produced a Gandhi and a Mandela and a Harriet Tubman, an Eleanor Roosevelt and a Martin Luther King, Jr., and each of us to guide the Earth toward peace rather than conflict.

I believe that protecting today's children—tomorrow's Mandelas and Mother Teresas and Aung San Suu Kyis—is the moral and common sense litmus test of our humanity in a world where millions of children's lives are ravaged by the wars, neglect, abuse, and racial, ethnic, religious, and class divisions of adults.

Something is awry when the net worth of the world's 476 richest billionaires exceeds the combined income of the poorest 2.5 billion people and when the income gap between the top and bottom fifth of the world's population has more than doubled in the last generation. Something is awry when, in the United States, the combined income of over 9 million families was less than that of a single health insurance executive last year. The United States is first among industrialized nations in defense expenditures, military exports, gross domestic product, the number of millionaires and billionaires, and the cost of our health technology. But we're twelfth in living standards for the poorest fifth of our children; seventeenth in the percent of children living in poverty; nineteenth in preventing low birth weight; and twenty-third in avoiding infant mortality. We're last in protecting our children against gun violence: Since 1979, firearms have killed 90,000 children in our homes, schools, and neighborhoods, more than the toll of all our combat deaths in Vietnam.

What legacies, principles, values, and deeds will we stand for and send to the future through our children and to a world desperately hungering for moral leadership and community? Few human beings are blessed to experience the beginning of a new millennium. How will progress be measured over the next thousand years if we survive them? By the kill power and number of weapons of destruction we can produce and traffic at home and abroad, or by our willingness to shrink and destroy the prison of violence we've constructed in the name of peace and security? Will we be remembered by how many material things we can manufacture, advertise, sell, and consume, or by our rediscovery of more lasting, nonmaterial measures of success—a new Dow Jones for the purpose and quality of life in our families, neighborhoods, cities, and national and world communities? Will we be remembered by how rapidly technology and corporate merger mania and greed can render human beings obsolete, or by a better balance between corporate profits and corporate caring for children, families, communities, and the environment? Will we be remembered by how much a few at the top can get at the expense of the many at the bottom and in the middle, or by our struggle for a concept of enough for all? Will we be remembered by the glitz, style, and banality of too much of our culture, or by the substance of our efforts to rekindle an ethic of caring, community, and justice in a world driven too much by money, technology, and weaponry?

A thousand years ago the United States was not even a dream. Copernicus and Galileo had not told us the Earth was round or revolved around the sun. Gutenberg's Bible had not been printed, Wycliffe had not translated it into English, and Martin Luther had not tacked his theses on the church door. The Magna Carta did not exist, Chaucer's and Shake-speare's tales had not been spun, and Bach's, Beethoven's, and Mozart's miraculous music had not been created to inspire, soothe, and heal our spirits. European serfs struggled in bondage while many African and Asian empires flourished in independence. Native Americans peopled America, free of slavery's blight, and Hitler's holocaust had yet to show the depths human evil can reach when good women and men remain silent or indifferent.

A thousand years from now, will civilization remain and humankind survive? Will America's dream be alive, be remembered, and be worth remembering? Is America's dream big enough for every sixth child who is poor, every sixth child who is black, every sixth child who is Latino, and every twelfth child who is mentally or physically challenged? Is our world's dream big enough for all of the children God has sent as messengers of hope and life?

What to do about priorities that bring good news to the rich and bad news to the poor, defy the prophets and the gospels, and mock American values of fair play and opportunity? How do we reorder these priorities for our children's and nation's sake?

Here are some suggestions:

Have a positive vision for our children and nation. It is not enough just to be against the dismantlement of (and cuts to) children's programs that still don't reach all children who are eligible or need them. We must demand what all children need. A lot of people say it's unrealistic to seek $75 billion per year, as the Children's Defense Fund is doing in supporting a comprehensive federal bill that would ensure that every child has enough to eat, provide access to better education, and give more children a place to call home. The bill would also expand tax relief to help low-wage working families escape poverty and support other initiatives aimed at giving each and every child a safe, fair, and healthy start in life. Some say our nation cannot afford this. I say nonsense. The annual investment for this bill would equal less than seven-tenths of 1 percent of our nation's 2003 gross domestic product and less than the 2001 Bush administration tax breaks alone will give to the wealthiest one-in-a-hundred Americans each year. But the tax cutters and the war profiteers don't ever stop asking for or getting far more. Our nation does not have a money problem. We have a values and priorities problem. If we can find the billions of dollars needed to fight a war in Iraq and give three sets of irresponsible tax cuts targeted overwhelmingly to the least needy, we can find the money to educate and protect our children.

Believe we can save all of our children and then do it. We can transform our nation's priorities if we truly believe we can. Don't ever give up insisting that children be protected first whatever the political or economic weather. An anonymous sage whose words I keep above my kitchen sink wrote: "If you think you are beaten, you are. If you think that you dare not, you don't. If you'd like to win, but you think you can't, it's almost a cinch that you won't. If you think you'll lose, you're lost, for out in the world you'll find success begins with a person's will. Life's battles don't always go to the stronger or faster ones. But sooner or later the one who wins is the one who thinks she can. It's all in the state of mind."

Have faith and act without ceasing. There's a biblical story about a judge who neither feared God nor had respect for people. In his city there was a widow who kept coming to him saying, "Grant me justice against my opponent." For a while he refused; but later he said to himself, "Though I have no fear of God and no respect for anyone, yet because this widow keeps bothering me, I will grant her justice, so that she may not wear me out by continuously coming." And the Lord said, "Listen to what the unjust judge says. And will not God grant justice to his chosen ones who cry to him day and night? Will he delay long in helping them? I tell you, he will quickly grant justice to them" (Luke 18:1–7). Like the powerless widow, we must wear down our powerful leaders through persistent witnesses all over America until they hear and do right by our children. We must call, write, visit, hold prayer vigils, take our leaders on Child Watches and make them see and feel the suffering of children. We must tie our children to community, state, and national budget and policy choices and tell those who represent us what they can and must do to help. And we must hold our leaders accountable with our votes for what they actually do. More people committed to children need to run for office and not forget about children when they win.

Don't be intimidated or silenced by budget experts or political spin-masters. Don't let anyone label us unpatriotic or unrealistic or say we're engaging in class warfare or are bashing any political party or leader when we share the facts—the truth—about unjust national budget and policy priorities. Unless we reverse our course, the recent lavish tax cuts for the wealthy, huge military increases, and war in Iraq will starve our national government of the resources needed to serve our vulnerable young, elderly, and disabled and to sustain our public infrastructure for decades to come. You do not need to be able to debate the technicalities of budget and tax policy to know it's disingenuous for the White House or Congress to plead no money to invest in children while simultaneously giving trillions of dollars in tax cuts to the wealthiest Americans. You don't need a Ph.D. in philosophy or theology to know it's morally wrong and hypocritical for leaders to say that no child will be left behind while leaving millions of children behind in poverty, without health coverage, in crumbling schools and understaffed classrooms, and alone after school without supervision.

Be strong and courageous and leave the results to God. "Plant the seed of hope and caring and leave the garden to God," Henry David Thoreau wrote. Many dismissed him as a crank or a social deviant. But Leo Tolstoy read Thoreau's essay "Civil Disobedience"; Gandhi learned about it from Tolstoy; Martin Luther King, Jr., read Gandhi; and the civil rights movement made history. Don't be afraid to be a voice in the wilderness for children and the poor. It's the moral and sensible thing to do.

Trust and serve God and recognize that every single one of us can make a difference. Let God use us, unworthy, weak, and inadequate as we are. God used a stutterer, Moses, as spokesperson to Pharaoh. God took a one-hundred-year-old man, Abraham, to create a people so numerous as to cover the face of the Earth. God used a boy with a slingshot to slay a giant who had paralyzed the king's army armed to the teeth with the best military weapons. God gave a young girl, Esther, courage to go ask the king to protect her people, saying if I die, I die. God heard aging and barren Hannah's ceaseless prayers for a child and gave her a son, Samuel, whom she rededicated to God. And God used five women—Moses's mother and sister, Pharaoh's daughter, and two midwives—to save a slave baby named Moses, who liberated the Hebrew people. If these five very unlikely female social revolutionaries were God's instruments for transforming history, then let us believe we can be God's instruments to save our children today. If those of us who call ourselves Christians really believe God sent a poor baby to save the world and to challenge the unjust political order of his day, why are we silent today when so many poor babies are suffering?

Assign ourselves right now to be a voice for justice for children in these scary and turbulent times of war and terrorism and greed and economic uncertainty. Wendell Phillips, the abolitionist, fervently condemned slavery in the 1840s as a "moral outrage" when his cause seemed hopeless. A friend asked him after a speech, "Wendell, why are you so on fire?" Phillips replied: "I am on fire because I have mountains of ice before me to melt." John Woolman did not wait for Abraham Lincoln, the Civil War, or the Emancipation Proclamation to speak and act against slavery. He traveled by horseback to home after home of individual Quakers to discuss the incompatibility of slavery with Quaker principles and urged them to stop being slave owners. Harriet Tubman didn't wait for President Lincoln and the Civil War either. She ran away from slavery and returned again and again to deliver others from slavery to freedom. Just do the right thing for children—right now—whatever the risk.

Never give up. Making our nation and world fit for our children and grandchildren is a task for marathoners—not sprinters. It is a complex and long-term struggle that must be pursued with both urgency and persistence. The playwright Bertold Brecht said: "There are those who struggle for a day and they are good. There are those who struggle for a year and they are better. There are those who struggle all their lives. These are the indispensable ones." Be an indispensable one for our children's and world's sake.

Recognize and honor the sacredness of each and every child. One of the reasons I believe so many millions of children are left behind—in the United States and in our globalizing world—is that too many in power and of privilege distinguish between their own children and other people's children. Yet as Mahub Ul Haq, a creator of the World Human Development Index, once presciently reminded us, "Abolishing poverty in the 21st century must become a collective responsibility since human life is not safe in the rich nations if human despair travels in poor nations. Let us recognize that consequences of global poverty travel across national frontiers without passport in the form of drugs, AIDS, pollution, and terrorism." Children—all children—are the world. Children are hope and life. Children are our immortality. Children are the seeds and the molders of history and the transmitters of our values—good and bad. When are we going to wake up and open our hearts? When are we going to act to build a nation and world fit and safe for and worthy of our children and grandchildren? When is our moral reach going to match our military and economic reach in a world in desperate need of hope and peace and justice?

Organize, mobilize, and hold our leaders accountable. It's time for children's advocates and all people of conscience to wake up, ask hard questions, act boldly, and hold ourselves accountable for holding our leaders accountable for taking children out of harm's way. It's time to close the adult hypocrisy gap between word and deed for children. It's time to compete with those who would destroy, neglect, and lead our children astray. The soul snatchers have been busy at work turning family and child dreams into drugs and violence and greed and consumption. The budget cutters have been relentless and swift in pursuing their special interests and turning child hopes into cold despair and grinding child futures into dust. Child advocates must get better and tougher at reclaiming our children's birthright to freedom from fear and want by working together and with more disciplined messages and priorities. We must set aside our personal and organizational egos for the greater good of saving children. We must seek and welcome new voices and make new alliances whose bottom line is the economic, social, and environmental well-being of children. If our nation and world are fit for children they are fit for everyone.

A Prayer to the God of All Children

O God of the children of Afghanistan, Pakistan, and India
Of Israel, Iraq, and Iran, Jerusalem, and Jericho
Of South and North Korea, Burundi, and Rwanda
Of South Africa, South Carolina, San Francisco, and San Antonio
Help us to love and respect and act now to protect them all.

O God of black and brown and white and albino children
and those all mixed together
Of children who are rich and poor and in between
Of children who speak English and Russian and Hmong and
Spanish and Chinese and Hebrew and Arabic and languages
our ears cannot discern
Help us to love and respect and act now to protect them all.

O God of the child prodigy and child prostitute,
of the child of rapture and the child of rape
Of run or thrown away children who struggle every day
without parent or place or friend or future
Help us to love and respect and act now to protect them all.

O God of children who can walk and talk and hear
and see and sing and dance and jump and play and
of children who wish they could but can't
Of children who are loved and unloved, wanted and unwanted
Help us to love and respect and act now to protect them all.

O God of beggar, beaten, abused, neglected, homeless,
AIDS-, drug-, violence-, and hunger-ravaged children,
Of children who are emotionally and physically and mentally fragile, and
Of children who rebel and ridicule, torment and taunt
Help us to love and respect and act now to protect them all.

O God of children of destiny and of despair, of war and of peace,
Of disfigured, diseased, and dying children,
Of children without hope and of children with hope to spare and to share
Help us to love and respect and act now to protect them all.

Galileo: Admonition, Defense, and Recantation (1616 and 1633)

Admonition (Injunction?) of Galileo (February 26, 1616)

The original admonition document is missing. A transcribed report exists in the Inquisition file. It is a key matter of dispute whether Galileo was actually enjoined from discussing Copernican theory, as the transcribed report—discovered in 1633—indicates. Scholars have questioned the authenticity of the report, arguing that the procedures described did not comport with established forms and that the substance was not consistent with what we know of events of 1616. (Translated from Latin.)

[The file report begins with a reference to the Pope's decree of February 25, 1616:]

Thursday, 25 February 1616. The Lord Cardinal Mellini notified the Reverend Fathers, the Assessor, and the Commissary of the Holy Office that the censure passed by the theologians upon the propositions of Galileo—to the effect that the Sun is the centre of the world and immovable from its place, and that the Earth moves, and also with a diurnal motion—had been reported; and His Holiness has directed the Lord Cardinal Bellarmine to summon before him the said Galileo and admonish him to abandon the said opinion; and, *in case of his refusal to obey*, that the Commissary is to enjoin on him, before a notary and witnesses, a command to abstain altogether from teaching or defending this opinion and doctrine and even from discussing it, and, if he does not acquiesce therein, that he is to be imprisoned.

Friday, the twenty-sixth. At the palace, the usual residence of Lord Cardinal Bellarmine, the said Galileo, having been summoned and being present before the said Lord Cardinal, was, in the presence of the Most Reverend Michelangelo Segizi of Lodi, of the order of Preachers, Commissary-General of the Holy Office, by the said Cardinal, warned of the error of the aforesaid opinion and admonished to abandon it; and immediately thereafter, before me and before witnesses, the Lord Cardinal being present, the said Galileo was by the said Commissary commanded and enjoined, in the name of His Holiness the Pope and the whole Congregation of the Holy Office, to relinquish altogether the said opinion that the Sun is the center of the world and immovable and that the Earth moves; nor further to hold, teach, or defend it in any way whatsoever, verbally or in writing; otherwise proceedings would be taken against him by the Holy Office; which injunction the said Galileo acquiesced in and promised to obey. Done at Rome, in the place aforesaid, in the presence of R. Badino Nores, of Nicosia in the kingdom of Cyprus, and Agostino Mongardo, from a place in the Abbey of Rose in the diocese of Montepulciano, members of the household of said Cardinal, witnesses.

Less than two weeks after Galileo received his admonition, the Church took the formal step of suspending or prohibiting publication and distribution of books suggesting that the Earth revolved around the Sun:

Decree of General Congregation of the Index

March 5, 1616

. . . And whereas it has also come to the knowledge of the said Congregation that the Pythagorean doctrine—which is false and altogether opposed to the Holy Scripture—of the motion of the Earth, and the immobility of the Sun, which is also taught by Nicolaus Copernicus in *De revolutionibus orbium coelestium*, and by Diego de Zuniga [in his book] on Job, is not being spread abroad and accepted by many—as may be seen from a certain letter of a Carmelite Father, entitled *Letter of the Rev. Father Paolo Antonio Foscarini, Carmelite, on the Opinion of the Pythagoreans and of Copernicus concerning the Motion of the Earth, and the Stability of the Sun, and the New Pythagorean System of the World, at Naples, Printed by Lazzaro Scoriggio*, 1615: wherein the said Father attempts to show that the aforesaid doctrine of the immobility of the sun in the centre of the world, and of the Earth's motion, is consonant with truth and is not opposed to Holy Scripture. Therefore, in order that this opinion may not insinuate itself any further to the prejudice of Catholic truth, the Holy Congregation has decreed that the said Nicolaus Copernicus, *De revolutionibus orbium*, and Diego de Zuniga, *On Job*, be suspended until they be corrected; but that the book of the Carmelite Father, Paolo Antonio Foscarini, be altogether prohibited and condemned, and that all other works likewise, in which the same is taught, be prohibited, as by this present decree it prohibits, condemns, and suspends them all respectively. In witness whereof the present decree has been signed and sealed with the hands and with the seal of the most eminent and Reverend Lord Cardinal of St. Cecilia, Bishop of Albano, on the fifth day of March, 1616.

Galileo's Defense (May 10, 1633)

When asked if I had signified to the Reverend Father, the Master of the Holy Palace, the injunction privately laid upon me, about sixteen years ago, by the order of the Holy Office, not to hold, defend, or "in any way" teach the doctrine of the motion of the Earth and the stability of the Sun, I answered that I had not done so. And, not being questioned as to the reason why I had not intimated it, I had no opportunity to add anything further. It now appears to me necessary to state the reason, in order to demonstrate the purity of my intention, ever foreign to the practice of simulation or deceit in any operation I engage in.

I say, then, that, as at that time reports were spread abroad by evil-disposed persons to the effect that I had been summoned by the Lord Cardinal Bellarmine to abjure certain of my opinions and teachings and also to submit to penitence for them, I was thus constrained to apply to his Eminence and to solicit him to furnish me with an attestation, explaining the cause for which I had been summoned before him; which attestation I obtained in his own handwriting, and it is the same that I now produce with the present document. From this it clearly appears that it was merely announced to me that the doctrine attributed to Copernicus, of the motion of the Earth and the stability of the Sun, must not be held or defended; but that, beyond this general announcement affecting everyone, there should have been ordered anything to me in particular, no trace thereof appears in it.

Having, then, as a reminder, this authentic attestation in the handwriting of the very person who informed me of the command, I made no further application of thought or memory with regard to the words employed in orally announcing to me the said order not to hold or defend the doctrine in question; so that the two articles of the order—in addition to the injunction not to "hold" or "defend" it—to wit, the words "not to teach it" and "in any way whatsoever"—which, I hear, are contained in the order enjoined on me, and registered—struck me as quite novel and as if I had not heard them before; and I do not think I ought to be disbelieved when I urge that in the course of fourteen or sixteen years I had lost all recollection of them, especially as I had no need to give any particular thought to them, having in my possession so authentic a reminder in writing. Now, if the said two articles accompanying attestation, there is no doubt that the injunction contained in the latter is the same command as that contained in the decree of the Holy Congregation of the Index. Hence it appears to me that I have a reasonable excuse for not having notified to the Master of the Holy Palace about the command privately imposed upon me, it being the same as that of the Congregation of the Index.

Now, if so be my book was not subject to a stricter censorship than that made binding by the decree of the Index, it will, it appears to me, be sufficiently plain that I adopted the surest and most becoming method of having it guaranteed and purged of all shadow of taint, inasmuch as I handed it to the Supreme Inquisitor at the very time when many books dealing with the same matters were being prohibited solely by virtue of the said decree. After what I have now stated, I would confidently hope that the idea of my having knowingly and deliberately violated the command imposed upon me will henceforth be entirely banished from the minds of my most eminent and wise judges; hence those faults which are seen scattered throughout my book have not been artfully introduced with any concealed or other than sincere intention but have only inadvertently fallen from my pen, owing to a vainglorious ambition and complacency in desiring to appear more subtle than the generality of popular writers, as indeed in another deposition I have confessed; which fault I shall be ready to correct with all possible industry whenever I may be commanded or permitted by Their Most Eminent Lordships.

Lastly, it remains for me to beg you to take into consideration my pitiable state of bodily indisposition, to which, at the age of seventy years, I have been reduced by ten months of constant mental anxiety and the fatigue of a long and toilsome journey at the most inclement season—together with the loss of a greater part of the years to which, from my previous condition of health, I had the prospect. I am persuaded and encouraged to do so by the faith I have in the clemency and goodness of the most Eminent Lords, my judges; with the hope that they may be pleased, in answer to my prayer, to remit what may appear in their entire justice the rightful addition that is still lacking to such sufferings to make up an adequate punishment for my crimes, out of consideration for my declining age, which, too, humbly commends itself to them. And I would equally commend to their consideration my honor and reputation, against the calumnies of ill-wishers, whose persistence in detracting from my good name may be inferred from the necessity which constrained me to procure from the Lord Cardinal Bellarmine the attestation which accompanies this.

Recantation of Galileo (June 22, 1633)

I, Galileo, son of the late Vincenzo Galilei, Florentine, aged seventy years, arraigned personally before this tribunal, and kneeling before you, Most Eminent and Reverend Lord Cardinals, Inquisitors-General against heretical depravity throughout the entire Christian commonwealth, having before my eyes and touching with my hands, the Holy Gospels, swear that I have always believed, do believe, and by God's help will in the future believe, all that is held, preached, and taught by the Holy Catholic and Apostolic Church. But whereas—after an injunction had been judicially intimated to me by this Holy Office, to the effect that I must altogether abandon the false opinion that the sun is the center of the world and immovable, and that the earth is not the center of the world, and moves, and that I must not hold, defend, or teach in any way whatsoever, verbally or in writing, the said false doctrine, and after it had been notified to me that the said doctrine was contrary to Holy Scripture—I wrote and printed a book in which I discuss this new doctrine already condemned, and adduce arguments of great cogency in its favor, without presenting any solution of these, and for this reason I have been pronounced by the Holy Office to be vehemently suspected of heresy, that is to say, of having held and believed that the Sun is the center of the world and immovable, and that the earth is not the center and moves:

Therefore, desiring to remove from the minds of your Eminences, and of all faithful Christians, this vehement suspicion, justly conceived against me, with sincere heart and unfeigned faith I abjure, curse, and detest the aforesaid errors and heresies, and generally every other error, heresy, and sect whatsoever contrary to the said Holy Church, and I swear that in the future I will never again say or assert, verbally or in writing, anything that might furnish occasion for a similar suspicion regarding me; but that should I know any heretic, or person suspected of heresy, I will denounce him to this Holy Office, or to the Inquisitor or Ordinary of the place where I may be. Further, I swear and promise to fulfill and observe in their integrity all penances that have been, or that shall be, imposed upon me by this Holy Office. And, in the event of my contravening, (which God forbid) any of these my promises and oaths, I submit myself to all the pains and penalties imposed and promulgated in the sacred canons and other constitutions, general and particular, against such delinquents. So help me God, and these His Holy Gospels, which I touch with my hands.

I, the said Galileo Galilei, have abjured, sworn, promised, and bound myself as above; and in witness of the truth thereof I have with my own hand subscribed the present document of my abjuration, and recited it word for word at Rome, in the Convent of Minerva, this twenty-second day of June, 1633.

I, Galileo Galilei, have abjured as above with my own hand.

[Galileo's Recantation excludes two points included in the original formula for abjuration presented to him by the Cardinals. These two points, objected to by Galileo, would have had him declare that he was not a good Catholic and that he deceived others in publishing his book.]

One Body (2008)

Margaret Gibson

I am born in a field
of cornflowers and ripe wheat
wind in the black gum trees
late afternoon before the storm
and the men are cutting the field
working the mower in circles
coming in and in
toward the center of the field
where I crouch down
with the rabbits, with the quail
driven into this space by the clackety mower
because I want to see
how the body goes still
how the mind, how the lens of the eye
magnifies to an emptiness
so deep, so flared wide
there is everywhere field and the Source
of field, and only
a quiver of the nose
or the flick of a top-knot feather, a ripple
so faint I may have imagined it, says
yes, says *no*
to the nearing rustle in the last stand of wheat—
and now it's quiet, too quiet
a soft trample
a click, the cocking sound, a swish
as the men steal in to take
what they want
they are clever, they are hungry
and because this one body is
my birthplace
my birthright, my only homeplace
my nest and burrow and bower
I understand
my mother is wheat, my father is wind
and I rise in a tall gust

of rage and compassion
I rise up from the mown and edible
debris of the world
wrapped in a bright
net of pollen and stars, my thighs
twin towers of lightning
and my voice
I am a storm of voices, snipe and wolf
snow goose, dolphin, quail, and lark—
Stop this. Stop it now
I say to the men, who stalk closer
keen on the kill, late light
on the steel of their rifles
and they are my brothers—they are my brothers
and I love them, too
Look into my eyes
I tell them. *See for yourself the one shining field*
Look into my eyes
before you shoot

from On the State of Nature (1651)

Thomas Hobbes

Of the Natural Condition of Mankind as Concerning Their Felicity, and Misery

Nature hath made men so equal, in the faculties of the body, and mind; as that though there be found one man sometimes manifestly stronger in body, or of quicker mind than another; yet when all is reckoned together, the difference between man, and man, is not so considerable, as that one man can thereupon claim to himself any benefit, to which another may not pretend, as well as he. For as to the strength of body, the weakest has strength enough to kill the strongest, either by secret machination, or by confederacy with others, that are in the same danger with himself.

And as to the faculties of the mind, setting aside the arts grounded upon words, and especially that skill of proceeding upon general, and infallible rules, called science; which very few have, and but in few things; as being not a native faculty, born with us; nor attained, as prudence, while we look after somewhat else, I find yet a greater equality amongst men, than that of strength. For prudence, is but experience; which equal time, equally bestows on all men, in those things they equally apply themselves unto. That which may perhaps make such equality incredible, is but a vain conceit of one's own wisdom, which almost all men think they have in a greater degree, than the vulgar; that is, than all men but themselves, and a few others, whom by fame, or for concurring with themselves, they approve. For such is the nature of men, that howsoever they may acknowledge many others to be more witty, or more eloquent, or more learned; yet they will hardly believe there be many so wise as themselves; for they see their own wit at hand, and other men's at a distance. But this proveth rather that men are in that point equal, than unequal. For there is not ordinarily a greater sign of the equal distribution of any thing, than that every man is contented with his share.

From this equality of ability, ariseth equality of hope in the attaining of our ends. And therefore if any two men desire the same thing, which nevertheless they cannot both enjoy, they become enemies; and in the way to their end, which is principally their own conservation, and sometimes their delectation only, endeavour to destroy, or subdue one another. And

474

from hence it comes to pass, that where an invader hath no more to fear, than another man's single power; if one plant, sow, build, or possess a convenient seat, others may probably be expected to come prepared with forces united, to dispossess, and deprive him, not only of the fruit of his labour, but also of his life, or liberty. And the invader again is in the like danger of another.

And from this diffidence of one another, there is no way for any man to secure himself, so reasonable, as anticipation; that is, by force, or wiles, to master the persons of all men he can, so long, till he see no other power great enough to endanger him: and this is no more than his own conservation requireth, and is generally allowed. Also because there be some, that taking pleasure in contemplating their own power in the acts of conquest, which they pursue farther than their security requires; if others, that otherwise would be glad to be at ease within modest bounds, should not by invasion increase their power, they would not be able, long time, by standing only on their defence, to subsist. And by consequence, such augmentation of dominion over men being necessary to a man's conservation, it ought to be allowed him.

Again, men have no pleasure, but on the contrary a great deal of grief, in keeping company, where there is no power able to over-awe them all. For every man looketh that his companion should value him, at the same rate he sets upon himself: and upon all signs of contempt, or undervaluing, naturally endeavours, as far as he dares, (which amongst them that have no common power to keep them in quiet, is far enough to make them destroy each other), to extort a greater value from his contemners, by damage; and from others, by the example.

So that in the nature of man, we find three principal causes of quarrel. First, competition; secondly, diffidence; thirdly, glory.

The first, maketh men invade for gain; the second, for safety; and the third, for reputation. The first use violence, to make themselves masters of other men's persons, wives, children, and cattle; the second, defend them; the third, for trifles, as a word, a smile, a different opinion, and any other sign of undervalue, either direct in their persons, or by reflection in their kindred, their friends, their nation, their profession, or their name.

Hereby it is manifest, that during the time men live without a common power to keep them all in awe, they are in that condition which is called war; and such a war, as is of every man, against every man. For war, consisteth not in battle only, or the act of fighting; but in a tract of time, wherein the will to contend by battle is sufficiently known: and therefore the notion of *time*, is to be considered in the nature of war; as it is in the nature of weather. For as the nature of foul weather, lieth not in the shower or two of rain; but in an inclination thereto of many days together: so the nature of war, consisteth not in actual fighting; but in the known disposition thereto, during all the time there is no assurance to the contrary. All other time is PEACE.

Whatsoever therefore is consequent to a time of war, where every man is enemy to every man; the same is consequent to the time, wherein men live without other security, than what their own strength, and their own invention shall furnish them withal. In such condition, there is no place for industry; because the fruit thereof is uncertain: and consequently no culture of the earth; no navigation, nor use of the commodities that may be imported by sea; no commodious building; no instruments of moving, and removing, such things as require much force; no knowledge of the face of the earth; no account of time; no arts; no letters; no society; and which is worst of all, continual fear, and danger of violent death; and the life of man, solitary, poor, nasty, brutish, and short.

It may seem strange to some man, that has not well weighed these things; that nature should thus dissociate, and render men apt to invade, and destroy one another: and he may therefore, not trusting to this inference, made from the passions, desire perhaps to have the same confirmed by experience. Let him therefore consider with himself, when taking a journey, he arms himself, and seeks to go well accompanied; when going to sleep, he locks his doors; when even in his house he locks his chests; and this when he knows there be laws, and public officers, armed, to revenge all injuries shall be done him; what opinion he has of his fellow-subjects, when he rides armed; of his fellow citizens, when he locks his doors; and of his children, and servants, when he locks his chests. Does he not there as much accuse mankind by his actions, as I do by my words? But neither of us accuse man's nature in it. The desires, and other passions of man, are in themselves no sin. No more are the actions, that proceed from those passions, till they know a law that forbids them: which till laws be made they cannot know: nor can any law be made, till they have agreed upon the person that shall make it.

It may peradventure be thought, there was never such a time, nor condition of war as this; and I believe it was never generally so, over all the world: but there are many places, where they live so now. For the savage people in many places of America, except the government of small families, the concord whereof dependeth on natural lust, have no government at all; and live at this day in that brutish manner, as I said before.

Howsoever, it may be perceived what manner of life there would be, where there were no common power to fear, by the manner of life, which men that have formerly lived under a peaceful government, use to degenerate into, in a civil war.

But though there had never been any time, wherein particular men were in a condition of war one against another; yet in all times, kings, and persons of sovereign authority, because of their independency, are in continual jealousies, and in the state and posture of gladiators; having their weapons pointing, and their eyes fixed on one another; that is, their forts, garrisons, and guns upon the frontiers of their kingdoms; and continual spies upon their neighbours; which is a posture of war. But because they uphold thereby, the industry of their subjects; there does not follow from it, that misery, which accompanies the liberty of particular men.

To this war of every man, against every man, this also is consequent; that nothing can be unjust. The notions of right and wrong, justice and injustice have there no place. Where there is no common power, there is no law: where no law, no injustice. Force, and fraud, are in war the two cardinal virtues. Justice, and injustice are none of the faculties neither of the body, nor mind. If they were, they might be in a man that were alone in the world, as well as his senses, and passions. They are qualities, that relate to men in society, not in solitude. It is consequent also to the same condition, that there be no propriety, no dominion, no *mine* and *thine* distinct; but only that to be every man's, that he can get; and for so long, as he can keep it. And thus much for the ill condition, which man by mere nature is actually placed in; though with a possibility to come out of it, consisting partly in the passions, partly in his reason.

The passions that incline men to peace, are fear of death; desire of such things as are necessary to commodious living; and a hope by their industry to obtain them. And reason suggesteth convenient articles of peace, upon which men may be drawn to agreement. These articles, are they, which otherwise are called the Laws of Nature.

Beloved Community (1995)
A WORLD WITHOUT RACISM

bell hooks

Some days it is just hard to accept that racism can still be such a powerful dominating force in all our lives. When I remember all that black and white folks together have sacrificed to challenge and change white supremacy, when I remember the individuals who gave their lives to the cause of racial justice, my heart is deeply saddened that we have not fulfilled their shared dream of ending racism, of creating a new culture, a place for the *beloved community*. Early on in his work for civil rights, long before his consciousness had been deeply radicalized by reistance to militarism and global Western imperialism, Martin Luther King imagined a *beloved community* where race would be transcended, forgotten, where no one would see skin color. This dream has not been realized. From its inception it was a flawed vision. The flaw, however, was not the imagining of a *beloved community*; it was the insistence that such a community could exist only if we erased and forgot racial difference.

Many citizens of these United States still long to live in a society where *beloved community* can be formed—where loving ties of care and knowing bind us together in our differences. We cannot surrender that longing—if we do we will never see an end to racism. These days it is an untalked-about longing. Most folks in this society have become so cynical about ending racism, so convinced that solidarity across racial differences can never be a reality, that they make no effort to build community. Those of us who are not cynical, who still cherish the vision of *beloved community*, sustain our conviction that we need such bonding not because we cling to utopian fantasies but because we have struggled all our lives to create this community. In my blackness I have struggled together with white comrades in the segregated South. Sharing that struggle we came to know deeply, intimately, with all our minds and hearts that we can all divest of racism and white supremacy if we so desire. We divest through our commitment to and engagement with anti-racist struggle. Even though that commitment was first made in the mind and heart, it is realized by concrete action, by anti-racist living and being.

Over the years my love and admiration for those black and white southerners in my hometown who worked together to realize racial justice deepens, as does their love of me. We have gone off from that time of legalized segregation to create intimate lives for ourselves that include loving engagement with all races and ethnicities. The small circles of love we have managed to form in our individual lives represent a concrete realistic reminder that *beloved community* is not a dream, that it already exists for those of us who have done the work of educating ourselves for critical consciousness in ways that enabled a letting go of white supremacist assumptions and values. The process of decolonization (unlearning white supremacy by divesting of white privilege if we were white or vestiges of internalized racism if we were black) transformed our minds and our habits of being.

In the segregated South those black and white folks who struggled together for racial justice (many of whom grounded their actions not in radical politics but in religious conviction) were bound by a shared belief in the transformative power of love. Understanding that love was the antithesis of the will to dominate and subjugate, we allowed that longing to know love, to love one another, to radicalize us politically. That love was not sentimental. It did not blind us to the reality that racism was deeply systemic and that only by realizing that love in concrete political actions that might involve sacrifice, even the surrender of one's life, would white supremacy be fundamentally challenged. We knew the sweetness of *beloved community*.

What those of us who have not died now know, that generations before us did not grasp, was that *beloved community* is formed not by the eradication of difference but by its affirmation, by each of us claiming the identities and cultural legacies that shape who we are and how we live in the world. To form *beloved community* we do not surrender ties to precious origins. We deepen those bondings by connecting them with an antiracist struggle which is at heart always a movement to disrupt that clinging to cultural legacies that demands investment in notions of racial purity, authenticity, nationalist fundamentalism. The notion that differences of skin color, class background, and cultural heritage must be erased for justice and equality to prevail is a brand of popular false consciousness that helps keep racist thinking and action intact. Most folks are threatened by the notion that they must give up allegiances to specific cultural legacies in order to have harmony. Such suspicion is healthy. Unfortunately, as long as our society holds up a vision of democracy that requires the surrender of bonds and ties to legacies folks hold dear, challenging racism and white supremacy will seem like an action that diminishes and destabilizes.

The misguided idea that one must give up cultural allegiance to create harmony positively emerged from religious freedom fighters whose faith urged them to let go of attachment to the things of this world (status, ethnicity, national allegiances) in order to be one with God. Negatively, it has been appropriated by the enemies of anti-racist struggle to further tensions between different racial groups, to breed fundamentalist and nationalistic feelings and support for racial separatism. Since the notion that we should all forsake attachment to race and/or cultural identity and be "just humans" within the framework of white supremacy has usually meant that subordinate groups must surrender their identities, beliefs, values and assimilate by adopting the values and beliefs of privileged-class whites, rather than promoting racial harmony this thinking has created a fierce cultural protectionism. That conservative force that sees itself as refusing assimilation expresses itself in the call for cultural nationalism, for disenfranchised groups to embrace separatism. This is why black leaders who espouse black separatism are gaining political power. Many black people fear that white commodification and appropriation of blackness is a neo-colonial strategy of cultural genocide that threatens to destroy our cultural legacy. That fear is not ungrounded. Black people, however, are misguided in thinking that nationalist fundamentalism is the best or only way to either preserve our heritage or to make a meaningful political response to ending racism.

In actuality, the growth of nationalist separatist thinking among black people is an extreme expression of collective cynicism about ending white supremacy. The assumption that white folks will never cease to be racist represents a refusal to privilege the history of those whites (however few) who have been willing to give their lives to the struggle for racial justice over that of white folks who maintain racist thinking—sometimes without even knowing that they hold racist assumptions. Since white supremacist attitudes and values permeate every aspect of the culture, most white folks are unconsciously absorbing the ideology of white supremacy. Since they do not realize this socialization is taking place, many of them feel that they are not racist. When these feelings are rooted in denial, the first stage of anti-racist struggle has to be breaking that denial. This is one of the primary distinctions between the generation of white folks who were raised in the midst of white supremacist apartheid, who witnessed firsthand the brutal dehumanization of black people and who knew that "racism" permeated the culture, and this contemporary generation that either engages in historical amnesia or does not remember. Prior to desegregation, few whites would have been as arrogantly convinced that they are not racists as are most whites today, some of whom never come into contact with black people. During the civil rights struggle, it was commonly understood that whites seeking to live in an anti-racist world measured their progress and their commitment by their interactions with black people. How can a white person assume he or she is not racist if that assumption has not been concretely realized in interaction? It was precisely the astute recognition on the part of freedom fighters working for racial justice that anti-racist habits of being were best cultivated in situations of interaction that was at the heart of every vision of non-racist community.

Concurrently, most white Americans who believed or believe that racism is ethically and morally wrong centered their anti-racist struggle around the desire to commune with black folks. Today many white people who see themselves as non-racist are comfortable with lives where they have no contact with black people or where fear is their first response in any encounter with blackness. This "fear" is the first sign of the internalization in the white psyche of white supremacist sentiments. It serves to mask white power and privilege. In the past the affirmation of white supremacy in everyday life was declared via assertions of hatred and/or power (i.e., public and private subordination and humiliation of black folks—the white wife who sits at her dining table eating a nice lunch while the maid eats standing in the kitchen, the white male employer paying black workers less and calling them by obscene names); in our contemporary times white belief in black inferiority is most often registered by the assertion of power. Yet that power is often obscured by white focus on fear. The fear whites direct at blacks is rooted in the racist assumption that the darker race is inherently deprived, dangerous, and willing to obtain what they desire by any means necessary. Since it is assumed that whenever fear is present one is less powerful, cultivating in whites fear of blacks is a useful neo-colonial strategy as it obscures the reality that whites do much more harm to blacks daily than vice versa. It also encourages white people to believe that they do not hold power over blacks even as their ability to project fear when there is no danger is an act of denial that indicates their complicity with white supremacist thinking. Those white people who consciously break with racist thinking know that there is no concrete reality to suggest that they should be more fearful of blacks than other people, since white folks, like blacks, are likely to be harmed by people of the same race. Let me give a useful example. When I worked as an assistant professor at an Ivy League university one of my white female students was raped by a black man. Even though she had been deeply committed to anti-racist work before the rape, during her period of recovery she found that she was fearing all black men. Her commitment to anti-racist struggle led her to interrogate that fear, and she realized that had she been raped by a white male, she would not have felt all white males were responsible and should be feared. Seeing her fear of all black males as a regressive expression of white racism, she let it go. The will to be vigilant emerged from both her commitment to ending racism and her will to be in loving community with black folks. Not abandoning that longing for community is a perspective we must all embrace if racism is to end.

More than ever before in our history, black Americans are succumbing to and internalizing the racist assumption that there can be no meaningful bonds of intimacy between blacks and whites. It is fascinating to explore why it is that black people trapped in the worst situation of racial oppression—enslavement—had the foresight to see that it would be disempowering for them to lose sight of the capacity of white people to transform themselves and divest of white supremacy, even as many black folks today who in no way suffer such extreme racist oppression and exploitation are convinced that white people will not repudiate racism. Contemporary black folks, like their white counterparts, have passively accepted the internalization of white supremacist assumptions. Organized white supremacists have always taught that there can never be trust and intimacy between the superior white race and the inferior black race. When black people internalize these sentiments, no resistance to white supremacy is taking place; rather we become complicit in spreading racist notions. It does not matter that so many black people feel white people will never repudiate racism because of being daily assaulted by white denial and refusal of accountability. We must not allow the actions of white folks who blindly endorse racism to determine the direction of our resistance. Like our white allies in struggle we must consistently keep the faith, by always sharing the truth that white people can be anti-racist, that racism is not some immutable character flaw.

Of course many white people are comfortable with a rhetoric of race that suggests racism cannot be changed, that all white people are "inherently racist" simply because they are born and raised in this society. Such misguided thinking socializes white people both to remain ignorant of the way in which white supremacist attitudes are learned and to assume a posture of learned helplessness as though they have no agency—no capacity to resist this thinking. Luckily we have many autobiographies by white folks committed to anti-racist struggle that provide documentary testimony that many of these individuals repudiated racism when they were children. Far from passively accepting it as inherent, they instinctively felt it was wrong. Many of them witnessed bizarre acts of white racist aggression towards black folks in everyday life and responded to the injustice of the situation. Sadly, in our times so many white folks are easily convinced by racist whites and black folks who have internalized racism that they can never be really free of racism.

These feelings also then obscure the reality of white privilege. As long as white folks are taught to accept racism as "natural" then they do not have to see themselves as consciously creating a racist society by their actions, by their political choices. This means as well that they do not have to face the way in which acting in a racist manner ensures the maintenance of white privilege. Indeed, denying their agency allows them to believe white privilege does not exist even as they daily exercise it. If the young white woman who had been raped had chosen to hold all black males accountable for what happened, she would have been exercising white privilege and reinforcing the structure of racist thought which teaches that all black people are alike. Unfortunately, so many white people are eager to believe racism cannot be changed because internalizing that assumption downplays the issue of accountability. No responsibility need be taken for not changing something if it is perceived as immutable. To accept racism as a system of domination that can be changed would demand that everyone who sees him—or herself as embracing a vision of racial social equality would be required to assert anti-racist habits of being. We know from histories both present and past that white people (and everyone else) who commit themselves to living in anti-racist ways need to make sacrifices, to courageously endure the uncomfortable to challenge and change.

Whites, people of color, and black folks are reluctant to commit themselves fully and deeply to an anti-racist struggle that is ongoing because there is such a pervasive feeling of hopelessness—a conviction that nothing will ever change. How any of us can continue to hold those feelings when we study the history of racism in this society and see how much has changed makes no logical sense. Clearly we have not gone far enough. In the late sixties, Martin Luther King posed the question "Where do we go from here." To live in anti-racist society we must collectively renew our commitment to a democratic vision of racial justice and equality. Pursuing that vision we create a culture where beloved community flourishes and is sustained. Those of us who know the joy of being with folks from all walks of life, all races, who are fundamentally anti-racist in their habits of being, need to give public testimony. We need to share not only what we have experienced but the conditions of change that make such an experience possible. The interracial circle of love that I know can happen because each individual present in it has made his or her own commitment to living an anti-racist life and to furthering the struggle to end white supremacy will become a reality for everyone only if those of us who have created these communities share how they emerge in our lives and the strategies we use to sustain them. Our devout commitment to building diverse communities is central. These commitments to anti-racist living are just one expression of who we are and what we share with one another but they form the foundation of that sharing. Like all beloved communities we affirm our differences. It is this generous spirit of affirmation that gives us the courage to challenge one another, to work through misunderstandings, especially those that have to do with race and racism. In a beloved community solidarity and trust are grounded in profound commitment to a shared vision. Those of us who are always anti-racist long for a world in which everyone can form a *beloved community* where borders can be crossed and cultural hybridity celebrated. Anyone can begin to make such a community by truly seeking to live in an anti-racist world. If that longing guides our vision and our actions, the new culture will be born and anti-racist communities of resistance will emerge everywhere. That is where we must go from here.

I Have a Dream (1963)

Martin Luther King, Jr.

Five score years ago, a great American, in whose symbolic shadow we stand today, signed the Emancipation Proclamation. This momentous decree came as a great beacon light of hope to millions of Negro slaves who had been seared in the flames of withering injustice. It came as a joyous daybreak to end the long night of their captivity.

But one hundred years later, the Negro still is not free. One hundred years later, the life of the Negro is still sadly crippled by the manacles of segregation and the chains of discrimination. One hundred years later, the Negro lives on a lonely island of poverty in the midst of a vast ocean of material prosperity. One hundred years later, the Negro is still languishing in the corners of American society and finds himself in exile in his own land. So we have come here today to dramatize a shameful condition.

In a sense we have come to our nation's capital to cash a check. When the architects of our republic wrote the magnificent words of the Constitution and the Declaration of Independence, they were signing a promissory note to which every American was to fall heir. This note was a promise that all men, yes, black men as well as white men, would be guaranteed the unalienable rights of life, liberty, and the pursuit of happiness.

It is obvious today that America has defaulted on this promissory note insofar as her citizens of color are concerned. Instead of honoring this sacred obligation, America has given the Negro people a bad check, a check which has come back marked "insufficient funds." But we refuse to believe that the bank of justice is bankrupt. We refuse to believe that there are insufficient funds in the great vaults of opportunity of this nation. So we have come to cash this check—a check that will give us upon demand the riches of freedom and the security of justice. We have also come to this hallowed spot to remind America of the fierce urgency of now. This is no time to engage in the luxury of cooling off or to take the tranquilizing drug of gradualism. Now is the time to make real the promises of democracy. Now is the time to rise from the dark and desolate valley of segregation to the sunlit path of racial justice. Now is the time to lift our nation from the quick sands of racial injustice to the solid rock of brotherhood. Now is the time to make justice a reality for all of God's children.

It would be fatal for the nation to overlook the urgency of the moment. This sweltering summer of the Negro's legitimate discontent will not pass until there is an invigorating autumn of freedom and equality. Nineteen sixty-three is not an end, but a beginning. Those who hope that the Negro needed to blow off steam and will now be content will have a rude awakening if the nation returns to business as usual. There will be neither rest nor tranquility in America until the Negro is granted his citizenship rights. The whirlwinds of revolt will continue to shake the foundations of our nation until the bright day of justice emerges.

But there is something that I must say to my people who stand on the warm threshold which leads into the palace of justice. In the process of gaining our rightful place we must not be guilty of wrongful deeds. Let us not seek to satisfy our thirst for freedom by drinking from the cup of bitterness and hatred.

We must forever conduct our struggle on the high plane of dignity and discipline. We must not allow our creative protest to degenerate into physical violence. Again and again we must rise to the majestic heights of meeting physical force with soul force. The marvelous new militancy which has engulfed the Negro community must not lead us to distrust of all white people, for many of our white brothers, as evidenced by their presence here today, have come to realize that their destiny is tied up with our destiny and their freedom is inextricably bound to our freedom. We cannot walk alone.

As we walk, we must make the pledge that we shall march ahead. We cannot turn back. There are those who are asking the devotees of civil rights, "When will you be satisfied?" We can never be satisfied as long as the Negro is the victim of the unspeakable horrors of police brutality. We can never be satisfied as long as our bodies, heavy with the fatigue of travel, cannot gain lodging in the motels of the highways and the hotels of the cities. We can never be satisfied as long as a Negro in Mississippi cannot vote and a Negro in New York believes he has nothing for which to vote. No, no, we are not satisfied, and we will not be satisfied until justice rolls down like waters and righteousness like a mighty stream.

I am not unmindful that some of you have come here out of great trials and tribulations. Some of you have come fresh from narrow jail cells. Some of you have come from areas where your quest for freedom left you battered by the storms of persecution and staggered by the winds of police brutality. You have been the veterans of creative suffering. Continue to work with the faith that unearned suffering is redemptive.

Go back to Mississippi, go back to Alabama, go back to South Carolina, go back to Georgia, go back to Louisiana, go back to the slums and ghettos of our northern cities, knowing that somehow this situation can and will be changed. Let us not wallow in the valley of despair.

I say to you today, my friends, so even though we face the difficulties of today and tomorrow, I still have a dream. It is a dream deeply rooted in the American dream.

I have a dream that one day this nation will rise up and live out the true meaning of its creed: "We hold these truths to be self-evident: that all men are created equal."

I have a dream that one day on the red hills of Georgia the sons of former slaves and the sons of former slave owners will be able to sit down together at the table of brotherhood.

I have a dream that one day even the state of Mississippi, a state sweltering with the heat of injustice, sweltering with the heat of oppression, will be transformed into an oasis of freedom and justice.

I have a dream that my four little children will one day live in a nation where they will not be judged by the color of their skin but by the content of their character.

I have a dream today.

I have a dream that one day, down in Alabama, with its vicious racists, with its governor having his lips dripping with the words of interposition and nullification; one day right there in Alabama, little black boys and black girls will be able to join hands with little white boys and white girls as sisters and brothers.

I have a dream today.

I have a dream that one day every valley shall be exalted, every hill and mountain shall be made low, the rough places will be made plain, and the crooked places will be made straight, and the glory of the Lord shall be revealed, and all flesh shall see it together.

This is our hope. This is the faith that I go back to the South with. With this faith we will be able to hew out of the mountain of despair a stone of hope. With this faith we will be able to transform the jangling discords of our nation into a beautiful symphony of brotherhood. With this faith we will be able to work together, to pray together, to struggle together, to go to jail together, to stand up for freedom together, knowing that we will be free one day.

This will be the day when all of God's children will be able to sing with a new meaning, "My country, 'tis of thee, sweet land of liberty, of thee I sing. Land where my fathers died, land of the pilgrim's pride, from every mountainside, let freedom ring."

And if America is to be a great nation this must become true. So let freedom ring from the prodigious hilltops of New Hampshire. Let freedom ring from the mighty mountains of New York. Let freedom ring from the heightening Alleghenies of Pennsylvania!

Let freedom ring from the snowcapped Rockies of Colorado!

Let freedom ring from the curvaceous slopes of California!

But not only that; let freedom ring from Stone Mountain of Georgia!

Let freedom ring from Lookout Mountain of Tennessee!

Let freedom ring from every hill and molehill of Mississippi. From every mountainside, let freedom ring.

And when this happens, when we allow freedom to ring, when we let it ring from every village and every hamlet, from every state and every city, we will be able to speed up that day when all of God's children, black men and white men, Jews and Gentiles, Protestants and Catholics, will be able to join hands and sing in the words of the old Negro spiritual, "Free at last! free at last! thank God Almighty, we are free at last!"

The Third and Final Continent (1999)

Jhumpa Lahiri

I left India in 1964 with a certificate in commerce and the equivalent, in those days, of ten dollars to my name. For three weeks I sailed on the SS *Roma*, an Italian cargo vessel, in a cabin next to the ship's engine, across the Arabian Sea, the Red Sea, the Mediterranean, and finally to England. I lived in north London, in Finsbury Park, in a house occupied entirely by penniless Bengali bachelors like myself, at least a dozen and sometimes more, all struggling to educate and establish ourselves abroad.

I attended lectures at LSE and worked at the university library to get by. We lived three or four to a room, shared a single, icy toilet, and took turns cooking pots of egg curry, which we ate with our hands on a table covered with newspapers. Apart from our jobs we had few responsibilities. On weekends we lounged barefoot in drawstring pajamas, drinking tea and smoking Rothmans, or set out to watch cricket at Lord's. Some weekends the house was crammed with still more Bengalis, to whom we had introduced ourselves at the greengrocer, or on the Tube, and we made yet more egg curry, and played Mukesh on a Grundig reel-to-reel, and soaked our dirty dishes in the bathtub. Every now and then someone in the house moved out, to live with a woman whom his family back in Calcutta had determined he was to wed. In 1969, when I was thirty-six years old, my own marriage was arranged. Around the same time I was offered a full-time job in America, in the processing department of a library at MIT. The salary was generous enough to support a wife, and I was honored to be hired by a world-famous university, and so I obtained a sixth-preference green card, and prepared to travel farther still.

By now I had enough money to go by plane. I flew first to Calcutta, to attend my wedding, and a week later I flew to Boston, to begin my new job. During the flight I read *The Student Guide to North America*, a paperback volume that I'd bought before leaving London, for seven shillings six pence on Tottenham Court Road, for although I was no longer a student I was on a budget all the same. I learned that Americans drove on the right side of the road, not the left, and that they called a lift an elevator and an engaged phone busy. "The pace of life in North America is different from Britain as you will soon discover," the guidebook informed me. "Everybody feels he must get to the top. Don't expect an English cup of tea." As the plane began its descent over Boston Harbor, the pilot announced the weather and time, and that President Nixon had declared a national holiday: two American men had landed on the moon. Several passengers cheered. "God bless America!" one of them hollered. Across the aisle, I saw a woman praying.

I spent my first night at the YMCA in Central Square, Cambridge, an inexpensive accommodation recommended by my guidebook. It was walking distance from MIT, and steps from the post office and a super-market called Purity Supreme. The room contained a cot, a desk, and a small wooden cross on one wall. A sign on the door said cooking was strictly forbidden. A bare window overlooked Massachusetts Avenue, a major thoroughfare with traffic in both directions. Car horns, shrill and prolonged, blared one after another. Flashing sirens heralded endless emergencies, and a fleet of buses rumbled past, their doors opening and closing with a powerful hiss, throughout the night. The noise was con-stantly distracting, at times suffocating. I felt it deep in my ribs, just as I had felt the furious drone of the engine on the SS *Roma*. But there was no ship's deck to escape to, no glittering ocean to thrill my soul, no breeze to cool my face, no one to talk to. I was too tired to pace the gloomy corri-dors of the YMCA in my drawstring pajamas. Instead I sat at the desk and stared out the window, at the city hall of Cambridge and a row of small shops. In the morning I reported to my job at the Dewey Library, a beige fortlike building by Memorial Drive. I also opened a bank account, rented a post office box, and bought a plastic bowl and a spoon at Woolworth's, a store whose name I recognized from London. I went to Purity Supreme, wandering up and down the aisles, converting ounces to grams and com-paring prices to things in England. In the end I bought a small carton of milk and a box of cornflakes. This was my first meal in America. I ate it at my desk. I preferred it to hamburgers or hot dogs, the only alternative I could afford in the coffee shops on Massachusetts Avenue, and, besides, at the time I had yet to consume any beef. Even the simple chore of buy-ing milk was new to me; in London we'd had bottles delivered each morning to our door.

In a week I had adjusted, more or less. I ate cornflakes and milk, morn-ing and night, and bought some bananas for variety, slicing them into the bowl with the edge of my spoon. In addition I bought tea bags and a flask, which the salesman in Woolworth's referred to as a thermos (a flask, he informed me, was used to store whiskey, another thing I had never consumed). For the price of one cup of tea at a coffee shop, I filled the flask with boiling water on my way to work each morning, and brewed the four cups I drank in the course of a day. I bought a larger carton of milk, and learned to leave it on the shaded part of the windowsill, as I had seen another resident at the YMCA do. To pass the time in the evenings I read the Boston Globe downstairs, in a spacious room with stained-glass windows. I read every article and advertisement, so that I would grow familiar with things, and when my eyes grew tired I slept. Only I did not sleep well. Each night I had to keep the window wide open; it was the only source of air in the stifling room, and the noise was intolerable. I would lie on the cot with my fingers pressed into my ears, but when I drifted off to sleep my hands fell away, and the noise of the traffic would wake me up again. Pigeon feathers drifted onto the windowsill, and one evening, when I poured milk over my cornflakes, I saw that it had soured. Nevertheless I resolved to stay at the YMCA for six weeks, until my wife's passport and green card were ready. Once she arrived I would have to rent a proper apartment, and from time to time I studied the classified section of the newspaper, or stopped in at the housing office at MIT during my lunch break, to see what was available in my price range. It was in this manner that I discovered a room for immediate occupancy, in a house on a quiet street, the listing said, for eight dollars per week. I copied the number into my guidebook and dialed from a pay telephone, sorting through the coins with which I was still unfamiliar, smaller and lighter than shillings, heavier and brighter than paisas.

"Who is speaking?" a woman demanded. Her voice was bold and clamorous.

"Yes, good afternoon, madame. I am calling about the room for rent."

"Harvard or Tech?"

"I beg your pardon?"

"Are you from Harvard or Tech?"

Gathering that Tech referred to the Massachusetts Institute of Technology, I replied, "I work at Dewey Library," adding tentatively, "at Tech."

"I only rent rooms to boys from Harvard or Tech!"

"Yes, madame."

I was given an address and an appointment for seven o'clock that evening. Thirty minutes before the hour I set out, my guidebook in my pocket, my breath fresh with Listerine. I turned down a street shaded with trees, perpendicular to Massachusetts Avenue. Stray blades of grass poked between the cracks of the footpath. In spite of the heat I wore a coat and a tie, regarding the event as I would any other interview; I had never lived in the home of a person who was not Indian. The house, surrounded by a chain-link fence, was off-white with dark brown trim. Unlike the stucco row house I'd lived in in London, this house, fully detached, was covered with wooden shingles, with a tangle of forsythia bushes plastered against the front and sides. When I pressed the calling bell, the woman with whom I had spoken on the phone hollered from what seemed to be just the other side of the door, "One minute, please!"

Several minutes later the door was opened by a tiny, extremely old woman. A mass of snowy hair was arranged like a small sack on top of her head. As I stepped into the house she sat down on a wooden bench positioned at the bottom of a narrow carpeted staircase. Once she was settled on the bench, in a small pool of light, she peered up at me with undivided attention. She wore a long black skirt that spread like a stiff tent to the floor, and a starched white shirt edged with ruffles at the throat and cuffs. Her hands, folded together in her lap, had long pallid fingers, with swollen knuckles and tough yellow nails. Age had battered her features so that she almost resembled a man, with sharp, shrunken eyes and prominent creases on either side of her nose. Her lips, chapped and faded, had nearly disappeared, and her eyebrows were missing altogether. Nevertheless she looked fierce.

"Lock up!" she commanded. She shouted even though I stood only a few feet away. "Fasten the chain and firmly press that button on the knob! This is the first thing you shall do when you enter, is that clear?"

I locked the door as directed and examined the house. Next to the bench on which the woman sat was a small round table, its legs fully concealed, much like the woman's, by a skirt of lace. The table held a lamp, a transistor radio, a leather change purse with a silver clasp, and a telephone. A thick wooden cane coated with a layer of dust was propped against one side. There was a parlor to my right, lined with bookcases and filled with shabby clawfooted furniture. In the corner of the parlor I saw a grand piano with its top down, piled with papers. The piano's bench was missing; it seemed to be the one on which the woman was sitting. Somewhere in the house a clock chimed seven times.

"You're punctual!" the woman proclaimed. "I expect you shall be so with the rent!"

"I have a letter, madame." In my jacket pocket was a letter confirming my employment from MIT, which I had brought along to prove that I was indeed from Tech.

She stared at the letter, then handed it back to me carefully, gripping it with her fingers as if it were a dinner plate heaped with food instead of a sheet of paper. She did not wear glasses, and I wondered if she'd read a word of it. "The last boy was always late! Still owes me eight dollars! Harvard boys aren't what they used to be! Only Harvard and Tech in this house! How's Tech, boy?"

"It is very well."

"You checked the lock?"

"Yes, madame."

She slapped the space beside her on the bench with one hand, and told me to sit down. For a moment she was silent. Then she intoned, as if she alone possessed this knowledge:

"There is an American flag on the moon!"

"Yes, madame." Until then I had not thought very much about the moon shot. It was in the newspaper, of course, article upon article. The astronauts had landed on the shores of the Sea of Tranquillity, I had read, traveling farther than anyone in the history of civilization. For a few hours they explored the moon's surface. They gathered rocks in their pockets, described their surroundings (a magnificent desolation, according to one astronaut), spoke by phone to the president, and planted a flag in lunar soil. The voyage was hailed as man's most awesome achievement. I had seen full-page photographs in the *Globe*, of the astronauts in their inflated costumes, and read about what certain people in Boston had been doing at the exact moment the astronauts landed, on a Sunday afternoon. A man said that he was operating a swan boat with a radio pressed to his ear; a woman had been baking rolls for her grandchildren.

The woman bellowed, "A flag on the moon, boy! I heard it on the radio! Isn't that splendid?"

"Yes, madame."

But she was not satisfied with my reply. Instead she commanded, "Say 'splendid'!"

I was both baffled and somewhat insulted by the request. It reminded me of the way I was taught multiplication tables as a child, repeating after the master, sitting cross-legged, without shoes or pencils, on the floor of my one-room Tollygunge school. It also reminded me of my wedding, when I had repeated endless Sanskrit verses after the priest, verses I barely understood, which joined me to my wife. I said nothing.

"Say 'splendid'!" the woman bellowed once again.

"Splendid," I murmured. I had to repeat the word a second time at the top of my lungs, so she could hear. I am soft-spoken by nature and was especially reluctant to raise my voice to an elderly woman whom I had met only moments ago, but she did not appear to be offended. If anything the reply pleased her because her next command was:

"Go see the room!"

I rose from the bench and mounted the narrow carpeted staircase. There were five doors, two on either side of an equally narrow hallway, and one at the opposite end. Only one door was partly open. The room contained a twin bed under a sloping ceiling, a brown oval rug, a basin with an exposed pipe, and a chest of drawers. One door, painted white, led to a closet, another to a toilet and a tub. The walls were covered with gray and ivory striped paper. The window was open; net curtains stirred in the breeze. I lifted them away and inspected the view: a small back yard, with a few fruit trees and an empty clothesline. I was satisfied. From the bottom of the stairs I heard the woman demand, "What is your decision?"

When I returned to the foyer and told her, she picked up the leather change purse on the table, opened the clasp, fished about with her fingers, and produced a key on a thin wire hoop. She informed me that there was a kitchen at the back of the house, accessible through the parlor. I was welcome to use the stove as long as I left it as I found it. Sheets and towels were provided, but keeping them clean was my own responsibility. The rent was due Friday mornings on the ledge above the piano keys. "And no lady visitors!"

"I am a married man, madame." It was the first time I had announced this fact to anyone.

But she had not heard. "No lady visitors!" she insisted. She introduced herself as Mrs. Croft.

M y wife's name was Mala. The marriage had been arranged by my older brother and his wife. I regarded the proposition with neither objection nor enthusiasm. It was a duty expected of me, as it was expected of every man. She was the daughter of a schoolteacher in Beleghata. I was told that she could cook, knit, embroider, sketch landscapes, and recite poems by Tagore, but these talents could not make up for the fact that she did not possess a fair complexion, and so a string of men had rejected her to her face. She was twenty-seven, an age when her parents had begun to fear that she would never marry, and so they were willing to ship their only child halfway across the world in order to save her from spinsterhood.

For five nights we shared a bed. Each of those nights, after applying cold cream and braiding her hair, which she tied up at the end with a black cotton string, she turned from me and wept; she missed her parents. Although I would be leaving the country in a few days, custom dictated that she was now a part of my household, and for the next six weeks she was to live with my brother and his wife, cooking, cleaning, serving tea and sweets to guests. I did nothing to console her. I lay on my own side of the bed, reading my guidebook by flashlight and anticipating my journey. At times I thought of the tiny room on the other side of the wall which had belonged to my mother. Now the room was practically empty; the wooden pallet on which she'd once slept was piled with trunks and old bedding. Nearly six years ago, before leaving for London, I had watched her die on that bed, had found her playing with her excrement in her final days. Before we cremated her I had cleaned each of her fingernails with a hairpin, and then, because my brother could not bear it, I had assumed the role of eldest son, and had touched the flame to her temple, to release her tormented soul to heaven.

The next morning I moved into the room in Mrs. Croft's house. When I unlocked the door I saw that she was sitting on the piano bench, on the same side as the previous evening. She wore the same black skirt, the same starched white blouse, and had her hands folded together the same way in her lap. She looked so much the same that I wondered if she'd spent the whole night on the bench. I put my suitcase upstairs, filled my flask with boiling water in the kitchen, and headed off to work. That evening when I came home from the university, she was still there.

"Sit down, boy!" She slapped the space beside her.

I perched beside her on the bench. I had a bag of groceries with me—more milk, more cornflakes, and more bananas, for my inspection of the kitchen earlier in the day had revealed no spare pots, pans, or cooking utensils. There were only two saucepans in the refrigerator, both containing some orange broth, and a copper kettle on the stove.

"Good evening, madame."

She asked me if I had checked the lock. I told her I had.

For a moment she was silent. Then suddenly she declared, with the equal measures of disbelief and delight as the night before, "There's an American flag on the moon, boy!"

"Yes, madame."

"A flag on the moon! Isn't that splendid?"

I nodded, dreading what I knew was coming. "Yes, madame."

"Say 'splendid'!"

This time I paused, looking to either side in case anyone were there to overhear me, though I knew perfectly well that the house was empty. I felt like an idiot. But it was a small enough thing to ask. "Splendid!" I cried out.

Within days it became our routine. In the mornings when I left for the library Mrs. Croft was either hidden away in her bedroom, on the other side of the staircase, or she was sitting on the bench, oblivious to my presence, listening to the news or classical music on the radio. But each evening when I returned the same thing happened: she slapped the bench, ordered me to sit down, declared that there was a flag on the moon, and declared that it was splendid. I said it was splendid, too, and then we sat in silence. As awkward as it was, and as endless as it felt to me then, the nightly encounter lasted only about ten minutes; inevitably she would drift off to sleep, her head falling abruptly toward her chest, leaving me free to retire to my room. By then, of course, there was no flag standing on the moon. The astronauts, I had read in the paper, had seen it fall before they flew back to Earth. But I did not have the heart to tell her.

Friday morning, when my first week's rent was due, I went to the piano in the parlor to place my money on the ledge. The piano keys were dull and discolored. When I pressed one, it made no sound at all. I had put eight one-dollar bills in an envelope and written Mrs. Croft's name on the front of it. I was not in the habit of leaving money unmarked and unattended. From where I stood I could see the profile of her tent-shaped skirt. She was sitting on the bench, listening to the radio. It seemed unnecessary to make her get up and walk all the way to the piano. I never saw her walking about, and assumed, from the cane always propped against the round table at her side, that she did so with difficulty. When I approached the bench she peered up at me and demanded:

"What is your business?"

"The rent, madame."

"On the ledge above the piano keys!"

"I have it here." I extended the envelope toward her, but her fingers, folded together in her lap, did not budge. I bowed slightly and lowered the envelope, so that it hovered just above her hands. After a moment she accepted, and nodded her head.

That night when I came home, she did not slap the bench, but out of habit I sat beside her as usual. She asked me if I had checked the lock, but she mentioned nothing about the flag on the moon. Instead she said:

"It was very kind of you!"

"I beg your pardon, madame?"

"Very kind of you!"

She was still holding the envelope in her hands.

On Sunday there was a knock on my door. An elderly woman introduced herself: she was Mrs. Croft's daughter, Helen. She walked into the room and looked at each of the walls as if for signs of change, glancing at the shirts that hung in the closet, the neckties draped over the doorknob, the box of cornflakes on the chest of drawers, the dirty bowl and spoon in the basin. She was short and thick-waisted, with cropped silver hair and bright pink lipstick. She wore a sleeveless summer dress, a row of white plastic beads, and spectacles on a chain that hung like a swing against her chest. The backs of her legs were mapped with dark blue veins, and her upper arms sagged like the flesh of a roasted eggplant. She told me she lived in Arlington, a town farther up Massachusetts Avenue. "I come once a week to bring Mother groceries. Has she sent you packing yet?"

"It is very well, madame."

"Some of the boys run screaming. But I think she likes you. You're the first boarder she's ever referred to as a gentleman."

"Not at all, madame."

She looked at me, noticing my bare feet (I still felt strange wearing shoes indoors, and always removed them before entering my room). "Are you new to Boston?"

"New to America, madame."

"From?" She raised her eyebrows.

"I am from Calcutta, India."

"Is that right? We had a Brazilian fellow, about a year ago. You'll find Cambridge a very international city."

I nodded, and began to wonder how long our conversation would last. But at that moment we heard Mrs. Croft's electrifying voice rising up the stairs. When we stepped into the hallway we heard her hollering:

"You are to come downstairs immediately!"

"What is it?" Helen hollered back.

"Immediately!"

I put on my shoes at once. Helen sighed.

We walked down the staircase. It was too narrow for us to descend side by side, so I followed Helen, who seemed to be in no hurry, and complained at one point that she had a bad knee. "Have you been walking without your cane?" Helen called out. "You know you're not supposed to walk without that cane." She paused, resting her hand on the banister, and looked back at me. "She slips sometimes."

For the first time Mrs. Croft seemed vulnerable. I pictured her on the floor in front of the bench, flat on her back, staring at the ceiling, her feet pointing in opposite directions. But when we reached the bottom of the staircase she was sitting there as usual, her hands folded together in her lap. Two grocery bags were at her feet. When we stood before her she did not slap the bench, or ask us to sit down. She glared.

"What is it, Mother?"

"It's improper!"

"What's improper?"

"It is improper for a lady and gentleman who are not married to one another to hold a private conversation without a chaperone!"

Helen said she was sixty-eight years old, old enough to be my mother, but Mrs. Croft insisted that Helen and I speak to each other downstairs, in the parlor. She added that it was also improper for a lady of Helen's station to reveal her age, and to wear a dress so high above the ankle.

"For your information, Mother, it's 1969. What would you do if you actually left the house one day and saw a girl in a miniskirt?"

Mrs. Croft sniffed. "I'd have her arrested."

Helen shook her head and picked up one of the grocery bags. I picked up the other one, and followed her through the parlor and into the kitchen. The bags were filled with cans of soup, which Helen opened up one by one with a few cranks of a can opener. She tossed the old soup in the saucepans into the sink, rinsed the pans under the tap, filled them with soup from the newly opened cans, and put them back in the refrigerator. "A few years ago she could still open the cans herself," Helen said. "She hates that I do it for her now. But the piano killed her hands." She put on her spectacles, glanced at the cupboards, and spotted my tea bags. "Shall we have a cup?"

I filled the kettle on the stove. "I beg your pardon, madame. The piano?"

"She used to give lessons. For forty years. It was how she raised us after my father died." Helen put her hands on her hips, staring at the open refrigerator. She reached into the back, pulled out a wrapped stick of butter, frowned, and tossed it into the garbage. "That ought to do it," she said, and put the unopened cans of soup in the cupboard. I sat at the table and watched as Helen washed the dirty dishes, tied up the garbage bag, watered a spider plant over the sink, and poured boiling water into two cups. She handed one to me without milk, the string of the tea bag trailing over the side, and sat down at the table.

"Excuse me, madame, but is it enough?"

Helen took a sip of her tea. Her lipstick left a smiling pink stain on the inside rim of the cup. "Is what enough?"

"The soup in the pans. Is it enough food for Mrs. Croft?"

"She won't eat anything else. She stopped eating solids after she turned one hundred. That was, let's see, three years ago."

I was mortified. I had assumed Mrs. Croft was in her eighties, perhaps as old as ninety. I had never known a person who had lived for over a century. That this person was a widow who lived alone mortified me further still. It was widowhood that had driven my own mother insane. My father, who worked as a clerk at the General Post Office of Calcutta, died of encephalitis when I was sixteen. My mother refused to adjust to life without him; instead she sank deeper into a world of darkness from which neither I, nor my brother, nor concerned relatives, nor psychiatric clinics on Rash Behari Avenue could save her. What pained me most was to see her so unguarded, to hear her burp after meals or expel gas in front of company without the slightest embarrassment. After my father's death my brother abandoned his schooling and began to work in the jute mill he would eventually manage, in order to keep the household running. And so it was my job to sit by my mother's feet and study for my exams as she counted and recounted the bracelets on her arm as if they were the beads of an abacus. We tried to keep an eye on her. Once she had wandered half naked to the tram depot before we were able to bring her inside again.

"I am happy to warm Mrs. Croft's soup in the evenings," I suggested, removing the tea bag from my cup and squeezing out the liquor. "It is no trouble."

Helen looked at her watch, stood up, and poured the rest of her tea into the sink. "I wouldn't if I were you. That's the sort of thing that would kill her altogether."

That evening, when Helen had gone back to Arlington and Mrs. Croft and I were alone again, I began to worry. Now that I knew how very old she was, I worried that something would happen to her in the middle of the night, or when I was out during the day. As vigorous as her voice was, and imperious as she seemed, I knew that even a scratch or a cough could kill a person that old; each day she lived, I knew, was something of a miracle. Although Helen had seemed friendly enough, a small part of me worried that she might accuse me of negligence if anything were to happen. Helen didn't seem worried. She came and went, bringing soup for Mrs. Croft, one Sunday after the next.

In this manner the six weeks of that summer passed. I came home each evening, after my hours at the library, and spent a few minutes on the piano bench with Mrs. Croft. I gave her a bit of my company, and assured her that I had checked the lock, and told her that the flag on the moon was splendid. Some evenings I sat beside her long after she had drifted off to sleep, still in awe of how many years she had spent on this earth. At times I tried to picture the world she had been born into, in 1866—a world, I imagined, filled with women in long black skirts, and chaste conversations in the parlor. Now, when I looked at her hands with their swollen knuckles folded together in her lap, I imagined them smooth and slim, striking the piano keys. At times I came downstairs before going to sleep, to make sure she was sitting upright on the bench, or was safe in her bedroom. On Fridays I made sure to put the rent in her hands. There was nothing I could do for her beyond these simple gestures. I was not her son, and apart from those eight dollars, I owed her nothing.

• • •

At the end of August, Mala's passport and green card were ready. I received a telegram with her flight information; my brother's house in Calcutta had no telephone. Around that time I also received a letter from her, written only a few days after we had parted. There was no salutation; addressing me by name would have assumed an intimacy we had not yet discovered. It contained only a few lines. "I write in English in preparation for the journey. Here I am very much lonely. Is it very cold there. Is there snow. Yours, Mala."

I was not touched by her words. We had spent only a handful of days in each other's company. And yet we were bound together; for six weeks she had worn an iron bangle on her wrist, and applied vermilion powder to the part in her hair, to signify to the world that she was a bride. In those six weeks I regarded her arrival as I would the arrival of a coming month, or season—something inevitable, but meaningless at the time. So little did I know her that, while details of her face sometimes rose to my memory, I could not conjure up the whole of it.

A few days after receiving the letter, as I was walking to work in the morning, I saw an Indian woman on the other side of Massachusetts Avenue, wearing a sari with its free end nearly dragging on the footpath, and pushing a child in a stroller. An American woman with a small black dog on a leash was walking to one side of her. Suddenly the dog began barking. From the other side of the street I watched as the Indian woman, startled, stopped in her path, at which point the dog leapt up and seized the end of the sari between its teeth. The American woman scolded the dog, appeared to apologize, and walked quickly away, leaving the Indian woman to fix her sari in the middle of the footpath, and quiet her crying child. She did not see me standing there, and eventually she continued on her way. Such a mishap, I realized that morning, would soon be my concern. It was my duty to take care of Mala, to welcome her and protect her. I would have to buy her her first pair of snow boots, her first winter coat. I would have to tell her which streets to avoid, which way the traffic came, tell her to wear her sari so that the free end did not drag on the footpath. A five-mile separation from her parents, I recalled with some irritation, had caused her to weep.

Unlike Mala, I was used to it all by then: used to cornflakes and milk, used to Helen's visits, used to sitting on the bench with Mrs. Croft. The only thing I was not used to was Mala. Nevertheless I did what I had to do. I went to the housing office at MIT and found a furnished apartment a few blocks away, with a double bed and a private kitchen and bath, for forty dollars a week. One last Friday I handed Mrs. Croft eight one-dollar bills in an envelope, brought my suitcase downstairs, and informed her that I was moving. She put my key into her change purse. The last thing she asked me to do was hand her the cane propped against the table, so that she could walk to the door and lock it behind me. "Good-bye, then," she said, and retreated back into the house. I did not expect any display of emotion, but I was disappointed all the same. I was only a boarder, a man who paid her a bit of money and passed in and out of her home for six weeks. Compared to a century, it was no time at all.

At the airport I recognized Mala immediately. The free end of her sari did not drag on the floor, but was draped in a sign of bridal modesty over her head, just as it had draped my mother until the day my father died. Her thin brown arms were stacked with gold bracelets, a small red circle was painted on her forehead, and the edges of her feet were tinted with a decorative red dye. I did not embrace her, or kiss her, or take her hand. Instead I asked her, speaking Bengali for the first time in America, if she was hungry.

She hesitated, then nodded yes.

I told her I had prepared some egg curry at home. "What did they give you to eat on the plane?"

"I didn't eat."

"All the way from Calcutta?"

"The menu said oxtail soup."

"But surely there were other items."

"The thought of eating an ox's tail made me lose my appetite."

When we arrived home, Mala opened up one of her suitcases, and presented me with two pullover sweaters, both made with bright blue wool, which she had knitted in the course of our separation, one with a V neck, the other covered with cables. I tried them on; both were tight under the arms. She had also brought me two new pairs of drawstring pajamas, a letter from my brother, and a packet of loose Darjeeling tea. I had no present for her apart from the egg curry. We sat at a bare table, each of us staring at our plates. We ate with our hands, another thing I had not yet done in America.

"The house is nice," she said. "Also the egg curry." With her left hand she held the end of her sari to her chest, so it would not slip off her head.

"I don't know many recipes."

She nodded, peeling the skin off each of her potatoes before eating them. At one point the sari slipped to her shoulders. She readjusted it at once.

"There is no need to cover your head," I said. "I don't mind. It doesn't matter here."

She kept it covered anyway.

I waited to get used to her, to her presence at my side, at my table and in my bed, but a week later we were still strangers. I still was not used to coming home to an apartment that smelled of steamed rice, and finding that the basin in the bathroom was always wiped clean, our two toothbrushes lying side by side, a cake of Pears soap from India resting in the soap dish. I was not used to the fragrance of the coconut oil she rubbed every other night into her scalp, or the delicate sound her bracelets made as she moved about the apartment. In the mornings she was always awake before I was. The first morning when I came into the kitchen she had heated up the leftovers and set a plate with a spoonful of salt on its edge on the table, assuming I would eat rice for breakfast, as most Bengali husbands did. I told her cereal would do, and the next morning when I came into the kitchen she had already poured the cornflakes into my bowl. One morning she walked with me down Massachusetts Avenue to MIT, where I gave her a short tour of the campus. On the way we stopped at a hardware store and I made a copy of the key, so that she could let herself into the apartment. The next morning before I left for work she asked me for a few dollars. I parted with them reluctantly, but I knew that this, too, was now normal. When I came home from work there was a potato peeler in the kitchen drawer, and a tablecloth on the table, and chicken curry made with fresh garlic and ginger on the stove. We did not have a television in those days. After dinner I read the newspaper, while Mala sat at the kitchen table, working on a cardigan for herself with more of the bright blue wool, or writing letters home.

At the end of our first week, on Friday, I suggested going out. Mala set down her knitting and disappeared into the bathroom. When she emerged I regretted the suggestion; she had put on a clean silk sari and extra bracelets, and coiled her hair with a flattering side part on top of her head. She was prepared as if for a party, or at the very least for the cinema, but I had no such destination in mind. The evening air was balmy. We walked several blocks down Massachusetts Avenue, looking into the windows of restaurants and shops. Then, without thinking, I led her down the quiet street where for so many nights I had walked alone.

"This is where I lived before you came," I said, stopping at Mrs. Croft's chain-link fence.

"In such a big house?"

"I had a small room upstairs. At the back."

"Who else lives there?"

"A very old woman."

"With her family?"

"Alone."

"But who takes care of her?"

I opened the gate. "For the most part she takes care of herself."

I wondered if Mrs. Croft would remember me; I wondered if she had a new boarder to sit with her on the bench each evening. When I pressed the bell I expected the same long wait as that day of our first meeting, when I did not have a key. But this time the door was opened almost immediately, by Helen. Mrs. Croft was not sitting on the bench. The bench was gone.

"Hello there," Helen said, smiling with her bright pink lips at Mala. "Mother's in the parlor. Will you be visiting awhile?"

"As you wish, madame."

"Then I think I'll run to the store, if you don't mind. She had a little accident. We can't leave her alone these days, not even for a minute."

I locked the door after Helen and walked into the parlor. Mrs. Croft was lying flat on her back, her head on a peach-colored cushion, a thin white quilt spread over her body. Her hands were folded together on top of her chest. When she saw me she pointed at the sofa, and told me to sit down. I took my place as directed, but Mala wandered over to the piano and sat on the bench, which was now positioned where it belonged.

"I broke my hip!" Mrs. Croft announced, as if no time had passed.

"Oh dear, madame."

"I fell off the bench!"

"I am so sorry, madame."

"It was the middle of the night! Do you know what I did, boy?"

I shook my head.

"I called the police!"

She stared up at the ceiling and grinned sedately, exposing a crowded row of long gray teeth. Not one was missing. "What do you say to that, boy?"

As stunned as I was, I knew what I had to say. With no hesitation at all, I cried out, "Splendid!"

Mala laughed then. Her voice was full of kindness, her eyes bright with amusement. I had never heard her laugh before, and it was loud enough so that Mrs. Croft had heard, too. She turned to Mala and glared.

"Who is she, boy?"

"She is my wife, madame."

Mrs. Croft pressed her head at an angle against the cushion to get a better look. "Can you play the piano?"

"No, madame," Mala replied.

"Then stand up!"

Mala rose to her feet, adjusting the end of her sari over her head and holding it to her chest, and, for the first time since her arrival, I felt sympathy. I remembered my first days in London, learning how to take the Tube to Russell Square, riding an escalator for the first time, being unable to understand that when the man cried "piper" it meant "paper," being unable to decipher, for a whole year, that the conductor said "mind the gap" as the train pulled away from each station. Like me, Mala had traveled far from home, not knowing where she was going, or what she would find, for no reason other than to be my wife. As strange as it seemed, I knew in my heart that one day her death would affect me, and stranger still, that mine would affect her. I wanted somehow to explain this to Mrs. Croft, who was still scrutinizing Mala from top to toe with what seemed to be placid disdain. I wondered if Mrs. Croft had ever seen a woman in a sari, with a dot painted on her forehead and bracelets stacked on her wrists. I wondered what she would object to. I wondered if she could see the red dye still vivid on Mala's feet, all but obscured by the bottom edge of her sari. At last Mrs. Croft declared, with the equal measures of disbelief and delight I knew well:

"She is a perfect lady!"

Now it was I who laughed. I did so quietly, and Mrs. Croft did not hear me. But Mala had heard, and, for the first time, we looked at each other and smiled.

I like to think of that moment in Mrs. Croft's parlor as the moment when the distance between Mala and me began to lessen. Although we were not yet fully in love, I like to think of the months that followed as a honeymoon of sorts. Together we explored the city and met other Bengalis, some of whom are still friends today. We discovered that a man named Bill sold fresh fish on Prospect Street, and that a shop in Harvard Square called Cardullo's sold bay leaves and cloves. In the evenings we walked to the Charles River to watch sailboats drift across the water, or had ice cream cones in Harvard Yard. We bought an Instamatic camera with which to document our life together, and I took pictures of her posing in front of the Prudential building, so that she could send them to her parents. At night we kissed, shy at first but quickly bold, and discovered pleasure and solace in each other's arms. I told her about my voyage on the SS *Roma*, and about Finsbury Park and the YMCA, and my evenings on the bench with Mrs. Croft. When I told her stories about my mother, she wept. It was Mala who consoled me when, reading the *Globe* one evening, I came across Mrs. Croft's obituary. I had not thought of her in several months—by then those six weeks of the summer were already a remote interlude in my past—but when I learned of her death I was stricken, so much so that when Mala looked up from her knitting she found me staring at the wall, the newspaper neglected in my lap, unable to speak. Mrs. Croft's was the first death I mourned in America, for hers was the first life I had admired; she had left this world at last, ancient and alone, never to return.

As for me, I have not strayed much farther. Mala and I live in a town about twenty miles from Boston, on a tree-lined street much like Mrs. Croft's, in a house we own, with a garden that saves us from buying tomatoes in summer, and room for guests. We are American citizens now, so that we can collect social security when it is time. Though we visit Calcutta every few years, and bring back more drawstring pajamas and Darjeeling tea, we have decided to grow old here. I work in a small college library. We have a son who attends Harvard University. Mala no longer drapes the end of her sari over her head, or weeps at night for her parents, but occasionally she weeps for our son. So we drive to Cambridge to visit him, or bring him home for a weekend, so that he can eat rice with us with his hands, and speak in Bengali, things we sometimes worry he will no longer do after we die.

Whenever we make that drive, I always make it a point to take Massachusetts Avenue, in spite of the traffic. I barely recognize the buildings now, but each time I am there I return instantly to those six weeks as if they were only the other day, and I slow down and point to Mrs. Croft's street, saying to my son, here was my first home in America, where I lived with a woman who was 103. "Remember?" Mala says, and smiles, amazed, as I am, that there was ever a time that we were strangers. My son always expresses his astonishment, not at Mrs. Croft's age, but at how little I paid in rent, a fact nearly as inconceivable to him as a flag on the moon was to a woman born in 1866. In my son's eyes I see the ambition that had first hurled me across the world. In a few years he will graduate and pave his way, alone and unprotected. But I remind myself that he has a father who is still living, a mother who is happy and strong. Whenever he is discouraged, I tell him that if I can survive on three continents, then there is no obstacle he cannot conquer. While the astronauts, heroes forever, spent mere hours on the moon, I have remained in this new world for nearly thirty years. I know that my achievement is quite ordinary. I am not the only man to seek his fortune far from home, and certainly I am not the first. Still, there are times I am bewildered by each mile I have traveled, each meal I have eaten, each person I have known, each room in which I have slept. As ordinary as it all appears, there are times when it is beyond my imagination.

On Not Winning the Nobel Prize (2007)

Doris Lessing

I am standing in a doorway looking through clouds of blowing dust to where I am told there is still uncut forest. Yesterday I drove through miles of stumps, and charred remains of fires where, in '56, there was the most wonderful forest I have ever seen, all now destroyed. People have to eat. They have to get fuel for fires.

This is north-west Zimbabwe in the early eighties, and I am visiting a friend who was a teacher in a school in London. He is here "to help Africa," as we put it. He is a gently idealistic soul and what he found in this school shocked him into a depression, from which it was hard to recover. This school is like every other built after Independence. It consists of four large brick rooms side by side, put straight into the dust, one two three four, with a half room at one end, which is the library. In these classrooms are blackboards, but my friend keeps the chalks in his pocket, as otherwise they would be stolen. There is no atlas or globe in the school, no textbooks, no exercise books, or biros. In the library there are no books of the kind the pupils would like to read, but only tomes from American universities, hard even to lift, rejects from white libraries, or novels with titles like *Weekend in Paris* and *Felicity Finds Love*.

There is a goat trying to find sustenance in some aged grass. The headmaster has embezzled the school funds and is suspended, arousing the question familiar to all of us but usually in more august contexts: How is it these people behave like this when they must know everyone is watching them?

My friend doesn't have any money because everyone, pupils and teachers, borrow from him when he is paid and will probably never pay him back. The pupils range from six to twenty-six, because some who did not get schooling as children are here to make it up. Some pupils walk many miles every morning, rain or shine and across rivers. They cannot do homework because there is no electricity in the villages, and you can't study easily by the light of a burning log. The girls have to fetch water and cook before they set off for school and when they get back.

As I sit with my friend in his room, people drop in shyly, and everyone begs for books. "Please send us books when you get back to London," one man says. "They taught us to read but we have no books." Everybody I met, everyone, begged for books.

I was there some days. The dust blew. The pumps had broken and the women were having to fetch water from the river. Another idealistic teacher from England was rather ill after seeing what this "school" was like.

On the last day they slaughtered the goat. They cut it into bits and cooked it in a great tin. This was the much anticipated end-of-term feast: boiled goat and porridge. I drove away while it was still going on, back through the charred remains and stumps of the forest.

I do not think many of the pupils of this school will get prizes.

The next day I am to give a talk at a school in North London, a very good school, whose name we all know. It is a school for boys, with beautiful buildings and gardens.

These children here have a visit from some well known person every week, and it is in the nature of things that these may be fathers, relatives, even mothers of the pupils. A visit from a celebrity is not unusual for them.

As I talk to them, the school in the blowing dust of north-west Zimbabwe is in my mind, and I look at the mildly expectant English faces in front of me and try to tell them about what I have seen in the last week. Classrooms without books, without textbooks, or an atlas, or even a map pinned to a wall. A school where the teachers beg to be sent books to tell them how to teach, they being only eighteen or nineteen themselves. I tell these English boys how everybody begs for books: "Please send us books." I am sure that anyone who has ever given a speech will know that moment when the faces you are looking at are blank. Your listeners cannot hear what you are saying, there are no images in their minds to match what you are telling them—in this case the story of a school standing in dust clouds, where water is short, and where the end of term treat is a just-killed goat cooked in a great pot.

Is it really so impossible for these privileged students to imagine such bare poverty?

I do my best. They are polite.

I'm sure that some of them will one day win prizes.

Then, the talk is over. Afterwards I ask the teachers how the library is, and if the pupils read. In this privileged school, I hear what I always hear when I go to such schools and even universities.

"You know how it is," one of the teacher's says. "A lot of the boys have never read at all, and the library is only half used."

Yes, indeed we do know how it is. All of us.

We are in a fragmenting culture, where our certainties of even a few decades ago are questioned and where it is common for young men and women, who have had years of education, to know nothing of the world, to have read nothing, knowing only some speciality or other, for instance, computers.

What has happened to us is an amazing invention—computers and the internet and TV. It is a revolution. This is not the first revolution the human race has dealt with. The printing revolution, which did not take place in a matter of a few decades, but took much longer, transformed our minds and ways of thinking. A foolhardy lot, we accepted it all, as we always do, never asked, What is going to happen to us now, with this invention of print? In the same way, we never thought to ask, How will our lives, our way of thinking, be changed by this internet, which has seduced a whole generation with its inanities so that even quite reasonable people will confess that once they are hooked, it is hard to cut free, and they may find a whole day has passed in blogging etc.

Very recently, anyone even mildly educated would respect learning, education, and our great store of literature. Of course, we all know that when this happy state was with us, people would pretend to read, would pretend respect for learning. But it is on record that working men and women longed for books, and this is evidenced by the founding of working men's libraries and institutes, the colleges of the 18th and 19th centuries.

Reading, books, used to be part of a general education.

Older people, talking to young ones, must understand just how much of an education reading was, because the young ones know so much less. And if children cannot read, it is because they have not read.

We all know this sad story.

But we do not know the end of it.

We think of the old adage, "Reading maketh a full man"—and forgetting about jokes to do with over-eating—reading makes a woman and a man full of information, of history, of all kinds of knowledge.

But we in the West are not the only people in the world. Not long ago a friend who had been in Zimbabwe told me about a village where people had not eaten for three days, but they were still talking about books and how to get them, about education.

I belong to an organisation which started out with the intention of getting books into the villages. There was a group of people who in another connection had travelled Zimbabwe at its grass roots. They told me that the villages, unlike what is reported, are full of intelligent people, teachers retired, teachers on leave, children on holidays, old people. I myself paid for a little survey to discover what people in Zimbabwe want to read, and found the results were the same as those of a Swedish survey I had not known about. People want to read the same kinds of books that we in Europe want to read—novels of all kinds, science fiction, poetry, detective stories, plays, and do-it-yourself books, like how to open a bank account. All of Shakespeare too. A problem with finding books for villagers is that they don't know what is available, so a set book, like the *Mayor of Casterbridge*, becomes popular simply because it just happens to be there. *Animal Farm*, for obvious reasons, is the most popular of all novels.

Our organisation was helped from the very start by Norway, and then by Sweden. Without this kind of support our supplies of books would have dried up. We got books from wherever we could. Remember, a good paperback from England costs a month's wages in Zimbabwe: that was before Mugabe's reign of terror. Now with inflation, it would cost several years' wages. But having taken a box of books out to a village—and remember there is a terrible shortage of petrol—I can tell you that the box was greeted with tears. The library may be a plank on bricks under a tree. And within a week there will be literacy classes—people who can read teaching those who can't, citizenship classes—and in one remote village, since there were no novels written in the language Tonga, a couple of lads sat down to write novels in Tonga. There are six or so main languages in Zimbabwe and there are novels in all of them: violent, incestuous, full of crime and murder.

It is said that a people gets the government it deserves, but I do not think it is true of Zimbabwe. And we must remember that this respect and hunger for books comes, not from Mugabe's regime, but from the one before it, the whites. It is an astonishing phenomenon, this hunger for books, and it can be seen everywhere from Kenya down to the Cape of Good Hope.

This links improbably with a fact: I was brought up in what was virtually a mud hut, thatched. This kind of house has been built always, everywhere there are reeds or grass, suitable mud, poles for walls. Saxon England for example. The one I was brought up in had four rooms, one beside another, and it was full of books. Not only did my parents take books from England to Africa, but my mother ordered books by post from England for her children. Books arrived in great brown paper parcels, and they were the joy of my young life. A mud hut, but full of books.

Even today I get letters from people living in a village that might not have electricity or running water, just like our family in our elongated mud hut. "I shall be a writer too," they say, "because I've the same kind of house you lived in."

But here is the difficulty, no?

Writing, writers, do not come out of houses without books.

There is the gap. There is the difficulty.

I have been looking at the speeches by some of your recent prizewinners. Take the magnificent Pamuk. He said his father had 500 books. His talent did not come out of the air, he was connected with the great tradition.

Take V.S. Naipaul. He mentions that the Indian Vedas were close behind the memory of his family. His father encouraged him to write, and when he got to England he would visit the British Library. So he was close to the great tradition.

Let us take John Coetzee. He was not only close to the great tradition, he was the tradition: he taught literature in Cape Town. And how sorry I am that I was never in one of his classes, taught by that wonderfully brave, bold mind.

In order to write, in order to make literature, there must be a close connection with libraries, books, with the Tradition.

I have a friend from Zimbabwe, a Black writer. He taught himself to read from the labels on jam jars, the labels on preserved fruit cans. He was brought up in an area I have driven through, an area for rural blacks. The earth is grit and gravel, there are low sparse bushes. The huts are poor, nothing like the well cared-for huts of the better off. A school—but like one I have described. He found a discarded children's encyclopaedia on a rubbish heap and taught himself from that.

On Independence in 1980 there was a group of good writers in Zimbabwe, truly a nest of singing birds. They were bred in old Southern Rhodesia, under the whites—the mission schools, the better schools. Writers are not made in Zimbabwe. Not easily, not under Mugabe.

All the writers travelled a difficult road to literacy, let alone to becoming writers. I would say learning to read from the printed labels on jam jars and discarded encyclopaedias was not uncommon. And we are talking about people hungering for standards of education beyond them, living in huts with many children—an overworked mother, a fight for food and clothing.

Yet despite these difficulties, writers came into being. And we should also remember that this was Zimbabwe, conquered less than a hundred years before. The grandparents of these people might have been storytellers working in the oral tradition. In one or two generations there was the transition from stories remembered and passed on, to print, to books. What an achievement.

Books, literally wrested from rubbish heaps and the detritus of the white man's world. But a sheaf of paper is one thing, a published book quite another. I have had several accounts sent to me of the publishing scene in Africa. Even in more privileged places like North Africa, with its different tradition, to talk of a publishing scene is a dream of possibilities.

Here I am talking about books never written, writers that could not make it because the publishers are not there. Voices unheard. It is not possible to estimate this great waste of talent, of potential. But even before that stage of a book's creation which demands a publisher, an advance, encouragement, there is something else lacking.

Writers are often asked, How do you write? With a wordprocessor? an electric typewriter? a quill? longhand? But the essential question is, "Have you found a space, that empty space, which should surround you when you write?" Into that space, which is like a form of listening, of attention, will come the words, the words your characters will speak, ideas—inspiration.

If a writer cannot find this space, then poems and stories may be stillborn.

When writers talk to each other, what they discuss is always to do with this imaginative space, this other time. "Have you found it? Are you holding it fast?"

Let us now jump to an apparently very different scene. We are in London, one of the big cities. There is a new writer. We cynically enquire, Is she good-looking? If this is a man, charismatic? Handsome? We joke but it is not a joke.

This new find is acclaimed, possibly given a lot of money. The buzzing of paparazzi begins in their poor ears. They are feted, lauded, whisked about the world. Us old ones, who have seen it all, are sorry for this neophyte, who has no idea of what is really happening.

He, she, is flattered, pleased.

But ask in a year's time what he or she is thinking—I've heard them: "This is the worst thing that could have happened to me," they say.

Some much publicised new writers haven't written again, or haven't written what they wanted to, meant to.

And we, the old ones, want to whisper into those innocent ears. "Have you still got your space? Your soul, your own and necessary place where your own voices may speak to you, you alone, where you may dream. Oh, hold onto it, don't let it go."

My mind is full of splendid memories of Africa which I can revive and look at whenever I want. How about those sunsets, gold and purple and orange, spreading across the sky at evening. How about butterflies and moths and bees on the aromatic bushes of the Kalahari? Or, sitting on the pale grassy banks of the Zambesi, the water dark and glossy, with all the birds of Africa darting about. Yes, elephants, giraffes, lions and the rest, there were plenty of those, but how about the sky at night, still unpolluted, black and wonderful, full of restless stars.

There are other memories too. A young African man, eighteen perhaps, in tears, standing in what he hopes will be his "library." A visiting American seeing that his library had no books, had sent a crate of them. The young man had taken each one out, reverently, and wrapped them in plastic. "But," we say, "these books were sent to be read, surely?" "No," he replies, "they will get dirty, and where will I get any more?"

This young man wants us to send him books from England to use as teaching guides.

"I only did four years in senior school," he says, "but they never taught me to teach."

I have seen a teacher in a school where there were no textbooks, not even a chalk for the blackboard. He taught his class of six to eighteen year olds by moving stones in the dust, chanting "Two times two is . . ." and so on. I have seen a girl, perhaps not more than twenty, also lacking textbooks, exercise books, biros, seen her teach the A B C by scratching the letters in the dirt with a stick, while the sun beat down and the dust swirled.

We are witnessing here that great hunger for education in Africa, anywhere in the Third World, or whatever we call parts of the world where parents long to get an education for their children which will take them out of poverty.

I would like you to imagine yourselves somewhere in Southern Africa, standing in an Indian store, in a poor area, in a time of bad drought. There is a line of people, mostly women, with every kind of container for water. This store gets a bowser of precious water every afternoon from the town, and here the people wait.

The Indian is standing with the heels of his hands pressed down on the counter, and he is watching a black woman, who is bending over a wadge of paper that looks as if it has been torn from a book. She is reading *Anna Karenin*.

She is reading slowly, mouthing the words. It looks a difficult book. This is a young woman with two little children clutching at her legs. She is pregnant. The Indian is distressed, because the young woman's head-scarf, which should be white, is yellow with dust. Dust lies between her breasts and on her arms. This man is distressed because of the lines of people, all thirsty. He doesn't have enough water for them. He is angry because he knows there are people dying out there, beyond the dust clouds. His older brother had been here holding the fort, but he had said he needed a break, had gone into town, really rather ill, because of the drought.

This man is curious. He says to the young woman, "What are you reading?"

"It is about Russia," says the girl.

"Do you know where Russia is?" He hardly knows himself.

The young woman looks straight at him, full of dignity, though her eyes are red from dust, "I was best in the class. My teacher said I was best."

The young woman resumes her reading. She wants to get to the end of the paragraph.

The Indian looks at the two little children and reaches for some Fanta, but the mother says, "Fanta makes them thirstier."

The Indian knows he shouldn't do this but he reaches down to a great plastic container beside him, behind the counter, and pours out two mugs of water, which he hands to the children. He watches while the girl looks at her children drinking, her mouth moving. He gives her a mug of water. It hurts him to see her drinking it, so painfully thirsty is she.

Now she hands him her own plastic water container, which he fills. The young woman and the children watch him closely so that he doesn't spill any.

She is bending again over the book. She reads slowly. The paragraph fascinates her and she reads it again.

> Varenka, with her white kerchief over her black hair, surrounded by the children and gaily and good-humouredly busy with them, and at the same time visibly excited at the possibility of an offer of marriage from a man she cared for, looked very attractive. Koznyshev walked by her side and kept casting admiring glances at her. Looking at her, he recalled all the delightful things he had heard from her lips, all the good he knew about her, and became more and more conscious that the feeling he had for her was something rare, something he had felt but once before, long, long ago, in his early youth. The joy of being near her increased step by step, and at last reached such a point that, as he put a huge birch mushroom with a slender stalk and up-curling top into her basket, he looked into her eyes and, noting the flush of glad and frightened agitation that suffused her face, he was confused himself, and in silence gave her a smile that said too much.

This lump of print is lying on the counter, together with some old copies of magazines, some pages of newspapers with pictures of girls in bikinis.

It is time for the woman to leave the haven of the Indian store, and set off back along the four miles to her village. Outside, the lines of waiting women clamour and complain. But still the Indian lingers. He knows what it will cost this girl—going back home, with the two clinging children. He would give her the piece of prose that so fascinates her, but he cannot really believe this splinter of a girl with her great belly can really understand it.

Why is perhaps a third of *Anna Karenin* here on this counter in a remote Indian store? It is like this.

A certain high official, from the United Nations as it happens, bought a copy of this novel in a bookshop before he set out on his journey to cross several oceans and seas. On the plane, settled in his business class seat, he tore the book into three parts. He looked around his fellow passengers as he did this, knowing he would see looks of shock, curiosity, but some of amusement. When he was settled, his seat belt tight, he said aloud to whomever could hear, "I always do this when I've a long trip. You don't want to have to hold up some heavy great book." The novel was a paperback, but, true, it is a long book. This man is well used to people listening when he spoke. "I always do this, travelling," he confided. "Travelling at all these days, is hard enough." And as soon as people were settling down, he opened his part of *Anna Karenin,* and read. When people looked his way, curiously or not, he confided in them. "No, it really is the only way to travel." He knew the novel, liked it, and this original mode of reading did add spice to what was after all a well known book.

When he reached the end of a section of the book, he called the air hostess, and sent the chapters back to his secretary, travelling in the cheaper seats. This caused much interest, condemnation, certainly curiosity, every time a section of the great Russian novel arrived, mutilated but readable, in the back part of the plane. Altogether, this clever way of reading *Anna Karenin* makes an impression, and probably no one there would forget it.

Meanwhile, in the Indian store, the young woman is holding on to the counter, her little children clinging to her skirts. She wears jeans, since she is a modern woman, but over them she has put on the heavy woollen skirt, part of the traditional dress of her people: her children can easily cling onto its thick folds.

She sends a thankful look to the Indian, whom she knew liked her and was sorry for her, and she steps out into the blowing clouds.

The children are past crying, and their throats are full of dust.

This was hard, oh yes, it was hard, this stepping, one foot after another, through the dust that lay in soft deceiving mounds under her feet. Hard, but she was used to hardship, was she not? Her mind was on the story she had been reading. She was thinking, she is just like me, in her white headscarf, and she is looking after children, too. I could be her, that Russian girl. And the man there, he loves her and will ask her to marry him. She had not finished more than that one paragraph. Yes, she thinks, a man will come for me, and take me away from all this, take me and the children, yes, he will love me and look after me.

She steps on. The can of water is heavy on her shoulders. On she goes. The children can hear the water slopping about. Half way she stops, sets down the can.

Her children are whimpering and touching it. She thinks that she cannot open it, because dust would blow in. There is no way she can open the can until she gets home.

"Wait," she tells her children, "wait."

She has to pull herself together and go on.

She thinks, My teacher said there is a library, bigger than the supermarket, a big building and it is full of books. The young woman is smiling as she moves on, the dust blowing in her face. I am clever, she thinks. Teacher said I am clever. The cleverest in the school—she said I was. My children will be clever, like me. I will take them to the library, the place full of books, and they will go to school, and they will be teachers—my teacher told me I could be a teacher. My children will live far from here, earning money. They will live near the big library and enjoy a good life.

You may ask how that piece of the Russian novel ever ended up on that counter in the Indian store?

It would make a pretty story. Perhaps someone will tell it.

On goes that poor girl, held upright by thoughts of the water she will give her children once home, and drink a little of herself. On she goes, through the dreaded dusts of an African drought.

We are a jaded lot, we in our threatened world. We are good for irony and even cynicism. Some words and ideas we hardly use, so worn out have they become. But we may want to restore some words that have lost their potency.

We have a treasure-house of literature, going back to the Egyptians, the Greeks, the Romans. It is all there, this wealth of literature, to be discovered again and again by whoever is lucky enough to come upon it. A treasure. Suppose it did not exist. How impoverished, how empty we would be.

We own a legacy of languages, poems, histories, and it is not one that will ever be exhausted. It is there, always.

We have a bequest of stories, tales from the old storytellers, some of whose names we know, but some not. The storytellers go back and back, to a clearing in the forest where a great fire burns, and the old shamans dance and sing, for our heritage of stories began in fire, magic, the spirit world. And that is where it is held, today.

Ask any modern storyteller and they will say there is always a moment when they are touched with fire, with what we like to call inspiration, and this goes back and back to the beginning of our race, to the great winds that shaped us and our world.

The storyteller is deep inside every one of us. The story-maker is always with us. Let us suppose our world is ravaged by war, by the horrors that we all of us easily imagine. Let us suppose floods wash through our cities, the seas rise. But the storyteller will be there, for it is our imaginations which shape us, keep us, create us—for good and for ill. It is our stories that will recreate us, when we are torn, hurt, even destroyed. It is the storyteller, the dream-maker, the myth-maker, that is our phoenix, that represents us at our best, and at our most creative.

That poor girl trudging through the dust, dreaming of an education for her children, do we think that we are better than she is—we, stuffed full of food, our cupboards full of clothes, stifling in our superfluities?

I think it is that girl, and the women who were talking about books and an education when they had not eaten for three days, that may yet define us.

Original Text of Speech to Be Delivered at the Lincoln Memorial (1963)

John Lewis

We march today for jobs and freedom, but we have nothing to be proud of. For hundreds and thousands of our brothers are not here. They have no money for their transportation, for they are receiving starvation wages . . . or no wages, at all.

In good conscience, we cannot support the administration's civil rights bill, for it is too little, and too late. There's not one thing in the bill that will protect our people from police brutality.

This bill will not protect young children and old women from police dogs and fire hoses, [for] engaging in peaceful demonstrations . . .

The voting section of this bill will not help thousands of black citizens who want to vote. It will not help the citizens of Mississippi, of Alabama, and Georgia, who are qualified to vote, but lack a 6th Grade education. "One man, one vote," is the African cry. It is ours, too. (It must be ours.)

• • •

We are now involved in . . . revolution. This nation is still a place of cheap political leaders who build their careers on immoral compromise and ally themselves with open forms of political, economic and social exploitation. What political leader here can stand up and say, "My party is the party of principles"? The party of Kennedy is also the party of Eastland. The party of Javits is also the party of Goldwater. Where is *our* party?

In some parts of the South we work in the fields from sun-up to sun-down for $12 a week. In Albany, Georgia, nine of our leaders have been indicted not by Dixiecrats but by the Federal Government for peaceful protest. But what did the Federal Government do when Albany's Deputy Sheriff beat Attorney C. B. King and left him half dead? What did the Federal Government do when local police officials kicked and assaulted the pregnant wife of Slater King, and she lost her baby?

It seems to me that the Albany indictment is part of a conspiracy on the part of the Federal Government and local politicians in the interest of expediency.

I want to know, which side is the Federal Government on?

The revolution is at hand, and we must free ourselves of the chains of political and economic slavery. The non-violent revolution is saying, "We will not wait for the courts to act, for we have been waiting for hundreds of years. We will not wait for the President, the Justice Department, nor Congress, but we will take matters into our own hands and create a source of power, outside any national structure that could and would assure us a victory." To those who have said, "Be Patient and Wait," we must say that, "Patience is a dirty and nasty word." We cannot be patient, we do not want to be free gradually, we want our freedom, and we want it now. We cannot depend on any political party, for both the Democrats and Republicans have betrayed the basic principles of the Declaration of Independence.

We all recognize the fact that if any radical social, political and economic changes are to take place in our society, the people, the masses, must bring them about. In the struggle we must seek more than civil rights; we must work for the community of love, peace and true brotherhood. Our minds, souls, and hearts cannot rest until freedom and justice exist for *all the people*.

The revolution is a serious one. Mr. Kennedy is trying to take the revolution out of the street and put in the courts. Listen, Mr. Kennedy, listen, Mr. Congressman, listen, fellow citizens, the black masses are on the march for jobs and freedom, and we must say to the politicians that there won't be a "cooling-off" period.

•   •   •

We won't stop now. All the forces of Eastland, Barnett, Wallace, and Thurmond won't stop this revolution. The time will come when we will not confine our marching to Washington. We will march through the South, through the Heart of Dixie, the way Sherman did. We shall pursue our own "scorched earth" policy and burn Jim Crow to the ground nonviolently. We shall fragment the South into a thousand pieces and put them back together in the image of democracy. We will make the action of the past few months look petty. And I say to you, WAKE UP AMERICA!

Message to the Grassroots (1963)

Malcolm X

We want to have just an off-the-cuff chat between you and me, us. We want to talk right down to earth in a language that everybody here can easily understand. We all agree tonight, all of the speakers have agreed, that America has a very serious problem. Not only does America have a very serious problem, but our people have a very serious problem. America's problem is us. We're her problem. The only reason she has a problem is she doesn't want us here. And every time you look at yourself, be you black, brown, red or yellow, a so-called Negro, you represent a person who poses such a serious problem for America because you're not wanted. Once you face this as a fact, then you can start plotting a course that will make you appear intelligent, instead of unintelligent.

What you and I need to do is learn to forget our differences. When we come together, we don't come together as Baptists or Methodists. You don't catch hell because you're a Baptist, and you don't catch hell because you're a Methodist. You don't catch hell because you're a Methodist or Baptist, you don't catch hell because you're a Democrat or a Republican, you don't catch hell because you're a Mason or an Elk, and you sure don't catch hell because you're an American; because if you were an American, you wouldn't catch hell. You catch hell because you're a black man. You catch hell, all of us catch hell, for the same reason.

So we're all black people, so-called Negroes, second-class citizens, ex-slaves. You're nothing but an ex-slave. You don't like to be told that. But what else are you? You are ex-slaves. You didn't come here on the "Mayflower." You came here on a slave ship. In chains, like a horse, or a cow, or a chicken. And you were brought here by the people who came here on the "Mayflower," you were brought here by the so-called Pilgrims, or Founding Fathers. They were the ones who brought you here.

We have a common enemy. We have this in common: We have a common oppressor, a common exploiter, and a common discriminator. But once we all realize that we have a common enemy, then we unite on the basis of what we have in common. And what we have foremost in common is that enemy, the white man. He's an enemy to all of us. I know some of you all think that some of them aren't enemies. Time will tell.

In Bandung back in, I think, 1954, was the first unity meeting in centuries of black people. And once you study what happened at the Bandung conference, and the results of the Bandung conference, it actually serves as a model for the same procedure you and I can use to get our problems solved. At Bandung all the nations came together, the dark nations from Africa and Asia. Some of them were Buddhists, some of them were Muslims, some of them were Christians, some were Confucianists, some were atheists. Despite their religious differences, they came together. Some were communists, some were socialists, some were capitalists despite their economic and political differences, they came together. All of them were black, brown, red or yellow.

The number-one thing that was not allowed to attend the Bandung conference was the white man. He couldn't come. Once they excluded the white man, they found that they could get together. Once they kept him out, everybody else fell right in and fell in line. This is the thing that you and I have to understand. And these people who came together didn't have nuclear weapons, they didn't have jet planes, they didn't have all of the heavy armaments that the white man has. But they had unity.

They were able to submerge their little petty differences and agree on one thing: That though one African came from Kenya and was being colonized by the Englishman, and another African came from the Congo and was being colonized by the Belgian, and another African came from Guinea and was being colonized by the French, and another came from Angola and was being colonized by the Portuguese, when they came to the Bandung conference, they looked at the Portuguese, and at the Frenchman, and at the Englishman, and at the Dutchman, and learned or realized the one thing that all of them had in common—they were all from Europe, they were all Europeans, blond, blue-eyed and white skins. They began to recognize who their enemy was. The same man that was colonizing our people in Kenya was colonizing our people in the Congo. The same one in the Congo was colonizing our people in South Africa, and in Southern Rhodesia, and in Burma, and in India, and in Afghanistan, and in Pakistan. They realized all over the world where the dark man was being oppressed, he was being oppressed by the white man; where the dark man was being exploited, he was being exploited by the white man. So they got together on this basis that they had a common enemy.

And when you and I here in Detroit and in Michigan and in America who have been awakened today look around us, we too realize here in America we all have a common enemy, whether he's in Georgia or Michigan, whether he's in California or New York. He's the same man—blue eyes and blond hair and pale skin—the same man. So what we have to do is what they did. They agreed to stop quarreling among themselves. Any little spat that they had, they'd settle it among themselves, go into a huddle—don't let the enemy know that you've got a disagreement.

Instead of airing our differences in public, we have to realize we're all the same family. And when you have a family squabble, you don't get out on the sidewalk. If you do, everybody calls you uncouth, unrefined, uncivilized, savage. If you don't make it at home, you settle it at home; you get in the closet, argue it out behind closed doors, and then when you come out on the street, you pose a common front, a united front. And this is what we need to do in the community, and in the city, and in the state. We need to stop airing our differences in front of the white man, put the white man out of our meetings, and then sit down and talk shop with each other. That's what we've got to do.

I would like to make a few comments concerning the difference between the black revolution and the Negro revolution. Are they both the same? And if they're not, what is the difference? What is the difference between a black revolution and a Negro revolution? First, what is a revolution? Sometimes I'm inclined to believe that many of our people are using this word "revolution" loosely, without taking careful consideration of what this word actually means, and what its historic characteristics are. When you study the historic nature of revolutions, the motive of a revolution, the objective of a revolution, the result of a revolution, and the methods used in a revolution, you may change words. You may devise another program, you may change your goal and you may change your mind.

Look at the American Revolution in 1776. That revolution was for what? For land. Why did they want land? Independence. How was it carried out? Bloodshed. Number one, it was based on land, the basis of independence. And the only way they could get it was bloodshed. The French Revolution—what was it based on? The landless against the landlord. What was it for? Land. How did they get it?

Bloodshed. Was no love lost, was no compromise, was no negotiation. I'm telling you—you don't know what a revolution is. Because when you find out what it is, you'll get back in the alley, you'll get out of the way.

The Russian Revolution—what was it based on? Land; the landless against the landlord. How did they bring it about? Bloodshed. You haven't got a revolution that doesn't involve bloodshed. And you're afraid to bleed. I said, you're afraid to bleed.

As long as the white man sent you to Korea, you bled. He sent you to Germany, you bled. He sent you to the South Pacific to fight the Japanese, you bled. You bleed for white people, but when it comes to seeing your own churches being bombed and little black girls murdered, you haven't got any blood. You bleed when the white man says bleed; you bite when the white man says bite; and you bark when the white man says bark. I hate to say this about us, but it's true. How are you going to be nonviolent in Mississippi, as violent as you were in Korea? How can you justify being nonviolent in Mississippi and Alabama, when your churches are being bombed, and your little girls are being murdered, and at the same time you are going to get violent with Hitler, and Tojo, and somebody else you don't even know?

If violence is wrong in America, violence is wrong abroad. If it is wrong to be violent defending black women and black children and black babies and black men, then it is wrong for America to draft us and make us violent abroad in defense of her. And if it is right for America to draft us, and teach us how to be violent in defense of her, then it is right for you and me to do whatever is necessary to defend our own people right here in this country.

The Chinese Revolution—they wanted land. They threw the British out, along with the Uncle Tom Chinese. Yes, they did. They set a good example. When I was in prison, I read an article—don't be shocked when I say that I was in prison. You're still in prison. That's what America means: prison. When I was in prison, I read an article in *Life* magazine showing a little Chinese girl, nine years old; her father was on his hands and knees and she was pulling the trigger because he was an Uncle Tom Chinaman. When they had the revolution over there, they took a whole generation of Uncle Toms and just wiped them out. And within ten years that little girl became a full-grown woman. No more Toms in China. And today it's one of the toughest, roughest, most feared countries on this earth—by the white man. Because there are no Uncle Toms over there.

Of all our studies, history is best qualified to reward our research. And when you see that you've got problems, all you have to do is examine the historic method used all over the world by others who have problems similar to yours. Once you see how they got theirs straight, then you know how you can get yours straight. There's been a revolution, a black revolution, going on in Africa. In Kenya, the Mau Mau were revolutionary; they were the ones who brought the word "Uhuru" to the fore. The Mau Mau, they were revolutionary, they believed in scorched earth, they knocked everything aside that got in their way, and their revolution also was based on land, a desire for land. In Algeria, the Northern part of Africa, a revolution took place. The Algerians were revolutionists, they wanted land. France offered to let them be integrated into France. They told France, to hell with France, they wanted some land, not some France. And they engaged in a bloody battle.

So I cite these various revolutions, brothers and sisters, to show you that you don't have a peaceful revolution. You don't have a turn-the-other-cheek revolution. There's no such thing as a nonviolent revolution. The only kind of revolution that is nonviolent is the Negro revolution. The only revolution in which the goal is loving your enemy is the Negro revolution. It's the only revolution in which the goal is a desegregated lunch counter, a desegregated theater, a desegregated park, and a desegregated public toilet; you can sit down next to white folks—on the toilet. That's no revolution. Revolution is based on land. Land is the basis of all independence. Land is the basis of freedom, justice, and equality.

The white man knows what a revolution is. He knows that the black revolution is world-wide in scope and in nature. The black revolution is sweeping Asia, is sweeping Africa, is rearing its head in Latin America. The Cuban Revolution—that's a revolution. They overturned the system. Revolution is in Asia, revolution is in Africa, and the white man is screaming because he sees revolution in Latin America. How do you think he'll react to you when you learn what a real revolution is? You don't know what a revolution is. If you did, you wouldn't use that word.

Revolution is bloody, revolution is hostile, revolution knows no compromise, revolution overturns and destroys everything that gets in its way. And you, sitting around here like a knot on the wall, saying, "I'm going to love these folks no matter how much they hate me." No, you need a revolution. Whoever heard of a revolution where they lock arms, as Rev. Cleage was pointing out beautifully, singing "We Shall Overcome"? You don't do that in a revolution. You don't do any singing, you're too busy swinging. It's based on land. A revolutionary wants land so he can set up his own nation, an independent nation. These Negroes aren't asking for any nation—they're trying to crawl back on the plantation.

When you want a nation, that's called nationalism. When the white man became involved in a revolution in this country against England, what was it for? He wanted this land so he could set up another white nation. That's white nationalism. The American Revolution was white nationalism. The French Revolution was white nationalism. The Russian Revolution too—yes, it was—white nationalism. You don't think so? Why do you think Khrushchev and Mao can't get their heads together? White nationalism. All the revolutions that are going on in Asia and Africa today are based on what?—black nationalism. A revolutionary is a black nationalist. He wants a nation. I was reading some beautiful words by Rev. Cleage, pointing out why he couldn't get together with someone else in the city because all of them were afraid of being identified with black nationalism. If you're afraid of black nationalism, you're afraid of revolution. And if you love revolution, you love black nationalism.

To understand this, you have to go back to what the young brother here referred to as the house Negro and the field Negro back during slavery. There were two kinds of slaves, the house Negro and the field Negro. The house Negroes—they lived in the house with master, they dressed pretty good, they ate good because they ate his food—what he left. They lived in the attic or the basement, but still they lived near the master; and they loved the master more than the master loved himself. They would give their life to save the master's house—quicker than the master would. If the master said, "We got a good house here," the house Negro would say, "Yeah, we got a good house here." Whenever the master said "we," he said "we." That's how you can tell a house Negro.

If the master's house caught on fire, the house Negro would fight harder to put the blaze out than the master would. If the master got sick, the house Negro would say, "What's the matter, boss, we sick?" WE sick! He identified himself with his master, more than his master identified with himself. And if you came to the house Negro and said, "Let's run away, let's escape, let's separate," the house Negro would look at you and say, "Man, you crazy. What you mean, separate? Where is there a better house than this? Where can I wear better clothes than this? Where can I eat better food than this?" That was that house Negro.

In those days he was called a "house nigger." And that's what we call them today, because we've still got some house niggers running around here.

This modern house Negro loves his master. He wants to live near him. He'll pay three times as much as the house is worth just to live near his master, and then brag about "I'm the only Negro out here." "I'm the only one on my job." "I'm the only one in this school." You're nothing but a house Negro. And if someone comes to you right now and says, "Let's separate," you say the same thing that the house Negro said on the plantation. "What you mean, separate? From America, this good white man? Where you going to get a better job than you get here?" I mean, this is what you say. "I ain't left nothing in Africa," that's what you say. Why, you left your mind in Africa.

On that same plantation, there was the field Negro. The field Negroes—those were the masses. There were always more Negroes in the field than there were Negroes in the house. The Negro in the field caught hell. He ate leftovers. In the house they ate high up on the hog. The Negro in the field didn't get anything but what was left of the insides of the hog. They call it "chitt'lings" nowadays. In those days they called them what they were—gut-eaters. That's what you were—gut-eaters. And some of you are still gut-eaters.

The field Negro was beaten from morning to night; he lived in a shack, in a hut; he wore old, castoff clothes. He hated his master. I say he hated his master. He was intelligent. That house Negro loved his master, but that field Negro—remember, they were in the majority, and they hated the master. When the house caught on fire, he didn't try to put it out; that field Negro prayed for a wind, for a breeze. When the master got sick, the field Negro prayed that he'd die. If someone came to the field Negro and said, "Let's separate, let's run," he didn't say "Where we going?" He'd say, "Any place is better than here." You've got field Negroes in America today. I'm a field Negro. The masses are the field Negroes. When they see this man's house on fire, you don't hear the little Negroes talking about "our government is in trouble." They say, "The government is in trouble." Imagine a Negro: "Our government"! I even heard one say "our astronauts." They won't even let him near the plant—and "our astronauts"! "Our Navy"—that's a Negro that is out of his mind, a Negro that is out of his mind.

Just as the slavemaster of that day used Tom, the house Negro, to keep the field Negroes in check, the same old slavemaster today has Negroes who are nothing but modern Uncle Toms, twentieth-century Uncle Toms, to keep you and me in check, to keep us under control, keep us passive and peaceful and nonviolent. That's Tom making you nonviolent. It's like when you go to the dentist, and the man's going to take your tooth. You're going to fight him when he starts pulling. So he squirts some stuff in your jaw called Novocain, to make you think they're not doing anything to you. So you sit there and because you've got all of that Novocain in your jaw, you suffer—peacefully. Blood running an down your jaw, and you don't know what's happening. Because someone has taught you to suffer—peacefully.

The white man does the same thing to you in the street, when he wants to put knots on your head and take advantage of you and not have to be afraid of your fighting back. To keep you from fighting back, he gets these old religious Uncle Toms to teach you and me, just like Novocain, to suffer peacefully. Don't stop suffering—just suffer peacefully. As Rev. Cleage pointed out, they say you should let your blood flow in the streets. This is a shame. You know he's a Christian preacher. If it's a shame to him, you know what it is to me.

There is nothing in our book, the *Koran*, that teaches us to suffer peacefully. Our religion teaches us to be intelligent. Be peaceful, be courteous, obey the law, respect everyone; but if someone puts his hand on you, send him to the cemetery. That's a good religion. In fact, that's that old-time religion. That's the one that Ma and Pa used to talk about: an eye for an eye, and a tooth for a tooth, and a head for a head, and a life for a life. That's a good religion. And nobody resents that kind of religion being taught but a wolf, who intends to make you his meal.

This is the way it is with the white man in America. He's a wolf and you're sheep. Any time a shepherd, a pastor, teaches you and me not to run from the white man and, at the same time, teaches us not to fight the white man, he's a traitor to you and me. Don't lay down a life all by itself. No, preserve your life, it's the best thing you've got. And if you've got to give it up, let it be even-steven.

The slavemaster took Tom and dressed him well, fed him well and even gave him a little education—a little education; gave him a long coat and a top hat and made all the other slaves look up to him. Then he used Tom to control them. The same strategy that was used in those days is used today, by the same white man. He takes a Negro, a so-called Negro, and makes him prominent, builds him up, publicizes him, makes him a celebrity. And then he becomes a spokesman for Negroes—and a Negro leader.

I would like to mention just one other thing quickly, and that is the method that the white man uses, how the white man uses the "big guns," or Negro leaders, against the Negro revolution. They are not a part of the Negro revolution. They are used against the Negro revolution.

When Martin Luther King failed to desegregate Albany, Georgia, the civil-rights struggle in America reached its low point. King became bankrupt almost, as a leader. The Southern Christian Leadership Conference was in financial trouble; and it was in trouble, period, with the people when they failed to desegregate Albany, Georgia. Other Negro civil-rights leaders of so-called national stature became fallen idols. As they became fallen idols, began to lose their prestige and influence, local Negro leaders began to stir up the masses. In Cambridge, Maryland, Gloria Richardson; in Danville, Virginia, and other parts of the country, local leaders began to stir up our people at the grass-roots level. This was never done by these Negroes of national stature. They control you, but they have never incited you or excited you. They control you, they contain you, they have kept you on the plantation.

As soon as King failed in Birmingham, Negroes took to the streets. King went out to California to a big rally and raised I don't know how many thousands of dollars. He came to Detroit and had a march and raised some more thousands of dollars. And recall, right after that Roy Wilkins attacked King. He accused King and CORE (Congress Of Racial Equality) of starting trouble everywhere and then making the NAACP [National Association for the Advancement of Colored People] get them out of jail and spend a lot of money; they accused King and CORE of raising all the money and not paying it back. This happened; I've got it in documented evidence in the newspaper. Roy started attacking King, and King started attacking Roy, and Farmer started attacking both of them. And as these Negroes of national stature began to attack each other, they began to lose their control of the Negro masses.

The Negroes were out there in the streets. They were talking about how they were going to march on Washington. Right at that time Birmingham had exploded, and the Negroes in Birmingham—remember, they also exploded. They began to stab the crackers in the back and bust them up 'side their head—yes, they did. That's when Kennedy sent in the troops, down in Birmingham. After that, Kennedy got on the television and said "this is a moral issue." That's when he said he was going to put out a civil-rights bill. And when he mentioned civil-rights bill and the Southern crackers started talking about how they were going to boycott or filibuster it, then the Negroes started talking—about what? That they were going to march on Washington, march on the Senate, march on the White House, march on the Congress, and tie it up, bring it to a halt, not let the government proceed. They even said they were going out to the airport and lay down on the runway and not let any airplanes land. I'm telling you what they said. That was revolution. That was revolution. That was the black revolution.

It was the grass roots out there in the street. It scared the white man to death, scared the white power structure in Washington, D.C., to death; I was there. When they found out that this black steamroller was going to come down on the capital, they called in Wilkins, they called in Randolph, they called in these national Negro leaders that you respect and told them, "Call it off." Kennedy said, "Look, you all are letting this thing go too far." And Old Tom said, "Boss, I can't stop it, because I didn't start it." I'm telling you what they said. They said, "I'm not even in it, much less at the head of it." They said, "These Negroes are doing things on their own. They're running ahead of us." And that old shrewd fox, he said, "If you all aren't in it, I'll put you in it. I'll put you at the head of it. I'll endorse it. I'll welcome it. I'll help it. I'll join it."

A matter of hours went by. They had a meeting at the Carlyle Hotel in New York City. The Carlyle Hotel is owned by the Kennedy family; that's the hotel Kennedy spent the night at, two nights ago; it belongs to his family. A philanthropic society headed by a white man named Stephen Currier called all the top civil-rights leaders together at the Carlyle Hotel. And he told them, "By you fighting each other, you are destroying the civil-rights movement. And since you're fighting over money from the liberals, let us set up what is known as the Council for United Civil Rights Leadership. Let's form this council and all the civil-rights organizations will belong to it, and we'll use it for fund-raising purposes." Let me show you how tricky the white man is. As soon as they got formed, they elected Whitney Young as its chairman, and who do you think became the co-chairman? Stephen Currier, the white man, a millionaire. Powell was talking bout it down at Cobo Hall today. This is what he was talking about. Powell knows it happened. Randolph knows it happened. Wilkins knows it happened. King knows it happened. Every one of that Big Si— they know happened.

Once they formed it, with the white man over it, he promised them and gave them $800,000 to split up among the Big Six; and told them that after the march was over they'd give them $700,000 more. A million and a half dollars—split up between leaders that you have been following, going to jail for, crying crocodile tears for. And they're nothing but Frank James and Jesse James and the what-do-you-call-'em brothers.

As soon as they got the setup organized, the white man made available to them top public-relations experts, opened the news media across the country at their disposal, which then began to project these Big Six as the leaders of the march. Originally they weren't even in the march. You were talking this march talk on Hastings Street, you were talking march talk on Lenox Avenue, and on Fillmore Street, and on Central Avenue, and 32nd Street and 63rd Street. That's where the march talk was being talked. But the white man put the Big Six at the head of it; made them the march. They became the march. They took it over. And the first move they made after they took it over, they invited Walter Reuther, a white man; they invited a priest, a rabbi, and an old white preacher, yes, an old white preacher. The same white element that put Kennedy into power—labor, the Catholics, the Jews, and liberal Protestants; the same clique that put Kennedy in power, joined the march on Washington.

It's just like when you've got some coffee that's too black, which means it's too strong. What do you do? You integrate it with cream, you make it weak. But if you pour too much cream in it, you won't even know you ever had coffee. It used to be hot, it becomes cool. It used to be strong, it becomes weak. It used to wake you up, now it puts you to sleep. This is what they did with the march on Washington. They joined it. They didn't integrate it, they infiltrated it. They joined it, became a part of it, took it over. And as they took it over, it lost its militancy. It ceased to be angry, it ceased to be hot, it ceased to be uncompromising. Why, it even ceased to be a march. It became a picnic, a circus. Nothing but a circus, with clowns and all. You had one right here in Detroit—I saw it on television—with clowns leading it, white clowns and black clowns. I know you don't like what I'm saying, but I'm going to tell you anyway. Because I can prove what I'm saying. If you think I'm telling you wrong, you bring me Martin Luther King and A. Philip Randolph and James Farmer and those other three, and see if they'll deny it over a microphone.

No, it was a sellout. It was a takeover. When James Baldwin came in from Paris, they wouldn't let him talk, because they couldn't make him go by the script. Burt Lancaster read the speech that Baldwin was supposed to make; they wouldn't let Baldwin get up there, because they know Baldwin is liable to say anything. They controlled it so tight, they told those Negroes what time to hit town, how to come, where to stop, what signs to carry, what song to sing, what speech they could make, and what they couldn't make; and then told them to get out of town by sundown. And every one of those Toms was out of town by sundown. Now I know you don't like my saying this. But I can back it up. It was a circus, a performance that beat anything Hollywood could ever do, the performance of the year. Reuther and those other three should get an Academy Award for the best actors because they acted like they really loved Negroes and a whole lot of Negroes. And the six Negro leaders should get an award too, for the best supporting cast.

Eight Levels of Charity (1180)

Maimonides

There are eight degrees of charity, one higher than the other.

The highest degree, exceeded by none, is that of one who assists a poor person by providing him with a gift or a loan or by accepting him into a business partnership or by helping him find employment—in a word by putting him in a situation where he can dispense with other people's aid. With reference to such aid it is said, 'You shall strengthen him, be he a stranger or a settler, he shall live with you' (Lev. 25: 35), which means: strengthen him in such a manner that his falling into want is prevented.

A step below this is the one who gives alms to the needy in such a way that the giver does not know to whom he gives and the recipient does not know from whom he takes. This exemplifies doing a good deed for its own sake. One example was the Hall of Secrecy in the Temple, where the righteous would place their gift clandestinely and where poor people from noble families could come and secretly help themselves to aid. Close to this is dropping money in a charity box.

One step lower is where the giver knows to whom he gives, but the poor person does not know from whom he receives. Thus the great sages would go and secretly put money into poor people's doorways . . .

A step lower is the case where the poor person knows from whom he is taking, but the giver does not known to whom he is giving. Thus the great sages would tie coins in their scarves, which they would fling over their shoulders, so that the poor could help themselves without suffering shame.

Lower than this, is where someone gives the poor person a gift before he asks.

Lower still is one who gives only after the poor person asks.

Lower than this is one who gives less than is fitting, but does so with a friendly countenance.

The lowest level is one who gives ungraciously. (*Mattenot Ani'im* 10: 7–14)

Jimmy Carter's Eyes (2006)

E. C. Osondu

When she was three the girl accidentally upturned the boiling pan with which her mother was frying bean cakes on herself. The hot oil left two thick lumps of scar tissue across her eyes, blinding her. Her mother had told everyone who came to sympathize with her that she believed that a nurse had said they'd cut off the scar tissue in the hospital and the girl would be able to see again. Actually, she had not been told this by a real nurse but by a doll-baby nurse. This was the name given to auxiliary nurses in the general hospital where she had stayed with the child for three months, watching the eyes covered by gauze and gentian violet.

No one blamed her for what happened to the child. No one in the village spent all their days watching their children. A woman had thousands of chores—fetching water and firewood, washing clothes, cooking for the family—and looking after the children somehow fitted itself around these activities. She had left the child by the boiling oil and had run inside to fetch her salt container. She needed to sprinkle a pinch of salt into the boiling oil to know if it was time to dunk the ground beans into it. By the time she ran back out, the little girl had grabbed the boiling pan of oil. She had screamed and a crowd had gathered quickly. As is traditional in the village when such things happen, many took a look at the child and ran back to their homes to bring different medications, some useful but most useless. Some came with an expired bottle of gentian violet, another came with a smelly black bottle filled with the fat from the boa constrictor killed five years back. One came with a lump of wet cassava which she said would cool the skin and leave no scars. All these were dumped on the girl's face. Someone screamed for the Midwife. The Mid ran the village dispensary. She did more than deliver babies: she wrote prescriptions, sold drugs, and gave injections. Mid took a look at the child and ordered that she be taken to the General Hospital in the local government headquarters which was a good ten miles away. A commercial motorcycle taxi was called, and the woman, holding the child close to her, rode away to the hospital. The crowd gathered around the fire which had grown cold and began to talk about the incident.

"It is always money, money, money for the young women nowadays. In my time this would not have happened."

"It was not her fault. She has to take care of herself and the baby. You know her husband simply woke up one morning and walked away."

"I have seen worse burns in my time. She is young and the skin will heal very nicely. You'll be shocked when you see the same child many years hence. There will be no single blemish on her skin."

"My boa oil can heal anything. They need not have taken her to the hospital—just a drop of the oil every morning and she would heal perfectly."

"Oh the oil from the boa constrictor that was killed years back, I remember it was so big people thought it was a log of wood that had fallen across the road. From the black marks on its back you can tell it had lived for close to forty years."

"I have a bottle of the oil myself. I simply forgot to bring it."

"I wonder why Mid told her to take the child to the General Hospital. With the different medications we have applied even if the skin was burnt by the fires of purgatory she should heal."

"You know she is the eyes and ears of the government among us here. Her job is more than giving babies with running stomach salt and sugar solution to drink. They sent her here to speak as the voice of the government. If you disobey her you could get into trouble."

"You know since she got here the tax collectors now know the best days to come, they now come on days when everyone is at home. Who do you think tells them?"

People in the crowd looked at each other as if they had spoken too much and began to disperse. Towards evening, the driver of the motorcycle taxi came to tell the woman's neighbors that she had asked that they bring a few of her clothes to the hospital. She also told them to search under her sleeping mat and bring all the money there to the hospital.

The people in the village gathered and drew up a roster of people who would take food to her in the hospital. Some volunteered to go pass a night with her in the hospital but were told not to bother by the woman. The hospitals were overcrowded and families of patients slept in the open verandah of the hospital. Those who had gone to the hospital said the place stank of carbolic acid and death. They said that because of frequent power outages, the ice melted from the bodies of the corpses in the mortuary and the corpses stank like decomposed frozen mackerel. They said the doctors and nurses had their own private clinics and preferred that patients came to consult them there rather than in the general hospital.

They said the child's eyes were covered with gauze and that she could not swallow and had to be fed through a straw.

The woman and her daughter stayed in the hospital for a long time. Longer than people stayed in the hospital when they went to have their hernias removed. No one followed the roster anymore; the villagers became busy with planting of their crops. Another woman began to fry *akara* by the roadside and people began to buy from her. Occasionally people spoke of the woman and her daughter and then looked away embarrassedly.

One day the woman returned with the little girl who had by now grown a bit. Two thick layers of scar tissue now covered the girl's eyes. She was blind, which was rather odd. A blind little girl was unheard of. In the village, people became blind when they grew old. They said everyone chooses the part of his body that would age more than the other parts. Some chose their ears and became deaf as they grew old. Others chose to age in their teeth and lost all of them.

The girl's mother smiled and did not say much. She did not complain that she had been abandoned in the hospital. She soon went back to her business of frying akara by the side of the road. There was no animosity between her and the other woman who had also started frying akara. She said the sky was wide enough for birds to fly without their wings touching each other.

The child sat by her mother and would sometimes pass salt and other items to her. The mother would leave her to go into the house and people would come and buy akara and the girl would collect their money and give them the correct change. This was very strange because the girl had not been to school and even if she had she was blind, so how could she distinguish between one currency note and another?

One day a little girl went missing in the village. Sometimes children would go missing but they would normally be found within a few hours. This was different. No one had seen the girl. When a child went missing, the mother of the child would tie her headscarf tightly around her waist and go around the village crying and asking *Who has seen my child*? It was generally believed that by the time she lost her voice, the missing child would be found. By the second day the child was still missing. The mother had lost her voice but the child was not yet found. When the mother walked past the woman frying bean cakes, crying and screaming, "Who has seen my child?", the blind girl spoke for the first time.

"I know who stole the missing girl."

"Be quiet and don't get us both into trouble."

"I saw him give the girl a piece of candy; he tied her mouth with a rag, and threw her into a jute bag and rode away on his motorcycle."

The woman had never heard the child say that many words. Whenever the child chose to speak, she spoke in a whisper. Many people assumed she never spoke at all.

The mother called out to the woman. She said out loud what the child had said. The villagers gathered. There was only one man they knew who rode a motorcycle and had a jute bag: the man who bought cocoa beans from the villagers. They sent some young men after him. They caught him with the child two towns away. He had cut a hole in the bag through which he fed the girl. He had kidnapped the child for juju money-making rituals. It was rumored that little virgin girls could be charmed and made to vomit money through juju. He cried and said the devil made him do it.

The parents of the kidnapped girl brought a gift for the blind girl and her mother. There was no attempt to explain how the girl arrived at the knowledge she had. Some people said she must have heard something. They said her blindness had sharpened her ears. Her mother suspected something but said nothing.

One day the girl said softly to the mother, "Father is never coming back."

"Why do you say that? I am not sure you remember your father, you were so tiny when he left."

"He ran away with the Catechist's wife's younger sister."

"How do you know that?" the woman asked, puzzled and frightened.

"They were traveling to Mokwa. He was going to start a new life with her, the car in which they were traveling broke down on the way; all the passengers came down while the driver opened the bonnet to find out what was wrong. He was crossing to the other side of the road to ease piss, and a car coming from the other side knocked him down."

"Oh my child how do you know these things?" the woman asked.

"They buried him by the roadside, his grave is overgrown with weeds, he's never coming back."

The woman was quiet for a while. Everything about the story sounded true. She began to cry quietly to herself.

All things eventually come to light. People in the village sensed the girl's true powers and began to come to her for answers.

"Will there be plenty of rain this year so I can plant cassava instead of yams?"

"My black sheep did not come home with the rest of my sheep last night. Where could it be?"

"My son who lives in the city has not come home for five years. Is he dead or in prison?"

"My son who died three years ago: was his death a natural death or did my husband's other wife poison him while I was out of the house?"

"Is the price of cocoa going to rise or fall this year?"

"My husband has been sick for years now; do you think he will recover?"

The girl answered all their questions in a whisper, she answered honestly. Her answers sometimes caused trouble, tore families apart. Her mother would sometimes speak to her by way of signs to be quiet but she spoke up all the time. The answers flowed out of her mouth like a gentle stream. She said what she had to say and was quiet.

Prosperity began to come to the village because of her. People planted the right crops at the right time and got very rich harvests. Evil was rare. People stopped stealing because they knew she would find them out. More farmers bought motorcycles. Life had never been better.

The mother stopped frying akara. She made a comfortable living from the gifts the girl received. She was happy for once in all her life. She always felt the girl's eyes on her and sometimes shivered slightly when she felt the girl was looking at her. The girl's voice did not change, her breasts were small. The mother was happy when she began to bleed in tiny drops every month. *Thank goodness she is a woman* she said to herself.

People said different things about the source of her power but no one denied it.

"Her power is from the river goddess. When she speaks it is the river goddess speaking."

"It is the Holy Virgin that gives people such gifts, that is why she is called the voice of the dumb and the eyes of the sightless."

"She is not Catholic, not even Christian—she does not mention the name of God."

"God who took away her eyes gave her the gift of sight, and now she sees more than those of us with two eyes."

People said all sorts of things but still came to her for answers. On occasion the mother would say the girl was tired and needed to rest, but the girl would come out of her room and provide answers to whomever needed them. People reminded the mother that she could now afford to take the child to the Baptist Missionary Hospital in the big city. The mother acted as if she did not hear them. She did not think it was wise to tamper with the will of God, she told those who were bold enough to ask her. Besides, if the girl thought it was such a good thing she would have said so. Quite a few agreed with the Mother; after all, those of them with two eyes did not see as much as she did.

At about this time, the former American President Jimmy Carter launched his River Blindness Eradication Program. The program sent doctors and nurses to villages to distribute drugs for the prevention of river blindness. They did eye examinations and distributed glasses which the villagers referred to as Anya Jimmy Carter—Jimmy Carter's Eyes. The frames of the glasses were second-hand, gifts and donations from affluent Americans. This time around though, it was going to be slightly different; they were coming with eye surgeons to help remove cataracts. The bearer of this piece of news was the Midwife. She told the villagers that she had made it happen, that the village was not originally in the plan for the cataract surgery; she had lobbied for them to be included.

People were excited about this piece of good news. One of the old men in the village said the former President was kind because he had been a groundnut farmer before he became a President.

They had already been to the nearby village and had sent a notice to the chiefs that they were coming. The Midwife said they would be moving from house to house.

At first everyone looked forward to the visit until the woman mentioned that this would be an opportunity for her daughter to have the scar tissue covering her eyes removed. It was free and the girl was bleeding, she was now a woman and needed to get married. She had only said this to a few people. It soon got round the village that the girl was going to undergo surgery. There was anger, there were complaints, there was resentment and then people began to complain aloud.

"This program is not for people like her, it is for people losing their eyes to river blindness."

"She lost her eyes due to her mother's carelessness. Her mother should bear the cost of her surgery in a proper hospital."

"What guarantee is there that she will see again? Even if the skin is lifted, I hear the eyeballs are dead and blank. Please, no one should make the poor child suffer for nothing."

"They say her mother wants a husband for the girl, I know many men that will gladly marry her the way she is, she is a bag of wealth."

"It is the mother that needs a husband. Why did she never remarry after her husband ran away, as we all know the husband is dead, the girl said it herself."

"The girl belongs to the entire village now, not to her mother alone. She ceased being the mother's property as soon as she received her gift."

"You are right you know—if the gift was for her alone she would have stopped at telling her mother about her father's disappearance."

"You are right, she sees things for everyone, she was sent to prosper the village."

"Why are the Americans sending the eye doctors to us? Do they mean to tell us they have cured all the blind people in America?"

"The Elders should meet and tell the woman what to do just in case she does not know."

Words got to the ears of the Elders and they being people who acted in the interest of the inhabitants of the village decided to prevail on the mother of the girl to do the right thing. They made their points—they told her that her daughter's gift was for the good of all, that if it was for her mother alone she would have been seeing things for the mother alone. They spoke to the woman for a very long time. The woman told them that the girl was already bleeding and was a woman. She wanted her to marry and have children. Midwife came along with the Elders. She explained the difference between a cataract and the girl's condition. It was very possible that the girl would not recover her sight after the surgery, this might traumatize the girl and she may even lose the gift of speech which would be a double tragedy. They talked to the woman for a long time. The elders told her that they would gladly marry the girl off to any of their sons. She cried, and then she nodded and agreed with them.

On the day the American eye doctors came, the woman and her daughter locked their doors and remained inside till they left. Some people got new glasses; some had surgery. Everyone was happy. The girl and her mother were referred to as heroes who had put the interest of the town above their own interest.

When the planting season began, people came to the girl with their questions but alas she had no answers. The stream had dried up.

"It was not our fault. We should not blame ourselves for it," one of the villagers said.

"Whatever has a beginning must have an end; even the deepest ocean has a bottom. She was bound to stop seeing things one day anyway."

"It is the white man's strong juju that did it, or don't you know that white people are powerful?"

"The blind girl and her mother should consider themselves lucky, if it were in some other village they would have stoned them to death for possessing witchery powers."

And so life returned to normal in the village and everybody's conscience was at peace. Occasionally when a sheep went missing, the owner would be heard to bite his fingers and mutter, "If only that blind girl still had her powers."

Crito (360 B.C.E.)

Plato

Socrates. Why have you come at this hour, Crito? It must be quite early.

Crito. Yes, certainly.

Soc. What is the exact time?

Cr. The dawn is breaking.

Soc. I wonder that the keeper of the prison would let you in.

Cr. He knows me because I often come, Socrates; moreover. I have done him a kindness.

Soc. And are you only just come?

Cr. No, I came some time ago.

Soc. Then why did you sit and say nothing, instead of awakening me at once?

Cr. Why, indeed, Socrates, I myself would rather not have all this sleeplessness and sorrow. But I have been wondering at your peaceful slumbers, and that was the reason why I did not awaken you, because I wanted you to be out of pain. I have always thought you happy in the calmness of your temperament; but never did I see the like of the easy, cheerful way in which you bear this calamity.

Soc. Why, Crito, when a man has reached my age he ought not to be repining at the prospect of death.

Cr. And yet other old men find themselves in similar misfortunes, and age does not prevent them from repining.

Soc. That may be. But you have not told me why you come at this early hour.

Cr. I come to bring you a message which is sad and painful; not, as I believe, to yourself but to all of us who are your friends, and saddest of all to me.

Soc. What! I suppose that the ship has come from Delos, on the arrival of which I am to die?

Cr. No, the ship has not actually arrived, but she will probably be here to-day, as persons who have come from Sunium tell me that they have left her there; and therefore tomorrow, Socrates, will be the last day of your life.

Soc. Very well, Crito; if such is the will of God, I am willing; but my belief is that there will be a delay of a day.

Cr. Why do you say this?

Soc. I will tell you. I am to die on the day after the arrival of the ship?

Cr. Yes; that is what the authorities say.

Soc. But I do not think that the ship will be here until to-morrow; this I gather from a vision which I had last night, or rather only just now, when you fortunately allowed me to sleep.

Cr. And what was the nature of the vision?

Soc. There came to me the likeness of a woman, fair and comely, clothed in white raiment, who called to me and said: O Socrates—

"The third day hence, to Phthia shalt thou go."

Cr. What a singular dream, Socrates!

Soc. There can be no doubt about the meaning Crito, I think.

Cr. Yes: the meaning is only too clear. But, O! my beloved Socrates, let me entreat you once more to take my advice and escape. For if you die I shall not only lose a friend who can never be replaced, but there is another evil: people who do not know you and me will believe that I might have saved you if I had been willing to give money, but that I did not care. Now, can there be a worse disgrace than this—that I should be thought to value money more than the life of a friend? For the many will not be persuaded that I wanted you to escape, and that you refused.

Soc. But why, my dear Crito, should we care about the opinion of the many? Good men, and they are the only persons who are worth considering, will think of these things truly as they happened.

Cr. But do you see. Socrates, that the opinion of the many must be regarded, as is evident in your own case, because they can do the very greatest evil to anyone who has lost their good opinion?

Soc. I only wish, Crito, that they could; for then they could also do the greatest good, and that would be well. But the truth is, that they can do neither good nor evil: they cannot make a man wise or make him foolish; and whatever they do is the result of chance.

Cr. Well, I will not dispute about that; but please to tell me, Socrates, whether you are not acting out of regard to me and your other friends: are you not afraid that if you escape hence we may get into trouble with the informers for having stolen you away, and lose either the whole or a great part of our property; or that even a worse evil may happen to us? Now, if this is your fear, be at ease; for in order to save you, we ought surely to run this or even a greater risk; be persuaded, then, and do as I say.

Soc. Yes, Crito, that is one fear which you mention, but by no means the only one.

Cr. Fear not. There are persons who at no great cost are willing to save you and bring you out of prison; and as for the informers, you may observe that they are far from being exorbitant in their demands; a little money will satisfy them. My means, which, as I am sure, are ample, are at your service, and if you have a scruple about spending all mine, here are strangers who will give you the use of theirs; and one of them, Simmias the Theban, has brought a sum of money for this very purpose; and Cebes and many others are willing to spend their money too. I say, therefore, do not on that account hesitate about making your escape, and do not say, as you did in the court, that you will have a difficulty in knowing what to do with yourself if you escape. For men will love you in other places to which you may go, and not in Athens only; there are friends of mine in Thessaly, if you like to go to them, who will value and protect you, and no Thessalian will give you any trouble. Nor can I think that you are justified, Socrates, in betraying your own life when you might be saved; this is playing into the hands of your enemies and destroyers; and moreover I should say that you were betraying your children; for you might bring them up and educate them; instead of which you go away and leave them, and they will have to take their chance; and if they do not meet with the usual fate of orphans, there will be small thanks to you. No man should bring children into the world who is unwilling to persevere to the end in their nurture and education. But you are choosing the easier part, as I think, not the better and manlier, which would rather have become one who professes virtue in all his actions, like yourself. And, indeed, I am ashamed not only of you, but of us who are your friends, when I reflect that this entire business of yours will be attributed to our want of courage. The trial need never have come on, or might have been brought to another issue; and the end of all, which is the crowning absurdity, will seem to have been permitted by us, through cowardice and baseness, who might have saved you, as you might have saved yourself, if we had been good for anything (for there was no difficulty in escaping); and we did not see how disgraceful, Socrates, and also miserable all this will be to us as well as to you. Make your mind up then, or rather have your mind already made up, for the time of deliberation is over, and there is only one thing to be done, which must be done, if at all, this very night, and which any delay will render all but impossible; I beseech you therefore, Socrates, to be persuaded by me, and to do as I say.

Soc. Dear Crito, your zeal is invaluable, if a right one; but if wrong, the greater the zeal the greater the evil; and therefore we ought to consider whether these things shall be done or not. For I am and always have been one of those natures who must be guided by reason, whatever the reason may be which upon reflection appears to me to be the best; and now that this fortune has come upon me, I cannot put away the reasons which I have before given: the principles which I have hitherto honored and revered I still honor, and unless we can find other and better principles on the instant, I am certain not to agree with you; no, not even if the power of the multitude could inflict many more imprisonments, confiscations, deaths, frightening us like children with hobgoblin terrors. But what will be the fairest way of considering the question? Shall I return to your old argument about the opinions of men, some of which are to be regarded, and others, as we were saying, are not to be regarded? Now were we right in maintaining this before I was condemned? And has the argument which was once good now proved to be talk for the sake of talking; in fact an amusement only, and altogether vanity? That is what I want to consider with your help, Crito: whether, under my present circumstances, the argument appears to be in any way different or not; and is to be allowed by me or disallowed. That argument, which, as I believe, is maintained by many who assume to be authorities, was to the effect, as I was saying, that the opinions of some men are to be regarded, and of other men not to be regarded. Now you, Crito, are a disinterested person who are not going to die to-morrow—at least, there is no human probability of this, and you are therefore not liable to be deceived by the circumstances in which you are placed. Tell me, then, whether I am right in saying that some opinions, and the opinions of some men only, are to be valued, and other opinions, and the opinions of other men, are not to be valued. I ask you whether I was right in maintaining this?

Cr. Certainly.

Soc. The good are to be regarded, and not the bad?

Cr. Yes.

Soc. And the opinions of the wise are good, and the opinions of the unwise are evil?

Cr. Certainly.

Soc. And what was said about another matter? Was the disciple in gymnastics supposed to attend to the praise and blame and opinion of every man, or of one man only—his physician or trainer, whoever that was?

Cr. Of one man only.

Soc. And he ought to fear the censure and welcome the praise of that one only, and not of the many?

Cr. That is clear.

Soc. And he ought to live and train, and eat and drink in the way which seems good to his single master who has understanding, rather than according to the opinion of all other men put together?

Cr. True.

Soc. And if he disobeys and disregards the opinion and approval of the one, and regards the opinion of the many who have no understanding, will he not suffer evil?

Cr. Certainly he will.

Soc. And what will the evil be, whither tending and what affecting, in the disobedient person?

Cr. Clearly, affecting the body; that is what is destroyed by the evil.

Soc. Very good; and is not this true, Crito, of other things which we need not separately enumerate? In the matter of just and unjust, fair and foul, good and evil, which are the subjects of our present consultation, ought we to follow the opinion of the many and to fear them; or the opinion of the one man who has understanding, and whom we ought to fear and reverence more than all the rest of the world: and whom deserting we shall destroy and injure that principle in us which may be assumed to be improved by justice and deteriorated by injustice; is there not such a principle?

Cr. Certainly there is, Socrates.

Soc. Take a parallel instance; if, acting under the advice of men who have no understanding, we destroy that which is improvable by health and deteriorated by disease—when that has been destroyed, I say, would life be worth having? And that is—the body?

Cr. Yes.

Soc. Could we live, having an evil and corrupted body?

Cr. Certainly not.

Soc. And will life be worth having, if that higher part of man be depraved, which is improved by justice and deteriorated by injustice? Do we suppose that principle, whatever it may be in man, which has to do with justice and injustice, to be inferior to the body?

Cr. Certainly not.

Soc. More honored, then?

Cr. Far more honored.

Soc. Then, my friend, we must not regard what the many say of us: but what he, the one man who has understanding of just and unjust, will say, and what the truth will say. And therefore you begin in error when you suggest that we should regard the opinion of the many about just and unjust, good and evil, honorable and dishonorable. Well, someone will say, "But the many can kill us."

Cr. Yes, Socrates; that will clearly be the answer.

Soc. That is true; but still I find with surprise that the old argument is, as I conceive, unshaken as ever. And I should like to know whether I may say the same of another proposition—that not life, but a good life, is to be chiefly valued?

Cr. Yes, that also remains.

Soc. And a good life is equivalent to a just and honorable one—that holds also?

Cr. Yes, that holds.

Soc. From these premises I proceed to argue the question whether I ought or ought not to try to escape without the consent of the Athenians: and if I am clearly right in escaping, then I will make the attempt; but if not, I will abstain. The other considerations which you mention, of money and loss of character, and the duty of educating children, are, I fear, only the doctrines of the multitude, who would be as ready to call people to life, if they were able, as they are to put them to death—and with as little reason. But now, since the argument has thus far prevailed, the only question which remains to be considered is, whether we shall do rightly either in escaping or in suffering others to aid in our escape and paying them in money and thanks, or whether we shall not do rightly; and if the latter, then death or any other calamity which may ensue on my remaining here must not be allowed to enter into the calculation.

Cr. I think that you are right, Socrates; how then shall we proceed?

Soc. Let us consider the matter together, and do you either refute me if you can, and I will be convinced; or else cease, my dear friend, from repeating to me that I ought to escape against the wishes of the Athenians: for I am extremely desirous to be persuaded by you, but not against my own better judgment. And now please to consider my first position, and do your best to answer me.

Cr. I will do my best.

Soc. Are we to say that we are never intentionally to do wrong, or that in one way we ought and in another way we ought not to do wrong, or is doing wrong always evil and dishonorable, as I was just now saying, and as has been already acknowledged by us? Are all our former admissions which were made within a few days to be thrown away? And have we, at our age, been earnestly discoursing with one another all our life long only to discover that we are no better than children? Or are we to rest assured, in spite of the opinion of the many, and in spite of consequences whether better or worse, of the truth of what was then said, that injustice is always an evil and dishonor to him who acts unjustly? Shall we affirm that?

Cr. Yes.

Soc. Then we must do no wrong?

Cr. Certainly not.

Soc. Nor when injured injure in return, as the many imagine; for we must injure no one at all?

Cr. Clearly not.

Soc. Again, Crito, may we do evil?

Cr. Surely not, Socrates.

Soc. And what of doing evil in return for evil, which is the morality of the many—is that just or not?

Cr. Not just.

Soc. For doing evil to another is the same as injuring him?

Cr. Very true.

Soc. Then we ought not to retaliate or render evil for evil to anyone, whatever evil we may have suffered from him. But I would have you consider, Crito, whether you really mean what you are saying. For this opinion has never been held, and never will be held, by any considerable number of persons; and those who are agreed and those who are not agreed upon this point have no common ground, and can only despise one another, when they see how widely they differ. Tell me, then, whether you agree with and assent to my first principle, that neither injury nor retaliation nor warding off evil by evil is ever right. And shall that be the premise of our agreement? Or do you decline and dissent from this? For this has been of old and is still my opinion; but, if you are of another opinion, let me hear what you have to say. If, however, you remain of the same mind as formerly, I will proceed to the next step.

Cr. You may proceed, for I have not changed my mind.

Soc. Then I will proceed to the next step, which may be put in the form of a question: Ought a man to do what he admits to be right, or ought he to betray the right?

Cr. He ought to do what he thinks right.

Soc. But if this is true, what is the application? In leaving the prison against the will of the Athenians, do I wrong any? or rather do I not wrong those whom I ought least to wrong? Do I not desert the principles which were acknowledged by us to be just? What do you say?

Cr. I cannot tell, Socrates, for I do not know.

Soc. Then consider the matter in this way: Imagine that I am about to play truant (you may call the proceeding by any name which you like), and the laws and the government come and interrogate me: "Tell us, Socrates," they say; "What are you about? Are you going by an act of yours to overturn us—the laws and the whole State, as far as in you lies? Do you imagine that a State can subsist and not be overthrown, in which the decisions of law have no power, but are set aside and overthrown by individuals?" What will be our answer, Crito, to these and the like words? Anyone, and especially a clever rhetorician, will have a good deal to urge about the evil of setting aside the law which requires a sentence to be carried out; and we might reply, "Yes; but the State has injured us and given an unjust sentence." Suppose I say that?

Cr. Very good, Socrates.

Soc. "And was that our agreement with you?" the law would say, "Or were you to abide by the sentence of the State?" And if I were to express astonishment at their saying this, the law would probably add: "Answer, Socrates, instead of opening your eyes: you are in the habit of asking and answering questions. Tell us what complaint you have to make against us which justifies you in attempting to destroy us and the State? In the first place did we not bring you into existence? Your father married your mother by our aid and begat you. Say whether you have any objection to urge against those of us who regulate marriage?" None, I should reply. "Or against those of us who regulate the system of nurture and education of children in which you were trained? Were not the laws, who have the charge of this, right in commanding your father to train you in music and gymnastic?" Right, I should reply. "Well, then, since you were brought into the world and nurtured and educated by us, can you deny in the first place that you are our child and slave, as your fathers were before you? And if this is true you are not on equal terms with us; nor can you think that you have a right to do to us what we are doing to you. Would you have any right to strike or revile or do any other evil to a father or to your master, if you had one, when you have been struck or reviled by him, or received some other evil at his hands?—you would not say this? And because we think right to destroy you, do you think that you have any right to destroy us in return, and your country as far as in you lies? And will you, O professor of true virtue, say that you are justified in this? Has a philosopher like you failed to discover that our country is more to be valued and higher and holier far than mother or father or any ancestor, and more to be regarded in the eyes of the gods and of men of under-standing? Also to be soothed, and gently and reverently entreated when angry, even more than a father, and if not persuaded, obeyed? And when we are punished by her, whether with imprisonment or stripes, the pun-ishment is to be endured in silence; and if she leads us to wounds or death in battle, thither we follow as is right; neither may anyone yield or retreat or leave his rank, but whether in battle or in a court of law, or in any other place, he must do what his city and his country order him; or he must change their view of what is just: and if he may do no violence to his father or mother, much less may he do violence to his country." What answer shall we make to this, Crito? Do the laws speak truly, or do they not?

Cr. I think that they do.

Soc. Then the laws will say: "Consider, Socrates, if this is true, that in your present attempt you are going to do us wrong. For, after having brought you into the world, and nurtured and educated you, and given you and every other citizen a share in every good that we had to give, we further proclaim and give the right to every Athenian, that if he does not like us when he has come of age and has seen the ways of the city, and made our acquaintance, he may go where he pleases and take his goods with him; and none of our laws will forbid him or interfere with him. Any of you who does not like us and the city, and who wants to go to a colony or to any other city, may go where he likes, and take his goods with him. But he who has experience of the manner in which we order justice and administer the State, and still remains, has entered into an implied contract that he will do as we command him. And he who disobeys us is, as we maintain, thrice wrong: first, because in disobeying us he is disobeying his parents; secondly, because we are the authors of his education; thirdly, because he has made an agreement with us that he will duly obey our commands; and he neither obeys them nor convinces us that our commands are wrong; and we do not rudely impose them, but give him the alternative of obeying or convincing us; that is what we offer and he does neither. These are the sort of accusations to which, as we were saying, you, Socrates, will be exposed if you accomplish your intentions; you, above all other Athenians." Suppose I ask, why is this? they will justly retort upon me that I above all other men have acknowledged the agreement. "There is clear proof," they will say, "Socrates, that we and the city were not displeasing to you. Of all Athenians you have been the most constant resident in the city, which, as you never leave, you may be supposed to love. For you never went out of the city either to see the games, except once when you went to the Isthmus, or to any other place unless when you were on military service; nor did you travel as other men do. Nor had you any curiosity to know other States or their laws: your affections did not go beyond us and our State; we were your especial favorites, and you acquiesced in our government of you; and this is the State in which you begat your children, which is a proof of your satisfaction. Moreover, you might, if you had liked, have fixed the penalty at banishment in the course of the trial—the State which refuses to let you go now would have let you go then. But you pretended that you preferred death to exile, and that you were not grieved at death. And now you have forgotten these fine sentiments, and pay no respect to us, the laws, of whom you are the destroyer; and are doing what only a miserable slave would do, running away and turning your back upon the compacts and agreements which you made as a citizen. And first of all answer this very question: Are we right in saying that you agreed to be governed according to us in deed, and not in word only? Is that true or not?" How shall we answer that, Crito? Must we not agree?

Cr. There is no help, Socrates.

Soc. Then will they not say: "You, Socrates, are breaking the covenants and agreements which you made with us at your leisure, not in any haste or under any compulsion or deception, but having had seventy years to think of them, during which time you were at liberty to leave the city, if we were not to your mind, or if our covenants appeared to you to be unfair. You had your choice, and might have gone either to Lacedaemon or Crete, which you often praise for their good government, or to some other Hellenic or foreign State. Whereas you, above all other Athenians, seemed to be so fond of the State, or, in other words, of us, her laws (for who would like a State that has no laws?), that you never stirred out of her: the halt, the blind, the maimed, were not more stationary in her than you were. And now you run away and forsake your agreements. Not so, Socrates, if you will take our advice; do not make yourself ridiculous by escaping out of the city.

"For just consider, if you transgress and err in this sort of way, what good will you do, either to yourself or to your friends? That your friends will be driven into exile and deprived of citizenship, or will lose their property, is tolerably certain; and you yourself, if you fly to one of the neighboring cities, as, for example, Thebes or Megara, both of which are well-governed cities, will come to them as an enemy, Socrates, and their government will be against you, and all patriotic citizens will cast an evil eye upon you as a subverter of the laws, and you will confirm in the minds of the judges the justice of their own condemnation of you. For he who is a corrupter of the laws is more than likely to be corrupter of the young and foolish portion of mankind. Will you then flee from well-ordered cities and virtuous men? and is existence worth having on these terms? Or will you go to them without shame, and talk to them, Socrates? And what will you say to them? What you say here about virtue and justice and institutions and laws being the best things among men? Would that be decent of you? Surely not. But if you go away from well-governed States to Crito's friends in Thessaly, where there is great disorder and license, they will be charmed to have the tale of your escape from prison, set off with ludicrous particulars of the manner in which you were wrapped in a goatskin or some other disguise, and metamorphosed as the fashion of runaways is—that is very likely; but will there be no one to remind you that in your old age you violated the most sacred laws from a miserable desire of a little more life? Perhaps not, if you keep them in a good temper; but if they are out of temper you will hear many degrading things; you will live, but how?—as the flatterer of all men, and the servant of all men; and doing what?—eating and drinking in Thessaly, having gone abroad in order that you may get a dinner. And where will be your fine sentiments about justice and virtue then? Say that you wish to live for the sake of your children, that you may bring them up and educate them—will you take them into Thessaly and deprive them of Athenian citizenship? Is that the benefit which you would confer upon them? Or are you under the impression that they will be better cared for and educated here if you are still alive, although absent from them; for that your friends will take care of them? Do you fancy that if you are an inhabitant of Thessaly they will take care of them, and if you are an inhabitant of the other world they will not take care of them? Nay; but if they who call themselves friends are truly friends, they surely will.

"Listen, then, Socrates, to us who have brought you up. Think not of life and children first, and of justice afterwards, but of justice first, that you may be justified before the princes of the world below. For neither will you nor any that belong to you be happier or holier or juster in this life, or happier in another, if you do as Crito bids. Now you depart in innocence, a sufferer and not a doer of evil; a victim, not of the laws, but of men. But if you go forth, returning evil for evil, and injury for injury, breaking the covenants and agreements which you have made with us, and wronging those whom you ought least to wrong, that is to say, yourself, your friends, your country, and us, we shall be angry with you while you live, and our brethren, the laws in the world below, will receive you as an enemy; for they will know that you have done your best to destroy us. Listen, then, to us and not to Crito."

This is the voice which I seem to hear murmuring in my ears, like the sound of the flute in the ears of the mystic; that voice, I say, is humming in my ears, and prevents me from hearing any other. And I know that anything more which you will say will be in vain. Yet speak, if you have anything to say.

Cr. I have nothing to say, Socrates.

Soc. Then let me follow the intimations of the will of God.

The Ring of Gyges (380 B.C.E.)

Plato

Book 2

With these words I was thinking that I had made an end of the discussion; but the end, in truth, proved to be only a beginning. For Glaucon, who is always the most pugnacious of men, was dissatisfied at Thrasymachus' retirement; he wanted to have the battle out. So he said to me: Socrates, do you wish really to persuade us, or only to seem to have persuaded us, that to be just is always better than to be unjust?

I should wish really to persuade you, I replied, if I could.

Then you certainly have not succeeded. Let me ask you now:—How would you arrange goods—are there not some which we welcome for their own sakes, and independently of their consequences, as, for example, harmless pleasures and enjoyments, which delight us at the time, although nothing follows from them?

I agree in thinking that there is such a class, I replied.

Is there not also a second class of goods, such as knowledge, sight, health, which are desirable not only in themselves, but also for their results?

Certainly, I said.

And would you not recognize a third class, such as gymnastic, and the care of the sick, and the physician's art; also the various ways of money-making—these do us good but we regard them as disagreeable; and no one would choose them for their own sakes, but only for the sake of some reward or result which flows from them?

There is, I said, this third class also. But why do you ask?

Because I want to know in which of the three classes you would place justice?

In the highest class, I replied, among those goods which he who would be happy desires both for their own sake and for the sake of their results.

Then the many are of another mind; they think that justice is to be reckoned in the troublesome class, among goods which are to be pursued for the sake of rewards and of reputation, but in themselves are disagreeable and rather to be avoided.

I know, I said, that this is their manner of thinking, and that this was the thesis which Thrasymachus was maintaining just now, when he censured justice and praised injustice. But I am too stupid to be convinced by him.

I wish, he said, that you would hear me as well as him, and then I shall see whether you and I agree. For Thrasymachus seems to me, like a snake, to have been charmed by your voice sooner than he ought to have been; but to my mind the nature of justice and injustice have not yet been made clear. Setting aside their rewards and results, I want to know what they are in themselves, and how they inwardly work in the soul. If you, please, then, I will revive the argument of Thrasymachus. And first I will speak of the nature and origin of justice according to the common view of them. Secondly, I will show that all men who practise justice do so against their will, of necessity, but not as a good. And thirdly, I will argue that there is reason in this view, for the life of the unjust is after all better far than the life of the just—if what they say is true, Socrates, since I myself am not of their opinion. But still I acknowledge that I am perplexed when I hear the voices of Thrasymachus and myriads of others dinning in my ears; and, on the other hand, I have never yet heard the superiority of justice to injustice maintained by any one in a satisfactory way. I want to hear justice praised in respect of itself; then I shall be satisfied, and you are the person from whom I think that I am most likely to hear this; and therefore I will praise the unjust life to the utmost of my power, and my manner of speaking will indicate the manner in which I desire to hear you too praising justice and censuring injustice. Will you say whether you approve of my proposal?

Indeed I do; nor can I imagine any theme about which a man of sense would oftener wish to converse.

I am delighted, he replied, to hear you say so, and shall begin by speaking, as I proposed, of the nature and origin of justice.

They say that to do injustice is, by nature, good; to suffer injustice, evil; but that the evil is greater than the good. And so when men have both done and suffered injustice and have had experience of both, not being able to avoid the one and obtain the other, they think that they had better agree among themselves to have neither; hence there arise laws and mutual covenants; and that which is ordained by law is termed by them lawful and just. This they affirm to be the origin and nature of justice:—it is a mean or compromise, between the best of all, which is to do injustice and not be punished, and the worst of all, which is to suffer injustice without the power of retaliation; and justice, being at a middle point between the two, is tolerated not as a good, but as the lesser evil, and honoured by reason of the inability of men to do injustice. For no man who is worthy to be called a man would ever submit to such an agreement if he were able to resist; he would be mad if he did. Such is the received account, Socrates, of the nature and origin of justice.

Now that those who practise justice do so involuntarily and because they have not the power to be unjust will best appear if we imagine something of this kind: having given both to the just and the unjust power to do what they will, let us watch and see whither desire will lead them; then we shall discover in the very act the just and unjust man to be proceeding along the same road, following their interest, which all natures deem to be their good, and are only diverted into the path of justice by the force of law. The liberty which we are supposing may be most completely given to them in the form of such a power as is said to have been possessed by Gyges the ancestor of Croesus the Lydian. According to the tradition, Gyges was a shepherd in the service of the king of Lydia; there was a great storm, and an earthquake made an opening in the earth at the place where he was feeding his flock. Amazed at the sight, he descended into the opening, where, among other marvels, he beheld a hollow brazen horse, having doors, at which he stooping and looking in saw a dead body of stature, as appeared to him, more than human, and having nothing on but a gold ring; this he took from the finger of the dead and reascended. Now the shepherds met together, according to custom, that they might send their monthly report about the flocks to the king; into their assembly he came having the ring on his finger, and as he was sitting among them he chanced to turn the collet of the ring inside his hand, when instantly he became invisible to the rest of the company and they began to speak of him as if he were no longer present. He was astonished at this, and again touching the ring he turned the collet outwards and reappeared; he made several trials of the ring, and always with the same result—when he turned the collet inwards he became invisible, when outwards he reappeared. Whereupon he contrived to be chosen one of the messengers who were sent to the court; where as soon as he arrived he seduced the queen, and with her help conspired against the king and slew him, and took the kingdom. Suppose now that there were two such magic rings, and the just put on one of them and the unjust the other; no man can be imagined to be of such an iron nature that he would stand fast in justice. No man would keep his hands off what was not his own when he could safely take what he liked out of the market, or go into houses and lie with any one at his pleasure, or kill or release from prison whom he would, and in all respects be like a God among men. Then the actions of the just would be as the actions of the unjust; they would both come at last to the same point. And this we may truly affirm to be a great proof that a man is just, not willingly or because he thinks that justice is any good to him individually, but of necessity, for wherever any one thinks that he can safely be unjust, there he is unjust. For all men believe in their hearts that injustice is far more profitable to the individual than justice, and he who argues as I have been supposing, will say that they are right. If you could imagine any one obtaining this power of becoming invisible, and never doing any wrong or touching what was another's, he would be thought by the lookers-on to be a most wretched idiot, although they would praise him to one another's faces, and keep up appearances with one another from a fear that they too might suffer injustice. Enough of this.

Now, if we are to form a real judgment of the life of the just and unjust, we must isolate them; there is no other way; and how is the isolation to be effected? I answer: Let the unjust man be entirely unjust, and the just man entirely just; nothing is to be taken away from either of them, and both are to be perfectly furnished for the work of their respective lives. First, let the unjust be like other distinguished masters of craft; like the skilful pilot or physician, who knows intuitively his own powers and keeps within their limits, and who, if he fails at any point, is able to recover himself. So let the unjust make his unjust attempts in the right way, and lie hidden if he means to be great in his injustice (he who is found out is nobody): for the highest reach of injustice is: to be deemed just when you are not. Therefore I say that in the perfectly unjust man we must assume the most perfect injustice; there is to be no deduction, but we must allow him, while doing the most unjust acts, to have acquired the greatest reputation for justice. If he have taken a false step he must be able to recover himself; he must be one who can speak with effect, if any of his deeds come to light, and who can force his way where force is required by his courage and strength, and command of money and friends. And at his side let us place the just man in his nobleness and simplicity, wishing, as Aeschylus says, to be and not to seem good. There must be no seeming, for if he seem to be just he will be honoured and rewarded, and then we shall not know whether he is just for the sake of justice or for the sake of honours and rewards; therefore, let him be clothed in justice only, and have no other covering; and he must be imagined in a state of life the opposite of the former. Let him be the best of men, and let him be thought the worst; then he will have been put to the proof; and we shall see whether he will be affected by the fear of infamy and its consequences. And let him continue thus to the hour of death; being just and seeming to be unjust. When both have reached the uttermost extreme, the one of justice and the other of injustice, let judgment be given which of them is the happier of the two.

Heavens! my dear Glaucon, I said, how energetically you polish them up for the decision, first one and then the other, as if they were two statues.

I do my best, he said. And now that we know what they are like there is no difficulty in tracing out the sort of life which awaits either of them. This I will proceed to describe; but as you may think the description a little too coarse, I ask you to suppose, Socrates, that the words which follow are not mine.— Let me put them into the mouths of the eulogists of injustice: They will tell you that the just man who is thought unjust will be scourged, racked, bound—will have his eyes burnt out; and, at last, after suffering every kind of evil, he will be impaled: Then he will understand that he ought to seem only, and not to be, just; the words of Aeschylus may be more truly spoken of the unjust than of the just. For the unjust is pursuing a reality; he does not live with a view to appearances—he wants to be really unjust and not to seem only:—

His mind has a soil deep and fertile,
Out of which spring his prudent counsels.

In the first place, he is thought just, and therefore bears rule in the city; he can marry whom he will, and give in marriage to whom he will; also he can trade and deal where he likes, and always to his own advantage, because he has no misgivings about injustice and at every contest, whether in public or private, he gets the better of his antagonists, and gains at their expense, and is rich, and out of his gains he can benefit his friends, and harm his enemies; moreover, he can offer sacrifices, and dedicate gifts to the gods abundantly and magnificently, and can honour the gods or any man whom he wants to honour in a far better style than the just, and therefore he is likely to be dearer than they are to the gods. And thus, Socrates, gods and men are said to unite in making the life of the unjust better than the life of the just. . . .

[We pick up the discussion in Book 9.]

Book 9

"Now that we've gotten this far," I said, "let's go back to that statement made at the beginning, which brought us here: that it pays for a man to be perfectly unjust if he appears to be just. Isn't that what someone said?"

"Yes."

"Then since we've agreed what power justice and injustice each have, let's have a disucssion with him."

"How?"

"By molding in words an image of the soul, so that the one who said that will realize what he was saying."

"What kind of image?"

"Oh, something like those natures the myths tell us were born in ancient times—the Chimaera, Scylla, Cerberus, and others in which many different shapes were supposed to have grown into one."

"So they tell us," he said.

"Then mold one figure of a colorful, many-headed beast with heads of wild and tame animals growing in a circle all around it; one that can change and grow all of them out of itself."

"That's a job for a skilled artist. Still, words mold easier than wax or clay, so consider it done."

"And another of a lion, and one of a man. Make the first by far the biggest, the second second largest."

"That's easier, already done."

"Now join the three together so that they somehow grow."

"All right."

Next mold the image of one, the man, around them all so that if someone who can't see what's inside but looks only at the container it appears to be a single animal, man."

"I have."

"Then shall we inform the gentleman that when he says it pays for this man to be unjust, he's saying that it profits him to feast his multifarious beast and his lion and make them grow strong, but to starve and enfeeble the man in him so that he gets dragged wherever the animals lead him, and instead of making them friends and used to each other, to let them bite and fight and eat each other?"

"That's just what he's saying by praising injustice."

"The one who says justice pays, however, would be saying that he should practice and say whatever will give the most mastery to his inner man, who should care for the many-headed beast like a farmer, raising and domesticating its tame heads and preventing the wild ones from growing, making the lion's nature his partner and ally and so raise them both to be friends to each other and to him."

"That's exactly what he means by praising justice."

"So in every way the commender of justice is telling the truth, the other a lie. Whether we examine pleasure, reputation, or profit, we find that the man who praises justice speaks truly, the one who disparages it disparages sickly and knows nothing of what he disparages."

"I don't think he does at all."

"Then let's gently persuade him—his error wasn't intended—by asking him a question: 'Shouldn't we say that the traditions of the beautiful and ugly have come about like this: Beautiful things are those that make our bestial parts subservient to the human—or rather, perhaps, to the divine—part of our nature, while ugly ones are those that enslave the tame to the wild?' Won't he agree?"

"If he takes my advice."

"On this argument then, can it pay for a man to take money unjustly if that means making his best part a slave to the worst? If it wouldn't profit a man to sell his son or his daughter into slavery—to wild and evil men at that—even if he got a fortune for it, then if he has no pity on himself and enslaves the most godlike thing in him to the most godless and polluted, isn't he a wretch who gets bribed for gold into a destruction more horrible than Eriphyle's, who sold her husband's life for a necklace?"

"Much more horrible," said Glaucon.

". . . [E]veryone is better off being ruled by the godlike and intelligent; preferably if he has it inside, but if not, it should be imposed on him from without so that we may all be friends and as nearly alike as possible, all steered by the same thing."

"Yes, and we're right," he said.

"Law, the ally of everyone in the city, clearly intends the same thing, as does the rule of children, which forbids us to let them be free until we've instituted a regime in them as in a city. We serve their best part with a similar part in us, install a like guardian and ruler in them, and only then set them free."

"Clearly."

"Then how, by what argument, Glaucon, can we say that it pay for a man to be unjust or self-indulgent or to do something shameful to get more money or power if by doing so he makes himself worse?"

"We can't," he said.

"And how can it pay to commit injustice without getting caught and being punished? Doesn't getting away with it make a man even worse? Whereas if a man gets caught and punished, his beastlike part is taken in and tamed, his tame part is set free, and his whole soul acquires justice and temperance and knowledge. Therefore his soul recovers its best nature and attains a state more honorable than the state the body attains when it acquires health and strength and beauty, by as much as the soul is more honorable than the body.

"Absolutely."

"Then won't a sensible man spend his life directing all this effort to this end?"

Selected Suras (610–620)

Qur'ân

from The Chapter of the Merciful

In the name of the merciful and compassionate God.
The Merciful taught the Qur'ân;
He created man, taught him plain speech.
The sun and the moon have their appointed time;
The herbs and the trees adore;
And the heavens, He raised them and set the balance, that ye should not be outrageous in the balance;

But weigh ye aright, and stint not the balance.
And the earth He has set it for living creatures; therein are fruits and palms, with sheaths; and grain with
chaff and frequent shoots;
Then which of your Lord's bounties will ye twain deny?
He created men of crackling clay like the potters. And He created the ginn from smokeless fire.
Then which of your Lord's bounties will ye twain deny?
The Lord of the two Easts, and the Lord of the two Wests!
Then which of your Lord's bounties will ye twain deny?
He has let loose the two seas that meet together; between them is a barrier they cannot pass!
Then which of your Lord's bounties will ye twain deny?
He brings forth from each pearls both large and small!
Then which of your Lord's bounties will ye twain deny?
His are the ships which rear aloft in the sea like mountains.
Then which of your Lord's bounties will ye twain deny?
Every one upon it is transient, but the face of thy Lord endowed with majesty and honour shall endure.

Then which of your Lord's bounties will ye twain deny?

The Opening Chapter
(I. Mecca)

In the name of the merciful and compassionate God.

Praise belongs to God, the Lord of the worlds, the merciful, the compassionate, the ruler of the day of judgment! Thee we serve and Thee we ask for aid. [5] Guide us in the right path, the path of those Thou art gracious to; not of those Thou art wroth with; nor of those who err.

The Chapter of the Land
(XC. Mecca.)

In the name of the merciful and compassionate God.

I need not swear by the Lord of this land, and thou a dweller in this land!

Nor by the begetter and what he begets!

We have surely created man in trouble.

[5] Does he think that none can do aught against him?

He says, 'I have wasted wealth in plenty;' does he think that no one sees him?

Have we not made for him two eyes and a tongue, and two lips? [10] and guided him in the two highways? but he will not attempt the steep!

And what shall make thee know what the steep is? It is freeing captives, or feeding on the day of famine, [15] an orphan who is akin, or a poor man who lies in the dust; and again (it is) to be of these who believe and encourage each other to patience, and encourage each other to mercy,— these are the fellows of the right!

But those who disbelieve in our signs, they are the fellows of the left, [20] for them is fire that closes in!

107. al-Ma`un: The Daily Necessaries

1   Hast thou observed him who belieth religion?

2   That is he who repelleth the orphan,

3   And urgeth not the feeding of the needy.

4   Ah, woe unto worshippers

5   Who are heedless of their prayer;

6   Who would be seen (at worship)

7   Yet refuse small kindnesses!

A Handful of Dates (1964)

Tayeb Salih

I must have been very young at the time. While I don't remember exactly how old I was, I do remember that when people saw me with my grandfather they would pat me on the head and give my cheek a pinch—things they didn't do to my grandfather. The strange thing was that I never used to go out with my father, rather it was my grandfather who would take me with him wherever he went, except for the mornings when I would go to the mosque to learn the Koran. The mosque, the river and the fields—these were the landmarks in our life. While most of the children of my age grumbled at having to go to the mosque to learn the Koran, I used to love it. The reason was, no doubt, that I was quick at learning by heart and the Sheikh always asked me to stand up and recite the *Chapter of the Merciful* whenever we had visitors, who would pat me on my head and cheek just as people did when they saw me with my grandfather.

Yes, I used to love the mosque, and I loved the river too. Directly [after] we finished our Koran reading in the morning I would throw down my wooden slate and dart off, quick as a genie, to my mother, hurriedly swallow down my breakfast, and run off for a plunge in the river. When tired of swimming about I would sit on the bank and gaze at the strip of water that wound away eastwards and hid behind a thick wood of acacia trees. I loved to give rein to my imagination and picture to myself a tribe of giants living behind that wood, a people tall and thin with white beards and sharp noses, like my grandfather. Before my grandfather ever replied to my many questions he would rub the tip of his nose with his forefinger; as for his beard, it was soft and luxuriant and as white as cotton-wool—never in my life have I seen anything of a purer whiteness or greater beauty. My grandfather must also have been extremely tall, for I never saw anyone in the whole area address him without having to look up at him, nor did I see him enter a house without having to bend so low that I was put in mind of the way the river wound round behind the wood of acacia trees. I loved him and would imagine myself, when I grew to be a man, tall and slender like him, walking along with great strides.

I believe I was his favourite grandchild: no wonder, for my cousins were a stupid bunch and I—so they say—was an intelligent child. I used to

564

know when my grandfather wanted me to laugh, when to be silent; also I would remember the times for his prayers and would bring him his prayer-rug and fill the ewer for his ablutions without his having to ask me. When he had nothing else to do he enjoyed listening to me reciting to him from the Koran in a lilting voice, and I could tell from his face that he was moved.

One day I asked him about our neighbour Masood. I said to my grandfather: 'I fancy you don't like our neighbour Masood?'

To which he answered, having rubbed the tip of his nose:

'He's an indolent man and I don't like such people.'

I said to him: 'What's an indolent man?'

My grandfather lowered his head for a moment, then looking across at the wide expanse of field, he said: 'Do you see it stretching out from the edge of the desert up to the Nile bank? A hundred feddans. Do you see all those date palms? And those trees—*sant*, acacia, and *sayal*? All this fell into Masood's lap, was inherited by him from his father.'

Taking advantage of the silence that had descended upon my grandfather, I turned my gaze from him to the vast area defined by his words. 'I don't care,' I told myself, 'who owns those date palms, those trees or this black, cracked earth—all I know is that it's the arena for my dreams and my playground.'

My grandfather then continued: 'Yes, my boy, forty years ago all this belonged to Masood—two-thirds of it is now mine.'

This was news to me for I had imagined that the land had belonged to my grandfather ever since God's Creation.

'I didn't own a single feddan when I first set foot in this village. Masood was then the owner of all these riches. The position has changed now, though, and I think that before Allah calls me to Him I shall have bought the remaining third as well.'

I do not know why it was I felt fear at my grandfather's words—and pity for our neighbour Masood. How I wished my grandfather wouldn't do what he'd said! I remembered Masood's singing, his beautiful voice and powerful laugh that resembled the gurgling of water. My grandfather never used to laugh.

I asked my grandfather why Masood had sold his land.

'Women,' and from the way my grandfather pronounced the word I felt that 'women' was something terrible. 'Masood, my boy, was a much-married man. Each time he married he sold me a feddan or two.' I made the quick calculation that Masood must have married some ninety women; Then I remembered his three wives, his shabby appearance, his lame donkey and its dilapidated saddle, his *galabia* with the torn sleeves. I had all but rid my mind of the thoughts that jostled in it when I saw the man approaching us, and my grandfather and I exchanged glances.

'We'll be harvesting the dates today,' said Masood. 'Don't you want to be there?'

I felt, though, that he did not really want my grandfather to attend. My grandfather, however, jumped to his feet and I saw that his eyes sparkled momentarily with an intense brightness. He pulled me by the hand and we went off to the harvesting of Masood's dates.

Someone brought my grandfather a stool covered with an ox-hide, while I remained standing. There was a vast number of people there, but though I knew them all, I found myself, for some reason, watching Masood: aloof from that great gathering of people he stood as though it were no concern of his, despite the fact that the date palms to be harvested were his own. Sometimes his attention would be caught by the sound of a huge dump of dates crashing down from on high. Once he shouted up at the boy perched on the very summit of the date palm who had begun hacking at a clump with his long, sharp sickle: 'Be careful you don't cut the heart of the palm.'

No one paid any attention to what he said and the boy seated at the very summit of the date palm continued, quickly and energetically, to work away at the branch with his sickle till the clump of dates began to drop like something descending from the heavens.

I, however, had begun to think about Masood's phrase 'the heart of the palm.' I pictured the palm tree as something with feeling, something possessed of a heart that throbbed. I remembered Masood's remark to me when he had once seen me playing about with the branch of a young palm tree: 'Palm trees, my boy, like humans, experience joy and suffering.' And I had felt an inward and unreasoned embarrassment.

When I again looked at the expanse of ground stretching before me I saw my young companions swarming like ants around the trunks of the palm trees, gathering up dates and eating most of them. The dates were collected into high mounds. I saw people coming along and weighing them into measuring bins and pouring them into sacks, of which I counted thirty. The crowd of people broke up, except for Hussein the merchant, Mousa the owner of the field next to ours on the east, and two men I'd never seen before.

I heard a low whistling sound and saw that my grandfather had fallen asleep. Then I noticed that Masood had not changed his stance, except that he had placed a stalk in his mouth and was munching at it like someone surfeited with food who doesn't know what to do with the mouthful he still has.

Suddenly my grandfather woke up, jumped to his feet and walked towards the sacks of dates. He was followed by Hussein the merchant, Mousa the owner of the field next to ours, and the two strangers. I glanced at Masood and saw that he was making his way towards us with extreme slowness, like a man who wants to retreat but whose feet insist on going forward. They formed a circle round the sacks of dates and began examining them, some taking a date or two to eat. My grandfather gave me a fistful, which I began munching. I saw Masood filling the palms of both hands with dates and bringing them up close to his nose, then returning them.

Then I saw them dividing up the sacks between them. Hussein the merchant took ten; each of the strangers took five. Mousa the owner of the field next to ours on the eastern side took five, and my grandfather took five. Understanding nothing, I looked at Masood and saw that his eyes were darting about to left and right like two mice that have lost their way home.

'You're still fifty pounds in debt to me,' said my grandfather to Masood. 'We'll talk about it later.'

Hussein called his assistants and they brought along donkeys, the two strangers produced camels, and the sacks of dates were loaded on to them. One of the donkeys let out a braying which set the camels frothing at the mouth and complaining noisily. I felt myself drawing close to Masood, felt my hand stretch out towards him as though I wanted to touch the hem of his garment. I heard him make a noise in his throat like the rasping of a lamb being slaughtered. For some unknown reason, I experienced a sharp sensation of pain in my chest.

I ran off into the distance. Hearing my grandfather call after me, I hesitated a little, then continued on my way. I felt at that moment that I hated him. Quickening my pace, it was as though I carried within me a secret I wanted to rid myself of. I reached the river bank near the bend it made behind the wood of acacia trees. Then, without knowing why, I put my finger into my throat and spewed up the dates I'd eaten.

When I Heard the Learned Astronomer (1900)

Walt Whitman

When I heard the learn'd astronomer,
When the proofs, the figures, were ranged in columns before me,
When I was shown the charts and diagrams, to add, divide,
    and measure them,
When I sitting heard the astronomer where he lectured with
    much applause in the lecture-room,
How soon unaccountable I became tired and sick,
Till rising and gliding out I wander'd off by myself,
In the mystical moist night-air, and from time to time,
Look'd up in perfect silence at the stars.

The Mercer Ethic

Jesse Mercer (1769–1841)—Baptist clergyman, co-founder of the Georgia Baptist Convention, and founder of Mercer University—was the earliest and primary advocate of education for lay Baptists and Baptist ministers throughout the state. Mercer faced significant and strenuous opposition within the Georgia Baptist Convention to his plan for a Baptist University. A considerable number of the Convention argued that God had "never designed the Baptists to have a learned ministry," calling higher education a Tower of Babel—unbiblical and not in the best interests of the denomination. These Baptists were proud of their uneducated ministers on principle, since in their view a man needed only the Holy Spirit to be a Baptist minister; education, they alleged, only hindered its expression. Argued one opponent, "If learning is to help the preacher, why not pray to learning instead of to the Lord?" The following address was given before the Georgia Baptist Convention at Indian Creek Meeting House in Morgan County, Georgia in an effort to win support for Baptist higher education.

Knowledge: Indispensable to a Minister of God (1834)

Jesse Mercer

I. What knowledge is necessary to a minister of God.

To this inquiry we unhesitatingly answer—THE KNOWLEDGE OF THE TRUTH. For we know of no truth, the knowledge of which, would be unimportant to a minister of God. We should like, dear friends, that you would now throw your thoughts over the universe, and see if you can discover any truth, which would be unnecessary to be known by a gospel minister. If it should be said by any, that it ought to be restricted to the knowledge of the truth as it is in Jesus, then we answer again, that we know of no truth which is not in Christ Jesus. The scriptures declare, "It pleased the Father that in him all fullness should dwell." He it is "that filleth all in all." "He is head over all things to the church." And "by him all things consist."—Then we ask, what truth is not in Christ Jesus? But the whole may be summed up in the knowledge of God and his works.—Nay, God is only to be known through his works of nature, grace and providence. . . .

II. How it is attainable.

This knowledge then we say, is to be attained only by a close application to the study of the works of God. The proof of this question is clearly implied in the scriptures, which enjoin its attainment. Our Lord commanded his ministers, Math. X, 16, saying, "Be ye wise as serpents, and harmless as doves." This we have seen already, involves the study and acquisition of much pious knowledge. . . .

We have it laid down in Psa. Cxi, 2–8, "That the works of the Lord are great, sought out of all them that have pleasure therein—He hath made his wonderful works to be remembered—The works of his hands are verity and judgment. They stand fast forever and ever, and are done in truth and uprightness." Here the phrases, "sought out," and "to be remembered," mark the duty to be done in acquiring the knowledge of the works of God. They cannot be sought out and remembered, without effort—without much study and tenacious care. But this duty is laid down with too much force to be mistaken in, Pro. Iv, 1, 2, 5, 7, "Hear, ye children, the instruction of a father, and attend to know understanding. For I give you good doctrine, forsake ye not my law—get wisdom, get understanding: forget it not; neither decline from the words of my mouth. Wisdom is the principal thing; therefore, get wisdom; and with all thy getting get understanding." But in chapter ii, 1–11, if possible this duty is made plainer still, and enforced by most encouraging motives.—"My son, if thou wilt receive my words, and hide my commandments with thee; so that thou incline thine ear unto wisdom, and apply thy heart to understanding; yea, if thou criest after knowledge, and liftest up thy voice for understanding; if thou seekest her as silver, and searchest for her as for hid treasures; then shalt thou understand the fear of the Lord, and find the knowledge of God. For the Lord giveth wisdom; out of his mouth cometh knowledge and understanding. He layeth up sound wisdom for the righteous; he is a buckler to them that walk uprightly. . . . When wisdom entereth into thy heart, and knowledge is pleasant unto thy soul; discretion shall preserve thee, understanding shall keep thee." Here we are taught, that though the Lord gives wisdom, and out of his mouth comes knowledge and understanding, yet it is to be attained by close study and persevering effort. It is to be sought as silver. How do men act, when they lay themselves out to get money? Why, they engage in some mechanism, profession, merchandize or agricultural pursuit, in which they ply themselves with untiring diligence to gain their object; so all good men, but especially ministers of God, ought to apply themselves to the acquisition of knowledge. But Solomon uses a bolder comparison. He says, it must be searched for as for hid treasures. Here reference is had to the anxious solicitude—the patient and indefatigable perseverance, with which men dig after the precious metals and other valuable substances, hid in the bowels of the earth; which can be better conceived than described. But as knowledge is more precious than silver, or gold, or rubies, it ought to be sought not only with equal, but superior application and untiring diligence; and then we have the encouraging promise of attaining the precious boon. And here we would ask, why God hid his most precious natural treasures in the bowels of the earth, or rather why he did not spread them over its face, so that the inhabitants of the world might just go out and gather up what they needed, like the children of Israel did the manna round their tents? Why, for this simple reason, it did not suit his plan. He formed man for labor, and constructed every thing accordingly: so that if man obtained them, he should dig deep for them: and the harder for the more precious.—And thus, says Solomon, in the acquirement of knowledge, "This sore travail hath God given to the sons of man to be exercised therewith." And it is evident, that the most deep and valuable treasures of wisdom and knowledge are gained by the most patient and persevering efforts of the mind. . . .

Let none say, that God caused Moses, Daniel and Saul of Tarsus, to be educated by men of the world, and if he now wants learned men, he can call them from the ranks of those who have been already taught. But let such remember, that the Lord's people were in circumstances in those days, which forbid these men's receiving the education necessary from them. But now the people of God are able—have abundant means; and shall they throw off this duty, because God once furnished himself and them with men qualified read to their hand? No. This would be the same as to say, because God once fed his prophet Elijah by ravens, now if God wants his ministers supported, he can send ravens to feed them. But who will dare to indulge in such a thought!

Lastly—A general examination of the views and characterics of the scripture writers, will show them to have been men of understanding and sound learning, speaking what they knew to be the truth—teaching the excellency of wisdom and knowledge, and deprecating the want of it as a real evil. Their writings will justify this declaration. The Bible is a learned book, abounding in the richest figures of speech, and the most refined erudition. But false Teachers, Prophets and Apostles are in these respects beautifully contrasted with the true. These are represented as brutish in knowledge, and speaking falsehoods out of the imagination of their own evil heart. Read Jer. Xxiii; and the xiii of Ezek. But to be a little particular. In Isa. Lvi, 10, of Israel it is said "His watchmen are blind; They are all ignorant;" or knowing nothing, (perhaps the scribes and pharisees are intended, whom Christ condemns as blind guides.) In verse 11, they are said to be "shepherds that cannot understand." Paul says of the false teachers of his day, that they desired to be teachers of the law, understanding neither what they say, nor where they affirm.—Tim. I, 7. And in chapter vi, 4, 5, he speaks of such as "proud, knowing nothing, but doting about questions, and strifes of words, whereof cometh envy, strife, railings, evil surmisings, perverse disputings of men of corrupt minds, and destitute of the truth." Peter in his second Epistle, chapter ii, 12, speaking of the same class says, "But these, as natural brute beasts, made to be taken and destroyed, speak of the things they know not." Jude in describing these same persons says, verse 10, "These speak evil of those things which they know not; but what they know naturally, as brute beasts, in those things they corrupt themselves."

Here observe, these false teachers are reproached for knowing nothing, but what they know naturally, as brute beasts.—In order, brethren, to perceive the full force of the contempt and derision thrown on these pretended teachers by the apostles, it is necessary to conceive rightly, how natural brute beasts acquire knowledge—namely, by instinct, or the force of habit.—Now, then, it is plain that these apostles thought it ridiculous for any man to pretend to be a teacher who knows nothing, but what he knows naturally as brute beasts, by infusion or force or custom; without an effort of the understanding, or the exercise of reason. 'Tis true, a man residing in a learned community, will drink in the knowledge of the society he keeps, and may seem to be learned; at least he may use many learned words; but not having exerted his understanding and reason in obtaining it, but having received it as a brute beast does, cannot use his knowledge understandingly, but rather as parrots do, and therefore, is ever subject to expose himself, and the cause he attempts to advocate, to contempt, and his hearers to deception. The Lord save us from an ignorant ministry!

After Jesse Mercer, Adiel Sherwood (1791–1879) reigns as the most influential architect of Mercer University. Sherwood pioneered the first Georgia temperance society and created the first Baptist Sunday school in the state. But it was his fierce advocacy of education for ministers that set him against many in his denomination. Sherwood's vision that manual-labor might be used as a means of providing tuition for higher education meant that the first students at Mercer Institute worked in the fields at least three hours a day, often alongside their professors. Sherwood, sometimes called the spiritual father of Mercer University, here argues that separation of church and state and religious liberty are the most important gifts Baptists gave to America and the world.

The Influence of the Baptist Denomination on Religious Liberty (1838)

Adiel Sherwood

The history of religious liberty, as it has been developed in the settlement of these United States, is a subject of deepest interest. It is not designed in this paper, to write that history, but merely to glance at a few facts revealed in its progress. We regret to say, that no one can do this, without discovering how much bigotry and selfishness exists in our nature, and how unsafe a depository of power, under any circumstances, is man. In this glance, too, we shall be convinced to how high a pitch of moral courage our species may be elevated, and what clear light, in the science of government, may be elicited from the oppressed and persecuted. Kings and ecclesiastics, for so many centuries, had held undisputed sway over the mind and conscience, that the people generally seemed to regard them as inheriting the authority, not only to control their property, but also to mould their civil and religious opinions. To call in question this authority was considered a most flagrant act of rebellion; and he who dared do it was punished for his temerity, either by death or banishment. . . .

Our Puritan ancestors, who had forsaken the homes of their fathers, "in order to enjoy religious liberty," were as intolerant in their enactments, as the government from which they fled. We have seen them *taxing*, *persecuting*, and *disfranchising* Episcopalians, and we have seen Episcopalians repaying them in good measure: while both Episcopalian and Puritan have taxed, persecuted, imprisoned and banished the Baptists and the

Quakers. Some of the latter have been publicly executed, and many, of both denominations, have died of the inhuman treatment received at the hands of their misguided persecutors. This is indeed a sad picture, and out of respect to the descendants of those deluded persons who enacted the laws referred to, we would cover it with the veil of oblivion. But truth and justice forbid that such facts should be forgotten. Let that picture stand out in bold relief, not to shame the present, but to serve as a beacon to future generations. . . .

We now turn our attention to the efforts of the Baptists in producing an entire revolution in public opinion. It is not affirmed, that they alone have labored to wrest from the magistrate the power to regulate religious concernments. The Quakers, everywhere, and in some States, other sects, have fought manfully by their side.

In the proposals for amending the form of government for Providence, Rhode Island, in 1640, we find this article: "We agree, as formerly hath been the liberties of the town, so still to hold forth, *liberty of conscience*." This State, it will be remembered, was settled by Baptists.

The second charter for Rhode Island, granted by Charles II, in 1663, and probably sketched by Roger Williams, allows "every person and persons freely and fully to have and enjoy his own and their judgments and consciences in matters of religious concernments." In alluding to this, some years after, Williams observes . . . "To suffer a civil magistrate to intrude his powers into the field of opinion, and to restrain the profession or propagation of principles. . . . destroys all religious liberty. No man shall be *compelled* to frequent or support any religious worship or ministry whatsoever. . . ." Rhode Island, settled by this denomination, has, from its commencement, been the asylum for the oppressed. And it may be asked, if, in a State, the receptacle of the discontented from the four quarters of the earth, there be any religion and any law? And whether the dominant party did not here also learn the art of persecution?

In regard to religion, it may be observed, that in 1811, there were about ninety religious societies in the thirty-one townships, while the whole population is less than 90,000: so that there is a place of worship for every thousand persons. In 1834, the biographer of Williams, who was a native of the State, says, "It is believed, that at this present time, there are as many religious societies in Rhode Island as in other States, in proportion to the inhabitants, and that the ministry is as well supported, though it is done by the voluntary liberality of the respective societies. The state of morality and religion would, it is believed, bear a favorable comparison with that in other States." The laws are as much respected as in other commonwealths,—she has never been agitated by an insurrection, nor often, if ever, witnessed a mob. Not a law infringing the liberty of conscience has ever been passed by her Legislature,—none to support religion, —for it has been thought wisest to leave this matter to the good sense of each particular neighborhood. In this respect, she forms an enviable contrast with her sister [states]. She stands out in the midst of them, unstained with the blood of heretics,—an object of the world's wonder and admiration,—giving to the old maxim, that "all sects will persecute if they have the power," a triumphant, though, alas, a solitary refutation. . . .

In February, 1785, a law for the establishment and support of religion was passed in Georgia, through the influence of the Episcopalians. It embraced all denominations, and gave all equal privileges; but in May, the Baptists remonstrated against it,—sent two messengers to the Legislature, and the next session it was repealed. In both ministers and members, they were much more numerous than any other denomination. Their preachers might have occupied every neighborhood, and lived upon the public treasury; but no,—they knew that Christ's "kingdom is not of this world," and believed that any dependence on civil power for its support tends to corrupt the purity and pristine loveliness of religion. They therefore preferred to pine in poverty, as many of them did, and prevent an unholy marriage between the church of Christ and the civil authority. The overthrow of all the above named odious laws is to be attributed to their unremitting efforts: they generally struck the first blow, and thus inspired the other sects with their own intrepidity. It is owing to their sentiments, chiefly, as the friends of religious liberty, that no law, abridging the freedom of thought or opinion, touching religious worship, is now in force to disgrace our statute books. . . The Baptists have successfully propagated their sentiments on the subject of religious liberty, at the cost of suffering in property, in person, in limb and in life. Let the sacrifice be ever so great, they have always freely made it, in testimony of their indignation against laws which would fetter the conscience. . .

The question may be asked, how should this denomination, in its sentiments of religious liberty, be so much in advance of the age? The form of church government established by the Puritans, was a pure democracy, and essentially that of the Baptists. True; but in the reception of members the two denominations differ widely: while a large portion of the former come into the church by birth, the latter enter of their own responsibility. They feel that they have rights, and prize them. One feature in the policy of the former renders it a kind of parental government, authorized to mould the opinions of its subjects before they are able themselves to discern them. But from the first, the Baptists seem to have perceived the truth on this subject. Whether they derived it from particular texts, or from the general principles of the Bible, it is not now for us to inquire. Their knowledge on this subject is coeval with their existence as a distinct people. Religious liberty is a Baptist watchword, a kind of talisman, which operates like a charm, and nerves every man for action. . . .

Involuntary respect goes forth to the man who brings to light some great and useful truth in the sciences or in the arts. Such was the discovery of the art of printing,—the power and uses of steam,—the true theory of the solar system: but what are these in comparison with the great moral truth which the Baptists have held forth before the public eye for centuries?— a truth, without which life would be a burden, and civil liberty but a mockery. Nor is this all. While the Baptists have always defended the principles of religious liberty, they have never violated them. They have had but one opportunity of forming a civil government, and they so formed it as to create an era in the history of civilization. In the little Baptist State of Rhode Island was the experiment first attempted of leaving religion wholly to herself, unprotected and unsustained by the civil arm. The principles, which were here first planted, have taken root in other lands, and have borne abundant fruit. The world is coming nearer to the opinions of Roger Williams; and so universally are his sentiments now adopted in this country, that, like other successful philosophers, he is likely himself to be lost in the blaze of his own discovery.

Howell Cone was a senior at Mercer in 1900. His essay was published in The Mercerian, *Mercer's first student publication.*

Redeeming Features of Industrial and Religious Change (1900)

Howell Cone

There is one belief, around which all systems of thought revolve. Whether expressed or not, whether understood or not, whether believed or not, it is yet the inspiration of human endeavor. This belief is that the present age is superior to every preceding age, that the standards of today are higher than they have ever been before. This universal belief in the ceaseless growth of man is the basis of all optimism, the origin of all faith, the foundation of all hope. . . .

Tradition, the mouthpiece of the past, is forever conning the lessons already learned, forever recounting the deeds already performed. Our civilization is the product of time, the result of countless years of experience. But, directly, that progress which goes beyond the present—which "stands upon the heights of life and longs for the heights that are higher;" is little affected by all the wisdom of experience, by all the "momentum of tradition." For growth ceases when tradition guides. . . .

The past yields to the historian knowledge, to the poet, she gives the dreams, the pictures and the jeweled words; but to the reformer, she gives the *cross* and the crown of thorns; him alone she crucifies. He who would take the next step in advance is bound by forms, shackled by old ties, crushed by the memory of an imaginary happiness in which is thought to exist the youth of every individual and every age, but which is the contentment and cheerfulness of the unthinking mind, the curtain with which a kind of providence veils the eyes of the incapable from the deep waters of life. Yet in the face of this natural weakness, man is optimistic; and the few leaves of human history rescued from oblivion would justify this belief. During all the eras of his existence man has never yet been able to resist the *Spirit of Activity*. From the ruins of Cities, from the ashes of Empires, from the shadows of change man has ever risen with a sweep grander than before. He has resisted the march of ideas, fought the drift of onward-moving principles. He has given to blank time all the culture of centuries of civilization; and has turned backward in his race life to grovel in the darkness of retrogression and decay. But through all the drifts and changes, through all the turmoil and the darkness, the *germ* in the *soil* still lived, and, in its own good time, the breaking clod has left it free to climb anew to its world of light and life. . . .

Man's growth is continuous; only the methods of man harden like shells, and must be broken by every succeeding age. The present is a transition period. We live in a new age and all our paths are new paths. We move on the crest of a world-change. So rapid is the advance that few realize what a day, a year, a decade may bring forth in national and racial life. Our temples are being destroyed. Our images are being broken. One half stands appalled, fearful before the dust of their broken shrines. The other half are slowly raising the new structures, more pure, broader, deeper, grander than even before. The iconoclast, the anarchist of yesterday becomes the constructive statesman of today. The forerunners of the next age are calling men to duty, and, as a reward, are reviled as innovators, pitied as castaways, because they have dared to differ from accepted dogmas. They are giving a new interpretation to old truths—teaching to all the children of men their new beauty and their unsearchable riches. . . .

The church also changes. The infallibility of theology is a reminder of feudalism and slavery; the numerous *isms* of the protestant church are the manifestation of individualism. The church cannot be higher than the life it expresses. None are so bold as to declare that it does not change, but many are so fearful as to ignore that change; some would repress it altogether. The church is of slow growth, for the eternity of the relations between man and his creator, the tremendous import of his belief concerning God, reinforce all the native conservatism of man, and produce that profound mistrust with which the world greets a change in the expression of religion. The State changes with the years; the Church, with the centuries. The slowness of change by which the Church in a new age expresses the life of that has its restraining influence, not upon the radicalism and heresy which it would check, but upon the spiritual growth of the race.

The Church is an organization whose purpose is to promote the growth of Christianity, but to some the sacredness of Christianity extends to the Church itself, and any change in its organization becomes a sacrilege. Theology is the science of religion, but by some the sanctity of religion is transferred to the science, so that theology becomes as sacred as religion. To such any dissent from their creed becomes, in their sight, an expressed disbelief in God and man. To them a change of interpretation instead of indicating a growth, a step in advance from the physical and sensual interpretation of the childhood of the individual and of the race, becomes a direct attempt to undermine the fundamentals of religion. Christ rebuked tradition when He exclaimed; "Ye can discern the face of the earth and of the sky, but how is it that ye discern not the signs of the times?" The same answer is applicable to the aforesaid devotees of tradition.

Religion is more than theology, Christianity is more than creed, higher than all the methods of man. . . The inertia of creeds, the strength and hardness of the external and medium of Christianity produce two kinds of thinkers: the reformer and the atheist. Both are iconoclasts, both destroyers. The reformer would destroy the old shell, the old form, and would erect a new structure expressing a new growth and a new life. The atheist too would destroy, raze from the earth, leaven not a rack behind. To him the evil has outmastered the good and the punishment of the whole should be death. But here his work must end, for he has destroyed in his thought that which is the source of life, and henceforth his system building is upon the sands and the spoils of chance. The Church has never realized that it is negatively productive of skepticism as well as reformation. The Church forgets that Luther and the Reformation was an expression of skepticism towards an old theology. The Church has been substituted for the religion of the Christ, and the Reformation was merely a shattering of the old shell. . . Likewise the Church of today refuses to bear any responsibility for modern infidelity. I do not mean that the *Modern Church* is entirely responsible. For the infidel too misjudges the spirit of Christianity. He too substitutes the creed for the God, substitutes the theology for the religion, substitutes the unprogressive expression for the continually progressive life. The infidel would transfix with sarcasm and ridicule the creeds of three hundred years ago, and think himself destroying the beliefs of the high souls of the nineteenth century. . . The Church has been indifferent to the dizzying rapidity with which all knowledge has progressed. It has opposed the progress of science, charging the foremost men of all the world with Satanic alliance. The same spirit which once imprisoned Galileo, and forced him with the threat of death to deny that the earth was forever turning to receive the kisses of the sun—that same spirit lived through modern life. Small wonder then that such a host of progressive men in all ages have denied to the Church the rights of censorship over their beliefs in the laws of nature! But today that dogmatism of creed which brands as aliens and outcasts all men who think beyond its pale, together with that dogmatism of science which refuses to recognize the mystic touch of an all-pervading and eternal spirit—both have lost the significance of authority, both have failed to satisfy the higher aspirations of the human soul.

By the time he arrived at Mercer in 1927, John D. Freeman (1864–1943) was one of the most renowned Baptists in the world. He had written eight devotional works, including several novels, worked as chaplain to Canadian troops in World War I, and led some of the most prestigious congregations in America, Canada, and England. A native Canadian, Freeman was chosen in 1905 to give the inaugural keynote address to the World Baptist Congress in London, where he underscored the core Baptist belief of freedom of conscience in the service of Christ. In 1939, a group of 13 fundamentalist Mercer students, along with a group of Georgia Baptist ministers, had Freeman tried for heresy at the age of 74.

The Place of Baptists in the Christian Church (1905)

John D. Freeman

In the last analysis Christianity means to us the union of a human life with Jesus Christ; this union, involving on the one hand a relation of personal saviourhood and sovereignty, and on the other a relation of personal trust and love and loyalty. This is Christianity stated in terms of its irreducible minimum.

Now, this conception is one that carries with it, inseparably, the *radical and far-reaching Baptist doctrine of individualism*. To Christ, and to Christ alone, the individual must stand or fall. There can be no proxy in the matter. There can be no sponsorial performance of religious obligations. It is no more possible for one person to believe or disbelieve in another's behalf than to go to heaven or hell for him. There must be personal repentance, personal faith, personal confession of Christ's name . . .

From Anti-Ritualistic People.

From first to last we have uttered our steady protestation against all soul reliance upon ceremonial observances. We could do no other. Our fundamental principle lays the axe at the root of all sacramentalism and sacerdotalism. The undelegated sovereignty of Christ renders it forever impossible that His saving grace should be manipulated by any system of man mediation. That union with Christ which is the soul of Christianity is a union effected by the sovereign operation of the Holy Ghost in the immediate bestowment of Divine grace. Any interposition of ecclesiastical

583

machinery, whether sacraments or priesthoods, or discipline or ritual, is a manifest impertinence. It is necessarily and always a usurpation and a wrong. . . . Hierarchies there have been and are, whose colossal pretensions obscure this truth, and whose far-flung shadows fall dark upon the paths of men. As long as the last shade of a shadow of the doctrine of man-mediated grace lingers on the earth, our Baptist mission remains unfulfilled.

In the second place, our doctrine of individualism, under the sovereignty of Christ, has made us the unswerving and strenuous, if sometimes lonely . . .

Champions of Soul Liberty.

In our postulate of soul-liberty we affirm the right of every human being to exemption in matters of faith and conscience from all coercion or intimidation by any earthly authority whatsoever. Our demand has been not simply for religious toleration, but religious liberty; not sufferance merely, but freedom; and that not for ourselves alone, but for all men. We did not stumble upon the doctrine. It inheres in the very essence of our belief. Christ is Lord of all. Any attempt to put conscience in thrall to human authority is *Lese-Majeste* to the King of kings, and a negation of the privileges and responsibilities conferred by Him upon the individual soul.

The conscience is the servant only of God, and is not subject to the will of man. This truth has indestructible life. Crucify it and the third day it will rise again. Bury it in a sepulchre and the stone will be rolled away, while the keepers become as dead men.

With reference to this great principle we can clearly claim a thorough-going consistency. Steadfastly refusing to bend our own necks under the yoke of bondage, we have scrupulously withheld our hands from imposing that yoke upon others. Baptists are the one considerable religious body in the world, with three centuries of history behind them, who can claim to have been a non-persecuting people from first to last. Of martyr blood our hands are clean. We have never invoked the sword of temporal power to aid the sword of the Spirit. We have never passed an ordinance inflicting a civil disability on any man because of his religious views, be he Protestant or Papist, Jew or Turk or infidel. In this regard there is no blot on our escutcheon.

It has been in behalf of soul-liberty, primarily, that we have ever stood for . . .

Separation of Church and State.

In our deep conviction, the union of these two institutions represents the most baneful misalliance of the ages. Whether the State be grafted upon the Church or the Church upon the State, the fruit therefrom is alike "Ate with impoisonment and stung with fire."

"One of the anomalies of history is that Protestants, coming out of the Roman Catholic Church, with loud complaints against her tyrannies, so speedily and so greedily copied and emulated her repressive measures." Over the whole field swept by the Reformation movement, Protestant State Churchism soon reigned supreme. Luther and Melancthon imposed it upon Germany; Zwingli and Calvin riveted it upon Switzerland; Knox and his associates fastened it upon Scotland; Thomas Cromwell and Henry the Eighth bound the accursed incubus upon the life of England, to which it clings relentlessly and oppressively until this day. . . . The brightest chapter of Baptist achievement has, however, been enacted, not in the Old World, but in the New. The old spirit of religious intolerance crossed the Atlantic in the *Mayflower*. The Pilgrim Fathers were no lambs fleeing from the slaughter. With them it was a question of whose ox was being gored. Their own ox had been gored long enough. They would provide him with a new pasture and an exclusive stomping ground. But they had no thought of dehorning him in the interest of universal soul-liberty. The Puritans who settled the Massachusetts Bay colony in 1628 were another people, but of a similar spirit, and the two soon blended. Together they established, not a State Church so much as a Church State, in which citizenship was conditioned upon Church membership. There, then, for a season, was the spectacle of Congregationalism established by law, coercing all into conformity therewith, forbidding dissent, and enforcing its prohibitions by penalties of disfranchisement, fine, imprisonment, scourging and banishment. But the monstrosity was short-lived. The mixture of iron and clay soon crumbled. By nothing was its downfall hastened so much as by the "passive resistance" of Baptists within the colony, and their constructive work beyond its bounds. In 1636 Roger Williams, fleeing from oppression in Massachusetts, settled Providence, and obtained a charter which provided that no person was to be in any wise molested, punished, or called in question for any religious opinion. . . . Suffice it to say that owing to the lynx-eyed vigilance with which the Baptist people watched against the possibility of a State connection with the Church, the Constitution of the United States, as adopted in 1787, declared: "No religious test shall ever be required as a qualification to any office in the United States." Lest this should prove inadequate as a safeguard of liberty, it was amended, upon the petition of the Virginia Baptists, to read: "Congress shall make no law respecting an establishment of religion, or prohibition of the free exercise thereof." This is America's chiefest contribution to the art of government and the science of politics. It is, to a very large extent, a Baptist achievement.

The world must not be permitted to forget what the Baptist doctrine of soul-liberty, broadening into the conception of personal liberty and finding expression in the ordinances of civil liberty, has wrought for the political emancipation of mankind.

In March of 1939, a group of thirteen fundamentalist students, led by John Birch and Reid Lunsford, accused professors from the Christianity, Astronomy, Biology, and English departments of heresy. They demanded that only professors who agreed with the Georgia Baptist Convention's creedal statements, teaching only Georgia Baptist Convention-approved textbooks, should teach at Mercer University. Derided as the "unholy thirteen" by the Mercer student body, the accusers mailed hundreds of copies of their allegations to Georgia Baptists all over the state, creating a controversy that eventually pressured President Spright Dowell to hold a heresy trial for the professors in March, 1939. Although the professors were cleared of wrongdoing by the Mercer trustees, John D. Freeman resigned that spring.

Mercer Heresy Trial
Exerpts (1939)

from The Trial of Professor John D. Freeman (1939)

Professor John D. Freeman, at 74 years old, was the primary target of the thirteen ministerial students. The students found fault with his views on demons, Genesis, hell, the inerrant Bible, and the efficacy of Christ's blood as a literal, rather than figurative, agent of salvation.

THE CHAIRMAN: The meeting will come to order. The 13 ministerial students who have prepared affidavits and signed letters sent out to the pastors of Georgia making charges against six members of the faculty are requested to remain in this hearing. All the pastors, ordained ministers here in Macon and those visiting, are privileged to sit in. Others who may be witnesses will be called by the respective sides. The men making the charges, if they have any evidence in connection with those charges, will be notified to come in and keep yourselves where you can be identified. All of the faculty against whom charges are made are expected to remain in this hearing . . .

[DR. JOHN D. FREEMAN: Taking the witness stand in his own behalf, testified in connection to the charges against him—]

JOHN FREEMAN: I will just state that this is quite a surprise party, as far as I am concerned. I was not aware of the fact that the ministers in Macon and of the Rehoboth Association and from elsewhere had been summoned against me for a trial. I have not requested to come and speak on my behalf any ministers and I am just here under the circumstances that have developed. . . .

THE CHAIRMAN: Any question for Dr. Freeman?

REV. SEABORN WINN: Did I understand that he was going to make a statement?

CHAIRMAN: Yes.

DR. JOHN D. FREEMAN: It is simply this: that my purpose and endeavor has been to help the students, who come to my classes to be better informed, more joyous, trustful, Christians and Christian workers. I have taught what I believe to be the truth and I am prepared to stand by my teachings, some of which has been misrepresented in these affidavits, misrepresented in this issue here, in the easy culling of a sentence or a part of a sentence and taking it out of its larger context. Now, I want to say this, all that is here in these affidavits of these students is but a small dust in the balance, compared with what has been charged against me now for a good many years, here and there throughout the state, charges that I taught the exact opposite of what I do teach . . . I do not know how many students are present here from my classes but I will ask them to stand. . . How many of them are ready to affirm that I have told the truth—

REV. SEABORN WINN: Now brother Chairman, he has the right to put these witnesses up one at a time and then they would be subject to cross-examination but . . . I don't think this is proper.

JOHN FREEMAN: Will the members of my class come forward?

SEABORN WINN: Before that, I want to ask if Dr. Freeman is through with his statement. I will ask Brother Tyner and Brother Nelms to ask him the questions.

REV. TYNER: What do you consider the duties and responsibilities of a teacher?

JOHN FREEMAN: To teach in a Christian college, in this institution?

REV. TYNER: As a teacher whether he is in Christian college or wherever he is teaching?

JOHN FREEMAN: I teach the truth and love my students and seek to help them; I pray for them, try to be a friend to them and to seek always to be their guide, philosopher and friend.

REV. TYNER: Then, is it the teacher's business to impart the truth so that the student will understand it as true?

JOHN FREEMAN: Yes sir.

REV. TYNER: Why do you say then, doctor, what is your reaction to this disturbance that arises in the mind of so many of these boys from year to year?

JOHN FREEMAN: My answer to that will be given when you hear the other side, the other reaction. Here are 23 students in a class in New Testament. Three only of these students make any charges against my teachings. Twenty of them are prepared to tell you that they have the exact opposite reaction.

REV. TYNER: I just wanted your reaction as to why this general impression was created?

JOHN FREEMAN: I would like to answer that—May I ask you this question: how many persons does it take to set a forest afire?

SEABORN WINN: Brother Chairman, we do not understand that the interrogator is to be interrogated from the stand.

JOHN FREEMAN: Well, who is the interrogator here? And why do you have official standing? Are you the interrogator? How many interrogators do I have?

REV. SEABORN WINN: Brother Tyner is interrogating Dr. Freeman—he was questioning you and not you him. . . . Isn't it your opinion, Dr. Freeman, that it is safer in a Baptist College in Macon to have as a textbook one that is accepted as orthodox by that denomination?

JOHN FREEMAN: I would say, yes—safer.

REV. SEABORN WINN: You do not feel that any book that is not accepted as orthodox by the Southern Baptists should be used in a Southern Baptist school?

JOHN FREEMAN: . . . Any one who teaches theology in the South had better use a Baptist textbook.

[Outburst of applause]

REV. SEABORN WINN: Dr. Freeman. Do you believe in the Genesis account of the creation?

JOHN FREEMAN: Yes.

REV. SEABORN WINN: As it is given in the English Bible?

JOHN FREEMAN: As I understand it, yes.

REV. SEABORN WINN: How do you understand it?

JOHN FREEMAN: I understand that the purpose of the writer is to affirm the creatorship of God, God the creator of all things; that he is not undertaking to give a complete, scientific statement regarding creation but that he sets forth the creation as having taken place during periods of time for six days. It was all the work of God. That was his concern, the concern of the writer, to affirm the Divine Authorship of Creation.

REV. SEABORN WINN: Do you believe that the Genesis account of the creation of a woman from the rib of man, direct by the power of God, is correct?

JOHN FREEMAN: Now, that is a question that I would like to know about.

[Several laugh]

REV. SEABORN WINN: But do you believe that really is correct as to God's statement of it?

JOHN FREEMAN: Well, as to God's statement, you say? As to Genesis' statement?

REV. SEABORN WINN: Do you teach your pupils that God created woman out of the rib of man, as is told specifically in the Genesis account of the creation?

JOHN FREEMAN: I do not teach the Old Testament—

REV. SEABORN WINN: Dr. Freeman, in these allegations—?

JOHN FREEMAN: I am not so much concerned about how woman was made as I am about how she was redeemed and brought into fellowship with Christ and made an heir of God.

REV. SEABORN WINN: Just what do you mean by the expression you gave in your statement as to your belief that [the Bible] was infallible for its purposes?

JOHN FREEMAN: Its purpose was to give us an authoritative and sufficient revelation of God and a way of salvation for man through Jesus Christ, God's Son. It is not written as one of my old professors used to say, to teach us how the Heavens go, but to teach us how to go to Heaven.

REV. SEABORN WINN: What is your teaching to your classes concerning hell?

JOHN FREEMAN: My teaching is that it is an awful fact proclaimed in the scriptures and that is the doom of every unrepented soul, who are doomed to separation from God, everlasting separation from God. I do not feel that it is a place, located down in the center of the earth and that the fires are material fires.

REV. SEABORN WINN: You do not feel that it is a place?

JOHN FREEMAN: Not a locality, no.

REV. SEABORN WINN: A literal place?

JOHN FREEMAN: No.

REV. SEABORN WINN: But a condition?

JOHN FREEMAN: Yes.

REV. SEABORN WINN: . . . Dr. Freeman, I am asking you this final question, if all your teachings to the students are as vague and indefinite as the answers you have given here this afternoon?

THE CHAIRMAN: I think that is a rather unfair question.

REV. SEABORN WINN: I withdraw the question and I have no further questions.

JOHN FREEMAN: I consider that a most offensive insinuation and highly unwarranted.

REV. SEABORN WINN: It was not intended that way.

REV. KILGORE: Brother Chairman, I think that this investigation here has gone far enough.

from The Trial of Professor Josiah Crudup, Astronomy and Biology Professor

Though beloved by the student body, those bringing charges against Professor Josiah Crudup objected to an implication in an Astronomy lecture that Genesis might be read figuratively rather than literally and scientifically.

REV. SEABORNE WINN: Do you believe the Bible record of Adam and Eve?

JOSIAH CRUDUP: Yes sir, and in my work, I intend to harmonize astronomy with the beautiful scripture of the First Chapter of Genesis, feeling it my duty here to harmonize them.

REV. SEABORNE WINN: And if, Dr. Crudup, they do not harmonize and you cannot harmonize them, do you tell your classes to let their preference be with the scriptural statements, if they make such connections?

JOSIAH CRUDUP: Oh, I leave that to them. Every man has to make his own decision on that.

REV. SEABORNE WINN: Do you leave the impression that the Bible statements on all matters are to be taken in preference to any other teachings from any other book?

JOSIAH CRUDUP: Well, I frankly haven't taken the obligation in the teaching of Astronomy to teach the scriptures also.

REV. SEABORNE WINN: You signed the statement though, didn't you Dr. Crudup, as held by the Southern Baptists?

JOSIAH CRUDUP: You say I have signed that?

REV. SEABORNE WINN: I am asking you the question, did you?

JOSIAH CRUDUP: Oh no, I have not . . . that I know of.

REV. SEABORNE WINN: Would you ever say anything in your Astronomy class that might lead your students to doubt Genesis without adding that you prefer the Bible to anything that might be said about Astronomy?

JOSIAH CRUDUP: Oh, in my Astronomy, if there ever comes any statement as to whether or not the student should believe in God or some scientific theory, I always tell the student that my own life has chosen to be convinced first of Deity.

REV. SEABORNE WINN: According to the Bible?

JOSIAH CRUDUP: Yes, as represented by the scriptures.

REV. SEABORNE WINN: Well, then do you believe the Bible account of Adam and that there was a person described in the Bible named Adam as the first created man?

JOSIAH CRUDUP: I have paused over that a long time and have tried to get a picture in my mind of how those things might have been. I have been assured by some of my great teacher colleagues that there have been at times or there is in the Greek, original Greek, the article before the word "Adam." So, that leaves me in my own mind to not know definitely whether the teachers are speaking of an individual or a group of individuals.

REV. SEABORNE WINN: Dr. Crudup, you know in the scriptural account, it says "God said that all the other animals and so on, all the animal kingdom,—but said for man there was no help-mate for him, and then God said it is not good for man to be alone, I will make him a help mate; and then the Lord God caused a deep sleep to fall upon Adam, and he took one of his ribs and made woman." Do you believe that?

JOSIAH CRUDUP: That thing had puzzled me also. I don't know what to say about that. I hope there will be no laughter when I make this remark because it has puzzled me as much as the hen and the egg proposition.

REV. SEABORNE WINN: Well, you are aware of the fact that Baptist beliefs are that as accepted amongst Southern and Georgia Baptists, of which Mercer University is an educational institution, are you not?

JOSIAH CRUDUP: Aware of all of the statements that have been made?

REV. SEABORNE WINN: That I have made concerning the creation of man and of woman, the Bible, Genesis story of the creation of the world and man—You are aware that Baptists do believe that?

JOSIAH CRUDUP: Yes sir, but I wouldn't know what proportion of Baptists.

REV. SEABORNE WINN: But that is the accepted belief?

JOSIAH CRUDUP: I have never read a declaration of Baptists beliefs that incorporated those statements.

REV. SEABORNE WINN: You are not familiar with the articles of faith of Baptists at the Philadelphia Convention or the New Hampshire Convention?

JOSIAH CRUDUP: Yes, I have read those.

REV. SEABORNE WINN: Well, do you accept those as a professor of this institution?

JOSIAH CRUDUP: Yes sir.

REV. SEABORNE WINN: You would not consciously teach anything that conflicted with those, to be received in preference to those, as a professor in a Baptist institution?

JOSIAH CRUDUP: No, I wouldn't feel that I have any business here if I did that.

from The Trial of James Wallace

James Wallace, a graduate student who served as laboratory instructor in Comparative Anatomy and Embryology, stood accused of teaching the theory of evolution in his biology class. The class used a textbook which suggested that human tail-bones may be vestigial remains of longer tail-bones.

REV. GROVER TYNER: Why did this question of children born with tails ever arise?

WALLACE: As a textbook for this course we are studying Walter, and in the book by Weimer.

REV. GROVER TYNER: I think you misunderstand my question: Why did that question come up?

WALLACE: I am coming to that. There are pictures in here of children with tails. [The students] asked me why such a thing would be in there and if such a thing would ever happen.

REV. GROVER TYNER: Did the question of evolution arise in that discussion?

WALLACE: I do not remember.

REV. GROVER TYNER: It was not then being taught that man evolved?

WALLACE: No sir, it was definitely not. It was merely an explanation of the pictures they asked me about . . . in the two textbooks being taught then, Walter's and Weimer's [General Biology].

REV. GROVER TYNER: In the teaching then, you do not feel that all men at one time or that all of mankind had tails and through evolution lost it?

WALLACE: That is not my department. I have nothing to do with that at all.

REV. GROVER TYNER: You do not teach that?

WALLACE: No.

REV. GROVER TYNER: You do not believe that?

WALLACE: That, I think, I have preference to myself.

REV. GROVER TYNER: Answer the question, yes or no, do you believe it or do you not?

WALLACE: Do I have to answer such a question? I refuse to answer.

REV. GROVER TYNER: Do you teach in a Baptist school of Georgia?

WALLACE: I do.

REV. GROVER TYNER: Are you a Baptist?

WALLACE: I am not.

REV. GROVER TYNER: You do not then believe the Bible statement regarding the creation of man?

WALLACE: I did not say that.

REV. GROVER TYNER: You did not say that?

WALLACE: I did not.

REV. GROVER TYNER: Do you think Adam was created with tail or without?

WALLACE: I have no definite knowledge of how Adam was created and I don't believe that any of you gentlemen have any. . . .

CHARIMAN: Your position is Assistant under Professor Carver?

WALLACE: Yes sir.

MR. T. HOYT DAVIS: Are you also a student?

WALLACE: I am a student, a graduate student.

REV. SEABORN WINN: Do you believe the Bible?

WALLACE: Naturally.

REV. SEABORN WINN: Alright, you believe that God made man of the dust of the ground and breathed into his body the breath of life, and man became a living soul. You do believe that story of the creation of man and not that he evolved through millions of years?

WALLACE: May I ask that the prosecutor stick to the accusations?

REV. SEABORN WINN: I will read it over again.

WALLACE: I believe the Bible as I told you before.

REV. SEABORN WINN: Do you believe that that is the Baptist declaration of faith under which this institution operates? And I repeat that I have been advised that the members of this faculty have signed it. So, I ask, do you believe in the articles of faith of the Baptist church?

WALLACE: To my own knowledge, I have never seen the articles of faith of the Baptist Church. I was not asked to sign them.

REV. SEABORN WINN: If evolution teaches one theory concerning the creation of man or the origin of man and the Genesis account seems to teach something else, would you prefer the theory of evolution or the theory in Genesis?

WALLACE: Well, let me elucidate upon the word that you have used there, the word "theory." We definitely teach theory, not facts, when we come to evolution. Theory is not a law. It is merely a proposition and the fact that it is a theory is emphasized.

REV. SEABORN WINN: Did you ever say this, "Evolution is true and any one is a conceited fool and an ass who doesn't believe in it?"

WALLACE: Don't you think that that is rather rare language to use in the classroom?

REV. SEABORN WINN: I ask you the question, did you or did you not?

WALLACE: I did not, if that was said in the classroom.

REV. SEABORN WINN: I am asking you the question, did you or did you not say: "Buddhism and [Islam] are just as good as the Christian religion. Some respects better and a man who lives up to either of them will be saved?"

WALLACE: I did not say that some Buddhists and some [Muslims] and some Confucianists are as good as Christians; what I did say is that I have known some B uddhists and some Confucianists who are better than some I know who profess Christianity.

REV. SEABORN WINN: Do you believe it is necessary to believe in Christ to be saved?

WALLACE: I do not think I have to answer that, do I?

REV. SEABORN WINN: You are a teacher in a Baptist Institution?

WALLACE: Yes.

REV. E. A. KILGORE: I think he ought to answer some of those questions.

WALLACE: I believe that if you have had the opportunity of learning of Christ, of hearing of Him—I believe that I have to believe in him to be saved, because I have known about Him.

REV. SEABORN WINN: Do you believe the Bible teaches any other way of salvation except through the faith in Jesus Christ as Lord and Savior?

WALLACE: I do not.

REV. SEABORN WINN: That that is the only way?

WALLACE: I believe that the Bible teaches Christ is the way.

REV. SEABORN WINN: The truth and the light, that no man cometh unto the Father but by Him?

WALLACE: I believe that Christ is the way.

REV. SEABORN WINN: And there is no other way?

WALLACE: I said, "the way."

REV. SEABORN WINN: I asked the question: did you believe there was any other way of salvation?

WALLACE: Not that I know of.

REV. SEABORN WINN: Then you do not believe, as far as you know, there is any other way of salvation?

WALLACE: Not as far as I know. If I may, I did not get a chance to finish my statement. There is one statement here where He said "I am the Way, the Truth and the Life. No man cometh unto the Father but by me." That was made and I made this statement afterwards: I said that although I didn't know, I imagined that God in his Goodness or mercy would surely have not let Christ die for merely one-third of the population of the world and let the other two-thirds out. I said that Christ was the way as a ticket agent, I mean as a ticket taker is the way into the theater; you have to go by that ticket taker before you can get in and you have to pay the price at the gate. Well, Christ paid the price for us.   I said that Christ paid the price for the world and he surely must have meant all the people that are in it. . . . God in his goodness would surely forgive and admit people into Heaven, people who had never heard or had never had a chance to hear him.

REV. E. A. KILGORE: Young man, you had better not try to teach theology.

The day after the heresy trial concluded, Mercer's student newspaper, The Cluster, *addressed the specter of outside forces attempting to curtail the freedom and scope of a Mercer education.*

Schism and Heresy (1939)

It is with genuine sorrow that *The Cluster* is forced to enter another fight. Usually *The Cluster* doesn't mind a nice clean fight; this time it is with sorrow because it has learned that certain persons posing as the traditional spirit of Mercer University have taken it upon themselves to foist their own conceptions of Christianity (more properly, narrow denominationalism) on others to the extent of controlling the hiring and firing of the faculty at Mercer.

We learn with amazement that such crass, medieval bigotry exists on campus.

It is reported on good authority that this group mailed out over 800 letters to Georgia ministers alleging various heresies and infidelities on the part of certain members of the Mercer faculty. The reaction of the student body alone should be enough to convince any purposeful Baptist minister of the absurdity of the charges, and it is primarily to report this reaction on the part of the students that *The Cluster* sees fit to print news of action of this group.

Apparently anti-everything in character, this small group of students has finally forced the campus into recognizing them, however unfavorable the recognition may be. What price glory!

The methods they have adopted might possibly be taken as a manifestation of the Holy Spirit as they claim, but we know many reputable psychologists (and ministers, as well!) who would be inclined to list their multifarious activities under the general heading of sensational exhibitionism. And their reputed connections to certain well-known persons at present outside the realm of recognized Baptistry, only makes the allegation more binding.

Because they are sincere in their accusations makes them at least honest in their conscious motives, but it no more prepares them for being students in this twentieth century than attending Mercer prepares one for deep-sea diving.

This group claims to be led by the Holy Spirit after much prayer, and the tendency is, of course, for one to be overawed by this solemn declaration until we realize the leaders of the Spanish Inquisition also thought they were led by the Holy Spirit—after ceaseless prayer. This analogy is not unfortunate, for indeed, with all this talk about heresy we could well imagine our unfortunate professors being toasted at the stake. . . .

The Cluster stands for something which at once leaps above argument: something for which we hope our ancestors who founded this supposedly democratic state, staining the black earth with their life's blood, have not died in vain: tolerance.

It appears that not only must we fight dictatorships and intolerance outside our borders, but we must be ever on our guard against petty intolerances and attempted dictatorships from within.

The irony of it all is that the group of professors on the list to be purged is almost without exception a group of MEN whose lives transcend any narrow sectarian belief—who are gentle and kind to their enemies as well as their friends; in short, men who embody in the flesh the principles of a dynamic Christianity, men who speak the same language as one Jesus of Nazareth. Needless to say, these men were profoundly shocked when they learned (without being forewarned by their accusers) that they were recusants and accused in words whose denotative value was obsolescent before the Declaration of Independence was signed.

It has been thought by some that publicizing the matter would make martyrs of the accusers, at least in their own minds. It is comparatively easy to be a martyr amid threats and jeers, but martyrdom is extremely untenable when satirical laughter is directed against it. Just as Don Quixote, rendered the coup de grace to the Knighthood-in-Flower Age, just so might the laughter of the campus prove to be the lean, boney knight who destroys the "You're-going-to-hell-if-you-aren't-a-Baptist" philosophy on this campus. For almost all the students are laughing, thank our good Lord.

In the 1950s, Mercer had strictly enforced rules for "lady-like" behavior among female students, including a prohibition against men sitting within twelve inches of women in the parlor of MEP. There were not similarly restrictive rules for Mercer's male students. Carolyn Martin, a student in the 1950s, explained that female students had to sign out on date cards, but "this was not true of the men—the guys got all the privileges. The rules were so one-sided: they just felt that they had to protect females." Mary Wilder, a student in the early 1950s and later one of Mercer's first feminist faculty members, shared the same memories: "the putting on raincoats over your shorts when you went to play basketball or volleyball—that was not true of the men. They were totally free to do anything they wanted to do any time they wanted to, but we were treated like little girls and protected." Mercer's female students did not try to gain redress for the double-standard in the fifties. "It never occurred to protest our situation at Mercer," Wilder explained. "I know you think that's crazy, but it never did. Wearing those raincoats [over our shorts] was like wearing a veil, and it never occurred to us that it was ridiculous." In the late 1960s, Mercer women staged a successful protest of the rules, camping out in the quad to break their early curfews. The rules were changed shortly thereafter.

from The Mercer University Women's Student Handbook (1950–1951)

Life at Mercer dormitories for women is organized in certain patterns that are designed to allow freedom of life in a large group. This freedom can be realized only through the cooperation of all members of the group.

Rules and Regulations

I. Call-downs

1. Call-downs may be given to any girl in the Dormitory by the faculty members in charge, any member of the Council, and monitors.
2. 3 minor call-downs equal one major call-down.

II. Campus

1. A major call-down requires two nights' campus.
2. Campus hours are observed from 7:00 PM to 7:00 AM.
3. The Campus must begin at once and may not be delayed to suit the individual. When campused, a girl may not leave the campus for any reason unless she has special permission from the faculty member in

charge, and then only to see a doctor, or her family. In case of the family, her parents shall be notified that she is campused before she sees them. When permission is granted for these emergencies, one extra day shall be added to the campus. If campus is broken without permission, a double major shall be added.

4. A "Campus" sign will be posted on the door to inform others that they are not to enter. A sign "Campus" should be respected by all residents, as neither the girls in campus nor her roommate can have visitors from 7:00 PM to 7:00 AM. Breaking a Campus sign carries a penalty of one major call-down. Riding in cars during Campus is considered breaking campus also.

IV. Conduct

A major call-down shall be given to a girl for unlady-like conduct.

V. Co-Op, Drug Store, Fruit Stand, Library

1. The Co-op, Tatnall Square Drug Store, and the Fruit Stand may be visited any time before 8:00 PM and between 10:00 and 10:30 PM and does not count as going off campus. If a girl goes from the Dormitory to the Co-op, Drug Store, or Fruit Stand between 8:00–10:00 PM, she must take a date privilege.

2. During 8:00–10:00 PM, girls may get permission from a Council member in the Library to go from the Library to the Co-op, Drug Store or Fruit Stand, but must return with 15 minutes to the Library. If girls go from the Library and return to the Dormitory, the time limit is 30 minutes, and on leaving the Library girls must get permission to go from a Council Member in the Library.

VI. Dates and Privileges

1. Boys may come into the Parlors at 1:30 PM. At all other hours before the above mentioned, boys must wait in the Foyer. Residents are responsible for their date's behavior.

Date Privileges Per Week

Seniors:	B Average	4 dates
Seniors:	C Average	3 dates
Juniors:	B Average	3 dates
Juniors:	C Average	2 dates
Sophomores:	B Average	2 dates
Sophomores:	C Average	1 date
Freshman:	B Average	1 date

Freshman: C Average   0 date

Any student: D Average   0 date

Penalty for going out without a date privilege is one major call-down.

2. Weekend date privileges are unlimited. Weekend date privileges cannot be exchanged for week-day privileges except in very special cases. Special Permission must be secured from the Resident Counselor.

   Girls with averages below C can never exchange a weekend date for a week date.

   All girls, whether they have a date privilege or not, are permitted to attend one mid-week Basketball game a week. They will sign out on the Book and will be in by 10:30 PM.

3. There shall be no dating on the Campus proper or in Tatnall Square Park at night. Penalty—one major call-down.

4. Remaining outside of M.E.P. with your date at night for a period longer than 5 minutes, whether in a car or standing outside the door, is considered loitering, and the penalty is one minor call-down.

VIII. Dining Hall

It is expected that you cooperate with Mrs. Nickerson and the dining hall girls by being prompt to meals and by conducting yourselves in a lady-like manner. Lady-like conduct includes proper dress, consideration for other people, quiet manner, and no excessive noise.

Dressing for dinner on Wednesday evenings and Sunday noon means that girls do not wear the informal clothes used for school, but in order to make the occasion a little more festive they wear "Sunday dresses" and shoes with heels.

In the dining hall, there will be no visiting between tables.

During an announcement in the dining hall everyone should stop eating.

IX. Dress

No sun-back dresses are to be worn in the dining hall or on campus without a bolero.

Gym suits or shorts may be worn to the gym, provided a raincoat or a long coat is worn over them. Blue jeans, slacks, or pedal pushers cannot be worn in the Co-op if remaining in the building. Blue jeans, slacks, or pedal pushers cannot be worn in the parlors for any length of time.

Girls are not to wear raincoats or long coats to breakfast, and hair curls that show under a kerchief are to be taken down.

Girls should be properly dressed for all meals. Penalty—one minor.

XV. Lights

On school nights and Sundays, lights will be out at 12:00 AM and on Friday and Saturday nights at 12:30 AM.

Light rules apply to sorority suites also.

XXIII. Signing Out

1. Girls must sign out in the Dormitory Register at all times when leaving the campus and after 8:00 PM whenever they leave dormitories to go to other buildings on campus. Girls are not to go out of M.E.P. after dinner at night alone.
   Failure to sign out and in—one major.
2. When a student has a date or is taking a date privilege, she must sign out on the date cards.
3. When students are leaving the city, or spending the night away from the Dormitory, they sign out on the home cards.

XXVI. Town Privileges

The number of town privileges on Monday through Thursday are listed below:

Freshmen—1	Juniors—3
Sophomore—2	Seniors—Unlimited

Penalty for over-cut: one minor call-down.

XXVII. Visiting out the Window

Students do not carry on conversations out the window. Girls may speak to someone out of the window if necessary, and monitors and Council members will be the judge of the necessity. Conversations out of the window result in one minor call-down. Visitors should call for girls at the Information Desk.

G. McLeod Bryan, Christianity professor at Mercer from 1948–1956, was among the first faculty members to be outspoken and politically active in his opposition to segregation, both inside the classroom and in the Macon community. Energized by his teaching, a group of his students broke segregation laws, reached out to the surrounding community in service to the poor, and lobbied Mercer to desegregate as early as the 1950s. McLeod Bryan, called "Mac" by his students, left Mercer in 1956 after he was pressured by Baptist authorities to stop teaching the writings of Martin Luther King, Jr., in his classes. One of his students, Harris Mobley, later worked with Mac to desegregate Mercer, convincing Sam Oni, an African missionary convert, to apply to Mercer in 1963. This 2001 interview was conducted at Mac's home in Winston-Salem, North Carolina: a rustic, wooded farmhouse standing as a rebuke to the finely manicured subdivision of suburban McMansions that completely surround it. Mac had simply refused to sell his untamed land to the subdivision developer.

Interview with
G. McLeod Bryan (2001)

What was the atmosphere regarding race in Georgia when you came to teach in 1948?

There's no way you can breathe in Georgia—you can't go to get a hamburger, you can't go to the drugstore, you can't take a bus-ride, you can't go to a ballgame, you can't go to church, can't go anywhere, without race. That's stifling. You can't live it. I mean, why do you have to listen to this endless nonsense? Let's take a good illustration of that. My next door neighbor's a policeman. We were living there on Adams street in a shotgun house, and the black section is just beyond us. And he's a policeman living next door. He's a Baptist, he's a deacon at a church, and all of this sort of thing. We have no television. . . . So I want to see the ball games—like the world series—and I have to go over to his house to see them. I'm sitting there on the back porch during the playoff season, and he gets up and leaves every now and then. And his wife—she's conscious of the fact that I'm noticing that he's leaving—and she says, "Oh well Mac," she says, "you have to understand Leo. He has to go out to spit every time Jackie Robinson comes up to bat." Now that's the kind of hellish cloud that hangs over you.

605

Let me give you another illustration: his son is the same age as my children—I had four children—and his little boy comes over and says, "Let's go out and beat some niggers." And he has a bicycle chain. And so I'm faced with the problem—what do I say to my children? So I say to him, "What do you want to beat them up for?" He says "well they're bad, we got to beat them in line." I said "oh well, let's do something tonight." I said to my boys, "let's go down the street and invite some black boys up to our house and let them see that these kids are just like they are."

And what happened?

Oh well, that little boy's embarrassed at that moment because he's looking at kids that play ball, skate, do the same—talk about the same things they do, but they're just down the street. So you know, everything is just one endless battle.

How did you get your students to begin to address the problems of segregation in Macon?

Macon had almost the worst housing of any city in the United States. And so it was really easy for me to take these students into these areas where housing was absolutely dilapidated, and we would take them there, and we would patch up an old house for an old lady who was dying—a black woman who was dying. And they'd get to see that she had no refrigerator and no food in the cupboard, and the neighbors all came around to watch us, and these kids all had nothing to buy hamburgers and that sort of thing. And living with them a day, they experienced poverty.

And so my students were doing *unusual* things. They were going to black churches, they were socializing with blacks, they were doing endless things together. We were painting buildings together, we were going on weekend retreats together, we were going to Koinonia [an interfaith commune in Americus run by Clarence Jordan], we met every Wednesday night, we went to conferences, we went to Buckeye Cove in the summer and built cottages, we went to Morehouse. We were just going everywhere. It was an extra university. It was a university that didn't have courses or grades. We had no recompense. We were living on the edge. We had our own bank account; we shared with people in need. It was the old Hebrew concept that we belong together. We lend money without interest, take what we need, and build up a community of faith.

Joe Hendricks said that Mercer has tried to be prophetic to culture. What does it mean to be prophetic?

You know, all my life I've wrestled with that question. . . In the Hebrew tradition the priest and the king and the prophet are your three role models, right? So how is it that the prophet got higher than the priest and the king? Because the prophet has *direct* inspiration. See, the prophet doesn't have to have a tradition. As I say, a prophet is a nobody coming from the woods. Amos says, "I'm a nobody. I came from the woods. I have no village. I have no degrees. I speak. Who do I speak for? Yahweh." And what the prophet is doing is reviving the best in the law. A prophet is a person who doesn't particularly respect the normal credentials and institutional structures because he or she thinks they can *break through* those traditional structures and find the true law or will of Yahweh underneath it. And that means automatically that he or she is opposed to the culture that is. You have to be an outsider.

Another characteristic of a prophet is he must suffer with his people to the nth degree. He cannot leave. Dietrich Bonhoeffer said, when he was in New York City and had the chance to be free, "I've got to go back to Germany." And all those people in New York said, "You don't have to go back; you can live like an American, free." He said, "I must go back." And what'd he do? He went right back into the concentration camp and died, with Hitler killing him, April 1945. See, but that's a prophet. The prophet must go to the people he's prophesied against, he must live with those people and suffer with them, and he must die with them. It's a hard road, brother. That's the reason they're barefoot.

What is the prophetic idea of justice?

I say to my wife "I love you, love you, love you!" And I grab her and hug her and throw her up in the air, and before she hits the ground she says, "who gets the car keys?" See, you have one car. And that's justice, see. You know, it's very simple. Justice is a very simple: all you have to do is ask who gets the car keys? Amos says "the rich sell the dirt on the poor man's head." Isn't that a great line? Who would write that? "The rich *pine* to sell the real estate on the poor man's head." How much dirt is here on my head and your head now? And somebody at this moment is pining to sell it as real estate? Amos is good. I mean, you read him—he's good.

Listen to the first law. It has moved me so many times. The first part of the Mosaic law is that if you cheat a poor man of his clothing, and you take it away from him, you give him a debt and you take his clothing for security, and the poor man is lying there in the night, shivering and freezing in the night—this is the law! Mosaic law!—God says, "I will hear his cry, and I will come down and punish the man and his wife and his children for what he has done against that poor man." Doesn't that scare you? It scares the living daylights out of me. You want to borrow a dollar from me. Right? "I gotta have a dollar to get gas back to the motel," right? Now I say "ok, give me your shirt for security." Simple transaction that goes on *billions* of times all over the world. God is not the least concerned about the transaction. He's concerned about you being without a shirt. Now who says that? [smiles.] I say it. And you say it too.

Well, what about Jesus? After all, there's a book called *Jesus: CEO.*

You've got *all* these books written with Jesus as a capitalist. I've got a whole shelf of them up there. It's laughable, and it's sick. . . . Can Jesus ride in a red Ferrari? Jesus was simply a peasant who always sided with the poor. He's a barefooted peasant with no property, and he died like Gandhi without a single piece of property.

I was in a feedstore yesterday buying feed for my animals, and the woman says "how're you getting along with all of those rich people around you?" She owns this [subdivision], and she's always teasing me about all these rich people around me. I said "well, I grew up never wanting to be rich." And she says, "that's the way I grew up. My father taught me never to envy the rich." So we agreed. Then I said, "But I have a prejudice against the rich." She said "Wait a minute, you're prejudiced against rich people?" She says, "You're a Christian aren't you? You're prejudiced against the rich?" I said "Yes." And she's a very strong Jesus follower. I said "You understand that Jesus was also prejudiced against the rich." She said "Where?" I said "Well, he said 'a rich man cannot enter the Kingdom of heaven.'" And then I quoted in Luke 16:19–30. Dives lived in a rich house with a gate and dog, just like these here [in this sub-division], and there was a poor man at the gate eating the crumbs off his table—I imagine eating dog food. This is a Jesus story. When they died, the rich man went to hell, and the poor man went to the bosom of Abra-ham. And the rich man says in hell, "why is the poor man in the bosom of Abraham?" And he prays to God, "please send a prophet to my broth-ers who are going to end up in hell like I am if they don't have somebody to tell them." And Jesus says that God said, "There's a chasm fixed between you and me that no person can cross. And besides, I've already sent prophets to your brothers, and to you and you would not listen." Now what a great parable! I was preaching this in Macon, Georgia in a mill church and a man came up to me at the end of the service, and he said, "Preacher do I understand you to say that poor man went to heaven just because he was poor, and the rich man went to hell because he was rich?" I said, "I didn't make up the story, sir." Now what do you call that? There's no moral superiority, no theological correctness, no circumcision, no baptism. You got it? What do you call that?

If there is an unjust law, do you break it?

Well, I do, and King brought this out for all of us, and then he taught us how you decided. If the law was made by the majority in which the minority has no voice, in which the minority is victimized, then the law is automatically unjust. If the law is made by the majority, and the minority has no voice in the making of the law, and they're the victims of the law, then that law is automatically unjust.

Now let's take the example of the Hitler party who came together at Wahnsee and set up the "Final solution" [to exterminate Jews]. Now look, there was no Jew in the movement. They made the law: who were the victims? Whenever that happens, that's an *immediate* unjust law. Alright, the second thing King said was when those who enforce the law are also in the majority and do not allow an equal representation, then that law is unjustly executed. Thirdly, if the law is adjudicated in the courts, and the minority people are not in the jury or in the judgeship, then the law is unjust. He went right down the line. And I don't see how anybody can argue with that.

What of order? Isn't it important to respect the law? I spoke with a police officer who said that he would have obeyed segregation laws and kept African Americans out of the park in order to keep order, even though he himself was African American. His job wasn't to question the law, he said, because that would lead to chaos. His job was to enforce the law.

I say he can hold to that as a solid social principle until the conflict comes to his doorstep, and then he has to decide whether the chaos that may come will borne a better social structure. And he has to choose. And at every one of those junctures—in Montgomery, in Birmingham, King and the Civil Rights movement chose chaos. And the chaos was, "we'll walk; we'll not ride the buses; we'll defy every police order; we'll do everything we can." I mean, the Montgomery police did everything in the *book* they could to control them, and they said, "we will not cooperate in any form or fashion with that." And that was amazing to me. There comes a juncture when you cross over that line. You have to move sometime. The reason for that is very simple: because the social structure between social order and social chaos comes to a breaking point. And when it comes to a breaking point as in Montgomery, you have to choose sides.

So at that time, we were breaking with the Civic book morality. You know, the civic book morality that we taught to white people was that the law is proper, and only bad people go to jail, and good people don't go to jail, and the courts handle the process even-handedly, and only the bad guys end up in the electric chair, and the good guys get off. And that's the civic book morality. And King was the first one to say *"phooey* on that!" There's such a thing as a statutory law which can be dead wrong, inhumane, and do exactly like Hitler's laws did in Germany. You know, they can be very civil laws but they're discriminating against a whole part of your culture. And King was the first one in many ways, in the South, to say, "look, if a Jew is being persecuted, then I stand up for the Jew. I have to stand up for that part of the culture which is being victimized." And those Christians in Germany who stood up, like Bonhoeffer, they went to concentration camps. Those that didn't had prominent jobs.

And that was the situation with Baptists in Georgia. See, Baptists *never* took a stand, and what was happening, these were all Baptist Mercer students for the most part, and they were saying *why is our denomination* the largest, most prominent denomination—not saying a word! See, that's the conspiracy of silence. Nothing in their literature, nothing in the Sunday-school lessons, nothing in the Sunday sermons, nothing in the theological courses. . . . And what was happening at that time in colleges of the South was also a conspiracy of silence, in which *nobody* brings up race. Period. Nobody. And whoever does as a college professor is at once in danger of his job, or in danger of not being promoted, in danger of reduction in salary, and all kinds of retribution. But students were eager to break through that conspiracy of silence.

In "Letter from a Birmingham Jail," Martin Luther King, Jr., is critical of people who were called moderates in the sixties. What's wrong with the word moderate?

The trouble with the term moderate, as you're using it, and with regards to race, is there were not two extremes. There was only one extreme, and that was a person who believed in genuine human relations. There was nobody else. Because a moderate was not saying "get rid of Jim Crow." The moderate was not saying "let's move speedily." The moderate was not saying any of those things. The moderate was saying, "I'm in the middle, between two extremes.". . . They all said, "King, we want you to go out of town." King, sitting in jail, wrote a letter saying "you all are wrong. Jesus is extremist, I'm an extremist, and you all are cheap moderates." "Moderate" is a deliberately chosen word to mislead the public.

The Georgia Baptist Convention put you on trial for heresy in the 1950s, and yet you're still a Baptist? Why?

The radicalness of Baptists means that an eight-year-old child like me can be Baptized, and then my vote is equal to an eighty-eight year old person. That's the most radical democratic structure in the world. I remember the day they called the role and my name was called after I was baptized, and I could vote along with the most revered eighty-eight-year-old man with a beard in that church. I can see him right now. And it dawned on me that my vote counted *exactly* the same as his. Now that's the radicalness of the Baptist polity. That's good. That's so good that it's scary. It scares the living daylight out of you. I would always take my side with the people.

But what if they're worshiping what you call a "local culture religion"? What if they're misinformed?

Then it's your and my business to inform them. And so if we haven't informed them, we take the blame every time they vote that way. We take the blame—those of us who know better. Chaos and democracy go together, but our last hope, our last best hope, is still in that Greek city-state model.

Let's take the women's issue. Baptists see it backward on the women's issue. There's a Mercer professor and his wife retired up here in the mountains of North Carolina, and I go up to visit them. So I was up there one Sunday afternoon, and he said "you want to go to church with me tonight? We're going to vote on women as deacons." Vote!

We get there, and I said, "now look, Zeb, do not tell them *any* form or fashion that I am *any* person, an expert on the Bible. I don't know anything about it. You just consider me an invisible, a guest." So we were sitting there, and the argument got hot and negative, and the preacher was all against women, and Zeb kept on botherin', botherin', botherin', and he jumped up and says: "We have a famous authority on this question sitting with us tonight, and I want you all to hear him!" I gave him a good punch in the ribs and I said, "Zeb, you really betrayed me right now."

So I get up, you know, without anything, and I say "well, I've got to have a Bible. I didn't bring my Bible." I knew *exactly* what I was going to do then. I turned around—some teenagers in back of me had Bibles, you know, and I looked at one, and it was a modern translation, and I said, "I have the wrong Bible." And they said "what do you see?" I said "These teenagers of yours have the wrong bible." They said, "Wooooow! You mean, it's not a King James version?" I said "No sir." I said, "The devil must have slipped in here and given these teenagers the wrong bible." I said, "well let me read you what this Bible says. I'll read you Romans 16th chapter."—I knew *exactly* what it says. Paul is writing to the leaders of the church in Rome, and Paul says, "I commend *Phoebe*, who is a ruler in the church." And I read from the Bible, "I want to read you what the Bible says, Phoebe is the *ruler* in the church." Now you know how the King James Bible translates that? "A *servant* in the church." See, there are your controllers. The word is quite clearly, "the ruler," not "servant." King James never wanted a woman to have a place. He had scholars, and scholars knew exactly what he wanted, they translated exactly how he wanted, and that's the way it's been. So the argument then turned into a whale of an argument over whether they should have the King James version of the Bible or any other version in the church. And I left.

See, you have this radicalness of Baptist freedom and voting and leading, but you have to have people like you and me to say, "look, I *know* the difference." And you don't think those people remember that? Every young person in that church is still arguing with their pastor, "can I read what I want to read?" [laughs] That was one of the greatest moments of my life.

Don't you get tired?

No, no, no. Life is exciting. There's no such thing as being tired.

What should students today do to overcome continuing racism and separation at school?

You have to have white students who are willing to make friends and join black organizations. Now at Wake Forest, I've been blessed by having a few students join the black gospel choir, join the black fraternities. . . . And they say, "look, how much will I enjoy, and how much will I gain?" Not: "how much I'm going to be a martyr," but "how much am I going to gain by this?" Think of that white guy and gal in the gospel choir. Think of how much music they've learned they sing all over the East coast. They've learned so much you know. Somebody has to be an agent all the time, a catalyst. That's not a hard job.

The Mercer Cluster *printed this editorial the day after the trustees of Mercer University voted to open Mercer's doors to all students "without regard to race." Many had pressured Mercer's president, Rufus Harris, to keep Mercer segregated, and the Christian Index had recommended admitting Oni as a foreign student, rather than opening Mercer's doors to African Americans as well—an idea lambasted by* The Cluster *in the weeks before the publication of the following editorial.*

Trustee Decision Shows Sense of Leadership (1963)

Time will judge the far-reaching effect of yesterday's trustee resolution, but already the decision has demonstrated a new spirit of leadership and decisiveness that has long been absent from Southern Baptist Schools.

At a time when many of our sister colleges struggle to avoid the desegregation issue, Mercer's trustees have taken their own initiative and made the decision that rightly belongs only to themselves.

The critics of the trustees will be loud and angry, but derision is to be expected. A clear-cut policy on a controversial issue can never be popular.

It would be naïve to think that the application of the Ghana student, Sam Jerry Oni, had no direct effect on the trustee action. Oni's application placed the only real issue before the university, the issue of Christian relevance to our social character.

But while Oni's application presented the issue, it was the trustees who made the issue vital. They could have easily avoided the basic question and admitted Oni as a foreign student, but they chose instead to draw the lines of policy clearly by ruling on the entire desegregation issue.

The strength and directness of the resolution testifies to purposefulness of the action. There was no blinking at the shadow of the state convention. There was no frantic concern over alumni reaction. In the words of trustee member Dr. Walter L. Moore, "each member made his own evaluations of the facts and acted with his own conscience."

This attitude toward an avenue of responsible leadership is a precious thing. Its demonstration marks a high point in Mercer's history.

Joe Hendricks graduated from Mercer in 1955, after writing Mercer's student honor code as the president of the Student Government Association. He returned to his alma mater in 1959, acting first as the Director of Religious Activities and then the Dean of Men until 1970. As President Rufus Harris's trusted advisor, he was the engineer of desegregation at Mercer, pushing Mercer to become the first private college in Georgia to desegregate, combing Georgia in an energetic and unparalleled effort to recruit African American students, and then mentoring students and championing integration once African Americans arrived at Mercer. He was a white leader in Macon's largely peaceful desegregation, he helped build the upward bound program at Mercer, and he was instrumental in the formation of the First Year Seminar experience. A legend at Mercer, Hendricks was at once spiritual mentor and father-figure to the student body for the latter half of the twentieth century. The students simply knew him as "Papa Joe."

Interview with Joe Hendricks (2001)

When did you first become aware of race?

Well I think the real awakening was right here in Groover Hall when I was an undergraduate at Mercer. . . [Christianity Professor] McLeod Bryan is a name you'll hear over and over again. If there ever was a prophetic teacher he was one; he just wouldn't let us off. I mean every opportunity on the national scene he'd remind us [of segregation]. I remember the circus came through here one time sponsored by General Electric, way back in 1951. . . It wasn't so much a circus, it was just a bunch of rolling exhibits, like "The World of Tomorrow." And next Monday he's up there, saying "did you all notice something different?" Well, it was a desegrated staff coming down, which was just unheard of. Here were people working together—black and white. So he'd just get every kind of opportunity like that he could to just sort of punch the elephant's butt, the elephant being segregation in the south. He just saw himself as sort of a Christian Socrates, you know. He didn't worry about getting all worked up about it—if he could just wake somebody up. And he was successful. I think the great credit actually belongs to those people back there. They didn't get anything desegregated, but they sure laid the soil. The professors were relentless. What they were about was really revolution, of course not with sticks and guns and bombs, but they were taking on every establishment.

There hasn't been any subversion in the last few years that equals what they were doing.

So the majority of Mercer students were politically energized against segregation by their experience at Mercer?

No. Getting a term from the Hebrew bible, there was a remnant. There was a remnant in Babylon or Assyria. You're talking about five percent of the student body who were operating that way. I'll give you an example. 1960 it may have been. There was an occurrence at Tatnall Square Park right across from Willingham over there. As I remember rightly what had happened was some little black kids had wandered into Tatnall Square Park. So a white man was enraged about it. Just any little thing could set things off. And a black man named Louis Wynne went out there and this white man stabbed him, in the park. Now in the front of Mercer, now, this is something you need to remember about this—all the way to the corner—were filled with Mercer students cheering the man with the knife. In other words, they were ridiculing the blacks for being in that park. I'm sure that a predominant Mercer student body at that time saw these black people in that park as a threat.

Let me understand. Black children came into the park?

That's right, they wandered in—they were banned from the park.

And how old were these kids?

Pre-school. At least elementary. Oh yeah, they were little tots.

And these little tots wander in and the police are called out?

Oh sure, sure. And Louis Wynne was just coming to rescue the kids.

But he was out of his place.

Out of his—there you go. He was in a world he was not supposed to be in in the South.

And so the white guy stabbed him?

That's right.

What happened to Louis Wynne?

I think he had—I don't want to exaggerate—but he had a whole bunch of stitches put in, and he was a war veteran. He wasn't a stranger to combat.

And there was a group of people cheering all of this on?

On the campus. They were stacked up at least two or three deep all the way down the front.

How do good people do this sort of thing?

They're culture-bound. Let me just give you a way of looking at that. When you're coming out of a culture of complete segregation in the church, everywhere else, when the political clout of blacks is practically nothing, minimal except for maybe Atlanta, and when you've been fed by the political machine, who actually believed everything they were saying, that all of this was Northern agitation, all of this was subversion. . . You manage to blend all of that together, and it's pretty easy to develop a mindset that these people are dangerous folks that are trying to change a way of life. Every politician from Virginia to Florida over to Louisiana and Texas—every politician reinforced that view. And churches were everywhere across the South in favor of segregation. And they believed that. It was important to them that they *could* believe all of that so the institution could go on. Galatians 3:28 says that "neither Jew nor Gentile, slave nor free, male nor female" and all of that. But, they didn't read that verse. [laughs]

When you're in a situation that's controlled culturally, politically, and socially, everywhere you go, then you have the option to be a good Nazi or to be a subversive. You can choose whichever one you want.

So there was no information for people to get?

No of course not. None. None. None. None. Not until King comes along. We owe so much to people like Lillian Smith up in North Georgia. But these were really small populations. Most of Mercer's sister colleges, Christian colleges, just get F's on all of this. They were worse than the state schools for the most part.

When you worked to desegregate Mercer in the 1960's, were you ever threatened?

When I got back here in 1959, I ended up being co-chair of the Macon Council on Human Relations with a black preacher, and we issued some kind of little painless statement calling for a "a conservative transition to desegregation," and I think we even euphemized "race" somehow, but it was clear what we were talking about. Next night, when that came out in the morning papers, they burned a cross over here at an apartment building where McCorkle Music Hall stands now. In front of my house, about six foot high. Right over where the music building stands. I wasn't at home, and I came back, and here were all of the people who lived in that apartment building over there standing around that cross, including my wife and children. And the older faculty—Miss Plinell, English teacher, Riley Plinell, her husband, the mathematician—they were both rabid segregationists, and they were ticked off at me. Not only did they not like what I was doing on race but they sure didn't like this violent response that took place. So I just took a hose and put out the fire, and, you know, went on. But it got a little touchy. It was a little ticklish.

And they all knew why the cross was burning.

Oh, absolutely, oh, absolutely. There wasn't any question about that. Here's the summation of it: They knew clearly that what I was doing violated their view of the world. And secondly, it violated their view of order—that you just didn't do stuff to disrupt academic business, and colleges ought to stay out of politics and stick to reading literature.

Did you ever think when you were teaching here that your life was in danger?

I just didn't have sense enough to care. You're young, and to hell with them. I guess if I have to be honest about it, I had the McLeod Bryan legacy going. He had moved on. But I'd come back here to work, and these people had liberated me and taught me, and some of them were still around. And so, there was just sort of a mandate to carry on. It wasn't like I started something. It was ongoing. This was Mercer's identity, and we felt some responsibility to keep that alive and express it. This was what it meant to be a Mercer faculty member or a Mercer student. Mercer was defined and vocationalized by the Judeo-Christian ethic—

What's the Judeo-Christian ethic?

Mercer very well was served by faculty members who had come out of the prophets, the Amoses, the Hoseas, and all of those, and that informed this around here more than any politics—that the Bible calls for justice. Now over in some other Baptist schools they might not have been playing it that way. They saw it differently. They were still evangelizing and all sorts of things. But we're playing it right. If you're going to serve Yahweh, there's a certain justice that emanates out of that. Well, that was heavy through here. And so that's what created the dialectics of the culture, coming primarily out of the Christianity department and sociology, but in other departments too. We just thought that this is what the radical Judeo-Christian tradition calls for. It was hugely important. It gave us a confirming context that justice is what we ought to be doing. And we ought to be doing it if it puts the institution into a little trouble. Any institution that's not in some kind of trouble with the culture is not doing its job. Look at the prophets: what they were saying along the way was a critique of the institution just like what we thought we were doing was a critique. You've got the Jerusalem hierarchy and all of that going, but then you've got the Amoses, and the Hoseas, the Isaiahs and the others. And that's really what's so great about what becomes of Judaism. You've got this conservative institution thing going, but you've got the prophets at work. It's when the prophets grow quiet that you need to get worried. And that's where we are right now.

The prophets are quiet now?

That is correct. Somewhere pedagogy and action have to merge. Go back to the heresy trials: this place has always been in trouble when it was doing well. It's not in trouble now, so I worry about it.

Sam Oni, from Ghana, was the first black student admitted to Mercer University in 1963. He graduated in 1967.

Sojourner's Truth (1994)

Sam Oni

I have often fantasized that Hoagie Carmichael wrote his immortal song, "Georgia On My Mind", with just me in mind. Of course, I know, as everyone does, that that song was in all probability inspired by some special lady, the object of Carmichael's affection. All the same, each time I hear that song, I am filled with such an extraordinary welter of emotions. They are emotions at once delicate and difficult. These emotions, in fact, continue to animate and illuminate my every experience here during my brief sojourn at Mercer University some thirty short years ago.

How marvelous it is, then,—I nearly said how sweet it is—for me to return to this place, this piece of God's good earth, this Georgian soil, borne on the wings of these self-same emotions! Our reunion this day and in the especial place owes its significance, in my view, not so much to events which shaped some of us here at Mercer and in Georgia some three decades ago. Rather, I believe this occasion to be exceptional because it accords each of us here assembled that rare opportunity both to celebrate the human spirit and to honor one another as the children of God. Above all, this moment is truly unique precisely because we owe it to ourselves and, most specifically, to this younger generation of Mercerians, the responsibility to bear witness to truth.

In deference to this younger generation, I do not intend to reduce this discourse to an escapist indulgence in bland reminiscences. Instead, I propose that we engage one another in a lively dialogue, even if I end up doing much of the talking. To set the ball rolling, then, let me sketch for you, in broad strokes, something of a backdrop.

I am a product of the missionary enterprise in Africa. Perhaps I should mention, in passing, that my parents, too, had been Christian converts. They were Anglicans, that is to say, of the Church of England. Not unexpectedly, I grew up an Anglican as well—until my mid-teens, that is. About this time, I fell under the spell of Southern Baptist missionaries, who had little difficulty in convincing me that the baptism I had received as an Anglican child was worse than useless. To guarantee myself a place in heaven, the Baptist missionaries persisted, I had not only to be born again, I had to be baptized by total immersion. I acquiesced.

My embrace of the Southern Baptist brand of the Christian faith was total. By my late teens, I had become reasonably strong in the faith, working as an interpreter for missionaries at church services, revivals and conventions. At the same time, I took on the added responsibility of pastoring my own church. I was soon to be rewarded with a Baptist scholarship to pay for my secondary school education.

However, this act of Christian benevolence came not without some strings attached. In this case, the missionaries reckoned that their proselytizing endeavors among our people would be greatly enhanced and, indeed, facilitated with the active intervention and involvement of well-educated Africans. They began to seek out such Africans to train. I was thus made an offer I could not refuse, a quid pro quo, if you like. Missionary scholarship would secure for me higher education, including retraining in a theological seminary. In exchange, I would undertake to return as a missionary/evangelist to work among my own people.

In the event, however, matters did not quite turn out according to the script. My dreams of acquiring higher education were shattered without ceremony. I was kicked out of Sadler Baptist Secondary School, Kumasi, Ghana, barely two years after my enrollment. What had been my crime? I had led a student protest against overweening ineptitude and egregious insensitivity on the part of the missionaries, a fact that put at peril our chances of success in our final examinations. In those days, failing those exams was just about tantamount to a death sentence. Seven assumed student ringleaders were summarily expelled. Of course, among them was a certain Sam Oni, singled out by the missionaries as the ingrate who had "bitten the fingers that fed him." And that, as they say, was that: the good Lord obviously did not intend me to become the Billy Graham of Africa; even achieve a college education, for the matter of that.

Though devastated, I remained constant in my faith. I, however, could not bring myself to break the news to my mother. By the time I mustered the courage to return home a week or so later, she had already heard. She was disconsolate. I, for my part, was clearly at a dead end. I had no clue as to what to do or where to turn. Moreover, I bore the enormous burden of not knowing whether my mother would ever forgive me for squandering a rare opportunity to attain higher education. I was the first in my family to get such a chance.

A few weeks prior to the dramatic events at Sandler Baptist Secondary School, a young missionary couple had arrived in Ghana. Before settling down at their own station to embark on the business of spreading the gospel, the couple, as was customary, first visited all other Southern Baptist missionary stations in the country. Apparently, at virtually every stop, the missionaries were fulsome in their commendation of one particular young African Christian. Such had been the praises that the new arrivals could hardly wait to meet this model convert.

Did divine intervention inspire the choice of Sekondi, my hometown, as the home-base of this rookie missionary couple? Perhaps it was no more than a fortuitous coincidence. No matter. As soon as the fact became known to me, it did not take much prompting for me to decide to seek out the newcomers and welcome them into our community. It was an act of faith. These new missionaries would either accept my hand of fellowship or they would reject it out of hand. I had nothing to lose.

The memory of that first encounter with Harris and Vivian Mobley I will cherish for as long as I live. Our meeting, though brief, was memorable for the immediate, spontaneous interest and evident concern that both Vivian and Harris showed in me and my predicament. The news of my expulsion had, of course, spread like harmattan fire in the relatively small Baptist community in Ghana. The Mobleys had received the news with subdued incredulity. They seemed totally at a loss reconciling this unexpected action of their fellow missionaries with the glowing notices of me that had been given by the same missionaries. In an act of Christian compassion, totally unexpected by me, Harris and Vivian Mobley promptly offered me a scholarship to enable me to complete my secondary school education.

The rest of the story, as they say, is history. I graduated top of my class at Fijai Secondary School, Sekondi. Before I knew it, Harris had applied on my behalf to a number of Southern Baptist universities in the United States. The applications were turned down one after the other by all but one school. Mercer University was later to achieve the dubious distinction of being the only school foolhardy enough to give me, a black man, a chance. I need not tell you what an epoch-making chance it has turned out to be.

A few weeks ago, a brief announcement in a Lagos newspaper caught my attention. BAOSA, that is an acronym for Baptist Academy Old Student Association, was about to commemorate the 138th anniversary of their school in Lagos, Nigeria. Founded by Southern Baptist missionaries in 1855, Baptist Academy is not only one of the oldest schools in the country, it remains one of the finest. To state that Baptist Academy has, over the years, contributed in no small way towards the spiritual, economic, political and social development of Nigeria and its people is to labor the obvious.

As every Mercerian should know, our alma mater was founded in the year 1833, thus predating Baptist Academy by a mere two decades, give or take a year or two. What every Mercerian might not realize is that by the time I arrived in 1963 as the first black student to be enrolled at Mercer University, Southern Baptist missionaries had been preaching the gospel among our people in Nigeria for some 113 years. The first missionary, the Rev. Thomas Bowen, had arrived in 1850. It is noteworthy, moreover, that both Ghana and Nigeria, my countries of birth and parentage respectively, lie on the West Coast of Africa. Even more germane is the fact that this part of Africa, the notorious Slave Coast, was the main source of African slaves that ended up on the plantations and labor camps of the New World between the 16th and 17th centuries.

The choice of West Africa as the theatre of missionary operations by the Southern Baptists remains for us in my part of the world a matter of supreme irony, prompting a number of intriguing questions: Was the choice of West Africa by accident or design? Was the choice, in any way, compensatory—even on a subliminal level? Faced with slavery and incipient colonialism, did Southern Baptist missionaries take a stand for human freedom and against human subjugation? Or did they play it safe and find refuge in remaining neutral? These are, by no means, idle questions. However we address the questions, it is highly unlikely to influence our people's deeply entrenched attitude on these matters. Africans have long identified as co-conspirators and, indeed, collaborators the emissary of the State and the missionary of the Church in the colonization and exploitation of our people across the African continent. The view is widely held among our people that when the white men came, we had the land and they had the Bible. They taught us to pray. We closed our eyes in fervent prayer. When we opened our eyes, the white men had our land and we were stuck with their Bible.

Ostensibly, the main reason for my coming to Mercer was to acquire a university education. However, I have to confess to what Harris Mobley and I considered a higher motive and a nobler objective. We were both convinced that nothing could be more pernicious to the Christian faith as the lazing incongruity between Christian preachment and praxis at home and in the mission field. My role, we conceived it, was by breaking the color bar at Mercer, I would be challenging our Southern Baptist brothers and sisters in America to confront the gross contradictions in their Christian witness at home and abroad. It was our conviction that I, an African Christian, converted by Southern Baptist missionaries, provided the most compelling and unassailable argument against the continuation of racial segregation as practiced in Southern Baptist churches, schools, colleges, hospitals and other establishments across southern United States.

I belong to that generation of Africans that came of age, politically speaking, in the late fifties and early sixties, as the sun began to set, so to speak, on the British Empire. My secondary school years coincided with that watershed in African colonial history. It was an invigorating period charged with ferment and agitations for political independence across our continent. The winds of change sweeping through colonial Africa left in its wake one independent nation after another. In 1957, Kwame Nkrumah, the charismatic and visionary Ghanaian leader, had achieved independence for his country, the then Gold Coast. He was, without a doubt, my generation's greatest cultural and political hero. He inspired us to dream fabulous dreams and see extravagant visions.

For my generation, especially in Ghana, it was our season of awakening, of political consciousness raising, of discovering other worlds beyond our frontiers. For us the solidarity of the tribe began to evolve into the solidarity of the race, of the oppressed and of the exploited. We were confronted with apartheid in South Africa and soon realized that the liberation struggles in the Congo, Algeria, Southern Africa and Vietnam were, indeed, our struggles, too.

By the time I was graduating from high school in 1962, the civil rights movement in the United States was rapidly gaining momentum. Rosa Parks and the bus boycott in Montgomery, Alabama; the demonstrations in Little Rock, Arkansas; the sit-ins in Nashville, Greensboro, Atlanta; the Freedom Riders from the North; and the police dogs and fire hoses in Birmingham, Alabama; all were making headlines in Ghanaian and African newspapers. You can well imagine my consternation as I read these extraordinary developments taking place in that "land of the free and home of the brave." How could these appalling events be happening in the same country that produced the missionaries?

In my bewilderment, I naturally turned to Southern Baptist missionaries for some plausible explanation. I might have been naive, but I had wondered out loud why black people and white people in America could not live together in harmony just as white missionaries and black Africans were doing in my part of the world. There were no easy answers, which is to say there were no answers at all. The missionaries, behaving out of character, prevaricated and appeared genuinely ill-at-ease whenever I raised the issue of race relations in America. I was, to say the least, dumb-founded.

Relief, however, was at hand. Where the veteran missionaries had appeared rather circumspect, Harris Mobley had been almost disarming in his candor. Racial discrimination was a past and present reality among Southern Baptists in and across the southern United States, Harris had informed me. According to him, all Baptist institutions were operated on strictly segregated bases, that is to say, for whites only. He pointed out, moreover, that the sort of inter-racial fellowships that we had come to accept as a matter of course in Africa were strictly taboo among Southern Baptists in the United States. The more Harris and I discussed the matter—and we did discuss it frequently—the more we felt a compelling need to do something to ring to an end this age-old anomaly and culturally-induced debasement of the Christian faith.

"I believe you should go to America, Sam," Harris said to me matter-of-factly one day. "I believe the Lord can use you to touch the hearts of our Christian brothers and sisters in America." I accepted the proposition with equanimity. An editorial in the now defunct New York *Herald Tribune*, reacting to the controversy surrounding my enrollment at Mercer, was not too far off the mark when it referred to me as "a missionary in reverse." Believing that was precisely what the Lord would have me to do, I embraced the challenge.

In the event, however, my brief stint as a missionary at Mercer was not what one would call a signal success. Instead of being a missionary in reverse, I was actually hampered by far too many reverses. I became a naive victim of crass racism. The racial mountain proved for me too formidable and insurmountable. I was sorely tested. Loneliness, that oppressive, paralyzing incubus, became my constant companion. I endured enervating mental and psychological anguish. My faith in God took a severe battering. It was, in the final analysis, a faith-shattering experience. And as if all that were not grim enough, my mother upped and died on me. My father's death followed a few months later. I had no idea how much longer I could hang on.

At the end of my four years at Mercer, I was certain of only one thing: I owed my sanity—what was left of it—and my survival to my guardian angels. No, I am not speaking of those winged heavenly beings. I refer, instead, to the handful of women and men, black and white in this place, in this city, in this state, who cared for me, nurtured me, protected me, consoled me and, above all, LOVED me. Among these, Charles and Eunice Davis occupy a very special place in my heart. I shall never forget my first visit to their home. After dinner, Charles simply handed me a key and said, "Our home is your home." I have remained a member of the Davis family ever since. Does anyone still wonder why "Georgia on my Mind" remains and always will be my song?

I am reminded of one poignant moment at my graduation here in 1967. One of my guardian angels, a dear lady, put her arms around me, congratulated me and added, "Sam, after all you have been through in Georgia in these last four years, you are a good man to hate every white person you ever meet." She paused, and before I could utter a word, she added, "But the remarkable thing about you is, I know you won't." Mrs. Edwards was absolutely right. In four years I had come face-to-face with the racial monster and I had found it utterly repugnant. My experience had taught me, moreover, that racism is a two-edged sword. It cuts as savagely the victim as it does the racist himself. Heaven forbid that I should then allow myself to be violated by the same noxious virus.

I began these remarks by pointing out that we have a responsibility to bear witness to truth. After all is said and done, we really have little choice but to embrace the elemental truth that we are, all of us, the children of one God. It follows, therefore, whether we like it or not, that we are brothers and sisters one to the other. In light of this truth, racism becomes an obnoxious hoax, an obscene fraud. The recognition, moreover, that one's skin color is nothing more than a pigment of one's imagination is a wondrous catharsis, a deliverance. It inspires in us the motive force to enable us to get on with the vital business of honoring one another as brothers and sisters.

James Baldwin's poignant words have an especial resonance for us at this precise moment, as racism waxes ever odious, and its side-kick, ethnic cleansing, rears its monstrous head on many fronts in our world: "For the sake of one's children, in order to minimize the bill they must pay, one must be careful not to take refuge in any delusion, and the value placed on the color of one's skin is always and everywhere and forever a delusion."

Let me conclude, almost as I began, by making a public confession. My life, I'm afraid, is not working out; at least not according to the script proffered by the missionaries. And if those same missionaries could see me now they would no doubt shake their heads forlornly and conclude that I had lost my way. I would not blame them; for as far as they are concerned, I have been, at best, a let-down; and, at worst, a ne'er-do-well. I did not, after all, make it as a missionary, nor did I answer the call to evangelism. Moreover, I gave up a life as a preacher. Let's face it, anyone who left the pristine serenity of Mercer University in the late sixties, only to end up in the spiritual, cultural miasma that was the University of California, in Berkeley, it must be admitted, had clearly lost his way.

However, if it is any consolation to my missionary friends, I would like to say that all has not been a total loss, as every now and again, I reflect on what I am going to be when I grow up. In the meantime, I am alive to life and with life. My life pulsates to the syncopated rhythms, colors and shapes of the eternal present. Mine is a life that transcends frontiers, embraces the mutuality of opposites and holds as an article of faith that "it is more blessed to give than to receive." Yes, mine is a life, which, in the language of Abraham Lincoln, strives to bring forth in my fellow human beings, my brothers and my sisters, "the better angels of our nature." And so long as I shall walk in His grace, revel in the splendor of children's laughter and relish the aroma of music, poetry and artistic expressions, my renewal and my wholeness shall remain on-going, a work-in-progress.

I am thankful to you all. I honor you all.

Gary Johnson attended Mercer University from 1966–1970, later returning to Mercer to become the college's first African American professor.

Interview with Gary Johnson (2001)

What are your memories of growing up in a segregated society?

As a kid you're not *completely* aware of it. I remember as a kid, less than ten, drinking out of the wrong fountain, and the entire store came screaming toward me, including my parents, saying "you can't drink at that fountain! What are you doing?" You know, as a kid you don't know. The fountain for colored people looked horribly filthy and dirty, and then there was a clean fountain, so hey, you obviously take the one that's clean. And all over the cities there were separate facilities. We had colored bathrooms, colored fountains, and I remember sitting in the back of the bus. And you'd have to be very respectful of white people. You'd have to honor them in the sense that you were not a first class citizen. I thought all that was weird as a kid, but you do what your parents say, and once you're back in your own little world it's all just fun and games, for the most part. You know, it didn't hit home with me until college.

How did you become one of the first African American students at Mercer?

Joseph Hendricks recruited me for Mercer. I remember him coming into the high school. Joe was always a committed person, but we always were aware that we were dealing with a white Southern man at the time. And Joe, when you first meet him, you don't really see him as any different, because he had a Southern drawl—he looked like a white man [laughs], but he was a person who always was—he just simply just walked right into the middle of a storm. He was *comfortable*. Joe was actually striking out on new territory. Very few colleges in Georgia were recruiting black students, and they were not doing this in any kind of fashion the way Mercer was doing at one time. There were a good number of us, and ain't no question, Joe single-handedly is [to credit for our presence]. And then he protects us after we got there. He was our number one advocate and kind of considered us his children.

How did the white students treat you at Mercer?

It was pretty primitive. I had an English class in Willingham Chapel, and I never will forget that—that really truly affected me throughout my entire four years. I walked into this class. I was kind of late, and there was one seat on the front row, and I sat in that seat. I was the only black student in that class. And the next day I was going to make sure that I was on time, so I was actually there early. I sat in that very same seat, and the students filter in, and nobody sits near me. Nobody sits in my row. The entire class sat behind me. I will *never* forget that. The entire class decided not to sit next to me. I remember I called mother the first week I was there, and I told her, "I'm comin home, this is crazy, this doesn't make any sense." It was, I don't know, you thought you had gone to hell. So there's fear, there's self-doubting, and all of the black kids' parents were saying, "You're not leaving, you're going to do better than I did in life."

Did African American and white students interact at all?

The only amount of communication we had with our white colleagues was scribbling on the bathroom walls, and that was usually about some kind of sexual mythology. They didn't have a *clue* as to who we were, and in a way we were I guess in a way a little in awe of them. But it was a whole question of ignorance on both sides.

What sorts of things were you writing on the walls to each other?

Oh they thought that black men were ah these sexual giants, you know, and that we definitely wanted to *rape* white women. And we were just basically degrading white men, calling them eunuchs. It was just primitive in some senses. It was just crazy. It was a question of examination up close for the first time, I believe, for a lot of them, and for us, of people of a different race. It was just sort of like, "gosh you brush your teeth like I do? Or you comb your hair, you take a bath?" You know, it was just those kind of basic questions that we had to get the understanding that, "Yeah, that's a human being."

And plus, they were trying to get rid of a lot of things that white parents had sort of pumped into them too. So they had to test all that stuff out and discover "that ain't true." And what happened a lot too is kids pulling away from their white parents basically because they told them lies. They found the truth that this is a person who should be treated just like I am, and all that stuff you told me is not true. And the only way you could do it is to put them into the mix in order for them to get it. There was no way to tell them, there was no way to teach integration. You actually had to *experience* it.

Did religion play a part in this process?

The Georgia Baptists were anti-Mercer in a lot of ways, anti-Joe Hendricks, anti-integration. So the school was actually in front in terms of integration or race relations compared with the parent organization like the Georgia Baptist Convention. The churches have always been behind social movements—behind the times. I mean you'd think that they'd be a leader in it, but churches have been the last places to actually get on board with social movements, and it was same thing with the civil rights in the nation. White churches, it took a very long time for them to become even associated with civil rights.

But Mercer at that time had some kind of reputation of being a great school in addition to the fact that it was religious, and its religious base had a lot to do with what happened in terms of the blacks and whites eventually coming together in some kind of way. Strangely enough, had it not been a Baptist school, I'm not really sure things would have proceeded the way they did. There was religion everywhere—all over the place—and a lot of it was hypocrisy. But with religious Southern Baptist people, your *conscience* begins to bother you a little bit, you know? It's funny how eleven o'clock Sunday morning can be one of the most segregated hours in America, and yet you're talking always about the questions of love and brotherhood. And the Civil Rights movement really used that as a mirror, basically saying "this is you—look at yourself. How is it that you call yourself a Christian and yet you're acting like that?" Now up front close and on an everyday basis, I think that begins to wear on you. And we basically had whites crossing that line because their consciences basically began to mess with them. And I think ultimately that just wears on you, especially if you're committed to a religion or to a faith. And that actually empowered black students too to challenge the old ways, the old institutions. I think that we basically had decided to that we going to show people exactly who they were in terms of conscience, and that they couldn't call themselves Christians treating us like this.

R. Kirby Godsey served as the seventeenth president of Mercer from 1979–2006, presiding over the construction of the Mercer Medical School, Pharmacy School, School of Theology, Engineering School, Business School, School of Education, Nursing School, and School of Music. His presidency was marked by an inclusive vision of a Baptist university in which faith and learning can be mutually supportive, rather than mutually destructive.

The Baptist Journey of Faith and Learning (1996)

R. Kirby Godsey

I am a Baptist. My vocation is education. And my vocation has allowed me to bring together my life of learning and my life of faith.

Neither journey has been without its troubles and its turmoil: neither the life of faith nor the life of learning.

In my journeys within education I have seen Baptist schools and secular universities up close. And I have been part of a Baptist university as it has struggled to shape its character. I have weighed in on the side of making Mercer a Baptist university. But the struggle is never-ending.

My journey of faith has carried me through the dead-heat of Baptist turmoil. I have mourned our losses and been preoccupied with our defeats. But I see a new day coming.

I am learning that being Baptist is a much larger world, a much higher calling than being a *Southern* Baptist. My journey has taken me beyond the boundaries of Southern Baptists. But I have no quarrel with Southern Baptists. I have no quarrel with those brothers and sisters who need to hold onto the mantle of being a Southern Baptist. It is their comfort zone. But out of the mourning called grief, I have come to the dawning of a new morning called light. For me, being Baptist is a higher calling.

Southern Baptists continue to be a large denomination. They continue to be powerful. They continue to be rich. They have achieved giant corporate status and they wield real political clout. But in the process, they seem to have buried the treasure of being Baptist.

We have witnessed, first hand, a religious debacle of one more denomination suffering from decay, losing its soul in search of political power and religious prestige.

But it would be self-centered to lose heart. Baptists are not, after all, the hope of the world. God's universe is not somehow waiting silently to see what in the world happens to Baptists. To think that the hope of humankind depends upon politics in Nashville is myopic and arrogant. Baptists have never been the source of all truth and we have not become the center of God's universe.

Our only reason for being is to serve as instruments of hope and grace. More simply put, Baptists were not called to become one more corporate giant in neon lights. Baptists were called to be simple priests, bearers of light, a family of faith living out the reality of God's presence in our world.

We do the best we can, but when it comes to religious organizations, we can usually recognize the signs of decay. We become rigid and exclusive, confident that we have a corner on God's truth. We become preoccupied with the contours of the denomination. We reorganize and streamline. We begin to squabble over the boundaries—whether here or there, a little to the left or a little to the right.

We should have seen it coming. We began to look to our feuds and to our close votes to add excitement and stamina to our meetings. We began to squabble about who had the truth and whose truth and message would prevail. It was mostly nonsense. Surely we do not believe that God is really interested in our petty disputes. . . . We are not here to fight. We are here to minister. We are not here to shout or demean one another. We are here to preach and to teach. We are not here to recite the right religious ideology. We are here to forgive. We are not here to eclipse the gospel with our mindless bickering. We are here to embody the gospel in our own honest caring. We are not enforcers. We are not the Gestapo for some misguided form of Calvinism. You and I are here to give flesh and blood to the gospel. We are not here to make sure that people recite the right language. We are here to be God's people. We are not here to require that people embrace the latest version of fundamentalist orthodoxy. We are here to give people hope, to bear light amidst the shadows, to teach, to live out grace. We are here to help people in Jesus' name and to ask questions later.

Caring is not something grandiose. It is not a theological proposition. It is certainly not a denominational posture. Caring is not a skyscraper. It is not a new organizational structure. Caring is not about getting a patent on the name of Lottie Moon.

Caring means to heal the sick, to help the poor, to shelter the homeless, to teach the ignorant. It means setting people free of disease and setting them free of prejudice. It means looking out for people who are lonely and taking up for people who are powerless.

The fact is that Southern Baptists became like most other denominational organizations, less Baptist and more authoritarian, less grace and more hype. Over and over again, churches and the denominations become servants of the culture. Power and popularity. The rhythms of Saturday night become the beat of Sunday morning. Jesus slips out the back door unnoticed to go look after the hungry.

My journey teaches me that as Baptists grow and succeed, they inevitably become enamored with their own success. The first thing you know we find ourselves trying to manipulate denominational politics, fundamentalists and moderates alike, while the homeless are sleeping under bridges and violence and abuse run rampant in our streets.

Being Baptist is a higher calling. Being Baptist is about caring, and caring is a different calling. It is God's call. It means bringing water to the thirsty in Jesus' name, pushing back the shadows of ignorance in Jesus' name. So being Baptist calls us back to our beginnings. Our birthright lies in lifting people up in Jesus' name. And unless helping people in Jesus' name prevails, our rhetoric and our proclamations and our political convocations, called Baptist conventions, are nothing more than a noisy charade that veils the skeletal remains of a dead denomination. . .

My Baptist journey has also carried me to the towers of academia. Success in academia is just as enchanting as success in the denomination. I watched and listened as colleagues would have Mercer to be done with our Baptist connections. Shake the Baptist dust from our feet. It was an enchanting idea. It was a road I could not and would not take. As a Baptist university, I believe that we must be a force for preserving our Baptist identity and our Baptist principles.

When I studied Baptist history, I have been astonished by the historical significance of education in the rise of the missionary impulse. The missionary force in the early 19th century was awash on the shoals of Baptist conflict. Almost dead. Opposition to missions was fierce. Some associations in Georgia struggled against the notion of a Baptist general convention precisely because it would encourage missions and education. In 1822, in Georgia, a motion to extend the gospel by missions met this response, "A motion was made to lay the matter on the table, amended by a motion to throw the matter under the table, and then by another, to kick the bearer of the motion out of the house." Historians record that the motion was carried by a rising vote, some of them leaping up and down and afterwards escorting the motion maker to the door, threatening physical harm if he ever again pronounced the word "missions," in the presence of that body.

Study Baptist history and you will discover that it was in the formation of a commitment to Christian education that the anti-missionary spirit was overcome. We have largely lost our connection to those roots. In so doing, we have lost our bearings. And what has become of us? In a work that began together, a great divide has emerged between missions and education, with enormous tension between the priests and scribes. But unless the preachers and the teachers, the priests and the scribes, the men and women of letters, and the men and women of the spirit can sit down together, our cooperative efforts, be they a convention or a fellowship, will flounder in a sea of pettiness and triviality. Evangelism that is content to paint "Jesus Saves" on all the rocks in public parks will fail. Education that presumes to separate the mind from the spirit will fail. Witness that is uninformed and uncaring will fail.

Missions and evangelism desperately need resources of education, and education desperately needs the power and the presence of honest faith. My journey has taught me that while churches and denominations may speak of Christian education, their real passion is for college football. But being Baptist has taught me that we cannot separate missions and education. We cannot separate thinking and believing.

Just as a denomination can lose the soul of being Baptist, a Baptist college or university or seminary can surely abandon their Baptist heritage. For our Baptist schools, it has been a double siege, a double-edged sword. There is the siege of those without who want to control our schools, to mandate our textbooks, to prescribe creeds to which teachers must give assent. There is the siege of those within who wish to abort any identity with the church.

On both fronts, we cannot be a good Baptist university, a good Baptist college, or a good Baptist seminary if either siege prevails. Within our institutions, we must bear witness to our faith and make clear to our students that the real trouble of our world is not that people don't know enough. It is that they are not good enough.

From without, we must overcome the fear of open inquiry and intellectual freedom. The mind and the spirit are not in conflict. We need not be defensive. God needs no defense and truth will be its own protection.

Now permit me a final word about my journey. For me, being a Baptist by faith and being an educator by vocation, converges in Mercer's decision to undertake theological education.

My journey of faith and my journey of learning have come together as we join hands with Baptists to create the McAfee School of Theology.

At Mercer, our journey has brought us here because it is where we began in 1833. Jesse Mercer established Mercer University in order to influence and to foster "pious intelligence." So, Jesse Mercer's lamp, Jesse Mercer's vision, has become a light for our path.

Piety means knowing that you cannot understand your life and that I cannot understand my life without reference to God. Piety means finding life's center. Piety is not sentimental or foolish. It is not about public prayer or giving out tracts. Piety is about finding a guiding light for our path. Piety means finding the purity of heart to will one thing. You and I are many people. We are distracted and scattered among many allegiances. Piety means finding a center for devotion that can bring order and meaning out of the chaos of our lives.

Yet, piety alone is not enough. A School of Theology should bring piety and thought together. The mind is a gift of God. Any notion that being devout means to turn away from thought is a caricature of truth and holiness. Speaking without thought leads to arrogant ignorance. Arrogance and ignorance are a lethal combination. It will numb the mind and kill the spirit.

So I say, let us never fear the search for truth. Let the teachers teach and let the preachers preach. God's truth will prevail.

Education that is controlled and limited by creedal boundaries is not education at all. Education that has been purified in the sieve of doctrinaire orthodoxy is not education at all. It is not even good training. We want to build a school where people can teach without fear of doctrinal listeners outside the door and where students can study without fear of intimidation and religious demagoguery. . .

One final lesson I have learned from my Baptist journey is that we do not go alone. The best evidence that God is with us is that we hold on to one another.

I believe that if we hold onto one another, God will be with us and we will find our way to the Promised Land. There will be twists and turns. There will be sharp curves and steep hills. We will stumble and someone will have to pick us up and brush us off. But if we walk together and follow God's light, we will find the Promised Land where faith and learning can stand together. And we will be Baptists, not because we believe the same doctrine, but because we serve the same Lord.

Bryan Whitfield is an Associate Professor of Christianity at Mercer University.

Sometimes I Can See You Singing: The Witness of Tom Holmes (2006)

Bryan Whitfield

Micah 4:1–5

Revelation 7:9–17

I'm from Georgia, and so I don't hear very well. That's right. I'm from Georgia, and so I don't hear very well. Now understand, when I say I'm from Georgia, I really mean that. I was born here, my parents were born here, their parents were born here, and their parents were born here, and we can keep going. And when my ancestors first came to Georgia, they came from generations spent in exotic places like Tennessee and North Carolina. And before that, from the British Isles and Northern Europe. All of them, in some sense, from one tribe and people and language, singing the same song. The white one.

Except, of course, my Cherokee ancestors. And they had been in Georgia, or what we call Georgia, the earliest of all. But nobody ever told me about them until I was over forty, and had my father's aunt not been tipsy on her pain meds, I don't know that I would ever have heard that story. But, like I said, I'm from Georgia, and so I don't hear very well.

It was Mrs. Nan McClure, my first grade teacher, good Nazarene elder that she is, who realized it first. If I could see her, I could follow directions, but if she stood behind me or off to the side, I had no idea what she was saying. When my parents first took me to see Dr. Harrison, the ear-nose-and-throat doctor, the diagnosis was clear: severe hearing loss. But I had compensated, you see, by learning to read lips. If I could see what you were saying, I was fine. But if I couldn't, then you were the teacher in a Charlie Brown television special.

But tubes in the ear (off and on from first grade through college), a major operation over Christmas break in seventh grade, and lots of crossed fingers later, I can usually hear. But the eardrum can't stand up to surgery again, so every severe cold raises the specter that I may need to brush off my now-dormant lip-reading skills.

But I'm from Georgia, and so I don't hear very well. I'm from Georgia. From Smyrna, the Jonquil City. Cobb County. Not Atlanta, though these days I say as much to people who don't know Georgia. But not Atlanta. Cobb County, where all directions begin, "Well, you go to the Big Chicken and turn." Cobb County. Home to Lockheed, Dobbins Air Force Base, Lester Maddox, J. B. Stoner, and Leo Frank. Stoner's headquarters were in the last bend in Cherokee Street before Dr. Harrison's office, down the hill from the hospital where I was born. Kennestone Hospital, and J. B. Stoner a stone's throw away. Leo Frank's blood spilled right down the road. That was all there from day one. Looming on the horizon to the northwest, there was historic Kennesaw Mountain, where the bad Yanks met the good Rebels, a favorite destination for our Cub Scout field trips. And other historic markers punctuated the highways: Cheatham Hill, Kolb Farm, Ruffs Mill, and, of course, the Battle of Smyrna, the Confederacy's last stand before crossing the Chattahoochee for the Battle of Atlanta. One nation, one tribe, one people, one language. That much was clear.

They integrated the Cobb County Schools the year I entered first grade, a decade after the Brown decision. But that didn't make any difference for us. Where we lived, everybody was white. W-H-I-T-E white. Everybody. At Belmont Hills Elementary School, diversity was Tali Gibeon, our student from Israel whose father was on special assignment at Dobbins Air Force Base. But that was it. A slice of Jewish rye in the midst of our white wonderbread sandwich. Our neighbors were white, our teachers were white, our playmates were white, our preachers were white. And we made sure that everybody in our pews was white as well. I don't remember it—I was in the nursery, I suppose—but our church, the First Baptist Church of Smyrna, Georgia, proudly voted in conference that as a matter of policy only whites could enter its doors to worship its God, who, of course, was also white. Every picture of Jesus we ever saw, Holman Hunt's chief among them, made sure we understood that Jesus was white and had blue, blue eyes. He was one of us. And we were singing the music of the tribe—one nation, one tribe, one people, one language.

There in the shadow of Confederate battles, was it any wonder that our junior high school teams were named "The Rebels"? That we wore Confederate grey hats to show our school spirit, that our school colors were blue and grey, that the band played Clare Grundman's "The Blue and the Grey"? We wore the clothes of the tribe, and we played the music of the tribe.

After my seventh grade year, our band director, Mr. Caldwell, who had been at the junior high and the senior high for at least fifty years, retired. My parents sat me down before school started and explained that this year, we would have a new director, Mr. Witherspoon. It was very important that I showed him the same respect that I would give to any teacher, that I listen to him and do what he said. I was puzzled. Why did we need to have this talk? Why would my parents be so worried that I would fail to show him respect?

Why? Because Mr. Witherspoon was not part of our tribe. He was unlike any teacher I had had before. Indeed, he would be unlike any teacher I would ever have throughout high school, college, and way too many stints in graduate school. He was my only African-American teacher. I have no idea of what it must have been like for Mr. Witherspoon to walk into that white, white school, full of white teachers and white students and white administrators and white parents. Looking back, he was a man who brought forth music from us crackers with amazing courage and grace.

But I didn't hear it. I grew up in the white doughnut, that belt of white-flight suburbs surrounding Atlanta in the sixties and seventies. No one ever talked about race—with one exception—missions. We Royal Ambassadors had a Great Commission to share our white Jesus with those children red and yellow, black and white about whom we sang. But when we looked around, all the little children Jesus loved, the ones we knew, were clearly white. The other-colored children lived far away, in places like China. They were the objects of our curiosity and our pity. But they didn't live close by; they were never the recipients of our love, nor we of theirs. And so we sang the music of the tribe—one nation, one people, one language.

Yes, I heard about the children of China, about Miss Lottie Moon and Dr. Bill Wallace. But I never heard about the children of Davenport Town. Oh, I eventually learned that such a black neighborhood existed in Smyrna. I knew my parents went there to campaign against Lester Maddox, urging the residents there to vote instead for Ellis Arnall. But I had no idea where Davenport Town was, or how to get there. All I knew was the music of the tribe—one nation, one tribe, one people, one language.

I never heard that I was living through one of the greatest non-violent revolutions in the history of the world. Oh, I read the Marietta and Atlanta papers. I read *Life* magazine as a ten-year old. I remember puzzling over why an entire issue was devoted to James Earl Ray, who seemed to have done nothing no more noteworthy than kill a black man by the name of Martin King. Before he was killed, I had never heard

King's name. I grew up less than eighteen miles from Ebenezer Baptist Church in Atlanta. But it might as well have been half a world away. One nation, one tribe, one people, one language.

Half the students from Davenport Town did attend my high school. But understand, it was my high school, not theirs. The school system neatly divided their neighborhood in half between my school and our crosstown rivals. And ability grouping insured that there was never more than one black face in any classroom I entered as a college prep student.

The percentages only went down when I left Smyrna for Athens, where Charlayne Hunter and Hamilton Holmes had integrated the campus of the University of Georgia less than twenty years before. African-American enrollment hovered somewhere below 4%. But it seemed less. I do not remember hearing one African-American voice speaking in any classroom I attended.

But I'm from Georgia, and so I don't hear very well. Two years at Yale Divinity School helped me start to hear. I met African-American students who challenged my stereotypes. A Lutheran friend from the Midwest slipped me a book: "Here's a book by a Baptist from the South. I think you'll like it."It was the week before exams at the end of the semester— but I couldn't stop reading, even through exam week. The title—*Brother to a Dragonfly*. By a fellow Baptist Yalie, Will Campbell. Campbell taught me things about the South, about me, that I'm not sure I would have heard otherwise. One nation, one tribe, one people, one language? Campbell taught me to put a question mark there. And my fellow students tried to teach me a bit of harmony to accompany the monotone I'd heard most of my life. The song was deeper, richer, more complex than I had imagined, with voices more varied than those I had known in Smyrna, Georgia.

Another year of study, this time in Louisville. Some friends of mine from UGA lived across the hall and worked in an inner-city church in German-town. After a semester went by, I joined them there. We talked about our model for ministry in inner-city Louisville—our fellow Georgian, fellow graduate of UGA, fellow graduate of the Southern Baptist Theological Seminary, fellow student of the Greek New Testament, Clarence Jordan. Those experiences, too, helped me to hear something of the richness of that song John once heard around the heavenly throne. When we sang together "red and yellow, black and white," the faces we saw and the hands we held were a better fit to the words we sang.

Then one April afternoon, when I was trying to find a summer job, I received a call from the truest Mercerian I have ever met. Why do I say he was the truest Mercerian I have ever met? He played a pivotal role in the two most crucial turning points of Mercer's history in the twentieth century: the heresy trials and the desegregation of the campus. In Mercer's employ, he raised over twenty million dollars, saving the pharmacy school from closure.[1] At one point, many thought him poised to become Mercer's next president. But that is not the reason I describe him as true. No, it is simply this. More than anyone else, he would help me hear; he would teach me that one tribe alone does not and cannot sing the song of that salvation that belongs to God and to the Lamb. One people, one language alone is insufficient to bear the tune. The music of the tribe is idolatry that leads to damnation, not to the worship of the true God and the Lamb. He would teach me that lesson, not simply by what he said, but by what he did.

That afternoon I stood, looking out my window one floor above the WMU's Lottie Moon Memorial Chapel in Carver Hall, and I heard these words of introduction: "I have a reputation as a bit of a maverick," he said. "But I've always simply tried to love people like Jesus loved them. Of course, that didn't work out so well for Jesus."

By the end of the conversation, he'd invited me to come to interview at the Central Baptist Church of Newnan, Georgia, where he was the interim pastor. I would, in fact, get the job, and for one remarkable summer I would work in the long and gracious shadow of Thomas J. Holmes.

But I was curious. What did he mean, he was a maverick? What kind of reputation did he have? I made my way to the library and located a copy of his book, *Ashes for Breakfast.* And there I read for the first time the story irretrievably wed to this building on the Mercer campus. Forty years ago, this structure was not called Newton Chapel; it was the sanctuary of the Tatnall Square Baptist Church. And its pastor was Tom Holmes. He had left a job as Mercer's director of development and alumni relations to accept Tatnall Square's call to be their pastor in December 1964. The previous year, Sam Oni had come from Ghana to be the first African student at Mercer. And the deacons of Tatnall Square had sent their previous pastor to Sam Oni's dorm room to instruct him that he would not be welcome to worship at the church on Mercer's campus. Sam Oni, acquiescing to their instructions, joined Vineville Baptist Church. When he was presented for membership at Vineville, it was Tom Holmes who lept to his feet and moved that the congregation accept Oni as a member.[2]

But that motion would only be the first stage in the relationship between the two men. With his wife Grace, Tom would invite Sam Oni to dinner in their home, the first such invitation he would receive from a white couple.

In July 1965, after Tom was called to be the pastor at Tatnall Square, he appointed a committee of deacons to make recommendations regarding seating African Americans, but they chose to take no action. The next summer, Tom began preaching a series of sermons on the book of Acts. The example of those early believers reaching out beyond ethnic barriers to form an inclusive fellowship sounded an unmistakably clear message to segregated ears. Then two African-American students participating in the summer Upward Bound program at Mercer attended Sunday morning worship. Grace made a special effort to greet them and shake their hands. That evening, one of the deacons informed Tom he would be removed as pastor for allowing them to worship at Tatnall Square. Sam Oni, reading of the impending vote in Ralph McGill's column in the Atlanta Constitution, returned to Macon to support Tom. The morning that he tried to attend worship at Tatnall Square, one deacon seized him in a headlock on the steps, a second helped carry him down the stairs, and a third called the police, who, stationed nearby, took him into custody. That same morning, the church voted to fire Tom and his two associates by a vote of 259–189. One nation, one tribe, one people, one language, 259 said. But 189 said, no.

Your ministry is finished, 259 said. But 189 said, no! And the minority was right. Tom's ministry was not done. It was different, always different, after that vote. The first place he would speak after his dismissal would be the synagogue here in Macon. He would forge new friendships with African Americans, being welcomed in their pulpits as one who took a stand for equality and justice. And on that dark day in April 1968 when Martin was shot, he and Grace would visit his friend Daddy King, who embraced him with the words, "Tom, they've killed my boy!," and they would weep together.[3]

And through those years, Tom served as the interim pastor of scores of congregations. He had a special knack for bringing reconciliation and healing to churches in the midst of turmoil and grief. I know. I saw him sow the seeds for a Habitat for Humanity chapter in affluent Coweta County by distributing Millard Fuller's books in a few key hands. I remember his preaching about koinonia. I still recall his anger at the fundamentalists he saw misdirecting the energies of his fellow Baptists—it brought back memories of his student years when he led the support for faculty members whom Birch charged with heresy. He railed against the 1984 SBC resolution declaring that Eve was first in the Edenic fall, and he swore he was going to write a book about fundamentalism entitled, "The Last Stagecoach to Nashville."

He never got the chance. After his interim pastorate at Central, he began another, at Rainbow Park in Decatur. That December, I was home from seminary for the holidays. Early one Sunday morning, two days before Christmas, I got another phone call from Tom. "I've never done this before," he said. "But I'm not feeling well, and I need you to come preach for me this morning." I was a seminarian with a total of two sermons to my credit, and neither of them was a fit for the Sunday before Christmas. But somehow, that sermon on Hebrews became a fit; it had to. I had been given that opportunity as a sacred trust. By week's end, Tom was dead. In the decades since, I've tried to keep that trust, and so, today, in this place where he and Grace bore such costly witness for Jesus, I preach for him still.

"I have a reputation as a bit of a maverick," he said. "But I've always simply tried to love people like Jesus loved them. Of course, that didn't work out so well for Jesus." I have come to hear, in that wry understatement, the summing up of a remarkable ministry and witness. I hear that following Jesus is costly. And I hear of grace and redemption on the far side of tragedy and pain.

Like I said, I'm from Georgia, and so I don't hear very well. In fact, most of the time, I don't hear very well at all. But Mercer's broad welcome for diversity, its room for difference, its heritage of striving for racial justice—which I see every day in every classroom I am blessed to enter and teach, being grafted in to that heritage and hope, helps me hear that music of the Apocalypse. And even on those days I do not hear well, when sounds come over me without meaning, I sometimes remember my first-grade lip reading skills. On those difficult days when I cannot hear, I look. I look in the Mercer mirror, and I can see faces. Faces like Tom and Grace Holmes. Faces like Carolyn Martin and the others in that faithful 189. Faces like yours. And sometimes, I can see you singing, from every nation, from all tribes and peoples and languages, and I can read your lips: "Salvation belongs to our God who is seated on the throne, and to the Lamb." Yes, sometimes, sometimes, I can see you singing. And I say, "Thanks be to God."

Notes

1. Grace Bryan Holmes, "Tom Holmes Remembered," in Thomas J. Holmes, *The Christian's Vital Breath:Thomas J. Holmes on Prayer*, ed. Grace Bryan Holmes, typescript, 1990.

2. I have drawn the details of these events primarily from the account of Grace Bryan Holmes, *Time to Reconcile: The Odyssey of a Southern Baptist* (Athens: The University of Georgia Press, 2000).

3. Grace Bryan Holmes, *Time to Reconcile.*

The Mercer Triangle Symposium was approved as a student organization by a vote of the Student Government Association in October of 2002. Its stated purpose was to provide a forum for discussion and debate about sexuality and sexual orientation. MTS sponsored lectures and forums for two years without incident, but in its third year, students sponsored a forum on sexual orientation to correspond with National Coming Out Day on October 11, 2005. Prior to the forum [meeting], MTS printed an advertisement in The Mercer Cluster *signed by 118 students, faculty, and staff, expressing their support for GLBT (gay, lesbian, bisexual, transgendered) students, faculty, and staff members at Mercer. On November 10, the Georgia Baptist Convention's newspaper, the* Christian Index, *printed a front-page article critical of the MTS—"What's Up with the Mercer Triangle Symposium?" Mercer President Kirby Godsey explained that MTS was approved by the Student Government Association and that the university recognized "the right of students to assemble and discuss wide-ranging social and religious issues." Within weeks, the Convention broke its 172-year ties with the university, citing long-standing governance issues, the trustee selection process, and the presence of the Mercer Triangle Symposium.*

Mercer Leaders Want More 'Baptistness,' Despite Loss of Convention Affiliation (2006)

John Pierce

In the first major event since the Georgia Baptist Convention unilaterally voted to break a 173-year-old relationship with its flagship university, Mercer University officials welcomed more than 150 church leaders to the campus Jan. 19–20 to explore ways to sustain and enhance the schools Baptist identity.

"We reaffirm that Mercer is a Baptist university," said Mercer president Kirby Godsey, "That reality, of course, can never be changed by a state convention."

Godsey, who will retire in June after 27 years as Mercer's president, said the university faces the dual challenges of evaluating "how the Baptist identity informs the Mercer experience" and how to "sustain relationships with Baptist people."

Godsey called the Georgia Baptist Convention's decision in November—
to sever ties with the university by pulling scholarship funds for Baptist
students—an action based on frustration over a lack of control, rather
than the publicized issue of homosexuality. Unlike three other Georgia
Baptist colleges, Mercer trustees are not selected by the convention.

"The abuse of the university in the *Christian Index* was unwarranted and
uncivil, and our critics know it," said Godsey, referring to a cover story in
the GBC-owned newspaper just prior to the November meeting.

The story focused on a meeting of the Mercer Triangle Symposium held
on what is nationally promoted by homosexual advocates as "Coming
Out Day."

"Did Mercer have a 'coming-out day?'" asked Godsey. "The answer is no.
This nation has a "coming-out day."

Godsey said some Mercer students held a forum—"not a novel idea at a
university"—to discuss sexual orientation. "What better place to discuss
such issues?" Godsey asked. "Otherwise, we leave such conversations to
the backrooms and hallways."

Godsey said he would rather students dialogue about gay and lesbian
issues in a university forum than get their information from the Internet
and *Will and Grace.* The stated purpose of the symposium, he added, was
"to provide an open forum for issues related to sexuality."

"Mercer will not be an advocate for alternative lifestyles," said Godsey.
"We will be an educational institution."

While the university has a different role than the church, Godsey said, Mercer is "keenly aware of our church constituency." However, said Godsey,
"our students will be permitted to discuss sexuality. We're more freeing
than some churches."

The university, he added, will act with respect and civility toward all persons. He suggested that Mercer has "about the same percentage of gay
students . . . as you have as members of your congregations."

Godsey said Mercer is exploring ways to move ahead as a Baptist university free of formal ties with the GBC. "Our challenge is that we can't
ultimately live out our Baptist identity in isolation," said Godsey. "How
do we join hands with Baptist people?"

The university serves churches through many functions, Godsey said,
including ministry preparation through the undergraduate program in
Christianity and graduate studies at McAfee School of Theology, the

resources of the Center for Baptist Studies and Mercer University Press, and the expansive Baptist archives collection.

Godsey tossed out a few ideas for expanding Mercer's role as a Baptist resource, such as producing a new hymnal or Bible study curriculum. And he suggested Mercer affiliate with other like-minded Baptist groups.

Godsey asked participants to meet in groups to consider new ways the university might assist Baptist congregations. "We need your best thinking, insights and highest wisdom," he said.

Mercer is appealing to churches for financial support to replace Georgia Baptist Convention funding for Baptist student scholarships. Godsey said the convention provides $3.5 million of the $11.5 million in aid to Baptist students, who make up more than half of the student population.

"The students entering Mercer this fall will receive no Baptist money unless it comes from you and your churches," Godsey told the gathering.

Godsey said he is very grateful for what Georgia Baptists have done in creating and supporting Mercer, but described current leaders as "walking around in three days of darkness."

Church historian Walter Shurden of Mercer, who also addressed the summit, called for formal action to ensure that at least half of the board of trustees and all future presidents be active Baptists. He suggested that at least 10 percent of the trustees be Baptist ministers from across the nation in order to keep the university connected with congregations.

Shurden urged Mercer to establish ties with Baptist organizations like the Cooperative Baptist Fellowship, Baptist World Alliance, Progressive National Baptist Convention and American Baptist Churches, USA. But he advised those should be "dotted-line" connections rather than "hardwired" as in the past with the GBC.

Reports from discussion groups showed various opinions about the degree to which the university should connect with other Baptist groups, the potential for including direct funding to Mercer in church budgets, and which resources would be most useful.

Overwhelmingly, participants called for a more aggressive effort to get Mercer faculty and staff visible in churches and to get Baptists—especially potential students—to visit the campuses.

Some voiced support for retaining an active campus ministry program. Currently, the Baptist campus ministry program is directed by convention employee Chris Fuller. Godsey said the future of that position is not clear but that the university will continue to have a Baptist Student Union.

Shortly after The Christian Index *printed its article, and wishing to prevent a break with the Georgia Baptist Convention as well as to protect GLBT students from backlash if a break were to occur, the faculty advisers of MTS and the Provost voluntarily disbanded the organization with the provisio that the group's right to exist could be revisited. April Trussell, the President of the Triangle Symposium, supported the advisers' actions but felt she would be betraying the principles of MTS to sign the disbanding statement on behalf of students. Her letter to her family, discussing the importance of her Baptist heritage in supporting the MTS, was printed in* The Cluster.

Building Character through Challenges (2005)

April Trussell

Dear Momma,

I am not sure what you've heard about me and my activism over the course of this semester, so I wanted to write to tell you, in my own words, what I've been doing and why.

The "what" is pretty easy to explain. I have spent the bulk of this semester as the President of Mercer Triangle Symposium. MTS was an alliance of GLBT (gay, lesbian, bisexual, and transgendered) and straight students at Mercer that promoted open, educational discussion of issues relating to sexuality and sexual orientation. We sought to validate and affirm the personhood and worth of all people on Mercer's campus—regardless of who we are or whom we love.

On October 11, we sponsored a forum for National Coming Out Day. It was one of the most uplifting experiences of my life. About 100 people showed up to discuss GLBT issues with our panelists. The issues were serious but the atmosphere was light, and people actually heard each other. I wish you could have seen it. In addition to the forum, we sponsored a statement in *The Cluster* and invited anyone who wanted to sign it to do so. We were amazed when 118 Mercerians, including faculty, students, and staff signed on.

The Cluster published an article about the forum two weeks later, and it was amazing! Emily Hill knew exactly how to characterize the forum and wrote about it in its educational context rather than sensationalizing it. I

647

could not believe the positive atmosphere at Mercer and the changes I could see on the horizon for GLBT individuals here.

Then, as we were trying to come up with new ways to expand the positive climate, *The Christian Index* published its article about National Coming Out Day. . . . At best, the article was a complete misunderstanding of the purpose of our group and of the event. The article caused enough stir, however, to make it obvious that Mercer needed to respond in some way to the accusations leveled against it. In support of our University and in the hopes of avoiding a split between Mercer and the GBC, which would cause financial hardships for Baptist scholarship students and a backlash against the very people we were advocating for, the Provost and the faculty advisors of MTS decided to disband MTS. The decision was heart wrenching. No good options on either side. I chose not to sign the request to disband, though, because someone had to stand up for the GLBTs at Mercer. We disbanded Monday, November 14, and the GBC voted to break ties with Mercer anyway on the next day.

Why I have spent the past few months working so hard for this cause is a much more complicated issue. Many factors have led to such a stand on my part.

First and foremost, you have taught me by your words and example that I must stand up for what I believe is right. You have shown me that it is okay not to go with the crowd. You have taught me to seek out for myself an understanding of truth. You taught me to love all people and to think for myself. Without your example, Momma, I would never have been able to take the kind of stand I have been taking all semester.

Second, my Baptist heritage will not allow me to take what has been fed to me as fact without investigating for myself. I cannot believe that an unexamined faith is a faith worth practicing. And I cannot believe that a faith not put into practice in the form of social activism is a real faith at all.

Without Sisters Baptist Church and my family, I would not be the person I am today. I am proud of the work I have done, and I plan to continue doing it even though Mercer Triangle Symposium has been disbanded . . .

Thank you for the example you have set for me. Thank you for teaching me to think for myself. Thank you for laying the foundation for me to become a strong activist for positive social change. Thank you for teaching me that to be Baptist is to claim the freedom of my soul and my beliefs from the enforcement of any creed or dogma.

I hope that you can see how much you have influenced me and how hard I am trying to do what I think is right in light of everything I have learned from you. I hope, also, that you can be proud of what I have become and of the stand I am making for my beliefs.

I love you.

April

Days after the Georgia Baptist Convention voted to sever its 172-year ties to Mer-cer University, hundreds of Mercer students, faculty, and staff gathered in Jesse Mercer plaza for a rally in support of their alma mater. A broad cross-section of the Mercer community spoke at the "We Are Mercer" rally, including those who favored GBLT rights and those who opposed them. All spoke of the need to hear dif-fereing opinions on sensitive issues at the university, and all spoke in defense of a community of respect and the right of the Student Government Association to approve or reject student groups without reference to authorities outside the uni-versity. Timothy Durski, a Mercer senior, offered this closing prayer at the rally.

Concluding Prayer, "We Are Mercer" Rally (2005)

Timothy Durski

God, we recognize You as sovereign over us, as the Author of peace in our lives. The hope we have in You can unite us as a community. Though we often miss the mark, we know You love us and give us strength enough to do what You have demanded of us. May we be a community of peace and of progress. We ask in humility that we may be agents of light in this dark world, sharing in Your work—inwardly that we might seek harmony with and understanding of each other, in the classroom and out; and outwardly in the larger community, that we might seek justice and be agents of peace and charity. Let Your work begin in this community and through this community, and may we be mindful of Your presence over us and in us. All praise is Yours, Almighty God. We pray this in Your Name, for our sake, and for Your glory. Amen.

Acknowledgments

p. 3: The Metropolitan Museum of Art, Catharine Lorillard Wolfe Collection, Wolfe Fund, 1906 (06.1234) Photograph copyright © 1995 The Metropolitan Museum of Art. Reprinted by permission.

p. 5: Copyright © 2006 C. Herscovici, Brussels / Artists Rights Society (ARS), New York. Reprinted by permission. Image provided by Art Resource.

pp. 15–29: From *The Message in the Bottle* by Walker Percy. Copyright © 1975 by Walker Percy. Reprinted by permission of Farrar, Straus & Giroux, Inc.

pp. 30–31: From *Generations* by Pattiann Rogers. Copyright © 2004 by Pattiann Rogers. Used by permission of Penguin, a division of Penguin Group (USA) Inc.

p. 32: From *House of Light* by Mary Oliver. Copyright © 1992. Published by Beacon Press.

pp. 33–34: From *The Selected Poems of Wendell Berry*. Copyright © 1999 by Wendell Berry. Reprinted by permission of Counterpoint.

p. 35: From *Collected Poems* by W. H. Auden. Copyright © 1940 and renewed 1968 by W. H. Auden. Used by permission of Random House, Inc.

pp. 38–49: From *The Lone Ranger and Tonto Fistfight in Heaven* by Sherman Alexie. Copyright ©1993, 2005 by Sherman Alexie. Used by permission of Grove / Atlantic, Inc.

pp. 85–101 From *Through the Safety Net: Stories by Charles Baxter*. Copyright © 1985. Published by Pantheon, a division of Random House, Inc.

pp. 110–111: From *The Flagrant Dead* by Stephen Bluestone. Copyright © 2009. Published by Mercer University Press.

pp. 112–126: From *Cathedral* by Raymond Carver. Copyright © 1981, 1982, 1983 by Raymond Carver. Used by permission of Alfred A. Knopf, a division of Random House, Inc.

pp. 127–139: From *An Account of My Hut* by Kamo no Cho⁻mei, translated by Donald Keene. Copyright © 1976. Published by Banyan Press.

pp. 145–147: From *The Prophet* by Kahil Gibran. Copyright © 1971. Published by Alfred A. Knopf, a division of Random House, Inc.

pp. 472–473: From *One Body* by Margaret Gibson. Copyright © 2008. Published by Louisiana State University Press.

pp. 478–484: From *Killing Rage: Ending Racism* by bell hooks. Copyright © 1995 by Gloria Watkins. Reprinted by permission of Henry Holt and Company, LLC.

pp. 485–488: Reprinted by arrangement with the Estate of Martin Luther King, Jr., c/o Writers House as agent for the proprietor New York, NY. Copyright © 1963 by Martin Luther King, Jr., copyright renewed 1991 by Coretta Scott King.

pp. 489–507: From *Interpreter of Maladies* by Jhumpa Lahiri. Copyright © 1999 by Jhumpa Lahiri. Reprinted by permission of Houghton Mifflin Harcourt Publishing Company. All rights reserved.

pp. 508–519: From the Nobel Lecture by Doris Lessing, December 7, 2007. Copyright © 2007 by the Nobel Foundation. Reprinted by permission.

pp. 522–532: From a speech given by Malcom X in Detroit, Michigan, November 10, 1963. Copyright © by CMG Worldwide.

pp. 534–541: As appeared on AGNI Fiction Online. Copyright © 2006 by Boston University.

pp. 564–568: From *The Wedding of Zein & Other Stories* by Tayeb Salih, translated by Denys Johnson-Davies. Copyright © 1985. Published by Heinemann Publishers, Ltd.